PRAISE FOR *LIGHT EMERGING*

"All we need for healing is light and love, and Barbara Brennan understands this so clearly. *Light Emerging* takes us to new depths of healing knowledge. I highly recommend it!"

—LOUISE HAY, author of *You Can Heal Your Life*

"Barbara Brennan is a pioneer in the interface between science and the healing arts. Her book is filled with deep knowledge and wisdom springing from direct experience and practice. It is destined to become a classic."

—KYRIACOS C. MARKIDES, author of *Fire in the Heart: Healers, Sages and Mystics*

"Barbara Brennan is that rare and vital combination of scientist, healer, and teacher. Her book is a powerful tool for all of us to live at the new norm of optimum wellness."

—BARBARA MARX HUBBARD, author of *The Revelation*

"Having personally experienced Barbara Brennan's healing gifts, I am honored to endorse her book. She combines the research methods of her extensive scientific background with her intuitive powers and her inherent wisdom. Modern 'medicine' is thereby enlarged and made human by this remarkable union."

—ROLLO MAY, PH.D., author of *Love and Will* and *The Cry for Myth*

AND FOR *HANDS OF LIGHT*

"This book is a must for all aspiring healers and health-care givers, an inspiration to all who want to understand the true human being."

—ELISABETH KÜBLER-ROSS

"Barbara Brennan's work is mind opening. Her concepts of the role disease plays and how healing is achieved certainly fit in with my experience."

—BERNIE S. SIEGEL, M.D., author of *Love, Medicine and Miracles*

This book is dedicated to
everyone on the path Homeward
to the True and Divine Self.

LIGHT EMERGING

The Journey of Personal Healing

BARBARA ANN BRENNAN

Illustrated by
Thomas J. Schneider and Joan Tartaglia

BANTAM BOOKS
NEW YORK · TORONTO · LONDON · SYDNEY · AUCKLAND

LIGHT EMERGING
A Bantam Book/December 1993

The poem quoted on page 139, "Through the Gateway," is from *The Pathwork of Self-Transformation,* by Eva Pierrakos, and is reprinted with the permission of her publisher, Bantam Books.

Book design by Richard Oriolo.

Library of Congress Cataloging-in-Publication Data

Brennan, Barbara Ann.
   Light emerging : the journey of personal healing / Barbara Ann Brennan.
      p.   cm.
   Includes bibliographical references and index.
   ISBN 0-553-35456-6
   1. Force and energy—Therapeutic use.
2. Imposition of hands—Therapeutic use.
3. Aura.   I. Title.
RZ999.B65   1993
615.8′52—dc20   92-31473
                                                      CIP

Published simultaneously in the United States and Canada

PRINTED IN THE UNITED STATES OF AMERICA

CWO   30 29 28 27 26 25

CONTENTS

PART IV
CREATING A HEALING PLAN

PART V
HEALING AND RELATIONSHIPS

PART VI
HEALING THROUGH OUR HIGHER SPIRITUAL REALITIES

LIST OF FIGURES

A New Paradigm:
Healing and the Creative Process

Since the publication of *Hands of Light,* my first book, I have continued to study the relationship of our life energies to health, illness, and healing. I have become very interested in the deeper questions of why we get sick. Is "getting sick" part of the human condition, with some deeper meaning or lesson behind it? How does living a "normal" life in our culture lead to illness? I wondered what life rhythms were most healthy for us to follow. How do our day-to-day choices and actions affect our health? How does the shifting of our consciousness moment to moment affect our health? I wondered if and how our illness could be related to our creativity and our evolutionary process.

I stopped my healing practice to get more time to create the Barbara Brennan School of Healing, and I continued to observe energy phenomena in class and group situations as well as within individual students. As I continued to teach and lecture, a very interesting pattern started to be revealed. At the beginning of the year, my guidance told me I would be lecturing on the creative process. When I finally was able to have several of these lectures transcribed, edited, and put together, I discovered a whole new connection between the evolutionary plan of the earth, our life task, our creativity, our health, and living in what Heyoan, my guide, calls the unfolding moment.

In order to understand the new material, it is necessary to enter into a new paradigm. Webster defines the word *paradigm* as "a pattern, example, or model." It is the way we perceive the world. A paradigm is a shared set of assumptions that explain the world to us and help us predict its behavior. We take these assumptions for granted. We define them as basic reality and don't think about them further. Does a fish notice the water?

"Most of our notions about the world come from a set of assumptions which we take for granted, and which, for the most part, we don't examine or question," observes Werner Erhard, creator of est and the Forum Workshops. "We bring these assumptions to the table with us as a given. They are so much a part of who we are that it is difficult for us to separate ourselves from them enough to be able to talk about them. We do not think these assumptions—we think from them."

Medical paradigms determine how we think about our bodies. Over the years, western medicine has identified evil spirits, humors, germs, and viruses as causes of disease and has designed treatments accordingly. As technologies in medicine advance and as we learn more about our mind-body connections, our medical paradigms are shifting. New paradigms give rise to new possibilities.

In the past, the auric field has been known to be associated with health and healing, but in a rather "esoteric" way. Knowledge of the field has been a mixture of real observations, assumptions, and fantasies.

Now, as we learn more about bioenergy in our laboratories and clinics, the idea of a human energy field that is directly connected to our health is becoming more acceptable within the western medical paradigm.

In this book, I present a new view of health, healing, and illness. Part I includes a scientific background, based on both energy field and holographic theories of why and how laying on of hands works.

In Part II, I describe what a healer can and cannot do for a person, the basic format of a healing session, and how a healer-physician team can work. Part II presents the concept of the internal balancing system, an automatic—usually unconscious—system that keeps us in top shape if we listen to and follow it. Part II also shows how we can create dis-ease in our lives and bodies if we don't follow our balancing system.

Through a series of interviews with patients in Part III, I present the stages of personal experience that take place during the healing process from the patient's point of view. I discuss what a patient can do to get the most out of that process, including how to work with a healer and a physician to create a healing plan. Case studies help bring the process of healing into everyday terms.

Part IV gives detailed healing plans and very useful healing meditations and visualizations that will help your personal healing process.

Part V describes how relationships affect your health in both positive and negative ways. Practical ways of creating healthy relationships are described, as well as the auric field interactions that occur in relationships. Ways to re-establish healthy auric field energy exchanges and connections are given.

Part VI describes the higher spiritual realities and deeper dimensions of creative energies and relates health, dis-ease, and healing to the creative process.

Appendix A presents a transcript of a healing session; Appendix B, a list of types of health-care professionals, what they do, and the national organizations through which you can find them; and Appendix C, a description of the Barbara Brennan School of Healing, which trains men and women healers for professional work and sends out lists of healers who have graduated. Plus the Bibliography provides resources for further study and reading.

Acknowledgments

I would like especially to thank my husband, Eli Wilner, for his loving support and encouragement of the natural unfoldment of my personal development.

I give a heartfelt thanks to the teachers of the Barbara Brennan School of Healing for walking with me through the development of the material that came together to form this book; to Roseanne Farano for her dedicated friendship, open listening, and clear advice; and to the clerical staff at the Barbara Brennan School of Healing for preparation of the manuscript.

PART I

AN OVERVIEW OF HEALING IN OUR TIME

"A new idea is first condemned as ridiculous and then dismissed as trivial, until finally, it becomes what everybody knows."

—William James

O N E

The Gift of Healing

The gift of healing rests within everyone. It is not a gift given only to a few. It is your birthright as much as it is mine. Everyone can receive healing, and everyone can learn to heal. Everyone can give healing to themselves and to others.

You already give yourself healing, even though you may not call it that. What is the first thing you do when you hurt yourself? You usually touch the hurt part of your body. You may even grab it to help stop the pain. This physical instinct also sends healing energy to the hurt part. If you relax and keep your hands on the injury longer than you normally would, you will find an even deeper healing taking place. Every mother touches, holds, kisses, or caresses her children when they are in pain. She does the same for her other loved ones. If you take these simple reactions and begin to study them, you will find that when you touch someone whom you love very much, there will be a stronger effect than if you are touching someone you don't know. Most likely you have given your touch a special essence—the essence of the love you have for that person. You see you knew healing all the time but were unaware of it.

When you are joyful, happy, energized, or in any other kind of good mood, your touch will be more pleasant to others than when you are in a bad mood.

The energy within a bad mood touch is not the same as that within a joyous one. How you are in any given moment is expressed through your energy. When you learn to regulate your moods and therefore the nature of your energy and your energy flow, you will soon be using your energy for healing. That is what healers do. They simply learn to perceive and regulate their energy in order to utilize it for healing.

These personal everyday experiences, which I'm sure have taken place since we were cave dwellers, have grown into the basis of laying on of hands healing. It has been around as long as there have been human beings. The ancients were aware of healing power coming from hands. Each culture explored and utilized this power from within the framework of its knowledge and traditions. In his book *Future Science*, John White lists ninety-seven different cultures over the face of the globe, each of which has its own name to refer to the healing or life energy fields. Life energy fields have been known in China and India for over five thousand years.

I call the life energy that surrounds and interpenetrates everything the universal energy field, or UEF. I call the life energy associated with human beings the human energy field, or HEF. It is more commonly known as the human aura.

Perceiving and Regulating the HEF

Many people can perceive the human energy field, and *everyone* can learn how to perceive it. In fact, we already do so—maybe not consciously, maybe disregarding it, or maybe calling it something else. For example, you know when someone is staring at you when you are not looking because you feel it; or you immediately like a stranger to whom you are introduced, and know that you will get along fine; or you have a vague sense that something good is going to happen, and it does. You are sensing the human energy field with the use of what I call Higher Sense Perception (HSP). HSP simply refers to our senses expanded beyond the normal ranges we are used to, sometimes referred to as the sixth sense. Other terms used for this ability are: clairvoyance, or being able to see meaningful things others cannot; clairaudience, or being able to hear things others cannot; and clairsentience, or being able to feel things others cannot.

I have been developing, studying, and utilizing HSP for many years. I have found more specific ways to differentiate between the types of HSP. It includes all our normal five senses—sight, hearing, touch, taste, and smell—as well as additional senses. One of these senses, our intuition, is a vague sense of knowing, such as knowing that something good is going to happen but you don't know what it is. Another example of intuition is when you know someone is going to call—you may even know who it is—but you don't know exactly what it is about.

Another of these senses is what I call *direct knowing*. This sense gives us complete and specific direct information. For example, we know a certain person is going to call, when they are going to call, and what they are going to say. Or, if asked a question about something that we think we know nothing about, we know both the overall concept and the specifics of the answer. Usually with direct knowing, we don't know how we know the information. We simply know it.

Another higher sense is our ability to sense our own and each other's emotions. We know what each other is feeling, even though we may not communicate it in words. We simply pick up the energy of the other person's feelings.

I distinguish between the sense of feelings and the sense of love. So another high sense is our ability to sense love. Sensing love includes a much deeper connectedness to others than does the sensing of the other emotions. It is in a category of its own.

In addition to our five senses of sight, sound, taste, smell, and touch, we have intuition, direct knowing, the sense of emotions, and the sense of love. When all of these senses function, we are able to become fully aware of being here now.

Our senses serve our awareness, and our awareness brings us into the present. Being in the present is an experience that many people achieve through meditation. This state of being is a doorway out of the bounds of time and space that limit us. Meditation quiets and clears the mind for high sensitivity.

HSP rests within the range of very subtle information that our brains normally filter out as unimportant. Consider the analogy of listening to music. When the music is loud, it is more difficult to hear the softer notes within it. If you turn down the volume, the softer notes and subtler nuances become meaningful. You can hear rhythms within the rhythms. The same is true of HSP and the human energy field. You can learn to turn down the internal noise in your head and pay attention to the softer rhythms and subtler nuances of life. When you practice this for some time, you find that these subtler rhythms *are the foundations* of your moment-to-moment experience of life itself. They are connected to the powerful life energy with which we all function.

Put your hand on your child's knee next time he or she bumps it. Let yourself feel your love for your child. Your hand will get hot. Why? Because the healing energy of your energy field is flowing from your hand and helping the knee heal. You will feel the healing energy as heat, pulses, or an electriclike tingling. This type of perception is called the kinesthetic sense. You are perceiving the human energy field kinesthetically, through touch.

Since you can perceive the human energy field, you can learn to interact with it and regulate it with your intent. Try changing the energy flow through your body by following these instructions. You can do it next time you feel tired or strained.

Lie down, and imagine the nice pleasant sun inside the solar plexus (stomach area) of your body. Pretty soon, you will feel much better, and your stomach will feel warm. Probably even your breathing will slow down as you begin to relax more. If you want to expand this relaxation to include your spirit, remember a wonderful religious or spiritual experience you have had, perhaps as a child. Remember that special, wonderful time when you knew that God (whatever that means personally to you) existed and that being alive was a most natural and holy experience—so natural that it wasn't a concern. You didn't give God a second thought. Let yourself float into that experience and be held peacefully in the arms of the creator. By doing this, you have changed your energy flow. You have put yourself into a powerful healing state. Feel your energy now. Do you like it?

The relaxed healing state you feel corresponds to your energy field as it becomes more coherent, as well as to a slowing down of your brain waves. They can be measured with an electroencephalograph, or EEG. It will probably show that your brain is in alpha rhythm, about 8 Hz or cycles per second, which is known to be a healing state. A magnetic field detector would show that your energy field is pulsating at 7.8 to 8 Hz. This is a very natural energy state for everyone.

Most likely, as a child, in a very natural unplanned way, you let yourself go fully into whatever was at hand. That is what you still do, in those wonderful moments of creative abandon when you have given over to the life energy that flows out of you from an internal source. Then the colors are brighter, the tastes sweeter, the air more fragrant, and sounds around you create a symphony. You are not the exception; everyone has these experiences.

Perhaps your best ideas come when you are not even thinking about a solution to a problem. You're trekking in the woods or watching a beautiful sunset, and suddenly it's there. It has emerged from deep within you. Or you look into the eyes of a tiny baby and see wonder, and you are filled with the wonder of the mystery of life. Again, the feelings have emerged from deep within you. They have come from a deep inner fountain that I call the central core of your being. It is from this deep inner source that your light emerges. It is your divine inner spark.

Tapping the Creative Healing Energies

All people can learn to tap into this deeper source within them. It takes practice to release the creative energies at will. The process is more one of getting inner obstacles out of the way than one of pulling up the creative energies. Once the blocks are gone, creativity flows up from deep inside like an artesian well. Any artist or writer knows the struggle to get over the creative or writer's block. Once the block is cleared, the painting or writing flows like a stream. It happens to scientists trying to solve problems. All the data are put into the rational mind. The rational mind struggles to find the answer but cannot. After a good sleep, some

dreams, and some right-brain activity, the answer is simply there. The creative force has been released by an internal process of letting go, getting out of the way, and allowing energy to flow.

The creative force is also released in times of crisis. It is then that we walk into the heroic. Everyone has heard of great feats being accomplished under crisis conditions, like a man lifting a car off a loved one after an accident. Or the mother who gets a strong urge to return home and arrives in time to save her children from danger.

The release of this creative force brings us to mastery in whatever is at hand. The process of healing is a process of releasing our creative force for the mastery of health and well-being. In fact, from my point of view and as we shall see in this book, much of illness is a result of blocking the natural flow of an individual's creative energies.

Why We Block Our Creative Energy

As we go through the painful experiences of our lives, we automatically try not to feel the pain. We have done this since childhood. We cut off our physical pain by withdrawing our consciousness from the part of our body that is in pain. We cut off our mental and emotional anguish by tensing our muscles and repressing it into our unconscious. To keep it depressed in the unconscious (or sometimes just below the level of our conscious awareness), we create all kinds of distractions in our lives that take our attention away from it. We may keep ourselves very busy and become workaholics. Or we take the opposite route to couch-potato heaven. Lots of us become addicted to drugs, cigarettes, chocolate, or alcohol. Many of us become addicted to being perfect, to being the best or the worst. We project our problems onto someone else and worry about them rather than trying to solve our own problems. We either misdirect or depress great amounts of energy in order to keep ourselves from feeling pain, including what we feel in the moment and being who we are in the moment. We think it works. We think that we can get away with not feeling or being who we are, but it doesn't work. The price is great, but we even deny that there is a price. The price is our life.

We think the only possible way to stop all this pain is to stop the energy flow that contains the pain. There are specific energy flows that contain physical pain, emotional pain, and mental pain. Unfortunately, this energy flow also contains everything else. Pain is only part of it. When we stop the negative experience of pain, anger, or fear of any negative situation, we also stop the positive experience, including the physical, emotional, and mental aspects of that experience.

We may not even be aware of this process, because by the time we have reached the age of reason, we do it habitually. We wall off our wounds. By walling off our wounds, we also wall off our connection to our deeper center or core. Since the creative process comes from the creative core within us, we have also walled off our creative process. We have literally walled off the deeper part of ourselves from our conscious awareness and our exterior life.

Frozen Psychic Time Conglomerates

The pain we have repressed started very early in our childhood, many times even before birth, in the womb. Each time since early childhood when we stopped the flow of energy in a painful event, we froze that event in both energy and time. That is what we call a block in our auric field. Since the auric field is composed of energy-consciousness, a block is frozen energy-consciousness. The part of our psyche associated with that event also froze in the moment we stopped the pain. That part of our psyche remains frozen until we thaw it out. It does not mature as we do. If the event happened when we were one year old, that part of our psyche is still age one. It will continue to be one year old and act as a one-year-old person when evoked. It will not mature until it is healed by getting enough energy into the block to thaw it and initiate the maturation process.

We are full of such energy-consciousness time blocks. How long, in any given day, does one human being act out of the adult self? Not long. We are continually interacting with each other from different frozen psychic time blocks. In any intense interaction, in one minute each person could be experiencing reality with the inner adult, and in the next, either or both people could have switched to an aspect of the wounded child of a particular age. This constant switching from one aspect of internal consciousness to another is what makes communication so difficult.

A powerful aspect of such frozen psychic time blocks is that they coagulate together according to like energy, forming a frozen psychic time conglomerate. For example, the energy may be of the nature of abandonment. Consider a man in middle age named Joe. (He's really a fictional character, but his story illustrates those of many people I've worked with. To illustrate what

happens at birth and can continue to build throughout life, I'm going to use Joe throughout this chapter. He could be any of us.)

When Joe was born, he was disconnected from his mother because she had a rough time in labor and was given anesthesia. He was separated again when he was a one-year-old and his mother went to the hospital to have another baby. From these two life experiences, the child, who loves his mother very much, expects abandonment from the one he loves most. Whenever any degree of abandonment happens later in life, it is experienced with the same force of devastation as the first time.

From such deep trauma, we form an *image conclusion*. An image conclusion is based on experience—in this case, the experience of abandonment. It is based on child's logic that states, "If I love, I will be abandoned." This image conclusion then colors all similar situations. Obviously, one-year-old Joe is not conscious of having such an opinion. Instead, it is unconsciously held in his belief system and is carried throughout life. In terms of the psyche, the two early events also directly connect to an event when Joe was ten and his mother left on vacation. When any similar event occurs in his life, his reaction will be from the standpoint of the image conclusion rather than the immediate situation. This causes all kinds of emotional reactions that are overexaggerated given the present situation.

As we will see in later chapters, our image conclusions initiate our personal behavior, which actually tends to re-create traumas similar to the original one. Thus, Joe would have a lot to do with creating a situation where, for example, he is abandoned by a wife or girlfriend. His actions, based on his unconscious negative expectations, have helped set up the situation. Since he unconsciously expects to be abandoned, he will treat his wife or girlfriend like someone who would abandon him. He may place excessive demands on her to prove her love, or even accuse her of planning to abandon him. This unconscious behavior will provoke her and actually help push her out the door. The real, deeper issue is that in treating himself as if he deserved to be abandoned, he has actually abandoned himself.

As we shall see, we should never underestimate the power of our image conclusions. Finding our images holds the key to the transformation process into health and happiness. We are full of such images, around which our frozen psychic time conglomerates assemble. We all have a lot of clearing to do.

Frozen psychic time blocks coagulate around like energy that composes an image, which confuses someone who thinks these experiences should be as separate emotionally as they are in time. It doesn't work that way. Each smaller segment of the frozen psychic time conglomerate is composed of the energy-consciousness that was frozen during a particular past experience. But like experiences are directly connected no matter how much time may have elapsed between them.

Through healing work, one of the small frozen psychic time blocks is released. The increased energy released into the auric field then, in turn, automatically starts releasing the other, small segments of the time conglomerate because they are of like energy. Going back to Joe's story, as each time block is released, he experiences it as if it were happening to him right now. Thus, he may be experiencing pain from when he was thirty years old, and as soon as that pain is released, he suddenly finds himself to be ten years old. Soon the ten-year-old becomes a one-year-old.

Once these pieces of the human psyche that have not matured with the rest of the personality are released, they begin a rapid maturation process. This process can take from a few minutes up to a couple of years, depending on how deep, strong, and pervasive the frozen energy-consciousness was.

As these energies integrate evenly throughout the HEF and are released back into the creative process of an individual's life, whole life changes occur. Joe's life begins to restructure itself from the new consciousness that is now active in the creative process. He will no longer abandon himself in an unconscious effort to get taken care of. Instead, he will abide with himself, because he now believes that he is worthy of and can create companionship. Once he has developed this new relationship with himself, he will attract a girlfriend who does not carry the energy of abandonment. Thus the new relationship will be a stable one in this area. Of course it may take several practice runs before the "right woman" comes along

Pain from Past Lives

A great deal of "past life" research has been done, both through literature search and through hypnotic regression. This research traces the origin of most chronic psychological pain back through previous life experiences. One extensive account is in Roger Woolger's *Other Lives, Other Selves*. In his past life regression therapy, Dr. Woolger finds that once a client has relived and cleared the pain from a past life experience, they are able to clear similar present life circumstances that other types of therapy could not touch.

Past lives are also held within our frozen psychic time conglomerates. They also attract and connect with each other by similar energy. They are not separated by time, so they are directly connected to events in this lifetime as well as other lifetimes. It takes a bit more energy to break into a frozen event from a past life because it has been there longer and is covered with more debris, but it can be done in healing sessions. It happens automatically when the person is ready.

According to my observations of the human energy field during healing sessions, past life traumas always underlie the chronic present-day problems that are difficult to resolve. When traumas from this life are cleared to a certain extent through laying on of hands healing, the past life trauma that is buried under them arises to the surface to be cleared. This type of healing work is very effective in transforming a client's life as well as his or her physical condition. Great changes always occur as a result of releasing past life trauma through hands-on healing. In this work, it is always important for the client to clearly relate past life work to present life situations, so that the entire conglomerate is released and is not used to avoid the issues of this life.

The Origin of Pain—Your Original Wound

The origin of pain, from my perspective, is even deeper than energy blocked from personal pain or the phenomena called past lives. It comes from the belief that each of us is separate; separate from everyone else and separate from God. Many of us believe that in order to be individual, we must be separate. As a result, we separate ourselves from everything, including our own families, friends, groups, nations, and the earth. This belief in separation is experienced as fear, and out of fear, all other negative emotions arise. Once we have created these negative emotions, we separate ourselves from them. This process of separating goes on creating more pain and illusion until the negative feedback loop is broken or reversed in personal process work. How to reverse this vicious cycle to create more and more pleasure and clarity in our lives is what this book is about. The key is love and connectedness to all that there is.

Love is the experience of being connected to God and to everything else. God is everywhere, in everything. God is above us, below us, all around us, and within us. The divine spark of God is uniquely individual in each of us. It is God individually manifested. We experience it as our inner fountainhead, or the core of our being. The more we are connected to God outside of ourselves, the more we are connected to and bring forth the individuality of the God within. When we are connected to the universal God and the individual God within, we are completely safe and free.

The Creation of the Mask Self to Mask Our Original Pain

When we are born, we are still very connected to great spiritual wisdom and power through our core. This connection to our core and therefore to spiritual wisdom and power gives the feeling of complete safety and wonder. During the maturation process, this connection slowly fades. It is replaced by parental voices intended to protect us and make us safe. They speak of right and wrong, of good and bad, how to make decisions, and how to act or react in any given situation. As the connection to the core fades, our child psyche tries desperately to replace the original innate wisdom with a functioning ego. Unfortunately, the overlay or internalized parental voices can never really do the job. Instead, what is produced is a mask self.

The mask self is our first attempt to right ourselves. With it, we attempt to express who we are in a positive way that is also acceptable to a world that we are afraid will reject us. We present our mask self to the world according to our beliefs of what we think the world says is right, so that we can be accepted and feel safe. The mask self strives for connection with others because that is the "right" thing to do. But it cannot accomplish deep connection because it denies the true nature of the personality. It denies our fear and our negative feelings.

We put our best into the creation of this mask, but it doesn't work. The mask never succeeds in producing the internal feeling of safety for which we strive. In fact, it produces the internal feeling of an impostor because we are trying to prove we are good, and we aren't good all the time. We feel like fakes, and we become more afraid. So we try harder. We use the best in us to prove that we are good (again, according to internalized parental voices). This produces more fear, especially because we can't keep it up all the time, more feeling of fakery, more fear, in a building cycle.

The intention of the mask is to protect us from an assumed hostile world by proving that we are good. The intention of the mask is pretense and denial. It denies that its purpose is to cover up pain and anger, because it denies that pain and anger exist within the personality. The mask's intent is to protect the self by not taking responsibility for any negative actions, thoughts, or deeds.

From the perspective of our mask, pain and anger exist only outside the personality. We don't take any responsibility. Anything negative that happens must be somebody else's fault. We blame them. That means it must be somebody else that is angry or in pain.

The only way to maintain this masquerade is to always try to prove that we are the good ones. Inside, we resent the constant pressure we place on ourselves to be good. We try to go by the rules. Or if we don't, we try to prove we are right and they are wrong.

We resent having to live according to somebody else's rules. It's a lot of work. We just want to do what we feel like doing. We get tired, we get angry, we don't care, we blurt out negative complaints and accusations. We hurt people. The energy that we have held in with the mask twists, pushes, leaks, and strikes out at others. And of course we deny that as well, since our intent is to maintain security by proving we are the good ones.

Somewhere inside, we enjoy lashing out. Letting out the energy is a relief, even if it isn't clear and straight, even if we are not acting responsibly when we do it. There is a part of us that enjoys dumping our negativity on someone else. This is called negative pleasure. Its origin is in the lower self.

Negative Pleasure and the Lower Self

I'm sure you can remember feeling the pleasure in some negative action you have done. Any energy movement, negative or positive, is pleasurable. These actions carry pleasure because they are releases of energy that has been stored up inside. If you experience pain when the energy first begins to move, it will always soon be followed by pleasure, because as you release the pain, you also release the creative force, which is always experienced as pleasure.

Negative pleasure originates in our lower self. Our lower self is the part of us that has forgotten who we are. It is the part of our psyche that believes in a separated, negative world and acts accordingly. The lower self is not in denial of negativity. It enjoys it. It has the intention to have negative pleasure. Since the lower self is not in denial of negativity as the mask is, it is more honest than the mask self. The lower self is truthful about its negative intent. It doesn't pretend to be nice. It is not nice. It puts its self first and makes no bones about it. It says, "I care about me, not you." It cannot care both about itself and about another because of its world of separation. It enjoys negative pleasure and wants more of it. It knows about the pain within the personality, and it has no intention whatsoever of feeling that pain.

The intention of the lower self is to maintain separation and to do anything it wants to do, and to not feel pain.

The Higher Self

Of course, during the maturation process, not all our psyche is separated from the core. Part of us is clear and loving without any struggle. It is directly connected to our individual divinity within. It is full of wisdom, love, and courage. It has connection to great creative power. It is the facilitator of all the good that has been created in our lives. It is the part of us that has not forgotten who we are.

Wherever there is peace, joy, and fulfillment in your life, that is where your higher self has expressed itself through the creative principle. If you wonder what is meant by "who you really are" or your "true self," look to these areas of your life. They are an expression of your true self.

Never take a negative area of your life to be an expression of your true self. Negative areas of your life are expressions of who you are not. They are examples of how you have blocked the expression of your true self.

The intention of the higher self is for truth, communion, respect, individuality, clear self-awareness, and union with the creator.

The Importance of Intention

The major difference between the higher self, the lower self, and the mask self is found in the foundation of underlying intent upon which each is based, and in the quality of energy present in any interaction that results from the underlying intent.

What is so confusing about a lot of human interactions is that they are different according to the intent behind them. The words that we speak can come from any of the three places of intent—our higher self, lower self, or mask self. The words themselves may say one thing but mean another. The higher self means it when it says, "We are friends." The mask self means, "We are friends as long as I am the good one, and you must never challenge the illusion that I am the good one." The lower self says, "We are friends only to the degree I allow. After that, watch out! Don't tread too closely because I will use you to get what I want and to avoid my pain. If you get too close to me or my pain, or try to stop me from getting what I want, I will get rid of you." (In this case, *get rid of* means anything that it takes to stop the person. It might mean simply not talking to them or overpowering them in an argument or a power play, or it may go as far as getting rid of them physically.)

Defending or Denying Your Original Wound Creates More Pain

The more our actions that arise out of the core are distorted by the mask, the more we must justify our actions by blame. The more we deny the existence of our lower self, the more we de-power ourselves. Denial holds back the power of the creative source within us. This creates a greater and greater cycle of pain and helplessness. The larger this vicious cycle of pain and helplessness gets, the greater the original pain or wound appears to be. It becomes covered with illusory pain of such imagined intensity that we become unconsciously terrified of it and will stop at nothing to defend ourselves against experiencing it. In our imagination, it becomes complete torture and annihilation. The more we justify staying away from it and not healing it, the more completely the original wound is buried and is not at all what we think it to be.

From my experience as a healer and teacher, I have concluded that we create much more pain and illness in our lives and bodies by avoiding the original wound through our habitual defense patterns than the original wound created in the first place.

Our Habitual Defense System

In my experience, the way we constantly distort our energy field into our habitual defense system causes more pain and illness in ourselves than any other cause.

When I describe the human energy field later in the book, we will see how this avoidance creates dysfunction in our fields, which then creates disease in our bodies. Our habitual defense patterns can be seen in our energy fields as an energetic defense system. Our energetic defense system is our habitual pattern of distortion in our fields, to which we retreat over and over again. It correlates with the mask self.

The more we succeed in holding the pain and anger down inside through this defense system, the more our positive feelings are also held down inside. We get dull. Life doesn't go the way we expected—it gets mundane and boring. Eros dies. We get caught in habitual vicious cycles and are unable to create what we long for in life. This also takes a toll on our body. We begin to lose faith in life.

Through our habitual process of walling out the pain, we also habitually wall out our deeper core. We have forgotten what it feels like. We have forgotten our essence. We have forgotten who we are. We have lost contact with our essential energies with which we create our lives. It is as if we expect ourselves to create our lives the way we want them to be, when we don't know who the "we" is that is wanting.

The Road Back to the Original Wound

The only way to remember who we are, to create our lives the way we want them, to create health and to feel safe, is to connect fully once again with our core. There is only one way to do this. We find and observe our images and release the frozen psychic time conglomerates associated with them, so that we can go to the source of all images, our original wound. We must uncover our original wound. To do this means going through our defense system and clearing the negative feelings and all the layers of imagined pain around the original wound. Once we reach our original wound, all of life is different, and we heal ourselves and our life. This is the transformation process.

There are many techniques to find the original wound. Regression using autosuggestion and using body posturing are two. Both of these techniques are taught in the classes during the training program at the Barbara Brennan School of Healing. By using these techniques, we are able to help students go to their original wounds together.

In one particular group exercise, the students let go of their defenses by taking the body posture that expresses what they think their wound is. To find the posture of their wound, they need only to bring their attention to the major emotional issues and pain they have now in their life and let their body react to them. This technique works because the pain is connected by like energy in the psychic frozen time conglomerate.

By intensifying their bodies' reaction and by keeping their attention focused inward, the students' pain is brought out and becomes progressively clearer. The result is always a roomful of very vulnerable people in pain. Their twisted and distorted postures clearly show their pain. Sometimes people stand on one leg with the other leg and both arms twisted up in front. Many have their heads bowed, while others lie on the floor curled up like small children.

In this exercise it becomes clear that the pain around present life issues is indeed the same as the pain experienced earlier in life. As the present pain is brought out, it also releases the older pain. To do this, the students

continue posturing, while maintaining an intent to constantly focus inward and backward in time to the original wound.

They automatically regress, layer by layer, through the pain associated with the image around the wound. Even though this pain is strong and frightening, it is basically illusory because it is based on the illusion held in the image. To explain what I mean by illusory pain, let us look back at our example of ten-year-old Joe, who is devastated when his mother goes away for a week's vacation. That is the way he feels, but it is not that situation that really devastates him.

By continuing to traverse through the illusory pain that is coagulated around their original wound, the students eventually go into their original wound. As they sink closer to the original wound, they are surprised that their pain decreases.

Once they are in their original wound, we ask them to keep its posture while moving close to another person, in order to make contact with another wounded human being. This always brings a reverence into the room. Everyone is wounded. Everyone is equal. The contact with each other creates a great deal of love in the room.

After the exercise is complete and it is time for sharing, interesting discoveries come forth. Students are usually surprised to see that their wound is not at all what they thought. They find that most of their pain comes not from the original wound itself but from defending the original wound. Very early on in their lives, they began defending against what they expected life to bring them according to their early image conclusion. Every time they defended against that image conclusion, they added more energy to their psychic frozen time conglomerate. Each time this was done, the illusion of the pain got bigger until they lost track of what the pain really was. All that was left was some unknown terrifying pain that was unbearable.

The most profound part of this exercise, according to the students, is to see how much time and energy we waste throughout our lives in defending our original wound. The deepest pain is self-betrayal. By doing this exercise, students can feel their very early decision to not act upon the truth of who they are, not to acknowledge and live by who they are. They can see that they made that decision time and time again throughout their lives, until it became an unconscious habit. That is a regular part of their defense system.

This experience gives them great freedom and an entirely different outlook on life. Life becomes a constant challenge to live by the truth and not betray the self. The greatest challenge in life is to stay connected to and express the core of our being, no matter what circumstances we find ourselves in.

This pain is not just in a few people—it exists in all of humanity to varying degrees. Some people are more aware of their pain than others.

The Human Condition: Living in Dualism

Each day we express our core to a certain degree. The degree of our expression is directly proportional to how firmly and clearly we are connected to and allow our core essence to come forth. The areas of our lives that flow smoothly, without problems, and satisfy us fully are those where we are directly connected to our core. Energies that come uninhibited directly from the core create great human works and great human lives. Energies that come uninhibited directly from the core create great health. They are the expression of our higher selves, the part of us with which we are born and that never loses its connection to the core.

We are usually quite shy about this part of us. Most of the time we do not show how much we care, how much we love, and how much we long for in life. We cover it, we label it, we squelch it to a "reasonable" degree of expression (according to internalized parental voices) and settle for less. This is "appropriate" behavior, or so we believe.

Sometimes when we are not vigilant we let go, and out comes the creative force! A sudden act of kindness or expression of love or friendship that happens before we think about it is an expression of this core essence. A moment of close connection is made, and love is released.

Then, not being able to tolerate the light and love, we become shy and pull away. It takes only a few seconds for us to catch ourselves in embarrassment and close off a bit. A sudden fear emerges seemingly from nowhere that says "Oh, maybe I did the wrong thing." That is the parental voice speaking, replacing the core. Under it lies the defense. It really means, "If you don't stop this energy flow, you will probably feel everything, including the pain that I am burying for you." So we stop the flow of our life-force, we contain it and dampen it. We bring ourselves back to the "normal" level of "safety" where we won't rock any boats—least of all our own.

This is the human condition. We live in the duality of choice, no matter what our life circumstances. Each moment we choose to say yes to a balanced, powerful, and safe undefendedness that brings about our full experience of life, or we choose to say no. In our no, we defend against true balanced life experience and block out our aliveness.

Most of us choose to kill some of our aliveness most of the time. Why? Because unconsciously, we know that to let the life-force flow would knock loose the old pain, and we are afraid of it. We don't know how to handle it. So we retreat from the defense and go back to the old, seemingly adequate mask definitions of who we are. The internalized parental voices of the mask get stronger, and we continue to retreat: "Who did you think you were anyway? God?" "Do you really think you can change things?" "Come on, be realistic! People don't change. Settle for what you have." "You're greedy." "You never appreciate what you have." Or "If your parents had only treated you better . . ." "If your husband hadn't done that . . ." "If only you would have been born more beautiful . . ." And so on! There are a million ways the mask can speak to keep you in your place. To a certain extent, it keeps you from feeling your pain. But in the long run, it creates more pain and eventually disease.

Illness comes from shrouding and disconnecting a part of ourselves from the core of our being. As we disconnect, we forget who we really are and live our lives according to our forgetting—that is, according to our mask, our lower self, and our defense system. Healing is remembering who we truly are. It is reconnecting to our core in the areas of our psyche where we have disconnected from it, and living accordingly.

To the exact degree we suppress our positive energies, we also suppress our creativity and our ability to maintain a healthful life or to heal ourselves.

It is the work of each of us to reconnect to our core and to heal ourselves.

The Spiritual Purpose of the Original Wound

We might ask, what is the cause or purpose of the original wound? The original wound is created by the fading of the connection between the newborn and its deeper spiritual wisdom within its core. Why, from the evolutionary perspective of humankind, would this take place? The answer lies in the difference between the core connection in early life and the connection gained through life experience. The early connection to the core is unconscious. The connections to the core that are made during the process of living are conscious. Adults' connection to their core, which is brought about through life experience, creates conscious awareness of their inner divinity. Adults become aware that they are a spark of divine light in the universe. They are localized divinity. This evolutionary process creates more conscious awareness in our species. We are finding out that we are co-creators of the universe. The purpose of incarnation is the creation of awareness of self as divine co-creator of the universe.

Following Our Longing Leads to Our Life Task

Each of us longs to be, to understand, and to express ourselves. This longing is the inner light that leads us along our evolutionary path. Taken to the personal level, this means that each of us is born with a life task to reconnect to the core of our being. In order to do this, we must remove the blocks between our conscious awareness and our core. This is called our personal life task. As we accomplish this, the release of our creative energies brings forth gifts from the core that we first receive and then share with the world. The gifts we give to the world bring about the accomplishment of our life task in the world. This world task unfolds only as we release our creative energies from our core. Thus we can accomplish what we wish to do in the world only by attending to our personal transformation process.

We Are All Wounded Healers

We are all wounded healers. We are all very reluctant to become *undefended*, to become unveiled, and to show what we have inside, whether it is positive or negative. We hesitate to show the pain or the wound that we each carry in our own way. We hide it in shame. We think we are the only ones, or that our pain is more despicable than anyone else's. It is just very difficult for us, unless we feel very safe. This is our human condition. It will take time for all of us to come out. And it will take a lot of love. Let's all give each other plenty of space, time, and loving affirmation. It is through this wound that we are all learning how to love. This internal wound we all carry is our greatest teacher. Let us recognize who we truly are inside. We are our beautiful core essence, despite the layers of pain and anger shrouding us. We are each individually unique, and it is great that that is the way it is. Let us become wounded healers, helping each other to share the truth of our inner being.

We can find ourselves within a benign, abundant, life-supporting universe that is holy. We are carried in the arms of the universe. We are surrounded by a universal health field that supports and sustains life. We can reach out and connect to it. We can be, and indeed are always, nourished by it. We are of it, and it is of us. The divine mystery of life is within us, and it is all around us.

You Are Your Healer

It is you and only you who will heal yourself. You are completely capable of that. The process of healing a personal illness is, in fact, an act of personal empowerment. It is a personal journey, a rite of passage, designed by yourself as one of the greatest learning tools you will ever encounter. Your healing journey will, of course, include a consideration and use of all the best tools modern medicine can offer you, as well as the best tools holistic healing can offer you.

From a deeper perspective, illness is caused by unfulfilled longing. The deeper the illness, the deeper the longing. It is a message that somehow, somewhere, you have forgotten who you are and what your purpose is. You have forgotten and disconnected from the purpose of your creative energy from your core. Your illness is the symptom: The disease represents your unfulfilled longing. So above all else, use your illness to set yourself free to do what you have always wanted to do, to be who you have always wanted to be, to manifest and express who you already are from your deepest, broadest, and highest reality.

If indeed you have discovered yourself to be ill, prepare yourself for change, expect your deepest longing to surface and to be brought to fruition. Prepare yourself to finally stop running and turn and face the tiger within you, whatever that means to you in a very personal way. I suggest the best place to start to find the meaning of your illness is to ask yourself:

"What is it that I have longed for and not yet succeeded in creating in my life?"

I suggest that you will eventually find a direct link between this unfulfilled longing and your illness.

It is within this fundamental picture of health and healing that you can regain your health. I speak here not just of the health of your physical body, because that is actually secondary, but of the health of the spirit, the health of the soul. It is within this framework or metaphor of reality that all life and health issues can be dealt with. For life in the physical is to be lived in love, to develop our higher qualities, and to become one with the divine. No matter what the circumstances of your life right now, that is what life is about. No matter what the pain, the problem, or the disease, it is a teacher. It is a teacher of love and a teacher that reminds you that you are divine. It is the process of your *Light Emerging*.

T W O

The Four Dimensions of Your Creative Energies

Understanding the nature of your creative energies, what they do, and how they function helps release your creative energies for health, healing, or creating something new in your life. It is also important to understand the relationship between your creative energies and the natural ebb and flow of the universal creative process within you. The life energy fields are the vehicle for the creative process. It is through life energy fields that your life situations, events, and experiences, as well as your material world, are created.

The creative forces have several dimensions. Our language is too limited to adequately describe the differences in these dimensions, which are experienced personally as you go through the creative process. For lack of better ones, I use the terms *energy* and *dimension*, in a nonscientific way, as I move through these explanations. As more individuals become consciously aware of these creative experiences, I'm sure that we will add the words we need to communicate better about them.

From my perspective, there are at least four dimensions within each human being. Each of these levels can be perceived with HSP and can be directly worked on for healing by a trained healer. Figure 2–1 shows these four dimensions of our humanness; the physical level, the auric level, the haric level, and the core star level.

The first dimension is the familiar *physical world*. Our physical world is held intact by underlying worlds of energy and consciousness.

Directly under the physical world is the dimension of the universal or life energy fields in which the *aura* or *human energy field* exists. This level is the energetic framework or grid structure upon which the physical world rests. Everything that is created in the physical world must first exist or be created in the world of life energy. Every form that exists must first be formed in the structured levels of the energy fields. This dimension also carries the energies of our personality. Every feeling that we have exists in the level of the life energy fields. The physical body expresses the fluid levels of the field in such things as smiles of love, or frowns of disapproval, the way we walk, sit, and stand.

Beneath the human energy field lies the *haric level*, in which we hold our intentions. Our intentions have a tremendous importance in the creative process. When we have unconscious, mixed, or opposing intentions, we fight against ourselves and disrupt the creative process. When we learn to align our intentions not only within ourselves but with the immediate group of people with whom we work, then align the intentions of our immediate group with the larger group that serves it, and so on, we tap into tremendous creative abilities.

Beneath the haric level is the dimension of the central core of our being, or what I call the level of the *core star*. This is the level of our inner source, or the localized divinity within us. It is from this inner source that all creativity from within arises.

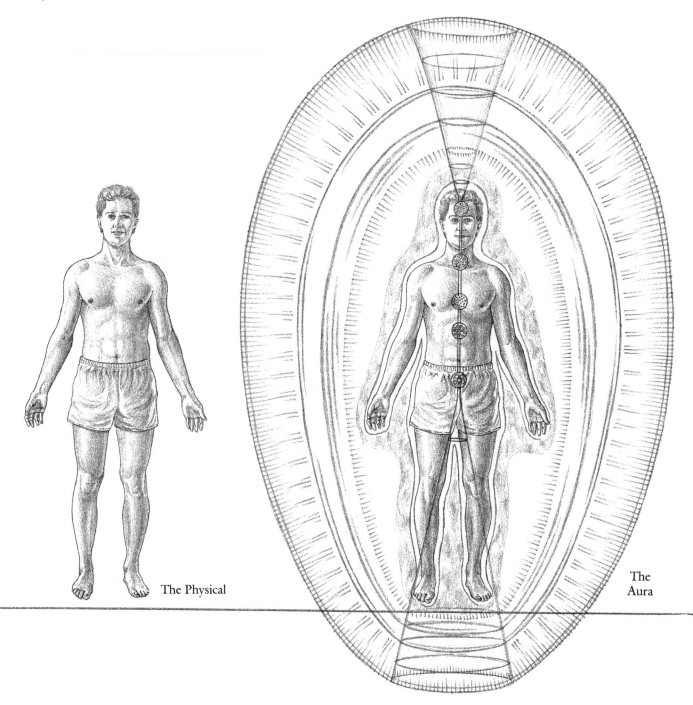

The Physical

The Aura

Figure 2–1 Four Dimensions of Humankind

The full natural creative process requires the emergence of energies and consciousness from the core star up through all these four dimensions. Permanent change in any one dimension requires a change in its foundation, which lies in the dimension beneath it. Therefore, from the perspective of healing, if we wish to change our bodies or any part of them, such as an organ, from an unhealthy state into a healthy one, we must work with the underlying energies that are the foundation for our bodies. We must work with each of the four dimensions. In order to do this work, we will first explore each of the four dimensions. We begin with the auric level, the human energy field.

This life energy field has been explored, investigated, and utilized for different purposes throughout history. This exploration began long before we learned the scientific method and has continued ever since.

Figure 2–2 lists historical references to a universal energy field that go back as far as 5,000 B.C. Figure 2–3 is a list of twentieth-century observers of the human

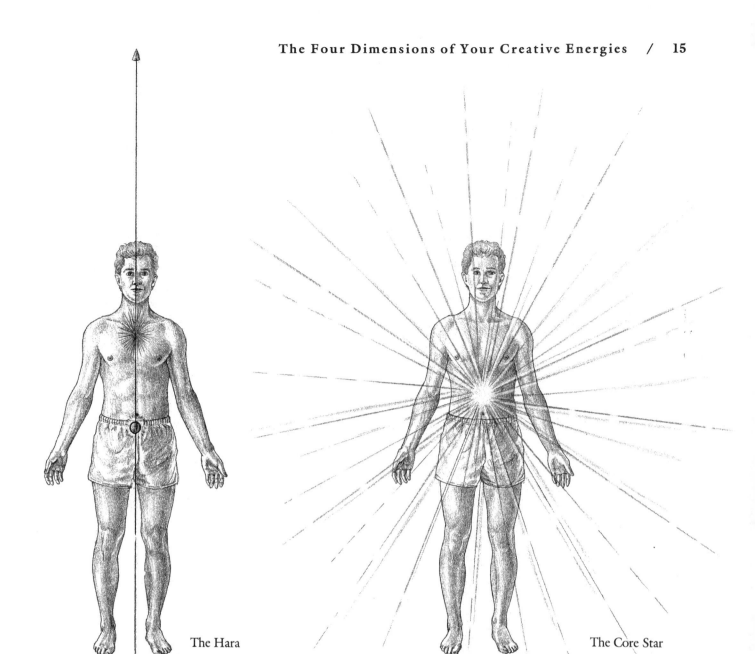

The Hara

The Core Star

fields." On the other hand, the terms *aura* and *human energy field* are used by healers to describe these life energy fields. It is important to make a distinction here because bioenergy fields have been measured in laboratories, while the aura or human energy fields are known through personal and clinical observations done by people using Higher Sense Perception. In the first case, measured information is limited by the state of the instrumentation, while in the second, information is limited by the clarity and consistency of the HSP observer. From my perspective, bioenergy field measurements correlate strongly with HSP observations. There are a few experiments that clearly correlate the two. They will also be discussed here, but first the scientific perspective.

energy field, the names they have used to refer to the life energy field, qualities that they have attributed to it, and how they used it.

Present-day scientists call the measurable energy fields associated with biological systems "bioenergy

The Physical World and Its Bioenergy Field

The energy fields associated with the human body have been measured by devices like the electroencephalograph (EEG), electrocardiograph (EKG), and the superconducting quantum interference device (or SQUID, a very highly sensitive magnetometer). Many studies have shown that a dysfunction or abnormality in the bioenergy field will leave room for infection in the body. For example, Dr. Harold Burr at Yale found that by measuring the energy field (which he called the life field) of a seed, he could tell how strong the plant would be. He found that a weakness in the life field of a living creature would predate disease.

Other researchers like Dr. Robert Becker, an orthopedic surgeon in New York, have measured patterns of direct currents of electricity that flow over and through the body. The bioenergy field is directly related to the functioning of the physical body. Dr. Becker showed that the pattern shapes and strengths of the body's complex electrical field change with physiological and psychological changes.

Dr. Hiroshi Motoyama of Tokyo, founder of the International Association for Religion and Parapsychology, has electrically measured the state of acupuncture meridians. He uses the results to diagnose for acupuncture treatment. Dr. Victor Inyushin of Kazakhstan University is one of the many scientists there who have measured the energy field with light-sensitive devices for many years. He is able to show the state of

FIGURE 2–2   HISTORICAL REFERENCES TO A UNIVERSAL ENERGY FIELD

Time	Place/Person	Name of Energy	Properties Attributed to It
5,000 B.C.	India	prana	The basic source of all life
3,000 B.C.	China	ch'i	Present in all matter
		yin and yang	Composed of 2 polar forces; balance of 2 polar forces = health
500 B.C.	Greece: Pythagoras	vital energy	Perceived as a luminous body that could produce cures
1500s	Europe: Paracelsus	illiaster	Vital force and vital matter; healing; spiritual work
1600s	Gottfried Wilhelm von Leibnitz	monads	Centers of force containing their own wellspring of motion
1700s	Franz Anton Mesmer	magnetic fluid	Could charge animate and inanimate objects; hypnosis; influence at a distance
1800s	Wilhelm von Reichenbach	odic force	Comparison to electromagnetic field

FIGURE 2–3 TWENTIETH-CENTURY OBSERVERS OF THE HUMAN ENERGY FIELD

Date	Person	Observed	Properties Found
1911	Walter Kilner	aura human atmosphere	Used colored screens and filters to see 3 layers of the aura; correlated auric configuration to disease
1940	George De La Warr	emanations	Developed radionics instruments to detect radiation from living tissues; used it for diagnosis and healing from a distance
1930–50	Wilhelm Reich	orgone	Developed a mode of psychotherapy utilizing the orgone energy in the human body; studied energy in nature and built instruments to detect and accumulate orgone
1930–60	Harold Burr and F.S.C. Northrup	life field (LF)	LF directs organization of an organism; developed idea of circadian rhythms
1950s	L.J. Ravitz	thought field (TF)	TF interfered with LF to produce psychosomatic symptoms
1970–89	Robert Becker	electromagnetic field	Measured direct current control systems on the human body; correlated results with health and disease; developed methods to enhance bone growth with electrical current
1970–80s	John Pierrakos, Richard Dobrin, and Barbara Brennan	HEF	Correlated clinical energy field observations with emotional response; low-light-level darkroom measurements correlated to human presence
1970s	David Frost, Barbara Brennan, and Karen Gestla	HEF	Laser bending with HEF
1970–90	Hiroshi Motoyama	ch'i	Electrically measured the acupuncture meridians; used for treatment and diagnosis of disease
1970–90	Victor Inyushin	bioplasma	HEF has a bioplasma composed of free ions; fifth state of matter; balance of positive and negative ions = health
1970–90	Valerie Hunt	biofield	Electronically measured the frequency and location of the biofield on human subjects; correlated results with aura readers
1960–90	Andria Puharich	life-enhancing field	Measured life-enhancing alternating magnetic fields (8 Hz) from healers' hands; found that higher or lower frequencies are detrimental to life
1980–90	Robert Beck	Schumann waves	Correlated healers' magnetic pulses with pulsations of the earth's magnetic field, the Schumann waves
1980–90	John Zimmerman	brain waves	Showed that healers' brains go into right/left synchronization in alpha, as do patients'

acupuncture points through coronal discharge photography. This photography uses a very high frequency, high voltage, and low current sent through the subject. The high frequency does not harm the subject because the current is low and high frequencies only travel over the skin of the subject.

There have been a few experiments to show the correlations between the measured "biofield" and the perceived "human energy field." The best that I know of are those done by Dr. Valerie Hunt at UCLA and by Dr. Andria Puharich in his private laboratory. Dr. Hunt's experimental results show direct correlations between the frequency and wave patterns of alternating electrical currents measured on the body surface and specific colors perceived by an "aura" reader. Dr. Hunt has performed the same measurements with twelve different "aura" readers using HSP. And in each case, for each color read she found a specific wave-form and frequency pattern. Dr. Puharich was able to consistently measure an 8 Hz (eight cycles per second) magnetic pulse coming from the hands of healers. He found that healers who produce a more intense signal have a greater effect of healing.

Dr. Robert Beck, a nuclear physicist, traveled the world measuring the brain waves of healers. He found that all healers exhibit the same brain-wave pattern of 7.8–8 Hz during the times they are giving healings, no matter what their customs or how opposed to each other their customs were. Beck tested charismatic Christian faith healers, Hawaiian kahunas, practitioners of wicca, santeria, radesthesia, and radionics, as well as seers, ESP readers, and psychics. They all tested the same.

He then asked to what drummer they were marching. And indeed, why. He found the answer in the fluctuations of the earth's magnetic field. It fluctuates between 7.8 and 8 Hz. These fluctuations are called Schumann waves. Upon further investigation, he found that during healing moments, the healer's brain waves became both frequency- and phase-synchronized with the Schumann waves. That means the healer's brain waves pulse not only at the same frequency but also at the same time as the earth's Schumann waves. It could be assumed that healers are able to take energy from the magnetic field of the earth for the healing of patients. This process is called field coupling.

Dr. John Zimmerman, founder and president of the Bio-Electro-Magnetics Institute of Reno, Nevada, has extensively studied the literature of many works on field coupling and correlated it with healers' experiences. It is clear that what healers call grounding into the earth is the action of linking up with the magnetic field of the earth, both in frequency and in phase. He has found that once healers have linked up with the Schumann waves, the right and left hemispheres of their brain become balanced with each other and show a 7.8–8 Hz alpha rhythm. After they link with the patient for some time of laying on of hands healing, it has been shown that patients' brain waves also go into alpha and are phase-synchronized with the healers', as well as right-left balanced. The healer has, in effect, linked the client with the earth's magnetic field pulses and has thereby tapped into a tremendous energy source for healing.

The Human Energy Field: The Vehicle That Carries Your Energy

As a healer and sensitive using Higher Sense Perception, I have observed the energy field around people for many years. After many studies of the energy fields of many plants, animals, and humans, I have concluded that the human energy field provides an energy matrix structure upon which cells grow. What I mean is that the energy field exists before the physical body.

A phenomenon that supports this idea is the phantom limb effect. The phantom limb effect occurs when people who have amputated limbs still continue to feel them. The residual feelings are usually explained by irritation of the nerve endings that have been cut. However, the phantom limb is still visible with HSP in the auric field of the patient. Since feelings are carried in the auric field, it makes sense to the HSP observer.

In one case, a friend of mine, Dr. John Pierrakos, founder and director of the Core Energetics Institute in New York City and author of the book *Core Energetics*, was working with a patient who was suffering from the phantom limb effect. The woman kept feeling that her missing leg was tied up under her so that she sat on it each time she sat down. Dr. Pierrakos could see the auric field of the limb bent up into the same position she felt it to be. He worked with her field to straighten the energy-leg so that it was in normal walking position. This relieved her symptoms. Later, he checked with the surgeon who had removed the leg. It turned out that the surgeon had tied the leg in that position for surgery. I believe this client was feeling her energy field.

This means that the basic energetic structure for the limb was still there. Thus, the field exists prior to the physical body. This is a fundamental difference from many scientific researchers. They assume that the field emanates from the body, rather than that the body is created by the field. If the field is indeed proven to exist before the physical, this implies that someday we may regenerate limbs as salamanders do.

Coronal discharge photography offers further evidence to support my hypothesis that the field is primary rather than the physical. It is called the phantom leaf effect. If you cut part of a leaf off just before taking a picture of it in this way, the whole leaf (including the missing piece) appears on the photographic plate in a brilliant display of color and light. Since the picture of the entire leaf appears, it is concluded that the picture of the missing piece of the leaf is caused by the energy field, which remains intact even though the physical aspect is missing. Thus the energy field could not arise from the physical; rather, the physical arises from the energetic.

This conclusion makes the energy field much more important to health and the growth process than was previously suspected. Since the physical body arises out of the energy field, an imbalance or distortion in this field will eventually cause a disease in the physical body that it governs. Therefore, healing distortions in the field will bring about healing in the physical body. Healing is a matter of learning how to heal the field by restructuring, balancing, and charging it.

Furthermore, as I showed in *Hands of Light,* energy events within the auric field are primary to and always precede a physical event. They precipitate it. That means that any illness will show in the field before it shows in the physical body and can therefore be healed in the field before it is precipitated into the physical body.

The auric field is a quantum leap deeper into our personality than is our physical body. It is at this level of our being that our psychological processes take place. The aura is the vehicle for all psychosomatic reactions. From the viewpoint of a healer, all disease is psychosomatic. A balanced functioning of our auric field is necessary to maintain our health.

Yet the auric field is not the source of the event. It is the vehicle through which the creative consciousness from the core reaches the physical.

All of the healing that I do and teach is based on a knowledge of the structure and function of the human energy field and the configurations that lie beneath it on deeper dimensions. In *Hands of Light,* I described the human energy field thoroughly: its anatomy and physiology, and its place in the disease and healing process. I also taught healing methods based upon it. I will briefly describe the human energy field again here and expand on areas briefly mentioned in that book.

Seven Levels of the Human Energy Field

The human energy field is composed of seven levels. (See Figure 2–4.) Many people have the erroneous idea that this field is like the layers of an onion. It is not. Each level penetrates through the body and extends outward from the skin. Each successive level is of a "higher frequency" or a "higher octave." Each extends out from the skin several inches farther than the one within it of lower frequency. The odd-numbered levels are structured fields of standing, scintillating light beams. The first, third, fifth, and seventh levels of this field are structured in a specific form. The even-numbered levels—the second, fourth, and sixth—are filled with formless substance/energy. The second level is like gaseous substance, the fourth is fluidlike, and the sixth is like the diffuse light around a candle flame. It is the unstructured level of the energy field that has been related to plasma and dubbed bioplasma. Remember, these are not scientific terms we use here because experimentation has not yet proven what it is. But for lack of a better term, we shall use the word *bioplasma.* The bioplasma in all three of the unstructured levels is composed of various colors, apparent density, and intensity. This bioplasma flows along the lines of the structured levels. It correlates directly with our emotions.

The combination of a standing light grid with bioplasma flowing through it holds the physical body together in its form, nurtures it with life energy, and serves as a communication and integration system that keeps the body functioning as a single organism. All of these levels of the human energy field act holographically to influence each other.

These levels, or energy bodies as many people call them, cannot be considered less real than our physical body. If all of your energy bodies are strong, charged, and healthy, you will have a full life in all areas of human experience. If your energy field is weak at any level, you will have difficulty having experiences that are associated with that level, and your life experience will be limited. The more levels or bodies that you have developed, the fuller and broader your life experience will be.

We have the tendency to assume that all life experience is the same as it is in the physical dimension. It is not. Rather, life exists on many vibrational levels. Each level is different according to the makeup of energy-consciousness in that level. This gives us a wide variety of life experience from which to learn. The seven levels of the auric field correspond to seven different levels of life experience. Each level is different in vibrational frequency range, intensity, and composition of bioplasma. Each therefore responds to stimuli according to its makeup.

It reminds me of how exciting it was, in applied mathematics, to derive equations of fluid motion under different conditions. I was surprised to see that the same equations worked for air in fluid motion as for water. The difference was that certain factors in the equations were more influential than others as the medium changed. The same was true for the equations that describe the movement of air close to the surface of the earth and the movement of air higher up. Air movement close to the ground is more influenced by the friction of the trees and shrubs than the air mass above it. As you move up away from the ground, it is necessary to decrease the friction factor in the equation that describes air movement. Results show a shift in direction of air flow. This shift of direction is called the wind shear. I'm sure you have noticed that clouds at one level usually move in a different direction from the clouds at a higher level. Micrometeorology describes short-distance movements of air in small local conditions that were very different from the macro-movements of air across the oceans, where the motion of the earth comes into play through the Coriolis force. Yet the same equations function for all. Different parts of the equations become more influential with different conditions.

I applied the same ideas and general principles when trying to make sense of auric field interactions. The energy-consciousness of the auric field flows differently and is influenced by different factors on different levels of the field. That is, the composition of the energy-consciousness of each of the field levels is unique, different from all the other levels. Each responds differently to different factors. Another way to surmise what is going on is to say that the bioplasma of each level of the field probably has its own frequency range, intensity of charge, and composition. So it most naturally responds to stimuli accordingly.

Another type of study, used in astrological as well as earth observations, influenced the way I looked at the auric field. It is common practice for science to build instruments that filter out extraneous wavelengths and then to make observations within only a narrow wavelength band. Observing the sun in this way yields pictures of the solar atmosphere at different heights. That is how we get pictures of sunspots, or of solar flares, which look very different from the energy deeper within the sun or in its outer layer, the corona. The same principles can be very useful in auric field observations. By changing one's HSP to different auric vibrational levels, different levels of the auric field become more clearly defined. Once these levels are clearly defined, it is easy to work directly with them.

The following description of the configuration of the levels of the auric field, and the life experience associated with each, arises from my observation, study, and experience during twenty years of healing and thirteen years of teaching. Figure 2–4 shows the seven levels of the auric or human energy field.

First Level of the Human Energy Field

Within this level you feel all physical sensations, painful and pleasurable. There are direct correlates between the energy flow, field pulsation, and configuration in the first level of your field and what you sense in your physical body. Wherever there is pain in your body, there is a direct correlate of dysfunction within the first level of the auric field.

Robert Becker, M.D., performed experiments that showed that a local anesthetic given, say, to make your finger numb so that you can have stitches, stops the stream of subatomic particles flowing along the sensor nerves of the finger. When the energy flow resumes, you are then able to feel again. I have observed the same phenomenon in the auric field. Numbness correlates to no flow of energy along the lines of the first level of the field. When a healer works to start a flow of energy there, the feeling sensation returns.

The first level of the field tends to be fine, thin, and of a light aqua-blue color for quiet, sensitive people. It is thick, coarse, and a darker blue-gray for strong, robust people. The more you connect to your body, take care of it, and exercise, the stronger and more developed the first level of the field will be. Athletes and dancers tend to have a very highly developed first layer. It has more lines of energy, they are thicker, more elastic, more charged, and bright blue.

If your first level is strong, you will have a very strong, healthy physical body and enjoy all the pleasurable physical sensations that go with it. This includes the pleasure of feeling your body, the feelings of vitality, of physical activity, physical contact, sex, and sleeping. It includes the pleasures of tasting, smelling,

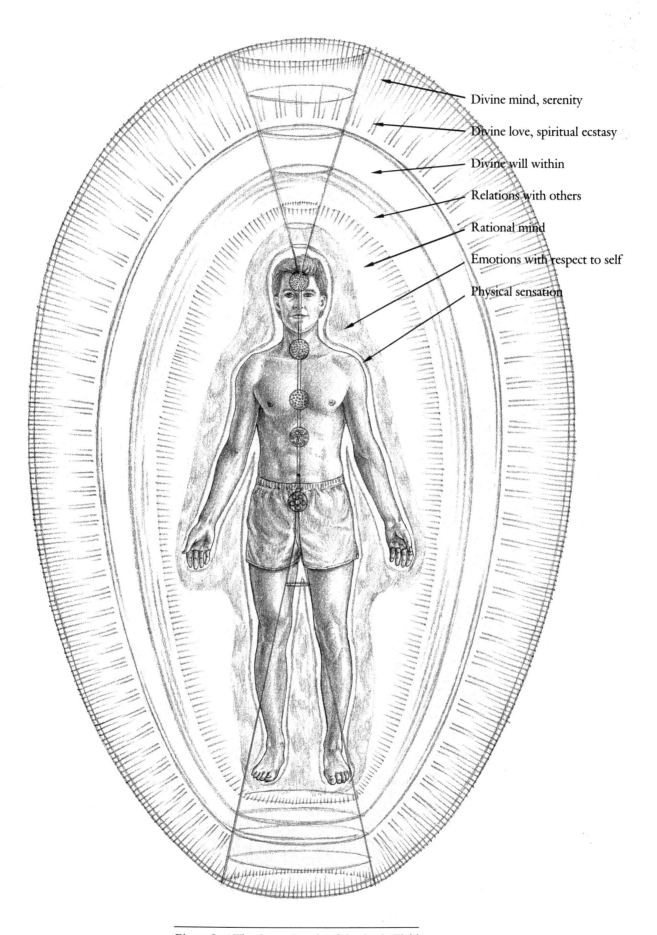

Divine mind, serenity

Divine love, spiritual ecstasy

Divine will within

Relations with others

Rational mind

Emotions with respect to self

Physical sensation

Figure 2–4 The Seven Levels of the Auric Field

listening, and seeing. This means you will most likely continue to use all the functions of your first level, thereby keeping it charged and healthy. Using it will tend to recharge it.

On the other hand, if you don't take care of your body, your first level will also become weak, the lines broken, tangled, or undercharged. They become thinner and sparser in the parts of your body that are the least cared for.

If your first level is weak, you will experience your physical body as weak and will not like to connect with all of the pleasures of sensation associated with it. You will then tend to keep it weak from lack of use. Most likely you will be connected to some of the lines of energy but not to all of them. In fact, some won't be experienced as pleasure at all. Rather, you will experience them as something you have to put up with. For example, you may hate physical activity of any kind. You may love to eat, but not to be touched. You might like to listen to music, but not to have to eat to keep your body going.

Second Level of the Human Energy Field

The second level is associated with your feelings or emotions about yourself. Every energy movement there correlates to a feeling you are having about yourself. Bright colors of cloudlike energy are associated with positive feelings about yourself. Darker, dirtier shades are associated with negative feelings about yourself. All colors can be found in this level. These clouds of energy flow along the structured lines of the first field level.

If you allow the feelings about yourself to flow, whether they are negative or positive, the aura keeps itself balanced. And the negative feelings and the negative energies associated with your feelings are released and transformed. If you stop yourself from having emotions about yourself, you stop the flow of energy in the second level that corresponds to those emotions. And your second level becomes stagnant, eventually creating undercharged, dark, dirty clouds of various colors related to the inexperienced feelings toward yourself.

Wilhelm Reich, M.D., called bioenergy orgone energy. He named the undercharged energy found in the field on the unstructured levels DOR, or "dead orgone energy."

The dark, stagnant clouds act like stagnation in other parts of your body. They clog up the system and disrupt healthy functioning. This stagnation will also eventually cause stagnation in the first and third levels of the field, which are adjacent to it. Most of us do not allow all our feelings about ourselves to flow. As a result, most of us have stagnated energy in our second levels and have interfered with our health to varying degrees.

If the second layer is strong and charged, you enjoy your emotional relationship to yourself. This means that you have a lot of feelings about yourself, but they are not bad. It means that you like and love yourself. You enjoy being with yourself and feel comfortable with yourself. If both your first and second levels are charged, you will love yourself and feel good about yourself when you are also enjoying all the physical pleasures that your body brings to you.

If your second level is weak and undercharged, either you will not have many feelings about yourself or you won't be aware of them. If your second level is charged but is dark and stagnant, you will not like yourself, possibly even hate yourself. You are holding down the negative feelings about yourself, so you may be depressed from disliking yourself.

Third Level of the Human Energy Field

The third level is associated with our mental or rational world. The lines of structure in this level are very delicate, like the finest thin veil. This level's light lemon-yellow energy lines pulsate at a very high rate. (Its brightness, fullness, and energy flow along standing lines of light that correspond to our mental processes and our states of mind.) When this level is balanced and healthy, the rational and intuitive mind work together in harmony as one, and we experience clarity, balance, and a sense of appropriateness. When the first three levels of our field are synchronized, we feel self-accepting, safe, and appropriate and have a sense of personal power.

If your third level is strong and charged, you will have a strong, clear mind that serves you well. You will have an active healthy mental life and be interested in learning.

If your third level is weak and undercharged, you will lack mental agility or clarity. You will probably not be very interested in academics or other intellectual pursuits.

When our thoughts are negative, the pulsations in the field are slower, the lines become dark and distorted. These "negative thought forms" are the form that corresponds to our habitual negative thought processes. They are difficult to change, because they appear to be logical to the person experiencing them.

If your first and second levels are weak and your third is strong and energized, you will tend to be someone who lives more in the mind than in your feelings or body. You will be much more interested in problem solving by reasoning things out than by considering your feelings in any decision. This will automatically limit your life experience.

Negative thought forms are also squeezed into action by stagnated emotions from the second and fourth levels just adjacent to them. In other words, when we try not to feel negative emotions about ourselves (second level) and/or about another person (fourth level), we stop the energy flow in the second and fourth levels. The energy flow in the third level then becomes distorted by this "squeeze."

Another way to understand this is to remember that the natural state of energy is constant movement. When the movement of energy is stopped in the second and fourth levels in order to stop negative emotions, some of that momentum is transferred into the third level. The momentum that moves into the third level causes mental activity. The activity is distorted because it is not free to move naturally and it is squeezed in by the energies just below and just above it.

I think the habit of maintaining negative thought forms is supported in our culture. It is more acceptable in our society to have negative thoughts about people and to malign them behind their back, than it is to express negative emotions to their face. We don't have an appropriate model in which to do this. It would be much more appropriate to look inside and find the negative emotions we have toward ourselves. Usually, we have negative feeling toward another because interacting with that person evokes some sort of negative feeling toward the self.

Fourth Level of the Human Energy Field

The fourth level of the field carries our whole world of relationships. From this level, we interact with other people, animals, plants, inanimate objects, the earth, the sun, the stars, and the universe as a whole. It is the level of the "I-Thou" connection. Here are all our feelings about each other. The energy of the fourth level seems thicker than that of the second, even though it is a higher vibrational level. In contrast to the energy of the second, which is like colored clouds, the energy of the fourth is more like colored fluid. It too contains all colors.

If the fourth level has undercharged energy, or what healers call energy of low vibrations, this energy will be experienced as dark, thick, heavy fluid. I call it auric mucus. It acts just like the mucus you accumulate in your body when you have a cold. This auric mucus has a very strong negative effect on your body, causing pain, discomfort, a feeling of heaviness, exhaustion, and eventually dis-ease.

The energy of the fourth level can be extended across the room to another person. Whenever two people interact, either overtly or covertly, great streams of colored fluidlike bioplasma reach out from each to touch the other's field. The nature of the interaction corresponds with the nature of the energy-consciousness of these energy streams. For example, if there is a lot of love in the interaction, there will be a lot of sweet rose energy that flows in soft waves. If there is envy, it will be dark, gray-green, slimy and sticky. If there is passion, the rose will have a lot of orange in it, with a stimulating effect. The waves will be faster, with higher peaks. If there is anger, it will be harsh, sharp, pointed, penetrating, invasive, and dark red.

The fourth level contains all the love and joy, as well as all the struggle and pain, of relationship. The more we interact with someone, the more energetic connections we make with that person.

If you have a strong, healthy, and charged fourth level, you will tend to have a lot of strong good relationships with others. Your friends and family will make up a big and important part of your life. You may like to be around people a lot and may be in a human service profession. Love and your heart are foremost in your life.

If your fourth level is weak and undercharged, your relationships with other human beings may be less important to you. You might be a loner. You may not have many intimate relationships with people. If you do, you may have trouble with them and feel that relationships are more trouble than they are worth. You may feel overwhelmed by others because many people will have a stronger fourth level than you, so your field literally gets overpowered by the energy in their fourth level.

We are born with cords in the auric field connecting us with our parents and ourselves, much like the umbilicus. These cords develop, as the aura does, through the stages of childhood development. (See *Hands of Light*, Chapter 8.) These cords represent our relationships with each parent. Each is a model of how we will continue to create relationships to either the men or the women in our lives. Each new relationship develops more cords. (See Chapter 14, "The Three Types of Auric Field Interactions in Relationships," for a more detailed description.)

The first three levels of the aura represent the physical, emotional, and mental experience of our world in the physical body. The fourth level of relationship represents the bridge between the physical and spiritual worlds. The higher three levels represent our physical, emotional, and mental experience of our spiritual world. They are the template for the three lower levels. That is, the seventh level is the template for the third level, the sixth is the template for the second, and the fifth level is the template for the first level. Each higher level serves as a pattern for the corresponding lower level.

Fifth Level of the Human Energy Field

The fifth level is the level of divine will. It is at first a bit confusing when you learn to perceive it because on the fifth level everything appears to be reversed, like a blueprint. What you normally experience as empty space is cobalt-blue light, and what you normally experience as solid objects are composed of empty or clear lines of energy. It is a template for the first level of the field. There is an empty slot or groove in the fifth level into which each blue line of light of the first level fits. The fifth level holds the first in place. It is as if space is filled with formless undifferentiated life. In order to have life take a specific form, it is necessary to first empty space to make room for it. The fifth level contains not only the form for your body but the form of all other life. The fifth level of the field contains the unfolding evolutionary pattern of life that manifests into form. Divine will is divine intent manifested into pattern and form.

The personal experience of this level is the most difficult to explain because we lack the words in our vocabulary to describe it. This divine will exists within you and all around you. You have free will to either align yourself with this divine will or not. Divine will is a template or pattern for the great evolutionary plan of humanity and the universe. This template is alive, pulsating, and constantly unfolding. It has a powerful, almost inexorable feeling of will and purpose. To experience it is to experience perfect order. It is a world of precision and a level of precise tones. This is the level of symbols.

If you are aligned with divine will, your fifth level will be strong, full of energy. Its pattern will fit the universal pattern of divine will, a pattern that also can be seen with HSP on this level. You will feel great power and connectedness with all that is around you because you will be in your place with your purpose and synchronized with all places and purposes. If you open your vision to this level, you will see that you are, in fact, co-creating this alive, pulsating template that determines world order. Your place in the universal scheme of things is determined and created by you on a deeper level within you, the haric level. It will be discussed in greater detail later in this chapter.

If your fifth level is strong, you are one of those people who understand and maintain order in your life. "A place for everything and everything in its place." Your house is neat, you are on time, and you do your job very well, no matter how detailed it is. Your will is functioning very well. It is aligned with divine will, whether or not you have ever heard of such a thing. You know order as a universal principle. You may be connected to the greater purpose or pattern in your life.

If, on the other hand, you are not aligned with divine will, the pattern of the auric field on your fifth level will be distorted. It will not fit with the great universal pattern, and you will not feel connected to what is around you. You will know neither your place in the universal scheme of things nor your purpose. In fact, the idea that there is such a thing may not make any sense to you. It will feel as if someone is going to lay a trip on you and define your place for you.

Of course, from this perspective, your place will not be something you will like or be comfortable with. You are probably intimidated by clear will and precision. You will probably either deny the importance of clarity, order, and place or rebel against it. If you have doubts about your self-worth, you may experience the fifth level as impersonal and unloving because on this level your purpose, not your feelings, is most important. If you have negative feelings about yourself as you bring your conscious awareness to this level, you may experience yourself as just another cog in the great wheel of life. All the above is the human experience that results from the fifth level of the auric field being out of alignment and distorted.

If your fifth level is not strong, you will not be orderly in your life. You are not interested in keeping everything neat and clean. In fact, it would be pretty hard to do so. Order may seem like a terrible hindrance to your freedom. In fact, you may even judge those who do keep order and say that it blocks creativity. You may not have much of a relationship to divine will or the greater purpose to your life. You may have difficulty understanding complicated systems or overall patterns of things.

If your second and fourth levels are weak, and the first, third, and fifth are strong, you may very well overpower your creative freedom with a dictatorial form of order. It's time to spend more time enhancing your emotional life.

However, if you can let go of your negative feelings and get through your resistance to such a perfect world by considering the possibility that you are co-creator of it, you have taken the first step to finding your purpose and your place and everything can change. You will begin to feel very safe because you are a part of a great divine plan. You can experience yourself as a spark of light within this great, alive, and pulsing web of light. You, in fact, generate the web from your light, as does everyone else. If you open your HSP on this level, you can feel and see the plan. You will experience yourself and the world to be clear light, almost like empty space on a cobalt-blue background.

Contemplation of this level and meditation on the great evolutionary plan help greatly to align your life with its purpose and ease your development. It means surrendering to who you are, not to what seems right according to social norms. Thus, in fact, you are not a cog in a wheel; rather, you are a fountainhead of creativity unlike any other in the universe.

Sixth Level of the Human Energy Field

The sixth level of the field looks like beautiful streamers of light radiating out in all directions, extending about two and a half feet from the body. It contains all the colors of the rainbow in opalescent tones. It is unstructured and is of very high frequency.

When the sixth level is healthy, it is bright and charged. The beams of energy stream out from the body in beautiful full straight beams of light. The brighter and more charged this level is, the more we are consciously aware of it in terms of human experience. This is the level of feelings within the world of our spirit; it is the level of our divine love. Sitting in this level of conscious awareness brings a great calming effect to the body for healing. It contains the ecstasy within our spirituality. It is experienced as spiritual love, as joy, elation, and bliss. We reach this level of experience by silencing the noisy mind and listening. We reach it through meditation, through religious or fine music, chanting or reverie. Here are great feelings of expansion where we commune in brotherhood with all the beings of the spiritual worlds of various heavens

as well as all of humanity, plants, and animals of the earth. Here each of us is like the halo around a candle. We are mother-of-pearl opalescent light beams stretching out from a central light.

If your sixth level is weak with not much energy, you will not have many spiritual or inspirational experiences. You may not even know what people are talking about when they discuss it. When the sixth level is undercharged and unhealthy, it is very difficult for us to experience anything on this level. We may have vague feelings either that God is sick or that God/heaven/spirituality simply doesn't seem to exist. Therefore, those that do experience it seem to be in fantasy, living in a Pollyanna world of their own making.

When this level is unhealthy, it is dark, thin, and undercharged and its beams of light sag. This is usually a result of lack of spiritual nourishment. Lack of spiritual nourishment can be caused by many things, such as: not being raised in an environment that includes it, so that it simply doesn't exist; having had a trauma about religion that results in rejection of that religion and of spirituality generally along with the religion; having had a trauma of some other personal nature that results in the person's rejection of God and religion. In the first case, the sixth level is simply undercharged, and the person doesn't know he or she needs spiritual nourishment. In the latter cases, not only is the sixth level undercharged, it is separated from the other levels of the field. One can actually see a gap between the levels, and the normal communication channels between the levels are closed.

If your sixth level is much stronger than all the other levels, you may use spiritual experience to avoid life in the physical. You may develop a childish view of life and expect life to take care of you as if you lived only in the spiritual world. You may use these experiences to make yourself special and prove that you are better than others because you have them. This is only a defense against the fear that you have to be in life in the physical. This defense doesn't work for long, and you soon will have a rude awakening that will throw you into disillusionment. Disillusionment is a good thing; it means to dissolve the illusion. In this case, it will bring you back into life now in the physical. You will learn that the physical world exists within the spiritual world, not outside of it.

The key to experiencing the spiritual world is to charge the sixth level of the field. This can be done through very simple meditation, like sitting quietly for five to ten minutes twice a day and focusing on an object such as a rose, a candle flame, or a beautiful sunset. Another way is to repeat a mantra, one sound or a set of sounds with no apparent meaning.

Seventh Level of the Human Energy Field

When the seventh level of the human energy field is healthy, it is composed of beautiful, extremely strong golden lines of energy that scintillate at a very high frequency. They are interwoven to form all the physical components of your physical body. They extend out from your body three to three and a half feet. At this distance, the seventh level forms into a golden egg that surrounds and protects everything within it. The outer edge of this egg is thicker and stronger, like an eggshell. It regulates a proper flow of energy out from the entire aura into the space beyond. It prevents energy leakage out of the field, as well as penetration by unhealthy energies from the outside. The seventh level serves to hold the entire field together. I am always amazed by the tremendous strength that exists at this level.

The seventh level golden threads of light also exist throughout and around everything. These threads knit everything together, whether they be the cells of an organ, a body, a group of people, or the whole world.

The seventh level is the level of divine mind. When it is healthy and we bring our conscious awareness to this level, we experience divine mind within us and enter into the world of the universal divine mind field. Here we understand and know that we are a part of the great pattern of life. Experiencing this truth of the universe makes us feel very safe. Here we know perfection within our imperfections.

On this level, with HSP we can see the golden grid system of truth as it interweaves itself through the universe. Here, with HSP we will eventually learn to communicate mind to mind. In the not-too-distant future HSP will be completely normal. Now we can sometimes access the universal mind for information beyond what we would be able to obtain through what are commonly regarded as the normal senses.

If the seventh level is strong, charged, and healthy, your two major abilities will be to have creative ideas and to clearly understand broad overall concepts about existence, the world, and its nature. You will create new ideas, and you will know where they fit into the great universal pattern of ideas. You will know how you fit into this pattern. You will have a clear and strong understanding of God. You may become a theologian, a scientist, or an inventor. Your ability to have a clear, integrated understanding may lead you to become a teacher of broad-scale, complicated subjects.

If the seventh level is not strongly developed, you will not come up with many creative new ideas. Nor will you have a good sense of the greater pattern of life. You won't know how you fit into it, since you won't know there is such a thing as this pattern. You may experience that nothing is connected and that the universe is random and chaotic in nature.

If the seventh level of our field is not healthy, the golden lines will be dull and weak. They will not hold their form and will be thinner in some places than others. They may even be torn open in some places, allowing energy to leak out of the system. If the seventh level is unhealthy, we do not experience divine mind or the connectedness of the truth held in the universal mind field. We will not understand the concept of perfection within our imperfections. Our imperfections will be very hard to tolerate. In fact, we may go into denial about them, claiming or striving for a perfection that is impossible to achieve in the human condition. We will not have access to the universal divine mind field. It will appear that our minds work in isolation and have very little to do with creation.

If your seventh level is stronger than all the rest, you may have the problem of making all your creative ideas practical.

The best way to strengthen the seventh level of the field is to continually search for higher truth in your life and to live by it. The best meditation I know to help strengthen the seventh level of the field is to use a mantra that repeats, "Be still and know that I am God." Doing this mantra brings energy to the seventh level and eventually brings the meditator to the experience of knowing he or she is divine mind and God.

It takes good functioning of all your bodies to bring your creative ideas into manifestation on the physical plane. This includes your health. If you want to have good physical health and a full life, it is necessary to clear, charge, and balance all your bodies and therefore all the areas of human experience. Therefore any healing process must include focused attention to and nourishment for all seven levels of your field.

The Chakras

Chakras are the configurations in the structure of the energy field with which healers work. *Chakra* is the Sanskrit word for "wheel." According to my HSP, the chakras look much more like vortices, or funnels, of energy. They exist on each of the seven levels of the

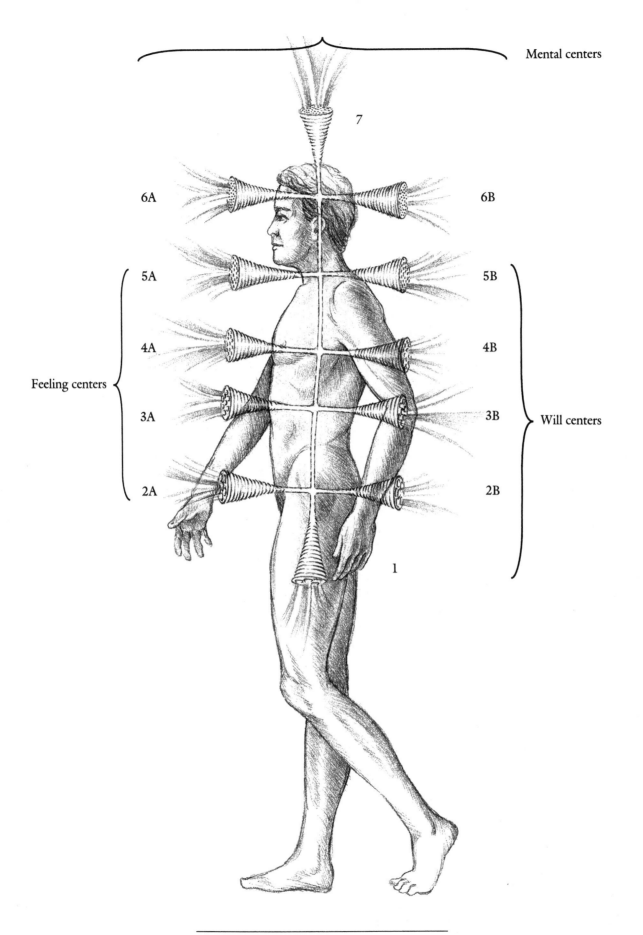

Mental centers

7

6A   6B

5A   5B

4A   4B

Feeling centers   3A   3B   Will centers

2A   2B

1

Figure 2–5 Location of the Seven Major Chakras

field, and chakras two through six appear on both the front and the back of the body. We label the chakras by their number and a letter: A for the front of the body and B for the back. (See Figure 2–5.)

Chakras function as intake organs for energy from the universal life energy field, which we can also call the universal health field all around us. The energy taken in and metabolized through each chakra is sent to the parts of the body located in the major nerve plexus area closest to each. This energy is very important for the healthy functioning of the auric field and the physical body. In eastern tradition that energy is called the *prana*, or the *ch'i*. If a chakra stops functioning properly, the intake of energy will be disturbed. This means that the body organs served by that chakra will not get their needed supply. If chakra dysfunction continues, normal functioning of the organs and other body parts in that particular area will be disrupted. That part of the body will weaken, as will its immune defenses, and eventually disease will occur in that part of the body.

There are seven major chakras. Each funnel has its wider opening on the outside of our body, about six inches in diameter, one inch from the body. The small tip is inside our body near the spine. The vertical power current lies through the center line of the body. It is the large channel of energy into which all the chakras release the energy they take in from the universal life or health field all around us. The energy from all the chakras laces up and down through the vertical power current. Each color is woven together, somewhat like a rope made of beautiful pulsating light of all colors. The vertical power current is about one inch wide in most people. However, in healers who have lifted to a high altered state of consciousness to heal, it can become as large as six inches in diameter.

The seven major chakras are located near the major nerve plexuses of the body. The first chakra is located between the legs. Its fine tip seats right into the sacral-coccyx joint. It is associated with the kinesthetic (sense of body position), proprioceptive (sense of body movement), and tactile (touch) senses. It is related to our will to live and supplies the body with physical vitality. It supplies energy to the spinal column, the adrenals, and the kidneys.

The second chakra is located just above the pubic bone on the front and back of the body. Its tip seats directly into the center of the sacrum, through which we sense emotions. It is related to our sensuality and sexuality. It supplies our sexual organs and our immune system with lots of energy.

The third chakra is located in the solar plexus area on the front and back of the body. Its fine tip seats directly into the diaphragmatic hinge, between thoracic vertebra twelve (T-12) and lumbar vertebra one (L-1). It supplies the organs in this area of the body—the stomach, liver, gall bladder, pancreas, spleen, and nervous system—with energy. It is associated with our intuition. It is related to who we are in the universe, how we connect to others, and how we take care of ourselves.

The fourth chakra, in the heart area, is related to love and will. Through it we sense love. The front aspect is related to love, the rear aspect to will. To keep this chakra functioning well, we live with a balance of love and will. Its fine tip seats into T-5. It brings energy to our heart, circulatory system, thymus, vagus nerve, and upper back.

The fifth chakra is located in the front and back of the throat. It is associated with the senses of hearing, tasting, and smelling. Its fine tip seats into cervical vertebra three (C-3). It supplies energy to the thyroid, the bronchi, lungs, and alimentary canal. It is related to giving and receiving and speaking our truth.

The sixth chakra is located on the forehead and the back of the head. Its tip seats into the center of the head. It supplies energy to our pituitary, lower brain, left eye, ears, nose, and nervous system. It is associated with the sense of sight. The front part of the chakra is related to conceptual understanding. The back part is related to carrying out our ideas in a step-by-step process to accomplish them.

The seventh chakra is located at the top of the head. Its fine tip seats into the middle of the top of the head. It supplies energy to our upper brain and our right eye. It is associated with the experience of direct knowing. It is related to the integration of personality with spirituality.

In general, the front aspects of the chakras correlate to our emotional functioning, the back to our will function, and the head chakras to our reason function. A balanced functioning of our reason, will, and emotion is necessary to maintain our health. Since the amount of energy flowing through a given chakra denotes how much that chakra is used, it also denotes how much the reason, will, or emotional aspect associated with that chakra is used. In order to create a balance of our reason, will, and emotions in our lives, we must balance, equalize, and synchronize our chakras.

In this book, we will describe how healers work with the human energy field during healing sessions and how you can work with your own field for self-healing. Later, we will relate the personal healing process to each of the seven levels of personal life experience found within each of the levels of the field. Self-healing can be accomplished by filling personal needs that are associated with each type of life experience on each level. (For more specifics about the aura and its chakras, please refer to *Hands of Light*, Parts II and III.)

The Haric Level: The Level of Your Intention, Your Purpose

The haric level is one quantum leap deeper into your nature and one dimension deeper than the aura. The haric level is the foundation upon which the aura rests. I call it the haric level because it is the level where the hara is. *Hara* is defined by the Japanese as a center of power within the lower belly. While the aura is related to your personality, the haric level is related to your intentions. It corresponds to your life task or your deeper spiritual purpose. It is the level of your greater incarnational purpose and your purpose in any given moment. It is here that you set and hold your intention.

The haric level is much simpler than the auric field, which has a very complicated structure. (See Figure 2–1.) It consists of three points along a laserlike line that is on the center line of our body. It is about one-third of an inch wide and extends from a point about three and one-half feet above our head, down deep into the core of the earth. The first point above the head looks like an inverted funnel. Its wide end pointing down is only about one-third of an inch wide. It represents our first individuation out of the godhead, when we first individuated from God in order to incarnate. It also carries the function of reason. It carries our reason to incarnate. It is through this place that we connect to our higher spiritual reality. I call this place the individuation point or ID point.

If we follow the laser line down into our upper chest area, we find the second point. It is a beautiful diffuse light. It corresponds to our emotion. Here we carry our spiritual longing, the sacred longing that leads us through our life. It brings the passion we have to accomplish great things in our life. This longing is very specific to our life task. We long to accomplish it. It is the thing that we want to do more than anything else in life. It is what we have come for. It is the longing each of us carries within, that lets us feel why we are here. I call this point the seat of the soul's longing, or soul seat, or SS.

The next point on the line is the *tan tien*, as it is called

in Chinese. It is the center from which all martial artists move when they perform. It is from this center that martial artists draw power to break concrete. It appears to be a ball of power or center of beingness, about one and one-half inches in diameter. It is located about two and one-half inches below the navel. It has a strong membrane around it, so it looks a bit like a rubber ball. It can be gold in color. This is a will center. It is your will to live in the physical body. It contains the one note that holds the physical body in physical manifestation.

It is with your will and this one note that you have drawn up a physical body out of the body of your mother the earth. It is from this center that healers can also connect to a great deal of power to regenerate the body, provided that the healer grounds the haric line deep into the molten core of the earth. When their haric line extends down into the earth, healers can gather great power. When used in healing, the tan tien can turn very bright red and become very hot. This is what is meant by being grounded on the haric level. When this happens and the tan tien turns red, healers feel intense heat all over their body.

When you have set a clear intention on the haric level, your actions on the auric and physical levels bring about pleasure. We will discuss dysfunction in the haric level (that is, your intention and your life task) with relationship to health throughout this book. For example, illness can be caused by unclear, mixed, or opposing intentions and disconnection from one's life task. Many people, especially in the modern industrialized part of the world, walk around in great spiritual pain because they do not know that they have a life's purpose. They do not understand why they are in pain. They don't know there is a cure for this kind of spiritual pain. The disconnection from their deeper life's purpose shows in the haric level. It can be healed from this level.

The Core Star Level: The Level of Your Divine Essence— The Source of Your Creative Energy

The core star level is a quantum leap deeper into who we are than the haric level and is related to our divine essence. Using HSP, on the level of the core star, everyone looks like a beautiful star. Each star is different. Each star is the internal source of life within. In this inner place, we are the center of the universe. Here is localized the divine individuality within each of us. It is located one and one-half inches above the navel on the center line of the body. (See Figure 2–1.) When one opens one's vision on the core star level and looks at a group of people, each looks like a beautiful star that radiates out infinitely yet permeates all the other stars.

Our core is the most essential nature of our being and is completely unique to each individual. It has been there within each of us since before the beginning of time. Indeed, it is beyond the limitations of time, space, and belief. It is the individual aspect of the divine. From this place within each of us, we live and have our being. We recognize it easily as that which we have always known ourselves to be since birth. In this place, we are wise, loving, and full of courage.

This inner essence has not really changed with time. No negative experiences have ever really tainted it. Yes, our reactions to negative experiences may have covered it, or shrouded it, but they have never really changed it. It is our most basic nature. It is the deeper goodness within each of us. It is who we really are. It is from this place within that all our creative energies arise. It is the eternal fountainhead within each of us from which all our creations come.

Your Creative Process and Your Health

The prime focus of this book is to help you understand the creative process originating within your core and its significance, especially with regard to health and healing. This creative process that originates within our core always begins with two ingredients. The first is positive intention, or divine intention; the second is positive pleasure.

Everything you have ever done in your life began not only with good intentions but also always with pleasure.

Every creative act you have done began within your core consciousness and upwelled through the deeper levels of your being until it reached your physical world. All the creations in your life take the same course. Every creative act takes the course in its journey into the physical: It manifests first as consciousness in the core, then as our intention in the haric level, then as our life energies in the auric level that later well up into the physical universe.

When these energies flow *directly* from the core through the haric level of our life task, through the auric level of our personality, and through our physical bodies, we create health and joy in our lives. It is upon this creative process that this book is based. It is with the "light emerging" from our core that we create our life experience on all levels of our being.

When we *block* the creative energies arising from the core star, we eventually create pain in our lives. The work that lies before us is to unveil our core so that our light and creations can emerge in joy, pleasure, and well-being. In that way, we can create a world of harmony, peace, and communion.

A New View of Healing— The Holographic Experience

In order to begin to understand and live holographic experience, we must take a look at our current way of understanding, which is not holistic.

The Metaphysics Underlying Our Scientific Models

Like the traditional belief systems of "primitive" cultures, our culture of the western scientific world is also shaped by its built-in assumptions. Many of these assumptions have remained unspoken and unchallenged until recently. What we consider to be our basic reality depends on the underlying metaphysics upon which we rest our science. Dr. Willis Harman, in his book *Global Mind Change*, notes three basic metaphysics— *M-1*, *M-2*, and *M-3*—that have been used during the history of human evolution. He defines them as follows:

M-1. Materialistic Monism (Matter Giving Rise to Mind)

In the first of these, the basic stuff of the universe is matter-energy. We learn about reality from studying the measurable world. . . . Whatever consciousness is, it emerges out of matter (that is, the brain) when the evolutionary process has progressed sufficiently. Whatever we can learn about consciousness must ultimately be reconciled with the kind of knowledge we get from studying the physical brain, for consciousness apart from a living physical organism is not only unknown, it is inconceivable.

M-2. Dualism (Matter Plus Mind)

An alternate metaphysic is dualistic. There are two fundamentally different kinds of basic stuff in the universe: Matter-energy stuff and mind-spirit stuff. Matter-energy stuff is studied with the present tools of science; mind-spirit stuff must be explored in other ways more appropriate to it (such as inner subjective exploration). Thus there develop, in essence, two complementary kinds of knowledge; presumably there are areas of overlap (such as the field of psychic phenomena).

M-3. Transcendental Monism (Mind Giving Rise to Matter)

Yet a third metaphysic finds the ultimate stuff of the universe to be consciousness. Mind or consciousness is primary, and matter-energy arises in some sense out of mind. The physical world is to the greater mind as a dream image is to the individual mind. Ultimately the reality behind the phenomenal world is contacted, not through the physical senses, but through the deep intuition. Consciousness is not the end-product of material evolution; rather, consciousness was here first!

Most of our cultural conditioning and heritage is based on the M-1 (mind out of matter) metaphysical model, which supports a mechanistic science. Our future is already seeded in the M-3 (matter out of mind) model, which leads to a holographic science.

Our Old Scientific Mechanistic Model in Health Care

To move into a holographic model for our health care, we must first explore our old ideas about health, healing, and medicine and find how they have limited us. Our old ideas come out of the old scientific, mechanistic model upon which our cultural conditioning is based. This old model, based upon the M-1 metaphysics (mind out of matter) contains the unspoken rational set of premises of this scientific age. Dr. Harman lists these assumptions:

1. The only conceivable ways in which we can acquire knowledge are through our physical senses, and perhaps by some sort of information transmission through the genes. [Or we can learn] through empirical science . . . the exploration of the measurable world through instrumentation which augments our physical senses.
2. All qualitative properties . . . are ultimately reducible to quantitative ones (for example, color is reduced to wavelength).
3. There is a clear demarcation between the objective world which can be perceived by anyone, and subjective experience which is perceived by the individual alone. . . . Scientific knowledge deals with the former; the latter may be important to the individual but its exploration does not lead to the same kind of publicly verifiable knowledge.
4. The concept of free will is a prescientific attempt to explain behavior which scientific analysis reveals is due to a combination of forces impinging on the individual from the outside, together with pressures and tensions internal to the organism.
5. What we know as consciousness or awareness of our thoughts and feelings is a secondary phenomenon arising from physical and biochemical processes in the brain.
6. What we know as memory is strictly a matter of stored data in the central nervous system.
7. The nature of time being what it is, there is obviously no way in which we can obtain knowledge of future events other than by rational prediction from known causes and past regularities.
8. Since mental activity is simply a matter of dynamically varying states in the physical organism (brain), it is completely impossible for this mental activity to exert any effect directly on the physical world outside the organism.
9. The evolution of the universe and of man has come about through physical causes. . . . there is no justification for any concept of universal purpose in this evolution, or in the development of consciousness, or in the strivings of the individual.
10. Individual consciousness does not survive the death of the organism; or if there is any meaningful sense in which the individual consciousness persists after the death of the physical body, we can neither comprehend it in this life nor in any way obtain knowledge about it.

These are the assumptions upon which our industrialized society and our health-care system are based. In some cases of health care they work beautifully. In others, they do not. In some areas of our lives, like the ability to purchase consumer products, they work for some of us. For some of us, who live trapped in poverty, they do not. To find more effective solutions for social problems and the diseases that "plague" the twentieth century, we must look deeper into our assumptions about reality.

In our culture, philosophy is based on the old mechanistic model of physics, which in turn is based on M-1 (mind out of matter) metaphysics, which maintains the world is made up of basic building blocks of matter such as electrons and protons. These tiny "things" or parts constitute everything that there is. Therefore if we divide the world into these things and study them, we should understand the world. Thus, we have been taught to trust and live by the rational mind. Our social system, schools, and medical system all emphasize the importance of solving problems rationally to understand the way things work, and then to find the cause of problems. To do that, we divide everything into separate parts and study them.

Unfortunately, in the past forty years or so, we have placed more and more emphasis on rationally dividing our world into separate parts and studying those parts as if they were isolated. Yet research shows that isolation simply is not true. For over twenty years our experiments in physics and biology have shown that everything is connected. It is impossible to separate the experimenter from the experiment. It is impossible to separate the individual from the whole. Yet in daily life we continue to think that things can be broken down and taken apart to be understood.

Why Isn't the Old Way Working?

·When we think in the mechanistic way we make statements like this:

"When are *they* going to do something about it?"
"*They* are destroying the planet."
"We'd be better off if executives (or workers) weren't so greedy."

These statements separate us from others by creating a fictional "they" or "them" on to whom we can shift responsibility for a problem or situation rather than do what we could do to change the situation. After all, we are co-creators of whatever situation we find ourselves in.

We have dealt with our own health and disease in the same way. We separate our organs from each other as if they were not working together in the same body. We separate our dis-ease from ourselves. We separate our body parts from our emotions about them, as if there were no effect in doing so. We compartmentalize them all with statements like:

"I caught your cold."
"I've got a bad back."
"My stomach is giving me trouble again."
"I hate my hips—they are too big for me."

We even try to get rid of the symptom rather than focusing on the cause of the problem. This can be very dangerous indeed. We make statements like:

"Doc, I want you to get rid of this knee problem once and for all."
"My head hurts. I need some aspirin to take the pain away."
"I'm getting rid of my gallbladder so it will stop bothering me."

Many times, we see illness as primarily caused by the invasion of some outside thing, like a microorganism or a tumor that needs to be removed. The major way of ridding ourselves of disease is to take a pill or have surgery. Prescribing the right medication to get rid of pain or to kill the invader is based primarily on research

and thinking that is founded on the premise of the world being composed of separate parts. These views do not deal with the cause of illness. The wonders of modern medicine are astounding, and yet as a people, we seem to be growing less able to personally maintain our health. When we finally get one thing fixed by the doctor, something else goes wrong. Sometimes the side effects from treatment lead to another ailment. Yet we tend to consider these ailments as separate occurrences. We have divided the world into so many parts that we get confused and begin thinking that the doctor is responsible for our health.

A great deal of pain has arisen out of the kind of thinking that sees a human being as a collection of separate parts rather than as a whole, integrated being. Such separatist thinking also leads to the abdication of responsibility for one's health to the doctor. We think a doctor can fix body parts as a mechanic fixes the parts of a car. I have been witness to a lot of this pain. Out of compartmentalization comes confusion. Many patients who have come through my office have been through a long list of health-care professionals, including physicians, therapists of all kinds, healers, psychics, acupuncturists, dietary specialists, and herbalists. From these treatments they have had minimal results, primarily because of the contradictory and confusing analysis of their condition. The patient simply doesn't know what to do or whom to believe because compartmentalization leads to contradiction.

Because of our cultural conditioning, we ask for a physical disease diagnosis. This is the equivalent of asking for basic building blocks of matter that don't really exist. We don't just ask for it—we demand it! And we get it. A concrete presentation of the "facts" of a physical disease diagnosis limits our ability to see the greater picture clearly because we take it out of the context of the interrelatedness of our whole being, in which the cause of our disease includes many levels of function and experience. We take it as the full answer and use it to (hopefully) make us feel safe. As a result, we put a lot of pressure on our physicians to take care of our health through diagnosis and treatment. We believe that if we name the disease and know it, we can control it, from a separated, disconnected place. Or better yet, the physician can control it.

Indeed, this method works very well for many diseases. It gets rid of the physical symptoms called disease, but it does not deal with the internal cause connected to the deeper reality within us. In the long run, the practice of diagnosis and treatment of physical symptoms is likely to separate us by one more step from ourselves and our deeper truth. I consider this a misuse of diagnosis. The problem isn't the system of diagnosis. The problem is that we stop with the diagnosis and its resulting treatment. We do not use it—as we could—as another piece of information in a large puzzle that leads to self-understanding and growth. Approaching disease from the point of view of separate symptoms also gives too much power to the diagnostic system and rigidifies it. This leads to another, more serious misuse of the diagnosis system.

The Mechanistic Model Produces Death-Sentence Diagnoses

The pain gets worse and the patients even more confused when they receive diagnosis and treatment recommendations that include threats such as, "If you don't follow our particular treatment program, you will get worse or even die." Of course physicians should give the information that they know about the patient's prognosis if the patient goes untreated, but physicians shouldn't imply that their way is necessarily the only way. Perhaps there are ways to treat the illness that they don't know about. In other words, the limitations of standard medical treatment techniques should be stated as such, and the door to other possibilities should always be clearly left open, whether or not the physician knows what the other treatments are. Rather than label a patient as "terminal," the physician needs to make it clear that it is western medicine that cannot treat the problem effectively.

One of the worst things I have seen newly diagnosed cancer patients go through is the terminal diagnosis. Yes, there are statistics about certain developments in certain diseases that show the probabilities of the course a given disease will take. But in no way does that mean it is true for any particular patient. Unfortunately, a patient who escapes the statistics is considered to have had an error in diagnosis, a "spontaneous remission," a "well-behaved disease," or even a "miracle." This discredits the method that was successful in helping the patient get well.

When western medicine uses the incurable or terminal diagnosis label for illnesses it cannot treat, it creates an additional problem for patients. It teaches patients that they cannot get well. It sets up a pathological belief within patients that they then act upon, thus enhancing their disease. That is, they not only have the disease to fight, they must also overcome the part of them that believes they cannot get well. A disease diagnosis induces a pathological view within the mind of the patient according to the beliefs of a medical system that

may not be able to help the patient because within its system there is no cure. In a way, western medicine covertly says, "Believe as we do, accept our metaphor of reality, that this illness (as we have diagnosed it) is the true and only reality (as we see it) and is incurable."

This covert statement brings us back again to the original issue: the roles our models of reality have in our lives, and our assumptions that they are the only reality. We don't consider the profound effect of this.

The Issue of Models or Metaphors of Reality

As the bag lady in Lily Tomlin's Broadway hit *The Search for Intelligent Life in the Universe* says, "Reality is a collective hunch."

What we tend to do is say that any model of reality that we accept *is reality*. We then get into trouble when what is doesn't fit the model. We blame ourselves or declare things to be impossible because they don't fit into the model. We tend not to see or say that the model is limited.

All models are limited. We need to remember that. If we do, then it is probably okay to accept a particular metaphor for reality in an unbiased fashion—for example, in the mechanistic case, that matter is the basic reality. But when it comes to incurable disease, that metaphor of reality is no longer working for us. Then it's time to find a more functional metaphor within which a cure is probable. It's time for the patient to find another medical system rather than go through painful invasive treatments that do not cure. Not only do these treatments fail to cure, they only make the cure by a different system, such as ayurvedic medicine, homeopathy, acupuncture, macrobiotics, or other such systems, much more difficult.

An untreatable diagnosis is a statement about the medical system, not the patient. If given as a statement about the patient's condition, it puts patients at a distinct disadvantage in their healing process. It leaves little if any room for the creative process of healing to come forth from the patient. It leaves no room for alternative care systems. It is far better when a physician says, "I have done all I can do for you. I am, at this time, unaware of any other treatments I can offer. If you wish, I will stand by you and keep you as comfortable as I can. Perhaps someone else knows another way."

This is all physicians are responsible for. They cannot take responsibility for other people's lives or their health. Physicians cannot play God. This ought to be a relief to them. Yes, physicians have the light of God within every cell of their beings. But so does every patient. Physicians are likely to have more access to healing power than any given patient at any given time. But patients have complete ability to learn to tap into that power, which also ought to be a relief to the physician.

The responsibilities we have placed upon our physicians, and that they have shouldered, are simply neither fair nor realistic. They are based on the mechanistic model. If a physician is supposed to give us a pill or do surgery to take away something separate from us that is bothering us, then he or she becomes the responsible one. It is as if we had nothing to do with it.

Moving Toward the Holographic Model

We as patients must take back responsibility for our healing. We must ask our physicians to help us do it. We must establish friendly working relationships among patient, healer, and physician to utilize the best in self-healing, healers, and the great service of healing that physicians offer.

A way to begin establishing friendly working relationships among patient, healer, and physician is to consciously move into the new M-3 (matter out of mind) metaphysics described at the beginning of this chapter. We need to consider that mind rather than matter is the basic reality. And that changes things a great deal. It leads us into holism.

The work presented in this book is based upon the M-3 metaphysics: Mind gives rise to matter; therefore mind or consciousness is the basic reality. Yet *mind* and *consciousness* are still limited terms in our culture. The broad expanse of human experience goes much beyond the mind. So I prefer to use the term *essence* to refer to the basic nature of human beingness. Essence is subtler and less limited than what we call consciousness. Essence underlies consciousness. Consciousness is subtler and less limited than what we call mind. Consciousness underlies mind. Therefore, it is essence that gives rise to consciousness, that gives rise to mind, that gives rise to matter.

That essence is found within the core star level of every living creature. It is found within everything. It is everywhere. Everything is ultimately interpenetrated with essence, consciousness, and mind. M-3 metaphysics, then, most naturally brings us to holism and the interconnectedness of all things, a very common experience of the healing state. By assuming M-3 metaphysics, we walk directly into the new science of holography, which shows a promising future by giving us

new answers to old questions about ourselves and our healing and creative processes.

Let's reorient ourselves to holism. What is it? How is it different from what we base our assumptions about reality on now? What would it be like to live within a holographic model of reality? What would it be like if we were to think and live holographically? How would our lives change?

Many of us have had experiences of wholeness either in meditation or in things as simple as a reverie on seeing a sunset. These experiences are very powerful. Most of the time, we wish we knew how to make them happen more often. We seem to have a great gap between the spontaneous experience of wholeness and the application of holism in daily life. It is this gap that we will seek to bridge in a step-by-step process in this book. At one end of our bridge is the physical world and our physical bodies. At the other is the expanded experience of holism where each of us is all that there is. So the question set before us is: How do we become holistic?

Experiencing the Universal Hologram

To explore what living within a holographic model would be like, on a personal experiential level, I asked several of my third-year healing students the following question: *"Imagine yourself a hologram. How does that un-limit you?"* Here are their answers.

MARJORIE V: In a hologram, we are both the observer and the creator. We are not just a part of a pattern, we are the pattern. A hologram is out of linear time and three-dimensional space. It is the interconnectedness of everything. It is un-limitation itself. It is total surrendering to all experiences—truly feeling one with everyone, everything, and every universe. It is instantaneous present, past, and future.

IRA G: Imagining myself as a hologram un-limits me because it permits the view that all the universe may be experienced or understood through one cell of my body and one experience of my life. Each part or component becomes a doorway of universal understanding.

SYLVIA M: If I am a hologram, then I have no limits. I can go into time and space into eternity and back again. I am the trees, the animals, and the homeless, and they are me. Maybe this is where that old saying comes from, "All for one, and one for all."

CAROL H: Imagining myself as a hologram un-limits me in that I recognize the interconnectedness with the whole of creation and that I am a reflection of the divine spirit. I also realize that all my thoughts, words, and deeds are experienced throughout the whole—which is an overwhelming thought! Also, I am experiencing all of creation as "receiver."

BETTE B: If I were a hologram, say of alcoholism, I would not only be the spouse of the alcoholic, but the husband, daughter, and son, and the alcoholic also. I could experience the alcohol going into the body and at the same time see and know how everyone else involved feels, thinks, and knows mentally, emotionally, physically, and spiritually. There would be no sides to take because I would be all of it at once and know that all of it is a part of God and the universe.

PAM C: I believe I am a hologram, but it's hard to let in what that means. It un-limits me because it means:

1. I am not separate, I am always in connection with the whole. In fact, I am the whole.
2. I can take whatever form I need to at any given moment. In fact, I am taking all of them all the time.
3. I am always in synchronicity with everything else that exists.
4. I am not restricted to my body. I have access to all the information in the universe, past, present, and future and other dimensions. I can be anywhere at any time. In fact, I can be several places at once. In short, it makes me very big and very connected. I am the whole as well as the parts.

ROSEANNE F: If I am a hologram, then I am not a part of the whole, I am *whole*. It un-limits me in every way, as I am not only connected to all things, I am all things and therefore am unlimited in my potential for understanding, knowing, seeing, learning, being, and doing (and much more, I'm sure).

In the inverse of "I am a whole" as a hologram, I am also in and of all else; so there is a balance of my unlimited self with all other things and beings.

JOHN M: This is a scientific metaphor for Christ's statement "I and the Father are One." It suggests for me that I am not an "outsider," that even as the prodigal son, I have held the fullness of the universe within me—or more accurately have had that fullness flowing through me. This thought reminds me of a sense of peace that has underlain my most scary and uncertain moments. It's as though, as I imagine the immensity of the whole, it looks back at me with something resembling a human face. The thought of myself as a hologram gives me courage and hope.

MARGE M: In this way I can see myself as everything that is. I need to learn to access those aspects of myself that I wish to access. As a hologram, anything is possible, all knowledge is accessible, and it is a matter of allowing this to happen.

LAURIE K: It gives me the wings with which to go and be anywhere I want at any time. It gives me creative responsibility in knowing who I truly am and, in that, changing the entire world. It provides me with unlimited access to all knowledge, all understanding. It frees me from the shackles of dualistic disharmony and propels me into a world of light, of unity, of knowing. I am inseparably connected to all.

SUE B: I found this hard to do because my mind says, "I am not." Instead, I find it easier to imagine myself as part of an interconnected web. When I do this, there is no "me" and "not me," but "I am." Time and space in this sense do not exist because "I am" everywhere at once.

JASON S: Imaging myself as a hologram seems to "un-limit" me to the extent that I allow it to. At some point it gets a little scary. For instance, when I imagine it, I feel somewhat more detached from my personality and life path and see all of it more as a series of interacting patterns. It gives broad vista to my view of myself. On the other hand—on the microlevel—I can see each aspect of my daily life as a full expression of who I am. I can see how I am "Jason-ing" through my life, with my talents, perspective, lack of perspective, problems, and strengths, all fully formed in every aspect. As someone who can get very detached as it is, I don't especially like the feeling of detachment when it gets too strong. I do like the feeling of all-one-time I get from looking at my life that way, though.

As a healer, when I look at patients that way, I feel the possibility of being completely in touch with their past, present, and possible future. It makes the moment of healing transcend this present moment.

The holographic experience requires expanded awareness. It requires great sensitivity to what is, both personally and interpersonally. It is possible to develop this expanded awareness in a step-by-step manner, as we shall see in the progression of this book.

The holographic experience is the experience of the healing moment. When linear time and three-dimensional space are transcended in the ways described above, healing automatically takes place. This is the true nature of the universe.

I'm sure such experiences as these are familiar to you. What we haven't done yet is learn how to bring them forth when they are needed and how to integrate them into normal life. Our real challenge is how to put them into everyday life in a practical way. In order to do this, we must understand holism better. So let's take a closer look at holography.

The Origins of Holism and Holography

In 1929, Alfred North Whitehead, a well-known mathematician and philosopher, described nature as a great expanding series of occurrences that are interconnected. "These occurrences," he said, "do not terminate in sense perception. Dualisms like mind/matter are false. Reality is inclusive and interlocking." What Whitehead meant by that is everything is relational, including our senses. We use our senses to get information about any given situation. Our senses affect the situation we perceive. The situation affects the senses with which we perceive it. In the same year, Karl Lashley published the results of his research on the human brain that showed that specific memory is not located in any one place in the brain. He found that destroying a portion of the brain does not destroy memory located there. Memory could not be located in specific brain cells. Rather, memory seems to be distributed all over the brain, probably as a field of energy.

In 1947, Dennis Gabor derived equations that described a possible three-dimensional photography that he called holography. The first hologram was constructed with the use of a laser in 1965 by Emmette Leith and Juris Upatinicks. In 1969, Dr. Karl Pribram, a renowned brain physiologist at Stanford University, proposed that the hologram worked very well as a powerful model for brain processes. In 1971, Dr. David Bohm, a well-known physicist who worked with Einstein, proposed that the organization of the universe is probably holographic. When Pribram heard of Bohm's work, he was elated. It supported his idea that the human brain functions as a hologram, collecting and reading information from a holographic universe.

What Is a Hologram?

So what are these men and their research saying? To understand their ideas, let's examine how a hologram works. No doubt, you have seen a hologram. It projects a three-dimensional image from seemingly nowhere into space. As you walk around this image, you see the different sides of it.

It takes a two-step process to create the three-dimensional hologram image. Figure 3–1 shows the first step. The beam from a laser is split in half by a device called a beam splitter. One half is focused through a lens onto an object such as an apple, then is

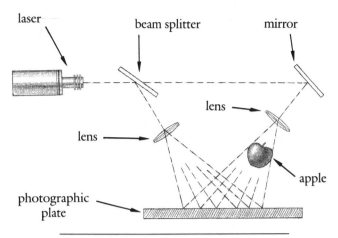

Figure 3–1 Making a Hologram of an Apple

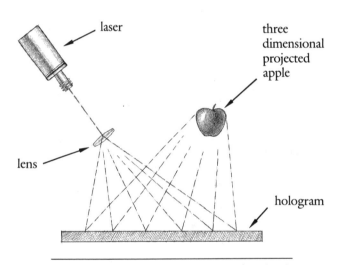

Figure 3–2 Projecting a Hologram of an Apple

reflected by a mirror onto a photographic plate. The other half is simply reflected by a mirror and focused through a lens onto the same photographic plate. A specific phase relationship is set between the two halves of the laser beam. A photograph is taken. The result is a photograph of an interference pattern that the two beams produce when they come back together on the photographic plate. This interference pattern looks like indiscernible squiggly lines.

The second step, Figure 3–2, is simply to remove the apple, the beam splitter, the second mirror, and the second lens. If you now take the laser and focus it through a lens and onto the photographic plate, you will find a three-dimensional image of the apple suspended in space! What is more surprising is that if you simply cut the photographic plate in half without changing anything else, you still get the image of the apple suspended in space, although it is a little hazier. If you cut another portion of the plate off, you will still get the whole image of the apple in space. This continues with smaller and smaller pieces of the photographic plate. You still get the whole apple, but it becomes a bit hazier each time!

The Holographic Model and Seven Premises about the Nature of Reality

As we enter the holographic era, we prepare for many changes. This era rests on the foundation of *seven basic premises about the nature of reality* that fall directly out of the holographic work and upon which the holographic model is based.

Premise 1: Consciousness Is the Basic Reality

To arrive at the premise that consciousness is the basic reality, let's follow Dr. Pribram's analysis. Dr. Pribram says that basic reality is the energetic signature that the brain picks up through our senses. Our brain then interprets the signature into the shape and color of an apple. What he means is that true reality is like the energy in the laser beams that carries information. What we see as reality is more like the projected three-dimensional picture of the apple in the hologram. The true reality is to be found in the energy that our senses pick up rather than in the objects we define as real.

Pribram states that our brain acts like the hologram that projects the true reality of the energy beams into an illusory apple. Our brain, using our five senses, picks up the energy field of whatever we bring our attention to in the moment and translates that energy field into an object. What this means is that the object we perceive represents the secondary reality. It is but a signature of the deeper reality (the energy beams) from which the projection of the object comes.

Pribram says that all our senses act together in a way to create the illusion of our world around us, much as a set of stereo speakers gives you the impression that the sound comes from the center of the room or a headset makes the music come from the center of your head. So far, only the hologram using the visible sense—light from the laser beam—has been built. Probably someday, holograms using the kinesthetic, auditory, olfactory, and gustatory senses will also be built.

Clearly, Dr. Pribram's research relates to our model of the human energy field. On the level of the aura, the basic reality is energy. However, if we go deeper, we find our intention, which results from our consciousness, upon which our energy flow is based. And even deeper than that, we find our essence and the core star level, the foundation of all reality. We have arrived at the M-3 metaphysics.

Implications of Premise 1 for our health and health-care system:

1. Probably the most profound implication for our health is that our consciousness, expressed as intention, and the energy in our auric field that results from that intention are the most fundamental factors in our health or dis-ease. This means that our intentions, both conscious and unconscious, and how they are expressed in our thinking, feelings, and actions are primary factors in our state of health. Any physical problem is only a physical manifestation of the true dis-ease that is to be found within consciousness. Consciousness founded the materialized statement of dis-ease.

2. Any science or health-care system based on the physical world is based on secondary causes, not primary ones.

Premise 2: Everything Is Connected to Everything Else

This connection is not dependent on spatial proximity or on time. An event in one location immediately, without time delay for communication (that is, faster than the speed of light and beyond Einstein's relativity theory) affects everything else.

Since there is no time delay, what we call cause and effect occur at the same time. Therefore our idea of cause and effect, which is so useful in our material world, is not applicable or valid in the primary reality.

Implications of Premise 2 for our health and health-care system:

1. According to the holographic view, it is impossible to take people, events, things, "no-things," or ourselves separately. The propagation of events works not only throughout their own specific areas of influence but profoundly affects other seemingly independent or unrelated areas of life. Our everyday experience, our science, our psychology, and our politics all point to the reality that nothing exists separately. An event, be it political, psychological, atomic, or subatomic, can never be taken as an iso-

lated occurrence, affecting only the immediate surroundings. Our science and our politics clearly show that whatever occurs now has an immediate effect everywhere. The development of nuclear weapons clearly shows this, as does the work of environmentalists.

2. Everything we do, say, think, and believe about health and disease affects everyone immediately.
3. By healing ourselves, we heal others. By helping heal others, we also heal ourselves.

Premise 3: Each Piece Contains the Whole

If we use the model of the hologram, we get a view of the nature of reality very different from the way our western culture has described it in the past. Since the whole three-dimensional image of the apple is still produced no matter how small a piece of the photographic plate is left, the hologram clearly demonstrates that each piece (of the holographic plate) contains the whole (apple).

Implications of Premise 3
for our health and health-care system:

1. Each part of us contains the whole pattern of us. This can be expressed in the physical world in our genes. In them, each cell contains our whole genetic makeup. Eventually, it may be possible to clone ourselves from a single cell!
2. On the energetic level, the energy pattern in the auric field of each cell contains our whole pattern of health. We can then tap into this health pattern to regain our health. We only need one healthy cell left to do so!
3. We are all that there is. Or another way to put it is: All that there is, is within each of us. By exploring our inner landscape, we also explore the universe.
4. By healing ourselves, we help heal the earth and the universe. (For further information and deeper understanding of how this works, see "What Can I Personally Do for World Peace?" channeled from my guide Heyoan, in Chapter 13.)

Premise 4: Time Is Also Holographic

Each aspect exists everywhere all the time and always (that is, both at all times and in all times). Each moment is whole, complete, and alive and coexists in a knowledgeable relationship with all other moments. Each moment is self-knowledgeable and self-intelligent and has access to all moments.

Implications of Premise 4
for our health and health-care system:

1. We now also know that an event in the past can be found broadly threaded through the tapestry of our present world makeup. What we do affects a broad range of people, perhaps much broader than we suspect at present. Our actions affect not only those around us but those at a distance, because these effects are not confined spatially or temporally. They are holographic—that is, these effects are not dependent on time or space.

   They act outside of such limitations, because in the primary reality, time and space do not exist.
2. On the personal level, each of us in this now has access to all other moments. Or: We are everywhere all the time, always.
3. Each of us is connected to the "I" that was very healthy before sickness and after getting well. We can access that experience of health and bring it into the now for healing.
4. In reverse, we can each continue to be connected to the lessons we learned from any illness to maintain the wisdom gained from the experience.
5. By entering into complete wholeness, it is possible to immediately heal ourselves.

Premise 5: Individuation and Energy Are Basic to the Universe

Each aspect is individual and not identical to any other aspect.

There is an experiment that proves that light is a particle and is also a wave of energy. However, another experiment shows that particles do not act like things. Rather, they are more like "individual events of interactions," which are also basically energy. Therefore: Every aspect of the universe is either a wave of energy or an individual particle of energy.

Implications of Premise 5
for our health and health-care system:

1. Each of us is composed of energy. By replacing our thoughts and assumptions that we are solid matter with the idea that we are light, we can change much more easily. So can our bodies, which are made of light. Our bodies are constantly changing. Each second, we have a different body.
2. Each of us is unlike any other being. What happens to each of us and what we experience is unique. It cannot be determined by a probability based on past statistics without the factor of creation, as stated in Premise 7, coming into play.

Premise 6: The Whole Is Greater Than the Sum of the Parts

If we reverse the process and connect the pieces of the photographic plate back together one by one, we get an increasingly clearer, more defined picture of the whole apple. Some of the major points that fall out of the sixth premise are:

1. Each aspect exists within a system greater than itself, which also exists within a system greater than itself, and so on.
2. Each aspect and system has knowledge of all other systems.
3. By connecting and integrating the smaller parts to the whole, we get a better, clearer understanding of the whole.

Implications of Premise 6
for our health and health-care system:

1. In holism, we say, as we connect our "parts" or "selves" together, we connect to and get a clearer picture of our greater, whole self.
2. Any group of people together create a greater whole that has more power, love, and creativity than each of those people taken separately or than the sum of their individual efforts.
3. Any individual within a group can tap into the power of that group. Each group within a larger group can access the power and energy in the larger group, and so on. This can be done for healing as well as for other creative endeavors.
4. We each, personally and in groups, have access to all the healing knowledge and power there is, ever was, and will be in the universe.

Premise 7: Consciousness Creates Reality and Its Own Experience of Reality

The seventh premise is based on Karl Pribram's model of the holographic brain. *Pribram states that the brain processes data consistent with what it is used to.* That means you will experience according to your expectations based on your beliefs and your heritage.

Since reality is created by consciousness, it also creates its own experience of reality, since that is part of reality.

Implications of Premise 7
for our health and health-care system:
In healing work we say: "We not only create our own reality and our own dis-ease, we also create our own experience of that reality, including our experience of our health or dis-ease."

This is a very controversial statement. The interpretation of this must be done very carefully, because it is fertile ground for misunderstanding and misuse. Having responsibility for a given situation is very different from being blamed for it. The latter implies that we have become ill because we are bad. On the other hand, if we accept the idea that we create our own experience of reality, it puts us into the powerful position of being able to find out how we created it the way it is, change our ways, and re-create another, more desirable one. There are two big catches to this.

The first is, from what level of our being is this creation stemming? From the divine essence, the consciousness level of intention, or the personality level of mind and feelings?

The second is, who is the we that is doing the creating? From the holographic view, we are all interconnected, are all connected to the greater creative power in the universe, and all affect each other always, everywhere.

People who constantly put themselves in stressful situations in their lives obviously have a great deal to do with creating the resulting heart disease on the personality level of the energy field that corresponds to thoughts and feelings. A great deal of personal choice is involved, and a lot of the creative energy is from the individual. However, these people are also products of their culture, which produces a great number of people with heart disease through stress, diet, and emotional lacks within the culture.

On the other hand, a baby born with AIDS certainly didn't exercise the same type of individual human choices on the level of personality that the above patients did. The creation of AIDS in a newborn can only be looked at from the holographic view, that this individual has arisen out of the collective whole of the society into which it was born. The "we" that is doing the creating here is all of us. We collectively have created a situation that gives rise to the condition of AIDS that is then expressed in some individuals in physical form. The condition of AIDS is expressed in all of us in some way. It may be expressed in our denial of its presence in our society or in our relationship to it, in our fear of it, in our negative reactions of wanting to get away from it, and even in our denial of the possibility that we could get it. The condition of AIDS in us may be expressed in our relationships with those who have it in physical form. The major expression of the condition called AIDS that we all have is in its challenge for us to choose love or fear. Each moment that we are faced with our condition that is called AIDS, which we have all created, we are faced with the challenge to choose love or fear.

Now, of course, one can include the deeper spiritual world of essence and intention within this metaphor and consider that before birth, an individual may have chosen to be born with AIDS as a gift to humanity. This gift challenges us to choose love rather than fear. We certainly have a great deal to learn about love in this age.

For myself, all of these statements could be true and helpful in the healing situation when used appropriately. The creation of one's reality needs to be explored on all levels for a complete healing.

Summary of a Holistic Health-Care Vision

The basic reality in the universe is essence. It includes our personal individual essence and the essence of everything else combined, which is called universal essence. All creation comes out of that essence: our consciousness, mind, feelings, and matter, including our physical body. Our health is a result of bringing our true unique essence through our consciousness, mind, feelings, and physical body. Our health or disease is created by us through this process. It is us.

Disease is the result of a distortion in our consciousness (our intent) that blocks the expression of our essence from coming through all the levels into the physical. Dis-ease is an expression of how we have tried to separate ourselves from our deeper being, our essence.

What we create arises holographically from both our individuality and ourselves collectively at the level of the groups to which we belong, from the most intimate to the universal scale. That is, our creations are not only our own doing but are strongly affected by and also arise (holographically) out of the people to whom we are most connected. Our creations are less affected by the people to whom we are less connected.

The cause of any particular illness is so multifold that it would be impossible to make such a list here. There are cases where the group source is very strong indeed. There are many cases now being manifested, such as those dear sweet babies born with AIDS, that arise out of the larger groups of humanity. This is a sign of the changing times. It is a manifestation of humankind's conscious awareness of the connectedness of all things. AIDS is a disease that will dissolve national boundaries and show human beings that love is the answer.

In this process of health or dis-ease, we cannot divide our interior self or separate ourselves from each other. We are all connected. Everything we think, feel, and do about health and dis-ease affects everyone else. By healing ourselves, we heal others. By expressing our essence, our uniqueness, we bring health to everyone by allowing them to express their essence.

Each part of us contains the whole pattern; every cell of our body contains the pattern of our whole body, and we also contain the pattern of humanity. We can tap into this great health pattern of power and light for healing. This pattern is real and alive.

We are this pattern. This pattern is in our auric field. We are energy, and we can change very rapidly. We live in a gelatinous body that is constantly changing and that is capable of great change.

Time is holographic. We can move through time frames for healing purposes and to gain information about the past or probable future. We can tap into all the wisdom of the ages for healing. We are this wisdom; it is within us as well as all around us.

Now let's rephrase those M-1 statements about our health (see p. 33) into the holographic view.

Instead of saying, "I caught your cold," we would say, "My cold is a signal that I need to balance myself. I've weakened my immune system, making it penetrable to a virus. Probably I didn't pay attention to what I needed. I need to take better care of myself. What do I need to bring back the balance? We are connected in that we both have created a cold. You probably need to take better care of yourself too!"

Instead of saying, "I've got a bad back," we might say, "My back pain tells me I'm backing out on myself again. Time to be clear about my intentions and keep in line with them. Out of these clear intentions will come a new relationship with my back that will include ways to take care of it as a 'good back.' The more I stand by myself in my truth, the more others will."

Instead of saying, "My stomach is giving me trouble again," we might say, "I'm being hard on myself again and putting all the tension into my stomach. Time to let go and give myself some TLC (tender loving care)."

Instead of saying, "I hate my hips, they are too big," we might say, "I keep dumping my hate into my hips and growing them bigger to hold it all."

This new way of relating to dis-ease does not stop us from having it treated by a professional. But it does put the emphasis on how we have been treating it all along and how that must be transformed to maintain a healthy state. It also opens new opportunities with which to gain the healthy state. Once we stop the old habits that are holding the disease in place and change our attitude, we automatically think differently about the problem in the first place. We are no longer an unconnected victim; rather, we had something to do with it in the first place. Thus we will, in our new freedom, make new avenues available to ourselves that we didn't have before. By doing this, we also help others open new avenues to themselves and others.

The Challenge of the Holistic Vision

The challenge with which we as patients and healers are presented is to accept the opportunities given by the holographic model, to understand what they are, and to learn to utilize them. Our true primary reality is the reality of consciousness and energy. Any science that focuses on the secondary or material reality of the physical world is based on illusion and is therefore illusory. If this is so, and there is evidence to support this theory, then our world is indeed very different from the way we surmise it to be from the three-dimensional definitions that we place upon it. It's going to take some getting used to because we are so accustomed to the definitions that we place upon our world.

First, we must personally change in order to accept the holographic view. It challenges our sense of identity and necessitates self-responsibility in a big way. This demands that we take a great deal of responsibility for what we do, both to ourselves and to others. In the realm of health, it makes us very responsible for taking care of our health. And at the same time it gives us unlimited resources with which to do that. At this stage of our development, it is impossible for us to imagine the tremendous potential power, knowledge, and energy that are available to us within this primary reality.

Re-Visualizing One's Old Diagnosis with the Holographic Model

The answers to what medical science calls "spontaneous remission" or "a miracle" lie in the holographic model. In the holographic model, a disease is equivalent to the image of the apple suspended in space that isn't really there. It is a signature of something else. It is a signature of the underlying imbalanced energies that created it. What traditional medicine calls the disease is a signature of the true imbalance held deeper in the human psyche. Or shall we say, from the healer's perspective, the disease is the physical manifestation of a deeper disturbance.

In the holographic model, everything is connected. For example, we connect the inability of a pancreas to function properly to our inability to absorb the sweetness in other areas of our lives. The pancreas is related not just to the digestion of the sweets we eat but to our ability to maintain the sweetness in life, in our relationships and in our personal nurturance. This may seem outrageous at first. But when one observes the workings of the human energy field, it becomes patently obvious. In a person with a healthy pancreas, we can observe direct energetic correlations between the energy field of the pancreas and that person's ability to connect with energy fields that correspond to universal sweetness.

When we think holographically, our symptoms are our friends. The true functional role of the symptom is to inform us that something within us is imbalanced. It is as if the symptom were the end of a string of yarn that is sticking out from under Grandma's couch. When we follow that string, we're led to the whole ball of yarn the kitten left there after playing. Within the ball is the cause of disease.

Especially in "incurable" cases, patients need to be directed to focus on the deeper inner reality and their other creative healing energies rather than the diagnosis. From the holographic standpoint, each person's natural predilection is to stay healthy or return to health in a most natural way. I call this natural process toward health the *balancing system*. Everyone has a balancing system. Most balancing systems are very strong, but they can be ignored and interfered with. It is each individual's responsibility to listen and respond to his or her balancing system.

Honoring Your Balancing System

Within you is a wonderful system of checks and balances that is designed to keep you, your auric field, and your physical body in perfect operating order. I call this system the balancing system. This balancing system holds your personal pattern of wholeness. Whenever anything is out of balance in your energy bodies or in your physical body, it automatically seeks to regain balance. Most of this system runs beneath the level of your conscious awareness. The wisdom held in this area of your being is probably much greater than you realize. We are just beginning to learn how to utilize it consciously.

In the past, we have not thought much about our balancing system, because it directly opposes the concept of entropy that falls out of M-1 metaphysics. The second law of thermodynamics shows that systems are continually breaking down and deteriorating and that you can't get more energy out of a system than you put into it. If you leave a piece of iron out in the rain, it will rust. Wood rots; leaves decay; and we get old and die. Energy is always lost out of a system. You can't build a perpetual motion machine. Within the M-1 system, we expect deterioration in everything.

But if this law applied to the entire world, it would mean a reversal in evolution, which, as we can see by simply looking around us, isn't true. Biological forms are continually evolving into more highly developed, intelligent, and specialized systems.

Rupert Sheldrake, Ph.D., a biochemist and author of *A New Science of Life*, *The Presence of the Past*, and *The Rebirth of Nature*, studied biological systems and developed the concept of morphogenetic fields and the theory of morphic resonance. His work shows that biological forms continually evolve through an underlying intelligent unified life field, the morphogenetic field. This life field automatically maintains health or seeks to return to it. This field is not only alive and constantly unfolding, but it has morphic resonance with all other life fields. That is, it is in contact with and communicates with all other life-forms. What happens to one creature will be communicated to all other creatures through morphic resonance. What one creature learns will eventually be transmitted to all other creatures.

Your balancing system is a morphogenetic field, based on the universal life principle of order that comes out of M-3 metaphysics and the holographic model. Evolution continually builds more complicated and highly evolved forms of life with more intelligence and capabilities. This continual building requires more order and balance within each more complicated system. Within every living organism is a predilection for balance and order. In terms of energy fields, this means a predilection toward balance and coherence within your field. Plus, it means that your field naturally tends toward synchronicity with all life energy fields. Your basic nature is to be in sync with all life.

On the physical level, your balancing system works automatically. If your stomach needs more acid, it doesn't bother to tell you about it—it just produces more. If you need more oxygen, your body simply breathes faster and deeper.

If, on the other hand, the body needs something it cannot give itself, the balancing system works through your senses to let you know to take care of it. In the first level of the field, you experience all body sensations. If you are thirsty, it is through the first level of the field that you will know it. Since everything in the energy field can be seen in terms of frequencies, when you are thirsty, the first level of your auric field will be low in the frequency of water. In other words, a lack of the water frequency at the first level of the field brings about the feeling of thirstiness.

When the first level of the field gets low in energy—say, from a lot of activity—its normal pulsations slow down and its lines get dull. You experience this change in your field by feeling tired. In this way, the first level of your field constantly tells you how to take care of your body. It tells you when you need exercise, sleep, food, and cooler or warmer clothes, when you need to change positions, clear your nasal passages, go to the bathroom, and so on. Feeling good, healthy, and energized corresponds to a charged, balanced, and coherent first auric field level.

As I began to delve into these processes with my patients, it became clear that directive messages telling patients what needed attending to were coming from all aspects of their lives. Your balancing system helps you take better care of yourself on all levels. When you do, feel, or think things that are not healthy for you, your balancing system will send messages to you in order to convince you to make your behavior healthier for you in all aspects of your life, including your personal relationships, your profession, your environment, and your spirituality. These messages come from the other levels of your auric field and will, again, be from the simple feeling of discomfort. The type of discomfort will correspond with the types of life experiences associated with each of the levels of the auric field, as was discussed in Chapter 2. Psychological discomfort or pain will come from imbalance in the levels associated with your psychological functioning, levels two and three. Pain or discomfort in relationship will come from imbalance in level four, while spiritual discomfort or pain will come from imbalance in levels five, six, and seven.

Keep an eye out for these different forms of messages from your balancing system. Stay tuned in and pay attention to how you feel in your various life situations. How do you feel about your psychological balance? How do you feel around the people you associate with? Do you feel spiritually connected and fulfilled?

You can change the situations in which you don't feel good, no matter what they are. They are unhealthy. You may need more nourishment in some areas. You may wish to spend less time in other areas. You may choose to leave behind certain situations, let go and let your life change. Once you learn the stages you will need to go through to change your health and your life (see Chapter 7) and the true, natural human needs that you do have that will bring about health once they are fulfilled (see Chapter 8), the rest of this book will give you the specific and detailed information you can use to balance your life. This will bring health and joy into your life.

How Imbalance That Leads to Disease Occurs in Daily Life

You may, however, convince yourself that it is easier to acclimate yourself to an unhealthy situation than to change it. Many people remain in denial about many areas of their lives because it seems either too difficult or impossible to change them. For some, the price seems just too high to take the chance of changing. It seems easier to convince yourself to accept less from life than you want or need than to pay a price that seems too high to take the chance of changing. This sort of denial can persist for years until life circumstances force a change, usually in terms of a personal crisis. Unfortunately, it is just this sort of thing that causes a great many of the physical difficulties that people have.

How and when you respond to an imbalance, and therefore to the discomfort signals from your balancing system in your auric levels, has a great deal to do with your body's health. The more you are able to respond to these requests, the better shape you will keep your body in and the stronger you will keep your immune system to fight off any possible illness.

To maintain your health, it is necessary to keep yourself aligned with your balancing system. If you find yourself in ill health, the work before you is to consciously align yourself with your balancing system, to reinstate its wisdom, and to follow its guidance. Most people ignore a great many of these messages when it is inconvenient to honor them. Let's look at a simple example of what happens when a message is ignored.

If you do not give your body the sleep it needs when it needs it, your body will go into an overdrive state. Your adrenals will give you the extra energy to continue your activity. If you make a habit of this, you will begin to experience the hyped-up state of adrenal overdrive as normal. That means that you will no longer be able to recognize the "I'm tired and need rest" message coming from your body's balancing system. If you continue to run on overdrive, your adrenal glands will become worn out, and you may go into a "burnout." What happens in a burnout, as a lot of therapists know, is that you simply lose most of your energy. And you cannot easily get it back. Even if you get a burst of energy, it will not last long, and you will have to rest. Sometimes it takes as much as three months to return to a normal work schedule. You have not only worn out your normal energy sources from your body's metabolic processes, but you have also worn out your reserve, which is drawn from the adrenals.

Find out the amount of rest your body needs and when it needs it. Remember, there are general guidelines for sleeping at night, but everyone is different. When does your body like to sleep? Are you an early bird or a night owl? Do you need seven, eight, or nine good hours of sleep at night? Set your own schedule.

Give yourself a break during the time of day that you usually get tired. In addition to getting the full night's rest that you need, I have found that a quick five-to-ten-minute rest as soon as you get tired is a big help. This is a must for anyone with back problems. Most reinjuries happen when a person is either tired or hungry. Find creative new ways to rest for short periods of time no matter where you are. For example, you can do a little simple meditation if you have five minutes to sit alone in your office or even in the bathroom. Do this by sitting still, with back straight and eyes closed, and breathing deeply while keeping your mind focused on a light in the center of your head. It will do wonders, and no one will miss you. If you have an office door you can close for a few minutes, bring a little rug or even a large beach towel to work. At break time, close your office door, put the towel on the floor, lie down on it with your legs, bent at the knees, up on the seat of your chair. The chair should be high enough to just give a little tug on the back of your knees so that it very

slightly lifts your back. Other ways to rest are to take frequent stretches or go for short walks. You will find your day going much smoother. If you are self-employed, then you have more control over your work schedule than if you have a nine-to-five job. But even people with full, regular schedules can train themselves to rest on breaks. If you work as a health-care professional or in consulting, be sure not to schedule appointments back to back for long periods of time. For example, I like to take a thirty-to-forty-five-minute nap right after lunch on the days when I teach long training programs. It completely refreshes me, and I come back to the work as if a new day were beginning. Most people do not realize how free they are to schedule these things. It's kind of like meditation or exercise; when you finally decide to do it, you have no difficulty finding the time.

Your balancing system works with food as well. When you need nourishment, you get hungry. You have an *appestat* within your system. It works much like the thermostat on your furnace, which turns the furnace on and off according to the temperature at which you set it. If you have been able to keep in touch with your appestat in a clear way, you will be hungry only when your body needs nourishment. And you will desire the kind of food that will give you exactly what your body needs each time you get hungry. You will also know how much your body needs. You will stop eating when your body has had enough, rather than "cleaning your plate," as if the food were more important than what it is for.

Here's how your appestat works in terms of the auric field. You get hungry because you are low on certain frequencies in your field that can be found in certain foods that you are usually accustomed to eating (assuming you have a full, balanced diet). The lack of such frequencies triggers hunger for the specific foods that contain those frequencies. When the frequencies are replaced, you are no longer hungry for the food that corresponds to the particular frequency, which is now fully charged in your field. You may, however, still be hungry for the frequencies that did not get replaced. Therefore, it is important to find that type of food to fill your frequency needs.

Why We Ignore Our Balancing Systems

Whenever anything needs extra attention and you ignore the message of discomfort from your balancing system, it will give you a louder message in the form of pain. If this message is not regarded as important, it will get louder still. How? The pain will get stronger. This will continue until you do something about it.

Ask yourself, Where is the discomfort or pain in my body? How long have I known about it? What have I done about it? If you ask yourself these questions, you will almost immediately be aware of discomfort within you that you have taught yourself to ignore, possibly for years. We all do it. The longer we ignore the messages and the symptoms, the louder the messages will get. The symptoms will become stronger. We even create disease by simply refusing to respond to these messages and take care of ourselves.

So why do we stay in this denial? There is one major reason. It is our fear. Under our denial lies our fear. We fear whatever we will have to face if we come out of the denial. I call fear the internal tiger.

Everyone has fears. What are yours? It is your fear that slows and blocks your *response-ability* to the messages from your balancing system. When you do not respond to your balancing system, you create more pain in your life. Your fear and your denial of it bring you closer to creating the very thing you fear in your life by blocking your natural ability to regain balance. This holds true for everyone, for all diseases, and even for people who don't consider themselves ill. (Physicians have stated that there are usually many diseases going on within normal human beings who consider themselves healthy.)

If you accept that your denial of your fear blocks your natural healing and growth process, it will be easier to remember that your symptoms are your friends. They keep you informed about your state of health. How well are you able to respond to them? What is your *response-ability*?

Denial can be a very costly thing. For example, a person came to me in a great deal of denial. She was overweight and wore very thick makeup, sunglasses, and a wig. I couldn't tell what she really looked like. She told me that she had just ended a relationship, lost her house, and had neither friends nor money. She had a large cancerous tumor growing in her jaw and throat area. It had been diagnosed two years earlier and treatment prescribed. She decided to "heal" it herself with no help because she had "healed" her cat. By the time she got to me, it appeared from my Higher Sense Perception that the tumor was impinging on her spinal cord in the neck area. Her arms tingled from the pressure on her nerves. Obviously, she needed more than I could give her. The probability of my being able to shrink the tumor in time to stop damage to her spinal column was extremely low. She had come too late to

me. She needed treatment from a physician, like surgery and chemotherapy, right away. I convinced her to go to another physician, one who worked with healers, but she didn't show for her appointment with him. Nor did she return for any more healings. I never saw her again. Most people do not stay in that kind of denial very long. Her fear was very great.

Denial can postpone a solution to a problem for so long that when the solution comes it is drastic. A friend of mine experienced a sudden change brought about by strong denial on the fourth level of the auric field. She was in denial about the state of her marriage. Her husband told her to come home for lunch on the day of her birthday because he had a surprise for her. When she got there, he told her that he was leaving her for another woman. In fact, he had spent the morning moving half the furniture out. He left, and that was that. She had had no idea there was a problem with their marriage. It was a very painful crisis to live through. Obviously, the shock changed her life quite a bit.

Why was she in denial? Because she was afraid that if she admitted to communication problems in her marriage, she would not be able to solve them. She feared she would lose her marriage. She did. It was hard. She may have been able to work it out with her ex-husband, or make the change in a less shocking way, if her denial had not been so strong and if she had been able to face her internal tiger. She is remarried now, in a much more communicative relationship. She is quite pleased with the final results.

Believe in Yourself—
You're Probably Right

It is important to believe in your balancing system and at the same time to be open to input from health-care professionals and friends you trust. If you get conflicting messages, keep pursuing an answer that will solve the conflict. If a physician says there is nothing wrong but your balancing system doesn't agree, get another opinion from another physician. Believe in and follow through on the messages coming from your balancing system. You will be grateful that you did.

For example, a friend of mine was told by a physician that the tumor growing in her mouth was not malignant. He even took a biopsy. However, she continued to have dreams about black strings of waste that needed to be pulled out of her mouth. She even had a dream about having cancer removed from her mouth. She didn't know what to do about the two different messages she was getting. She finally went for another biopsy that showed a malignancy. Fortunately, she did go back before the cancer had metastasized. Unfortunately, it was eight months later and radiation therapy was needed. It is several years now since her treatment, and she is fine.

In my fifteen-year practice as a healer, I found that most patients know the cause of their illness when they come. They speak about it in the first few moments of their intake interview. Many times, they also know what is wrong physically. They may not know the technical name for their problem, but they do know something is wrong. Usually they know what body organs are involved. I have found that the balancing system will very often give information about a disease before it is bad enough to show up on many of the tests that our medical system uses for diagnosis. This means the patient knows about it long before it is provable in our medical system. Here are some good examples where people believed themselves, even though they were unable to get answers right away.

David tried to get help for six years from many different physicians and health-care professionals for his symptoms of exhaustion and poor digestion. All the tests, including blood, urine, and hair analysis tests, showed him to be disease free. Many physicians told him that it was all in his head and that he should stop thinking about it and get on with his life. Apparently, his problem was what is called subclinical, meaning the tests weren't accurate enough to show it. David's symptoms of exhaustion and poor digestion persisted. Finally, he came to me. When he came, he was sure he had an infection in his liver, and he thought it was hepatitis. By examining his energy field, I was able to see that he had multiple infections throughout his abdomen. I was also able to psychically read a drug that would help his condition. David got a prescription from a physician who agreed with my findings. With a combination of the drug and healings, David's health was restored.

A woman I'll call Ellen came to me after seeing many physicians for about six months. Again her balancing system gave her information that was subclinical. They could find nothing wrong and told her she was a hypochondriac. That diagnosis, of course, didn't take her symptoms away. She continued to weaken every day. When she came to her healing, I was able to see "psychically" that she was being poisoned by fumes coming up through the floorboards of her home and that she

was also allergic to the dust from old carpets that had been there for years. I also "read" that she needed to take her children and herself to a psycho-immunologist to get checked out. I told her to get rid of the carpets and get the furnace inspected.

It turned out that she had just bought the house and moved in about six months earlier. Then she remembered that she kept thinking that her illness had something to do with her house, but she wasn't sure what. She returned home after the healing and had the furnace inspected. It indeed was leaking gas in several places. She replaced the furnace, threw out the old carpets, and immediately started getting better. She is quite well now. After examining her children, the psycho-immunologist said that if the leaks had continued for only a couple more weeks, both her children would have been brain damaged and she would have been very ill.

The Holographic Function of Your Balancing System

As I continued to delve into the processes of the balancing system with my patients, it became clear that the directive messages coming from all aspects of their lives had a similarity. These messages worked holographically. Their basic content was the same. If an individual was having problems with the pancreas, which plays an important role in the digestion of sweets, most likely they were having trouble with sweetness in other areas of their lives. And clear distress signals were being given in those areas as well. For example, people having trouble digesting sugar will also have trouble experiencing sweetness in other areas of their lives, such as in relationships to spouse or family, or in their work, or in their pastimes. Here we have another example of the holographic functioning of the universe.

Let's look at this phenomenon from the perspective of the auric field. Sweetness in the first level of the field is experienced as physical taste. In the second, it is experienced in the sweetness of a good relationship to oneself. In the third, it is a sweet thought; in the fourth, the sweetness that comes in intimacy; in the fifth, the sweetness in clear divine will; in the sixth, the sweetness of spiritual ecstasy; in the seventh, the sweetness of universal mind. And beyond that there is the cosmic energy of sweetness threaded throughout the tapestry of the universe.

Another way to look at the concept of a difficulty being threaded holographically throughout your life is to consider the relationships of frequency bands within the auric field. Since the levels of the HEF can be seen as frequency bands, each personal experience correlates to these energy frequency bands. A personal experience of sweetness can be seen as a different frequency or frequency band for each level of the field. These frequencies of sweetness of the different levels of the field relate to each other as harmonics, or overtones, do in music.

If an auric field has difficulty metabolizing a particular frequency into the auric field on one level, it will probably have a similar difficulty metabolizing its related harmonics on the other levels of the field as well. Health requires that a person be able to accept and assimilate (that is, metabolize) sweetness into all the levels of the auric field.

So now let us restate the basic questions from the holographic point of view. Where is the discomfort/pain in your life? How long have you known about it? And what have you done about it? The longer you have ignored or denied it, the more serious the situation probably is.

Once you have found the discomfort, check all the other areas of your life and find how the same thread of discomfort is there, woven through your whole existence. You see, that is the real problem—that which is woven through your whole life. It injures you in all areas of your life, not just the one that shows it most.

If you have back trouble, what other areas of your life are you backing out of? I immediately look for something the patient has always wanted to do and never thought they really could. This particular problem has a great deal to do with the deeper spiritual longing each of us carries within us. This longing directs our life from a spiritual level. It is usually on the edge of consciousness. Sometimes the person hasn't thought about it for years. Other times, they are just afraid to try, or they avoid it. Usually there are internal voices that say, "Who do you think you are?" or, "You're not good enough," or, "There's not enough _____ to do it."

One patient who was working for a large electronics machine company in sales was bed-ridden 80 percent of his time when he came to me. With HSP, I could clearly see that he had a lot of good inventive ideas that he was not putting forth to his company. His back improved to a certain degree in the healing work, but it didn't really get healthy until he put some time in on his special projects. The company is using them now, and

he is much better. He was able to devote part of his time to research and design work. It was something he had always longed to do.

If your legs are weak, how are you not standing up for yourself in all other areas of your life? Many times people with leg problems do not defend themselves. Or in other cases, they do not earn their own incomes. Sometimes, they just plain need to be taken care of, and this is the only way they can ask. When the original need or longing is filled, healing speeds up. One woman who was bed-ridden for ten years after an operation had her whole family taking care of her. She finally had her fill and had the bright idea of hiring a dog walker to walk with her. It worked, and she is much freer now.

If you have trouble assimilating foods, what else in your life that comes to you as nourishment do you have trouble assimilating? One particular patient, a middle-aged woman who had digestive problems, also had trouble receiving nourishment coming to her from friends. She was just afraid that whatever she received would be harmful. She had very bad eating habits and would simply not bother to have three meals a day. During her healing process, she found a good diet that nourished her body. With her strength growing, she was also able to allow others to give to her in ways she never had before. Her friends encouraged her to give herself things that she would never have bought for herself before. Her husband took her on vacations, something she had never done before. She got a new house and furnished it for the first time in her life.

If you have thyroid problems, how are you doing regulating the energy in your life? (The thyroid regulates energy metabolism in the body.) Joan, a busy businesswoman, worked all the time, for years, until she overtaxed her thyroid. She was unable to regulate where she spent her energy in her life, splurging it all in her work. When Joan read Louise Hay's book *You Can Heal Your Life*, she saw that a statement related to thyroid problems is, "When is it going to be my turn?" Joan said she really related to that. She always had the next job to do and never had time for herself. Joan finally quit her job and now lives a much more subdued life.

The liver is associated with how you "live" your life. I know a man who has a sluggish liver and the rest of his life is sluggish also. He never really got out there and did what he wanted. He has spent a lot of time smoking pot and wishing he could be a singer.

If you look from the perspective that these people simply didn't know how to metabolize the energies they needed directly into their fields, their experiences make sense. Working with people in this way helps them find and stop the lies they are living in their lives and promotes a great deal of healing.

Of course, one doesn't just tell somebody, "Oh, your legs are weak. You aren't standing up for yourself." This is not a statement of love. Rather, it is important to lead the person into self-knowledge. Healers not only fill in the missing frequencies in the field but teach clients how to metabolize them for themselves. The patients must learn that they are betraying themselves by not giving themselves what they long for in their lives. The healer shows them how their particular phys-ical problem is much more than just weak legs or a sluggish liver. It is a dissatisfaction of the soul that they really wish to heal.

The holographic model works well in such teachings. Disease is really a very simple thing. So is knowing its cause. But most people are not taught to recognize that kind of "knowing." Healers are. I would therefore say that the main job of any healer is to educate the patient back into a state of familiarity with his or her balancing systems, that deeper place within us that remembers who we are, what we need, and how we heal ourselves.

PART II

THE TECHNIQUES OF HEALING IN OUR TIME

"The real act of discovery consists not in finding new lands but in seeing with new eyes."

—Marcel Proust

My Personal Perspective As a Healer

I had a healing practice for some fifteen years. I've been a healing teacher for thirteen more years. One thing I know with absolute certainty is that healing and teaching must be approached with love, humility, courage, and power if they are to be effective. Healing and teaching must be done in the clear light of the deeper spiritual truths. Whenever a patient comes to me in need of healing, I am aware that the deepest need any person has is to find his or her way home, to the real self, the divine within. It doesn't matter what the presenting complaint is. The deeper inner need is always the same. In opening the way into the real self, patients heal themselves.

All healers and teachers must walk their talk. It takes a lot of self-development and self-transformation and a lot of training in the healing arts to be an effective healer. Humility and meticulous honesty with self are of utmost importance. The hard part about healing training is not the techniques but the personal growth one must go through to become ready to learn the techniques. Then the techniques come quite naturally. For example, in my years of teaching, I have seen beginners try to learn advanced techniques before they are spiritually ready to enter into the deeper spiritual

experience connected with the technique. What results is a lot of fantasy and sometimes temporary damage to their fellow students' energy fields. In other cases, I have seen people take a weekend workshop, get labeled or label themselves as healers, and begin a healing practice. Many times, these people give ineffectual healings and fantasy prognoses. Some even announce fantasy cures to very ill clients who end up back in the hospital.

The heart of healing is not the techniques but the states of being out of which those techniques arise. For example, when I first began healing, I accomplished less in a one-and-one-half-hour healing than I can now accomplish in a few minutes, because I can now enter into much deeper and more powerful spiritual states of being that transmit thousands of times more noninvasive healing energy that is extremely precise to what the client needs.

Healers do not work miracles. All healing can do is what the human body can do. It can do a lot, and there are things it can't do. To my knowledge, no human being has ever regenerated a limb—yet. But I'm willing to bet that every illness that has been labeled as "terminal" has been healed or "spontaneously remissed" by at least one person. "Terminal" is the present state of the human condition. We will all "die." That is, our physical body will die. But that doesn't mean we will die, as in "cease to exist," or even lose consciousness for very long, for that matter. The hardest part of physical death may be the fear of letting go into the unknown, of letting go of loved ones and in some cases the physical pain associated with death.

I say these things from life experience gained through what I call Higher Sense Perception. Many people call it being psychic. I prefer the term *Higher Sense Perception*, meaning the development of the senses beyond the ordinary ranges most human beings use. That's not as glamorous. All the five senses can be expanded beyond the normal ranges with good teaching and practice. As with any other skill, some people are more talented than others. When you develop seeing, hearing, smelling, tasting, and touching beyond the normal ranges, a whole new world opens up. It takes quite a bit of getting used to, but if you give yourself plenty of time, you can integrate this new world into your life. Of course your life will change, but it always does anyway.

When Higher Sense Perception opens, a person can see energy fields surrounding and interpenetrating everything, including the human body. These energy fields are intimately associated with all life functions and change constantly in accordance with life function, including physical, mental, and spiritual life functions. The human energy field, or aura, is composed of seven energy levels, as we have seen. Each level has constantly changing patterns of energy that pulse with the lifeforce. Each level is composed of higher vibrations or pulsations than the one it surrounds and interpenetrates. These patterns change with health, sickness, and the dying process.

When we learn about the human energy field and observe it for a while, a new idea dawns. The human energy field isn't just an energy field. It is the person. In fact, it is more the person than the physical body is. The levels of the human energy field are really energy bodies. They are you. You are energy. You are not in your physical body—your physical body is in you. From this perspective, then, when you die, something very different happens.

I can "see" a person after they leave their physical body at death. People who just died still have some of these energy bodies. They are composed of the higher four levels of their energy bodies, without a physical body inside them. The lower three levels, that hold the physical body in place, dissolve in the dying process. To me, death is a transition. It is a great change. It is a rebirth into another plane of reality. Unless they have had a long-term illness, people usually look pretty healthy shortly after death. Usually in hospitals, they rest on the "other side" of the curtain that separates what we normally call life and death. To me, that curtain is illusory; it only separates our physical self from our higher spiritual self, which does not die at physical death. Taken in this light, we can look at it as a curtain that separates who we think we are from who we really are.

These things may sound outrageous, but to stand by my reality, I must say them. It is real for me. If it is not real for you, then do not try to force my experience into your reality. You must build your reality out of your experience. In that building, consider the possibility that life is a greater mystery than you know, and whatever death turns out to be for you, it has the possibility of being a really wonderful surprise.

Another aspect of Higher Sense Perception is perceiving spiritual guides or guardian angels. This level of reality opens when one opens Higher Sense Perception to the fourth level of the human energy field and higher. In the beginning, I just thought I was having a vision or making something up. I would be giving a healing, and an angel would walk into the room. I knew they were angels because they had wings. The ones who didn't have wings, I called guides. Soon they were putting their hands through mine as I worked on people. I could see *and* feel their hands working. Then they started telling me where to put my hands, and what to do in a healing.

I still hung on to the idea that it was just a vision. Of course, people kept getting well when I did what they said. A big change came when I decided to ask the guides questions. They answered with things I did not or could not have known. Our interactions had become relational. I could see, feel, hear, smell, touch, and interact with them. They had become just as real to me as anyone in a physical body. This still takes some getting used to. It's not something everyone can do, at least not yet.

If guardian angels and spiritual guides are not part of your reality, consider the possibility that they could be. You may be pleasantly surprised by how your life struggles become easier by allowing the possibility that you can get help by simply asking for it and learning to recognize help when it comes. You can do this, even if you can't see, hear, talk with, or feel them. It is a way to open a door to your eventually perceiving them. That is what I did, and it worked.

After some time, I became friends with a particular

guide who has been with me many years. "His" name is Heyoan. He says he does not have a gender, but I like to use *he*. I have spent many years healing with Heyoan and the guides of each patient who walk into the healing room with the patient. Now Heyoan and I teach the healing classes. I lecture for a while, then go into an altered state and "channel" Heyoan. That means Heyoan gives a lecture through me. This always lifts the whole class to a much higher level of spiritual understanding than if I talk to the class without "channeling." In every class, new information, which builds on all that has gone before, comes through. Heyoan has contributed several meditations for healing that you will find throughout this book.

If, on the other hand, guardian angels or guides are not a reality for you or are not acceptable for you, perhaps you can call the phenomenon of guidance "getting information from an alter ego," "mind reading," or simply "psychic reading." For me, it is not the metaphor of reality that you use to describe this phenomenon that is important but the usefulness of the information that is gained through altered states of consciousness. I'm sure, as this phenomenon becomes more understood, we will find better metaphors with which to describe it.

From a holistic perspective, in which we all consist of energy fields in which our physical bodies live, what is healing? It is dissolving the veil between our personality self and our inner divine core. It is dissolving the veil between who we think we are and who we really are. It is dissolving the veil between life and death. If a patient comes to me and asks, "Am I going to die?" or, "Does healing mean I am going to get better physically?" I give the answer set within the context of the divine core within the patient and the spiritual reality I described above. One gets better whether or not one dies, and death is very different in the above context.

If a patient asks, "Will I ever be the same again?" the answer is no, but it is given in the context of life as constant personal change.

If the question is, "Am I going to get better?" the answer, within the above context, is always yes. For life is always moving toward unification with the divine whole.

The answer to "Will I walk again?" is usually "I don't know, but it is possible. Nothing is impossible."

QUESTION: How do I deal with this terrible pain?
BARBARA: Healing usually reduces the amount of pain, but don't feel bad about taking pain-killers; they are also a gift from God. Doing relaxation and visualization exercises helps reduce pain. Self-rejection and self-judgment increase pain. Go easy on yourself. You are not at fault here. This is a life lesson. You are not being punished. Spend several minutes a day doing the breathing, color, and loving-yourself exercises given in Part IV.

QUESTION: I am terrified. Help me. Tell me what to do.
HEYOAN, my guide, says:

~

Let fear be your ally. Fear has a great deal to teach you. Fear is the experience of being disconnected from who you truly are; it is the opposite of love. Fear can be an ally if you allow it to be, and just say, I'm afraid. In continually doing this, you begin to see that you are not fear itself, but that fear rather is a feeling. "I am afraid" becomes "I feel fear." It is the reaction of holding feelings because you believe they are coming too fast. These feelings are based on a great many assumptions of what might happen. Most fear is not of what is happening now but of what might be. If you are able to stay in the moment, fear will not find you. Fear is the projection of something that has happened in the past, into the future, through a large magnifying glass. So when you are in fear, you are not in reality. But rather than deny that you feel it, just say what you feel in the moment. This act alone will bring you into the moment, and thereby out of fear.

~

QUESTION: How will my life be different?
BARBARA: Because you are sick, you may no longer be able to function in what you thought your life's purpose was. It is necessary to change your self-definition. It is necessary to focus on inner values rather than outer goals. The outer goals will come again later. Now it is time to heal the inside. What your life is all about will begin to have a much deeper personal meaning to you. You will gain insights into the preciousness of life itself you never had before. You will gain love. That is always a lesson in illness. Your life will be affected in greater ways than you can imagine now. It is time to begin to surrender to the process of healing and let yourself be carried by your greater wisdom, which is connected to the divine.

A patient often first goes to a healer, hoping to find relief from pain or a certain symptom or to be cured from a specific disease, maybe have a tumor taken away. And *always* the patient receives much more than that. The focus of the healer is not only to eliminate the leg pain or the tumor but to also work with the patient to find and heal the root cause of the original symptom or disease. That will be found on a deeper level of the patient's inner being.

As a professional healer, I have been witness to healings of all kinds. At first some things surprised me. Later, I understood them to be part of the natural process of healing. As the inner corridors to the deeper self open within, the patient's experience of life changes. So does the rest of his or her life.

We've all heard about people who, after experiencing an illness, change professions. They don't do so because the illness required it—for example, because they couldn't physically drive a truck anymore—but because they find a different purpose. They desire change. The "simple" healing of an illness can bring about dramatic change. Personal relationships change. Some healings bring about marriages; others bring about dissolution of marriages that don't nurture the partners. In other cases, an illness will be the completion of a whole stage of life. And the patient will change just about everything—profession, home, geographic location, friends, spouse. Some healings mend long-term splits among family members. Through the healing experience, people gain a much greater respect and trust for their own inner knowing. Many people refer to this as a rebirth.

What Your Healer Will Do That Your Physician or Therapist Will Not

If you are considering going to a healer, it is important to know that healers work within a very different context than physicians. The two can be complementary if communication avenues are open and trust is created. Since I believe that in the future many physicians and healers will work together for the benefit of all, I've devoted the chapter after this one to that vision.

Many patients come to a healer wanting the same services a physician offers. Most of us see disease according to the medical system established in this country. People have been so used to going to a physician to get rid of a particular ailment, they expect healing work to alleviate pain and cure a specific illness as well.

The first thing healers must do when such a patient comes to them is to educate the patient as to what is being offered and what is not. To make this clearer, let's start with the basic structure of an office visit to the doctor, then compare it to what happens when you go to a healer.

1. The doctor checks the patient in an examination room.
2. The doctor orders tests to be done that will help figure out what is wrong.
3. After the examination, patient and doctor meet in another room, "the doctor's office," where the doctor sits behind a desk, to discuss what the doctor might think is wrong. The doctor does what he or she can for the patient until the rest of the tests come back.
4. The patient schedules another appointment for after the tests are completed.
5. In this appointment, the doctor does more examination, gives the results of the tests, and gives a diagnosis. The doctor prescribes a method of treatment based on the diagnosis or orders more tests if the first ones are not conclusive.
6. Treatment is usually some kind of medication or surgery to get rid of the problem.

When patients come to a healer, many times they expect the same six steps to be followed. They want a psychic examination. They ask the healer to take away (apparently magically) their problem, much as pills and surgery take away some physical problems. Many people expect to have a posthealing meeting in which the healer gives a diagnosis and a prognosis of how long it will take "to take it away."

Most healers do not use the six-step structure when working with patients. Usually, there is very little talking, no tests, no diagnosis, no prescribed medications, and many times no explanation of what is about to occur before the healing, what is occurring during it, or what has occurred afterward.

The steps in a healing session are very simple.

1. Healers usually begin with a short talk with a patient as to why the patient came. Some healers simply ask the patient to go in, take off their shoes, and get on the healing table or simply sit in a chair.
2. The healer works on the patient, either touching or not touching the patient, according to his or her healing techniques. The healer might give some explanation. There may be some discussion during the healing.
3. The healer finishes, leaves the room, and tells the patient to rest a few minutes before getting up.
4. There is very little discussion afterward, and the healer asks the patient to come back at the appropriate time.

Many patients are disappointed by their first healing experience because they don't understand what happened. They feel more relaxed and probably better, and they want to know why. They may have even walked into the office with a whole set of questions, all based on the system of illness (and M-1 metaphysics) that is accepted in this country.

They may have questions like:

"What disease is this?"
"Do I have a tumor? What kind of tumor?"
"Can you take it away?"
"How many healings will it take?"
"How much will this cost?"
"Is my Fallopian tube blocked and preventing pregnancy? Just open it please. The doctors say they can't."

After a healing, people say things like:

"Well, I don't really feel much different—just more relaxed."
"What did you do?"
"Now tell me exactly what you did."
"How long will it last?"
"Is it gone? Will it come back?"
"Shall I come back? How many more times?"

These are all important and valid questions that need to be addressed, but they arise out of the present-day medical and health-care system of this country. To answer them in a meaningful way for the patient, the healer must bring the patient into a different understanding of health and disease.

Whether or not healers are aware of the scientific holographic context and M-3 metaphysics explained in Chapter 3, their main focus is holistic—to help patients create health in all areas of life. They do this by clearing and balancing the patient's energy, by working to align his or her intent to heal, and by helping him or her connect to the deeper core of his or her being, creative force, and core consciousness. They direct healing energies into the patient's energy system. Many healers work completely intuitively, allowing their hands to move freely. They offer no explanation of what might be wrong with the patient or what is happening in the healing. That is why it is called faith healing.

Others try to offer explanations that may not make any sense at all to the patient. Some have complete systems of knowledge worked out. These systems may be known by other healers, such as the system of acupuncture, while others may have been worked out personally by the healer and be specific only to him or her. They describe what is going on in the patient and how the healing is working. These can be difficult for the patient who isn't trained in the particular system the healer is using to understand.

To educate patients, I first find a common ground of understanding within which to converse. Then I explain as best I can the healing process that is to be initiated by healings. I say that healing will continue to unfold within them and tell them how much it is going to affect their lives.

I remember one session when a new patient named Liz, who had an ulcer and wanted to prevent surgery, walked into my office and said, "Now tell me exactly what you do." I stopped for a moment at the question and thought, "I wonder if she asked her surgeon the same question, and what answer she got."

It would, of course, take years to explain what exactly I do. A patient such as Liz would have to be completely reeducated in the holographic view of reality, the causes of illness from that perspective, the human energy system, therapeutic techniques, and healing techniques.

So I asked myself, "What is the deeper question Liz is asking? What does she really want to know?"

Liz was obviously trying to take responsibility for her health and her healing. She genuinely wanted to understand what to expect in the healings. She wanted to know what I could give her. Her question was, "What are the possible outcomes of healings?" She had no idea of how broad the effect could be. She didn't know how much all that depended on her and her acceptance of personal change in her life. She didn't know that the human energy field exists and affects the physical body. And most of all, she didn't know she could heal herself with her intention to heal (haric level) and with her creative force from within (core star level). My challenge was to cover a vast ground of knowledge in a few minutes' time. I searched for a simple analogy to start with and remembered how a radio works. Of course, I would have time for more detailed explanations during the healing sessions that would follow.

So I said, "Have you heard of the human energy field, or aura?"

"No," said Liz.

"Well, there is an energy field that surrounds and interpenetrates the body. It is intimately associated with your health. When you become ill, it is because the normal functioning of this field has been disturbed. What I do is to realign this field, charge it, and repair it. It is a little like acupuncture. Have you heard of that?"

Liz said, "Yes, I've heard of it, but don't know much about it."

"Well, acupuncture is an ancient form of healing from the east, that works by balancing your energy field, which supplies bioenergy to the different systems of your body. This energy is very powerful. We actually bring more energy into our bodies through this field than we do by eating. Did you notice that on sunny days you have more energy than on cloudy days? That's because the sun charges the energy in the air. Then we take it in through our energy system. We don't think too much about it in our culture because we concentrate primarily on the physical body. But in China, Japan, and India, it is known to be most important to our health. Their systems are based on knowledge of these life energy fields."

Liz replied, "Where does this energy come from?"

"The source of this energy is inside you and all around you," I said. "It's like radio waves that are always there in the air. You just need to know how to receive them to get the benefit. Turn on the radio and tune it to the station you want. Your energy field is like a radio. I'm here to repair it and help you learn to tune it better. I'll help open up and balance your chakras."

"My what? My chakras?" Liz asked.

"The chakras in your aura are your energy receivers," I explained. "They look like vortices of energy that, by virtue of their spin, pull energy into them like any whirlpool. After the energy gets sucked into your body, it then flows along the energy lines in your field to your organs.

"Whenever there is disruption in your field, your organs don't get the energy they need, and they become weak, eventually allowing access for infection or other physical problems."

"That sounds simple enough," Liz agreed. "So

you're actually saying that I could get this ulcer because my energy lines are weak?"

"It is, of course, more complicated than that, but that's basically the idea. The way you react to stressful situations can be seen in your field. You habitually distort your field in a way that pulls healthy energy out of the stomach area and draws improper and therefore unhealthy energies to your stomach. When we've rebalanced your field, you will be able to feel what proper healthy energies in that area feel like. Now what you experience as 'normal' for you is not healthy."

"What do you mean by that?"

"Just bring your awareness to your stomach now," I said.

"It feels like it usually does."

"After the healing, it will feel different," I said. "Then you will understand what I mean. It's something you need to experience. It is a subtle difference, but a very powerful one as far as health goes. Eventually you will learn how to keep the proper balance of energies in your system, and you will be able to maintain a higher level of health. So when I rebalance your field, the energy flows properly to your body systems, and you regain your health. You will be able to tap into the energy fields all around you.

"I call these energy fields the universal health fields. They are there for everyone. They are not only available for your physical health but for your emotional, mental, and spiritual health as well. So now, when I work on your fields, we will also work on your emotional, mental, and spiritual aspects that relate to your having an ulcer. You see, it's not just a physical thing. Not only that, but whatever is healed for you personally will also heal whatever aspect of your life it is connected to."

"What do you mean by that?" Liz asked. "What connections do you mean?"

"From the healer's point of view," I went on, "everything is connected to everything else. It is the holistic view. It means that your ulcer, which is a result of overacidity in your stomach caused by your reaction to stress, not only affects your digestion and your nourishment but is a sign to me that you most likely have stress in every area of your life that concerns 'digestion' of personal nourishment. In other words, even when someone gives you something, it must be hard to take it in and let it make you feel good."

"Sounds familiar, but I don't see how that could be connected to an ulcer," she replied.

"Yes, well, let's just start where we are now, and let your experiences unfold. We'll take care of the connections as they come up. I'll make it clearer then."

"How long will it take to regain health?" she asked.

"How many sessions it takes depends on how well your system responds to the healing, how much change it (you) can take, and how long you are able to hold that change. Change isn't always so easy, you know, because it affects all areas of your life, as I said. It takes time to integrate changes. You see, we want to go for the deeper cause of the ulcer, not just the ulcer. We want you to be able to take in and enjoy what you receive. We want to find out why you may not think that is okay."

"I think it's fine to receive," she said. "But it's true— I always feel that I owe the person who gave me something. I don't like to owe people. Wow, I didn't know there was so much to this. Does this stuff really work?"

"Working with the human energy field is actually more useful in some illnesses than our regular medicine," I said. "I usually get the people with diseases that our medical system isn't very successful with. People with cancer, colitis, immune disorders, viruses, migraines, and so on."

"Well, I'm glad I'm here. This sounds interesting. Let's go for it."

Liz really wanted to know what the healing process was all about, and we were able to communicate clearly. This helped her as she went through the healing process. As we continued through several weeks, her ulcer disappeared and she regained her health. Not only that, she also changed her profession and began a new relationship.

The Skills of a Healer

I gently coaxed Liz into the holistic view by describing it in simple terms. As a healer, I work from a broader view to deal with disease. I agree with physicians that an infection due to a microorganism may occur and that usually a medication will remove it. But from my perspective, the microorganism is not the cause. Healers know that a weakness or imbalance in the patient's physical-energetic system allowed for the microorganism invasion that developed into a disease. The microorganism invasion is also another symptom. The cause must be dealt with from the holistic or holographic point of view before true health can be restored. The healer is more concerned with the underlying balance of energies, intention, and consciousness that support health or that become imbalanced and eventually allow for disease.

Healers must have the ability to work with all these aspects of a patient's human makeup. They focus on healing the physical body and seek to heal the patient's emotional, mental, and spiritual aspects as well.

The tools and training of a healer are very different from those of a physician. Although most highly skilled healers probably are capable of accessing information about an illness, perhaps even naming both it and an appropriate medication that would correspond to a physician's diagnosis, that is not their primary concern. Healers regard that information as part of the description of "Pribram's apple," not the primary reality and not of prime importance. Indeed, it is quite illegal for them to give such a diagnosis. That right has been reserved for those courageous and dedicated souls who have graduated from medical school and passed the state boards.

Liz did not ask me for a diagnosis; rather, she told me what it was when she came in. She filled out my client intake form that asks for the patient's disease history. I checked the information she had given me. With HSP I could see that part of the wall of the stomach tissue was worn away, and that the tissues that remained in that area were inflamed. They looked red. With that HSP information, I too would conclude that she had an ulcer. Yet I do not, as a healer, diagnose, any more than you do, when you can simply look and see that someone has just cut themselves or broken an arm.

How Healers Work with the Human Energy Field

There are specific healing techniques for each level of the human energy field. I usually concentrate on the lower levels of a patient's field when I work, starting on level one. The work includes sensing, cleansing, balancing, repairing, and charging the field. Most of the time, each layer has to be treated separately to make sure that all levels are healed. A full healing must include healing all levels of the field, or *all* the energy bodies in addition to the physical. Therefore, I move through levels of patients' energy fields that correspond not only to their physical, emotional, and mental nature but to their spiritual nature and their basic beliefs in reality as well. All need to be balanced. To do this, the healer taps into the universal health field held in the holographic universe. If this is not completed, the patient may very well recreate either the same or another disease.

Healers are usually born with a talent to be able to learn to perceive and work with the energy field. This talent is no different from another person's talent in music, math, or business. Most healers have had training, like other professionals, to develop these innate talents into a healing art. This training teaches the healer to develop Higher Sense Perception, with which to sense the levels of the human energy field and eventually the levels of the hara and core star beneath the aura. It will probably also include training in channeling.

By diligent practice of many exercises designed to increase the sensitivity of their senses, healers learn to use those senses beyond the normal range of human perception. Many healers can feel, hear, and see this energy field, as well as intuit other information about it. In addition to sensing the field, the healer also must learn a great deal about how to work with the field to heal through its levels, as well as about human anatomy, physiology, psychology, illness, and the ethics of healership.

With Higher Sense Perception, healers distinguish the many levels of the human energy field. Since each layer of this energy field also penetrates inside the body, healers also sense the field inside the human body. Well-trained healers also develop the ability to sense the energy field of the whole body, of a single cell, and sometimes even of smaller particles. With the use of HSP, healers can access a great deal of information to utilize in the healing process.

Above all, healers' greatest tool is love. All healing is done in the context of love. I believe that love is the connective tissue of the universe. It holds it together. Love can heal anything. Healers not only work from a place of love, they teach patients to love themselves. As we move through this book, it will be more and more apparent just how important loving is. Loving the self is a full-time job. Most of us have a lot to learn in this area.

Liz's healings slowly progressed through the levels of her aura. Her third chakra, located in the stomach area, was torn. I repaired it, and her ulcers began to heal. On the emotional level, that chakra is associated with connecting to other people and being able to receive nourishment from them in a healthy way. Her relationships became closer and more fulfilling as we worked to teach her to maintain a healthy balance of energy in that area of her body. On a deeper level of the psyche, that chakra is related to who you are in the universe, your place on earth and in this life. As those levels of her field became stabilized in a healthy way, she also became more self-confident about who she is.

The Mechanics of a Healing Session

The mechanics of a healing session are quite simple from the physical point of view. Of course they vary with each healer. The mechanics I describe here are those followed by the men and women who have graduated from the Barbara Brennan School of Healing.

If you choose to have a healing with such a graduate, you will first be asked to fill out an intake form, usually listing your history and presenting your complaints. The healer will interview you to make you feel comfortable and find a common ground of communication within which to speak. A main question will be, "Why are you here? What have you come to accomplish?"

From your answer, the healer will not only find what you want but will begin to find your level of experience with the healing work.

While the healer listens to you and finds a common ground of understanding, the healer is also using HSP to scan your energy field to find imbalances, tears, stagnations, and depletions. She watches your constantly changing flow of energy as you talk. She correlates those changes with your psychological state as you describe your problems. She reads your physical body with normal vision to discover the psychological environment of your childhood from your body structure and body language. She also scans your physical level with HSP to check internal structural alignment and organ functions. The healer usually takes about ten to fifteen minutes for this scan to find the major areas of difficulty in your body and energy system. She will sometimes share this information with you if she is sure of it and if giving it to you will not interfere with your healing process. In other words, she will speak in ways that do not frighten you, stop your energy flow, or decrease your ability to intake energy. All this information integrates into a holographic model, since all the levels of functioning affect each other.

After getting the overview, the healer will ask you to take off your shoes and socks and lie on the treatment table. Nothing else needs to be removed. Sometimes some jewelry or crystals may be interfering with your field, and she will ask you to remove them. The healer simply proceeds to put her hands on your feet and sends energy through your body. She slowly moves up the body, placing her hands in key positions and using various healing techniques, depending on what HSP revealed about your condition. Of course, with HSP, the healer is always observing the effects she is having on your energy fields. (She also carefully observes and regulates her own field—a very important part of healing training.) The healer continues this HSP scanning to see how well you are receiving the healing and to get more detailed information about the changes occurring in your field during the healing. With use of HSP, the healer can make sure that all necessary changes are accomplished and that nothing is missed.

As the healing progresses, the healing gets much stronger. More energy is poured through your system, and you will probably go into a very deep state of relaxation, which helps the healing process a great deal. At this time your brain becomes synchronized with the healer's. Both are in strong alpha waves (8 Hz), the healing state.

Other information obtained with HSP will include diet, vitamins, minerals, herbs, or even medications that could later be prescribed by a physician if appropriate. The HSP also reveals psychological problems that helped cause the illness. It reveals childhood traumas, your images of how you think reality is, and ultimately your belief system, which is the basic cause that keeps your illness intact. The healer directly works with all these through your energy field.

During the healing, the healer will also use HSP to receive guidance from spiritual teachers, guides, or guardian angels. This guidance comes in many different forms. The guides may tell the healer what to do next; they may tell the healer where to look for your physical difficulties; or they may even name the disease you have. The guides usually tell the healer the cause of the problem from both the physical and the psychological perspective. The guides may speak directly through the channel of the healer to you. When this occurs, the conversation that ensues is usually a very tender, personal one that brings you into a deeper understanding of what is going on with yourself, why it is going on from the perspective of cause, and the deeper spiritual and life lessons involved. These conversations are always supportive and truthful and make no false promises if the channel is clear. The guides also work directly through the hands of the healer to heal you. Other information received through HSP is either written down or taped for your further use.

It usually takes several sessions to get down to the cause in the belief system. By the time the healer has progressed through all layers of the field and brought closure to the healing, you will probably be in a state of deep relaxation and serenity.

Many healers encourage you to rest on the table for ten to thirty minutes to allow the fields to stabilize. This allows you to take full advantage of the healing and allows it to integrate into your energy system. The healer usually answers a minimum of questions at this time, because in order to ask a rational question, you must go out of the healing alpha brainwave state and into the "rational" beta or fast brainwave state, which will stop the healing process. When I was practicing healing, I always warned my patients before the healing

started about this very important posthealing quiet time and encouraged them to ask all the questions in the beginning of the healing before the alpha linkup occurs. Later, the healer will ask you to come back at the appropriate time and will assure you that the rest of your questions can be answered next time.

Common Questions and Answers

Can a Patient Resist a Healing? If So, How?

Many times people resist the healing process by trying to control the situation with an overactive mind. This is easy to do. All the patient needs to do is force a very active mind and refuse to relax and allow the healing to take place. If patients force their brains to remain rational, they will not go into an alpha state, 8 Hz, the healing state. Rather, they will stay in normal waking brainwave patterns, beta waves. (Patients, of course, can do this anytime, whether or not a healer is present.) If they continue to stay in such a state, they will interfere with the normal healing processes in their body. When patients' rational minds get out of the way and their brainwaves go into alpha, they are able to surrender to their natural healing process as enhanced by the healer.

How Are Healing Sessions Spaced?

Healings are usually scheduled once a week, to last one or one and one-half hours, for several weeks. Sometimes, especially for back problems, I would only work with people if they could come twice a week. That is because there is so much strain on the back from normal daily activity that inevitably patients would get tired, have low blood sugar, do one last lift, and restrain their backs again before a week was up. I found that diet was also very important for back problems. People would only strain their back again when they were overworked and hungry, with low blood sugar. I would instruct them to carry a bag of nuts and dried fruit around with them, to eat more often, and to eat complete meals. It is amazing how many overstressed, undernourished people our rich society produces!

The spacing of sessions for cancer patients who are on chemotherapy or radiation therapy should be at least weekly and always right after a treatment, even if that treatment is daily. Chemo and radiation cause debris in the physical body as well as the energy field. The debris from chemo is composed of the chemotherapy itself, as well as from the tissues it kills. The body must get rid of both. Chemotherapy causes low-frequency, mucusy, dark, thick bioplasma in the auric field that does not support life. It slows and interferes with the functioning of the auric field, causing a great deal of discomfort in the client. Radiation also causes debris in the physical body because it not only kills cells, it alters the normal biological processes that occur in many cells around those that are killed. This produces a lot of waste products that also must be gotten rid of. Radiation burns the auric field, much like putting a nylon stocking into a flame. This damage needs to be repaired. Radiation also causes the auric field to splinter like glass, thus causing a lot of debris in the field that needs to be cleared. The sooner the healer clears the debris caused by chemo or radiation out of a field, the fewer the side effects will be.

How Long Does It Take?

How long a series of healings lasts depends on the seriousness of the problem, on how long the patient has had the problem, and on the long-term effects of the healing. Usually the patient strongly feels the healing effects for about three days. Then the energy system will begin to resume its old habitual distortion to a certain extent. How much and for how long the energy system of the patient can maintain a clear, balanced state is completely individual and depends on so many factors that it would be impossible to enumerate them all here. Of course the severity of the problem, the patient's life circumstances, the patient's self-care and ability to carry out what activities or diets are required, and the skills of the healer are all factors.

With each succeeding healing session, the patient's energy system regains more and more of its original healthy configuration. The old habits of distortion are gradually dissolved. How fast permanent changes can occur is completely individual. Suffice it to say that some patients will finish in one healing, others in many months of healing. As the healing process unfolds, it becomes easier and easier for the healer to know how long it will take, because the healer observes the extent of the changes and how long they hold each time a healing is given. Sometimes a more advanced healer will give the approximate length of the healing series through guidance in the beginning session.

The healing process can continue, perhaps over weeks, months, or years. How long it lasts, in many cases, depends on what degree of health the patient accepts.

The Spiritual Healer's Greater Purpose

Many patients wish to continue the healing process long after the original presenting complaint is gone because what they settled for as "health" before entering a healing situation is simply no longer acceptable. This occurs because healing not only educates patients but helps them make much deeper connections to their internal longings. In this case, the process of healing becomes one of personal evolution and release of creativity. It becomes a spiritual experience.

From the holographic point of view, this means the healer will be working on the connection between the individual within a system, that is, within the greatest system, the Universal Being. On this level, an unacceptable state of health is seen as an apparent disconnection from or imbalance with the whole or the divine.

That leads to questions: "What is the patient's relationship with God-Goddess, the cosmos, or the Universal Being?" "How have her beliefs led her to the experience of disconnection from her essential connection with the Universal Being?" "How has he forgotten who he is, and how has his way of living that arises out of that forgetting led him into imbalance and vulnerability to infection?"

Healers work directly with the energy field of the patient to balance it with the highest spiritual reality to which the patient can expand.

Healers' greatest purpose is to help their clients connect with the greatest spiritual reality possible. They do this in very practical ways, stepping on each rung of the ladder from basic physical humanity, through the personality level of the human energy field, through the haric level of intentionality, and to the divinity within each human being, the core essence.

The healer first looks for the precise nature of the patient's energy field patterns that express the different aspects of his or her being. Since they act holographically to affect each other and the physical body, the healer's line of inquiry covers the overall physical and energetic patterns that correspond to the emotional, mental, and spiritual health of the patient. The healer helps the patient deal with his or her intention toward their health and their life's purpose. One of the main jobs the healer is faced with is to help patients find the cause of their illness. How do patients cause this illness in themselves?

All of these areas of inquiry and healing are necessary to restore full health and to prevent another occurrence of the disease, or the possibility of another disease. The healer and patient work together to explore these areas. Ultimately, the healer and patient come face to face with the ultimate cause of the patient's dis-ease.

Healers ask: "What are the patient's beliefs about divinity that help hold this dis-ease in place?" "How is God seen as a negative authority that would punish rather than love?" "How has this individual then taken upon himself the punishment that he thinks God has ordained for him?" "How does this patient mete it out and assume that God is doing it to her?"

We are speaking here not only about that which individuals create for themselves as punishment, but about how they meet greater cycles of events that do not seem to be immediately connected to their individual creation. These greater cycles are the long-term effects put into motion in times past, or "karmic cycles," as well as those events that come about as a result of the collective creativity of humankind. Each individual has the choice to meet these experiences with expectations of punishment for some terrible past deed, rather like a lesson chosen by the greater self, for the purpose of learning and soul growth.

The healer helps clients open a corridor to the deeper creative energies of their core, from which they create their experiences of reality.

Ethical Limitations of a Healer

We are left with this one very practical question of ethical limitations. This question has a broad range of aspects, and its answers depend on the healer involved. Here are some.

Untrained People Who Call Themselves Healers

First it is very important that healers be aware of their level of ability and be straightforward about it. One of the worst things I have seen happens a lot. Very ill people go to a healer or a healing circle and are told that they are cured. The healers jump to this conclusion because they felt so much energy and got such a spiritual high from the healing that they assumed it meant the patient was cured. At times, such people even get guidance that says this is so. They may even advise that patients stop treatments that the healers know nothing about. They are completely convinced that this is right and their guidance is true.

These healers are out of reality. They are not in touch with their patients or their conditions. They have "blissed out" on their own energetic high and have disconnected from the patient in the process. This is very serious. It is a Pollyanna escape into denial because such healers cannot deal with the reality of life, pain, and death. It is a misuse of spirituality and healing for denial of their own fear.

There is nothing wrong with a healing circle that brings love, hope, and support to people who are isolated in fear with their disease. But it is important to stay in reality about the amount of love, hope, and support that is needed for such a person. It is not a one-shot deal. It is a long ongoing process. The support groups and workshops of Bernie Siegel, M.D., and Louise Hay attest to the strong positive effectiveness of such groups.

To Charge or Not to Charge

I have found that there is a worldwide issue with people thinking it wrong for healers to charge money. This prejudice can be found in Great Britain, Russia, Europe, and Southeast Asia, as well as in the United States. I believe there are two ways to go with this. It depends on the healer's training and expertise.

If healers are trained in a religious tradition like the Christian charismatic movement, the healings are done in church service, and often donations are accepted. From my perspective, that seems appropriate.

If, however, healers have gone through a meticulous long-term training—at least four years, in my opinion—healers have the right to charge. This type of training includes anatomy, physiology, psychology, ethics, and professionalization of a practice, as well as the development of HSP and healing techniques. It is through this type of training that healership will gain its rightful professional role in our health-care system. These healers have the right to charge normal professional fees just like psychological therapists, massage therapists, home-care nurses, physical therapists, and physicians. These fees should be in the same range as those of any therapist. A no-fee policy for such a person is simply prejudice. If these healers didn't charge, they would have to work all day in a job for financial support and then give whatever is left to healing. That would simply keep badly needed healing services to a minimum.

No Diagnosis, Please

Healers should not diagnose and cannot prescribe drugs. They have not been trained to do so. A healer may, on the other hand, receive guidance as to what drug may be beneficial. The patient can take that information to a physician to check out. (See Chapter 6 for a fuller discussion of healer-physician cooperation.)

Are Healers Responsible to Tell All They Know?

This was a question that really disturbed me in the beginning of my practice. At first, I simply gave all the information I received through my channel to the person involved. I figured it was not my job to discriminate. If I got it, they got it. I got into trouble right away with this one. I freaked people out. They didn't really want to know, even though they claimed they did. They weren't ready for the answer.

I remember in 1978 I was at a healing conference in Washington. A member of the audience knew I had HSP and could see his neck vertebrae. He followed me the whole weekend, endlessly asking me to tell him what his neck looked like. I finally sat down on the steps of a large corridor in the hotel and drew the misalignment in his neck. He became very quiet and left with the picture. I saw him two years later at another conference, and he told me that he had been very upset for days after the incident. He had never seen a picture of how bones in the neck become misaligned, and he didn't understand the meaning of his misalignment. I had not taken the time to tell him how to take care of the problem and that it was not serious.

In another case, one of my best friends, Cindy M. from Washington, D.C., was studying in New York City for a few weeks and decided to have a healing. Her presenting complaint was that she had a little pain in her chest. During the healing I looked down into her chest with HSP and saw a black-gunmetal-gray shape like a three-dimensional triangle. At the same time I saw this, my guide Heyoan leaned over my right shoulder and said, "She has cancer and she is going to die."

I had a private argument with Heyoan. I was outraged that he could know of an imminent death and, even worse, that he would tell me about it. Needless to say, I kept it quiet. Right after the session, I went to a birthday party. I was so upset, I had to leave early. I didn't know what to do. Was my guidance off? Was it possible to be told of someone's death? Would I help her create it if I thought about it in that way when I was giving her healings? What should I tell her to do? Later I checked with advanced healers I knew to see if such a thing was possible. They said it was.

I did the only thing I could do. I told Cindy to stop school, go home, spend time with her husband, and get her chest checked out by a doctor. She came to two

more healings before leaving New York. In each healing, I would see the same dark form in her lung, and Heyoan leaned over my right shoulder and said, "She has cancer and is going to die."

I kept asking her to go home. I didn't tell her the specifics of my guidance. She finally did what I asked her to do. The tests were clear. I assumed my guidance was wrong. But she kept getting worse. Four months and three CAT scans later, the physicians at George Washington Hospital found the spot—same size, shape, and location. They said it was a blood clot. Again, I thanked God the guidance was wrong. She didn't respond to treatment but got worse. They opened her up and found mesothelioma—a lung cancer they did not know how to cure. She died eight months later.

About three days before she died, when I was in Washington helping Cindy separate from her friends, she called me into her room right after she had gone to the bathroom. She said, "I just pissed out a half truth for you. What was it?"

I explained why I hadn't told her what I'd seen when she first came for a healing.

She said, "Thanks for not telling me sooner. I wasn't ready. It's okay now."

What I learned was that, as a healer, and like any professional, I can access "privileged information." This information must be handled professionally, under a code of ethics that includes the right person and the right timing. I now only give "privileged information" that comes through guidance when the guidance says to do so, and to whom guidance indicates.

When Healers Should Disqualify Themselves

All healers encounter circumstances in which they should disqualify themselves. This is very important for both healers and patients to understand. This means any healer you go to may have to disqualify herself. One sign of good healers is that they make sure that they are qualified to treat you before taking you on as a patient. They may not openly discuss this with you if there is no problem. But usually by the end of the first session, they will know and tell you if there is a problem. The two major reasons for healers to disqualify themselves are their previous relationship with a patient or patient's spouse and because they are not qualified to handle the case.

In the first case, many people think they can go to a healer who is also a friend. This is fine, as long as both people know that it will change their relationship permanently. The two must make the decision of which is more important—the healing relationship or the personal one. Because healing is such a deep process, if the two try to maintain their personal friendship as it was, they will rather rapidly reach a point where the healings are jeopardized or the deeper healing process is compromised. In cases where a husband and wife want to go to the same healer, again, if the healing process continues over any length of time, relational problems may occur because of the depth of personal change involved in the healing process. For this reason, I recommend that healers use the same guidelines as therapists, who do not take both people in a marriage for individual counseling.

Healers must be able to know if they are qualified to handle any particular case. This may also have to do with the level of expectation from patients. If patients expect miraculous results, the healer must inform them that the probability is very low. Only one percent of cases heal instantly. Some healers may not be able to handle certain illnesses or types of cases. They may react to certain illnesses that affect their energy system in ways that make them sick or give them pain. They may not be able to handle someone who has received a "terminal" sentence and, if it happens, go all the way through the dying process with someone. They may not be able to work with the physicians involved. They may know someone who could do it better. If they are prejudicial about a certain treatment the patient is on, they need to deal with it honestly and let go of the prejudice. If they can't, they should refer the patient elsewhere.

I had to disqualify myself from a case several years ago with a young man who was paralyzed from the waist down. I could see what was wrong in the energy field, but I had absolutely no effect on it after trying for an hour and a half. I didn't charge him for the session and sent him home. I said I would call him if I found a way to help him or if I found someone who could. Several years later, I found someone to whom to refer him.

How to Get Straight Information About Expected Results

The best way to get straight answers is to ask straight questions. Ask the healer whatever you want to know—it's their job to find a way to answer from their framework of healing. It may not be the answer you want, but you ought to be able to get one. Even ask them about their cure rate, if you want to know. They must answer honestly. How many patients has the healer treated with this disease? What were the results? Healers must be clear as to what they are offering. This way you, the patient, can be clear as to what results you can expect and therefore what you are paying for. Of course, your healing is dependent on many other things, but you have the right to know about healers' experience and results, as well as how long they have been practicing and how well they are trained.

S I X

The Healer-Physician Team

As you consider working with both a healer and a physician, it is important to interview both to see if they are open to working together. Let both the healer and physician know how and with whom you are working. If they have not worked with each other before, talk with them to find out if they will cooperate. Let them know how they can help each other in helping you regain your health. The physician or healer may be too busy to spend much time consulting with the other. In most cases not much consultation time is really needed. If either one will not be in goodwill with the other, I suggest that you find another person to do the job.

It may come about that, in your treatment, there will be directly opposing points of view. Then it is very necessary for the two to converse. At such times, goodwill and understanding are of extreme importance. Your health treatment depends on it.

In my experience, two directly opposing points of view or conflict between physician and healer happens very rarely if both of them are in reality and open-minded. However, many people still carry the negative image that healers and physicians are opposed to each other. If people learn how the two systems complement each other, this negative image, fortunately for all, can be cleared.

There are five major ways that the healer-physician team works best together to gather a broader, deeper, and more useful set of information about a patient's condition and what to do about it. The five major objectives are:

1. *To obtain a clear understanding of the disease process going on in the patient.* In healers' terms this is called a dis-ease description; in physicians' terms it is called a diagnosis. Each is made in a different context. The healer uses Higher Sense Perception to describe the energy field and physical body function or dysfunction. The physician uses standard medical procedures to obtain a medical diagnosis.

2. *To bring about the patient's health on as many levels as possible.* The healer works through the process of directly laying on of hands to balance and repair the energy bodies and the physical body. The physician primarily works to restore health to the physical body.

3. *To obtain a broader, fuller, more informative, and more meaningful disease history.* The healer-physician team does this by combining information from the history of life experience that the healer obtains through the use of HSP with a standard medical history taken by the physician.

4. *To assist the patient to find the deeper meaning and cause of the illness.* Many physicians help patients deal with the mental and emotional causes of illness as well as the physical by listening to their patients and

giving advice. Healers help the patient deal with their illness on all levels of their being—the lower three auric levels that correspond to physical sensation, emotional, and mental; the three upper spiritual auric levels; the haric level of intention; and the core star level of the creative source.

5. *To create more effective treatment modalities, to reduce the time it takes to heal; to reduce discomfort; and to reduce the side effects from harsh medications.* Using HSP, the healer will obtain information on diet, herbs, homeopathic remedies, and other substances or techniques the patient can use. When specific medical techniques or medications are received through HSP, they can be given to the patient's physician for consideration. During the years of my practice, I regularly received, using HSP, specific medications or changes in dosages for patients. Their physicians later concurred with the information, and when prescriptions were changed, the patients recovered.

As we begin to develop the healer-physician team, much of the information from the healer may not make a lot of sense to the physician because it is not within his or her domain of expertise. In time, by working together, bridges of communication will be created and much more understanding about the body, the energy bodies, and the healing process will emerge. All five of these areas greatly facilitate the healing of the patient and will also help the physician gather more information about what is going on in the patient. Let's examine, in more detail, each type of information the healer can obtain.

Objective 1:
Getting a Clear Understanding of the Disease Process

When working with a physician or a group of health-care professionals, healers will describe the disease process occurring in the patient's physical and energetic bodies. She shares this description with the professional team for the sake of clarifying the disease process in the patient. To do this, the healer will use HSP to analyze the patient's condition. She will begin by checking the human energy field as follows:

- The patient's overall energetic pattern, with its balances and imbalances
- The pattern, in more detail, for each level of the auric field

The healer then focuses on the physical level to describe the unhealthy or imbalanced physiological processes going on in the patient's body. These, of course, are the result of the energetic imbalances she first described. To do this, she uses HSP to sense the functioning of the organs and the tissues on the physical level. The healer proceeds in several steps, checking:

- The general state of the human energy field
- The general functioning of each organ
- The general functioning of the organ systems
- The interactions between organ systems
- A more detailed functioning of each organ
- The state of the tissue of the organ

This disease description will, in many ways, correlate to a physician's diagnosis. All the senses can be used in the HSP mode. I will discuss the three most commonly used by healers: visual, auditory, and kinesthetic (touch). But the language will be different depending on the sense used to access the information. The language will most likely not be technical medical language.

The Healer's Dis-ease Description Using Visual HSP

When the healer uses the visual type of HSP, the organs of the body have particular colors that correlate to health and other colors that correlate to disease and dysfunction. The healer simply looks at organs in the body to see if they are weak or strong, underactive or overactive. When she finds the specific organs that need more attention by using this general type of scan, she can then focus on a more detailed examination of each dysfunctional organ.

Let me give some examples of how the visual sense works. When viewing the liver, the healer can first focus on the entire liver to find its relative size and to discover whether or not it's enlarged. She can also observe whether it looks too dense for its normal functioning. She can change her resolution—as you do when scanning a newspaper column, then focusing on one sentence—to find out whether certain portions of the liver are underfunctioning while others are overfunctioning, by simply watching the liver in process. If there are areas of the liver in which waste material is accumulating, the auric color of that waste material tells if the waste material is too acidic or too alkaline. The healer can see whether this waste material is too viscous to move out of the liver. She does this simply by looking at the thickness of the fluid and watching it move through the liver.

For example, many times I have seen an accumulation of stagnated green or yellow fluid in portions of the liver. This means toxins are piling up in the liver and there is an excess of bile. Sometimes the yellow color is left over from some drugs the person has recently taken that the liver has a hard time processing. The auric perception of hepatitis is always a band or layer of orange color. Sometimes, if someone has taken drugs for hepatitis, it shows in the liver as an area of thick, brownish mucus. Chemotherapy for breast and other cancers always appears as green-brown gunk in the liver. If the chemotherapy is given intravenously through the arm, the aura of the arm also turns brown-green. I have seen configurations that remained in the auric field as long as ten to twenty years when no healing was given.

The healer can view the effects of particular foods or drugs on the liver. Many times a combination of drinking wine and eating thick, gooey cheeses like brie causes a great deal of stagnation in the liver. It looks like stagnated mucus. That decreases the natural healthy life pulse of the liver and thereby reduces its ability to function.

To gather more information, the healer can increase her resolution and focus down to the cellular level so that she can view the cell condition. Many times the cells will be enlarged or elongated. Or the cell membrane may not be working in a way that is chemically balanced so that certain fluids that are not supposed to move through that membrane do. For example, long-term smoking usually breaks down the cell wall, making it flaccid so that the cell becomes enlarged and misshapen. The pollutants from smoking also form an acidic layer on the outside of the cell membrane, which then changes its permeability. With high or microscopic resolution, the healer can also view microorganisms inside the body and describe their appearance. All the information obtained through vision-type HSP will be described in terms of pictures using visual terms. All of this information is given in the healer's language in simple descriptive terms, as above, not in the technical terms to which a patient or physician may be accustomed.

The Healer's Dis-ease Description Using Auditory HSP

The healer can also use auditory-type HSP. There are two major types of auditory information—sounds (or tones) and words. The body, organs, and tissues all produce sounds that can be heard with HSP but not with "normal" hearing. These sounds give information about the health of the body and organs. A healthy body produces a beautiful "symphony" of sounds that all flow together. Whenever an organ is not functioning right, it gives off a discordant sound. By developing her sound vocabulary, the healer will be able to describe health and dis-ease within the physical and energy bodies in terms of sound.

For example, using auditory HSP, the healer may very well hear a high-pitched squealing sound coming from the pancreas of someone with diabetes. She will also see (using visual HSP) a dark vortex of energy over the pancreas that makes the squealing sound. These two pieces of information will tell her immediately that the person has diabetes. (The healer will, in turn, use sounds or tones for healing, as we will see later on.)

The other form of auditory HSP is the reception of words. If the healer is proficient in auditory HSP, she may be able to directly access the name of an organism, disease, or even a drug to be taken, including the amount and time. Most medical terms are quite long and complicated, making them very difficult to pick up through HSP. I have been able to do this only a few times. Most of the auditory information I get comes either as simple directives or as long discourses on the deeper meaning of existence or the way the world works. A few examples of auditory directives will pop up in the text as we move along. The healing meditations given in Part IV of this book are good examples of channeled discourses that are very useful in the healing process.

The Healer's Dis-ease Description Using Kinesthetic HSP

Each organ has a pulse. Certain organs pulsate faster than others. Using the kinesthetic (feeling sensation) type of HSP, the healer can feel the pulse from each organ. First the healer would feel the entire body system in general and find out general imbalances within organs. Then she feels within organ systems, and then cross-organ systems. For example, using kinesthetic-type HSP, the healer will check on the organ pulse of the liver to find if it is higher or lower than normal. The healer will then feel larger areas of the body to find if the liver pulse is synchronized with the other organ pulses of the body. If the liver is abnormal, the healer finds how its abnormal functioning affects organs in its vicinity and other areas within the body.

One typical question that arises in the dis-ease description given by a healer is, How does an under-functioning liver (abnormally low pulse, denoting hypofunction) affect the pancreas? My answer, from information taken with kinesthetic sensing, is that a hypofunctioning liver strains the pancreas and makes it work harder, which causes the pulse of the pancreas to increase, causing a hyperfunctioning pancreas. Eventually the pancreas will become too weak from overwork to function properly, and its pulse will also drop down below normal, causing a hypofunctioning pancreas.

Information gathered kinesthetically from infertile women who are trying to get pregnant is very interesting. In healthy bodies, the ovaries pulse synchronically with each other, with the thymus near the heart, and with the pituitary in the head. In many cases of infertility, the ovary pulses are imbalanced with each other and the other organ pulses. The ovaries have to be balanced with each other, the thymus, and the pituitary before they are able to produce a ripe egg and release it at exactly the appropriate time. When they are not pulsing synchronically, the egg will be released at the wrong time in the menstrual cycle. It may be premature or overripe, or not released at all. To reestablish balance, the healer sends energy to reestablish a synchronic pulse among all of these three endocrines. This is done through a series of techniques in laying on of hands. I have been able to assist many previously infertile women in this way. They are mothers now. (Of course, in some cases, other organs might very well be involved with this, so the healer would feel them and then balance them also.)

A good example occurred several years ago, when I was still practicing healing in New York City. The client, Barbara, wanted to get pregnant. She was forty-two.

Barbara had clinically died from hemorrhaging after giving birth to a daughter fifteen years earlier. She told me she could remember leaving her body and visiting her deceased father, who told her to return to earth. He said that she could bring all the love and peace to earth that she felt there with him. She could then feel herself being pulled back into her body. A doctor stood over her and said, "She's gone." The next thing she was aware of was a big nurse leaning over her, pumping her chest, screaming, "Breathe, damn you, breathe!"

After a long road of recovery, raising her daughter alone, then finally getting married again, Barbara wanted another child. There was a lot of concern about this. No one had ever found the source of the hemorrhaging, so it might happen again. Plus, Barbara had had cervical cancer four years before getting married. Her physicians were concerned that, because of the surgery, the cervix would not be strong enough to hold the fetus for nine months.

She had tried to get pregnant with no success for three years before she came to me. A brief inspection of her energy field showed a large tear in the second chakra. Her ovaries were not functioning properly, and they were not synchronized with the thymus or the pituitary. She would ovulate infrequently, and when she did, it was too late in the cycle for the egg. I also saw her weakened cervix and another place within her womb where an old wound had been. This was the source of the hemorrhaging.

First I cleared and cleaned the wound and restructured the first level of its field so it would heal. I then rebuilt the energy field of the cervix to make it strong. I made it extra strong so it could hold the fetus. Next, I repaired all the damage in the second chakra, then stabilized it. I then synchronized the ovaries with each other, then with the thymus, and then with the pituitary. As each system in the body began to function, Barbara's energy increased. This took one session in February 1984.

I called up Barbara in September 1990 to see how she remembered the event. Barbara said, "You found a black energetic hole at the source of the hemorrhaging, and you found also an energetic dysfunction at the cervix. You found both of the sources of prior medical concerns. Then I became pregnant in March. It was a miracle.

"Another interesting sidelight was that I came back to see you in my ninth month because Annie was in a breech position. You turned her. . . . Another interesting piece of this was that you prepared me for a cesarean. I can remember feeling your conflict. I remember trying to support you by saying it's okay, it's okay, you can tell me anything that is going on here. Well, I did have a cesarean. After twenty-four hours of labor, my cervix just wouldn't dilate and Annie went into distress."

When Barbara came for her second healing in her ninth month, I received guidance that she was going to have a cesarean. I didn't want to tell her in a way that would sound as if it would have to be that way. I wanted to leave plenty of room for the possibility of a natural birth, but I did manage to warn her that it was a good idea to accept it any way it came, that having the child was the most important thing, not doing it perfectly. As I remember, when I was working on her, it seemed that we had a choice between building a strong cervix and having a cesarean baby, or not building a strong cervix and chancing losing the baby.

Later Barbara said, "This never would have concerned me anyway. I never had any mindset about how you are supposed to have a baby. I think most New Age spiritual women have a lot of gunk about medical procedures. They can't quite handle the duality between that and being spiritually responsible for our own healing. I never had any trouble with that. It is their duality, not real duality.

"I think there is a mindset with many people generally about those issues. It feels as though you have to make a choice between your taking self-responsibility for your spiritual and physical well-being and medical technical know-how, knowledge, and expertise. In fact, every time you make such a choice, you are limiting reality because there really is no need to choose. It is only when they work together that it is complete. What we are all trying to do is to heal that duality on the earth."

Using the Visual, Kinesthetic, and Auditory HSP Together to Describe Dis-ease

Now, using visual, auditory, and kinesthetic HSP together, let us "focus on" (visual term), "tune into" (auditory term), and "connect to" (kinesthetic term) the pancreas to "see" (visual term) what information we can "get" (kinesthetic term). In people with problems in digesting sweets and sugars, the pancreas will "look" weak. Instead of being a bright, clear, peachy-brown color, the pancreas will have a very faded peachy-brown color. The pancreas may be enlarged due to its inability to function properly. Using visual HSP, the healer can "see" this. By increasing visual resolution, the healer may also see piles of yellowish-amber cells here and there in the pancreas. The anatomy book tells us that these are the islets of Langerhans. In some cases, there may be more of these piles of cells, or each islet may have more cells and be larger than normal, or each islet may be made up of enlarged yellowish-amber-colored cells. The excess numbers of the islets of Langerhans are the body's effort to produce more of the secretion that they make. Auditory HSP or a physiology book tells us that this secretion is the hormone insulin. Using the kinesthetic sense, the healer finds that the organ pulse of the pancreas is also lower than what the healer feels to be healthy. The pancreas is underfunctioning. Thus visual, auditory, and kinesthetic HSP together tell us that this patient needs healing work to reestablish normal pancreas function.

When a weakened pancreas begins pulsating more slowly than its normal healthy rate, it usually begins to affect the pulsation of the left kidney, located directly behind it. Soon this kidney pulsates at a rate that correlates with the slower pulses of the pancreas. This makes the kidney drop sugar into the urine. The kidney looks darker than normal. From the healer's perception, the functioning of both the pancreas and the kidney is decreased. Even the connective tissue wrapped around the organs, called the fascia, begins to harden, contract, and bind the organs together. The fascia is the physical medium that carries most of the energy flow of the first layer of the auric field through it. When it hardens, its ability to conduct energy greatly decreases. This in turn decreases the amount of energy flow the organ wrapped in the fascia can receive from the energy fields all around us.

I believe that this decreased conductivity through our fascia has a great deal to do with aging. When work is done to soften the hardened tissues, a great deal more energy flows to the organ or muscle surrounded by the fascia. That organ or muscle wakes up and becomes alive and healthy again. This type of work combined with healing energy work is effective even on very old injuries. It re-enlivens tissues that have been unusable for years. It takes lots of time and attention to repair old injuries, but to many people it is worth it. People who do body work or energy work that softens the fascia stay younger longer. Many such people look ten years younger than their age.

Healers use all the same HSP techniques mentioned above to describe problems in the haric and core star levels. This information will include description of any disfigurement or dysfunction in these levels. (The haric and core star levels and the five objectives of healing will be discussed in Chapters 16 and 17.)

Objective 2: Direct Hands-On Healing Work

As was described earlier, the healer acts as a conduit for healing energies from the universal health field, or universal energy field, all around us. The human energy field must be regarded as no less real than the physical body. There are several levels of bodies. The healer will work on each. The first, third, fifth, and seventh levels of the auric field are structured in a way such that they contain all of the organs that we know about in the physical body, plus the chakras, which are intake organs that metabolize energy from the universal energy field for the area of the body in which they are located. These structured levels appear to be composed of standing light beams. The even-numbered layers are not structured. They look like blobs or clouds of fluid in motion. The fluid flows along the standing light lines of the structured layers.

The healer's work on the structured levels is to repair, restructure, and recharge the energy bodies. The healer's work on the unstructured levels of the field is to clear stagnated areas, to charge weakened areas, and to balance overcharged areas with the rest of the field.

All this has a big effect on the functioning of the physical body. Even if the physical organ has been removed, rebuilding it on the structured layers of the field and charging it on the fluid layers of the field have a very strong healing effect on the body. In cases where the thyroid has been removed, I have consistently seen a restructured thyroid on the auric level reduce the amount of thyroid medication that a patient needs to take. Hands-on healing work usually decreases healing time by one-third to one-half the normal time, decreases the amount of medications needed, and greatly reduces side effects of invasive modalities.

A friend of mine who was highly allergic to drugs had a double cataract operation. She took drugs only during surgery. She took no pain-killers afterward, did self-healing several times a day every day, and healed twice as fast as the "normal" recovery time for a one-eye lens removal. Simple problems like sprained ankles, which normally require two weeks on crutches, can be healed in one-half to three-quarters of an hour if worked on immediately.

If it is not possible to give immediate hands-on healing, other healing methods developed in osteopathic medicine, Structural Integration (Rolfing), deep tissue work, unwinding, or *myofascia* work will still reduce healing time to a few days. Whenever such an injury occurs, the body recoils and twists itself away from the injury. The fascia and muscles sometimes remain in the twisted position. These methods are very useful in healing injuries resulting in misalignments, sprains, strains, bruises, fractures, and injuries to the spinal cord. By holding the body in certain tension positions and following body pulses, one can simply follow the unwinding of the twists that resulted from the injury.

Recently, a very heavy table collapsed on a healer-student's shin and foot. We immediately picked her up and worked on her for about forty-five minutes. She feared that her leg was broken. After careful visual HSP examination, we knew that it was not broken. It was badly scraped and bruised. We did laying on of hands techniques to restructure the energy field, and a structural unwinding technique simultaneously. At the end of forty-five minutes there was no swelling, very little bruising, and a few scratches. She rested a few hours

with ice on the area, and the next day she was walking normally. It looked as if she had bumped herself two weeks before.

I have seen benign "operable" tumors reduce to "not necessary to operate" in a few laying on of hands healings. I have seen heart patients avoid open heart surgery, cancer patients reduce the amount of chemotherapy needed, early stages of diabetes turned around, colonectomies prevented. In a few cases, I have seen cancer disappear. I have seen many lives completely reformed into the way the people longed for their lives to be.

The healer also does hands-on work on both the haric and core star levels. Once the healer has determined the state of the haric and core star levels, she can work directly on each of them. Haric and/or core star healing is advanced work. It requires a lot of training and practice to do it. (It will be discussed in Chapters 16 and 17.)

Objective 3: Obtaining a Fuller, Broader Disease History

The third area of work with the healer-physician team is the gathering of a disease history. A physician does this through the patient's personal and family health and medical records. The healer obtains historical information by psychically witnessing past events, which are both physically and psychologically related to the disease. The healer has the ability to go backward in time and to observe the sequence of events that have occurred to a particular organ, body part, or the whole body system on the physical or energy body levels. The healer does this first by kinesthetically connecting to the body part, then by consulting memory.

It is much the same process as when you activate your own memory. You automatically do it only for yourself. It feels like simply rolling time backward to witness a past event. Try it for another person by first connecting to them and then activating memory. You will be surprised. You can access their past also. You were just brought up to believe that the only past you could remember was your own.

On the physical level, the healer will use HSP to witness, in reverse sequence, the traumas that occurred to a particular body part. In my experience, most serious illness is not new. Rather, the disease configuration has built up over a long period of time and through several different forms and symptoms that are compiled into the present state. How you are now represents the sum total of your life experience.

A common example is hip problems in older people. Most hip problems in later years are activated by structural misalignment in earlier years in the spine or knees. Dietary deficiencies may also contribute to the degeneration process, until the elderly person falls and breaks a hip.

Many people notice that the same body part is repeatedly injured. Once an ankle is twisted and sprained on the tennis court, that same weakened ankle will most likely be sprained again. This misalignment in the ankle radiates throughout the entire structural system of the whole body and affects all parts of it. An early fall off a tricycle bumping the knee may lead to a later bicycle knee injury, which in turn leads to a jogging knee trauma, and so on. Each injury increases structural misalignment that then leads to more injury.

Usually by the time a serious problem erupts in the physical body, that part of the body has been traumatized many times. A problem in an organ is a sign that the problem has sunk deeply into the body. Effects of old childhood traumas are enhanced, carried forward, and maintained through repeated bad living habits on the physical, emotional, mental, and spiritual levels. People re-create and repeat problems in their lives over and over from their negative belief systems. These negative belief systems are usually unconscious. Using HSP, these re-created negative experiences can be read in sequence.

One patient named Tanya, who had the umbilical cord wrapped around her neck and had a forceps birth, repeated these neck and head traumas throughout life in different forms. In early childhood, she fell off a cannon in a park and landed on her head. Then she fell from trees more than once. Later, her brother accidentally hit her in the head with a baseball bat. She was standing behind him when he swung back to hit a ball. Each time she received a blow to the head, her neck also got worse. Her father repeatedly hit her whenever her mother reported that she was "bad." She wouldn't know it was coming because the punishment came many hours afterward, when her father came home from work. Sometimes he hit her with a yardstick while he held her upside-down by one foot. Next, there were repeated blows to the head from an abusive husband. This went on for almost ten years. During this time there was a whiplash accident in a motel room, when a man tried to pull off her swimsuit. Two years later, there was another whiplash and hairline skull fracture

from a car accident. The continued neck and head injuries led to more and more structural misalignment that weakened not only the areas directly involved but the whole structural system as well. The whole left side of her body was weakened. She said it came from being married to a right-handed man—it's the left side that gets hit. Through laying on of hands and unwinding, she was later able to heal most of her injuries.

Since organs all work together, chronic dysfunction in any particular organ will eventually affect all others. First the other organs may overwork to make up for the loss of function in one organ. Then later they may underfunction because they are unable to carry the extra load. To the healer, who sees the body functioning from the holographic point of view, anything occurring in any part of the body is always related to the rest of the body.

I witnessed an interesting case of earlier dietary deficiencies in a man who had shin splints. When I rolled backward in time, I saw that the cause was related to the fact that he drank a lot of milk as a fast-growing teenager. Milk was not the best source of calcium for his body. When his body grew bone cells, they became "too hard" and didn't allow the muscles to insert properly into the bone. Thus at the age of forty he got shin splints when he jogged.

Objective 4:
Assisting Patients to Find the Deeper Meaning and Causes of Their Illness

---

Through HSP, the healer helps the patient access general information about the patient's background on the psychological level. This includes information about possible childhood trauma, interaction with parents and the environment, the patient's mental attitude about life, and the patient's belief system.

A healer will also use HSP to "read" specific information about the psychological history that correlates to a given presenting complaint. To do this, the healer connects to the diseased body part and rolls backward in time *while tuned in to the psychological level* and witnesses the past experiences of the individual directly related to the physical problem. This also reveals a lot about the patient's personality, childhood psychological traumas, and reactions to them that create certain unhealthy life patterns that led to partial creation of the physical problems.

This information, when handled sensitively, can

greatly help the patient's personal healing process. It helps patients give up unhealthy habitual actions that cause imbalance in their energy system that eventually lead to disease in the physical body.

The idea that one might create accidents in one's life as a result of one's beliefs and earlier traumas is, of course, interesting and controversial. Some accidents are clearly the result of intent. I'm sure you have all witnessed children hurting themselves directly after being confronted about something they shouldn't have done.

Tanya's case is a good example. As Tanya worked to heal herself through hands-on healing and deep tissue work, she was able to find how she helped create her injuries, even the car accident in which she was not the driver. She connected with her intent to continue to be the "victim" of other people, which somehow, from the child's reasoning, meant she was "good." This is what I mean by a negative belief system. In order to remain "good" from the unconscious child's reasoning, she had to keep being the "victim." Her father hit her to punish her for being "bad." To her child's reasoning, the punishment then made her "good" again. She also remembered that when her father hit her, she felt connected to him. Besides being terrified, she could also feel his pain and could feel that his hitting her actually relieved some of his pain. This is the basis of martyrdom. In the incident of the car accident, her abusive husband was driving. You might ask, how could she take the "blame" for that one? She didn't take the blame, but she connected with an intent to hurt herself the night before. It was a way to stop the intense pain of her life. She said that the night before the accident, she was extremely upset. Her husband was trying to set her up with an old boyfriend, and she didn't know what to do. She remembers repeatedly looking at the large plate-glass window of her home, thinking how good it would feel to run across the room and hit it with her head. She said she felt totally crazy.

She was finally able to leave the marriage and create a new life for herself. After all the work on herself, it was only a year or so after the divorce that she began a very healthy, supportive relationship with her present husband of seven years.

During the reading and the unfolding of past information, the healer is also working directly to clear the energy field distortion that is correlated with those events and with those traumas. Work is being done on both levels at the same time. The information is being brought to consciousness, and the distortions in the field from those events are being cleared. This has a very positive effect on the healing for the patient.

The healer can then tune to higher levels in the patient that reveal thought patterns or habitual thought forms that take over and rule the patient's psyche at times. The healer will also eventually be able to help the patient find his or her negative, unhealthy belief systems that are the root cause of habitual unhealthy living patterns that create disease.

As Tanya connected with her unconscious efforts to remain a victim and therefore "good," she began changing her stance. She reached the haric level of intention. She intended to remain a victim so that she could remain the "good" one and also not have to go out into the world and take responsibility for herself.

She aligned with a positive intent to change. It was necessary to connect with a deeper part of herself that already knows she is good, her core. From the broadest perspective, the cause of illness is forgetting who you truly are (disconnection from the core), and healing is remembering the true self (connection to the core). Thus Tanya began to remember who she is. She connected with her inner basic goodness by building corridors of communication to her core star. She didn't have to prove her goodness anymore through victimization.

Objective 5: Creating More Effective Treatment Modalities

The fifth major objective of the healer-physician team is to bring about new combined treatment modalities. The results from the first four objectives—the new disease description, information about the body's functioning, the changes in the view of the causes and deeper meaning of illness, and the strong positive healing effects of laying on of hands—bring about great changes in treatment modalities and new guidelines to help us maintain our health.

Some major changes in treatment modalities are:

1. The entire approach to health and healing shifts into a new paradigm that includes all aspects of the broad expanse of human life experience. In this holistic view, where everything affects everything else, no area of patients' lives can be isolated as separate from health problems. Patients also are considered to have a lot to do with creating the problem.
2. By understanding how our life habits and our psychological environment affect our health, we change our attitude toward how to maintain health.

We focus our attention in those areas to maintain our health. We develop healthy psychological habits and learn to automatically process old emotional blocks and belief systems that cause us physical difficulties.

3. The need for prescribed medication and surgery decreases. I have had several patients for whom surgery was not needed. When they went to their presurgical checkup, their doctors canceled the surgery. I have helped people shrink tumors and thyroids, wash aberrant cells from a uterus to avoid a D and C or even a hysterectomy, avoid removal of the colon, and no longer need open heart surgery.

   Many prescribed medications have been reduced by the physicians because their patients got well sooner. The use of pain-killers has been greatly reduced in patients with chronic pain such as headaches, back pain, or pain in the ovaries.

4. Healers and physicians working together can provide more specific personal information for each patient as to which remedy or medication to take and as to exactly when to start and stop a particular medication. Healers can also provide information as to how much and when to decrease medication during the healing process. From the healer's point of view, no particular herb, remedy, or drug is bad or necessarily undesirable in and of itself. What is important here is for the patient to have the freedom to choose the method of treatment most useful and appropriate for him or her. As my guide Heyoan says, "The precise substance, in the precise amount, at the precise time acts as an alchemically transformative substance for healing."

   The healer can read the effects that any particular herb, homeopathic remedy, or medication is having on the body of the patient. It is possible for the healer to observe the patient taking homeopathic remedies to see the effect on the energy field, because remedies have both immediate and long-term effects on the field. If it is the incorrect homeopathic remedy, there will be no effect. If the remedy is not potent enough, it will not penetrate into the field and have a big effect. A higher potency will. A higher potency will reach higher levels of the field and may not immediately affect the lower ones. This information can be very helpful to the homeopath not only in choosing the correct remedy but in choosing where in the patient's energy bodies they wish it to have the most effect.

   I have found that healing will reduce the required amount of medication the body needs, even when a gland has been removed. I have experienced this many times with various people and different kinds of medications. It is an automatic result of the laying on of hands healing process.

   Reducing the amount of medication needed by patients going through the healing process is a step-by-step process. Normally, the guidance in the beginning is for the patient to continue on the medication they have. After some period of healing, perhaps only a few weeks, the guidance will suggest that the medication be reduced by a quarter. After a few more weeks or months, another reduction will be needed.

   Let me give an example. I was working with a young woman who had multiple physical disorders nearly from birth—many illnesses, many surgical operations. She was in her mid-twenties. Her progress was slow, but she steadily gained health and energy. After approximately six months of healing, she reached a plateau of health. The healings didn't seem to be having much effect. I asked for specific guidance, using auditory HSP, as to why she stopped progressing. I heard the following words: "Tell her to reduce her thyroid medication by one-third." At the time, I was completely unaware that she was taking it. In a rather embarrassed manner, I asked her about it. She confirmed that she was taking it. In the next few weeks, with the consent of her physician, she reduced her intake of the medication according to the guidance channeled and proceeded to regain more health. After five months it was necessary to make another reduction. Shortly thereafter, she left treatment, satisfied with her health, having decided to go to college.

5. Healers can help in choosing treatment modalities. For example, before Jennifer arrived in my office for her first appointment, I received information that said she should choose the type of chemotherapy that lasted three months and used two drugs, rather than the one that lasted two months and used three drugs. I had never met Jennifer and didn't know why she was coming to receive healing from me. When Jennifer told me her presenting complaint, she stated that just a week before, she had been given the choice by her oncologist of two different chemotherapies for her cancer treatment. One was to use three drugs and last two months, while the other was to use two drugs and last three months. She had come to me to help her make the decision. Needless to say, I already had the answer.

6. Working with a healer can help reduce the negative side effects of many harsh treatments, not only because less of the treatment is needed but because

laying on of hands reduces the negative side effects during treatment. It also reduces or removes long-term deterioration of the body caused by chemotherapy and radiation treatments. Chemotherapy pollutes the liver and weakens the body's natural immune system. Laying on of hands enhances liver function. Radiation therapy breaks the first layer of the energy field into splinters, like broken glass; laying on of hands repairs it.

Many times, ten to twenty years later, the radiated parts of the body will begin to dysfunction. One patient lost most of the use of her arms because the nerves deteriorated. She received very strong radiation treatments in the area of the brachial plexus (the area where the nerves that serve the arms come out of the spine) for Hodgkin's disease ten years earlier.

We found, by treating another patient with laying on of hands as soon after radiation therapy as was possible, that we were able to continually remove the fragmented auric field and rebuild it each time. That patient had very few negative effects from her radiation treatments.

Another patient had had spinal surgery ten years before I met her. When she came to healing, she was still primarily bed-ridden. She could only walk to the bathroom and back. I saw red dye still locked in her spine. Apparently it was used to view the spine with some hospital device. With healing treatments to remove the red dye, she became much stronger and started to walk again.

Postsurgical healings effectively reduce pain and repair what could become long-term side effects. A patient named Elizabeth still had pain in her right ovary and the abdominal region of her body one year after her cesarean section. I could see that the energy lines of the first layer of the field were tangled and blocking normal energy flow to that area of her body. In one healing, I was able to untangle, align, and reconstruct the energy lines of the first layer of the field. Her pain immediately went away and hasn't returned in two years. If the distortions in her field had remained, she probably would have eventually had infections in that area of her body since the lack of energy flow would eventually weaken the area.

In the case of Richard W. (see the transcript of the healing session in Appendix A), a vertical scar in his chest from open heart surgery interfered with the energy flow that served his heart and chest. Repairing it insured longer health in that area.

7. Information on the long-term negative effects of harsh treatment modalities used today will change the protocol for such use.

When we understand the long-term, negative effects that many harsh treatments have on our energy fields and our physical bodies, they will not be so readily used as they are today. I gave an example earlier of how a red dye stayed in the spine for ten years after treatment. I have seen other drugs still in the liver years after they were used for treatment of hepatitis. Many drugs are used in too strong doses for some people, who are more sensitive than others. When we can get more specific information as to just what dosage an individual can accommodate, we will be able to gauge the dosages better to suit the individual.

In some cases, the amount of medication needed can be reduced drastically by healing methods. For example, I was working with another healer to help a young woman who received a liver transplant. We prepared her energy field before the surgery. After the surgery, we connected her energy bodies to the new liver by reconstructing all the energy lines that had been cut to remove the old liver. We could tell that the new liver was actually larger than her original one. We tried to warn the hospital staff that she would need less of the medication that prevented her body from rejecting the liver. Unfortunately we couldn't get anyone to listen to us. They finally reduced the medication when she started having side effects. She is fine now.

8. Through HSP completely new treatment modalities never used before have been discovered. These, of course, will have to be researched and tested. Some have been beyond the possibilities of present-day technologies. For example, I once received information that a certain substance be fed by drip directly into the spleen of a child with leukemia; such technology did not exist. I have received information that describes machines to filter the blood of AIDS patients. Unfortunately, these machines do not yet exist at this writing. Someday machines will be built that send certain frequencies into the body to dissolve scar tissue. Other frequencies from the same device will explode cancer cells and not affect normal cells because of the difference between the normal and cancerous cell wall structure.

Since the dis-ease configuration always appears in the auric field before the physical body, we will develop treatment modalities and equipment that cure the disease in the energy field bodies before it has a chance to precipitate down into the physical body. This will prevent a lot of physical illness.

9. We will also become much more conscious of the physical environment we live in and how it affects our energy fields and our health. One of the most interesting areas that I have encountered when reading the functioning of physical systems with HSP is the highly sensitive chemical balances needed by the brain. Because of the pollution to which we are all subjected, many of these sensitive chemical balances within the brain are strongly affected. Many small groups of different kinds of cells, which I'm sure are well known to brain physiologists, produce various chemicals in the brain that regulate not only each other and different areas of the brain, but also the whole body functioning. Environmental pollution—such as food additives, extremely low-frequency radiation in electrical fields from high lines, and air pollution—disrupts these chemical balances. Over long periods of time the slow accumulation of internal pollution increases these imbalances and causes a great deal of ill health in the body. This kind of information can be gathered through HSP and hopefully will someday be tested in the laboratory for proof.

The life energy in food is also decreased by pollution. Because of the chemical poisoning of the soil, the plants themselves do not produce foods with high enough pulsatory rates to keep the human body healthy. Pulse rates of food intake must be within the range of organ life pulses, or they will drag the organ pulses down and the organs will eventually become unhealthy. We find many Americans taking vitamins and minerals because our foods are not full of the life-force. Our physical bodies can, through eating healthy, uncontaminated food, maintain pulsations that are synchronized with the pulsations of the earth itself. This is one of the reasons why organic foods are so important.

Remember, the earth as a whole has its own life pulses. One of these is the pulsation of the earth's magnetic field. It pulses eight times per second (eight Hertz, or 8 Hz). Since we have physically evolved within that magnetic pulse, it is very good for us. Before it was contaminated, our soil carried the healthy pulsations of the earth. The natural food we ate was healthy because it was synchronized with the earth pulsations. Now when we eat a carrot grown in poisoned and polluted soil, the carrot does not enter into the body with the same vibrational energy as a healthy carrot grown in healthy earth-synchronized soil. Many times such a carrot is poison to us, and we are better off not eating it. We have a great need for the health food industry. It is an attempt to give us the life-force-supporting food our bodies need and to reestablish the balance between us and the life-force of the earth that produced our bodies.

As healers and physicians do more work together, we will build bridges of communication. We will learn how to combine the information gathered, by the healer through HSP, with the information the physician gathers in his or her years of training and through the physical testing with advanced technologies. I'm sure that healer and physician will make a wonderful team. Eventually, physicians will develop their HSP. And healers will help in the laboratory to develop instrumentation that will verify and quantify the information healers gather. Someday we will have sensitive instrumentation that can do national screening of people's energy systems to prevent the imbalances in the field from being precipitated down into the physical body that later emerge as disease in the physical body.

PART III

THE PERSONAL EXPERIENCE OF HEALING

"The birth and death of leaves is part of that greater cycle
that moves among the stars."

—Rabindranath Tagore

Time to Take Care
of Yourself

When I was regularly seeing clients, it became clear to me that all my patients had to improve the way they took care of themselves. That meant they each had to take a lot of responsibility to follow through in all the different areas of self-care they needed. They had to reprioritize their lives to put themselves and their health first. To do this takes a great deal of effort, because usually they gave priority to something else.

For example, female cancer patients tended to have their priorities oriented around other people's needs, like husband and children. Many of them experienced a great deal of pressure from their families to get back into the house and take care of everyone as soon as possible. That this pressure was usually indirect or underground made it even harder for the client to see and deal with it directly. Family members would say, "We just want our life to get back to normal."

People with heart problems and burnout had oriented their priorities around work. Some of these people had to learn to trust others and delegate authority. Their healing process included asking themselves why they needed the control so much. Usually they found they didn't feel safe without the control. They lived by their will rather than by their heart.

To maintain your health properly, you must take care of yourself holographically—that is, in all areas and all levels of your life. The healing process requires great change. It does not work to go to a healer to get something fixed so that your life can "get back to normal." Rather, expect to move into new territory, new ways of caring for yourself, new life priorities, new ways to relate to your intimate partners, children, and friends. They will not all take it so easily as you would like; there will likely be some rough spots to get over, some differences of opinion. But in the long run, it will all work out for the betterment of everyone. Your job is to keep sticking to your truth.

You may say, "This sounds ridiculous. How can I do this when I am sick? Now I am supposed to rest."

My answer is that this is the time you have given yourself to do it. In fact, you have everything that you need to do it. As we go through the list of levels of self-care and the things that need to be attended to, you will be able either to do them for yourself or to get someone to help you with them. Your exact care plans, of course, depend on how incapacitating your illness is in any phase of it. Just remember, this is your *opportunity* for great change. It is a time of reorientation, of overviewing your life and its deeper meaning. You now have the personal time to do it.

How you do use this time is completely personal. You may just need to sleep for weeks to facilitate a deep connection to yourself. Sleeping gives you time to yourself that perhaps you could not manage any other way. You may spend the time asking for help. Perhaps you never gave yourself the opportunity before. You will definitely spend some of the time revamping your value system. The changes in your value system will thread holographically through your life and continue to create changes for years to come.

As you begin your changes, it is handy to have a road map of what to expect in your personal experiences. To help you recognize your path, I will discuss the path of the healing process from the viewpoint of two different frameworks. The first is the framework of the seven stages that you go through in your healing process. The second looks at the healing process in terms of the seven levels of healing. Each level relates to a level of the auric field of human experience.

The Seven Stages of Healing

As I watched people through the healing process, I noticed that the process is never a smooth, even curve upward into health. Most of the time, people experienced an immediate internal improvement. Then later, patients seemed to regress. At this point, they often questioned the treatment. Many times they thought they were worse off than before they came. Their energy fields clearly indicated that they were indeed better. The imbalances in their fields were much less; their organs were functioning better. Despite their more balanced fields, however, they were experiencing the imbalances they had more acutely. Sometimes they would even have worse pain. What was happening was they were becoming less tolerant of imbalances that at one time felt "normal" to them. In short, they were in better health.

I also noticed that people go through distinct phases during their healing process. These phases are part of the normal human transformation process. Healing requires changes of mind, emotion, and spirit, as well as physical change. Each person needs to reevaluate his or her relationship to the issues involved in a personal healing process and set them into a new context.

First, people must admit there is a problem and let themselves experience the problem. They need to come out of denial about the situation. I noticed that each time a person experienced "getting worse," he or she was coming out of denial and into consciousness about another aspect of the problem. Many times patients thought they were angry because they were getting worse. Actually, they were angry that there was more to deal with.

Most patients would then search for a way to make it easier; they wanted an easy out. Many would say things like "I've done enough work on it" or "Oh no, not that again." Finally, if the person decided to go deeper, there would be the willingness to go the next round, expressed in statements like "Well, okay, let's go for it."

Healing, like therapy, is a cyclical process that carries a person on a spiral of learning. Each cycle requires more self-acceptance and more change as one goes down deeper and deeper into the true, clear nature of the real self. How far and deep each of us goes is entirely our own free choice. How each of us takes the spiral journey and what road map we use is also a free will choice. Rightly so, for each path is different.

All dis-ease requires change within the patient to facilitate healing, and all change requires the giving up, surrender, or death of a part of the patient—whether it be a habit, job, life-style, belief system, or physical organ. Thus, you as patient/self-healer will experience the five stages of death and dying that Dr. Elisabeth Kübler-Ross describes in her book *On Death and Dying*. They are *denial, anger, bargaining, depression,* and *acceptance*. You will also go through two more stages: *rebirth* and *creation of a new life*. They are a natural part of the healing process. It is of utmost importance for the healer to accept whatever stage the patient is in and not to try to pull them out of it. Yes, the healer may need to lead them out of it because of a physical danger that may be involved. But it must be a gentle leading.

To help describe the personal experience of going through the seven stages of healing, I have chosen two cases where surgery was required in addition to laying on of hands healing. These cases offer a broader view of all aspects of healing. Of course, someone utilizing only laying on of hands and "natural" healing will also go through the same stages.

Bette B., the first patient, is about five feet five inches tall, has dark brown curly hair streaked with gray, and has a very loving personality. She is a professional nurse and dedicated student of healing. Bette is sixty-seven years old, married, and mother of two children. She lives in the Washington, D.C., area with her husband, Jack, a retired safety engineer. Bette had previously had pain, weakness, and tingling in the left leg that led to paralysis from her waist down in 1954. As a result, she had two lumbar disks removed. After eight months of personal healing work, consisting of water therapy, physical therapy, and a lot of praying, she was able to walk again—something the surgeons didn't expect. She had another back surgery in 1976, during which another disk was removed, along with scar tissue and bone splinters. She went to a pain and rehab clinic for recovery. In 1986, new symptoms of pain, weakness, and tingling in the left arm and pain in her neck began. In 1987, Bette went for more surgery, this time in the neck. I interviewed Bette a few months after her surgery.

Karen A., the second patient, is a tall, beautiful brunette in her midforties, married, with two stepchildren. She has no children of her own. Karen is a seasoned therapist. Her husband is also a therapist. At the time of this writing, they live in Colorado.

Karen's illness occurred when they lived in the Washington, D.C., area. Her physical problems began very early in her life, around puberty. She had chronic pain in her lower pelvic region for years. Later it was diagnosed as uterine fibroids and endometriosis on the right ovary. She became infected, the pain got worse, and she decided to go ahead with a hysterectomy. The experience of healing led her into a very deep self-revealing spiral of inner growth.

We will go through the stages one by one to find and explore the basic ingredients of each.

The First Stage of Healing: Denial

The need for denial exists in everyone at times. We all try to be or pretend that we are exempt from the more difficult experiences of life. We use denial to hold this pretense because we are afraid. We think we can't handle something, or we just don't want to.

If you become ill, you will probably use denial or at least partial denial not only in the first stage of your illness or following confrontation, but also later on, from time to time. Denial is a temporary defense that gives you time to prepare yourself for acceptance of what will come at a later stage. Especially if you need harsh treatment, you are likely able to talk about your situation only for a certain amount of time. Then you need to change the subject to more pleasant things or even fantasy. That is okay; it is perfectly natural. There is something that you fear that you are not yet ready to face; in time, you will be. Give yourself the time you need.

You will be able to speak comfortably and directly to some members of your family, friends, and health-care professionals about your condition. And you will not be able to discuss it at all with others. And guess what! You don't have to. This has a great deal to do with your trust of each person. It is of great importance to honor that in yourself. It also has a lot to do with these people's feelings about illness, their own bodies, and your illness. You may be reacting to what is going on in them. (It is always necessary for health-care professionals to examine their own reactions to illness when working with patients. Their reactions will always be reflected in the patients' behavior and can contribute a great deal to the patients' well-being or detriment.)

Remember, denial is a completely normal mode of behavior. Do not judge yourself when you find it in yourself. We all do it, not only with illness but in most areas of our lives. Denial serves to keep us from seeing what we don't feel prepared to see or feel. It is a defense system that keeps us from going nuts. If your system feels that it can handle it, you don't have to be in denial. As soon as you are ready to handle it, you will come out of denial.

Long-term denial can be very costly. Yet it needs to be dealt with kindly and compassionately. You will need love both from yourself and others to get through it. So it is important to surround yourself with people you love and trust. Open to their love and share with them whenever you can.

Bette used denial by ignoring the messages coming from her body and her balancing system:

> I remember having pain in my shoulder and down my arm over the elbow and thinking, "Oh, you're just getting a little bit old and maybe you have arthritis. Just ignore it; it'll go away." When I was painting, I would have difficulty using my left arm.
>
> The difficulty with my arm would come and go. I think it went on like that for about four years. The last year and a half before I actually went to the doctor to have the surgery, my hand and my arm were definitely losing strength. For the first time in my life, I had to ask my husband to open jars for me. I denied this away by saying to myself, "You've got a little arthritis in your hand. That's all it is. Don't get upset by it."
>
> I did ignore the weakness in my arm because that came and went also. I would get really, really panicky about losing the strength when it came to carrying packages in from the grocery store. But I wouldn't allow myself to feel the panic long. I would change from the left arm to the right arm and make the packages a lot lighter.
>
> I really believe, though, that part of this denial was almost necessary for the disease to get to the point where it was "operable." At least, that's the way it seems to me today. I don't think it would have been operable at that time. I don't think it had gone far enough. Had I known earlier, I would have been terrified. It was easier to deny it than to run to the doctor because I always had a saying as a nurse that I should know what was wrong with me before I went to the doctor, rather than going in ignorance and saying, "You're the doctor, what's wrong?" I felt I had to know the answer first.
>
> As a nurse, we were always taught that a lot of things are in your head. My fear, I think, was that because I was a nurse and the doctor was "God," he would tell me it was all in my head and that there was nothing wrong with me. That was a hard thing to overcome.
>
> As I'm saying this, I'm beginning to realize how important it was then for me to do this on my own, rather than having to go and get help from doctors. I think the purpose of this entire experience was to enable me to feel powerless and to be able to work with other people.

I asked Bette what she meant by powerless. She explained that what she meant was that she needed to learn to surrender and feel safe. This will become clearer as we go through the stages with her.

Karen's denial also took the form of ignoring messages from her balancing system that came in the form of pain. Being in the therapy profession, she spent a good deal of time "working on" the psychological issues involved. Unfortunately, it finally became clear that this was also a form of denial. Karen needed to deal with her problem on the physical level.

She states:

> I think I was in denial all along until I decided to have the operation. I was in more discomfort than I let myself know, and I kept telling myself that if I just worked this next piece through, then it would all be okay. I could heal it. The form denial took was in keeping me trying to work things through in therapy.

What is under everyone's denial is fear. The fear is of things they will have to face and go through because of their illness.

Karen was afraid that she couldn't heal herself. She was afraid of the hospital experience and of being physically helpless during and after the operation. She also feared that she might die during the operation, even though there really was no question about her going through it successfully. She avoided the treatment for a long time because of this fear.

Bette's fears were similar:

> I was afraid of an operation, to be dependent on others because I was not healing naturally and had to do surgery. Another fear was that I would lose my creativity in my hands and not be able to paint. Painting has become such a soothing, wonderful, creative experience for me that [to lose] it terrified me more than not being able to walk.

Many times we have fears that don't make any sense, but those fears feel very real and strong. Whether we label such a fear irrational or from a "past life experience," as many healers do, these fears must be acknowledged and dealt with.

Bette recalls:

> I feared that if anything was wrong in my neck, I was going to have my head chopped off. This was very, very terrifying to me. It came out of no place seemingly and was really very very frightening.
>
> I think there were two cycles of all these stages of denial/anger/bargaining/acceptance. One was prior to being diagnosed, and the other was after the doctor told me to go to the neurosurgeon. In fact, when the doctor first told me he was going to send me to the neurosurgeon, I said, "No, not that!"

I remember my husband saying to me, "Why are you so afraid of the surgery?" And I remember saying, "I don't know why." I've had two other spinal surgeries, but it's as though this were the vital part of my life. This was going to be terrifying because I truly believed inside me it was going to end my life.

I postponed it and postponed it and postponed it. I was just simply terrified. I can remember the morning of the first appointment. There again was that fear of having my head chopped off.

On the morning of going to the neurosurgeon, I remember getting up and crying bitterly to Jack, "I don't want to go. Let's forget the whole thing. This is more than I can handle. Why is this happening to me?" I was terrified and I cried for twenty-five minutes before I went to the neurosurgeon.

In Bette's healing process, she was able to share these fears with her husband and friends. It was important for her to feel them in the presence of another person, whether or not they were realistic. It is this sharing that allowed the fear to be transformed. When she did this, her fear turned into anger and she entered into the second stage of healing.

The Second Stage of Healing: Anger

If you go through the healing process, you will reach a time when you can't maintain the first stage of denial anymore. You will then probably have feelings of anger, rage, envy, and resentment. You may say, "Why me? Why not Joe Blow, who is an alcoholic and beats his wife?" Because this type of anger is displaced in all directions, you will probably project it onto your environment almost at random. Friends, family, healers, doctors—none of them will be any good, and all of them will be doing things wrong. When your family gets your anger, they may react with grief, tears, guilt, or shame and even may avoid future contact with you. This may increase your discomfort and anger. Bear with it; this is a stage.

Your anger is easy to understand since you have to interrupt your life activities with some things unfinished. Or you aren't able to do things other people can do, or you have to use your hard-earned money for healing rather than the vacations or travel that you expected.

Anyone going through the healing process will hit some anger. It will be different for each person. For some, it will be a big explosion like Bette's, especially if they haven't allowed themselves to be angry before. When Bette reached the second stage, her anger exploded and she went straight to the top:

I remember being very angry. I was very angry at God because I thought, "God put me through the paralysis of my legs and everything, and my legs still weren't back to totally normal." And I thought, "You can't take my arms as well as my legs, because my arms are connected to my spirituality and my creativity."

Anger, on the other hand, was just another emotion for Karen.

Anger was just one of any number of passing feelings that went through me. I may have been angry off and on in relation to how uncomfortable I was, but it doesn't feel like a big stage that I went through. I think that at different times I had different feelings, like anger, that I wasn't healed by people who were supposedly there to heal me or at some of the different doctors I went to. I would move between being angry for a while and then trying to make a deal with God.

Thus Karen moved back and forth between the second stage of anger and the third of bargaining.

Be prepared to find that you are much more interested in bargaining than you may have thought! Everybody does it.

The Third Stage of Healing: Bargaining

Since anger didn't get you what you wanted, you will probably, and quite unconsciously, try to bargain by being good and doing something nice so that you will get what you want. Most bargains are made with God and usually kept secret or mentioned between the lines, like dedicating a life to God or a special cause. Underneath there is usually an associated quiet guilt. You may feel guilty for not attending meetings of your religious choice more often. You may wish you had eaten the "right" food, done the "right" exercises, lived the "right" way. It is very important here to find and let go of that guilt because it only leads to more bargaining and eventually to depression. Find all of your "should-haves," and imagine them dissolving in white light. Or give them over to your guardian angel or God. When you have completed your journey through the seven stages, you will probably find a change you wish to make in your life, but it will not come out of fear, as this one does.

Bette tried to bargain her way out of the illness by trying to get someone else, anyone but the surgeon, to fix it:

> I was trying to get my husband to fix it. It was kind of like I wanted him to soothe me and say, "This is all going to get better." I don't think I actually realized I was bargaining, but I do know I said to myself, "If you just meditate more, if you do more baths, if you massage yourself more, and if you continue to use the white light, this will all go away and you will not have to go for surgery." I wanted to dedicate myself to being a more devoted person to meditation and hoping that somehow this would get me off the hook.
>
> I also went back and forth between accepting that, yes, I would have to go to surgery and hoping that somehow someone magically would wrap my spine in the gold light and everything would be taken care of. I asked for healings, but was never able to schedule one. I can remember Ann [a fellow student healer who offered healings to Bette] saying that she would come over, and I used a million different reasons why Ann should not come to my house. I didn't trust her, I didn't trust anybody, simply because I didn't trust myself.

For bargaining, Karen went straight to God:

> My bargaining took the form of my inner child that said, "Look, God. You make me better and I'll do anything if you let me get through this. Or if I live and get through this [which there wasn't much question about], I will make a deep commitment to give my life to the healing of this planet, in whatever form is required of me." The more I bargained the more depressed I would get afterward.

The Fourth Stage of Healing: Depression

Depression refers to the feeling state we experience when our energy is very low and we have lost hope of getting what we want the way we wanted it. We try to pretend that we don't care, but we really do. We are

sad, but we don't want to express the sadness. We enter into a state of gloom and usually don't want to interact with others. Depression means depressing our feelings.

From the point of view of the human energy field, depression means depressing the energy flow through your life field. Some of this energy flow correlates to feelings. Therefore, when we think of depression, we usually think of depressing feelings.

There are three causes for depression. One is denial from bargaining, mentioned above. That is trying to heal yourself through avoidance and rejecting yourself for the way things are, rather than a truthful seeking of a solution.

The second cause is depressing feelings of loss. All illness requires letting go of a way of life, a physical body part, or something like a bad habit. If you block your feelings of loss, you will get depressed. If you allow yourself to feel the loss and mourn it, your depression will lift. You will be in mourning, a totally different state. Mourning is an open flowing, a feeling of loss, rather than a depression of feelings. Whatever you lost, you need to mourn it. You may go through mourning at different times in your healing process. Just stay with the feelings of the loss whenever they come up for you. That will bring you to the stage of acceptance.

A third cause of depression is harsh invasive treatments like chemotherapy, anesthesia, and surgery that imbalance your body chemistry and make you go into depression. When your body resumes its physical balance, the depression will lift. From the point of view of the human energy field, the harsh treatments and drugs stop, slow down, or clog the normal energy flow through your energy field. Thus you become depressed. When the drugs wear off, the energy flow resumes, and the depression lifts. Hands-on healing clears the field in about half the normal length of time, and patients come out of postoperative depression sooner.

Bette's depression took the form of self-rejection. She withdrew into herself and did a lot of crying:

> I felt I was a bad person. If I had worked harder at the healing, if I had done my homework, if I had been a better God-person, then I would have been able to heal myself. It was almost as though I had to totally give in and heal my powerlessness in order to allow someone else to do the work. What was wrong with me? I could never be a healer. That was very, very scary to me, because inside, I truly believed I was meant to be a healer, and I still do. But going

through all this healing was very scary at the time. I felt I wasn't even a good wife anymore.

It's really pretty ugly when all of this negative stuff comes up and you kind of go back to the old God that you knew a long, long time ago, and you feel you're being punished for something because you're not good enough.

I had to let go of a lot of things. I simply couldn't do as much as I wanted to do around the house. I wasn't able to concentrate on the healing class homework. We had planned to go away, and I simply couldn't do it because I was in so much pain. I had to force myself in anything that I did. I had to force myself to get out of bed in the morning. I was uncomfortable in bed, but I was more uncomfortable when I got up. I really didn't know what to do. I didn't trust myself. I didn't trust anyone else. I had to go through a period of going for physical therapy to see if it would help, and actually the physical therapy made it worse. So I had to mourn the fact that that couldn't help before it was the right time for me to have the surgery. Part of me was hoping it would help and part of me kind of knew it wouldn't.

There's one more thing, Barbara. I had to mourn the loss of my ability to paint during that time. That was really, really hard for me, because that had always been a way of healing for me. It had been a way to get through things and to still feel creative, to still feel spiritual. I was not able to do it because I couldn't see, and that was a big loss, another loss. I was very depressed after the surgery, I couldn't do any self healing at all then, I just forced myself to listen to a few tapes.

Karen's depression was also full of self-judgments and self-rejection:

I just got bogged down under my own self-rejection. I felt I was failing at healing myself. I didn't know whether I would be giving up by going to a doctor. I just got totally balled up in that kind of thing.

Finally, I woke up one morning and I had real bad pain in the right part of my abdomen, and I just felt like "I can't take this anymore." I didn't know if it was psychological or physical, or what doctor to go to. I couldn't get in to see my gynecologist, and I just was over the edge and so I called you. And when Heyoan talked to me through you, he reminded me about my self-judgment. I didn't even know I had been in self-judgment. That was the turning point for me. I re-framed a lot around the operation at that point. I

began seeing it as letting go of self-judgments and getting my needs met. That became the theme for me. After I talked to you, something lifted and I called and got an appointment with a doctor really quickly. I just decided to have an operation, and from then on everything just started moving.

As soon as Karen let go of her self-rejection and made the decision to have the operation, her depression lifted and she entered the stage of acceptance.

The Fifth Stage of Healing: Acceptance

When you have had enough time, energy, and focus to process the four previous stages, you go into a stage in which you are neither depressed nor angry about your condition. You will have been able to express your previous feelings, your envy for the healthy, and your anger at those who do not have to face illness. You will have mourned the impending loss that your illness demands. You may wish to be left alone or to communicate in quiet, nonverbal ways of Being because you are preparing yourself for change. This is the time of really getting to know yourself better, of going inside and meeting yourself anew. You question the values you have lived by that have helped create your illness. You begin to feel your true needs and seek nurturance in ways that you haven't before. You gravitate to new friends and may separate from some old ones, who may not be part of the next phase of your life. You make the necessary changes in your life to facilitate your healing process. The process speeds up. You feel great relief, even though there may be a lot to do to complete your healing.

Once Karen reached acceptance, things completely changed. Everything was then taken within the context of meeting her needs. Out of Karen's acceptance came a way to take more control of her life by focusing on her needs. She learned how to ask for what she needed:

Speaking the truth, the truth of my needs, was the thing that released me. Just my needs without judgment. The minute I began saying them more, they began being answered. Lo and behold!

For Bette, it was the opposite. Rather than more control, for her acceptance meant deep surrender, something she had been terrified of before. As her healing process continued, the powerlessness that had been a symbol of weakness in Bette's old context became a symbol of strength in the new. It takes a great deal of faith and strength to surrender. What she thought was collapsing into powerlessness and neediness was actually a surrender to love and to the higher power within her and all around her. For her, acceptance came in stages. The first was before her operation.

She recalls:

> I really sensed deep within me that it was important that I have the surgery, I needed to go through the experience, number one, to learn to work with other medical people, to work with any other people, as a matter of fact. I needed to not be so independent. I needed to change this value of doing it all on my own.

> Acceptance did not come permanently. It came in small, easy doses. It came as, "Yes, Bette, you must have the surgery. This is necessary for you to go through, and you've got to do it." The other part was actually going into the hospital. I went back and forth through almost all of the stages. I again went through some denial. I was angry. I didn't like anybody in the hospital except one nurse. It seemed they were all much too busy. However, thank God for my supportive friends.

A large part of Bette's surrender was to ask for and to allow herself to receive a lot of support from her friends.

The Sixth Stage of Healing: Rebirth—A Time of New Light Emerging

---

Acceptance and healing lead to rebirth, a time to meet yourself in a new way. You will be delighted with who you find there. In this stage you need plenty of quiet alone time to get to know yourself. Be sure to give yourself this time. Perhaps even go on a silent retreat, or go fishing for a few days. You may need a few weeks or even a few months of private personal time.

In the process of your recovery, you discover that you have uncovered parts of yourself that have been buried for a long time. Perhaps new parts you have never seen emerge. There will be plenty of *light emerging* from within you. Look at it; see the beauty; smell the fragrance; taste and delight in the new you. You find new internal resources that you were not able to

bring out before. You may have always felt that they were there, but now they begin to flow to the surface. It can truly be a rebirth for you.

You experience everything in your life, both the present and the past, within a new context. This is a time of rewriting your history. This is when you understand that you can actually change your relationship to past events to heal them. It happens automatically because you have changed your stance in life. You have changed the context within which you experience your life. This is what is meant by true healing.

For Bette, rebirth began with humility:

> When I first became humble enough to ask for help, it was like becoming less and less defiant and accepting the need to work with my husband and my friends and to be dependent on them. And accept the fact that I couldn't do it all myself. It felt good to have the love and caring coming to me. It felt warm and comfortable and very reassuring.

> I attribute my healing to the tremendous surgery by the doctor, to my ability to heal myself, and to my friends in the spiritual community who helped me also.

> I'm not as afraid of being powerless anymore. Before, it was like being a ship without a rudder. So I had to be strong. I felt I needed to be isolated. I didn't trust my higher being or higher power to provide what I needed. I had to do it by my will. Now it is nice to know I can trust other people, and I don't have to be isolated. I feel safer trusting myself and others.

> It turned out that what I thought was to be powerless was actually the need for me to surrender to the higher powers, both inside and outside me. I know there is a universal power that is there to provide me with whatever I need. I am a part of it, and it is a part of me.

Karen also placed old experiences within a new context during her rebirth stage. In the earlier stage of bargaining, she had been willing to "give her life" to whatever was "required" of her to heal the planet. But when rebirth came, she found that being "required" to "give her life" was coming out of a place of fear within her. It was like saying, "God, you save my life, and then I'll give it up to save the planet."

In rebirth, she found a deep commitment to first heal herself and then the planet. That is the way it works. Healing starts at home and then holographically threads through the rest of life on the planet. In healing the self, one heals the planet. These commitments came out of her love. Karen felt that the whole experience of the healing helped her to focus on what she wanted and needed to do next in her life:

The outcome of the operation was that I really got more deeply committed in that way. I came out of it wanting to give my life over in service, but it didn't feel like the negative form of bargaining. What turns me on the most is helping healers find their unique mode of healing. It feels like a very important stage of looking at what I am about and taking a deeper level of responsibility for myself.

The Seventh Stage of Healing: Creating a New Life

All areas of your life will be affected as you move into health again. Many areas of change and opportunity that you have longed for, and that were blocked or seemingly unattainable, open to you. You live more honestly with yourself and find new areas of self-acceptance that you were unable to maintain in yourself before. You find more internal humility, faith, truth, and self-love. These internal changes automatically lead to external changes. They come out of your creative force and spread holographically throughout your life. You attract new friends. You either change your profession, or you change the way in which you approach your work. You may even move to a new location. All these changes are very common after a healing is completed.

Bette's life has changed tremendously. At the time of this writing, it's been two years since her operation. In the first year, she spent most of her time healing herself and reorienting herself to her new attitude toward life. A lot of her fear was gone. During the healing process, she had related to the irrational fear of having her head chopped off with a past life in France, where she was guillotined. Of course this cannot be proven, but opening to and allowing the feelings around it dissolved a great deal of her fear. During the year of internal adjustment, Bette's personal life began filling in. Her relationship with her husband became closer. Her sex life became more active. At the ripe age of sixty-seven, she says her sex life is better than it's ever been! Her husband is delighted.

About two years after the operation, in 1990, Bette started her healing practice. At first there were a few clients; then it slowly grew. I called Bette after her operation for a followup on the earlier interview. I asked her about her life changes that were initiated with the operation, and how her practice is.

She told me:

I had to go through it to get over that terrible fear that I was going to die. It all connected to that life with the guillotine when my head was cut off. Now I've lived through that terror. I've gained strength, and I can handle a lot more. When I was ready to help other people, they just started coming for help. Now they are coming out of the walls. As soon as I help one person, two of her friends show up for help.

My art work has taken a back seat—no time for it. But it changed in character. My paintings became a lot more spiritual. Everything is in a new dimension. It's as if when they cleared out my neck, it cleared out another layer of the—what did you call it?—the shroud around my core. I'm in a whole other dimension. My life is changed, everything is beginning to fall into place. I think the greatest thing is that I am beginning to know why I am here—that is, to heal myself and to heal other people, to help other people get well. I used to feel there were lots of limits, and now it seems the limits are gone. There is no boundary. I think it is up to me to help other people realize that they are boundaryless.

Karen's life changed also, but in a different way. She and her husband decided to end their therapy practices in the Washington, D.C., area and move up into some mountain land in Colorado. They spent plenty of time saying good-bye to their friends of fifteen years, sold their house, and moved. They spent the winter months in Colorado meditating, reading, and simply Being in a way they had never been able to in their very busy lives in the East. After a year of this personal internal reverie, Karen is now again starting a practice in Colorado.

EIGHT

The Seven Levels of the Healing Process

If we examine Bette and Karen's experiences as they progressed through the seven stages of healing, we find two primary ingredients that were keys to the unfoldment of their process. These two primary ingredients are required on the personal healing journey to get the most benefit from your personal healing process.

The first ingredient is the reframing of the personal healing process into a *personal life lesson*. Many times, our experience of an illness is colored by our early childhood ideas that being "sick" means there is something "wrong" with us. It is important to distinguish between the old negative ideas of illness with which we were raised and the internal experience through which we live during an illness. There is a great deal to be learned from illness if we look at it primarily as a learning process. Since the experience of being ill challenges us to fall into our old images of the past, it is important to keep reminding ourselves of the new framework out of which we seek to live.

We are "re-membering" ourselves, or bringing back our original connection to the deeper self when we go through the healing process. "Re-membering" is bringing our "members," or parts of ourselves, back together. It's much like putting the smaller pieces of the holographic plate back together to get a clearer, sharper image.

When we go through each level of the healing process, we will be tempted to fall back into the "old" way,

the old judgments, the old narrow vision. A lot of the work of healing is to keep choosing to walk into the new framework, no matter how loud the old voices within us are yelling danger.

The second of these ingredients is meticulous honesty with yourself *with particular regard to personal needs*. It is important to admit that you do have needs, to know that it is okay to have them, and to become aware of them. This requires searching for what those real needs are. Many of us are not aware of many of our needs. Finding our needs on all levels and meeting them is essential. It takes patience and self-search to uncover our real needs.

Meeting our needs on each level of our being is very important in the healing process because our unmet needs are connected directly with how we got ill in the first place. Remember in Chapter 1, we spoke of the basic cause of all illness as stemming from forgetting who we truly are and acting according to that forgetting? Not meeting our true needs is a direct outcome of not living according to who we truly are. Part of going through the healing process is to retrace some of our steps to address real needs that were not filled, to acknowledge those needs, no matter how painful that process, and to find a way to fill them now. Wherever and whenever our emerging creative process is stopped, there are unmet needs and pain. Uncovering these inner psychic spaces brings life energy to them.

Fulfilling the original positive creative intent that stems from the core of our being is what healing is all about. This dissolves the shroud around the core of our being, and we live in the truth of who we are. Meeting the needs of the moment brings us holographically to the healing of all past unmet needs. It brings us to our basic need—the creative expression of our core.

Let's look at this process from a very practical working point of view; through the levels of the human energy field and the needs that correspond to each level. As I worked with people, I found that each of a patient's needs was related to a specific level of the human energy field. As stated in Chapter 2, the human energy field is directly connected to and expresses human physical, emotional, mental, and spiritual levels of being. Each level of the field is associated with a human level of life experience. (See Figure 8–1 for a summary of the needs on each level.)

Remember, the first level of the field is associated with the functioning of our physical body and physical sensation. Our need on the first level is to enjoy a healthy body and all the wonderful physical sensations that go with it. The second level is associated with our personal emotional relationship to ourselves. Our need on the second level of the field is to love and accept the self as we are. The third level is associated with our mental activity and sense of clarity. Our need on the third is to have a well-functioning, agile mind full of clarity. The fourth is associated with our interpersonal emotional life, our "I-thou" connections. Our need on the fourth level of the field is to love and be loved by others, in many forms of relationships, such as friends, family, colleagues, and lover.

The fourth level, associated with the human heart and loving, is considered to be the bridge between the physical world, expressed in the first three levels of human functioning, and our spiritual world, expressed in the three levels of spiritual functioning.

The fifth level of the field is associated with the power of the word in the creative process. It serves as the template for all form on the physical level. It is the level at which speaking the word leads to creating form in the physical world. If you speak truth, you create truth and clarity in your life. If you do not speak honestly, you create distortion in your life. Thus, our need on the fifth level of the field is to speak and be in our truth.

The sixth level is associated with spiritual feelings, such as the feelings of ecstasy you may have in a religious ceremony, or when you hear inspirational music, or perhaps when you watch a sunset, sit on a mountain, meditate, or look into the eyes of a loved one. Our need

FIGURE 8–1 YOUR NEEDS ON EACH LEVEL OF THE AURIC FIELD

First	**Simple physical comfort, pleasure, and health.** We need to have many wonderful physical sensations.
Second	**Self-acceptance and self-love.** We need to relate to ourselves in a loving positive way.
Third	**To understand the situation in a clear, linear, rational way.** We need rational clarity that functions in harmony with our intuitive mind.
Fourth	**Loving interaction with friends and family.** We need to give and receive love in many types of relationships, with our spouse, family, children, friends, and colleagues.
Fifth	**To align with the divine will within, to make the commitment to speak and follow the truth.** We need our own personal truth.
Sixth	**Divine love and spiritual ecstasy.** We need our own personal experience of spirituality and unconditional love.
Seventh	**To be connected to divine mind and to understand the greater universal pattern.** We need to experience serenity and our perfection within our imperfections.

on the sixth level is for the spiritual nourishment that brings about spiritual experience.

The seventh level of the field is associated with divine mind. When you bring your conscious awareness to this level, and it is clear, strong, and healthy, you know the divine perfection in all that there is. You understand all the pieces of the puzzle of your life. You experience serenity.

This is the level that holds your beliefs, some of which are in accord with divine law and others of which are distorted. The negative beliefs you carry are the source of all your problems. From these negative beliefs or "images," you create dis-ease on whatever level it manifests within your life—physical, emotional, mental, or spiritual.

Our need on the seventh level of the field is to know serenity. Serenity comes from understanding the perfect pattern of life upon the earth. This comes from positive beliefs that are based on the truth.

Using Karen's process as a framework to guide us, we'll discover that by filling the two necessary primary ingredients—to go through the process of honestly meeting our needs and maintaining the point of view that this experience is another life lesson or even a life adventure—then our healing experience becomes both a personal transformation process and later a personal transcendental process. The process of transformation is one in which we use introspection to find out how we are functioning unconsciously.

It is sometimes a difficult thing to be meticulously honest with the self. To look at our shortcomings and find what is beneath them, and to choose to change, is just plain hard work. But it has great rewards. When we uncover the negative within ourselves, we also uncover the original positive creative force that was distorted into the negative aspect that we now wish to change. Thus, the transformation process brings us the gift of our original, true, clear, and loving self.

After we have done a certain amount of transformation process, the released original creative energy automatically lifts us into transcendental experience. We can then use both the transformational and the transcendental processes for healing. Not only do we heal our bodies and transform our lives, we transcend into higher personal spiritual experience. When we transcend the mundane, we learn to incorporate higher spiritual values into the practical aspects of our lives. We "spiritualize" matter. We bring our spirit into the physical aspects of life.

Here's what the healing transformational process looks like in a personal and practical way with respect to your auric field. To heal yourself on the first four levels of your being means to change your daily life in each of these areas. This requires going through a *personal transformation* process to change how you take care of yourself, first level of your auric field; how you love yourself, second level of your auric field; how you bring clarity to your life situation so that you can understand it better, third level of your auric field; and how you relate to others, fourth level of your auric field.

To heal yourself on the higher three levels requires the personal process of *transcendence*. You must transcend or reach up, out, or into these higher values and bring them into your life through an act of courage and faith. In both Bette and Karen's lives, it was the surrender to truth and the decision to live by it that helped them come out of denial. Each let go of the attitude that said, "It must be my way; I will do it by myself."

Each was trying to prevent or avoid a particular life experience that she needed. Each needed to face something within herself that, because of fear, she had been avoiding for a long time. Calling on their higher internal power gave the impetus to let go of trying to personally control the situation and trust in the deeper cycles of life change everyone goes through. As soon as this surrender came, the separation of the self from the greater internal "I am," which is associated with the source of life itself, ended. And healing began.

As you come to the higher three levels of the auric field, your transformation process automatically moves into a transcendent one. That is, you will deal with levels of your being that relate to your spiritual nature rather than your material nature of everyday living. In the transcendent process you begin to recognize parts of yourself to which you may not have paid much attention before, or that you did not think were very important. You will find a whole new world in these areas of your being. You will find yourself to be much greater than you thought yourself to be. You will begin experiencing the universal hologram. This process is an automatic one and unfolds out of every individual. Each individual's unfoldment is different. Enjoy yours.

The second road map for the healing process focuses on your process of healing as it relates to each of your needs, which correlate to a specific level of your auric field. As we move through each level of human experience associated with each level of the aura, we will clarify what needs are common for all of us on those levels of our being.

Transforming Your Health and Your Life

The key element in the transformational process is to set a very clear and firm positive intent. This is the first step in taking responsibility for your self-healing. Clearly align yourself with your goodwill, or the divine will within you, to find and speak your truth and to follow it. Be sure that you give yourself time to be alone and meditate to do this. Do your meditation in a special place, and acknowledge the beginning of change in your life. Meditate to find the divine will within you as it speaks within your own heart. Make your commitment to your healing process. By doing this, you are aligning the lower levels of your field that relate your physical life to the higher spiritual levels of your field so that you will follow the blueprint of your higher power. You activate "as above, so below." Once you have done this, you can begin work on the lower auric levels.

In finding your needs, it is extremely important to not turn medicine away just because you're into hands-on healing. Instead, find the best way to use it. Let go of the judging of any particular healing path. Karen and Bette's experience illustrates the importance of this. Both needed surgery. Your judgments have a strong negative effect in stopping your healing. Carlos Castaneda quotes Don Juan when he said to "choose a path with a heart." From the examples of both Bette and Karen, it has become clear that *the very act of self-judgment removes the heart. All paths can have a heart. You put the heart on the path that you choose, but as soon as you put in the self-judgment about your choice, then you take out the heart.* Acknowledging your needs, loving yourself, and meeting all of them takes away the self-judgments and puts the heart in the path. Yes, you are a human being and you have multiple levels of needs. If you fill your needs, you won't be as likely to let yourself sink into your negative expectations about what an experience (such as meeting your mother-in-law or receiving a particular type of treatment, like having an operation) may be like. Nor will you, with your negative expectations, react in the experience in such a way as to re-create another trauma. So you are really healing your negative image and your negative belief system, which are the cause of the problem in the first place.

Karen made a delightful discovery once she decided to fill her needs:

What I began realizing was that I had needs on every level. And as I decided to go into the operation, it got very clear that I just had to take all of them on. In deciding to act on what I needed, from the physical level on up, my needs got very clear. There were specific things I had to do in order to go into the operation and get the most out of it.

I think that if people knew that they could still get their needs met in going into an operation, they wouldn't fight it so much. Especially the kind of spiritual people who know about healing. Sometimes the ethos is that, "Too bad, you have to have an operation." But from my end it doesn't have to be that. The more people can realize their needs, the more they can get all of them fulfilled.

The needs are so much more creative and varied than I thought. The creativity's in solving them, but if you believe they can be solved you can have a zillion needs, and it's fun to solve them. They're not problematic.

Your Needs on the First Level of Your Auric Field

First-level needs are simple physical needs. It is important to regulate your environment and set the appropriate time and place for any activity so that you are constantly reminded of your internal personal transformation process. This places focus on the personal experience of healing as more important than the outer old definitions of sickness.

If you need to go for tests or an interview with a physician, be sure to create the most appropriate way to do this. Present yourself in a way that is aligned with, supports, and maintains your internal life source. Take charge of the situation in a gentle way. If a fast is not required for tests, make sure that you have eaten so that you do not have low blood sugar. Choose your clothes to express who you are. If possible, choose the best time of day for you to go. Ask a friend to come with you for support, if you're going to hear test results and they are potentially serious. Choose the best health-care professionals, clinics, or laboratories. You have many choices. Make good use of them. It is important.

A prime need on the first level of the auric field is to feel comfortable. *Surround yourself with things that will help you see reality from this new holographic viewpoint, even when there are not other people around or when you might forget.* If you are in a hospital, bring books you like and that remind you of the greater reality. If you get scared, open one and just read something on fear. *Emmanuel's Book* by Pat Rodegast is really good for this. If you like crystals or music tapes, have them at hand so if you forget your reality, you will have something to remind you of who you really are and of what is really happening. It will keep you focused on the deeper point of view. If you know what tapes get you into altered states, play them. You finally have time to lie around and listen. Those tapes can get you to some wonderful places. If the hospital has given you a mind-altering drug such as a tranquilizer or sedative, take advantage of it and have a free ride into deep relaxation.

After Karen's friends reminded her that she had a choice, she decided that she wanted a private room and she got one. That was very important to her. Karen brought music tapes and crystals to her room. Since she was not on a special medical diet, her husband brought her food. This she loved:

Everybody knows hospital food is really atrocious. I think I would have been really sick if I had eaten it. Ron just kept bringing me food from the health food store or the hfealth food café. I don't know what I would have done if I'd had to eat hospital food. So that's just another important physical need that got met because I knew about it and could ask for it.

After you leave the hospital and your treatment is completed, if you are still having healings or are in a therapeutic process, you may relive the more invasive parts of your treatment. This is a good way to clear your field of any leftover garbage from the drugs or the physical trauma. This garbage slows down your healing process. Many people will go through the process of reliving the trauma many years later. Whenever it comes up is fine. What is important is to let it happen when you are ready.

Karen did it right away, and quite unexpectedly:

After I was home from the hospital, I finally ran out of Demerol. I went down to less and less pills till I went off it. I felt terrible the next day. Ron was helping me to breathe, and I went into a kind of primal state in which I relived the operation. As I started breathing and crying, this horrible feeling that I didn't want to see something came, and then I realized I was reliving the operation. I felt awful physically and awful emotionally. My body was reliving it. It surprised me. That felt important because I started healing a lot faster, which I couldn't have done if the pain of the operation was still in me, in my cells.

Remember, if this happens to you, it is best to have someone there to support you. It is okay; you will be fine. Just let go and go through it. It will do you a lot of good.

Here are some good questions to ask yourself:
What kind of environment do I need to best suit my healing process?
Is the atmosphere in my bedroom good for me?
Is there plenty of sunlight and plenty of plants?
Is my favorite music playing?
Do I have pictures to remind me of things that I wish to be reminded of?
What other objects would help me remember the positive aspects of my life? (Perhaps certain pieces of jewelry, crystals, or some other favorite objects would help.)
Do I have reminders that will help all of my senses remember who I am?
What can I see and touch?
What odors help me feel better?

What are the things within my diet, that I could taste, that would help me feel pleasure during this time?

Your Needs on the Second Level of Your Auric Field

The needs on the second level are for self-acceptance and self-love. A big problem on this level is disliking the self, self-rejection, and even in a great many cases self-hatred. These are bad habits you will need to confront directly. What are your needs with regard to accepting and loving yourself? Make a list of the ways that you reject yourself during any given day. Begin to eliminate them one by one. Make a conscious effort to replace the self-rejection with a positive feeling. Write some affirmations stating positive feelings to yourself, and practice them several times a day. You can even post them where you can read them, like on your bedpost, refrigerator, or bathroom mirror.

Some good affirmations are:
I love myself.
I love myself in my imperfections.
I am a strong, creative individual with lots of love.
I love my spouse, child, family, animals.
I accept the life I have created for myself and can change the parts of it that I don't like.
I can continue to love those I strongly disagree with and also not betray myself by forcing myself to agree, or pretending I agree.
I am a beautiful, radiant being of light.
I am full of love.
I remember who I am.

These small reminders of who you are help build a very positive attitude toward the self.

Karen worked to clear her negative attitudes, and it helped her a great deal:

I think the operation helped me to love my body. It forced me to incarnate in ways that I hadn't and that helped me. I had to love and accept myself in new ways. I had to mean something to myself. I think probably one of the greatest pains people must go through in facing an operation is that they split from their bodies, and then this thing is done to their bodies. They just try to not be there and ignore it and wait for the body to recover, rather than being with it in ways that they can: loving your body, accepting it, talking to it about what is going to happen.

Some good questions to ask yourself are:

Which parts of my body do I dislike? Why?

How do I reject these parts?

I hate _____ because it is _____.

How do these body parts remind me of my self-rejection?

I hate my _____ because it reminds me of my _____.

How do I reject myself?

Your Needs on the Third Level of Your Auric Field

Your needs on the third level relate to your mind and your need to understand the situation in a clear, linear, rational way. This means getting all the information about whatever disease process is going on in your body and not limiting yourself to one view of it.

The first thing that you need to do to do this is to find out and clear your negative judgments about yourself and your illness. They block your way to finding solutions for your healing.

We have a lot of negative self-judgments. Negative self-judgments are different from self-rejections in that they are mental conclusions based on the negative way we feel about ourselves. Negative judgments perpetuate a negative feedback loop that regenerates more negative feelings to the self, which then prove our negative judgments correct. Many of us do this to ourselves much more than we realize. Listen in sometimes—you will be surprised at the extent of these internal parental voices we carry within. When negative judgments come up, you can choose one of two major ways of dealing with them.

The first is to express them aloud to yourself or to a friend. You will find that what you say inside to yourself is exaggerated both in kind and in time: Whatever the problem, you are worse than anyone else, forever. Such as:

You deserve to be sick because you are a _____.

The reason you are sick is because you always _____.

Now that you are sick, everyone knows that you are a _____.

Every time you try to do something, you mess it up, you idiot.

You will never be a good _____, so just forget it.

I knew you weren't going to make it. Just give up now and get out of everyone's way.

You are a pain in the _____ to everyone, so just shut up.

Once you have said these things out loud, especially to a friend, you will see how ridiculous they are. Your friend will also know the truth about you and can help put you straight. It is surprising how silly some of our self-judgments sound, once we say them out loud so that we can hear them.

The second way of dealing with them is to just allow your negative attitudes to be and quickly return to the positive as soon as you can, with no self-judgment. For example, if you say to yourself, "Boy, I'm stupid," you can just replace it with a positive statement like, "I'm smart," or "I understand _____." Maybe you catch yourself saying, "I'm not going to get better." You can replace it with, "I'm getting better every day" or, "My body is capable of healing itself."

Choose the method best for you, depending on the situation you are in at the moment your negative self-judgments arise.

Clearing your self-judgments will clear your way to find more ways to treat yourself, because you will be able to ask more questions. Self-judgments keep you from asking questions because you have filled in the answers with wrong information. Once you clear the wrong information, there is room for the right answers. This brings you to the next step—the search for the right modality of treatment.

Find out what different treatment modalities are available from which you can choose. If you can't get that information yourself, then have someone get it for you. If you are going to have an operation or if you need to go through certain treatments in the healing process, read all about those treatments. Find out what they do and what their side effects are.

Karen found out exactly what would happen with her operation. It was very, very helpful to her:

I knew enough to ask a lot of questions, and my friends also helped me know what to ask. The surgeon was a woman, and she answered all my questions. She told me everything that was going to happen. She talked about being examined, shaved, drugged, and wheeled down the hall. She even told me what it was going to be like, going into and coming out of the anesthesia.

This was very important to me, because I had a lot of bad ideas about hospitals, being treated like a piece of meat, and what might happen to me. I could have very easily gone into my image of being punished because I'd rejected the feminine in me and therefore had to have my uterus taken away. As it was, because I kept meeting every need, I didn't do that. Rather, the operation was really symbolic—even though I was losing my uterus—of reclaiming that part of myself, of reclaiming my feminine.

Of course, I also did go through a lot of grieving about losing my uterus. But it wasn't big, it didn't feel as if it was weighing me down or holding me back.

Some good questions to ask yourself are:
What are my negative ideas of what might happen?
How can I find out what will happen step by step?
What, if anything, can I change about this?
What choices do I have of alternative treatments, if any?
What will I need to let go of and grieve for?
What is the possible deeper meaning in all this?

Your Needs on the Fourth Level of Your Auric Field

The fourth-level need is the need for loving interaction with your friends and family. The fourth level of the auric field many times is called the "bridge" between the spiritual and the material worlds. You need support from your friends. Call them. Tell them your needs. Initiate some kind of a support system so that you will be well cared for. Or ask a friend to get together your support system. If you are away from home and can use the phone, make regular phone calls to close friends, or have people call you.

Of course, if you are weakened by your condition, you will want to place boundaries on those calls. You may want to limit the time friends visit. Choose the people who will support *your* healing process. Do not be afraid to set boundaries. It is essential to say no in the moment to people who do not enhance your healing process.

Your friends and people in your family may be distressed by the situation or may not agree with how you are taking care of it. You must make affirmations that you can love yourself and love your family without betraying yourself. You are not responsible for their upset. You are not responsible for their hurt. Their fear with regard to your situation or your illness is most likely not grounded in reality. Their fears are usually unconscious and are mentioned indirectly between the lines of conversation. Notice how you feel after someone has been to see you or called. If you feel better, keep up the communication. If you feel worse, set up your boundary till a more appropriate time to deal with them. Just say no. (See Chapter 13 for information on dissolving negative contracts with friends.)

Friends can bring things. If you are in a hospital and have difficulty with food, friends can bring you healthy food. They can also bring you those physical things—books, sacred objects, clothing—that you need to remind you of who you are. You need to be touched by friends. Ask for it if they hesitate.

Karen got a lot of help from friends. She says:

I just feel really blessed that everyone I knew who came to visit me is some kind of healer on some level. So they really knew what to give me. Friends would sit and meditate with me the first day. Pam came, and Sheila came and meditated. Ron was always there, on every level. Pam brought me homeopathic stuff. You know, for the rest of the week, everybody who came was really intuitive, and there were no people coming in and looking at me as if I were a person who was in a pitiable condition. Everybody would somehow pick up where I was and enable that moment to become a healing moment, all the way through the week.

Some good questions to ask yourself are:
Whom do I feel comfortable with?
Whom do I want to help me? How?
Whom do I not feel comfortable with?
How can I say no to them?

Using Transcendence for Healing the Three Highest Levels of Your Auric Field

---

Your Needs on the Fifth Level of Your Auric Field

The primary need on the fifth level is to align with the divine will within you, to make the commitment to speak and follow your truth. The fifth level of the auric field is the template through which all physical form comes. It's like the negative of a photograph. On this level the power of the word is very strong. The power of the word carries the creative force. The fifth level of the field relates to standing up for what you know. It is a level of will. It means aligning yourself with the divine will within you and following it. The fifth chakra is related to speaking your truth and to giving and receiving. The need here is to speak your truth and live by it. It also relates to sound or using sound to create form.

Karen related her experience of the fifth level:

The truths that I kept speaking before I went into the hospital were all of the needs I had. I began saying them more than I ever have in my life. It forced me to my knees that way.

I'll tell you the first thing that comes to my mind. I have a feeling that there is a connection between the blockage in my second chakra with the uterus and the ovaries and my voice. Singing is a level of my core expression that is coming out now. It feels like it comes directly from down there [lower pelvis]. I wasn't able to do that before. I had to go through the whole healing before I was ready to sing.

Start talking, and continue voicing your needs and your truth. This is the time to access the deepest truth within you. It may not at all agree with what the people around you are saying. State your reality in a positive, loving way, and continue to live by it even though relatives or old friends may disagree.

There will be times, especially if you are in a hospital, when there will be no one there but the staff, who may not know anything at all about the kind of reality in which you live. Make use of your reminders that are there to maintain your truth in a very positive way. Do not give space to others to voice their negative opinions about your reality. If they insist, tell them you will hear them later, after you are well, but not now. Do not let them use you to relieve their anxiety or guilt. You are not responsible for their discomfort. This will also help you to not fall into the negative fears that you have with regard to your illness.

When you do fall into fear and doubt, use one of these four ways to deal with it.

1. Express it to the appropriate people to transform it.
2. Replace it with a positive statement to transcend it.
3. Find the tension in your body where the fear is, and infuse it with the rose light of unconditional love.
4. Pray for help and surrender. Let go, let God. Help always comes within fifteen to thirty minutes. The fear will change into another feeling. What changes is your state of consciousness, not necessarily the outer situation.

All of the above are speaking your truth. If you feel fear, your truth in the moment is that you're afraid. If you have doubts, that's the truth of what you feel at that moment. It is as simple as that. The feelings are only feelings. They will pass. By speaking your truth in those moments to the people who are able to relate to it, you fill another need on the fourth level. It is extremely important to express your feelings by speaking to those who can understand. Do not share doubts in an inappropriate situation—that is, with people who

believe in the same doubts and have a stake in your maintaining yours. If you do, there is a good chance that those people will increase your doubts by telling you that, in fact, your doubts are true, that their way is better, and that you had better do as they say. Find ears that can hear and eyes that can see, and you will get the support you need.

It is of utmost importance to speak your truth.

Some good questions to ask yourself are:
What is it that I need to say?
What is it that I need to say to close friends who may disagree with me?
What have I kept quiet about for many years?
Why haven't I expressed what I believe?

Your Needs on the Sixth Level of Your Auric Field

The sixth level is the level of divine love or spiritual ecstasy. By speaking the truth of your needs whenever they come up and filling them, you automatically move to the sixth level. The sixth level has to do with feeling more than with understanding. You will simply be in states of ecstasy at times. They come and go. They change daily because you are constantly changing. Music helps you lift to these wonderful states of being. So do pictures of things that remind you of the holiness of life within you. There are no good words to express the experience of spiritual ecstasy. Everyone has his or her own personal description of it, all usually quite far from the experience itself. Words like, "living in the light," "floating in the arms of the Goddess," "being with God," or "being love" have all been used. What are your words for this experience?

It is from the sixth level of our being that we experience unconditional love. Karen shared her deeper feelings of the sixth level:

What it meant for me was going to the deepest access I could find, my divine nature, and letting it lead me through this. I've felt a sense of my life task for a long time. It is simply to deeply love and accept and live out of the feminine and align the masculine with it. The masculine had been quite rampant and off balance before.

In the last two weeks we said good-bye to over eighty people that we really love and had to separate from since we're moving to Colorado. We did it very lovingly. Even with all the reactions of those people, some of which have been very heavy, I've been able to keep open-hearted and be right there with it. You know, that feels like the higher feeling level of it.

Some good questions to ask yourself are:
What is the nature of my spiritual needs?
Do I give myself time to allow for my spiritual feelings to surface?
What is the nature of my spiritual feelings?
When and how do I feel unconditional love?
In what areas of my life do I need unconditional love?
How much time am I willing to spend daily allowing for unconditional love to infuse that area of my life in meditation or visualization?
Which music brings me to my spirituality?

Your Needs on the Seventh Level of Your Auric Field

The seventh level is the level of the divine mind where you begin to understand the greater universal pattern. The divine mind brings you to the reason for being—the soul's purpose in life, the great pattern that is unfolding within you and all around you. Within this level there is a deep sense of the soul's purpose, a reason for being here, a reason for the experience you are having, a feeling of trust. There's a constant kind of curiosity about what's going on rather than a dread. When you enter these levels of spiritual awareness, the entire experience is lifted to a higher or transcendent reality. You will know that all is right in God's world. In serenity there is no blame; all is unfolding in the most appropriate manner, just as it needs to.

We need to know and understand the divine pattern of all things: to see the perfect pattern held in gold light

of all that there is, and to know that everything is perfect in its imperfections. It is from this level that we experience serenity.

During the healing process, we can attain access to the seventh layer, and we are set free. Karen explains it this way:

I have a lot available to me internally, even when I forget. I have a deep sense of the meaning of my soul's purpose and my being here for a reason. Whatever was going on, there was a learning to be had. For me, the essential, bottom-line ingredient is knowing that there's hope. Hope gives a constant kind of curiosity about what's going on rather than dread.

Well, now I'm feeling a kind of serenity around all of the dealing with my leaving clients and people. I'm able to remain at a level of seeing it all from a much higher perspective. Like, if I'm working with clients and I'm leaving, I can see that there's something that we have to do together in the time that we have left. That, no matter what it is, whether it's clients or anybody, there's just some terrific symphony being played out. If I just do each step as it's there, then it will all still be in harmony. I'm not frantic around things that I would have been scared or frantic around in the past.

Some good questions to ask yourself are:
What are the greater patterns threaded through my life?
What is the nature of the deeper hope that leads me?
What is my symphony of life?

Part IV will help you create a very practical healing plan for each of the levels of your field to include all your personal needs.

PART IV

CREATING A HEALING PLAN

"Until one is committed there is hesitancy, the chance to draw back, always ineffectiveness. Concerning all acts of initiative (and creation), there is one elementary truth, the ignorance of which kills countless ideas and splendid plans: that the moment one definitely commits oneself, then Providence moves, too. All sorts of things occur to help one that would never otherwise have occurred. The whole stream of events issues from the decision, raising in one's favour all manner of unforeseen incidents and meetings and material assistance, which no man could have dreamt would have come his way. I have learned a deep respect for one of Goethe's couplets: 'Whatever you can do, or dream you can, begin it. Boldness has genius, power and magic in it.'"

—W.H. Murray, *The Scottish Himalayan Expedition*

Creating Your Personal Healing Plan

As I continued my practice and teaching and gained more experience with people, it became obvious to me that each person needed to have a specific personal healing plan based on his or her needs to improve total life quality, not on a general treatment procedure to cure a disease. Of course, healing the physical body or a psychological illness is of great importance, but this new broader perspective is essential. The healing plan is focused on healing the person, not curing the disease. The more the healing plan is focused in this way, the deeper and more profound the healing becomes. It seems that there is no limit to health. Once an individual starts on a comprehensive healing plan, healing becomes a lifelong process of growth and learning. It becomes a great adventure that takes one to ever deeper and fuller experiences of life.

As we create a healing plan, we must remember that spiritual truths formulate the background and purpose of our life in our physical bodies as well as on all our auric levels. If there is disorder in a particular level of our field, undoubtedly we are not fulfilling our spiritual purpose in that level. We are not getting what we need to create our life.

Therefore, when we enter into the healing of any level of the auric field, we must ask if that level is serving its purpose. We begin to formulate questions like these: Are our physical bodies serving their purpose to help us discern our divine individuality through action? Are our second levels providing us with the experience of our individual feelings and love for ourselves? Is level three of our auric field providing us with the ability to focus our conscious awareness, to differentiate and integrate our perceptions, so that we have clarity and a sense of appropriateness as individuals? Are we, through level four, making loving "I-Thou" connections that fulfill our needs? Are we experiencing our connectedness to all beings?

In creating healing plans for our daily lives, we must start with our most basic needs: those that integrate the physical and the spiritual aspects of our being.

In this section I will show you how to create a healing plan for each of the four lower levels of your auric field, each of which represents a different aspect of your human life and your human needs. The first level of your healing plan will focus on the personal care of your physical body and its template, the first level of your auric field.

One of the biggest changes you will experience in your healing process will be your sensitivity to the life energy fields all around you that flow through you. We will look at your environment in terms of the energy it provides for you. We will begin in Chapter 9 by focusing on the vastness of this environment and then focus down to the smaller scale of the many life energy fields in which you are continually immersed.

The Energies of the Earth As Foundation to Life

Different locations on the earth have different combinations of energy. The entire energy field of any particular location is very complicated. It consists of the energies of local geological configurations, including the energies of the combinations of all the organic and inorganic substances that make up the composition of the earth, such as mineral deposits; the energies of all the flora and fauna that exist there now and have ever existed there; the energies of the various societies of human beings and their activities in that location from time immemorial; and the energies of the human beings and their activities that exist there now.

In addition, every location on earth is also influenced by the energies from the solar system, as well as interstellar and intergalactic energies. These energies penetrate into, go through, or accumulate differently in different earth locations. The magnetic field of the earth plays a partial role in this configuration, as it directs certain bands of cosmic energies into certain locations on the earth.

Heyoan says that in the future we will have maps of these energy fields and that people will choose the locations of their homes and towns by them, somewhat like the geomancers of China. Through their very complicated system of divination, geomancers choose the building site and the location and orientation of houses on the building site. They also choose the location of important holy cities, such as the Forbidden City. Geomancers design both the exterior and interior of houses, as well as furnishings to control energy flow through the house. Much of their knowledge comes from traditional beliefs as well as the knowledge of energy flow, so it doesn't make much sense to westerners without a lot of study. Heyoan says in the future we will even choose the location to birth new nations according to the energy field maps of the earth as well as other planets. He suggests that there are places that are much more healthy for individuals to inhabit than others. Of course, there are general guidelines for this that we will put forth in this chapter, but he also reminds us that it varies with the individual.

For example, some people just naturally feel better near the ocean or another large body of water, while others feel better in the mountains or in a desert. These propensities are directly related to the combinations of energies that make up our human energy field. Each of us is different because the energies that make up each person's auric field are different, plus each of us is being permeated by the deeper essence of the core star in a different way. Usually people know where they belong geographically and express it in statements like "I'm a mountain person" or "I just have to live by a large body of water."

Some choose the area to live by climate or weather.

The Weather

Our preference for certain types of weather is directly related to the types of energies making up our auric field. Our preferences vary according to what is compatible with the energies in our auric field and how we like our energies to flow. Some of us prefer a change of season. Some prefer constant warmth and clarity in the desert without rain. Some of us prefer wet weather.

Electrical storms, prerain ozone, and rain all charge and help clear the auric field. The increased negative ions in the air excite and charge the auric field, causing energy to flow faster through it. Some of us like this; some of us are afraid of the increase in flow through our field.

The sun charges the atmosphere with *prana* or orgone energy. To see this energy, defocus your eyes and gaze softly at the sky. Tiny dots of light appear and move in curved trajectories. If you observe the movement of the whole field of dots, you will see that the whole field of dots pulses together. These dots can be bright or dull. When it is sunny, they are bright and move briskly about. This high-energy orgone makes you feel very good. It charges your field and gives you lots of energy. When it is cloudy, the small dots of light are not as bright, nor do they move as fast. Sometimes, after long cloudy periods, they look as if part of them is very dark or black. The longer the weather has been cloudy, the darker and slower the orgone, the less it charges your field, and the grumpier you get.

In sunny mountainous regions, the orgone is very light, bright, and highly charged. The most strongly charged orgone I have personally seen is in the Swiss Alps in the wintertime. There is a lot of snow, lots of sunlight, and fresh air. The orgone there is not only the most highly charged, it was also the thickest I've ever seen, with more dots per cubic foot. No wonder people go there for vacation to get rejuvenated.

Part of the problem of depression caused by light deprivation in the winter in the regions of higher latitudes is due to the steadily decreasing charge of the orgone in the atmosphere. This is why many people in the northern part of the United States go skiing in the sunny mountains or south to the sea for a winter vacation to get recharged. Sometimes it may take a week or so to rebuild the charge.

It is important, of course, not to overexpose yourself to the sun. Always use sunscreen. Start with a very high sunblock, and then slowly work your way down as you get acclimated. Once you are recharged, all you really need is about twenty minutes or so of sunlight a day to maintain a good charge. How much longer anyone can stay in the sun without experiencing the negative effects of exhaustion, sunstroke, burn, and skin disease depends on the individual's sensitivity. An overdose of sun strong enough to cause sunburn on our physical body burns the first level of the auric field as well. The sun's rays penetrate through this energy field, causing it to break and splinter into small fragments like shattered glass. It is no wonder that repeated overdoses of the sun's radiation causes cancer. Sunblock just screens out the harmful rays. It doesn't stop the sun from charging your auric field.

The sea charges the energy in the air also. The damp salt air charges the auric field and helps clear it of vibratory frequencies that are too low to sustain life. Walking along an ocean beach causes the auric field to expand. Sometimes the field doubles in size and extends out over the water.

On southern beaches year-round and on northern beaches in the summer, swimmers and sunbathers get a triple charge. The sun charges the auric field directly, the salt air charges and clears it, and a twenty-minute swim in the salt water deeply clears old stagnated mucus that may have accumulated through the dark winter months. Several days of these activities are great for the health of your auric field.

Nature: The Sea, Forests, Streams, Lakes, Deserts, Mountains, and Wildlife

It is impossible for us to even imagine what it must have been like for the Native Americans before Europeans disrupted the balance of nature in this country. People lived as integrated members of nature, a privilege we have deprived ourselves of. We have become more and more disconnected from the earth, and it shows everywhere on the planet as disease and natural disasters.

When nature is not disrupted, it stays in balance with the broad-scale whole earth energies. The energies of nature charge the auric field and put it into balance with its surroundings. In undisturbed, natural settings, we find our natural synchronicity with the planet's energies. When we are in balance with our surroundings, which are, in turn, in balance with the whole earth, we are a natural part of everything. What we eat from our surroundings will be nurturing to us because our energy fields are balanced and poised for assimilation. Spending several hours every week in an unspoiled setting reestablishes a balance between your auric field and earth energies. This is necessary for full health.

Calm lakes have a great soothing effect on us by relaxing the tension or hyperincoherent pulsations in our field caused by the stress of modern living. The auric pulsations from fast-flowing streams enhance the auric field, causing it to pulse faster in a coherent, healthy way. The auric energy near the bottom of a waterfall is tremendous. Broken tree branches caught in the energy stay alive much longer than they would without such energy.

The trees in a pine forest pulsate at a rate very similar to a human's auric field. Sitting in such a forest or simply leaning against the trunk of a pine tree in your back yard will recharge your field when you need it. Do this as long as you like. You might even get into contact with the consciousness of the tree while you are at it.

Mountains help us feel the power of the mineral kingdom of the earth and to ground into that power so that we can then stretch to great airy heights of our consciousness. The clear air of a bright desert invites us to expand our field out to great distances and feel larger and, for some, even more capable than we were before.

By spending time with wild animals in nature, we absorb their energies, which automatically brings us to a gut (not mental) understanding of our ability to synchronize with the natural world all around us. The ability to synchronize with natural and therefore planetary energy gives us access to great wisdom and teaches us to trust our basic human natures.

The energy of nature brings us to a greater understanding of life in all forms. Each species carries great wisdom, different from the wisdom of all other species. We can learn a great deal from the animals, not only from their behavior but also from the integrity with which they live. Healers commonly use healing tools they fashion from the bodies of animals found in the woods or "road kills." Each of these bodies is considered to be a gift from the "Great Spirit." Each is treated with honor and respect. The objects are made in ceremony in order to maintain the wisdom of the species from which they came. Such an object is used in the healing process to provide a direct holographic link to the wisdom of the species.

Our flower gardens and yards help us connect to the earth in ways that perhaps make up for our lost heritage of the wild. Here we have an interface between humans and nature, a blending of nature's will and human will. All manner of wondrous plants fill our senses with the splendor that nature brings in our own back yard, greenhouse, or living room. Plants supply different varieties and frequencies of energies in the energy field all around us that nurtures our field. House plants, especially, keep the energy of a home charged, clear, and healthy. The more contact we have with these plants, the greater the energy exchange that nurtures both the plants and us.

Organic gardens help us connect to the earth energies and provide food that is energy balanced to our needs. The more we work in the earth, the more connected and nurtured by earth energies we are. And, of course, we also get the added benefit of the organic food that we produce.

Population Density

In the late seventies and early eighties, over a period of about six years, I had the privilege of going to Holland once a year to help run intensive transformation groups. In the private sessions I gave during this time, I noticed a very curious thing. The clients (usually Dutch or from other European countries) would slide their chairs closer to mine as we sat facing each other to work. Without thinking about it, I would slide my chair back a little. During the session, clients would then slide up closer, and back I would go again. Usually by the end of the session, my chair would be squeezed up against the wall. I felt very uncomfortable about this. I had never experienced it in America.

Embarrassed about the whole thing, I began setting up the room ahead of time to try to give myself more space. But inevitably by the end of each session, I would be squeezed up against the wall. Under these conditions, I found it very hard to think and to separate myself from the client. I began thinking that something was really wrong with me. Perhaps I was just less friendly than these people. I tried to force myself to adjust to the new boundaries, but I could not. I began walking around the room to get some space. It only worked for a minute or two; then the client would follow me to get closer.

Finally I realized that the problem was that my aura extended out about one to two feet farther than theirs did. They were trying to make "normal" contact with me the same as they would with other Europeans. As I began observing the field interactions, I realized that these people (especially the Dutch, who had been squeezed up against the sea) had adjusted their auric dimensions to live with each other in smaller spaces than those I was used to.

Several years later, I noticed a large difference between the auras of Americans on the East Coast and those on the West. In general, people in the New York area have fields that do not extend out as far as those of the people who live in Southern California. I surmise that a person who lives in bigger spaces with fewer people will have an auric field that extends out from the body farther than someone who lives in smaller spaces with more people. In general, the auras of people in crowded cities are smaller than those of people in the country. The auras of people in highly populated countries are smaller than those of people in countries with sparser populations.

In addition to this, there is a difference in the boundaries that people create with each other with their auric fields. The people in the New York area who attend my training classes tend to have strong boundaries to keep separate from each other. It is almost as if their auras bounce off of each other at the seventh level, like two rubber balls bouncing off each other. In Southern California, I observed that people who attended my training classes like to let their auric fields simply diffuse through each other without interfering. They seemed to let levels four through seven interpenetrate in the same space, yet not really touch. Thus, people from California, even though they have larger auric fields, will want to stand closer together in order to communicate than will be comfortable to New Yorkers. The New Yorker may experience the communication as somewhat airy or not quite all there. The Californian, at the same time, may experience the East Coaster as harsh and rigid.

Of course there are other major factors in these differences. The main one is that we like to interact with people by intermingling the levels of our fields with which we are most comfortable. Each of us develops some levels of our auric field more than others, depending on our family and societal upbringing. Different societies focus on specific values. These values focus development on different aspects of human experience. For example, if truth is held as the highest value, than the third level of the field will get a lot of attention. If love is considered to be of highest value, then most likely the fourth level of the field will get developed more in that society.

Of course, the development depends on just how each society expresses its values. If spiritual values of divine love or divine will are considered of the highest, as they are in some religious societies, then the auric fields of the people in that society will reflect that value by being more highly developed. The sixth or fifth levels of the field will be most developed. People of that society would then tend to intermingle their auric fields on those levels when communicating.

Europeans tend to be highly sophisticated, with highly developed first and third levels, and they like to engage at the third level. New Yorkers like the second, third, and fourth levels, but they don't like to intermingle and prefer to have their fields couple in ways that create tension. The tension serves to let the people distinguish differences. Californians like the second and fourth levels and like to intermingle diffuse energies without a lot of engagement or coupling. Perhaps these Californians are looking for sameness with no tension. All these conclusions are based on people who have attended my training classes. Perhaps they represent only a certain proportion of the above-mentioned populations.

Cities

Large cities are places of high energy with a great variety of energy types. Heyoan says that large cities and civilizations form over places on the earth where vast amounts of life energies from outer space accumulate. These energies are a source of knowledge. He says that we unconsciously gravitate to these areas. Here, each of us is inspired to create, resulting in the rise of a civilization that materializes the knowledge in the accumulated energies of the place. The birthplaces of mathematics and language were once centered on such vortices of energy. The people who gravitated there became channels through which these forms of knowledge were brought into the world.

Heyoan goes on to say,

~

Thus, as you might imagine, those vast centers of learning that now exist upon the earth are locations of such energy vortices of knowledge. One of the reasons that centers of civilizations move about upon the face of the earth is that each is sourcing a particular knowledge [held in the energy fields] that is prominent in a given period of history. This is one of the less-known and more important factors in the progress of civilization. The world tends to focus on the prominent civilization and thereby does not interfere with the place that will be the source of the next rising civilization.

~

As cities bring creativity, invention, and knowledge, they produce a lot of waste material on both the physical and the auric levels. In cities, we learn how to live with each other in high energy. This high energy tends to knock loose negative blocks of energy that need to be cleaned out. Unfortunately, one of the major results of this process is that large cities not only accumulate vast quantities of the energy of higher knowledge, they also accumulate vast quantities of negative or DOR energies.

DOR, a term coined by Wilhelm Reich, stands for dead orgone energy. DOR energy vibrates well below the frequency needed for life and can be detrimental to health and well-being. When densely accumulated, DOR can be dangerous, even life-threatening. It causes illness to erupt in the weakest part of the body and energy field. In many large cities, these DOR energies permeate everything and penetrate deep into the earth. They affect everyone who lives in such a place, and many need to leave regularly to maintain their health. For example, I had a healing and teaching practice in New York City for about fifteen years. In order to ground down into good earth energies and tap into them for healing, it was necessary to go down through about forty yards of accumulated negative energy that looked like dark grayish-black goo. This goo exists throughout the entire base soil and rock of New York. There are, of course, places where it is not so dark or thick. But in general, it underlies all activity in this great city. Beneath the dark goo are normal clear earth energies that have not yet been affected by the polluted energies. The mass and depth of DOR seems to increase every year. *Ghostbusters II* was not far off!

I also noticed that the environmental pollution in the air of New York City increased terribly each year. With each succeeding year, I could see the increase of negative effects in the patients who lived there. Every year I saw people's immune systems wearing down more from the tremendous environmental pollution. The primary effect I saw was in the brain. According to my auric observations, the many different brain cells we have produce very minute quantities of various substances that are necessary for healthy brain and body function. These substances seem to act like triggers to control the functioning of the organ systems of the body. What I noticed over the years I practiced in New York City was a steadily increasing imbalance in the secretion of these substances. It seemed that a very small change in quantity and timing of the production of these substances made very large disruptions in the normal functioning of body processes. Even though I was able to rebalance the disturbed life energies in the brain, the patient would then return to a polluted environmental life energy field that would then again disturb healthy brain function. Everyone seemed to be completely oblivious to what was going on.

I then began noticing the general state of the elderly people who lived in New York City. Years of exposure to environmental pollution had taken its toll on them. They were much less energized and their fields much more imbalanced than the elderly people I saw who lived in the rural areas. I realized that the longer these people were exposed to DOR, the less sensitive they became. It's kind of like putting a frog in water and slowly heating it up. He doesn't notice the water getting hotter and eventually dies. On the other hand, he would jump out if you put him into hot water.

Choosing a Place to Live

We all have a wish of where we would live "if only we could." Many people wish they could live where they grew up because they fondly remember the landscapes of their youth. They long for the feelings, sights, sounds, textures, and fragrances of the flora and fauna in the areas of the earth where they grew up because they were more sensitive to their natural surroundings during childhood. These remembered experiences usually reproduce the mind-body connection we had in childhood and lost during the maturation process. This connection reestablishes a healthy, balanced auric field state of relaxation that brings about healing.

On the other hand, other people, with perhaps more disturbed, difficult childhoods, prefer to relocate in an entirely different climate and landscape. They find new horizons more conducive to healing than the old.

Our preference of where to live is directly related to our life energy field configuration that we call "normal." We are comfortable with a particular set of different types of energy from our environment—the sea, the woods, or the mountains. And we choose the places we live accordingly. We are also used to a range of energy and power running through us. What is normal for one person can be very low or very high energy for another. We are used to a specific degree of "openness," with a particular way we hold our boundaries.

We also choose our living places to help us feel normal. "Normal," you'll recall, is actually a particular habitual imbalance that we carry in our field. We tend to like environments that support the status quo. Usually we don't like too much change in our lives. We don't like anyone or anything to rock the boat on our normal energy levels. A lot of the time, we choose our living environments accordingly. It helps our holistic living if we make this choice conscious. If we really need to move on to a new environment to create the kind of change we would like in our lives, but are procrastinating, it may be a good idea to consider moving to a whole new area of the country. It sure worked for Karen, the woman, you'll recall, who moved cross country after her surgery.

The Ancient Art of Feng Shui

Feng shui is the ancient Chinese art of designing and creating a harmonious environment. Feng shui (pronounced "fung shway") is based on the belief that energy patterns are generated and affected by everything we do, build, or create. It teaches that our destinies and our lives are interwoven with the workings between the universal energy field and our human energy field. Feng shui uses the placement of buildings and objects as a means of managing and harmonizing the energies in our environment with our personal energies. For example, where your front door is placed and what it faces are very important. If it faces a wall, the wall will block the natural flow of earth energies into your home. Always having to move around the wall to enter your house will take more of your energy and disturb your natural flow. Always facing a wall when you approach your home blocks the natural flow of energy that you connect to your home when you approach it. This will interfere with your relationship to your home and may make you feel weak, defeated, and blocked in your life because you must struggle to get to your place of comfort. This may then create more struggle in your life.

According to feng shui, it is important to know the energetic influences of landscape, the position and flow of water with respect to your home, the stars, colors, the weather, animals, shapes, designs, and the like. Feng shui uses many different kinds of things to help set up a controlled energy flow in the places we spend our time. For example, it uses mirrors to reflect energy—putting a mirror on the wall opposite your front door reflects any negative incoming energies. It uses sound to change the energy or to direct positive energy into your home for health, well-being, and prosperity.

Feng shui can help you pick the place to build your house or office. It tells you where to position it with respect to the landscape, roads, and neighbors. It tells you where to put your driveway.

Several books on feng shui are listed in the Bibliography. To a westerner, many of the specific rules and principles that it teaches may not make any sense. This is partly because of the cultural differences in world-view and partly because it is a very old tradition. In what has been handed down, superstition may be completely mixed in with what actually works. But if you are interested in getting very specific about how you are affected by your home or office environment, pick up a book on feng shui and check it out.

I suggest that you use all the information in this chapter to review where you live. This country offers a vast array of choices of types of places to live, and it is possible to move to a place of your choice and find work there if you wish to. If you do wish to live in a city to take part in the high energy available to you there, be sure to take trips into the country regularly. Plus, clean your energy field regularly with the techniques described in the section on grooming your energy field in Chapter 10.

Some good questions to ask yourself about where you live:

Which type of landscape do you choose?

If you do not live in the kind of landscape you wish, what can you do to get to spend some time there on occasion?

Which area of the country offers you the type of boundaries you prefer, with the population density you prefer?

Where do the kinds of people you like to interact with live?

Have you always wanted to move somewhere, and never have?

What unfulfilled need do you think this move would fill?

Can you fill this need where you live now?

Is the need really something else?

Is staying where you are now avoiding something you are afraid to face?

If so, find out what that is, so that you can consciously choose to stay or move on if you wish.

The Energies of Spaces and Objects That Surround and Nurture Your Field

---

Living Spaces

The energy of the space you live in has a big effect on your auric field. All spaces have energy. The energy of a space depends on its shape, its colors, the materials it is built out of, and the energy of the creators of the space. Spaces accumulate the energy of people who use the space, the energy of what they do in the space, and the energy with which they do it. All these energies build up in a room, whether they are healthy or unhealthy. The more a space is used with the same energy, by the same people for a particular purpose, the more that space gets charged with the energy of that purpose.

I'm sure you have noticed the energy difference between a bus or train station and a cathedral or temple. For example, if you've been in New York City, compare the energy in places like the Port Authority terminal and Grand Central Station to the energy in St. Patrick's and St. John the Divine cathedrals and the Temple Emmanuel. The energies in the stations are harsh, chaotic, jagged, and usually full of dark polluted clouds. It is not pleasant to be there very long. It even feels dangerous, not just because of crime but because of the tremendous amount of accumulated negative energies there that it is possible to pick up in your auric field. The energies of the cathedrals and temples, on the other hand, are clear and of higher vibrations. The higher spiritual nature of the energy in these spaces positively affects anyone who enters.

Energies accumulated during religious services also contain the energies of the beliefs of the people who worship there. People who hold similar beliefs will feel supported when they are in such spaces because they are in an energy field of beliefs similar to their own. But the same energies may feel intimidating or stifling to someone who does not hold the same beliefs.

Spaces used for silent meditation or simple communion with God, such as Quaker meeting houses, have wonderful clear, clean energy of very high vibration. The clearest meditation space I have seen is the sanctuary in the spiritual community in Scotland called Findhorn. Findhorn is noted for its human-nature interface. Here the community comes to hold silent meditation several times per day. Over the years a wonderful clean and clear energy has built up, synchronic with the energies of nature.

The temperature and humidity regulation in a space also affect your energy. Forced-air heating systems lower the humidity in the space to that of desert air. It is difficult to humidify it in a healthy way. This dry air makes the auric field a bit brittle and vulnerable to invasion. Hot-water baseboard heat is the best because it doesn't dry out the air so much. Gas furnaces sometimes leak and cause a lot of damage before the leak is detected. If you have a gas furnace or stove, have it checked regularly or get a gas detector installed.

Aluminum has a vibration rate way below that needed to support human life. I wouldn't have it in my kitchen or my house. Aluminum siding on houses or trailers decreases the life energy vibration rate inside the house or trailer. It drains the energy of the people inside. Wood is very compatible with life energy vibrations and is healthy to live inside. Concrete has a neutral effect on the auric field. Some large apartment buildings have steel structures that interfere with the normal expansion of the auric field. If the rooms of an apartment are large with high ceilings, the steel probably won't affect it much. Large windows bring lots of light that charges the air for better health.

Objects You Live With

Objects also carry energy. They contain the energy of the materials they are made of, the energy that was placed in them by their creator (consciously or unconsciously), and the energy all their owners have placed in them. If the objects are antiques, they carry the energy of all the places they have been kept. The objects that you place in a room bring all these energies to add to the energy symphony of the room.

Crystals placed in specific locations within a home for the purpose of holding the energy of the home are very useful and do a terrific job. A friend of mine has several large crystals in each room placed in ceremony for this purpose. Every time I've visited, the energy in this home feels wonderful.

Healers place natural crystals in their healing rooms to bring added healing energy to the room, to keep their rooms free from DOR, to help keep grounded to the earth, and to enhance the rooms' beauty. They clean these crystals daily by placing them in direct sunlight and by soaking them in a bath of four tablespoons of sea salt to one quart of water for about twenty minutes.

Different types of crystals have different vibrations, and individual ones vibrate differently, even if they are composed of the same minerals. It is important to test each crystal to make sure it will do the job for which you have placed it. One simple test is to place the crystal where you would like it and leave it there for a few days. If you still like its energy, then leave it as long as you like it there. If you don't like it, move it to another location, and leave it a few days again. If that is not the spot, repeat the procedure. You may end up putting it outside. What is important is what you like. You live with it.

Artwork has an extraordinary effect on the auric field. This effect varies a great deal with each individual, but we can make some generalizations about its effect. Some pieces, such as Van Gogh's *Starry Night*, open the field into deep personal contemplation about the journey of life, its agony and its ecstasy. Beautiful impressionistic scenes, such as Monet's *Water Lilies,* charge the sixth level of our energy field and produce an experience of serenity. Rembrandt walks us into the longing for the light and enhances the core star light within. The excellence in any work of art inspires us to do our best by bringing our field into more coherency. An appropriate frame is one that vibrates on the same frequency as the painting. The painting on its own has a certain visual integrity. An inappropriate frame masks the visual potential of the artist's intent. An appropriate frame is one that equals the intensity of the painting when it is frameless at a minimum and ideally adds to the painting's essence. Thomas Cole, the famous nineteenth-century American painter, stated, "The frame is the soul of the painting." Hang your art to create appropriate moods according to what you want to be doing in the space you will see it in.

Sound in Your Environment

Sound has been used for centuries for healing by healers and medicine people of all traditions and cultures. The ancient tradition of chanting, popular again in this country since the sixties, changes the auric field so that we are brought into altered states of consciousness. Many contemporary healers use toning to alter the auric field of their clients to improve their health.

I have seen that sound has a very strong and direct effect on the auric field. During my fifteen years of practice as a healer in New York City, I used it for many different purposes. Using my voice, I toned directly into the physical bodies and auric fields of my clients. I recorded these sounds for each client so that they could play the tape of healing sounds specific to their bodies and fields once or twice a day. The client would simply play the tape while lying comfortably on a bed, or meditate to the tape. As the client improved, I would update the toning tape with a new set of sounds. In this way, the client was able to improve much faster through self-healing at home. I used different tones and tone combinations for different purposes, such as: loosening energy blocks, charging areas of the body, clearing specific energy lines of the auric field, enhancing tissue growth, stopping bleeding, moving fluids, herding parasites out of the body, exploding the eggs of parasites with their resonant frequencies, exploding microorganisms with their resonant frequencies, and spinning and charging chakras.

By toning the correct sound into a deformed chakra, the chakra takes the shape it ought to have. Using

FIGURE 9–1. CHAKRA TONES

Chakra	Color (Level 2)	Note
7	White	**G**
6	Indigo	**D**
5	Blue	**A**
4	Green	**G**
3	Yellow	**F**
2	Orange	**D**
1	Red	**G** (below middle "C")

HSP, I have done this regularly with clients in my practice. The effect is very powerful. Because my vision is so accurate, I am able to find the appropriate sound simply by watching the chakra respond to the variety of tones that I make. When I hit the right tone, the chakra simply stands up and spins correctly. It only takes a few seconds once it has taken the correct shape and spin on the first level of the field to become the correct color on the second level of the field. It is amazing how fast it works. When I continue to tone into the chakra for a few minutes, the chakra becomes stabilized.

The tones I use are a combination of many frequencies with overtones. We have not done a frequency analysis on these tones to find out just what frequencies are involved, as that would take sophisticated equipment that we do not have at this time. I have recorded these tones many times on different people. They are usually the same. The notes I have found in this way for each chakra are listed in Figure 9–1.

Another interesting thing about this type of toning is the immediate effect it has on a patient's ability to picture a particular color in his or her mind. Most people can do this quite readily. But if the client has a chakra that is not functioning properly, it will not be able to take in the color associated with it. And the client will not be able to picture the color in his or her mind. For example, if the third chakra is not functioning and all the others are, the client will be able to picture all the colors associated with all the other chakras except for yellow, which is associated with the third chakra. Toning into the third chakra will put it back into shape. As soon as the chakra "stands up and spins right" and turns the correct color, the client is then able to picture the color.

Sound affects not only the first level of the auric field that shapes the chakra, but also the second level of the field where the chakras are the rainbow colors—red, orange, yellow, green, blue, indigo, and white. I have affected on all levels of the field by toning techniques. The number of levels affected at once is dependent on the number of overtones the healer is able to produce at once. For myself, I noticed that as soon as I try to get in the overtones to affect the higher levels of the field for a particular chakra, I begin to lose the lower frequencies and have less effect on the lower levels of the field. To remedy this problem, I simply go through it twice. I do the higher levels of the field for each chakra with a higher set of toning pitches after I have gone through the chakras.

Two types of chakra toning tapes are available from the Barbara Brennan School of Healing. The first is the chakra tones produced verbally, as described above. The second is chakra tones produced mechanically.

A growing field of inquiry shows that sound is directly related to the creation of forms in nature. This field is called *cymatics*. In his book *Cymatics*, the late Dr. Hans Jening, of Basel, Switzerland, showed through experimentation that sound is directly related to form. When he placed fine grains of sand or lycopodium powder upon a metal plate and then sent a steady unbroken sound frequency through the plate, the fine grains of sand or powder would form into specific patterns. When he changed the sound, he got a different pattern. Repeat the first sound, and he got the original pattern back again. As long as he continued the same sound, the same pattern would hold; as soon as the sound stopped, the pattern would stop holding and the grains would slowly redistribute themselves according to gravity.

Dr. Guy Manners, a doctor of osteopathy who has his own clinic in Bretforton, Worcestershire, England, continued this work with Jening to try to create three-dimensional forms from sound. To do this, they began to use more than one frequency at a time. Two, three, and four frequencies combined did not create a three-dimensional image. But as soon as they tried five sound frequencies simultaneously, the small particles on the metal plate took a three-dimensional form.

Dr. Manners spent twenty years researching this phenomenon and found the tone combinations that are appropriate for each organ. He then made a machine called the Cymatics Instrument to produce these sounds to be used in clinical practice. At this point, they are in use all over the world. I visited Dr. Manners at the Bretforton Hall Clinic and observed these machines at work. They clearly had a strong effect on restructuring the auric field into its correct, healthy form. This effect should in turn decrease the time required for healing.

By now, you can see that whatever the sound around us, it directly affects our auric field, whether it is music, traffic noise, factory noise, or the unspoiled sounds of nature. We are only beginning to understand the broad-scale effects of sound on our health and well-being. Even though we don't understand it all, it is important to acknowledge this very strong effect and to regulate our sound environment accordingly.

If you live in a large city, take all the precautions you can to control the sound pollution coming at you. You may be able to sleep through city noise, but it is still affecting your field. I suggest that, if possible, you put in triple-pane windows and thick, sound-dampening drapes on your windows. Try to control the noise in your office as much as you can. If you have a private office, soundproof it so that noise from the rest of the office or outside does not enter. If you work in a large room with a lot of noise, soundproof your immediate area to dampen the sound there. And shield your ears if possible.

Music plays a very important role in health and healing. Many healers use music to help calm the auric field or bring it to high vibrational heights to help the client go into a healing state. The wide variety of music offers us a wide variety of effects. Some music is very soothing; some charges the field. Some music directly enhances altered states, and other music awakens the rational mind. There is a lot of New Age music out now that charges and opens each chakra in sequence as it is played. Some is wonderful for meditation. In the trainings given by the Barbara Brennan School of Healing, we use music all the time to bring students to different states of consciousness for healing. For example, drum music is very good for grounding down to connect with earth energies and to open the first and second chakras. Popular rock music opens our sexuality and gets the body and the auric field moving in a lively fast pace that increases the energy flowing through the field. Love songs open the fourth chakra to help us connect with each other. The many types of meditation music done on synthesizers are great to lift our spirituality. Any instrument can take us through all the levels of human experience if the musician knows how to do it. At the Brennan school we regularly use harp music to take us into the experience of the essence of the core.

A regular diet of music helps us remain healthy. The type of music you choose will be directly related to the types of energies that compose your energy field and what type of personal learning you are doing at any particular moment. Give yourself free range to choose which music you like, and to use it any way you want. This is a whole world of nourishment that is open to you. Don't deprive yourself of it. If you find you have old judgments about a certain kind of music, perhaps you ought to try it sometime and experience what it does to your field. You may be avoiding something. Or you may be finished with the phase of personal development that that particular music represents.

If your spouse loves music you hate, confine the music to one particular room, so that you have the choice to listen or not. Perhaps you need two different listening areas, so that each of you can play what you want. Perhaps one of you loves silence. Find which time of day you want it, and make some agreements in your household that can help everyone get their needs met. If you need to, put doors between more of the rooms in your house. Or ask your spouse to wear headphones.

If you have teenagers who play loud music, try to confine that music to their room with soundproofing materials, or ask them to use headphones also. It is better to protect yourself from this music/noise rather than try to get them to change. They may need the music for their transition into adulthood.

In the process of human development, when we enter into puberty, energies we have not experienced before, at least not in this lifetime, begin to unfold within our auric fields. New intellectual and spiritual energies of higher frequencies begin to flow through the entire field. There are new energies both in the heart chakra and in the sexual chakras. Integrating these new energies into our field is a real struggle. We are not only separating ourselves more from our parents, we are also learning to connect to others in ways we never have before. We find ourselves rather vulnerable to this auric unfoldment, as we move from being children wanting our parents to take care of us one day to rejecting our parents and being in puppy love with someone we hardly know the next. As teenagers, we used rock music to help us through the transition. It helped us separate from our parents by building a wall of sound between us and them. Rock music stirs up the energies in the auric field that are being released and developed during puberty. It charges our will to live, the first chakra, and our sexuality, our second chakra. It helps us begin to disconnect our dependency from our parents and connect to our peers (the third chakra). And of course, the romantic music opens the heart chakra. It connects us with love to those going through the same experiences. It frees us from parental dominance, while reorienting our dependency toward our peer group. In order to fill the many needs we will have as adults, we must cultivate the essential skills of connection to and cooperation with peers. If these skills have not been established

before puberty, we are now given a final push before adulthood to do so. No matter how much we as parents can't stand the noise now, at one time it was also the symbol of our movement into the outer world.

Energize Your Space with Color

Everything we just said about sound, we can also say about color. Both are created through a vibrational wave, and thus both have a wave structure and a frequency of vibration. Sound and colored light are very different. Sound is a longitudinal compression wave that travels through a material substance like the air or the wall of your house. *Longitudinal* means that it travels along the same path as its wave motion. The sounds that we hear do not exist in outer space or in a vacuum. They must have that material substance to be transmitted. Colored light, on the other hand, is an electromagnetic wave that vibrates perpendicular to its path of movement. It can travel through outer space or a vacuum. Both are ultimately manifestations of higher frequencies that exist beyond the physical world. Both are manifestations of the divine.

Color is essential to health. We need all the colors in our auric fields. If we are clear, we are attracted to the colors we need. Figure 9–2 lists different colors and the general effect they have on you. For example, red colors stir up our emotions, while blue cools and calms our emotions. This chart can be used when you are choosing colors to decorate your home, office, or healing room. Once you clearly determine the purpose for each living space, you can choose a color that supports that purpose.

Since every disease is associated with the dysfunction of certain chakras, and the dysfunctioning chakra needs to be nourished with the color it is lacking, color can be used for the treatment of different diseases. For example, a person who has an underactive thyroid needs the color blue. If the thyroid is overactive, they have too much blue and probably need green, which is a color that does general balancing of the field. Multiple sclerosis patients need red and orange because the first and second chakras are most affected. All cancer patients need gold, since all cancer has a torn-open aura on the seventh level, which is gold. Cancer patients also need the color of the chakra in the area that the cancer is located in the body. For example, liver or pancreatic cancer patients need yellow and peach, the colors of the third chakra on the second and fourth levels of the field respectively.

I have heard that painting the rooms of hyperactive children blue helps calm them down. Some mental

FIGURE 9–2 THE GENERAL EFFECT OF COLORS

Red	Increases your connection to the earth and gives strength to basic life-force urges such as the will to live in the physical world. Charges, protects, shields. Good for all organs in the first chakra area.
Maroon	Brings passion and will together.
Rose	Brings strong active love for others, helps you love. Very healing for heart and lung problems.
Pink	Brings soft, yielding love for others.
Peach	Brings a soft, yielding, expanding light spirit.
Orange	Charges your sexual energy and enhances the immune system. Good for all organs in the second chakra region. Increases your ambition.
Yellow	Gives more mental clarity, a sense of appropriateness. Good for all organs in the third chakra region. Clears the mind.
Green	Brings balance and a feeling of fullness: I'm OK, you're OK, and the world is OK. Good for all organs connected to the fourth chakra, like the heart and lungs.
Blue	Brings peace, truth, and quiet order. Helps you speak the truth, increases sensitivity, strengthens the inner teacher. Good for all organs in the fifth chakra area, like the thyroid. Used to cauterize wounds in spiritual surgery.
Dark Blue	Brings a strong sense of purpose.
Indigo	Opens spiritual perception, brings the feeling of ecstasy. Helps you connect to the deeper mystery of spiritual life. Good for any organ near the sixth chakra.
Purple	Helps you integrate and move into spirituality, brings a sense of royalty. Helps increase a sense of leadership and respect.
Lavender	Brings a lighthearted attitude toward life. Clears and purges invading microorganisms, brings a feeling of lightness.
White	Helps you connect to your purity and expands your field. Brings spiritual expansion and connection to others on the spiritual level; gives outward flow of energy. Reduces pain. Good for the brain.
Gold	Enhances the higher mind, understanding the perfect pattern, brings a sense of great power. Helps you connect to God and to the spiritual strength in you. Strengthens any part of the body.
Silver	Very strong purging of microorganisms, used directly after lavender in cleaning out debris. Helps you move faster and communicate better. Used to cauterize wounds in spiritual surgery.
Platinum	Clears and purges invading microorganisms, even stronger than silver light.
Brown	Enhances a rich connection to the earth and grounding.
Black	Helps you draw within and stay centered. Brings complete peace. If you use it well, it will help you enter into deep internal creative forces. Brings you into the void, the source of teaming unmanifest life, waiting to be born into manifestation. Brings you into Grace. Good to help deal with death. Good to heal bones.

hospitals paint their walls blue to help calm their patients. I would guess that someday hospitals will be painted the color that will help patients stay in a healing state of mind. Grass-green and rose will help any patient to charge and balance the heart chakra at the second and fourth levels of the auric field. The heart chakra is central to all healing because all healing energy must pass through the center of the heart chakra on its way to the body of the receiver. We might also make large panels of colored glass backed by full-spectrum halogen lighting that could be moved around from room to room as needed for healing. Each large panel could be made of the color of each chakra, so that the auric field could simply drink in the color. The chakra tones could be played so that any disfunctioning chakra could take its healthy cone-shaped form that stands up and spins clockwise to receive the color.

Of course, there are exceptions to the list of colors given in Figure 9–2. You could very well associate any color with a painful personal experience. In this case, the color would be associated with the experience and have a different effect on you. We love certain colors and hate others. Our relationship to color is also an expression of what is happening in our energy fields. If our first and second chakras, red and orange, are undercharged, meaning that we have dampened our physical will-to-live energy and our sensuality, we may want to keep it that way. In this case, we may need red in our field for our emotional and physical health. But at the same time, we may avoid increasing those colors because of our personal experience of them. We will refuse to wear reds and oranges because they increase those energies. When those energies are increased in our fields, they also bring forth any emotional issues we may have with those aspects of our lives with which they are associated.

Living with Scents That Make Sense

We seldom perceive things in a neutral fashion. Various sights and sounds make us happy, sad, or angry. Certain odors can make some individuals positively ecstatic. There is also a two-way connection between these emotional aspects of perception on the one hand and thoughts and memories on the other: Appropriate aromas can conjure up images of meals and wines consumed in the past, and the odor of various incenses can return us to the high spiritual experience we once had in a spiritual ceremony in which they were used. The fragrance of perfumes can carry us into pleasant memories of being with someone we loved who wore that perfume. Natural body fragrances can bring us into the erotic memory of lovemaking. When we enter into these positive emotional states, our auric field takes on the configuration of that positive state, and healing takes place. Such is the power of aromatic healing.

Our sense of smell was one of the first senses to develop as we evolved. Our sense of smell is registered by the olfactory system, which feeds into the midbrain area near the limbic system. As a result, the olfactory system has always been related to the limbic system. The limbic system is directly connected to our emotion-laden responses, what we might call animal instincts. These drive-related activities—feeding, defense, and sexual behaviors—are central to the preservation of individuals and the species of all human beings and all the animal kingdom.

For example, dogs use the smell of fear to help them survive. Do you know the smell of fear? Some human beings do. When a dog smells fear, he responds in several different ways, depending on who is afraid. If it is his pack, he will become alert and cautious, searching for the source of the danger. If it is an enemy that he is concentrating on, he will take advantage of his adversary's fear and probably attack. Do you react to the smell of fear? How?

The aromas that surround us make a great deal of difference in our lives. I'll bet you know the fragrance of your loved one. I'll bet that fragrance immediately affects your mood. The use of fragrance is as old as we are. Incense is burned in sanctuaries to help the congregation to enter into a holy state of mind. Men and women use fragrant perfumes to attract and turn on the person they desire to meet. Flowers attract the birds and bees with fragrance. If you wish to set a particular ambiance in your home, use fragrance in addition to lighting and other effects. Which scents do you like? What different moods do they put you in? Do you use different scents for different things? If not, try it—you will be surprised by the power of the sense of smell.

Since aromas act directly and very rapidly to affect physiological responses, when used properly they can help us create very fast healing responses. Aromatherapy has been used for healing for centuries. It was developed by the ancient Egyptians and used extensively in India and China. Our Native American medicine people have used it since their ancient past. It is becoming more popular now in America. You can purchase aromatic essential oils and aromatic plant essences for about any purpose you can think of. There are aromatics to calm you down and to perk you up; to relax muscles or energize you; to turn you on, or to turn you off. There are aromatics to take you into different states of being. There are different aromatics to energize and balance each chakra. And if they are made properly, they all work.

It has been known for centuries that oil placed upon the skin helps the healing energy enter. But according to my HSP vision, more than that is going on—and more than the limbic system response mentioned above. It appears to me that some of the aromatics used in healing are actual auric essences that go directly into the auric field, providing it with the energy it needs, much as homeopathic remedies do. Muscles relax at the mere touch of a "calming nutrient" laid upon them. There certainly wasn't time for the oil to be absorbed into the skin or muscle. I can see the colored energies of the aromatic entering the field. In fact, a corridor for energy flow begins to open at the moment one reaches for the bottle containing the essence.

So I suggest that you explore this area on your own: not only for healing, but also for setting the appropriate ambiance in your home, office, or healing room. Be sure to use natural fragrances that are derived from natural substances. Don't use synthetics—they do not work.

Creating an Energy-Wise Space

There are several things you can do to keep the energy in your living space clean. Make sure it gets plenty of sunlight. It will charge the life energy in the room and not allow dead orgone energy to accumulate. If low vibratory energy does start accumulating in the space, you can remove it by smudging the room by burning sweetgrass or sage. Or burn a combination of one capful of pure grain alcohol to one-fourth cup Epsom salts. I recommend that you keep plenty of plants in the room so that a fresh exchange of energy between plants and people is constant. Open the windows whenever possible for fresh air.

Cleanliness and order in the space will keep the energy clear as well. Order is very important to maintain good positive energy in a space. Find a place for everything, so that order is easy to keep. Disorder creates a psychic drag on your system and sucks your energy. Disorder is an expression of inner chaos. It speaks to you about your unfinished inner business. If you tend to collect things that you won't use or don't really like much, you had better check out why, because it is sure to be affecting many other areas of your life. Order is a divine principle. Order functions to hold a space for us in which to do our life's work. Order creates a safe space in which the creative force within us can come forth.

One patient who came to me because of a pain in her hip was not able to clean her apartment of all her old things, many of which had been left to her by her late mother. I gave as much healing as I could, but I continually received guidance that she needed to clean up her apartment to cure her hip. The hip pain was related to her not being able to let go of old leftover problems she had with her mother. She carried unrealistic guilt about this. When she finally let go of the unreal guilt and cleaned her apartment, her hip started to get better. It was amazing to watch. Every time she threw out another box of stuff, her hip got better.

Many building materials used in houses are toxic to us. Fluorescent lights beat against your auric field, causing it to become incoherent. They produce dead orgone energy that can make you sick. Just turn them off, put a piece of tape over the switch, and get some incandescent floor or table lamps. We are constantly adding pollutants to the air from our furnaces and gas appliances. Whenever people have their apartments exterminated, they breathe in some of the poison. Even the chemicals used to sterilize public places, like the toilets on a bus, are unhealthy to breathe. Even when toxins in the air are easy to detect, we still expect our bodies not to react when we breathe them. We slough it off, as if it were somebody else's problem.

There is not only a great deal of air pollution in all our cities now but a great deal of electromagnetic energy permeating everyone's living space. It is some-thing that is very hard to detect naturally. Dr. Robert Becker's book, *The Body Electric,* describes his studies showing the effects of these radiations on the body. Dr. Becker presents studies that show there is a higher incidence of autoimmune diseases like leukemia and other forms of cancer in people whose homes are near high-tension power lines.

We are waking up to the fact that we must do a lot to stop waste and pollution in our lives. The best place to start is at home. Recycle everything you can. It really isn't that hard. It is getting more organized every year. In fact, there is a great job market now in the new recycling industry.

Here are some things you can do about pollution in your personal spaces:

- Live far away from high-tension wires.
- Use a good humidifying system in your home, something that evaporates water into the air. Don't use ultrasonic humidifiers that throw fine particles into the air, on which diseases are carried.
- Get a negative ion generator.
- Filter the air with a home air filter.
- Filter your water with a good three-stage water filter. Use it for the whole house. Most home supply stores carry them now.
- To prevent winter light deficiency, add extra full-spectrum lights, preferably halogen. Or get a special light box of 2500 lux. Use it for an hour a day.
- Remove or turn off fluorescent lights.
- If you have gas appliances, get a gas leak detector.

Creating a Healing Space

It is very important to take care of your immediate environmental needs during an illness. Remember, you will be in a healing room, not a sick room. The more you surround yourself with the things that remind you of who you truly are, the more pleasant will be your time of illness. Make sure the room you are in is full of life, pleasure, and joy. Cover every detail of your physical needs, not only in the physical setting but in terms of light in the room, music, food, and favorite objects around you. Here is a list of things to have in your healing room:

- something to express all aspects of yourself
- plenty of light, if it doesn't hurt your eyes
- colored-glass pictures hung in the windows
- crystals hung in the windows that make rainbows from sunlight
- your favorite pictures or wall hangings
- plants and flowers

- bright-colored cloth of your favorite color
- your favorite objects
- your favorite music, within easy reach
- things that you like to eat that are within your diet limitations
- soft things to touch or hold if you get lonely
- fragrances that please you
- photos of your friends
- fresh air

Be sure the energy of your living space expresses who you are. The energy composite of your living space is very important to your health and well-being. When choosing your furnishings and your living space, remember, they all contribute to its energy makeup. The size of a shape is important to your auric field. I don't like low ceilings because I can feel my auric field running through them. They make me feel squeezed in. I also like large rooms for the same reason. Use all the information in the preceding sections to help you answer the questions below about your living space.

Some good questions to ask yourself about your living space are:

Is it comfortable and cozy for you?

Do you like the amount of light it has?

Are the colors right for you?

Do you need plants?

Does your space express all aspects of yourself? What do you need to add to include all of them?

How does your space express your health?

How does it express your illness?

What do your closets say about your inner psyche?

Does it clearly say who you are, or is it representing the part of you that needs attention, care, and love?

Is it arranged the way you like it, or has something bothered you for years that you have not fixed or changed?

Do you have things that you don't need or want and won't let go of?

What other areas of your life does this affect?

What else won't you let go of?

What fear underlies this hanging on?

How does your living space affect your relationships?

Does the energy of your space express who you are?

The same holds true for your working space, whether or not you own your business.

Some good questions to ask yourself about your work space are:

What is the energy of your work space like?

How do your desk/tools/equipment feel and look?

How does your work area feel and look?

Is it in order?

How does it express who you are?

Does it serve you well?

What else do you need to help you do your work?

Does the energy of your work space express who you are?

Your Physical Body As Spiritual Habitat

From the spiritual perspective, our bodies are vehicles with which to do a task. As we make the psychological adjustment to see our bodies as vehicles with which to accomplish one task in physical reality, taking care of our bodies in a new way becomes very important. Not only do we want to make them healthy, we want to keep them very clean and clear so that we can live in the highest possible balance with nature and with the highest possible sensitivity to Higher Sense Perception. What we at one time may have called healthy may not look so healthy anymore. For example, eating heavy meats, sugars, and stimulants like coffee dulls our senses. What we wear enhances or slows down the flow of energy through our bodies. Hygiene becomes very important to keep our energy fields unpolluted. Looking at these areas and more improves not only your health but also your sensitivity to your energy field and all the energy fields around you.

Personal Hygiene for the Physical Body

Remember, your skin is the largest excretory organ of your body, so it is important to keep it in full working order. Be sure to use natural and nontoxic soaps or skin cleansers that are pH-balanced for your skin. The skin has a natural acid mantle that helps prevent infection. If you use soaps that are too alkaline, you will remove the protective mantle and leave yourself open for invasion. We all naturally lose the top layer of our skin as the old cells die off and are replaced with new ones. A shower brush helps remove these old cells. If you use skin moisturizing cream or lotion, be sure it is natural and pH-balanced. The same goes for your makeup. Don't use shampoos or hair rinses that leave heavy residues on your hair. Make sure they are natural and nontoxic as well.

Be sure to brush your teeth twice a day and floss once a day. Use natural toothpaste, or a combination of one part salt to eight parts baking soda.

Change your toothbrush every two weeks, or sterilize the one you have. There are also teeth-cleaning devices on the market that remove plaque. Find out which one your dentist recommends and get it. They work very well for me.

If you are too ill to do these things for yourself, or if you haven't used natural products before, get someone to help you.

Grooming Your Energy Field

Your energy field needs grooming just as your physical body does. As you know, dark stagnated energy accumulates in the auric field when it is not functioning properly. This happens when you hold on to negative feelings, when you have been under a great deal of stress, when you are exhausted and run-down, and sometimes when you have been exposed to the heavy negative energies of others. Dark cloudlike masses accumulate in the second level of the field, and heavy gooey mucus accumulates in the fourth level. You will know that you have accumulated dark clouds or heavy mucus in your field because you can feel it in different ways. You may have pain in the area where it is accumulated, like a low-level muscle ache or a headache. You may feel logy, tired, irritable, or sick. You may even feel that you weigh more than normal or are toxic or polluted. You may feel as if you were getting a cold or the flu. All of these things are signals to clean your field as soon as possible so that you will not get sick. Here are several ways to clear the dark clouds or mucus out of your field.

Baths

One of the best ways I know to clear the field is to take a bath in sea salt and baking soda. You can use as much as one pound of each in a tub of water. This is a strong solution, so it tends to deplete your energy. But if you have picked up a lot of negative energy or have accumulated a lot of low vibratory energy from an illness, it is a good idea to try it this strong. Be sure that the water is not too hot. You will not be able to take the water as hot as you usually do without the salt and soda. If you have trouble with low blood pressure, be very careful, because in some cases people have been known to faint in this bath, and you don't want to take a chance with that. If you get dizzy, get out of the tub, and try it with cooler water. Soak for twenty minutes in the tub. Then lie in direct sunlight for ten to twenty minutes to recharge your field. Use sunscreen. You will be surprised at how much cleaner and clearer you feel after such a bath.

Other baths on the market today can clear the field. Check your local health food store for the ones they carry, and experiment with some of them. There are baths to pep you up, to help you sleep, and to help remove the lactic acid from sore muscles after exertion.

It is always nice to accompany your bath with music and candlelight. If you do this, you can go into a deep healing state and do some visualizations during your bath.

Smudging

You can also clear your field by smudging. Use a sage stick, sweetgrass, cedar, or any combination of these from your local health food store. Simply let the smoke from the stick diffuse through your auric field. It will take the DOR out of your field. Be sure you do this outdoors or with a door or window open. Some incenses also clear the field. Experiment with your favorite ones.

Crystals

Hold a clean, clear quartz crystal in your hand, find the low vibratory energy in your field, and direct it into the crystal. Do this with your intention. This will only work if you are able to keep your mind completely clear of anything else while you do it. The minute your mind and your intention go to something else, the clearing stops and the negative energy goes back into your field. If you are an experienced meditator and can find the low vibratory energy in your field, you should be able to do this. Clean the crystal after you are finished.

There are several ways to clean crystals. The easiest is to simply put them outside in the sunlight for a day or so. If you live near the ocean, you can bury them in the sand under the salt water for an afternoon or a day. Be careful—you may lose them doing it this way. You can soak them overnight in a solution of one-quarter teaspoon sea salt to one pint spring water. I have found all of the above methods work very well. I have heard that some people simply put them in dry sea salt for a day or so. I once observed Marcel Vogel clear them with a blast of energy from his third eye and a swipe of a well-energized hand. That, however, takes practice.

Auric Brush

Another good way to groom your auric field is with the simple auric brush. It is like brushing your hair, but now you will brush your aura. Do it with a partner. One person stands with legs spread to shoulder width, arms at the sides, with eyes closed. The other begins at the front of the body. With fingers spread wide, reach up as far above the head of your partner as you can. Imagine that your fingers grow six inches longer than they are. Begin now to use the elongated fingers of both hands as a brush. Make long continuous strokes from above the head down through the body, all the way to the ground. As you reach the ground, bell out the bottom of the field. Notice that your imaginary elongated fingers actually reach through the physical body. Make one long stroke down the body without stopping. Do not break your stroke. If you do, start over at the top of the head to prevent energy pile up. Now take a step around the body, and do the same thing so that you stroke right next to the last stroke. Continue all around the body, covering the entire body till you reach the place where you started. Make sure you do not leave areas undone. Now it's your turn to be stroked with the auric brush. This has a wonderful calming and grounding effect. Enjoy.

Clothing and Jewelry

Ever looked in your closet and there is nothing to wear, yet there are lots of clothes there? You may need a color that is not there. Your energy field responds to the colors you wear. Usually, you will want to wear the color that you lack or the one you feel harmonious with that day. For example, if you need more physical energy you may need red that day. However, anger makes the energy field dark red. If you are feeling angry and do not want to get angry at work, you'd better not wear red to work. It may help charge your anger. On the other hand, red will help protect your field by warding off negative energy. It also will help keep you from absorbing negative energy. Whatever color you or others around you wear affects your mood. In general, the colors listed in Figure 9–2 (see page 115) are effective in clothing as well.

If you are ill and in your pajamas without much choice of color, you may still want someone to pull some of your favorite things out of the closet so that you can see them and absorb their color. You could try to get different-colored pajamas. Or pick the color you need according to the chart, and get a friend to buy a yard or so of cotton cloth that color. Drape it on your bed. Colored light bulbs or a large green spotlight help a great deal. Flowers are also great to add color to cheer up your surroundings.

A healer friend of mine told me that her MS patient improved after she started wearing red socks to energize her legs. The client was sure the red socks had a lot to do with it.

Wear natural fibers. They have a strong positive effect on the energy field, enhancing and sustaining it. Cottons, silks, and wools are best. Fabrics that are mixtures are also fine. Be sure there is more of the natural fiber than the synthetic. It is best to avoid fabrics made from petroleum by-products, especially if you think you might be sensitive to them. These are acrylics, polyesters, and nylon. These synthetic fabrics interfere with the natural energy flow of the human energy field. Nylon stockings strongly interfere with the energy flow up and down the legs and are, in my opinion, related to many modern female illnesses. I recommend that you wear them only when you really have to. Find silk stockings somewhere if you can.

If you wear jewelry or crystals, make sure they are within the healthy vibrational range of your field. To test this, hold them firmly in the palm of your hand and feel the effect they have on your hand. Does their energy feel heavy or light? Sharp or soft? Does it pierce into your field, or gently soothe the outside of your field? Does it rev you up or calm you down? Does it charge you with the types of energies that you need, or does it pull energy from you because its vibrations are too slow for you? Find out where it feels more comfortable by feeling your energy as you place it on different places on your body. Are you comfortable with it? Perhaps you need a particular color in your auric field. Ask yourself for what purpose are you wearing this crystal. Does it do the job? Ask your guidance what you are to do with this crystal. Repeat this procedure with all your crystals and all your jewelry.

It is possible to get sick from wearing objects that belonged to other people whose energies are not compatible with yours. To prevent this from happening, if you are given or inherit an old piece of jewelry, soak it for a week in salt water. Use four tablespoons of sea salt to one quart of spring water. If possible, leave the bath with the object in it in the sun.

The Life Energy in the Food You Eat

All of the food that you eat is filled with life energy. Different foods carry different energy combinations. This means that when you eat food, you imbibe the energy in the food. If this energy is what your auric field needs, it will help your body and your health. If the energy in the food you eat is not what your field needs, then it will interfere with your health.

We need a lot of additional research to clarify how the life energy in our food affects us. The two major investigators I know of who have investigated life energy in our food are the famous Michio Kushi, who developed macrobiotics, and Dr. Hazel Parcelles, a naturopathic physician in Albuquerque, New Mexico, who studied the life energy in organically grown foods as compared to the life energy in foods that have been grown with pesticides.

Macrobiotics essentially divides foods by their energy into two basic groups: those that contain yin, or female, energy and those that contain yang, or male, energy. All foods can be designated on a line depicting a degree of either yin or yang, with neutral in the middle. According to macrobiotics, we need a certain combination of types of foods based on the energy that they carry. This combination varies with who we are, the season of the year, and the location we live in. Macrobiotics is very popular in this country now. I have seen many people get well from it. Other people have not done so well on it because their bodies could not adjust to it. It was a drastic change in their lifelong diet, or it simply wasn't what their bodies needed at the time.

Dr. Hazel Parcelles is a longtime healer who is 103 at the time of this writing and still practicing her art. She pioneered in the field of measuring the life energies in foods to determine if they had "life-supporting or life-enhancing" energy rates. (Energy rates means frequency of pulsations.) She devised a method to measure life energy rates in food with a pendulum. If any food measures below the life-supporting or -enhancing rate, she advises not to eat it. If eaten, it simply takes energy out of the system.

According to Parcelles, there are two major things that decrease the life energy rates in food. The first is pollution from such things as pesticides and acid rain. In order for food to be healthy, it must maintain an auric pulse rate that is at least as high as the human energy field pulse rate. Fresh, naturally grown foods always have higher energy than those that are polluted with pesticides. Organic food contains the life energy vibratory patterns we need for our health. Organic food is healthy not only because it maintains the normal energy pattern of the produce but because it maintains an intensity and vibration rate high enough to sustain life. It also contains more natural nutrients such as vitamins and minerals.

Drs. Patrick and Gael Crystal Flanagan of Flagstaff, Arizona, have been observing the effect of nutrients on the blood through a high-powered dark field microscope for many years. They have found that organic raw fruits and vegetables as well as their juices quickly affect the blood in a positive way. Raw fruits and vegetables provide trace minerals and live enzymes that are powerful blood catalysts. The fluid within the cells of organic fruits and vegetables has a high zeta potential or negative electrical charge. The zeta potential is the force that maintains the discreteness of the billions of circulating cells that nourish the human organism. Our blood cells are kept in circulation by it. If the zeta potential is low, toxins cannot be suspended for elimination, nutrients cannot be suspended for transporta-

tion to the cells, and the entire system becomes clogged.

The Flanagans have found that poisons and pollutants tend to destroy the zeta potential in the foods we eat, thereby making them very hard to utilize for the body's nutritional needs. Saturated fats and animal fats found in milk, dairy products, potato chips, processed foods and meats tend to cause blood clumping and stickiness. This interferes with the mobility and ability of the blood to transport nutrients to the cells. It also stops the body from eliminating toxins.

Certain positively charged ions like the aluminum ion are extremely destructive to the balance of the biological colloidal system. This is why we should not use aluminum pots and pans for cooking. We should carefully avoid aluminum-containing products such as antacids, baking powders, and deodorants.

Pesticides not only decrease the vibrational rate of produce to below that which sustains life, they disfigure the energy field pattern of the produce, thereby changing its nature. The more pesticides in foods, the more the energy field of the food is distorted and weakened. Parcelles has ways of removing the negative energy effects of poisons left in whole foods such as vegetables, fruits, and eggs. The formula may seem absurd because it is so simple, but it restores the original pattern and intensity of the life energy field of the produce. It works for vegetables, fruits, whole grains, and whole raw eggs. It does not work for any food that no longer has its energy field intact—such as meat, poultry, processed foods, milled grains, or dairy.

Simply fill your sink with cool water. Add a capful of Clorox. It must be plain Clorox, without anything added to it (not new and improved with special scents or anything). Put all the garden produce and eggs that you bring home from the grocery store to soak in the sink for twenty minutes. After twenty minutes, rinse everything in cool water, and you are finished. Simply store in the refrigerator as usual.

Dr. Parcelles states that the second major way food loses its energy is by spoiling. As foods spoil, they lose their frequency rate and vibrate at a frequency lower than life. If you eat these foods, they will simply decrease the rate of vibration of your field. Your field will have to make up for the decreased frequency by drawing energy from another source, such as the digestive organs, or discard it as waste energy. It is better not to eat them. Be sure your food is fresh. Overcooking food also decreases the life energy in it. So it is great to have lightly steamed vegetables rather than fully cooked ones.

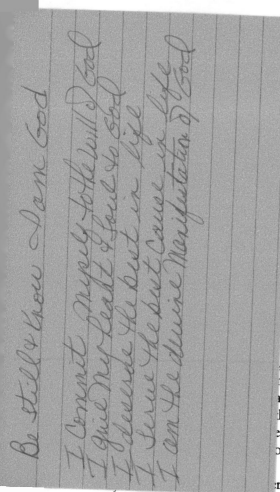

...fect the energy in ... are slaughtered in ...y configuration of ... grayish white with ... persons who eat it. ...f terror out of their ... one of the reasons ... slaughtering cattle

...an and synchronized ...erican people took ...eat. They did it in ...ould ask permission ...shment from the ani-...illed. By doing this, ...ntaining the fourth-..., whom they saw as ...n the ceremony there ...y the person would ...her forms of life and ... of life eating life to ...f staying within the

...rals do not have the normal energy field of natural vitamins and minerals that your energy field needs. Therefore, taking synthetic vitamins and minerals will not necessarily fulfill your energy field needs.

Medicines are not made with the energy field in mind. Many of them cause strong negative effects in the field such as decreasing or changing the normal vibration levels needed to maintain health. Homeopathic remedies, on the other hand, are energy medicine and work directly through the field to the physical body. The higher the potency, the higher the auric level they affect.

Your Eating Habits and Your Aura

Be sure to eat when you are hungry. When a field does not receive all the types of energy it needs or when there is no food available, the energy field gets very depleted. The longer hunger goes on, the more depleted the field gets. The field will get depleted in the areas of the field where the particular energies are lacking and where it is already weak. One of the hardest things about healing back problems is preventing reinjury. Reinjuries always occur when the client is hungry. I asked clients with back problems to carry little snack bags of fresh nuts and raisins with them to work. Every time they were late for a meal, they could eat to keep up their blood sugar level. They did not reinjure themselves then. Their blood sugar level was apparently affecting the strength of their muscles and also their physical awareness as to what was okay and what was not okay to do.

Overeating, on the other hand, can cause the vibrations of a field to decrease, and the person to go into depression. The aura of overeating looks dark and slimy. It is full of toxins.

When you do not drink when you need to, your energy field begins to contract. After a long time of thirst, it begins to get brittle. If your thirst continues and dehydration sets in, your auric field will begin to splinter.

Pay attention to your food when you eat it, and make it look appealing. Give yourself enough time to eat. Chew your food well. It is extremely important not to have a stressful meeting while you eat. Stress immediately affects the third chakra by closing it down or tightening it. The third chakra brings the life energies to your digestive organs. Remember, the food is going to nourish your cells and become you once it is inside your body.

Before you begin to eat, do a little meditation with your hands placed over your food to give it energy and synchronize with it. Visualize it nourishing you. Give thanks for it. Then, as you eat, follow your food all the way through your digestive system and into your cells. It will help you appreciate it.

General Guidelines for Good Food to Eat

Everyone needs a diet that is especially suited to him or her. This diet will change with the seasons and over time. If you are having any digestive problems such as intestinal gas, please get yourself checked out for what you may be allergic to or what digestive organs are not functioning properly. Exhaustion, dizziness, inability to think clearly, and even spinal misalignment can all be related to food allergies. Bloating after meals is very common for people of middle age in this country and often is related to the inability of the body to digest carbohydrates and polysaccharides. Many diseases such as Crohn's disease, ulcerative colitis, diverticulitis, celiac disease, cystic fibrosis, and chronic diarrhea have been cured or alleviated through a low-carbohydrate, or specific-carbohydrate diet.

If you are in good health, probably your diet is working for you. I hesitate to recommend any specific diet because everyone's needs are so individual. However, here are some good general guidelines for healthy ways to eat.

Eat Only Organic Food

Its energy field is stronger, and it has a vibration rate high enough to sustain and enhance life. If you can't get it, use Dr. Parcelles's cleaning methods to restore the original energy patterns. Choose unprocessed foods. If you buy packaged food, be sure to read the label to check what may have been added in processing. Drink only fresh spring water, bottled in glass, or get a very good water filtration system.

What to Eat

Your diet should consist mostly of whole grains, salad, and fresh organic vegetables in season. That means more root vegetables in the winter to synchronize you with winter earth energies. You can also eat fresh fish, organic lean meats like turkey or chicken breast, and some other meats like lamb, depending on your body's needs. Be sure to use cold-pressed polyunsaturated oils on your salad. Some studies have shown that certain oils, like cod liver oil and linseed oil, reduce the cholesterol in the blood. They are also high in vitamin A. You may want to add them to your diet.

Steam or roast your food whenever possible. Or eat it raw.

Choose fresh whole grains over bread and pasta. Whole grains retain life energy much longer than flour. Mixing grains, corn, and beans to get complete protein is good. Dried beans need to be cooked slowly and well so that they are easier to digest. Many people have trouble digesting soybeans. If you get gas from eating beans, it means you have not digested the food completely. Cut them out of your diet till you are stronger. Try tofu. It is partially digested for you.

Buy only fresh nuts and keep them in the refrigerator. When they go rancid, they are very hard to digest, and it is best not to eat them. Remember, nuts are high in oils, so be sure they are okay for you. Don't eat too many.

What Not to Eat

Cut out all foods that have preservatives or other chemical additives because their vibrational rate is not life-supporting. Keep your diet low in foods that have fat, cholesterol, sugar, salt, and dairy; low in acidic foods like tomatoes; and low in foods that have stimulants like coffee and chocolate. Dairy foods and sometimes wheat tend to produce mucus in the system. I suggest that you limit your dairy intake to very little or none. There are lots of nonfat, lactose-reduced dairy products on the market today. You may want to try them. Many people have negative reactions to nightshades, such as eggplant and green peppers.

Do not eat bottom fish, like sole or fluke, or the kinds that have been polluted. Each year, different fish in different areas of the world's seas get polluted in different ways. To keep informed as to what is clean enough to eat, ask your local health food store people or check with the FDA.

Read the Labels

On any packaged food, you get to find out what it is that you are buying. Do this especially in the health food stores on items that say they are protein snacks. Most of them really aren't. They are a New Age way of denying our intake of sweets. Most of that stuff is really just New Age junk food.

Watch Your Distribution of Calorie Intake

Get one of the many little books that are on the market that show the amount of calories and cholesterol and the different types of fat in different foods. Use it as a guideline to choose the foods you will eat. There are also some good books that give diets that balance specific ratios of protein, fruit, vegetables, carbohydrates, and fat. They even give specific meal plans and recipes. Read the labels of the food you buy to determine the grams of protein, carbohydrates, fat, and cholesterol. If the label doesn't tell you what you need to know, you may not want to purchase the product. Many labels are very misleading just to make a sale.

Food Combinations

It is easier for your body to digest certain combinations of food. Hard-to-digest food will stay in the system and dump toxins into your body. Mucus in the digestive tract is composed of long strings of undigested protein. If you follow simple guidelines in mixing food according to the digestive process, your body will more easily digest them. Grains and vegetables go together well. In general, we could say starches and vegetables go together well. So do proteins and vegetables, like meat and vegetables or nuts and vegetables. Oil and leafy greens or oil and acid or subacid fruits digest okay together. But oil with sweet fruits like bananas or dates does not. Remember, oil slows digestion. Things that are hard to digest together are protein and starch (meat and potatoes), oil and starch, or fruit and starch. Eat melon alone, and wait a couple of hours before eating anything else. Any fruit makes a great snack. Fruit is best eaten alone, as are fruit juices. If you have juice in the morning, drink it as soon as you get up. Wait a half to one hour, then have breakfast.

Drinking the Waters of Life

Water is very important to our health. Water is the carrier of all nutrients to the cells, including oxygen. We cannot even breathe without water. The human brain is composed of over 90% water, and the body is at least 70% water. Even bones are 60% water. Since our bodies are composed of mostly water, the type of water we drink has a profound influence on our well-being. There are several places on earth that have "special water" where people live to be 100 or more. The Flanagans have found that this special water is full of natural colloidal mineral clusters that are suspended by an electrical charge or zeta potential. This alters the surface tension of the water and makes it a more efficient solvent and wetting agent. It is the solvent nature of water that enables it to perform its functions in the living system. Certain minerals in this special water actually alter the structure of the water so that it closely resembles that found in the cells of living fruits and vegetables.

Aluminum salts are used to precipitate or coagulate organic colloids out of many municipal water supply systems. Free aluminum ions are sometimes found in city tap water. These aluminum ions neutralize the zeta potential in the water, and make it very unhealthy to drink because it will decrease our blood's capability to carry nutrients to the cells and toxins away from the cells. Therefore it is important to drink fresh spring water, or water that has been distilled or run through a reverse osmosis system.

Vitamins and Minerals

Take only natural vitamins and minerals. They carry natural earth energy. Many people have strong negative reactions to some of the vitamins they take because they are sensitive to the binders with which vitamins are made. If your diet is good, you may not need them. Be aware of the stress changes on your body as you go through your normal schedule. There are times when you need them and times when you don't. If you do eat foods that have been grown on weak soil, you may need vitamins to make up for the deficiencies in your food. If you are working in the health-care field and have a lot of personal contact with ill people, you need to supplement your diet with vitamins and minerals. Be sure to get a good

multimineral/vitamin natural product, and be sure to take extra amounts of calcium, potassium, magnesium, and vitamin C. Take liquid calcium so that it gets digested in the stomach rather than in the lower intestines. Never take vitamin C without taking vitamins A and E. Again, the amount depends upon your body. The algae on the market today is a very good source of minerals and vitamins.

The Flanagans have found that all natural raw vegetarian foods contain more than twice as much magnesium as calcium. In addition they contain at least five times as much potassium as sodium. The sodium/potassium balance controls blood mobility through electrical charge balance while the magnesium/calcium balance affects the output of hormones that control the mobility of these ions in and out of the bones and soft tissues. These hormones can directly affect blood balance. The Flanagans state that excess magnesium helps to move calcium away from soft tissue and into the bones where it belongs. When calcium is in excess to magnesium, hormones are released that move calcium away from bones and into soft tissue where the excess calcium ions destroy cells. For years I have observed this in the bodies of my clients. I was so pleased to see it verified scientifically that I wanted to mention it.

It is important to absorb nutrients over time in order for them to be effective. Therefore, do not take all of your vitamins at once; rather spread them out, so that your blood levels can be maintained at a healthy level throughout the day.

Creating Your Special Diet

If you have a serious illness, an important part of your healing plan must include planning your diet. Which diet is right for you depends on what your problem is and what treatment modalities you have chosen. Some physicians and healers have not been thoroughly trained in dietary healing. If yours are not, get someone who specializes in diet to work on your healing team. Be sure that they know something about the energy in food and food balancing as well as its physical nutrition. Work openly with your physician, your healer, and your other health-care professionals. Some health-care professionals may vary your diet week to week or month to month, depending upon your progress. The foods you eat must not only nourish you in specific ways according to your condition, they must also be easy for your system to digest. Most likely it will be important to regulate your protein, fat, and carbohydrate intake, as well as salt, sweets, and stimulants. You may have to have everything cooked to aid in your digestion. Remember, no matter what the diet is, you still should be able to find ways to choose the things you like to eat.

Macrobiotics is well known today. As I said earlier, I have found it very helpful for many of the people who follow it. Others were not helped. Some of the basic principles of food balancing in macrobiotics are very important. I have seen macrobiotic diets clear the energy field very nicely. If you are having any kind of radiation treatments, consider going macrobiotic. According to Michio and Aveline Kushi, macrobiotics is very effective in curing radiation sickness. In his book *Macrobiotic Diet*, Michio Kushi states:

At the time of the atomic bombing of Nagasaki in 1945, Tatsuichiro Akizuki, M.D., was director of the Department of Internal Medicine at St. Francis' Hospital in Nagasaki. Most patients in the hospital, located one mile from the center of the blast, survived the initial effects of the bomb, but soon after came down with symptoms of radiation sickness from the radioactivity that had been released. Dr. Akizuki fed his staff and patients a strict macrobiotic diet of brown rice, miso and tamari soy sauce soup, wakame and other sea vegetables, Hokkaido pumpkin, and sea salt and prohibited the consumption of sugar and sweets. As a result, he saved everyone in his hospital, while many other survivors in the city perished from radiation sickness.

Other healing diets, such as the Pritikin diet and Dr. Ann Wigmore's diets, have helped people who are ill. I have seen many people helped a great deal with a high protein diet set out for them by biochemists. The Fit for Life diet, which includes a lot of fruit in the morning, helped many people lose weight, feel lighter and healthier, and be more energized. But others, who had candida (yeast infections), got worse because of the high fructose in that diet. See the Bibliography for books about these diets. Be open to exploring, but pay attention to how the diet is working for you.

Some health-care professionals recommend special fasts, cleansing diets, or special purges like enemas, colonics, or liver flushes to clear the system. These are effective when used with care and consideration of your body and its tolerances. If you want to fast, get some guidance on what kind of fast is best for you. Don't do it without learning how because you could hurt yourself.

While enemas and colonics provide fast clearing of the body's toxins, they also wash away your natural digestive fluids, which you will need to replace. If you take too many of them, you can get weaker. Do not just get a few colonics on your own. If you do colonics, you need one health-care professional in charge of your overall program. It is best that the part of the colonic apparatus that is inserted into you has never been used before. If not, buy that part for yourself only to use. I have seen some patients greatly helped by colonics and others weakened from taking too many. If you are allergic to coffee, don't take a coffee enema. Use pure water instead. Coffee could send your body into convulsions. If you're not allergic to coffee, you may on the other hand feel very cleansed and get a high from it.

Once you have the specifics of what is best for you to eat, you can then utilize the General Guidelines for Good Food to Eat above to choose the foods that can make up that diet.

Energy Exercises for All Your Bodies

Studies show that if you exercise, you not only reduce your aging rate, you can reverse it. It is never too late to start. Recently in *Time* magazine there was a picture of an eighty-year-old grandmother who took up karate and became a black belt within two or so years.

The American Heart Association recommends at least a good twenty minutes of aerobic-type exercise a minimum of three times a week. You can work up to five times per week if you like. By *aerobic*, they mean any activity that works large muscle groups to continuously maintain an elevated heart rate of 60 to 65 percent maximum heart rate for fifteen minutes or longer. Your maximum heart rate is the absolute capability of your heart to beat. Of course, you don't want to exercise at that rate since it would severely strain your heart—perhaps to the point of death. You can determine your maximum heart rate by subtracting your age from 220. This includes aerobic workout or dancing, walking, biking, swimming, rowing, jumping rope, and cross-country skiing. Aerobic exercise keeps your circulatory system strong and usually does not build muscles or help you lose much weight. You start to lose weight only after the twenty-minute period is up. Therefore, you have to keep going longer. To build muscle you need to exercise in other ways. Find out how from your local health club.

The best way to lose weight is to exercise and to eat well, as described in the section on food. Studies have shown that it is much better to exercise and eat than to severely limit your food intake to lose weight.

Yoga is very good for the body, as well as for all the levels of the auric field, when done with a good instructor. It helps establish a strong body-mind connection and brings large amounts of smooth-flowing energy to your system. Some of the postures are designed to balance and charge acupuncture meridians. You will need to supplement it with the aerobic workout for your heart.

Regular swimming, dance, and aerobic exercises charge the first level of the field quite well, provided that all parts of the body are given attention. Exercise machines, such as the Nautilus, will increase the strength of the muscles of the first level of the field, and somewhat that of the organs, but not as well as faster movement exercises.

For levels one through three of your auric field, the energy bodies associated with the material world, tai chi and chi gong, give balance and charge and strength to the field on the first through the third levels. If done correctly according to individual needs, they can strengthen all parts of the body and bring about health. Tai chi and chi gong are wonderful for increasing your energy, your body-mind connection, and your grounding. I think such soft martial arts are the best types of body-mind trainings there are, provided the instructors are well trained. Tai chi and chi gong can strengthen more levels, depending how well the mind-body interface is focused. They can strengthen the higher levels if practiced with meditation. All of these exercises are done with specific breathing techniques that charge and balance the auric field.

Exercise: Energy Exchange

The following energy exchange exercise does great things for the fourth level of the field. These exercises are done with a partner. Put on some music you like, and stand face to face with a partner. Begin by putting your palms up together with your partner's palms, close but not touching. Now move to the music, keeping your palms synchronized. Notice how easy it becomes after some practice. When it becomes easy, try closing your eyes. Continue moving to the music. You may be surprised at how easy it is to synchronize with another's energy. Once you are synchronized, open your eyes again.

Now bring some of your focus to yourself. How are you doing this? What are you doing with your energy field to make this possible? Search for particular feelings in your field so that you will know how to re-create this state of communion again. Enjoy this exercise with another partner. How is it different? How is it the same? Continue as long as you like. Try the same exercise without music. How do you like it this way? Once

you have become used to the state of communion, you can apply it in other situations. If someone calls for help, try it. If you are about to get into an argument with someone, try it.

Breathing and Exercise

Through breath control we can regulate and direct the flow of energy through our body and auric field. Any good exercise includes breath regulation.

Healers breathe strongly and deeply to increase their energy and power for healing.

Many people in our culture do not breathe deeply and use only the upper-chest breathing. This keeps the energy field weaker than it could be. Deep diaphragmatic breathing is automatic in children, but we begin to cut our breath down as we block our feelings. Holding our breath or dampening our breathing is the best way to stop feelings and anesthetize ourselves. The lungs are associated with freedom. If we dampen our breathing or let the chest collapse, we feel sadness. Our shallow breathing in this culture is related to our feelings of being trapped in a world we cannot control and feel very unsafe and unfulfilled in.

Breathing fully and deeply with our diaphragms helps us feel the power to regain our freedom and works to release the spirit of fear in which we are all held in this nuclear age.

Here is a simple breathing exercise: Stand with your knees bent, legs at shoulder width, so that your knees come over your feet; or sit upright in a chair with only the lower part of your back supported. Relax. With your right index finger, hold your left nostril closed. Take a deep breath in through your right nostril. Hold it, close your right nostril with your right thumb. Now breathe out the left nostril. Then breathe in the left nostril. Hold your breath. Close your left nostril with your right index finger. Release your right nostril and breathe out. Repeat this breathing while pulling your diaphragm down so that your lower abdomen thrusts out on your breast. Fill your whole chest with air. Now you can add a simple mantra if you choose for each in-and-out breath—freedom, power, health. When you get used to the feeling of deep breathing, you can do it through both nostrils anytime. Hopefully, it will become a healthy habit.

In martial arts, the direction of strength and power is always the direction of the energy flow. A sharp outburst of energy directed at an opponent is always accompanied by a large forced-out breath and a loud cry.

Martial arts, in which two people interact with each other's energy fields, will charge and strengthen the fourth level of the auric field, the level of relationship. However, the best physical exercise I can think of to enhance the fourth level of your auric field is to dance. Dance is always done in relationship—if not to another person, then to the music itself!

The fifth, sixth, and seventh levels of the field are the energy bodies associated with the spiritual world. These levels of the field are charged, balanced, and strengthened by doing special exercises such as kundalini yoga and kriya yoga that combine yoga positions with the "breath of fire." It is best to learn these from a good instructor.

Breath of fire is a type of fast pant breath that uses the diaphragm as a pump. It gives a very powerful charge to the aura, very quickly. The last breath is taken deeply and held, then slowly let go. By doing this in different yoga positions, the exerciser first charges the field, then directs the energy to exactly where it is needed.

We all need exercise, even when ill. One patient of mine who was mostly bed-ridden for years from a spinal injury could walk only short distances with a walker or with help. She got tired of that and hired a person who walked dogs to walk her. At first it was a very short distance. Now it is several times around the block. This improved her health so much that she no longer needs a wheelchair.

Whatever your condition is, be sure to get whatever kind of exercise you can do. It is very important. If you are too ill to do much, do a little. O. Carl Simonton, M.D., in his book *The Healing Journey,* recommends a range of motion exercises in bed. I highly recommend these. Choose your type of exercise; if possible find someone who knows about exercise and get them to design some just for you in your condition. There are forms of tai chi and chi gong that are designed specifically for healing. They are designed to open each acupuncture meridian. If possible, have a good tai chi instructor come to your house to work specifically with you. A little walk will do you a world of good. If it's warm, get outside into the sunlight and get a breath of fresh air. As you recover, you will be able to walk farther. Eventually you can work up to a good one-half to one hour brisk walk.

Sleep and Rest

When you are tired, your auric field shrinks and is dull. Its colors are washed out. Its otherwise normally beautiful, bright sixth level rays of light stream out in all directions, sag, and droop. The longer you go without rest, the more dilapidated your field looks. The sooner you get rest when you are tired, the quicker the aura regains its normal fullness, brilliance, luster, and shape.

Some people need a good nine to ten hours' rest; some need eight; some less. Generally, we need less rest as we get older. Some people need the rest all in one shot; others need it more often in smaller amounts. Some people are night owls; some are morning people.

When and how much rest you need is highly individual. It's a good idea to listen to what your body wants and to try to follow it. During the fifteen or so years I had a healing practice, I struggled with this problem. I found that I became extremely tired between 1:30 and 2:45 P.M. It was very difficult to give healings during that time. I realized that it simply wasn't working for me—so I changed my schedule. Since I am a morning person, I began early. I gave four healings between 8:00 A.M. and 1:00 P.M. Then I ate from 1:00 to 1:30, slept from 1:30 to 2:45, and gave healings between 3:00 and 5:00 or 6:00 P.M. It took me only a couple of minutes to fall asleep at 1:30. Each time I would see myself going into a white light. Like clockwork I would wake up at 2:45 and be ready for a new day! It was like having two days in one and really worked for me.

There are no rules for how you ought to sleep—other than rest when you are tired and according to your body rhythms. Experiment with what works for you, and try it for a while. You will be surprised at how much more energy you have. Don't keep your rest schedule rigid over a long period of time, because it will change. Just go with your flow that keeps your aura bright and charged.

How You Use Your Time

How you spend your time on a daily and weekly basis is very important to your physical, emotional, mental, and spiritual well-being. Remember, each level of your auric field corresponds to specific aspects of your life. The only way to keep your field healthy and charged is by giving time and focus to each aspect. You probably won't be able to give equal time to all aspects of your life. But be sure to give at least several hours a week to all aspects. Things included in your time-activities budget are time for yourself alone, your mate, your family and friends, your work and social life, and your relaxation. If you tend to spend more time in one of these to the detriment of the others, schedule the forgotten activities on your calendar. If you are a workaholic type, be sure to schedule alone times and times with your spouse as thoroughly as you schedule your work time. Give adequate time to developing each aspect of your life in order to develop each aspect of your auric field. Let's go over them again. To keep your physical body and first level of the field in good condition, spend time doing physical activities and exercises and eat well. To keep your second level healthy is to love yourself.

Spend time giving yourself loving caring and doing whatever you feel like doing. You need time for yourself, at least one hour a day or one day a week that is devoted to you and whatever you want to do. That means that you are taking care of yourself that day, not other people. Play your favorite games or music. Be with your favorite people or be alone, your choice. Do things that you haven't given yourself time to do.

To keep your third level healthy, spend time using your mind. Read books, problem-solve, create new ideas. Your fourth level can be kept healthy by maintaining a good working intimate relationship and supportive friendships. The higher three levels of your field can be kept healthy by following spiritual practices that are right for you, such as meditation, prayer, working with divine will, and deep contemplation.

When you are ill, you can still maintain activities in all seven aspects of your life. Of course, they will be different from what you may consider to be normal. In fact, you are more likely to have more time to devote to the spiritual aspects of your life. This helps a great deal in your healing. In illness, some of the biggest changes in your time-activity budget will be in your work and your relationships. The time you once spent at your work or taking care of your family is now spent taking care of yourself. This may seem very strange at first if you aren't used to it. It may be especially hard if you have spent a great deal of your life doing your work and if work is one of the major ways you have felt good about yourself.

You may have used your work to define who you are. Suddenly, you no longer have that part of your life in an active way. This will be very threatening at first. Be sure to give these threatening feelings time and space. Meditate on it yourself, and discuss it with friends. Tell them exactly how you are threatened, and they will be able to help you. Remember, no matter how important your work, it is not more important than you are. As you learn to let go of that self-definition for the time your illness requires, you will find deeper areas of yourself that were pushed away in your busy life, and that

you may have not met for a long time. Your first order of business is to take care of yourself. Try it for a while—you might just find out that you like it! Whatever your work skills are, they will also come in handy now, because you can take what you have learned in the work area of your life and apply it to your new project—healing yourself. For example, if you have been a manager, you will be able to use your organizational skills to organize your healing team and your healing plan. On the other hand, it may be good for you to just let go and let someone else do it.

You will find your life rhythms changing during an illness. When you are healthy, your life rhythms will flow in ways you consider to be natural for you. For example, you probably wake up at a regular time most days and get sleepy at another—say, in the middle of the day. You may go to bed early, or maybe you are a night owl. You probably get hungry at regular times during the day and eat certain sized meals that you think are natural and healthy. You probably prefer to do exercises at a certain time of day and not at another time.

Don't get alarmed when all this changes. Don't try to force yourself to keep the old rhythm or to go back to it. That is not healthy. You are moving into different healthy rhythm cycles. Your appetite will change, your sleeping hours will change. You may even get to sleep when you always wanted to but had to work. You may have more energy when other people are dozing off, or vice versa. The healthy rhythm for you now is the one your body chooses. Now is the time to simply go with your body's new healing rhythms. Eventually they will settle into what you label as normal. You just need a little adjustment. Your rhythms may not ever revert back to what you called healthy and normal before you got ill. That's okay. You will probably like the new ones better.

Some Good Questions to Ask Yourself about Taking Care of Your Physical Body and Your Auric Field Are:

Do I need to improve any of my personal hygiene habits?

What is the best kind of exercise for me now?

What is the best diet for me now?

What clothing and jewelry best suit me now?

What colors do I need to wear now, considering my moods and my state of health?

Is my diet right for me?

Do I consider the life energy in the foods I choose?

Is my time budget the best for me?

ELEVEN

Healing Yourself with Love by Letting Go of Perfectionism

You are your primary healer. One of the most powerful paths of self-healing is to enter into a positive emotional relationship with yourself. Most of us need a lot of work in this area. We simply will not accept ourselves the way we are. For example, a guilt feeling is nothing but the rejection of the state in which we find ourselves in the moment, indicating that we are unwilling to accept ourselves as we are now. That is, if we feel guilty for something we have done or not done, then either we are procrastinating doing something to rectify it, we are still processing it, or we have made the choice to punish ourselves with guilt because our actions did not express our integrity. It is easier to feel guilty for something than to do what we must to keep our integrity. We fear whatever it is we must do. It is easier to feel guilty than to face our fear. Our guilt covers our fear, but it leads to self-rejection. We choose self-rejection over fear.

The most epidemic health problem we have is self-hatred. I understand that this may sound outrageous, especially to someone who has not felt self-hatred or who is in denial. But whenever you get to know anyone more deeply, you find a kernel of self-hatred inside them that runs very deep.

Rather than calling it self-hatred, we use the term *low self-esteem*. Inside each person is a constant struggle for self-esteem that covers the self-hatred. The struggle for self-esteem rarely stops. Everyone tries to be special in some way to prove their self-worth. It may not be conscious, but it shows in behavior, both underachieving and overachieving. There are those who try harder and those who don't even bother. We are in a vicious cycle. We try, or blatantly don't try, to prove we are worthy by a set of standards we laid out for ourselves in childhood. Yet when we do attain the goals laid out in those standards, we simply disregard them and pursue different ones.

We base our self-worth on what we expect of ourselves. We demand an impossible perfection from ourselves. Then we judge and reject ourselves when we do not achieve that perfection. We demand a never-ending list of accomplishments from ourselves. As we achieve each one, we ignore and devalue it. We immediately focus on the next hurdle to surmount. We don't allow time for the accomplishment to sink in or to congratulate ourselves for what we have done or for what we have become through our effort and struggle. We do not give ourselves the gifts that we have achieved or have given to others. Just ask healers to compare the number of their self-healings to the number of healings given to others. Ask musicians if they can listen to and enjoy their own music without being judgmental.

No wonder there are people who don't even try to

achieve anything. They see the folly in the whole game, so they refuse to play. Unfortunately, they kill their creativity, spirit, life energy, and sometimes their bodies in the process.

There are two levels of causes under all this striving or nonstriving. One is the level of psychological cause. The other is the deeper, spiritual cause.

The Cause of Self-Hatred
on the Psychological Level

On the psychological level, the cause of self-hatred is self-betrayal, which begins for us in early childhood. Since we were small children we have disliked ourselves when we couldn't do what we thought we ought to be able to do, whether it was something we initiated or something that was requested of us by a parent, teacher, or some other authority. Remember, we were small children. We had very little sense of what is possible.

What we do know is that, like all children, we were born with unconditional love for those around us. We want all those around us to be happy and loving. We expect unconditional love from those around us. Unfortunately, things rarely work out that way. Here's what happens instead.

When we see other people in our lives—almost all of them bigger than we are—expressing their negative feelings, it scares us. Many adults overpower us when they are angry or when we express our negative feelings. This happens even if we have a really good reason for negative feelings that are truly expressing our response to a bad situation. As small children, this overpowering feels life-threatening, so we suppress our justified response to a life situation.

In addition to the suppression of justified negative reactions, we have no way of dealing with the fact that people in our family aren't always loving to each other and that they express fear and hatred. So we do the logical—to a child—thing. We try to make the hurts go away and everything all better. We deny our own feelings, and betray ourselves in the process.

Of course, to take care of everyone in this way is an impossible task. But that doesn't stop us. The more we try to smooth things over and deny negative feelings in ourselves and others, the less true to ourselves and our original impulse of unconditional love we're being. The harder we try to make everything right, the more helpless we feel, and the more of an impostor—

betraying who we really are—we become. Underneath, we are trying to get the love we expected. The more we try and don't succeed to get the love, the more we become convinced that we are unlovable, and the less we are able to love ourselves. (See the development of the mask self, described in Chapter 1.)

There is another part of this vicious cycle that makes things even worse. As small children, when we do succeed and get praise or help on how to succeed even more, inside we feel something is wrong because we still didn't get the love we wanted. Instead, we got praise. Praise and love are not the same. So we try harder. Each time we go around this vicious cycle, to succeed and get more praise, the sequence proves to us ever more forcefully that there is something wrong with us.

Not only that, but when we do succeed in "being good" and get a reward, even if it is love and recognition, it is the impostor child, not the real child inside, who gets the love. The real child inside is covered by the impostor. Since the impostor gets the goodies, it proves even more that the real child inside is not worthy of love.

Every time we as children succeed in being good, somewhere within our psyche we get the message that our "real self" is not lovable. It is love that we need, and it is love that we can't get. Through this process we never learn how to love ourselves. Rather, we forget who we are. Our true need to be recognized and loved for who the "real child inside" is—not what the impostor does—never gets met. This painful cycle continues through adulthood.

The Cause of Self-Hatred
on the Spiritual Level

The other cause of self-hatred is actually the same as the psychological one, but it can be found in your spiritual life. If you are reading this book, you are probably consciously on a spiritual path of some kind. Being on such a path sometimes makes it even harder to accept the self, because much of your life's effort may be to get clear about yourself, understand, and improve yourself. Therefore, you are probably much more aware of your imperfections and the way you create the negative experiences in your life than you were before you actively began your spiritual work. Again, it is difficult to find imperfections within and accept yourself.

There is another aspect of spiritual work that makes the imperfections of physical life difficult to accept. When we do spiritual work, we are constantly moving from one level of consciousness to another. At the higher levels, this work is full of light and bliss. But when we come down into the physical level and try to integrate what we have experienced, it is sometimes even more difficult for us to accept the imperfections of our humanness. It is most difficult to live in a physical, finite reality and to know, at the same time, that our greater reality is infinite. It is most difficult to feel our fear and, on a higher level, know that there is no need for that fear, to feel confusion in our mind and to know, on a higher level of our being, that we are clarity and light.

The spiritual teachings themselves can also make it difficult for us to accept and love ourselves. Sometimes they seem paradoxical. It is difficult to be told that we must free ourselves from the prison of our humanness and, at the same time, that we must trust the human condition. It is difficult to be told that the material world is an expression of the divine, in fact *is* divine, and yet to see the chaos, anger, and hatred here. It is difficult to be told that to become more spiritual, we must spiritualize matter and that the only way to do that is to accept the material world as it is. It is most difficult to accept the basic nature of duality of our physical world, and yet try to move beyond that duality into a state of oneness with it.

The way to do this is through self-love and through the acceptance of the universe as it is, of our lives as they are, knowing that always and ever there is a guidance and a protection and that there is always a higher reason for everything that happens. And when this broad aspect of acceptance is incorporated into your conscious mind, into your conscious living, you will find your progress to be very rapid indeed.

The process of healing can seem more difficult from the spiritual perspective because it does not seem rational. We are told by our guidance that we are spiritual beings of light, and yet we feel trapped in a body that may be full of pain and dis-ease. We are told to lovingly accept that pain and disease as it is, to lovingly accept that we created it, and to even lovingly accept how we created it. That means to come out of denial that it is there and is there for a reason; to love and accept ourselves, who created it; and to accept all the thoughts and actions we have done to create it. If that is what we do, it means accepting the further creation of the disease.

Even though at first it may seem like it, please note:

Acceptance does not mean surrender to the disease or the disease process. It means deeply trusting, loving, and accepting our lives and ourselves, no matter what. It means really getting to know the deeper self, communing with it, identifying with it, and finding its divinity. In so doing, we find that the healthy body is an expression of that deeper self. We find that wherever the illness is in the body is where we have not allowed the deeper divine self to express itself. It is where we are confused between the real self and the impostor and have allowed the impostor to reign. It is where we have allowed the vicious cycle of self-hatred to spin.

Breaking Your Vicious Cycle of Self-Hatred

The only way to break out of the vicious cycle that holds self-hatred in place is to identify the impostor within and stop trying to rework yourself to please others. Begin to observe yourself to find out how much you become the impostor; how you manipulate, betray, and reject yourself according to *what you think others want from you*; and thereby how you lose connection to your true self. I bet it's similar to the way you have done it since childhood.

To find your vicious cycle of self-hatred, ask yourself:

How do I sell out and do what I assume authorities want?

How do I reject myself for such selling out?

What kind of self-hatred do I heap upon myself for doing it?

Do I reject myself before someone else can?

In what situations do I dislike and reject myself more (for instance, losing in competition)?

What do I do to myself when I lose?

Make a list. On one side of the page, write all the things you find wrong with yourself. On the other, write how you feel toward yourself about them. Through self-examination of this sort, you can become aware of your self-judgments and negative feelings about yourself. That is already a big part of the battle. Once they are found, you have the key to go deeper to the heart of the problem. The next step is to allow those feelings. I will use the auric field to illustrate why and how this works.

How Negative Emotions Toward Yourself Affect the Second Level of Your Field

Our emotional relationship with ourselves is found in the second level of the auric field. The second level of the auric field carries our positive and negative feelings about ourselves. It is the negative feelings about ourselves that cause lots of problems. The energy and consciousness associated with negative feelings in the second level are of a nature that is contrary to life. To make things worse, we hold this energy-consciousness still, not allowing our negative emotions to flow. This lowers the vibrational frequency to a vibration lower than that which supports life and health, causing stagnation in the second level. The stagnation then affects the first level of the field, blocking the life energy flow to the physical body.

The way we hold these emotions still is by transferring some of their energy-consciousness to the mental level for dissipation. There, the negative energy-consciousness is expressed as self-judgment. The self-judgment then suppresses the feelings even more.

Let me restate this, speaking simply of energy-consciousness transfer. We transfer the negative energy that would normally be expressed in terms of negative emotions up to the third level of the field, where it turns into self-judgments that in turn suppress the negative emotions of the second level even more. This negative feedback loop compresses the second level of the field, reducing its frequency to below what is healthy for life. This then causes an emotional depression in the person.

The auric field of such a person looks very narrow on the second level. The normally bright-colored clouds of energy that should be flowing along the lines defined by the first level are dark and dirty. Some people who have bright second levels may not at all comprehend the situation and may be very uncomfortable near someone like this. Others will be moved to help them out of their situation.

It is relatively easy to clear the second level of the field. Technically, it is a matter of transferring the energy-consciousness back down into the second level and getting it to move by charging it. The moving energy will bring emotional experience that will take the person deeper into themselves, to the root of the problem, and finally into the essence of self and the core. A healer can do this by working with the second level of the field to clear it and by encouraging the client to express feelings.

You can do it on your own, once you know the process. First you become conscious of your self-judgments and understand that they cover pain. But understanding is not enough. You must let down and feel. Let your energy-consciousness back down into the second level in order to feel. Feeling it is necessary, because feeling it returns the flow of energy to the second level of the field, which is stagnated. The flow of energy then clears the stagnation and recharges the field in a healthy way.

Practice changing judgments coming from the third level of the field, like "I'm no good because . . ." or "I should have done . . ." into feelings on the second level like "I hurt" or even "I hate myself." Let the feelings flow, no matter what they are. It really works. Immediately, the stagnant clouds of the second level of the auric field begin to move and start clearing. Through the clearing and movement, the second level charges. Soon "I hate myself" turns into "I hurt," which turns into "I love myself," "I'm sorry I treat myself this way," and so on. Emotional expression returns the field to its natural state of flowing, bright colors of the energy-consciousness of self-love.

A businessman I'll call Jeffrey was unable to break out of his vicious cycle of perfectionism until he began to express his feelings of pain. Jeffrey had been pushed by his family since birth to become well known in his field and financially successful. As an adult, he felt he could never do enough. No matter what his accomplishments, he simply could not find satisfaction within himself. Each success brought him less pleasure. He felt empty inside.

Jeffrey's auric field showed a great deal of rigidity in the third level, as well as stagnation in the second. His third level was compressing the second. He was unaware of feelings and rarely expressed them. The emptiness brought him to my healing table. As he sank into the emptiness, his second level began to charge and move. It turned from bright amber-yellow to bright red as he first expressed his self-judgments and then self-hatred. By reading and working with the field as he expressed himself, I guided him to stay on track. Soon the self-hatred melted into pain.

Here for the first time, he began to feel the pain of the inner child who had been put under the stress of trying to be perfect. At times he moved into self-judgment to stop the pain. When this happened, the flow of energy in the second level of the auric field would stop and give way to activity in the third level, primarily on the back of his body where chakra activity is an expression of will—that is, the will to make the pain stop. I described what it looked like and helped him direct his consciousness and energy flow back to the front of the body and to the second level of the field. As he did this, an automatic natural flow of energy-consciousness up the front of the body would release feelings again. As he learned to redirect this flow of energy through his body, it became easier to return to the feelings.

As this ebb and flow of expression continued, the feelings from the self-rejection of the present gave way to the pain from past self-rejection. Jeffrey realized he had been carrying it since childhood. He had tried so hard to do what his parents wanted, and he was still trying, whether or not he really wanted to. He felt himself the impostor, doing anything to get his parents' love. He got the message of what he was supposed to do to be "good," and in some way or other, he was still doing it today in the business world.

Thus he reached the source of his vicious cycle. He found it in the young child's conclusion that he must strive for perfection to attain his parents' love. Suddenly he had another view of his whole life. At first it was very discouraging. It seemed that everything he had ever done to succeed was for the wrong reason—to buy love.

Once again, he tried to take himself out of feeling that pain by going into more self-judgments. As I encouraged him to stay with that pain, he fell deeply into the reality of the inner child. The need in this inner child for love was very real indeed. He loved this inner child with all his heart. He felt and recognized the essence of this child and the essence of his core. He had finally come home.

Jeffrey's life had changed. From then on, he could see himself and every other human being in a different way. He would never be able to avoid his feelings as much as he had before. He would never be able to sustain his self-judgments as they were. He would catch himself striving for perfection, slow down, and ask his inner child what it wanted. He would let a few great deals pass by and choose being instead of overdoing.

The flow of energy through Jeffrey's second level continued to build over time. With continued work, his second level took on a normal state of bright flowing colors. His third level also became brighter, more flexible, and more balanced front to back. His first level became stronger and more charged. As a result, his physical body felt younger and more energized. These changes moved up into the fourth level of his field, and his relationships with others took on deeper meaning.

It is through this process of emotional expression that we learn just how much we have brutalized our inner child with our self-judgments. We have not allowed it to have its free range of emotional expression toward itself, which it needs to live within us in a healthy way. And as we have done it to ourselves, so we have done it to others. Once we stop doing it to ourselves, we stop doing it to others. When we accept our own limitations, the needs of our inner child and its imperfections, we accept them in others.

As we begin to accept ourselves the way we are and get to know the inner child, we see that we have made the assumption that the inner child should grow up. There are parts of the child that need to grow up, but primarily the inner child's spirit needs to be released into freedom. Rather, it needs to live fully within us. Our inner child fills our personality with a sense of wonder and joy of life. It gives us simple pleasure that can never be matched by adult activities. The inner child holds the keys to our "real self," for it is part of it. Our inner child is a doorway to the essence of our core. If you spend more time with your inner child, you will find out who your real self is. It is composed of many parts from all the life experiences you have had.

Getting to Know Your Inner Child

A good way to get to know your inner child is to play. It turns out that playing is also a great way to find out your needs, especially the ones you left behind you in your childhood. Playing will automatically bring them out. Once they are activated, some of them will mature into your true adult needs. Play is also a great way to find out that your needs are good and that what you are is valuable and unique. Playing is a great way to express positive feelings about yourself. It charges the second level of the auric field and makes it fluid.

To do this, I suggest that you find a chunk of time each day, perhaps an hour or so, to just do what you want to do and nothing that you don't want to do. Schedule the time as if it were a business appointment. Fill your desire, no matter how young the part of you is that wants it. For example, wear what you want to wear, no matter how outrageous it may seem. Eat what you want to, go where you want, play the music that you want. If you don't like it, stop immediately, but only because you are not having fun, not because some voice tells you you are not doing the right thing. See how fast you can change what you are doing according to what you want in the moment. Let go and enjoy yourself. Remember, that is what you did as a child. You will be surprised at the results.

After you get used to having regular playtime, you will notice that there is a connection between the inner child's needs and the adult's. Children's play has always expressed the deep teleological yearnings human beings carry. As the psyche matures, those yearnings are expressed in mature adult ways. Activities that begin in the child's realm may mature into adult activities. Or they may remain as they are. Allow them to be whatever they are. Do not place demands on your play.

When my daughter was young, we used to play together regularly. One of my favorite things was putting Celia to bed at night. I got to play the role of a naughty duck, using a hand puppet. Ducky never really wanted Celia to go to sleep and would jump under the covers with her, be silent for a few minutes, and then suddenly throw off the covers! Or Ducky would constantly ask her if she was asleep yet. It was great fun!

We also painted together fairly regularly. Celia was always painting moons and stars. One time, I couldn't figure out what to paint, so I painted an aura. Then I painted another one. Soon I had a whole bunch of them. Years later, a professional artist redid them for *Hands of Light*. (They are Figures 11–1 and 11–2 in that book.)

Play activates and releases the child's fantasy. Fantasy in the mature psyche becomes creative visualization.

When I first published *Hands of Light*, Dorian, one of my healing class students from Colorado, gave me a beautiful white bear who became known as Buddha Bear. Everyone agreed that if I was going into the world to teach, I would definitely need a bear. They were right. Buddha Bear has been a great help to my inner child ever since. In the beginning, he even traveled with me.

In recent channelings, Heyoan has suggested that once we give our child self space to be, we must also give our child space to grow into maturity, and to be integrated into our whole being.

Self-Love Exercises

It is also good to practice direct self-love. Here are some wonderful exercises to learn to love yourself. If you have problems generating love feelings with the first exercise, the next one might help. Try them all, and pick the ones you like. Spend some of your time each day actively loving yourself. You can do this by scheduling fifteen minutes each morning and evening. An-

other option is to schedule it for one minute on the hour every hour!

These exercises may not be as easy to do as they sound. Usually as soon as we begin concentrating on ourselves, we begin analyzing, accessing, placing shoulds, judging, and wreaking all manner of internal nasty behavior upon ourselves. This is not self-love. If you find yourself being negative, gently stop being negative and return to the positive. It is not selfish to love yourself. Rather, think of yourself as a cup that can be filled. When your cup runneth over, the love spills out to those around you. You must love yourself in order to give love to others. Remember that all the negative things you do to yourself, you also do to others, perhaps unconsciously, and all the good things you do to yourself, you also do to others.

Filling the body and the self with love:
You may first wish to start with only a part of your body, as it is easier. Choose a part of your body that needs help, or that you dislike, reject, or are ashamed of. Simply concentrate on that part of your body and direct love into it. Fill it with energy; talk to it kindly. If you are in pain in any part of your body, give it extra love. Instead of trying to get away from it (which we all do when we are in pain), enter into that part of your body with your consciousness. Occupy that part of your body with conscious awareness and loving kindness.

Now do the same for your whole self. Simply concentrate on yourself, and direct love to yourself, as you do to those you love. If you like to use colors, first use green, then rose, then gold and white. Fill your whole body with these colors.

Initiate the love feelings with something that is easy:
Concentrate on the thing or person, such as a rose, animal, or child, that is easiest for you to love. Enter into a state of love with it, and give it your love. For example, if it is a rose, look at and appreciate its beauty. Feel its texture. Enjoy its fragrance. Feel your connection to it. Feel how much you love and enjoy it.

After you have generated strong feelings of love within yourself, transfer those feelings of love toward yourself. Do the same thing with yourself as you did with the rose. Look directly at your body. Don't use a mirror. Appreciate your body. Look at your favorite part of the body, then at each other part of it. Touch it. Feel its texture. Feel yourself inside it. Stroke it gently. Smell the different parts of your body. Feel how much pleasure your body has given you. Love your body.

Speak kindly to it. Practice this daily until it becomes easy. It will.

The following exercise is a bit more difficult, but very effective. Do it in stages, and you will become a master in the art of loving yourself. Begin with a short time, and work your way up to ten minutes.

Loving the person in the mirror:

Sit in front of a mirror, and look into your eyes and love yourself. During this time, do not allow yourself to judge or hurt yourself. As you may know, most people look into the mirror and immediately see all the things that they think are wrong and judge them. If you find yourself doing this, immediately change the self-judgment into a loving thought and action to the self. Again, speak kindly to yourself. Look deeply into your eyes, and see the spirit, the longing, the love, and the life struggle there. Notice how beautiful your eyes are. Note the positive aspects of your hair and facial features. See how they are an expression of your spirit. Look for the child inside. See its joy, its wonderment, and its love. Now look for all the other aspects of this person. See what the person likes to do. See how these favorite pastimes have helped to shape this person into what you are today. See the knowledge of which you are caretaker. What has this person come to earth for? What are the deep longings of this person in the mirror? How can you help this person fulfill their longing? Love this person, and all that you are.

After succeeding with this one, you are ready to go to the fourth exercise.

Loving the person and body in the mirror:

Stand before a full-length mirror nude. Love and accept every part of your self and your body. Concentrate on each part of your body as you did before. Fuse your conscious awareness into it. Or imagine a tiny self just like yourself, enter into that part of your body, and simply be there. Stroke the part of your body you are concentrating on and looking at. Love it. Love the person in that part of the body. When your negative self-judgments arise, speak them out loud and feel your emotional response to them. This is what you do to yourself every time you make such a judgment. Now replace the negative judgment with a positive statement about the area of your body. Then fill it with simple loving kindness. Cover your entire body in this way. First, allow the negative to be spoken out loud so that you can become fully conscious of it and the feelings that it creates. Then replace it with the positive.

Remember, concentrate on the body part first and then on the person in that part of the body. As you do, check out how you have treated each part of your body and yourself about that part of your body. Have you been kind and appreciative? Or have you treated your body and yourself like a tyrant, demanding perfection and performance and disregarding the messages it has sent to you? You will find that there are parts of your body and yourself that you continually reject, probably many times a day. Heal this negative process in you by becoming aware of it and giving extra love to those parts of your body and yourself. Replace all the negative statements you find toward your body and yourself with positive ones.

Loving the parts of your body that are ill or deformed:

After you have covered every part of your body, bring your attention back to the parts that are ill or damaged. Give more loving attention here, accepting them exactly as they are, filling them with unconditional love and your core essence. Bring that part of your body back into the nation that is you. A key to doing this and to loving part of your body that you may feel has betrayed you is to find out what purpose in your life that part has served. I guarantee you that part of your body is teaching you a lesson or has taken some form or responsibility that you were not able to do. It has helped you survive. It has helped you tolerate some life experiences you could not tolerate without it. For example, tumors sometimes carry the energy-consciousness of filling a cavity or hole in a person's life. They fill people up when they feel empty. Weak legs help people sit down when they can no longer stand up for themselves. Misalignments in the back and neck help people control their anger because they dampen the amount of red energy that can roar up the spine in rage. When these types of problems put people in bed for a few weeks, it is because they need peace, quiet, and rest.

Once you have accepted this alienated part back into yourself and are at one with it, you can also give it a positive visualization. Tell it how it will get better. Be specific. If you have a tumor, and it has served the purpose of filling you up, tell the tumor you no longer need it to fill you up. Tell it that it can dissolve and integrate with the rest of your body. Tell the rest of the body around it to accept its integration back into the whole. Or if you have a broken bone that is having trouble healing, visualize it knitting together and growing normally, a most natural thing for it to do. If you have a chronic misalignment, visualize the muscles relaxing and getting strong in ways that hold the bones in place and clearing the fear or negative feelings associated with the physical problem.

A person I call Bob continually rejected his neck. He had a rather large neck and a double chin. This rejection went on for years. He had several neck injuries and also developed a hypothyroid. His neck was continually going out of alignment, causing a lot of pain and sometimes even mental confusion. Bob began with the mirror, and then later worked with himself as he lay in bed just before going to sleep at night.

As Bob began to heal his neck, he concentrated on loving all parts of his neck, including his double chin. Each evening when going to bed, he would put his fingers on his neck where it was weak or in pain and speak lovingly to it. He let the energy from his fingers run into his neck. As he opened up the energy blocks in his neck, he discovered many voices of fear and complaining there. In the second level of the field were all the things that he had not let himself say to others. Instead, when his block was activated, he would continually repeat the things he couldn't say to others to himself. In this way, he tried to find an acceptable way to say what he needed to say without evoking his fear, which was also held in the same place in his neck. It didn't work. It simply made the blocks in his neck stronger.

From the auric field perspective, he was continually taking energy from the fourth level, the "I-Thou" interaction level, that was in the things he wanted to say to others, and moving it down into the second level, saying them to himself. He was thereby clogging the second level.

During the healing process, Bob had to bring the energy back up to the fourth level and release it by shouting out what he had not allowed himself to say. In this way, he released the voices stuck in his throat. This, of course, also brought him into fear, which was released by feeling it. Some of the fear was from very early childhood, when he had not been allowed to "talk back" to his parents.

Under it all was an inability to ask for his needs. The throat chakra is related to speaking the truth. In Bob's case, it was to speak the truth of his needs. He realized that the only way he could get his needs met in childhood was to beg and beg for them. Then after a long wait, some of them would be met. Bob realized that his enlarged thyroid was related to filling the hole of hunger in his neck, which was there from having had to wait so long to be fed. As his healing process continued over several months, he was able to speak the truth of his needs, the energy blocks in his throat cleared, and his neck got stronger.

Then he discovered an interesting aspect he had never thought of. On several occasions he found himself in certain situations where he suddenly got extremely angry at someone. As his anger began to rise up his spine, he would stop it by squeezing his neck muscles so hard that it would throw his neck out. He then realized that the misalignment in his neck helped him to control his rage. It helped him to keep from hurting people. In other words, he chose to hurt himself rather than the person at whom he was angry. When he realized what a service his misaligned neck had given, he began to appreciate it more. He also developed better ways to control his rage by noticing how he created or got himself into situations that provoked it, by not asking for his needs and not taking care of himself. In each case, had he taken his needs seriously, he would not have been in the situation where that particular rage was provoked. His anger always emerged in situations where others were not respecting his needs. When he began to respect his own needs himself, the situations simply did not arise, or there was no rage to be provoked.

Each night, Bob touched his body and told the blocks to clear, the thyroid to shrink to normal size, and the neck to get stronger. The muscles in the neck got stronger. Soon he was able to do neck exercises that he hadn't been able to do for years. His neck quit going out of alignment. Bob took Synthroid for several months, and his thyroid function became normal. He hasn't had any neck injuries for years.

As you go through the mirror exercises, they will evoke many feelings. Allow them to flow; here is some help to do so.

Allowing Your Feelings to Flow

Allowing yourself to feel your feelings is perhaps one of the hardest things to do in healing yourself, if you haven't practiced it. Remember, the energy-consciousness of the second level is experienced as feelings about yourself. If you want the second level of the field to become balanced, clear, charged, and healthy, you must allow your feelings about yourself to flow. During an illness, your feelings will range from sadness to happiness to serenity to anger to fear to deep terror to weakness to guilt to disgust to demand to self-pity to loneliness to envy to love, and so on. All of these feelings have correlates to energy in the second level of the field, and the more you can just let them flow out of you, the more the field can clear. Part of the healing process is to simply let them flow out because they have been blocked for so long. It worked for Jeffrey and Bob, and it will work for you.

I have worked with many people, and I have never found anyone to whom this does not apply. We are all so agile at avoiding the unpleasant emotions we carry. Many of us just haven't realized how blocking the feelings blocks our creative force and actively makes what we fear more possible. On the other hand, facing the feelings and going through them releases us to create what we want in life.

Now is the opportunity to get them out. Accept them as they are. They are just feelings to let flow out and cleanse you. Do not be afraid to express negative feelings. People who are ill, who have studied positive visualization, sometimes get the idea that they should not have negative feelings, for fear the feelings or thoughts will become a negative visualization and make their illness worse. Because of this fear, they sometimes go into new levels of denial about their negativity. They may decide only a certain amount of it is allowed. After that's expressed, they go into denial about the rest of it.

I have not found the expression of negative thoughts or feelings to cause harm if it is done with certain parameters. The first is that the expression of the negativity must not be habitual. As soon as it becomes habitual, it is no longer cathartic. The other is that it must be done with a conscious positive intent for healing. If you allow all the negative thoughts to come forth into consciousness and the negative feelings to flow *with the positive intent to heal yourself*, then you will not get stuck in negativity that will harm you. The important point here is clear intention. Express the negative feelings with the intention to release them, let them go, and move on beyond them. This will help heal you. If you go into denial about your negative feelings, they will still be at work in you making you sick. They will not go away by sugar-coating.

The best way to replace the negative for positive growth is to combine the expression of the negative for release and the positive visualization. First clear the negative out of the field, and then, in the space that was emptied, replace it with the positive, bright colors of visualization.

What we want is usually the opposite of the very fear we avoid. In other words, there is a direct inverse connection between what we fear and what we want to create. The beautiful poem that follows states it clearly. It was channeled by Eva Broch Pierrakos in Pathwork Guide Lecture 190.

Through the Gateway

Through the gateway of feeling your weakness,
lies your strength.

Through the gateway of feeling your pain,
lies your pleasure and joy.

Through the gateway of feeling your fear,
lies your security and safety.

Through the gateway of feeling your loneliness,
lies your capacity to have fulfillment,
love and companionship.

Through the gateway of feeling your hate,
lies your capacity to love.

Through the gateway of feeling your hopelessness,
lies your true and justified hope.

Through accepting the lacks of your childhood,
lies your fulfillment now.

Healing Meditations

To help you continue your healing process, here are some meditations to do to heal the second level of the auric field. They are simple and easy to do and are very effective in clearing, balancing, and charging your field.

Color Breathing Meditation

Since the second level of the field contains all colors, a simple way to charge the second level is to do color breathing. You can use any colors you like. I suggest that you try the following ones: red, orange, yellow, green, blue, indigo, purple, lavender, and rose. You may wish to add white, silver, gold, and black. Get a sample of each of the colors you want to use—like a piece of cloth, paper, plastic, or glass. You may even use the rainbow colors created by the sun through a leaded-glass crystal in your window.

Be sure that you follow the instructions carefully. Do not just think about the color, or you will make yellow. By thinking, you activate the third level of your field and draw energy to it. Yellow is the color you make when you think. To keep the energy coming into the second level of the field, you must feel the color. You must become the color. You must be the color. To become a color you must enter into the feeling state of that color.

1. Hold the color in your hand, feel the color, look at it.
2. Breathe the color in. Fill your whole body with the color.
3. Become the color.
4. Now breathe the color out.
5. Breathe the color in again. This time fill your whole auric field with the color. Imagine that you are the color.
6. Feel what it feels like to be the color.
7. Now breathe the color out.
8. Repeat this several times.
9. Now breathe in the next color. Again fill your body and field with the color.
10. Repeat each color several times before you move on to the next.

As you do this, you will notice that different colors have different effects on your mood. Each color is associated with a principle or quality. If you need that attribute in your life, meditating on that color and bringing it into you will help you develop it in your life. Figure 11–1 gives a list of colors and the chakra and body parts they nourish.

FIGURE 11–1   THE CHAKRA COLORS ON THE SECOND LEVEL OF THE AURIC FIELD AND THE BODY AREAS THEY NOURISH

CHAKRA 1	red	lower part of body, adrenals, tailbone
CHAKRA 2	orange	lower pelvis, sex organs, immune system
CHAKRA 3	yellow	solar plexus area, stomach, spleen, liver, pancreas, kidneys
CHAKRA 4	green	heart area, circulatory system
CHAKRA 5	blue	throat, lungs, ears
CHAKRA 6	indigo	eyes, head, lower brain
CHAKRA 7	white	upper brain, eyes

Color Meditations for the Chakras

In Chapter 2, I gave a general description of the auric field and its chakras. Remember, the chakras serve as metabolizers of energy to the areas of the body in which they are located. If you are de-energized and weak in any particular area of the body, then it is good to wear that color or to do a little color breathing meditation. (To find out what color you need, see Figure 9–2. To do the chakra color meditation, use the drawing in Figure 2–5 to locate each chakra.)

Start with the first chakra. Bring your attention to the area of the body where the chakra is located. Imagine the chakra color on that part of your body, both the front and the back. Form the color into a six-inch-diameter disk. If you can visualize in three dimensions, turn the disk into a funnel by extending its tip into your body until the small point of the funnel touches your spine. Spin the disk or funnel in a clockwise direction on your body.* Pull the color of the disk or funnel into your body as you breathe in. As you breathe out, the color continues to come into your body. Imagine it flowing into the specific organs in that part of your body, as listed in Figure 11–1. Move on to the next chakra. Repeat several times for each chakra.

Be sure to cover all the chakras, starting with the first chakra, then continuing up the body in sequence. As you work your way up, give extra time to the areas of your body that are not well.

Self-Healing Meditation for Your Specific Dis-ease

Two wonderful books list specific meditations for specific diseases. The first is *Healing Visualizations* by Dr. Gerald Epstein. It is laid out in such a way that you can look up your particular problem and follow the visualization. He even tells you how often to do it. Another book I recommend is Louise Hay's *You Can Heal Your Life*. It gives simple mantras to be repeated for each problem you may have. These mantras are related to the belief system you probably have that is associated with your dis-ease. For example, for thyroid problems, the negative statement made by a person is "When is it my turn?" The positive visualization to change this problem is "I have all the time in the world for me."

---

* *Clockwise* as used here means as if you were outside your body looking at a clock on each chakra place. This holds for the front and back chakras. Another way to determine *clockwise* is to first curl the fingers of your right hand. Then point the thumb of your right hand into the chakra. The curled fingers point in the direction of chakra spin. Use the right hand for both the front and back of the body.

Introduction to Uncovering the Healer Within

Fantasy or myth is a very powerful healing tool that lifts us out of the ordinary reality and into a world of symbols that help us experience the broader expanses of life's journey. When we are faced with serious illness or sudden large changes in family structure, we need this help. Within such myths, we can associate ourselves with the power of the Gods, rise above the mundane, and accomplish heroic acts. Here is a metaphorical story that will help you tap enormous healing power and may even help answer questions that cannot be answered in terms of everyday reality.

In our work with this chapter, we have met the inner child who has been brutalized and wounded. We have played with that child and given it space for the expression of life. Now it is time for direct healing of this child. The wounds and illnesses of the physical body are those of the child. When we begin to walk deeply into these wounds, it may be overwhelming until we meet the healer within. Next to our inner child, we carry the healer within, who is completely capable of handling whatever we come up against in life. The healer within knows our history from the very beginning, knows our incarnational task, and deals with all our problems from that broad, wise perspective. Here is a visualization to meet the healer within you. It is a myth or fantasy for your personal healing.

~

UNCOVERING THE HEALER WITHIN
Channeled from
Heyoan

Once upon a time, aeons ago before time was known as it is today, there was a spark of light in the heart of the divine. That spark in the divine burst forth into millions of stars. Each star had a name that was written in the word of God. One of those stars is you. As a star, you grew and developed and sang across the heavens to the other stars.

In this time before you were born as a human, you knew light, love, and wisdom. Being unborn, of course you had no body, so there was a great deal of freedom. You were completely aware of the essence of your being. You had great freedom to move about the universe at your will. You moved in the direction that you focused in. With your intention, you began creating things. If you had a wish, you automatically created it.

You created stone and earth; tree and flower; star and planet; even cloud and wind. Your essence moved easily, changing from one form to another. You experienced being a cloud, a moon, a sun, or a fish, or a cat. You continued to move as your pleasure led you. As you moved from one form to another, creating more forms, you slowly became identified with form, and shadow was

born. You got so excited in the creating that memory slipped and you forgot who you were. You were so busy creating, you didn't even notice that you began to think you were form.

Shadow grew darker, and pain was born out of forgetting that the true self is essence. The true self is the creator, that which is beyond form. That is how you created shadow and pain. You forgot who you are. You split yourself in two: the part that forgot and the whole that remembers.

Within every human being, there is the spark of the divine in every cell of your body. It is the essence of self. Within that true essence of who you are is the healer within you who has all of the creative power of the universe. The healer within you is named according to the word of God. That is who you truly are.

Move your awareness now to your inner essence, your power and light that are completely unique. You are the word of God made manifest. Move your awareness to the total essence of your being—that is the healer within you. You have felt it your entire life. The golden threads of this power have been woven through the tapestry of your life since before you were born. You knew as a small child, as you know now, what this means. Feel the essence, the power, flowing through you. It is your uniqueness. It is your beauty. It is your love. It is the sweetness that you experienced life to be as a child.

Your power lies within the sweetness of who you are. It is within the sweet longings you have protected and shielded from others. You are like a flower unfolding in the sunlight. Feel the power and the nature of your divinity, unlike any other. Now ground that well in your body. That part of you is still free. That part of you can still move freely through space, time, and other realities. Feel yourself in this freedom now.

As you are moving through time and space to different types of reality, in the far distance you hear a cry. That cry wells up and becomes more audible, and you say, "Oh, what could that be?" You hear the longing in the cry for help. Then you spot it and you see the beautiful blue and white shimmering planet in the sky. You are drawn closer to that beloved planet by the cries of need. As you get closer, you say, "What can I do to help? How can I answer this cry, this call? How can I help heal the pain that is upon the earth?"

Then you have a great idea. You decide to create a physical form by drawing it up out of the earth and drawing the pain with it. You intend to use the physical form to heal the pain.

You descended into a tiny physical body. After nine months or so, you were born into this world as a human being. The longer you remained attached to that body, the dimmer the memory of your original essence became.

As a child, and perhaps way before that, you began taking on the pain. During the experience of the pain, you completely forgot who you were. When the pain would leave, you would remember. When the pain would come back, you would forget. The pain that you chose to heal grew inside of your body.

Look over your childhood. Find the deepest pain that you have carried in all those years. With that pain, you will find your deepest longing. What is it that you want to be? What is it that you longed to be as a child that you now and then thought you could never be? Did you want to move among the stars? Did you want to heal everyone on earth? Did you want to paint or to create beautiful music? Did you want to make everyone feel safe? What was it that you wanted

more than anything? If you could be or could have anything you wished on earth, have any fantasy come true, what is that fantasy? How is the unfulfillment of that related to your very deep pain?

Look backward over your life. As you moved through each moment of your life carrying that pain, there is one thread: a repeated cycle on the spiral of life, where that deepest pain from childhood has been repeated over and over and over again in the many different experiences that you have had. If you look at all of those experiences, you will find a common thread among them all. When you find that common thread, then allow yourself to begin feeling that pain. Allow your body to experience this pain. Where has it affected your body? When you feel it in your body, where does your body tense?

Explore now throughout your body where that pain has affected your psychic, your spiritual, your mental, your psychological, and your physical being. That thread runs holographically through every portion of your being, and as it runs through your body it hits in particular places that eventually become experienced as physical pain. Find it in your body. If you are sensitive to the auric field, then find it in the auric field.

As you find that pain, on whatever level it has manifested most profoundly—perhaps a fear, perhaps a problem with relationship, perhaps in a physical disorder, perhaps in your profession— then ask yourself a question: "What has this to do with my deepest longing? How is this particular problem associated with my deepest longing of who I wish to be, what I want to do with my life, where I wish to live?"

The first job you have is to heal that pain within the body. For it is by the pain in your body and life that you will learn the personal skills that you need to fill your longing, no matter what it is.

Find that pain within your body, and put your hands on it: that which you have carried for a lifetime, that darkest belief system that has the most profound forgetting, that one major, deepest pain, be it in your heart, your belly, or in your throat. Put your hand there now, and experience the consciousness there that believes in separation. It is the shadow. It believes it is separate and isolated from everything, isolated and separate with no hope. Find that pain that has been there from the earliest of days, and let that shadow begin to dissolve.

Enter into the shadow. Accompany yourself into the dungeon within the self that needs healing. Do not deny the human experience of that real pain from the human perspective. It is not a new pain. It has been there ever since you can remember. It is not the kind of pain that goes away easily, for it is deeply, deeply ingrained. Spend some time with the pain.

Then when you are ready, move your conscious awareness to the healer within you. Here is your wisdom. Here is your longing and your light with which you came here to heal the pain that is in your body.

Move back to the pain and feel the pain. Then move to the longing and feel the longing. Move back to the pain and then to the longing again. Continue moving from one to the other until you find the association between the two, until you can answer the question, "What does this pain in my life mean to me? What is it trying to tell me? What is the message it brings to me?"

While you are feeling that pain with your hands, from the human perspective, ask the essence of healer that you are what you need to do. What is the deepest cause of this pain? Ask for help to heal this pain. Ask the healer within for help to heal that which you have been unable to heal in yourself up until now. Truly ask, and it shall be answered. Ask very specifically what you can do. What is the cause? What is the belief system? What do you need to do every day?

Allow the essence of the healer within you to work through your hands to heal your body. Be a channel to heal the self. Let the light flow through you.

After you have received as much information as you can, reach for the highest spiritual reality you know; your higher self or your guides. Reach for the memory of who you are from that highest spiritual reality. You will find that the pain within you is precisely the pain that you were drawn to earth to heal, way back before you were born, when you were that wondrous spiritual being. That is who you truly are.

So reach up to that part of the self that has incarnated in order to heal the very pain that you carry within yourself and that you have carried since your birth. For it is precisely the pain you have come to heal, and it is you who have chosen to take on this pain and in doing so you chose to incarnate with precisely the best combinations of energies and wisdom and love to heal that particular pain.

That is what you have come to heal, and you are fully equipped to do so. You have fully equipped yourself to heal it. And that wondrous spiritual being that you were before your birth when you heard the cries and the longing from the earth and were drawn toward the earth is the healer within you. You are the person who knows how to heal that pain more than anyone else. That is your healer within. Be the healer within you, and heal that thread of pain that you have carried throughout your whole life. Touch your body in places you feel pain.

As you are working, move your consciousness back and forth between the healer within and the inner person who is in pain. As you continue to move back and forth, you begin to understand the relationship between the healer within you and the pain that it has come to heal. You have drawn this pain up from the earth to transform it. Give yourself plenty of time to complete this process. You are integrating the pain within, the longing that you carry within your heart, and the healer within that can heal you.

Let the healer within you draw out that pain and return you to wholeness. Move back and forth between the human with the deep pain, and the healer with universal power. Move them closer and closer together as you move back and forth until they merge. Continue the process until you become completely merged. When you feel satisfied that the merging is complete and has stabilized, I would like you to remain silent for at least an hour. Remain silent, sit in meditation, or simply get up and go for a walk in the woods.

～

As time progresses, all of the above will become easier for you. After practicing self-love and allowing feelings to flow, it is a good idea to see how it is changing your life. Do a quick self-check of how well you take care of yourself now by answering the questions given below. Then begin to nourish yourself in those areas of your life. If you are physically unable right now to do it, get someone to help you create a plan to begin after your health returns.

To assess your self-care, ask yourself:
In what areas are you lovingly nourished, and in which ones are you lacking?

How and where in your life have you not been giving yourself the love that you not only need but also deserve?

How do you neglect yourself in terms of your own health?

What have you been withholding from yourself that is possible to have or do but just seems to get put off?

What do you really want from life that you have not yet been able to create?

Is there a skill you have always wanted to learn?

How can you learn it now, or if not now, after you get well?

Healing Through Self-Awareness

Energy associated with our mental processes is found on the third level of the auric field. Remember, in the creative process through which we create our whole life, the creative energy from the core moves through the haric level, and then down through each level of the auric field on its way to the physical. In each level, it is infused with the aspect of human life existing on that level. In the third level of the auric field, the creative energy from our core is infused with individual mind. Through the individual mind, we become self-aware.

Heyoan says the main job of our minds is to focus conscious awareness. With our focused conscious awareness, we can use our perceptions to differentiate and integrate all the information coming to us. We receive clarity and understanding of ourselves and whatever situation we are in. We then can be appropriate with ourselves and the situation. Differentiation, integration, clarity, and appropriate being are essential to the creative process. When they are not present, our creations turn out to be not what we intended or else incomplete and therefore uncomfortable, embarrassing, or painful.

On the third level of the auric field, healing means increasing our conscious awareness of how we create the pleasure and joy or the pain and dis-ease in our lives. On this level, we need rational understanding of ourselves and our bodies. When we are in reality with ourselves, we place real limitations upon ourselves, and

we see what our true capabilities are. We do create unreal expectations of ourselves from our fantasy, for we do not create disappointment.

In order to be in reality with ourselves, the third level of the auric field must be healthy. When it is healthy, it is bright, lemon-yellow, clear, and well-structured. It is flexible and yet resilient. When we have a healthy third level, thinking becomes a full-life process. We integrate information flowing from the levels of the field below and above the third, in a way that does not rule over our thinking processes. In other words, balanced thinking allows input from our physical sensations and our feelings about ourselves from the lower levels of the field. It allows the input from relationships of the fourth level of the field to help us understand ourselves and, through connection with others, fill our thinking with love.

When energy flows freely from the higher, spiritual levels into the third level of divine mind, love, and will, it infuses creative principles, inspiration, and an unfolding model of purpose into our thinking. It makes our thinking holistic. Then we can understand and follow the messengers from our balancing system to reverse any dis-ease process and to create pleasure and joy.

By clearing your fears and self-judgments, you will be able to choose a healing team without their interference.

If you are afraid that you might have cancer, you may not go get tested. Or on the other hand, you may force yourself to hurry up and get it over with and not take time to choose your team. You may end up going to the most convenient, fastest place rather than the best. If you have self-judgments about being, say, overweight, you may be too embarrassed to go for help or you may deny that you need help. Overeating doesn't mean that you are bad. It is an emotional defense. There are many medical reasons for being overweight other than overeating.

But how rational are we really? One of the biggest problems we all have is our propensity for rationalizations. We convince ourselves that we are acting rationally. In fact, we are using our reason to make up excuses for unhealthy behavior that does not follow our balancing system. What is happening here, from the auric point of view, is that our emotions or will are overinfluencing our reason because of unconscious fears.

Any imbalance in the third level, or its integration of all information from other levels of our being in the third level, brings about irrationality.

When the third level of the field is rigid and inflexible, it turns from lemon-yellow to an amber color. It does not allow a healthy flow of information from the other levels of the field, and it becomes isolated. The result of this overrigidity is narrow-minded thinking, thinking that is cut off from broader aspects of aliveness. It creates set flows of energy that correspond to pigeonhole definitions of life. This type of thinking puts the mind as the primary experiencer of life. It actually becomes very irrational in its overrationality. This type of mind divides and overcomplicates everything and sees itself as the master.

On the other hand, the third level can become very light yellow, too weak, overly flexible, and too influenced by the other levels, especially the emotions. Then we have difficulty in separating out the exaggerated feeling of the moment with the longer-term reality. This results in the type of fantasy in which the individuals imagine themselves and life to be much better or worse than the one they actually are in in the present moment. They get the present mixed up with a possible future that they may be able to create through visualization, self-improvement, and a lot of work over a long period of time.

Of course, there are many different configurations in different people in which the third level is overinfluenced by certain other levels of the field and underinfluenced by certain others. It is important for us to find out how and why we become irrational. It is important for us to find out why we rationalize, what our rationalizations are, what their effect is, and what is under our rationalizations.

The Little Drunken Monkey's "Reasons Why Not"

A few years ago, I attended a short course on organizational planning. The speaker told us that in business you either get the results you want or you get "reasons why not." There are really only two categories. Our reasons why not are a tricky form of denial that we apply everywhere in our life. They give us excuses, alibis, rationalizations, justifications, or stories to explain why we didn't get the result we wanted. What they *never* give us is the results we wanted. Our mind is very good at giving us reasons why not and somehow convincing us that our reasons why not are almost as good as the results that we wanted!

Reasons why not serve to keep us in denial. With them, we avoid something in ourselves, something we are afraid of. Otherwise, there would be no need for our reasons why not. We would simply say we had no intention of doing it, whatever "it" happened to be.

Eastern mystics call the part of us from which reasons why not come, "the little drunken monkey." We all listen to the drunken monkey within our mind when we need a reason why not, especially when we have decided to maintain a diet or a formal set of exercises or pursue a different activity such as studying a new subject. Whatever our commitment, our needy child inside still "wants what we want when we want it." That's when we unconsciously call upon the little drunken monkey to give us some good rationalizations to help us get it.

The drunken monkey will be glad to tell us all the reasons why eating just one piece of chocolate doesn't "really" matter. We still claim to be on the diet. We don't admit that in fact we are not really on the diet. Or we got off it for a snack, then got back on it. Actually, although we think we've been dieting for days, we have only been on it perhaps a few hours! Smokers regularly take another cigarette and claim to have stopped smoking. I have even heard people exclaim, "I've stopped smoking. I'm down to only one pack a day." The drunken monkey serves denial. He will be glad to tell you that missing one day of exercises doesn't really matter.

Of course, many of us continue to miss even more days of exercise once we break our schedule. The drunken monkey is very careful not to mention that. In fact, if we completely forget to do it for a few months, he won't bother us. When we do remember or are reminded by someone, he will jump into action and supply us with an endless list of reasons why not. Some popular reasons why not:

"I don't have time."
"I'm too busy."
"I don't know how to do it."
"I'll stop if you stop."
"Well, you didn't stop, so I'm not going to."
"He/she made me do/not do it."
"I'm too weak."
"I don't care."
"It won't matter."
"I'm too dumb."
"I'm not good enough."
"I didn't know."
"I really didn't know there was a rule, or speed limit, or curfew."

We usually pick a few favorite reasons why not and use them for everything.

Our reasons why not work holographically throughout every aspect of our life. When we use a reason why not in one area, it automatically applies to all other areas in our life. It is habitual. For example, in the area of self-care, we may "not have time" to do our exercises or to cook, so we "just have to" eat some junk food. In another area of our life, we may "not have time" to answer our letters, call people back, reconcile our checkbook, finish a project at work, and so on.

Our denial, in the form of reasons why not, of the need to take care of our health also comes in a variety of statements. Say, for example, we haven't been feeling well for a while, and we haven't done anything about it. Our reasons why not may go something like this:

"There isn't anything wrong with me anyway."
"If I ignore it, it will just go away."
"The doctor will hurt me."
"I will heal myself."

But then, we never really take on the job of doing regular self-healing because there is no time.

Avoidance or denial keeps us away from our fear. It helps us put off facing our internal tiger. Unfortunately, it also keeps us disconnected from our balancing system and therefore will probably lead to disease.

To reconnect to our balancing system, we must face our fear. We must turn and face our internal tiger.

Exercise to Find the Fear That Keeps You from Following Your Balancing System

After spending some time learning to recognize that little drunken monkey in your head, let yourself uncover the fear that he helps you deny. This will help you learn to tell the difference between him and messages from your balancing system. Remember, denial is the first stage of healing. It is necessary to move out of denial to go to the next step in the healing process. Here is a good way to do it.

In Chapter 10, we went over the areas of daily physical self-care, and made a list of questions to ask yourself about taking care of your physical body and your auric field. Go over that list again, and note the areas with which you have the most difficulties. Now, make a list that has five columns, as shown in Figure 12–1. In the first column, put the messages from your balancing system, or the areas of physical self-care, with which you have difficulty. Then ask yourself why you are not able to take care of yourself in this way. The second column is for the desired result that you would achieve if you did take care of yourself in the way you have listed. If you flossed your teeth regularly, for example, you would have healthier teeth and gums. In the third column put the drunken monkey's reasons why not for each of your listed difficulties. For example, perhaps you don't floss your teeth at night because you are too tired. In the morning, you probably don't have time.

The fourth column brings in the holographic truth. If you scan the other areas of your life, you will notice that you habitually apply your favorite excuse to everything else. In this way, it becomes holographic.

Now, I understand that it may be that you don't have time to do certain activities because you have to take care of your kids or because of your job. But that is a matter of you choosing to balance your life according to what you want. Obviously, we all have to make choices to have all our needs met. But I'll bet you use the same "I don't have time" with your kids or in your job to avoid certain activities. Perhaps taking care of your kids is your excuse not to take care of yourself. Or perhaps you use your job as an excuse not to give yourself pleasure in other ways that you need. In that case, it is just another reason why not that you are using to avoid something within yourself.

So to fill in the fourth column, scan your life. In what

FIGURE 12–1 CHART FOR FINDING THE FEAR UNDER YOUR REASONS WHY NOT

Message from Balancing System	Desired Result	Reasons Why Not	Other Areas Affected	Fear Avoided

Health-Care Examples:

| Roger: pain in lower back | free of pain; rest | "I'm too busy to get help." | unable to complete work in all areas | fear of failure and success; fear of criticism |
| Emily: lumps and pain in breasts; time for a checkup | no lumps; no pain | "It wouldn't happen to me. I don't trust doctors." | feel unhealthy all over; feel dishonest in all areas; feel a vague sense of guilt | fear of cancer and its treatments; fear of death |

Other Life Area Examples:

| Pat: no leisure time | fun; pleasure | "I'm too busy." | intimate relationships | fear of being ostracized |
| George: blocked creativity in fine art painting | beautiful paintings; recognition for work | "I'm not good enough. I'm just too lazy." | discount everything else as not done well enough or not really important even if done well | fear of feeling self; fear of criticism; fear of deeper self that would come out in work |

other areas do you use this excuse? Observe yourself as you go through the day using your reason why not to avoid facing or doing something in various areas of your life—for example, with your spouse and children. What else do you not have time for or are too tired for? Playing with your kids? Making love? Notice how you use the same excuse for many areas in your life. List all the other areas of your life in which you use your favorite excuse in column four.

As you observe yourself using your excuse throughout other areas of your life, ask yourself, "What am I afraid of?" Let this question drop inside, and sit for several moments with your feelings. Keep sinking down into your feelings until you feel the fear. What is it that you are afraid to face? Put this fear in the fifth column. Scan all the areas of your life that are affected by this fear. The fear that you avoid facing affects all areas of your life in some way. You will find its strongest effect in the areas that are unfulfilled and that give you trouble. Explore the link between these areas and your fear. Let yourself sink into your feelings about this.

To illustrate how this works, look at the examples listed in Figure 12–1.

Roger, a construction worker, had chronic back pain from an old injury that he never gave a chance to heal. Whenever his back hurt, he ignored it, hoping the pain would go away. He knew that all he had to do was to lie down for a short time and the pain would go away. His reason why not was that he was just too busy. He had to work. He was the sole breadwinner and was proud of it.

He continued to ignore the messages of pain coming from his back. The back pain got worse. Finally one day he tried to lift a heavy suitcase. The next day he couldn't move and had to stay in bed for two weeks. His body had given him two weeks to simply lie there and feel himself. As he did so, he got in touch with feelings he never knew were there. He felt tremendous fear that if he didn't get up and work, his family would leave him. He feared that he would be criticized for being lazy and lying in bed. He knew the fear was irrational because he really couldn't move, but it came anyway. Then he realized that his parents had always criticized his older brother for being lazy. He remembered a childhood decision he had made to never be like his brother. Rather, he would be macho man! Thus, to face this childhood fear and heal his back, he had to stop being macho man.

Roger's two weeks in bed let him admit that he didn't have to be macho anymore. The first thing he did was to admit that his back needed to be taken care of. He took time to find out how to heal it. He found some very basic back care stretches and exercises and did them regularly. He went to a healer. For many months he was very careful about what he lifted. Whenever he did physical activity, he would lie down and ice his back for ten minutes. He ate only when he was hungry because he knew that low blood sugar increases the potential for reinjury.

This healing affected another area of Roger's life: his relationship with his brother. He could now drop his judgments of his brother's supposed laziness and be better friends.

The next case deals with a woman I'll call Emily, a physical therapist with lots of private clients. Emily had lumps in her breast but avoided going for a mammogram because cancer "wouldn't happen to me because I am on a spiritual path." She said that she didn't trust the doctors. She was, of course, afraid that she had breast cancer. As a result of her avoidance, she carried a constant feeling of fear and unhealthiness. She also carried a vague sense of dishonesty and guilt since she was a health-care professional. She projected the guilt for her dishonesty onto the doctor with her message of not trusting.

When she finally did go, it turned out not to be cancer. Her feelings of fear, unhealthiness, dishonesty, and guilt vanished. As a result, she had a lot more life energy and felt better about herself, especially in her work. Emily was then able to see where else in her life

she had been dishonest about herself. She stopped her constant overwork with her clients, which had given her the excuse that, since she was working to help people and was on a spiritual path, cancer wouldn't happen to her. She had actually been using overwork as an excuse to not take care of herself. She discovered that the cysts in her breasts were symbolic of her not nurturing her inner child. When she began nurturing herself, she went on a low-fat diet. Then the cysts in her breasts began to shrink. (Note that the breasts nurture the child. When she nurtured her inner child, the disease in her breasts disappeared.)

So from the broader perspective, the lumps in Emily's breasts were a result of her inability or unwillingness to take care of herself. So was her workaholism, which she used as the excuse not to take care of herself. The resulting fear, feeling of unhealthiness, and guilt were only part of the price she paid on the emotional level. The other part was that she stayed in a profession that was not right for her. Not nurturing her inner child kept her from knowing herself more deeply. When she did give her inner child more time, she changed her profession. She stayed in the health-care world but saw fewer people privately and was able to help more people through teaching.

Exercise to Clear the Denial Under Your Reasons Why Not

You can use Figure 12–1 again to do the same exercise for any area of your life in which you have difficulty—be it your profession, relationship, or leisure time. The same principle works. In the first column, state your area of difficulty. In the second, describe what you want. Give your reasons why not, then find the other areas affected and the fear avoided. Once you find the fear, face it, and clear it by feeling it, you will no longer need your denial.

A woman named Pat has no leisure time for fun. Her reason why not is that she is too busy. Other areas are affected—she has very few intimate relationships and is lonely. Her underlying fears are those of being ostracized and of intimacy. As a young child, she was not allowed to play with the other children in the neighborhood. Pat felt ostracized since she never made friends with them. The same is true now. Once she learns what the fear is under her denial, she can face that fear by purposively and regularly initiating relationships. This will be very scary for her at first, and she will probably feel rejected and ostracized several times in the learning process. But practice makes perfect. A whole new area of her life will open up. She will find the kinds of people she likes and the kinds of interests that she likes to share with others. She will learn a great deal from others. She will begin to have great pleasure from relationships and will find plenty of time for them. Eventually, she will probably even create an intimate relationship.

In another example, George wants to paint, but he blocks himself from doing it with the excuse that he is not good enough or is just too lazy. Other areas of his life that are affected are many. He does not consider anything else as important as painting. Therefore anything else he accomplishes is not really satisfying because it lacks value, even if it is done well. George considers himself lazy in other areas of work. Underneath all this is his fear of failure and criticism and, more important, his fear of his deeper self that will come out during the creative act of painting.

In order to succeed in such a creative act, a free flow of energy must be attained. The only way to attain a free flow of energy is to let everything out, including all the negative consciousness that is held in the blocked energy of the auric field. This is why many artists and writers are considered to be eccentric or to have unacceptable behavior. They do not live in the mask self of socially acceptable behavior. It is not possible to be creative and do so. In the movie *Amadeus*, the composer Salieri was appalled at Mozart's outrageous behavior and couldn't reconcile it with the beauty of Mozart's music. What Salieri didn't understand was that Mozart's way of keeping his creative force flowing was his outrageous behavior. It was Mozart's way of expressing his negative side.

Through expressive therapies, we now have better ways to attain free flows of energy, although many artists of the past did not. In therapy the expression of negative consciousness takes only a few minutes and need not be acted out. In expressive therapies people can simply yell into a pillow, pound a pillow with their fists, or chop wood while shouting all the awful things they would like to do.

Many times the undefended expressions of creative people are considered by society to be outrageous or dangerous behavior. Most of the time such behavior is not at all harmful but just breaks social rules that control people and maintain power over them. Breaking the rules brings fear to people because it initiates the transformation process and the dissolution of the mask, which leads to the uncovering of deep internal pain. What is not understood by many is that healing the uncovered pain leads to their personal light and power. The pain must be uncovered before it can be healed. It is the same principle as lancing a boil so that the infection can be cleaned out. Unfortunately, most people do not know this and therefore consider mask-dissolving behavior to be dangerous.

George is in the process of getting in touch with his denial and expressing the fear and rage beneath it. Once he starts to express the fear and rage, he will be able to begin to paint. As he continues to let go to the creative force within him, not only will his art develop, but each phase of it will bring out more fear and rage. As he clears the fear and rage from his system, it will clear more creative force so that he can paint more.

George may even be afraid of success. Because of that, the more he paints, the more he will have to clear to keep the creative energies flowing. He may even be afraid of what he might do with the power if he becomes very successful. Increased power in the world means increased power flowing through the energy field. The stronger the energy/power that flows through the field, the more the deeply and tightly held negative energy in the field is released. The only way to handle power well is to keep clearing the negative energy-consciousness that is released from deeper and deeper levels of the field (and the subconscious) as the increased power flows through.

This ongoing cycle will continue as long as George continues to clear. His creativity will never end. Of course, the process of clearing the negativity will become easier and quicker with the years and will take on new forms because as soon as one thing becomes habitual, it is no longer cathartic. If some of his rage is at his mother, expressing it will eventually become habitual. When this happens, he could very well be using it as a defense against what is beneath it. It will then be time to change his expression and go into new areas of his psyche that are perhaps even more frightening and unfamiliar to him.

A healer working with George in this process will help him clear his field through healing techniques that are not available to many therapists or body workers. The healer removes blocks that do not come out in the expressive work, charging areas that need to be charged and rebuilding parts of the field that are in distortion. The healer also teaches him how to detect the distortions and blocks produced in his field by denial and defensiveness and to return his field to normal clear functioning. Thus, his process will become much faster.

Each time George goes through a new cycle of painting, it will release creativity in other areas of his life,

FIGURE 12–2 CHART FOR CLARIFYING YOUR JUDGMENTS AND THEIR EFFECTS

Self-Judgment	What You Would Do	Good Feelings	Parental Voice	Fear Avoided	Other Areas Affected

Examples:

Self-Judgment	What You Would Do	Good Feelings	Parental Voice	Fear Avoided	Other Areas Affected
Roberta: I'm too fat.	be freer in my body; be more outgoing; be less defended; feel sexy; intimacy in life	feel beautiful; feel powerful; feel good about myself; I want sex	"Who do you think you are?" "You are arrogant. Others will know you want sex."	fear of attention fear of energy fear of sexuality	hold down sex feelings and creativity everywhere in life; not nourished in area of sex
Terry: I will never have a man/woman	have marriage, kids, house	feel full, happy, powerful	"He/she will betray me and take everything."	fear of intimacy fear of sharing fear of betrayal	no close relationships with men/women in other areas of life

such as his work and his relationship. He will find his work at a gallery more interesting. He will be surprised and happy to find that his ability to maintain deeper levels of intimacy is also growing. A lot of his denial—and the old fear and rage that were between him and the rest of the world—is gone.

If you have never done work releasing negative energy, I suggest that you try it with a healer or a body psychotherapist. It is very effective in getting through this stage of the clearing work. Once you know the technique of releasing negative feelings and thereby the negative energy-consciousness held in your field, you will be able to do it on your own when you need it without the help of a therapist. Be sure the windows are closed. It won't hurt anyone, but it will keep the juices flowing. If it is handled well, the energy released will change to great amounts of love very quickly.

Exercise to Clarify Your Judgments and Their Effects

Now let's become clearer about the areas in which you do not love yourself and have self-judgments. This time we will make a six-column chart, as shown in Figure 12–2. Make a list of all your self-judgments that came up when you were doing the self-love exercises before the mirror in Chapter 11. Put them in the first column. In the second column, make a list of all the things you would do or be like if these self-judgments were not true. Now imagine yourself doing these things. It will make you feel good. List the good feelings in column three.

Stay with the exercise and sink deeper into your feelings. If you do, your good feelings will diminish and you will eventually feel fear. This may not make any sense to you at first, but stay with it—it will. Inside, you will find your internalized parental voices, voices from other childhood authorities, or your own inner child's voice giving you negative warnings. These voices reflect your negative conclusions about reality, which are called negative images or negative beliefs. They warn you of the dire consequences that may happen if you continue to feel the pleasure of fulfilling your longing.

Remember, these voices are from your mask self, and their original purpose was to keep you good and safe—that is, safe according to your child's interpretation of what your parents or others told you would keep you safe. This may not have anything to do with reality.

If you still don't feel the fear, stay with it. These voices will eventually frighten you because they constantly remind you of what a dangerous thing life is. They tell you what you have to do to be safe. The catch-22 is you can never do everything they tell you to do. Therefore you are not safe! When you find the fear, list it in the fifth column.

As we discussed in Chapter 1, your internalized parental voices do keep you safe in a different way. They keep you safe from feeling your wound. Unfortunately, they also keep you safe from your creative energy! If you listen to and follow your internalized negative voices, your creative energy will remain locked in your mask self. If you do not follow these warnings, you will release energies within you that you have not experienced for a long time, perhaps since infancy. You may become like the artists discussed above. You may uncover your wound and have to deal with your deeper rage and pain. But it will free your life!

In addition to this, your actions may not take care of other people's masks. You may frighten them and make them angry. I am not advocating acting out your negative feelings or dumping them on someone. But I do mean claiming your independence. It may be right to stop curbing your actions because of what other people think. You may quit your job if it is not right for you or even leave your marriage if it doesn't nourish you.

Figure 12–2 also shows a couple of examples of the negative effects of self-judgments and the rewards of giving them up. Roberta's self-judgment was "I'm too fat." This self-judgment made her feel worse about herself, so she ate more. When she tried to get herself to go on a diet, another voice came up. It said, "You can't make me." She had hit her rebellion. When she worked on this in her sessions, she discovered that in her youth, her parents had tried to get her to go on a diet. It turned out that from her perspective, they tried to

make her do a lot of things. Eating was a way of claiming her freedom. The trouble was, as she grew up, she lost the ability to tell the difference between what she wanted to do and what her parents wanted her to do.

After spending time getting to know her inner child, Roberta began to be able to distinguish between what she did for herself and what she did out of rebellion. She decided she really did want to lose weight because she believed that she would be free in her body, more outgoing, and less defended.

Roberta went on a diet. As she lost weight, she began to feel that she was beautiful, powerful, good, and sexy. Then the healing crisis came. Her internalized parental voices, voices from her mask self, shouted more judgments at her: "Who do you think you are?" "You are arrogant," and "Others will know you want sex." She became afraid and, in her fear, started to eat again. The voices subsided as she again gained weight. She worked in her therapy sessions about the weight gain and recognized her fear. She went back on the diet and continued facing the fear in her process sessions. Under the fear were deeper fears: fear of attention; fear of her own energy and what she would do with it; and fear of her sexuality. (These fears are listed in column five.) Her deeper fears affected other areas of her life where she held down feelings, her sexuality, and her creative force. As she faced her fears, she was able to accept her sensitivity in being with other people so she was not so afraid of being the focus of attention. She found more pleasure in her sexuality and lost quite a bit of weight. Probably the most dramatic effect was the blossoming forth of her creativity. She became a prolific painter.

The second example, Terry, is common among both men and women, so it is written for both. These people have been single for a long time or have been divorced. The first self-judgment is that they will never have a spouse. They fear the right person will never come along. It just is never going to happen to them, and there is nothing they can do about it. They long for a full life with kids and home. They imagine that it will give them a feeling of fulfillment, happiness, and power. No matter how many people do come along, the right one never does. As soon as they begin to get intimate, all the internal parental voices warn of betrayal and loss. It is then that these men and women find something wrong with the person they have met and conclude that that person just wasn't their spouse-to-be. If these people go to therapy, they will uncover a deep-seated fear of intimacy. Their self-judgment that they will never have a spouse is really a denial of their deep fear of intimacy. Until they face this fear, these individuals never get close enough to anyone in their daily lives to create intimacy.

Exercise to Find the Truth Underlying Your Self-Judgments

Now you can see that you use your self-judgments to avoid your fear. Pretty tricky, eh? It's even trickier than you thought! Your judgments are really reasons why not. Now, using Figure 12–2, relabel the first and fourth columns "Reasons Why Not," and the second "Desired Results." Next time you have self-judgments, become aware that they are only reasons why not clothed in a nasty costume.

If you have self-judgments about going to a doctor or healer to get help, they are probably reasons why not to go and get the problem taken care of. Some common reasons why not in the form of self-judgments are:

"I'm just a hypochondriac."
"I just can't take a little pain."
"I'm a coward."
"I won't bother the doctor with my insignificant little complaints again."

These cover a fear of facing the truth of your situation so that you can do something about it.

With the help of these exercises, you will be able to stop the negative effects of your fears on your rational processes and move into clarity. Once you have gone out of denial, gone to a physician or healer, and received a diagnosis or disease description, you will need to go through the process again. Remember, this process will be even harder once someone has told you that there is something wrong, no matter what language they use. If you are physically feeling very bad, are disoriented, or do not have much energy, it will be even harder. Get someone close to you to help you.

Be sure to use the charts in Figures 12–1 and 12–2 to help you choose your health-care professional team. The charts will help make the practical information very valuable. Once you have the information you need, you will be able to sort out your reasons why not, know what to do, and figure out how to act appropriately to manage your dis-ease.

Getting a Rational Understanding of Your Illness and Your Healing Path

In Chapter 8, we discussed the importance of knowing what is going on in your body and auric field, as well as knowing the different kinds of treatment modalities available. It is good to do this before you get ill. But if you are already ill when you read this, now is the time to understand the mechanics of your illness and the healing process you will choose to go through. All of these things will help you focus on and give in to your healing process.

For example, if you hurt your back and know you need two weeks in bed, then you will be able to surrender to that schedule. You will be much better able to utilize your time for going deep inside in order to heal yourself of the deeper issue that lies under the back pain. Otherwise, every few days when your back feels better, you may assume you are well and stop resting. That is a good way to reinjure it.

Of course, it is important to know that everyone's healing process goes at its own pace. Your physician or healer can only give you general guidelines to help you understand what may be ahead of you. What you go through will be your own experience at your own pace. None of the information you get about what your healing process will be like, and how long it will take, is a promise that this is how it will be. Rather, it is how it usually is. It is very important to not set up rigid expectations of what your experience will be. This could be a setup to get upset when it doesn't turn out to be that way. Rather, the idea is to be able to get a good overview of your probable healing process so that you can adjust your life accordingly.

Finding the Health-Care Professionals Available to You

Remember, it is always better to know how to get information about illness and the different kinds of methods to treat it before you get ill. If you don't want to spend time doing this, at least make some connections now with people you know who have access to this information, just in case you need it someday. I suggest that you get a family physician and have a yearly checkup in which you can also check him or her out. Find out which hospitals serve your area. Do a little research on what other treatment methods—like acupuncture, homeopathy, deep tissue work, body psychotherapy, and naturopathy—do and whether they are available in your community. Check all of the health-care professional possibilities. It is a bit like getting insurance or learning first aid. Appendix B lists possibilities and how to locate them in your area. It also lists what they can do for you.

If you become ill, in addition to seeing your physician, I recommend that you get nutritional advice, body work of some kind, like hands-on healing, and some therapeutic work to deal with the psychological aspects of your dis-ease. Therefore, it's good to have at least four professional people on your healing team that are willing to work together.

Diseases are described in different ways depending upon the discipline used. To help you get a broader understanding of the dis-ease process going on in you, I suggest you read about it in at least four major disciplines. The Bibliography lists suggested reading about different disciplines that describe dis-ease from different points of view.

Now that you know whom to ask, where to find them, and how they look at disease, you can put together the mechanics of your healing plan with your team of health-care professionals. Here is an ideal list of the five major areas in which to get professional help. I realize you may not be able to do all five, but do as many as you can.

Five major areas of professional help in your healing plan:

1. Get a diagnosis from your physician (M.D., N.D., D.O., or homeopath), with prognosis and recommended treatment.
2. Get a disease description of your body and auric field from your healer, with prognostication and treatment program.
3. Get a nutritional analysis and dietary program.
4. Get a diagnosis of your problem from your other health-care professional—a structural body worker or an acupuncturist.
5. See a therapist to deal with the emotional issues related to your disease.

You may have to interview many candidates for your work. This may be a problem because most health-care professionals don't have time to devote to such interviews. And you may be too ill to do so. You or someone who is helping you will most likely have to ask their staff. Don't be afraid to. Remember, you are hiring them for a service. This requires that you be-

come as informed as possible about the services that they provide. Again, it is better to pick them out as your regular support system before you get ill. If you didn't do it before, then do the best you can now. Don't be afraid to ask for help. Your friends may be very helpful in this area. They may have had many experiences with physicians that they have never mentioned to you before, so just ask. It may not always work out, because everyone is different and your friends may like particular physicians' styles more than you do.

I've listed some questions below that are not usually asked by patients. Yet if we hired someone to do any other job for us, we would feel free to ask them. Since healing is a relatively new field in this country, people regularly ask me such questions. Asking them helps to set up clearer communications between the client and myself, and helps clarify what I could do for them. I have met some physicians and health-care professionals who are willing to answer questions like these. And if clients are willing to keep asking, more healers will accept it. You are not insulting anyone by asking such questions. Rather, you are showing your interest in getting the best care possible. That should be respected.

Some good things to find out about your health-care professionals' experience in their field:

What training do they have?

What are their skills?

What do they have to offer you?

What are the newest and best ways to treat what you have?

How long have they been doing health-care/healing work?

How many patients have they seen who have your illness?

What results did they get with them?

What results do they expect to get with you?

What type of information can/will they give you?

The field of medicine is so complicated now that you most likely will want someone who has spent some time working in the area of medicine in which you need care. Experience and keeping up with the latest developments and new treatments really do count in a lot of diseases. Remember, the quoted statistics are usually national and may not be at all true for the people or hospital you are considering going to. Asking specific questions, like the number of patients with your illness whom a health-care professional has seen, and their results, gives you grounded information about the reality of his or her experience in the area of health care that is most important to you. Some health-care professionals believe in giving a minimum of information. Some hold it back until they feel the client is ready to hear it, and some tell everything in a rather blunt way. Notice how the people you interview speak with you. Make sure you like their style before getting in too deep and being told serious information in a way that is not compatible with your emotional makeup.

All health-care professionals have a network from which to draw. Find out about this by asking the following questions.

Some good things to find out about the support system your health-care professional has:

What other connections or facilities do they have access to?

What is their support community?

Which hospital will you be going to if you need to go? What is its reputation?

What facilities does this hospital have?

Is this the right hospital for your disease? (Different hospitals specialize in different diseases, especially the rare or difficult-to-heal ones.)

How long have they been treating patients with your particular disease? Are they familiar with this disease?

Is there anyone on the hospital staff who understands your point of view and will support your way of healing?

Do you have to go to a special laboratory for tests? Where is it?

There are many different kinds of chemotherapy. The best kind for you may not be given at a local hospital. It is better to make the effort to travel for the best treatment. If you happen to be one of the people looking for a heart transplant, this matters a great deal. Since the first successful heart transplant, many hospitals have added facilities to provide that service. However, their success rates vary drastically. Make sure you get the statistics on survival rate and number of patients treated from that particular hospital rather than the national average. I realize that all of this may seem impossible once you are ill, but it will help a lot in the long run. Get someone to help you. If you can't explain it, show them this book.

Once your team is put together and you understand a bit more about how they view the disease process from their discipline, the next step is to put together your healing plan. You will need the following information to choose a treatment modality.

Good questions to ask about treatment modalities:

What are the steps of the treatment modality?

What is the treatment's effectiveness?

Where is the closest treatment facility?

What are the side effects?

How much will hands-on healing reduce these?

What is the cost of such programs?

How much does your insurance cover? (Ask your insurance company.)

What will you have to do to complete these programs?

What will it feel like?

How long will it take?

What is the length of convalescence after the treatment program?

How much does healing reduce this time?

How long, what kind of, and how much help will you need at home?

How much bed rest will you need?

How can you help clear your body of the drugs you will use by using cleansing diets, herbs, homeopathic remedies, vitamins, and hands-on healing?

Once you have this information, it will not be so difficult to choose your combined treatment plan. Remember, the success of the treatment plan depends a lot on your sticking to it and doing your part.

Laying Out Your Healing Plan with Your Health-Care Professional

After choosing your team, make the most detailed plan that you can, in terms of what will be needed as you move through the steps of the healing process. This plan should include diet, food supplements like vitamins and minerals, exercise, meditation, medications or herbs, and specific treatments. This level of treatment will be supported by your personal transformation process. Remember, you will go through the stages of the healing process as described in Chapter 7.

If you have found a healer and a physician who will work together, review Chapter 6 on the healer-physician team. Encourage the healer and physician to find a common language to discuss your case so that they can work together to create the most effective healing plan available to you.

Visualizations for Self-Healing

A big part of what you do besides getting the treatment will be healing visualizations like the ones given throughout this book. They deal with each level of your being, how to clear your field, how to work with specific areas of your body that are sick, and how to open your creative processes. Other sources for healing visualizations are suggested in the Bibliography.

It is well worth noting that the process of visualization, which requires that you continue to imagine how good you really want things to be and how good it will feel, will evoke negative reactions, as depicted in Figures 12–1 and 12–2. When these negative voices do arise, it is important to let them speak. Do not suppress the negative voices back into denial. You have worked hard to allow them space. Let them speak, but do not let them win. When you hear them, you will recognize them for what they are, which de-powers them. Of course, they may win more some days than others. Do not fear this. In the long run, they will lose. Your intention to heal yourself will help you pick yourself up and keep going forward into your real self, which will heal you. On those days when the negative voices seem to be winning, just surrender and do nothing but pray. Let go. Rest. You will move into peace. The next day will be better.

Once you have recognized the negative voices for what they are, replace the negative voices with a positive one. By returning to and staying with images of how good you want your life to be each time the negative voices and feelings arise, you create what you want. By sticking to it, you eventually get through and clear all the negative voices and the fears beneath them and replace them with positive images and creative energy. Essentially, think of visualization as being a means to direct the creative energy that is released through the process of clearing denial and negative feelings. You are creating another habitual behavior, but this time it is a positive one. An interesting thing about the human mind is that if something is repeated often enough, the mind acts as if it is true. That is how you started believing the habitual negative voices in the first place. Now you just need to replace them with positive voices. It really works! Thus the process of visualization is another very positive way to face your fears and feel your feelings.

HEALING AND RELATIONSHIPS

"When I look back, usually I'm sorry for the things I didn't do rather than for the things I shouldn't have done."

—Malcolm Forbes

The Importance of Relationships to Your Health

As I continued to work with and teach about health and the human energy field, I became increasingly aware of how important our relationships are to our health. In fact, our relationships are central to our health. Everything is relative and connected. Nothing is isolated, and nothing can be done in isolation. Not even our thoughts are isolated. Everything that we feel, think, and do is in relationship to each other, the planet, and the universe. As is well known in science, every event that occurs is always in relationship to all other events. All events are relational. We are holographically connected in relationship to everything else, as well as to all events. Therefore our health and well-being are always in relationship to everything.

As I began exploring our relatedness in healing, I found that the cause of every illness that we have is always connected to our relationships. Healing ourselves with respect to our relationships became the central theme of my work. I have devoted the next three chapters to showing how our relationships affect our health and how healing through the context of relationship and the human energy field changes our lives and our physical bodies in wonderful, fulfilling ways.

Creating Healthy Relationships

As we become clearer in our self-awareness, we can begin applying that self-knowledge to the relationships we create. We see that the same reasons why not that we apply to ourselves, we also apply to relationships. We have discussed how to clear our reasons why not to get the desired results in our lives. Now we can learn to do the same thing in terms of relationships. A simple tool to do this with is by using the concept of contracts.

The Unspoken Contracts We Create in Our Relationships

All our relationships with others can be viewed in terms of contracts. Contracts create boundaries that define and maintain acceptable relational behavior patterns. The contract of a relationship is made up of unstated, usually unconscious agreements between people about how they will act with each other, including what they will and won't say and do. Contracts can be made between two people, or they can be made within or between groups of people, where they are expressed as social norms.

We will concentrate here mostly on contracts between two people. However, everything that will be said can also be applied to contracts between an indi-vidual and a group and between groups, no matter how large they are. It also can be applied to your individual and humankind's relationship to the planet, on which I will focus a bit at the end of this chapter.

Healthy positive relationships are interdependent and have clearly established contracts of honesty, sup-port, and caring between friends. In them there is plenty of room for freedom, creativity, and self-expression, as well as healthy care and concern for each other. These positive contracts promote the growth of each person involved. On the other hand, codependent relationships are created through negative, unhealthy contracts that limit, trap, use, control, and even intimi-date the people in them. They block creativity, personal expression, and personal freedom and interfere with the natural personal growth of each person involved.

We all create both positive and negative contracts. Most of the time these contracts are unconscious and work automatically. The areas of our lives that flow smoothly and fulfill us are the areas where we have created positive contracts with others, based on mutual positive beliefs. For example, the experience of work-ing at a task with others in an easy manner that gets the job done is based on a positive contract that states that clear thinking, a willingness to work, and cooperation between individuals work best to accomplish the task. This contract is based on a positive belief, and on the belief that the world is a place that supports such positive mutuality.

In our problem areas, we create negative contracts with others. As we live within a limited view of reality, we adopt certain attitudes, stances in life, and ways of living that help substantiate our limited view. In doing so, we form negative psychological contracts to insure that others will behave in certain ways with us that reflect our limited view of reality. The primary reason for these contracts is to avoid certain feelings and experiences that we do not want to have. With our negative contracts, we freeze our life energies and thus also freeze a lot of creative energy within us.

Underlying a negative contract is not only our fear of life experience but our negative belief about how the world is. Usually this belief is unconscious and stems from childhood trauma. For example, a child whose father severely punishes or abuses her may grow up believing that men are cruel. Her early experience of the man in her life, her father, taught her that. As an adult, she may very well avoid men or have trouble in relationships with them due to her negative expectations. She will set up negative contracts that keep men away, or she will get into relationships with cruel men. These relationships will prove her belief that men are cruel.

Contracts, once set up, are placed in motion and remain in motion. Each time a negative contract is fulfilled, it serves to strengthen the negative attitude about life and reality that it supports. These negative beliefs grow stronger and limit us more in life each time we circle around through another negative experience. The auric configuration that corresponds to them gets more distorted each time. Another way to say this is that a negative contract strengthens a negative thought form or belief.

The energy-consciousness related to a negative belief shows up in the energy field as stagnation and distortions in the seventh level. These distortions slowly get transferred down through the other auric levels. At the relational or fourth level the distortions show up as stagnations or blocks in the field of a single person or as negative auric field interactions between people. Thus a field distortion at level seven, revealing a negative belief system, is transferred down to level four, where it expresses itself as a negative contract through fourth level field interactions with others. The more a negative contract is acted out in relationships, the greater the distortion on the fourth level of the field. The distortions continue to be transferred down through the lower levels of the field until they reach the physical body. Eventually, they are expressed as discomfort and illness in the physical body.

Since both positive and negative contracts work holographically, we habitually make the same type of contract with many people. Any process of healing requires an uncovering and dissolving of all of these negative contracts. As these negative forms or patterns in the auric fields of relationships are cleared through hands-on healing and personal process work, the psychological perspective of negative life stance, negative beliefs, and the actions or behavior patterns they exhibit dissolve and are replaced by positive ones.

Exploring Negative Contracts

First, we will explore how negative contracts come about, look at their format, and discover how to dissolve them. Then we will learn how to create positive contracts with intimate partners, friends, and health-care professionals.

A typical negative contract starts in childhood between parent and child, especially if there is hardship in the family. Consider the case of Gary, a boy whose mother has to work and is exhausted and preoccupied with money matters when she gets home. She will not be able to give her son what he needs. Gary will do all kinds of things to get her attention. When he finds one that works, he will use it again and probably keep using it as long as it works. He discovers that if he helps her or takes care of her when she feels bad, he gets her attention. He unconsciously confuses this attention with love. Thus he gets the message that he must take care of his mother to get her love. This, of course, is the reverse of how it ought to be. Unconsciously, Gary concludes that if he doesn't take care of Mom, then he won't get Mom's love. Thus he learns that love has a price. After the dynamic is repeated several times, it becomes habitual and continues into adulthood, where it takes the form of unhealthy, exaggerated caretaking. Whenever he gets involved in a relationship with a woman, he always ends up taking care of her in an exaggerated, unhealthy way, be it his wife, his business partner, or an employee. Deep inside, he believes this is necessary in order to get love. Of course, this reason is unconscious. He just knows that every time he gets into a relationship, he takes too much responsibility and gets sucked dry. He then begins to avoid relationships because they are just not worth all the work. This brings him into a vicious cycle of neediness, despair,

FIGURE 13–1 GARY'S NEGATIVE CONTRACT

PERSON'S NAME: *Mother*

If I Do/Don't	He/She Will/Won't	Unconscious Belief	Immediate Price	Supported Negative Belief	Other Areas of Life Affected	True Price
If I do take care of Mom . . .	She will love me.	I have to take care of Mom in order to get her to love me.	I take care of Mom, but I don't get her love.	Relationships suck energy and don't really fill my needs.	I pay for love everywhere in other forms, e.g., by giving money, gifts, personal time.	I am tired of this burden. I avoid relationships. The price is too high.

resentment, and then withdrawal. He will, at times, even choose to isolate himself.

The chart in Figure 13–1 helps clarify the steps in the negative contract that Gary habitually sets up. Remember that the caretaking in this negative contract is exaggerated caretaking. It is taking care of an adult when he or she doesn't need it, as if he or she were a child. The first column is labeled "If I Do/Don't." This refers to the actions that Gary unconsciously believes he must do in order to get what he needs. In this case, he believes he must take care of his mother, or any other woman with whom he is involved. The type of caretaking is all-inclusive, as if his mother or the other woman were a child. He takes responsibility for her and her life, as if she couldn't. Therefore in column one we put: *If I do take care of Mom.*

The second column, labeled "He/She Will/Won't," is for the results Gary believes he will get if he follows his unconscious belief. In this case, he believes he will get Mom's or another woman's love. We put: *She will love me.*

The third column, labeled "Unconscious Belief," is for Gary's unconscious belief about what he has to do in order to get what he wants: *I have to take care of Mom in order to get her to love me.*

The "Immediate Price" in column four is the short-term price Gary pays because his belief is erroneous. He not only has to take care of Mom or the woman in his life, he doesn't even get her love that way: *I take care of Mom, but I don't get her love.*

Column five, labeled "Supported Negative Belief," is for the broader negative unconscious belief that this proves through experience. For Gary, it is: *Relationships suck energy and don't really fill my needs.*

Column six, labeled, "Other Areas of Life Affected," is for the holographic effect of the broader negative unconscious belief in other parts of life: *I pay for love everywhere in other forms, e.g., by giving money, gifts, personal time.*

The last column, labeled "True Price," gives the results on the personal, psychological level for this unconscious belief. It gives the long-term effects on Gary's life. All the giving doesn't buy the love he was seeking to get in the first place. He may get attention and praise, but he will never get love. This causes disappointment, disillusionment, and a lot of resentment about relationships. He concludes: *I am tired from this burden. I avoid relationships. The price is too high.*

Gary is pretty unhappy by this time. His feelings probably fluctuate between being burdened and resentful and going into isolation. It is possible to get caught in a vicious cycle between exaggerated caretaking and isolation for many years.

To get out of this vicious cycle, Gary must take the chance of challenging his negative belief and facing the results he fears. He must reverse the behavior that is dictated by his unconscious belief. If he continues his caretaking long enough, he may get mad enough to stop being such a nice guy and stop the exaggerated caretaking of the women in his life—be they Mom, his wife, business partner, employee, sister, or friend. Most likely, more than one woman is involved here. He has developed this type of relationship with most of the women he knows. He may just start with one. But if he is successful, he will be able to transform his negative belief and his resultant actions in all the areas of his life affected by it. He will be surprised to see what the results turn out to be.

FIGURE 13–2   POSITIVE RESULTS FROM DISSOLVING GARY'S NEGATIVE CONTRACT

PERSON'S NAME: *Mother*

If I Do/Don't	He/She Will/Won't	True Result	Positive Belief Supported	Other Areas of Life Affected	Positive Results to Me	Positive Results to Other
If I don't take care of Mom . . .	She will not love me.	Mom still loves me. I don't have to buy her love!	I am lovable; love has no price.	I no longer have to buy love anywhere.	I give and receive more love and create fulfilling relationships.	Mom stands on her own two feet. She gets love rather than service.

Now let's use Figure 13–2 to dissolve Gary's old negative contract and create a healthy relationship with Mom and the other women in his life. The first column, labeled "If I Do/Don't," is for the reverse action that Gary will not take. In this case it is: *If I don't take care of Mom.*

The second column, labeled "He/She Will/Won't," is for the feared result when the action is reversed. In this case his fear is: *She will not love me.*

Gary's mother may complain at first. She may become more needy and demand the old status quo. Gary may fear that she will leave him or get sick. He may also feel bad about himself for a while. Usually this is not real, because the kind of exaggerated caretaking he has been doing is not what she needs. Of course, when someone is ill, the line between healthy and unhealthy caretaking is different and may be more difficult to find. (We will address this in the next section, "Creating Healthy Relationships with Your Family and Friends.") In the long run, all will work out. It will turn out that Gary's mom still loves him, even if he doesn't take care of her in the old unhealthy way. The third column, the "True Result" for breaking a negative contract, shows how well things turned out! In this case: *Mom still loves me. I don't have to buy her love!*

At first, Gary may not believe that it is true and will have to test it for a while. He will go back and forth between unhealthy and healthy caretaking. As he learns the difference between the two, he will find a new world opening up. He will see that his mother still loves him as he goes through the process of sorting his life out. Since she still loves him even though he is not taking care of her in the old unhealthy way, his life experience now supports a new positive belief. It is listed in the fourth column, under "Positive Belief Supported." He understands that: *I am lovable; love has no price.*

Gary understands that you really can't make anyone love you, no matter what you do. Love flows naturally from people who can love. It is a gift of life. Now the release begins. It snowballs into all the other areas of his life. He is also lovable in those areas, and love can't be bought nor need it be. This is shown in column five, "Other Areas of Life Affected." Gary figures out: *I no longer have to buy love anywhere.*

Gary has stopped buying love anywhere in his life because he knows he deserves it. He will not have to isolate himself anymore. He is now free to make relationships because they will no longer be a burden to him. He will be able to get his needs met in the relationships. Instead of the cycle of exaggerated caretaking, resenting, and isolating himself from his mother, he now freely gives love. There is a beautiful flow of love between him and the women in his life. Column six, "Positive Results to Me," shows the results for Gary, now relieved of his burden: *I give and receive more love and create fulfilling relationships.*

This has immediate wonderful positive effects for all the women in Gary's life. He no longer takes care of them in an unhealthy way. This leaves him free to love them. This challenges them to take their power and to take care of themselves. They also now get love rather than caretaking as a substitute for it. The women in his life now have the choice to also dissolve their side of the contract to stay in the relationship or to break the relationship. Column seven lists "Positive Results to Other." In this case, what the mother will most likely do is find real love within herself: *Mom stands on her*

FIGURE 13-3 CHART FOR CLARIFYING YOUR NEGATIVE CONTRACT

PERSON'S NAME: _____

If I Do/Don't	He/She Will/Won't	Unconscious Belief	Immediate Price	Supported Negative Belief	Other Areas of Life Affected	True Price

own two feet. She gets love rather than service. So do all the other women in his life.

Wow, what a deal! It's good for everyone! Of course, this works for a girl whose father is both caretaker and provider as well.

Creating Healthy Relationships with Your Family and Friends

You will need to change your interactions within the many intimate relationships you have. So during your healing process, you will find yourself changing friendships, some perhaps more substantially than others. If you learn how to distinguish what these contracts are, dissolving or breaking them and making new contracts will be smoother. The more conscious you are of this process, the less likely you will be to establish negative contracts again.

Have you noticed that in order to be with certain people, you have to play a certain role or be a certain way? This is the first sign of a negative contract. On the other hand, there are people with whom you can be yourself completely. You don't have to hide anything or convince them of anything. Yet you know that they will honestly tell you whatever they think of a given situation, even if you don't like it. That is a sign of a positive contract.

Exercise to Find Your Negative Contract

To check out your relationships, build a chart using Figure 13-3, like the one we used in Figure 13-1. This chart can show your negative contract. You can use it to observe any relationship you are in, whether it be a long-term relationship or a new one. I suggest you start with a particularly difficult relationship, with which you are having trouble. Choose the type of relationship in which you are uncomfortable, and find yourself acting in ways you don't like. Perhaps you are not even aware of these actions when you are in the presence of the person, but after he/she leaves, you are left with an uneasy or bad feeling. You may not know what is wrong, but you do know that something is wrong. Review how you acted with the person that is different from how you are in the presence of people with whom you are comfortable. What are you doing differently? That action is the action that you unconsciously believe you must do in order to get what you need from this person. Write your false action in the first column, labeled "If I Do/Don't."

To find out why you do such actions, you must find your underlying emotion. Usually it is fear. What are you afraid the person will or won't do if you do not act according to your negative belief? To find this fear, imagine yourself in the typical situation with the person with whom you are having trouble. Now imagine yourself doing an action opposite to the one you think you have to do. In your imagination, watch what the other person does in reaction to your action. List whatever you imagine they would do in column two, "He/She Will/Won't."

Now you understand that if you stop your false actions, you are afraid that the other person will do whatever is listed in column two. Therefore your false actions are to control the other person's behavior. They show what you believe you have to do in order to get the person to do what you want. Column three is for your "Unconscious Belief." It reflects the immediate result that you will have if you both keep your negative contract. Fill it in: *If I do/don't (your false action) then he/she will/won't (his/her imagined behavior toward you).*

For example, suppose that it is someone that you are afraid to contradict, disagree with, or challenge. You might write: *If I do not challenge (name), he/she will support me.* Or: *If I do challenge (name), he/she will not support me. Or he/she will undermine me, perhaps publicly.*

In another example, you are ill, and you are ashamed or afraid to ask for your needs to be met with your partner. You have been the caretaker, and now the tables are turning. Your partner just wants you to hurry up and get back to normal. But you have very real needs: *If I do not ask for (what you need), he/she will be nice to me.* Or: *If I do ask for (what you need), he/she will be angry.*

The next column is for the price you pay for this result. What is the effect on you of doing your false action, for not being who you naturally are? How have you not expressed yourself? How have you not been who you are? List what you find in column four, "Immediate Price."

In the first example, we have: *If I do not challenge (name of person), I do not speak my truth or act the way I believe. I do not express who I am. I do not create the power in myself that comes from living my truth. If I do not challenge (name of person), I will not be challenged back, and I will not give myself the opportunity to find out what needs to be changed inside me.* In the second example, we have: *If I do not ask for my needs when I am sick, I may get sicker.*

Because of these lacks in your life, you begin to see and feel yourself in a false way. You begin to believe you are less than who you truly are. Your false actions limit your expression, and you believe that the limited you is the real you. What do you think about yourself when you do this? How has this action stifled your creativity? Your life experience? Your life task?

If you relate to the first example above, you may see yourself as a coward. As a coward, you do not express your creativity because you are afraid someone will be challenged by it and undermine or attack you publicly. By not expressing your creativity, you do not create your life's dream. If you relate to the second example above, you may be disgusted with yourself for being sick. You may feel that you are a burden to everyone. You begin to believe that the world is a world that supports the falsely limited you. What is the general negative belief that says the world is a place where the

above limitations are good to have? In column five, list the "Supported Negative Belief," or thought form, that you give energy to every time you do this false action.

In the first example, the supported basic negative belief would go something like this: *Expressing my truth and my creativity is dangerous and leads to public attack.* In the second example, the supported basic negative belief is something like: *When I have needs or am sick, people will be angry. I must never get sick. Having needs is dangerous.*

Your negative belief hampers you holographically throughout your entire life. List all the "Other Areas of Life Affected" in column six.

If you relate to the first example, you may avoid challenge in many areas and many other ways in your life. You may avoid self-challenge. You may block your creativity everywhere whenever it is challenged. If you relate to the second example, you probably do not ask for your needs in many or all other areas of your life.

The price you pay is not just the immediate short-term price shown in column four. The true price is that your negative contract or negative belief limits you in all areas of your life and keeps your life from moving forward. List the "True Price" in the seventh column.

If you relate to the first example, the true price may be a life that is void of challenge, and therefore stagnant, dull, and unfulfilling. If you relate to the second example, the true price may be a life of unmet needs and deprivation. You may not even know what real needs are. You may not understand the needs of others.

Exercise to Dissolve Your Negative Contract

On the other hand, if you break the negative contract, then you will probably not like the reaction of your friend or the immediate result you will get. But in the long run it really pays off. Make another chart, using Figure 13–4, to show the results of breaking your negative contract. (It will be like Gary's, in Figure 13–2.)

The first column is "If I Do/Don't." Fill it in. The second column is "He/She Will/Won't," the feared price. It is the price you believe you would have to pay and are hoping to avoid paying. Fill it in.

In our first example, we have: *If I do challenge (name), he/she will not support me or he/she will undermine me, perhaps publicly.* In our second example we have: *If I do ask for (what you need), he/she will be angry.*

Now it is time to pay up. You don't want any debts carried over into your new way of being. You will be surprised at what the price turns out to be. Try doing your *true action* rather than your false action just to see

FIGURE 13–4 POSITIVE RESULTS FROM DISSOLVING YOUR NEGATIVE CONTRACT

PERSON'S NAME: _____

If I Do/Don't	He/She Will/Won't	True Results	Positive Belief Supported	Other Areas of Life Affected	Positive Results to Me	Positive Results to Other

what happens. Your true action may be the opposite of your false action, but not necessarily. You may find an even better one! Column three, labeled "True Results," refers to the actual result that occurs. Fill it in.

In our first example, your true action may be the opposite of your false action: you challenge the person you are afraid to disagree with. You state your opinion about something that may be directly opposed to his/hers. You do not need to do this in a combative way. Simply state your opinion without a negative energy charge. The person may do many different things. He/she may challenge you back, and you may have a lively discussion in which you both learn a great deal by listening to each other and by explaining what you are trying to communicate in several different ways. You will find that the situation is not as black and white as your inner child believes it to be. If the person does undermine you publicly, then you also challenge that. If you continue to speak your truth and be open-minded, you will learn a great deal and feel your power. Your creativity will be released through the challenge that you have given to yourself by doing this in the first place. You will learn through interaction. Therefore, the "True Result" is: *I can challenge (name of person) and be safe, and even learn something!*

In the first example, the feared price is not only the counterchallenge of the person you were afraid to challenge. You will also face the possibility of public undermining. You will be challenged to distinguish between true reality and your projection of reality that comes from your negative belief system.

If you try our second example of asking for your needs when sick, you will be surprised that the person

you ask will respond differently from what you expected. He/she may be very attentive to you. He/she may need to be reminded of what you need. He/she may immediately begin to think of other needs you have that need to be filled. He/she may become resentful if you are sick for a long time. But if you keep talking, you will both find solutions. You will begin to understand and know your needs in a different way. You will find that they are reasonable human needs. Therefore the "True Result" for our second example is: *When I ask, my needs get met.*

Column four is for the "Positive Belief Supported" through your new actions. Fill it in. To get an idea of what it could be, check out our two examples. For our first example, the positive belief that is supported is: *The world is a place of truth. Truth is safe, builds power, and opens creativity.* For our second example, the positive belief supported could be stated as: *My needs are natural human needs. I can know what they are, ask for help, and get them met. The world is a place in which needs are natural and can be filled.*

In column five, list the "Other Areas of Life Affected" by the positive belief that you have supported through your new actions and that challenge your fear. You will find that all parts of your life are affected. In our first example, if you began to challenge someone you did not challenge before, you probably will begin to challenge all parts of your life and the people in them in ways that you have not done before. You will challenge yourself to live in your truth and be more creative in all aspects of your life. In the second example, you will begin asking not only for what you need, but for what you want. You will be able to distinguish between the two. You will most likely do this in all areas of your life.

The "Positive Results to Me" (in column six) will be vast. If you relate to our first example, you will gain more self-confidence, more freedom, and more creativity in your life by taking on more challenges. You will greatly improve your self-esteem. In the second example, you will find more nurturance and fulfillment in your life as you learn more about your true needs and how to fill them. You will also learn about what you want and be able to go for it.

In the last column, list the "*Positive Results to Other.*" How have others benefited from your changing your behavior? List the benefits to others in the last column. In our first example, the first person to benefit from your changed behavior besides you may be the person whom you challenge. This challenge will help them grow if they wish to, because they can learn a great deal about themselves from it. Your immediate family will benefit from your increased power and creativity because you will not only challenge them to go for theirs but will set an example for them. Of course, you will probably challenge them on their habitual patterns also!

In our second example, the person whom you ask to help you fill your needs will immediately be given a chance to express his/her loving and giving. He/she may be challenged to find out how much he/she is able to give and love and find greater depths of love within. He/she will also learn how to communicate better, through the give-and-take of caring for someone who is ill. If he/she has not already done so, he/she will also learn how to recognize and fill his/her own needs. He/she will also learn how to ask for what he/she wants, because you are a model for learning to fill needs.

The Benefits of Breaking Negative Contracts

The more negative contracts you break in this way, the more freedom, creativity, and power you will have—and the safer you will feel. Once you have released yourself into a new way of being, your positive belief system will be activated. This will spread throughout your life holographically. You may be very surprised at the tremendous positive effects of breaking your negative contracts, not only on yourself, but on the person with whom you were holding them. Breaking such contracts frees a great deal of creative energy that you will now be able to use in your life in other areas. It will enhance your personal healing process a great deal. It will also free creative energy in your friend's life.

Some friends may insist on keeping the old contract. Since you will not keep it, that friendship may dissolve with the contract. Your old friend may find another person who is willing to make the old contract. Let go and let God. Your old friends will face those changes in their lives when they are ready. There are no judgments about this—everyone must be free to change and grow at their own pace. This may also happen in intimate relationships. It is, of course, much more difficult to lose an intimate relationship, but it does happen when people change rapidly.

In such cases, when grief for that old friendship or intimate relationship arises within you, it is helpful to remember that love and learning are always created in every kind of relationship. That which always remains from friendships and intimate relationships is the love. It is only the negative that dissolves. The pain and the distortion dissolve through time and through learning. The love that was created always remains and is never diminished. When your old friend goes through the necessary change in his or her life, you may happen to meet again and find the friendship rekindled. The love will still be there.

If you are ill and moving through the healing process, you will transform many old negative contracts with friends and your intimate partner. You will find that those people who will agree to the change in your mutual contract will also grow through the stages of healing with you. As you move through and transform each of the seven levels (as discussed in Chapter 8), you bring the people involved with you to a higher view of the entire process. When you go through deep changes in your life, so will the people around you. Their lives will change.

Creating Healing Relationships with Your Health-Care Professionals

It is very important to create positive contracts with your health-care professionals. The purpose of such a positive contract is to clarify your needs, find the right qualified people to help you fill them, and to carefully create a trustful, safe environment in which you will be able to do your work and surrender to the process of healing and to the wisdom and help coming from the health-care professionals you have chosen. The more carefully this is done the better, because at some time during the process, *you will be required to trust, let go, and live by faith and hope.* Be sure that you draw the right people to you and create the appropriate place and situation in which to do that.

Before entering into a relationship with a health-care professional, I suggest that you do the work in the previous section about your personal relationships. This will give you information about the structure of any negative contract that you might automatically, unconsciously set up with your health-care professional. You will then find it easier to go through the material that follows. Utilizing the information given in this chapter and in Chapter 12, let us use some important questions as guidelines to set up positive healing relationships with your healer, your physician, and any other health-care professional whose services you may wish to engage. The object is to create the best client-healer-physician team that you can. You can also use these guidelines if you wish to use a nutritionist, a therapist, or any other health-care professional.

If you are too ill to do this by yourself, then get someone to help you go through it. If, on the other hand, you are caring for someone, like a family member, who is too ill to work on this at all, then try to do it from the information you know about them. It will be a big help.

Use the chart in Figure 12–1, as you did in Chapter 12, to answer these questions.

Points to check out about yourself to make sure you are clear about which belief system you are coming from and what you need:

What is my desired result?

What is my reason why not—why I have not obtained this desired result before?

What is the fear I have avoided that I will have to face?

Upon what negative belief system is that fear based?

Your half of any negative contract with another person will always be based on your negative belief system. You will find that the negative belief system you list is one that is familiar to you. You use it in many areas of your life. You have probably already come up against it in doing the exercises in this chapter that explore negative contracts in relationships. You probably related to the two examples given. They are very apropos to the healing relationship. The first example says it is dangerous to challenge someone who disagrees with you. It is based upon the negative belief that the universe is not a place that supports the truth or the truth-finding process, or more personally said: *Expressing my truth and my creativity is dangerous.*

If this negative belief is operating within you when you interact with a health-care professional, you will have difficulty standing up for what you believe. If you do not like the attitude or stance that your health-care professionals take with regard to you and your healing process, you probably won't challenge them. You will refrain from expressing your doubts about the plan they are presenting to you. You will probably refrain from expressing your creative ideas about healing yourself. Unfortunately, such concerns, doubts, and creative ideas may be the key to your healing process.

If you wish to move through your healing process with the attitude of increasing your self-awareness and finding your truth each step of the way, then you need to get help from someone who is willing to work in that way. It can't be someone who simply tells you how it must be. You must find someone to work with who will lay out the healing plan on the table and speak with you openly about it. You need to know what your choices are and what consequences come with those choices, as best as any health-care professional can tell you. Many, many physicians are willing to do this now with an open heart.

Discerning whether a plan is right for you and challenging one that is not right for you will be much easier if you are clear that the positive belief system that you are coming from says that the universe supports truth, truth-finding, and the expression of creativity in problem-solving. The more you center yourself into this reality before you need to make a decision, the clearer you will be about making a decision when one is required of you.

In the second example above, to which you may have related, the supported basic negative belief is something like: *When I have needs or am sick, people will be angry. I must never get sick. Having needs is dangerous.*

Obviously this will interfere a great deal with your healing process and with your relationships with your health-care professionals. They will be much too busy to try to figure out what all your needs are. Nor could they, if they even had the time. It is up to you to begin to understand that you have real adult needs and that your needs are greater if you are ill than if you are not. It is perfectly reasonable to get help to fill them. If you know that you have a tendency not to ask for your needs to be met, you must concentrate on centering into the positive belief that we live in a world where everyone has natural human needs and where needs can be met. Therefore, you can ask your health-care professionals to fill these needs. Even if you are embarrassed, it is better to ask. If they cannot fill them, or if they feel that it is inappropriate to do so, you are still on the path to getting them filled. You can keep asking until you find the appropriate person to fill them.

Asking for what you need and challenging aggressive treatment modes for a life-threatening illness is very, very difficult. It requires clarity about where you are coming from. For example, nobody wants chemotherapy; nobody wants radiation. But is your resistance to it coming from the commitment to ask for what you need and stand up for your truth to heal yourself in a way that is right for you? Or is it a way to avoid a very unpleasant treatment and to thus stay in denial? These are the questions that many people face. They are not easy. Knowing on which belief system you tend to base your actions will come in very handy at such a time.

If you tend never to challenge, you probably ought to start. If, on the other hand, you are the sort of person that challenges everyone on everything, you are probably coming from a negative belief system that says people are not trustworthy. In this case, such actions would probably be detrimental to your healing. The big question is, are you coming out of love or fear? If it is not love, try again.

There are many variations on what I call the games people play with health-care professionals. Many patients want physicians or healers to be more than human, to have no flaws, and to take full responsibility for their health. For example, a negative belief system that supports not being able to ask for your needs to be met has its reverse side, in which the physician or healer is supposed to be all-knowing and all-caring. There is a part in everyone that wants to revert to the womb, where all needs are automatically cared for without their asking. But that is not the real world. Everyone is limited. Every one of us is human.

Be aware that health-care professionals' knowledge is necessarily limited. The knowledge of medicine is limited. Although it is very advanced scientifically, it knows much less than there is to know. After all, it was and still is being formulated by people who are simply trying to learn as much as they can within a certain framework of knowledge. So it is with healing. Healing is a path of knowledge that interfaces with the way of knowledge of medicine, and there are many paths of healing. Neither medicine nor healing can take responsibility away from the person who is born into that body in the first place. You always were and always will be responsible for your body.

As a teacher of healing, I run into this a lot from those who come to study with me. Since I am able to read the field and see into the body, some students think that that means I automatically read everything about their health whenever they are in one of my classes. I have had several people get angry at me because I didn't warn them ahead of time about something that showed up in their yearly physician's checkup. Once these people get over the initial shock, they find that they are actually avoiding knowing things about the workings of their own body. This avoidance is usually based on our fear of the human condition in which we live as vulnerable physical beings.

However, in the long run, the more we maintain our natural body-centered consciousness, the more we are able to follow the messages from our balancing system and keep it healthy on a daily basis. This is very empowering. With our balancing system, we remain awake to what is going on in our physical habitat as much as possible. Therefore the person (ourselves) who can do the most about it has first alert. We are always there inside the body!

Doing this makes a big difference. For example, I mentioned a case in an earlier chapter about healing back pain. I found it necessary for the client to carry small healthy snacks to maintain a good level of blood sugar so that he would not reinjure his back. This worked very well for him. He became much more conscious of what was going on in his body minute to minute. By being present and responding to his own need over time, he then healed his back. A female client with whom I was working at the same time refused to do this. She didn't want to maintain a high level of body awareness. She didn't eat what and when she needed to maintain her blood sugar level to prevent injury. She kept reinjuring herself. She had deeper issues of self-responsibility that she needed to deal with before reaching this practical way of handling the problem.

Once you have done the work in this chapter to find the types of negative contracts that you set up with people, you can check out how you might set up the same types of negative contracts with your health-care professionals. Consider the examples here, then ask yourself these four additional questions:

What negative contracts have I set up in the past that I may unknowingly use with my health-care professionals?

What is the positive belief system out of which I will now allow my actions to arise? (You will want it supported by whomever you choose to work with.)

What do I need from my healer, physician, or health-care professional to help create the desired result?

What simple mantra that expresses this positive belief can I find to use anytime? (For example, you could use a simple one-word mantra such as *health, creativity, peace, truth, ask, challenge, abundance, pleasure,* or *love.* You can use this mantra any time during the day. If you like to be precise, simply think of it a few times on the hour of every hour, or when you get up in the morning or go to bed. You could use it in a formal meditation, where you sit quietly with your spine erect and aligned. Or simply lie in bed and concentrate on one or two simple words that mean a lot to you.)

Now that you know what you need, you can apply it to the various health-care professionals you chose in Chapter 12. Create an imaginary contract with each. Be clear on what you want from each. This process will continue as you gather more information. You will definitely need a different contract for your healer from the one you have with your physician. Review Chapters 5 and 6 before you create the contracts. Remember, the more you do this before you get sick, the easier it will be if you do get sick. Do it as a preventive health-care measure to maintain your health now, and it will be that much easier to create healing relationships with those whose help you request if you do get ill. If you need help to clarify the process, do not hesitate to ask someone who will understand what you are doing.

Since most health-care professionals do not set up preliminary interviews, you will most likely not be able to present your ideas until your first appointment with a physician or your first session with a healer. Make sure that you do this during the initial part of the appointment. After a healing it will be too late. You will be in an altered state, and most likely it will not be appropriate to talk much.

Points to check out with your health-care professional to make sure you can create a positive contract with him or her:

Is he or she willing to give you the type of information you want, in as detailed a manner as you require to fill your need? (Be sure he or she describes choices of treatment plans.)

Is the person clear and honest about what he or she can give you and what his or her limitations are?

From what belief system is he or she working? Is it similar to the one that you wish to support? (This one may be too difficult to answer. If so, just skip it for now—it will eventually show itself.)

Do you both agree on the desired result?

What does the person want from you? What are your responsibilities to carry out the healing process?

Once you have set up your healing team, make sure someone makes a schedule of the many things that will need to be done and the help you will need in doing them—like going to appointments and getting someone to do your shopping so that you can maintain your diet. Get your friends to help you create your healing space. Be sure to have alone time, just for you to get to know yourself better.

Creating a Healing Relationship with the Earth

There is a holographic relationship between your personal healing and the healing of the earth. Many of us are concerned about the great deal of pain on the earth today. We want to know how we specifically have helped to create it and how we personally can help to heal it. As I said at the beginning of this chapter, everything that has been said about individual relationships can be applied to our relationship to the earth. Collectively, our negative contracts show in our treatment of our planet. On the personal level, any negative contracts that you have found operating in your personal relationships are also functioning holographically in your relationship to the earth.

It is on the fourth level of our field that we connect to the earth and create relationships with the earth like those we create with each other. From the auric perspective, the earth is a live sentient being, and we are part of its body. This idea makes sense in the M-3 metaphysics. Since all matter is created from mind or consciousness, then consciousness created the physical body of the earth. The physical earth, then, just like our bodies, arose out of the consciousness that created it. Just as our consciousness is connected to our body through the auric field, so the earth has consciousness that connects to it through the earth's auric field. Some of the earth's aura is known through our study of the magnetosphere and the Van Allen belts, which are parts of the earth's magnetic field. Many of you have seen the magnificent colors of the Northern Lights, which look very similar to the human aura.

Since our bodies are part of the earth, we are holographically connected to the earth. We are born out of it, and it is our mother. Native Americans honor this connection and maintain a humble respect for our dependence upon the earth.

Many people of our present culture like to forget our dependence upon the earth and our interconnections to all the beings that live upon it. We act as if we own it; indeed, we even believe we do own pieces of it. I thought Crocodile Dundee put it straight when he said in the movie, "It's rather like two fleas arguing over who owns the dog they live on." Much of our mistreatment of the earth comes from our personal pain, which our negative beliefs keep re-creating. Collectively, we hold ourselves in this pain, and collectively, we mistreat the earth.

Since we have learned from holographic theory that everything we do affects everything there is, then we must somehow, in perhaps some small way, be responsible for what is happening on the earth today. After all,

the smaller system within the greater system is directly connected to and immediately affects that greater system. Such a thought is overwhelming to most of us. We have quite a lot to deal with in our own lives without taking on planetary problems. Many people turn away from the immensity of the problems humanity as a whole faces now.

To deal with such an issue, someone once asked Heyoan, "What can I do for world peace?" The channeled answer I received not only clarified how we help create the problem but also gave a way for us to do our part without feeling so overwhelmed that we turn away.

Essentially what Heyoan said is that just as you hold negative belief systems that create pain in your life, you also help hold that negative belief system in the collective unconsciousness of humankind, out of which humanity's pain arises.

Here is the channeled answer and the step-by-step process to find your appropriate area of service.

~

WHAT CAN I PERSONALLY DO FOR WORLD PEACE?
Channeled from
Heyoan

This is a wonderful question, and I hope that more people will ask it of themselves. It is becoming more and more important that larger numbers of people begin taking responsibility for becoming world citizens. The first step toward that end is to consider yourself from the greater vantage point, and let your decisions and actions arise out of that broader knowing.

From our vantage point, since you are joint creators of the earth and all that exists there, you have made it as it is. You have created all that you experience in your life, and when there is pain, it is there only because you have made it so. This does not mean that you are bad; it simply means that you have not learned a lesson you have come here to learn, and so you have created a situation that not only arises out of that unknowing but that gives you precisely the tools that you need and the direction to look to in order to incorporate that learning.

Take our perspective and apply it to the world situation. First ask yourself the questions you would ask concerning any personal issues. What does this world situation mean to me personally?

What is the message the greater world (being a mirror to the self) is trying to tell me about what I need to learn? What is the nature of the pain I have helped to create? What needs to be done about it, and what is it that I can personally do? How have I personally contributed to the greater situation?

Now you might say, "I didn't do it." You might even blame others—"It was the politicians"—or you might choose some other nation or ethnic group to blame. But it is you who have participated in an election or refrained from voting. It is you who have carried prejudices within yourself regarding others who seem different from yourself. You do it with complete strangers as well as with people you know. These generalizations and assumptions that you make about others, you also automatically and often unconsciously place on yourself. This causes you a great deal of inner personal pain. When you hear yourself speaking negatively about another, ask yourself what effect it has on you when you say it about yourself.

The longings of the human soul do not limit themselves to national boundaries, languages, or creeds. But with these distinctions, the soul finds an appropriate classroom (or playground) in which to learn. It is precisely this variety that makes the earth such a wonderful choice for incarnation. Nations were created to bring diversity and excitement to your lives. They were never meant to be a battleground. Indeed, one could live many lives upon the earth in many environments and never get bored.

So what has happened? The things that brought you to earth for your schooling are precisely the things that cause the problems. Fundamentally, your belief in a separated reality beckons you to return each time to earth. That belief also causes you fear. So you have come here to dissolve fear, but it is through the fear that needs dissolving that you have brought more fear. So ask yourself: "Precisely what is it that I am afraid of, both in my personal life and on the world scale?" See how they are really the same fear. Do you know that these fears are precisely the same fears most humans have, and from which most humans act? These common fears, then, are the origin of world conflict.

You all fear loss, illness, death, and lack of freedom. You all fear that someone will take something of value away from you once you have established it in your life. But I tell you, the only person who can do that is you.

To the extent that you take away your own personal freedom out of fear, to that same extent you will try to take away another's freedom. To the extent that you create illness in your body, to that exact extent you would allow others to maintain it in theirs and stand aside offering no help. To the extent you create impoverishment of physical, emotional, mental, and spiritual nourishment in your life, to that extent you can tolerate impoverishment in others and even hope for company. As you have done it unto yourselves, so you have done it unto others.

So the first place to create world peace is at home. Create harmony at home, in the office, and in the community, and then extend it across national boundaries. Would you let your child go hungry? Then why let the next-door neighbor's, the African, or the Indian go hungry? Wherever you draw the line is where you have limited yourself: your self-definition, your love, and your power.

I recommend that you each devote ten percent of your time and energy to a private project for the purpose of bringing about world peace. This may be in the area of education, political activity, communication, or simply monetary contribution to a cause with which you are profoundly connected. Do this only from the perspective that you have helped create the situation as it is and therefore intend to heal it as the healer that you are and from the power available to you as co-creator. Thus, rather than working for world peace because you should, you will work because you want to. Rather than working out of fear or guilt, you will work from the point of view of a creator putting his or her work in order. Never, never approach world peace from the point of view that you are nearly powerless to do anything about it. That simply is not and never will be true. You are the co-creator of all you experience, including the world situation. If you do not like what you have created, find the lessons to be learned from your imperfect creations and re-create in another, more suitable way.

If you fear poverty, then your actions arising out of that fear—trying to stop personal poverty—will help create poverty on a world scale. Your fear helps maintain the mass belief in poverty. This mass belief in poverty causes a backlash reaction in which everyone strives to get more and to keep it for themselves. This greed leads to the struggle for economic gain that has, in turn, brought about the impoverishment of the world's resources. This creates more poverty and holds it in place in the physical world.

Consider this, my friends: The things you most abhor and fear are the very things that you create. Thus, not only are you to delve into your belief in your personal poverty and what that means to you, you are to take ten percent of your time to look into world poverty. The world solution will be the same as the personal one.

Greed is based on the fear of not having enough. What appears to be greed is really a result of fear of poverty. That, in turn, creates poverty, which in turn leads to the destruction of the earth's resources and challenges your very existence. Ultimately, therefore, your fear of poverty covers your existential fear, and ultimately, your greed rests upon the shaky foundation of your deeper existential fear.

Now, what can be said of this greed? *Greed* is a term you may never wish to apply to yourself. Let us soften it a little: If you look within, you find many "wants." Make a list of your "wants." You will find that many of them are designed to make you feel safe, which they can never do. Now ask yourself, "Which of these wants do I wish to create from my higher consciousness, based on my positive belief system? Which do I want to create to make myself feel safe, based on my negative belief system?" Divide the list in this way. Now focus on the positive list and ask yourself, "How does each of my wants serve the world as well as my personal self?" When that is completed, address each item designed to assuage fear and ask, "What fear am I trying to assuage, and how? If I act according to these wants, how will my actions affect the world?" As you know from the previous material, basically you are acting out of and thereby affirming fear in the world by following through with such action. Note that as you do this, you may find that some of the items are on the wrong list.

This exercise may give you a better understanding of just how responsible you are for creating not only your life experience but the world situation as well. You are very responsible! You have in fact a big effect!

So, dear ones, be aware of the very direct effect your belief system has both on your personal relationships and on the world situation. Because of this powerful direct effect, you can change both by discovering your negative belief systems and changing them to project love, caring, and trust into the world. Be in peace and in love.

~

Homework from Heyoan

1. List your fears on the personal level. List your fears on the world level. See the similarity.
2. List your wants. Divide the list between wants to assuage fear that stem from negative beliefs (negative wants) and those that come from positive beliefs (positive wants).
3. Find the fear out of which your negative wants arise. Find the higher consciousness out of which your positive wants arise.
4. What have you created on the personal level from each of these positive and negative wants? What in the world situation is similar to the personal one? That is what you have helped to create in the world, both positive and negative.
5. In what area of world service (according to your negative creations coming from fear) do you wish to give your ten percent toward world peace?

Results of Clearing Your Wants to Assuage Fear

Consider the person who is gluttonous because he fears starvation. He may overeat and even hoard food. Such a person helps hold the fear of starvation in the collective unconscious of the human race. When he works on his problem, he may choose to give by helping feed those on the planet who are starving.

A friend of mine I will call Mark did just this. He was overweight at the time I met him. I knew nothing about his background. But I knew he was very concerned about his weight and the health problems it caused. He was particularly concerned about the extra strain on his heart. He had worked on this problem in the past by going on diets of various sorts, losing a few pounds, and then immediately regaining the weight. He had to go into the deeper issues involved with his weight before he could lick the problem. He went to a healer to get help to stop his overeating. He shared his process of healing with me. He has given me permission to write about it.

Mark discovered that the first level of fear within him was simply the fear of hunger. He could not tolerate the inner feeling of hunger. This was a surprise to him, and he had no idea where such a fear would have come from. It certainly wasn't a reality in his life. He searched for where the fear of hunger came from and found that his parents had had terrible financial problems at the time of his birth, during the Great Depression of the late thirties. Although they were always worried about where the next meal was coming from, nobody ever went hungry. He had found the source of his fear of hunger. His early family heritage carried a fear of hunger, although it never happened. As a young child, he thereby learned that this unknown thing called hunger was a terrible thing to be feared. His young psyche could not distinguish between fantasy and reality. His early childhood solution was simply never to be hungry. It worked, but he gained weight.

In Mark's healing process, he began to practice tolerance of the fear of hunger by eating good healthy meals and cutting out his nearly constant eating throughout the day. Improving his diet in this way immediately increased his energy level and his level of self-

~

awareness. What was different about this process was that his motive was deeper than just the loss of weight, as it had been in his earlier dieting. It had become an exploration of his inner world.

At times, the fear would be too great, so he would have a snack. In this way he worked gently with himself. As he continued to explore his experience of the feeling of hunger, he found that he could begin to distinguish between the feeling of hunger and the feeling of inner emptiness. He found that he even enjoyed the feeling of inner emptiness because it gave him plenty of room inside. It was peaceful. It was just life without form. Now and then something new would arise out of his inner life without form. Many times, he experienced high spiritual ecstasy.

Then other things started coming out of this inner void. As he was sitting one day in the inner quiet, he experienced the rising feeling of the fear of starving to death. Then it broke full force. Quickly, he found himself in the middle of the experience of starving to death. It was another century. He was in a different body and a different life. He jumped up from his meditation in fear. Later in his healing session, he told his healer what had happened. Together during the healing they rolled backward in time to the past life experience that had arisen in his consciousness. The healer worked to clear his auric field of the auric debris left from that experience. He experienced himself living in a time of great hunger. According to his experience, he had actually helped cause this hunger through misuse of power. He and many others eventually lost family and life through starvation.

Of course, in this case, there is no way of proving that such a thing really did happen to him. But there are some very well-organized studies that support his experience, for instance, one by Ian Stevenson of the University of Virginia, who is verifying past life information from very young children. At any rate, our main focus here is on the healing effect of clearing this experience from Mark's auric field. First he lost his fear of hunger and starvation. Then he changed his life a great deal.

As Mark said:

When my energy field cleared, I finally understood that my fear was from something that had already happened rather than something that was going to happen. I then had a very overwhelming desire to stop the possibility of it happening again. I saw the mistakes I had made last time around and wished to try again.

I began to see eating as a pleasurable way of nurturing my body so that I could be free to be who I am and to do what I had come here to do, which is to deal with the real starvation that is happening on earth right now.

Mark no longer believes in the fear of hunger. He teaches meditation on inner emptiness as a path of self-discovery. He holds the belief that the experience of inner emptiness is a wonderful and necessary part of human life, leading to greater self-understanding and the connectedness of all things. He has lost fifty pounds. He is working for an organization that fights world hunger.

The Three Types
of Auric Field Interactions
in Relationships

One of the most interesting privileges that HSP (Higher Sense Perception) gives is the gift to watch auric field interactions between people when they are relating to each other. On the fourth level of the auric field, everything we do with each other shows up in a living, moving, constantly changing display of colored fluidlike light, or bioplasma. The interplay of the bioplasma reveals a great deal about relationships that I certainly never suspected before I saw these auric field interactions in detail. Bioplasmic displays reveal that we are connected to each other in many ways that our psychological and sociological theories have not included. They show an interdependence between all living creatures far beyond what we have previously understood.

No matter how much we may think we are independent and do things on our own, we never really are. This is a lesson that many human beings are relearning now. In the tribal communities of our past, we knew how much we depended on each other. But in the early twentieth century, the modern world gave us a false sense of freedom. Now with satellite views of the earth and modern communications technology, we get a broad view of what it means to be interdependent. We see that our individual actions combine into a powerful force that is changing the face of the planet. We see that what is done in one country can immediately affect all others. We see it in the world banking system, in the stock markets, in our weaponry, and in our pollution of the earth. The international concerns that the average American now has, spurred by something as simple as watching the evening news, indicate that the planetary holographic connection is beginning to be felt.

Everything we think, say, and do holographically affects everyone else through the life energy fields. Most of us are not conscious of the depth of this statement. Yet many are beginning to be. Many people feel it in a primitive way. We get a gut feeling that something terrible is happening, and we go to our TV sets to check out what it is. That is what many of us did on October 17, 1989, when our TVs told us that our gut feeling was right: The second-worst earthquake in recorded history had just hit San Francisco. This gut feeling that something is wrong is common in many people when a large calamity happens somewhere on earth. In other cases, we have a feeling of lightness and freedom that tells us that something wonderful is happening. For example, when the Berlin wall came down, we felt our connectedness to the Berliners in their striving for and standing up for freedom.

We felt connectedness not just because we saw it on TV but because we are energetically connected, through the fourth level of the auric field, to all people of the world. We resonate with those who hold freedom dearly in their hearts. Opening our conscious awareness on the fourth level means literally feeling others. It means feeling their presence and their deeper reality of feelings, hopes, joys, fears, and longings, as if we were them. On the fourth level, personal boundaries are very different from those in the physical world. Let's explore what that means.

On the fourth level of the field, energy-consciousness takes the form of what it believes itself to be. What it believes itself to be depends on its vibrational frequency and its energy content. When our energies are alike on the fourth level, we feel as if we were the same person, because we feel exactly what others are feeling. "Is it me or you?" we ask.

Yet, when our energies are different on the fourth level, we feel that we are not the same person. That is, we are not others because we have our own feelings, different from theirs. On the fourth level, we move back and forth between fusion or oneness with and separation from other people in an effort to become individuated.

In the process of life on the fourth level, we come together and fuse in communion. This communion then allows us to move apart into individuation. It is only through individuation that we can know our unique inner divinity. The more we know our inner divinity, the more we are able to come together in communion. Through this circular process of growing self-awareness, love is created.

This process can be very confusing when we try to clarify fourth level reality in the physical world, where boundaries are clearly defined by our skin. Reality simply is very different on the fourth level of the field from what it is on the physical level. I began describing this difference from the scientific perspective in Chapter 2. Now I will do it from the spiritual perspective. To understand why the process of life on the fourth level of the field is so different from that on the physical, let's explore the underlying process of creation that is functioning here.

Here is how the fourth level is created: The creative force from the core of our being projects down through the higher levels of the auric field and into the fourth, on its way to the physical world. As it does this, it splits in two and becomes relational. At this point a dualistic split occurs. It is in the fourth level of our field that we first become dualistic. The fourth level of our auric field is the bridge between the physical and spiritual worlds. We experience this bridge through relationships with others. Without this bridge of relationship, the physical and spiritual would appear to be divided and separate.

In the fifth, sixth, and seventh levels, which correspond to our spirituality, we do not experience duality. The main functions of duality are to explore differentiation and to define boundaries. As creation is stepped down through the levels below the fourth, then into the physical world, boundaries become more clearly defined. Each progressive level down has a more clearly defined duality. So it is on the fourth level that duality first begins to manifest in the back-and-forth movement between feeling that you are the same as another person and then feeling different from them.

Just beneath the fourth level is the level of the mind. Here, through clarity, we think about who we are: "I think, therefore I am. I think differently from you. Therefore, I am me, you are you." On the second level of the field, duality again expresses itself in a different way. "I have emotional feelings about myself, therefore I am. I feel differently about myself from the way I do about you, therefore we are different. We are not the same person." On the first level of the field, duality is clarified thus: "I feel myself through sensation. I sense my physical body. I sense your physical body. It is different, therefore I am different from you." On the physical level, our skin defines our shape. We look into a mirror and say, "Oh yes, there I am!"

But what, we might ask, is so important about differentiation and individuation if we are all one anyway? In dualism, we learn to individuate our conscious awareness, through the "I-Thou" relationship. *It is only through the dualism into which we descend that we can awaken our conscious awareness to individuality.* Through dualism we provide ourselves with a mirror to get a good look at ourselves. Without dualism, discernment of our individuality could not occur. I cannot overemphasize the importance of this fact.

Stylianos Atteshlis, who lives in Cyprus, is a world-renowned healer, known as Daskalos in the book *The Magus of Strovolos* by Kyriacos Markides. In his theological teachings, Atteshlis explains dualism in terms of the descent of man from the angels. He says that it is only through descent into the human experience of duality and free will that conscious awareness can exist. He says that we were all archangels who passed through the "idea of man" into duality in order to awaken to our inner divinity and to gain awareness of the evolution of consciousness. He says that archangels and angels are not individuated as we are; they have no consciousness of self as individual and are without individuality. Free will is automatically divine will; there is no free will. In other words, the idea of choice does not exist within a nonindividuated being. Human beings, on the other hand, who finish their rounds of birth and death on this planet and then transcend to higher worlds, are beings of great spiritual power who are also individuated.

Individuation is a process that begins with incarnation down through the fourth level of duality and then down deeper into duality in the physical world. It is a very long-term process of creation that continues through centuries in the physical plane. Then it moves into higher frequencies of life experience that apparently go on infinitely.

So even though many of us complain about duality and the difficulty of human relationship, *relationship is at the heart of spiritual growth and development.* The fourth level is a bridge between our spirituality and our physical nature. It is a bridge between heaven and earth. It is a bridge that is made of relationships. It is through relationships that we become whole. In the past, some may have considered it very spiritual to sit and meditate on a mountain somewhere. But that is no longer true. Once we've sat upon the mountain to know God, we must bring our learning back to humanity to be fulfilled. Can we still be loving, honest, and truthful? It is much harder in relationship than on a mountain.

Many of us get lost on the fourth level bridge because we don't know how to create relationships that fulfill our needs, both to give and to receive. Through relationship, our learning is put to the test. By making our relationships function better to fill our needs and the needs of others, we build the bridge between our personal self (levels one to three of the auric field), through the interpersonal self (level four of the auric field), to our transcendent unitive self (levels five to seven of the auric field). In the fourth level, we learn to know ourselves, each other, and eventually God better, through recognizing the God within us and within each other.

All the energy correlations to our interactions with people (individuals or groups of any size), animals, plants, minerals, and the planet are found within the fourth level of our field. It is the level at which we create and express love for all sentient beings. The fourth level of our field is a bridge of love. Whenever two people interact, a lot of field activity occurs in the fourth level of the auric field.

When HSP vision opens on the fourth level, a whole world of connectedness opens to us. There are three major types of field interactions in the fourth level of our fields. The first type is through harmonic induction of the frequencies of one field into the field of another person. The second, and most apparent, type is the streams of colored fluidlike energy, or bioplasma, that flow between the fields. And the third type is the cords of light through which we connect with each other's chakras.

Each type of auric interaction can be either positive or negative. The positive interactions serve to charge and nourish our fields. The more we have them, the fuller, more fulfilled, and happier our lives become. On the other hand, the negative interactions can cause damage to the auric field and lead to disease.

Communication Through Harmonic Induction of Field Pulsations

One major way we communicate through the auric field system is by influencing each other's field pulsation rates. The pulsation rates in one person's field induce a change in the pulsation rates of another's field. It works just as tuning forks do. Whichever auric field is stronger usually influences the other. That is why people travel long distances to sit in the field of their guru. The guru is usually someone who has spent a good deal of time in life meditating and increasing the frequency, size, and power of his or her field. Whenever disciples sit within range of the guru's field, their auric field is lifted to higher vibrations. And they feel wonderful. Of course, this also releases the people's personal process because the increase of power running through the field releases energy blocks that then have to be dealt with.

Harmonic induction is an important factor in relationship. If your field is strong, with more energy than your spouse's, and your pulsation rate is faster, your field will induce a faster pulsation rate in your spouse's field. If your field is a slower rate but you are still stronger—more energized—your field will slow your spouse's pulsations down. People like to maintain their fields within a certain range of pulsation rates. Couples usually match up within nearly the same range. Or individuals may pick spouses outside of their range to help speed them up or slow them down.

It is difficult to communicate through a very big difference in pulsation rates. Intimacy requires field coupling. In other words, the ability to either pulsate in the same frequency range or to synchronize fields using harmonics is necessary for communion.

When people are not within the same frequency range or cannot synchronize harmonically, it is extremely difficult to communicate. They just don't understand each other. It feels like talking to a brick wall. Your pulsations have no effect on theirs. Or it feels as if your words disappear into a cloud. Your pulsations are just absorbed into their field without producing any change, or they are deflected off into space. Like a mirror, your pulsations just bounced off with no effect. Or it just goes over their heads—your pulsations were too high in frequency, and their field is not able to pulsate that fast. For information exchange, one field must be able to have an effect on the other. Of course, many times it is possible to purposely not allow your field to be affected by another. One can become a mirror, a brick wall, a cloud, or just too dense on purpose—to prevent communion. We all do this at times to keep each other out.

When two people do commune, the fields affect each other in a beautiful way. The pulsations of one field cause changes in the other, which then build and create new changes in the first. This process continues in a positive feedback loop, creating new colors and frequencies in the two fields and creating a lot of pleasure for both people involved. Both people learn a lot in such communications.

We immediately feel uncomfortable in a relationship when we sense vibrations coming into our field through harmonic induction that we don't like. There are times when two people's auric fields beat against each other, creating a high-pitched screeching interference, much like feedback when a microphone accidentally gets too close to a speaker. These energy field interactions are very unpleasant, and we find them very hard to deal with. They register consciously as repulsion, dislike, fear, or even disgust. We simply don't like the person. This goes on until somebody changes. When they do, so does their auric field.

Relating Through Bioplasmic Streamers

Whenever two people interact, great streams of bioplasma flow between them. When people like each other, a great deal of energy is exchanged. The energy-consciousness in these bioplasmic streamers corresponds with the type of communication going on between the people involved. The colors and shapes of the bioplasmic streamers depict the nature of the interaction. In comfortable, pleasant communication, the streamers are smooth-flowing, with soft, bright colors that dance in an exchange of energy. As a streamer from one person's field reaches over and touches another's field, it fills the other's field with colors, feelings, and energy. In normal relational interactions, lots of different kinds of streamers of energy-consciousness are exchanged between the people involved. The streamers can be of any color of the rainbow, and any shape. The general effect of the colors follows the same guidelines as those in Figure 9–2. The brighter and clearer they are, the more positive, powerful, and clear the energy-consciousness. These are the kinds of communication where each person gives a lot to the other, and both get filled, having had their needs met.

The heart chakra on the fourth level of the field is rose. If there is a lot of love in the interaction, a lot of sweet rose energy flows in soft waves. When two people fall in love, the heart chakra on the fourth level becomes very active, training more rose energy into their auric field. (See Figure 14–1 in the color insert.) Soon their auras are overflowing with rose energy. Couples in love create a beautiful rose cloud of energy around them. Anyone who happens to be near or in this cloud feels wonderful. We all love lovers. When we are near them, our heart chakra on the fourth level begins to open more and pull in more rose light. And our auric fields also begin to produce a rose cloud. If there is passion, the rose will have a lot of orange in it, with a stimulating effect. The waves will be faster with higher peaks.

Probably one of the funniest things to watch is when people are pretending not to interact. They may not be looking at each other or overtly acknowledging each other's presence, but great streamers of colored bioplasma flow between them. Each person's field responds in bright scintillation. This can happen when two people first meet and are very attracted to each other. And it can happen when people are deeply involved, perhaps secretly, and are pretending not to know each other. They may or may not acknowledge the interaction openly, but the HSP observer is in on the secret!

When people do not like each other, they usually try not to exchange energy flow. Sometimes that doesn't work, and the friction builds up between them. Then, like a high-voltage gap that suddenly gets released through a spark of electricity, they will lash out at each other. Sometimes it is so powerful, it actually looks like a flash of lightning. In harsh communication, the relational energy streams are sharp, jagged, and dark in color, and they penetrate the other's field like spears or arrows. For example, anger is pointed, penetrating, invasive, and dark red. Envy is dark, gray-green, slimy, and sticky. If one person is trying to covertly get something from another, the streamers will be dense, slimy, and tentaclelike. They will grasp into the other's field to suck energy like a suction cup. Or they might be brittle and sharp and hook into the other's field and hang on in a desperate fashion. Remember, all these forms are possible, because on the fourth level energy-consciousness takes the form of what it believes itself to be.

Negative interactions actually feel like spears, arrows, or daggers that tear open the field. They feel like slimy sucking tentacles that steal or drain energy. They feel like parasitic hooks that drag the energy field down. They feel like that because that is exactly what they do.

Bioplasmic Streamers in Family and Other Close Relationships During Illness

Some common interactions occur through the bioplasmic streams when people are ill. People who are ill have a double problem where energy needs are concerned. They need extra energy to fight their illness, yet they have difficulty metabolizing even a normal amount of energy for themselves because their chakras most likely aren't functioning properly. That's how they got sick in the first place: Their fields are weaker. Remember that energy flows from a higher to a lower voltage. When one person is ill and another is healthy, the healthy person usually transfers a lot of healthy bioplasma to the ill person. They do this automatically.

In addition to that, when the ill person needs something, he or she will send out a bioplasmic streamer of supplication to the healthy person's auric field. These streamers suck the energy that is needed. This happens whether or not the person asks for it directly. This process is normal, natural, and unconscious. It is part of the give-and-take of family life. The energy exchange within family life is very good for the person who is ill because it gives strength to fight illness. All the family members, including children and pets, give life energy to the ill person in this way. That is one of the benefits of the holographic connection that each of us has within a family situation. People tend to get well more quickly in energetically supportive situations.

During the healing process, the ill person will at first need to be able to receive energy from others, then eventually learn to stand on his or her own two feet, and finally help supply energy to the family structure again. There are many variations of how this works. I'll cite the two extremes of the spectrum.

The ill person may have been sucking energy for years before the illness began manifesting physically. At an appropriate time in the recovery, he will need to learn how to metabolize all the energy he needs for himself. This will be a natural part of the healing process, as his chakras will be repaired and can function properly to supply him with all the life energy he needs.

In an opposite case, a family member who has been supplying a great deal of energy to the members of her family may need to receive a lot for herself. This may be very difficult for her and her family at first because the roles are reversed. She may be unable to receive and may need practice at it. Here is where the family can help her learn to receive by good, loving caretaking. They may even have to be pushy about it at times. On the other hand, in such a case family members may still try, through habit, to take energy from her when she needs it most. If you see this happening in your family, be very careful about protecting her. Taking energy from her at this time could have a negative effect on her health.

If the illness is long term, the family members will very likely begin to feel the psychic drain of the illness directly on their own fields. They are metabolizing energy not only for themselves but for their loved one. They most likely will not know what is happening to them, but they will get tired and grouchy and not want to take care of their loved one at times. It is essential for each family member or intimate partner of anyone who is ill to get away and off by themselves to get replenished. Otherwise, resentment and guilt over the resentment will grow, which could then lead to depression, exhaustion, and even physical breakdown and illness.

All family members need to find ways to gather energy for themselves. This can be done very well through meditation, pleasurable hobbies, sports, personal creative activities, healthy friends, and other pastimes. To stay at home for twenty-four hours a day, sitting by the side of a loved one who is ill, is the worst thing people can do, both for themselves and the ill person. Eventually everyone will be ill. Healthy people need to interact with other healthy people for a creative exchange of energy. People who are highly creative like to spend time with peers who are also creative because together they generate and exchange a lot of high-frequency, creative energy. The exchange then releases the creative force within each of them.

Bioplasmic Streamers in Public Work

The act of teaching or performing is one of feeding energy-consciousness to students in a way that helps lift them into another level of understanding. Great streams of bioplasma flow between a teacher or performer onstage and a class or audience. A teacher of healing needs to be able to carry the energy of a room so that the collective energy-consciousness of the students can be lifted and enlightened into an experience of higher understanding. Teachers must be able to hold the energy of what they are teaching while it is being taught.

For example, I must hold my energy at the fourth level of the auric field when I am leading a fourth level healing exercise, or the students will not be able to learn it. If I try to teach fourth level healing while holding my energy at the third level of the field (the level of the rational mind), the students will duplicate that. They will try to do the healing on the third level and not be able to hold the fourth level. The old myth that those that cannot do can always teach is simply not true. The teacher must not only know how to do but must also be able to do it while conveying it to others. That is even harder.

The same type of bioplasmic streamers of supplication occur in all forms of relationships when one person wants something from another. If there is a demand with the request, the streams associated with the request will suck energy. If there is a simple request, and then a letting go, the streamers will not suck energy. For example, since we are speaking about classroom activities, if a student decides to talk to a teacher personally and is determined to do so even if the teacher is very busy, he or she will throw a streamer of energy out to grasp the teacher's field. Sometimes students even do it before entering the classroom. Or they do it from the back of the room and then walk the length of the room along the path of the auric streamer. The teacher may be deep in a conversation with another person but will probably feel the intent the moment the student hooks on to her or his field.

Anyone who has ever been a public figure has experienced energy streamers from their public or their fans. In such cases, many people try to attach streamers all at once, and the psychic drag of it gets difficult to handle. The more people do this, the heavier is the drag. Since the fourth level of the field is independent of space, these connections can and do occur from all over the earth. It is a big responsibility to try to be loving in all these connections, which are also projections, demands, or requests of some sort. And that takes practice. When the public figure is tired, it is difficult to always respond in a loving, positive way. This is one of the reasons anyone in the public eye feels an extreme need for privacy. The need is just to get to be alone, to feel the self, and to get replenished.

Bioplasmic Streamers and Burnout

Everything that has been said about bioplasmic streamers in public work also goes for the more private work in the helping and healing professions. The professional's job is to hold an auric field of healthy vitality and balance while low-energy and low-frequency bioplasmic streamers of supplication are constantly pulling and dragging on them. This makes helping and healing very difficult work. The professionals must be persistent in self-care. They must create a daily schedule to revitalize their energy field and renew themselves, or they will burn out. That is why burnout is so common among these professionals. Most of them do not realize that they need more self-care than a person who is not in the helping professions.

Bioplasmic Streamers and Objects

Bioplasmic streamers also occur when we connect to inanimate objects. Remember, any action we do is preceded by thought and feeling that can be seen in the auric field before we follow through with the action. In other words, we do things energetically before we do them physically. If the action is to be relational, it will first be expressed in the fourth level auric streamers. The moment we decide to make a phone call, we send out a streamer of energy-consciousness to the phone. Then we reach for the phone. This phenomenon continues throughout the entire day. Each time we connect in this way to an object, some of our bioplasmic energy-consciousness is left in that object. The more we work with an object, the more of our energy it absorbs and the more connected we feel to it.

The type of energy-consciousness we place in an object through our bioplasmic streamers depends on how we feel about the object. If we like or love it, we fill it with love. If we dislike it, we fill it with the energy of the type of dislike we have for the object. If we are in a bad mood when we pick up the phone, some of it stays in the phone. If we are in a good mood, some of that stays in the phone. As we continue to fill the object with our energy, it contains more and more of the kind of energy with which we have filled it. The object will then give off that kind of energy to anyone who comes in contact with it.

Healers use this principle when they charge an object, such as a piece of cloth or a crystal, with healing energy and send it to a client. The cloth or crystal carries the healing energy from the healer to the client, who then absorbs the energy from it. What is more, the healer can continue to charge the object at long distance. It can then continue to be a source of healing energy for the client.

Essentially, talismans of power work on this principle. Shamans or magicians are taught how to empower objects by learning very clear, efficient ways of concentration to transfer their energy-consciousness into an object. Objects can be filled with energy-consciousness of any type. This energy-consciousness is made up of feelings and thoughts. Since this energy-consciousness is not pure thought, I do not use the popular term *thought form* for it. Rather, I call it a psycho-noetic thought form—*psycho* referring to feelings, and *noetic* referring to the mind or thought. Each psycho-noetic thought form takes on the form that corresponds to the feelings and thoughts that make it up.

Rituals traditionally were, and still are, used for this. Rituals set a form, practice, or procedure that is repeated at regular intervals. Rituals include not only set actions but set spoken words, and specific things to concentrate the mind on while the words and actions are repeated. In ritual, it is important to generate specific feelings at will, to fill the thought form with the power of feelings. In other words, a ritual is a way to recreate a particular type of bioplasmic streamer of energy-consciousness, or psycho-noetic thought form, at will for a specific purpose. Ritual is a conscious act of creation. Each time an individual repeats a ritual, he or she adds more energy-consciousness to the original psycho-noetic thought form, which was created the first time the ritual was performed. Since rituals are repeated through generations, they are a way of connecting to very powerful thought forms that have been built up over long periods of time. Each time people perform a ritual, they holographically tap into the power of the psycho-noetic thought form for their use. And in turn, they also reinforce the power object with the thought forms they are creating in the ritual.

Creative visualization works on this same principle. By concentrating on what you want to create, you create it in the psycho-noetic world first. Eventually, it automatically steps down into manifestation in the physical world. We are continuously doing this every moment of our lives. We just usually aren't aware of it. The more aware we become of this process, the more we can consciously choose what we create.

The Cords That Bind Us

Another type of auric interaction in relationship is through the cords of auric light that connect us to each other through our chakras. These cord connections occur between all like chakras. That is, people connect to each other with cords going from first chakra to first chakra, from second chakra to second chakra, from third chakra to third chakra, and so on.

When working as a healer, the first cords I ever noticed were the ones that connect between third chakras. It seems that in our culture, the cords between third chakras get the most damage as we go through life. Almost all the people I have worked with have damage to their third chakra cords. Therefore they came to my attention first. At first, I didn't understand the significance of the cords since I had never heard of them before. I just knew that in a great number of the clients on whom I worked, I would find myself digging out cords that were embedded in the third chakra. In other cases, the cords would be dangling out in space. Slowly, I realized that these cords connected to people with whom the client was in relationship.

I was instructed through guidance to untangle the cords, to repair them, and in many cases to strengthen the connection between the two people. Guidance also had me root some of the cords down through the client's chakra and through deeper dimensions down into the core star. Heyoan said,

~

You are rooting the cords of "who this person is in the universe" [which is the psychological function of the front of the third chakra], deep into the core of his being, and thus releasing an unhealthy entangled dependency.

~

As time went on, I began to get feedback from the clients about the profound effect changing the cords had on their relationships. Not only would a client change in a relationship; so would the other person involved. It was then that I started realizing the power of the cords in relationship and the powerful effect that working directly on them through the auric field had on changing people's relationships and their lives. Over time, I observed cords connecting all the chakras and worked with them.

Since the cords are connected on the fourth level of the field and higher, which exists before and beyond three-dimensional physical space, many cord connections actually occur before life in the physical dimension begins. They continue to exist even after the death of anyone involved. The cords remain connected to the deceased people, who have left their bodies and are in the astral or spiritual world. Once they are made, these cord connections never cease. They never dissolve. They are beyond the physical world. At physical death, the auric field of the fourth level and higher doesn't really go through much of a change. It simply isn't connected to a physical body anymore. Therefore, it is not surprising that the cord connections remain after physical death.

Heyoan says there are five major types of cords:

~

- **The soul cords that the ongoing soul carries from its original God connection and its monad within the spiritual world.**
- **The cords from past life experiences, on earth or elsewhere.**
- **The genetic cords that are gained by connecting to birth parents.**
- **The relational cords that grow through relationship with parents.**
- **The relational cords that grow through relationship with other human beings.**

~

The soul cords connect us always to God and home. Through these cords, we connect to our guardian angel or our personal guide.

The cord connections from past lives help us remember the connections we had with people before this life. Many times, we meet people and have the feeling that we know them from before. We feel connected to them in ways that may at first be difficult to describe but that feel real. We find that we like the same things or carry the same longing. After a time, we find that we are working together to fulfill that longing. We may have slight glimpses of possible past life experiences together, or a full-blown past life memory may surface.

Just a word of caution about past life phenomena. Past life memories can be very tricky. As soon as you find yourself using a past life as an excuse for negative behavior, watch out. You are probably on the wrong track. If you blame someone for your negative feelings toward them; or if you put yourself in a better position in the past than you are now with respect to someone (for example, if you were the boss then and now you are not, or if you were the teacher then and your present teacher was the student); or if you give yourself license for otherwise nonsocial behavior like extramarital sex, you are misinterpreting and misusing the past life connection and heaping up more karma. Usually whatever problems you have now, you had then. But they usually are not as bad now as they were then, since you've learned a few things in the ensuing lives.

The cords from past life experiences include past lives not only on earth but elsewhere. Not only have we incarnated as humans on earth in the past, we have also had life experiences in other forms and in other places in the universe. Some of us feel that connection now, as we are beginning to allow such a possibility to enter into our consciousness. Many people look up to the stars and recognize them as home.

The Genetic Cords

Our genetic cords first connect deep into the interior of the heart chakras of a mother-and-child-to-be *before conception takes place*! I have seen the field of the baby-to-be floating just outside the field of its mother-to-be. The effort to connect the first cord comes from the person who is incarnating. If the mother is afraid of pregnancy, she may not allow the place that is deep within her heart chakra to open in a way that the connection from the child-to-be can be made. She will not get pregnant until she does this. This can be a cause of infertility in women. She can pray and meditate to face her fear. Her fear will arise so that she can deal with it in process and thereby open that very deep place within her heart. This heart chakra opening will activate the thymus gland. Then, assuming that the other endocrines—especially the ovaries and pituitary—are balanced with it, she is ready for conception.

By deeper observation with higher resolution, I noticed that there are also cords that connect from the mother's heart chakra to her egg and from the father's heart chakra to his sperm. When the egg and sperm come together, these cords are then connected between each parent and to the child who results from the conception. In this way, the parents are also connected to each other through the child.

Once the initial genetic cord connections through the mother's heart chakra are made, genetic cord connections are made through all the other chakras. Thus, you are connected through all your chakras to your parents. They, in turn, are connected through all their chakras to all their children. In this way, you are connected to your siblings. This connection goes on through grandparents, aunts, uncles, and cousins. It continues through all your bloodline connections, through the great genetic tree of life dating back through time immemorial. It creates a great network of light cords connecting all human life back to the first humans on earth. This great life network exists outside of three-dimensional space and independently of it. In this way, you are intimately connected to everyone that has ever lived on earth. In fact, in this same way, if evolutionary theory is correct, you are connected to all life-forms that have ever evolved up out of and lived on the earth. It is through these original birth cords that we carry our genetic heritage on the auric level.

I also noticed that when congenital birth defects, inherited proclivities to different diseases, and miasmas occur, they are related to problems with the genetic cord connections. For example, problems with the genetic cord connections in the fourth chakra can result in a child being born with a hole between the two heart chambers.

The Relational Cords

The relational cords between parents and child develop between all the chakras. They remain connected whether or not the child stays with its original parents. If a child is adopted, new cords are grown between it and its new parents. The genetic cords and the first relational cords that are developed in the womb, during the birthing process and shortly thereafter, still remain. And biological parents continue to affect the child through them as it develops.

The relational cords represent different aspects of relationship, according to the chakra's psychological function:

- Cords from the first chakra, which also grow down deep into the earth, represent the stability of the will to live in the physical body in relationship to the earth and in relationship with another person.
- Cords from the second chakra represent the enjoyment of life's fecundity in sensual and sexual relationship.
- Cords from the third chakra represent the clarity and appropriateness of caretaking of the self and others in relationship.
- Cords from the fourth chakra represent loving and the mystery of the balance between loving and willing in relationship.

- Cords from the fifth chakra represent secure trusting in the higher will of the relationship. They also represent giving and receiving in truthful communication through sound, words, music, and symbols.
- Cords from the sixth chakra represent the ecstasy of seeing higher concepts in the exchange and interplay of ideas while at the same time experiencing unconditional love with whomever this exchange is taking place. They represent the pleasure of recognizing your loved one as a beautiful being of light and love. They represent the ability to love from a spiritual perspective, as did many religious figures such as the Christ and Buddha.
- Cords from the seventh chakra, which also connect up into the higher realms, represent the power to be within the divine mind of God in relationship to God, the universe, and another human being. They represent the ability to understand the perfect pattern of a relationship. They also represent the ability to integrate the physical and spiritual worlds in relationship.

The state of these cords represents the nature of the relationship we have with each parent. As the child matures through the developmental stages of growth, the cords mature also. With each new learning about relationship, the cords take on more strength and resiliency. The nature of the cords reflects the nature of the relationships the child creates. The cords reflect how established and healthy a relationship is. The patterns that children develop are repeated throughout life. They determine how well they are able to relate to other people. A child uses the model of each of its original relationships with its mother to create relationships with other women and with its father to create relationships with other men. This is one of the reasons why we tend to re-create the type of relationship we have had with our parents with our intimate partners.

The cords on the left side of all chakras always connect out to a female person. The cords on the right side of all chakras always connect out to a male person. Thus, by knowing on which side of anyone's chakra the problem is—whether the role is parent, child, or peer—a healer can immediately tell if the problem originated from the client's relationship with his or her mother or father and was then duplicated with another human being of like gender.

Each time we have any kind of relationship with another person, we create new cords. These cords change and grow as the relationship changes and grows. The cords can attach between chakras only if both people allow them to. Unhealthy entangled dependence or healthy interdependence is always a mutual agreement. The fuller and stronger the relationship, the fuller and stronger the cords. The more interactions in a relationship, the more cords for that relationship. The more relationships we create, the more cords we create.

The state of the cords represents the nature of the relationships we have and how we are connected. Some of them are healthy; some are not so healthy. In healthy interdependent relationships, these cords are alive, bright, pulsating, and flexible. They serve to maintain intimacy, trust, and understanding while making plenty of room for freedom and flexibility in the relationship.

In unhealthy, codependent relationships, on the other hand, the cords are dark, unhealthy, stagnated, heavy, and slimy, or stiff, dim, and brittle. These cords serve to maintain relationship in dependence and inflexibility, and to crowd out individuality. The more we become tied to a person with unhealthy cords, the more the probability for habitual interaction, rather than spontaneity.

In unhealthy relationships, we misuse the cords that connect us. If we use the cords to slow the relationship down, to keep it from changing, and to keep interactions slow and dull, the cords become thick, dense, heavy, and dull. The relationship probably becomes stuck in depressed resentment and anger. If one person is trying covertly to get something from the other—such as to be taken care of—but not admitting it, the first person will send out a long, sticky, tentaclelike stream of energy, reaching into the third chakra of the second person to suck energy. Such cords can also cling to or hook in to another person in an effort to control. If we make the cords brittle, stiff, and unyielding, that is how the relationship becomes. The cords can also be depleted, weak, and flimsy, like the relationship to which they correspond.

As a relationship becomes healthier, the cords become brighter, more charged with energy, more flexible and resilient. They are very beautiful with many colors in healthy relationships.

Each chakra grows cords that represent a particular aspect of relationship, as shown above. Each time we have a life experience with someone in that aspect, new cords are grown. If we interact with someone in all aspects as represented by the seven chakras, cords will be grown to connect all seven chakras. In intimate, long-term relationships, we build many cords that connect us through all our chakras. It is in this way that we build very deep intimate relationships and remain psychically connected to people no matter where they are on earth, and no matter how much time has elapsed since seeing them. For example, mothers know how their children are no matter where they are and no matter how long it has been since they have seen them.

Life Trauma and the Relational Cords

One of the most painful experiences in life is to lose a loved one through abandonment, divorce, or death. The cords usually get badly damaged in these experiences. I have seen all the chakras on the front of the body torn open, with the cords floating out in space, after such trauma. The personal experience of such a trauma is described as the feeling of being torn apart, or as if their better half is missing. Many people become disoriented and don't know what to do with themselves.

In a difficult divorce, the party who wants out usually tries to tear out as many cord connections as possible, leaving the other person a bit bewildered, as well as creating a lot of pain and havoc in his or her own field. When this is done, each person is in pain and left with the feeling of being disconnected from many aspects of his or her life, because it was all so involved with the partner. The damaged cords represent not only the old relationship but the activities that the couple did together. Many people who separate in this forceful way have a tendency to get involved on the rebound, to try to heal the pain caused by their drastic actions. Unfortunately they tend to re-create the same type of negative relationship with the same type of man or woman they had before, because they have not healed the relational cords. When a lot of cord damage is done in the process of forced separation, I have seen it take at least five years, sometimes seven, to reorient the new lives of couples who were long married and then divorced. It depends on how much damage was done and how well the person can heal it. Of course, a healer who can see and work with the cords can do it much faster.

What people do not understand about this phenomenon is that in any separation, certain cords must dissolve, while others remain. When one partner departs, what happens to the remaining partner depends on how he or she prepares for separation and lets go of the dependency in the old relationship. Unhealthy cords resist the change and try to maintain the status quo, while the healthy cords simply allow the transition. Healthy cords remain connected, no matter what happens. Once two people come together in love, the love remains, and so do the cords that represent that love.

Problems with the Relational Cords

Problems with First Chakra Cords

Cords from the first chakra (which also grow down deep into the earth) represent the stability of the will to live in the physical body in relationship to the earth and in relationship with another person.

The main causes of weakly developed or damaged first chakra cords I have seen are:

- a child's reluctance to incarnate
- a birth trauma that disrupts the newborn's ability to connect the cords to the earth at birth
- early physical hardship that impeded a child's growing relationship to the earth and prevented the normal development of cords down into the earth
- physical abuse at an early age in which the child felt its life threatened and caused the child to prepare to leave by disconnecting the cords from the earth
- the child's emulation of parents who were not connected to the earth
- some accidental injuries that caused damage to the coccyx that in turn damaged the inside of the first chakra and the cords

Damage to the first chakra cords causes problems in the client's will to live and function in the physical world. It causes problems with the client's grounding to the earth and ability to connect to others in a physically oriented life—such as sports, exercise, and the enjoyment of the natural world and the earth in general. The main result of this damage is an ungroundedness, an inability to absorb the dense earth energies. This, in turn, makes for a weakness in the overall energy field that cannot support a robust physical body. The physical body becomes weak as a result.

Lack of connectedness to the earth results in a great deal of fear about life in the physical world per se, such as fear of being in a physical body because it seemingly is separate from the apparently hostile physical world around it. The person feels like a prisoner in a terrible cage—the physical body—of frightening and painful torture. People in this state feel as if they were being punished for some terrible thing they have done. They spend time trying to find out what it is. If only they can make it right, they think, they will be released from their suffering. They never feel safe.

They may find that meditating, moving as much energy-consciousness as possible out the top of their heads, makes for a safe haven, if only they could do it all the time. Unfortunately, this meditation is the worst thing they could do for themselves because it only weakens the cords that connect to the earth. And in the long run, meditation makes them less able to deal with the physical world.

Common illnesses that result from damaged first chakra cords: Actually, weakness in the first chakra cords weakens the energy field and the physical body to such an extent that ultimately, all illness is, directly or indirectly, related to it. At first, the weakness may show as a lack of physical energy. Then it could show in the adrenals. Later, it could become cancer, AIDS, or an autoimmune disease like rheumatoid arthritis. Usually, how the disease manifests later has a great deal to do with the state of the other chakras and cords.

Examples of healings and their effects: Probably the most common healings I have done on first chakra cords are the ones with people who have had broken coccyxes or an early trauma in which they disconnected from the earth. During my healing practice, I regularly restructured the first chakra and then established new cords down into the earth. The results of these healings were a revival of the immune system, a strengthening of the physical body, and a doubling of physical energy available to the client. One particular case comes to mind, in which a woman had Epstein-Barr virus and could not get well. Her first, second, and third chakras were not functioning properly. Her healer kept working on the third chakra. That helped her to a certain extent, but she had relapses regularly. It was not until I repaired the second and, primarily, the first chakra, then connected the cords down into the earth, that she became and stayed well.

Problems with Second Chakra Cords

Cords from the second chakra represent the enjoyment of life's fecundity in sensual and sexual relationship. The clearer our relationship to our sensuality and sexuality, the healthier the cords that we will create. The better a couple is matched sexually, the better the sexual relationship, the healthier, stronger, and more beautiful the cords will be. Any disorder in the cords will be experienced as a disorder in these areas of our lives. Or if we have issues with our sensuality and sexuality, the cords that we grow between our second chakras with the person with whom we are in a sexual relationship will show our problems.

Each time we have sexual contact with another person, we create more cords and remain connected to that person throughout the rest of our lives. Sometimes this causes confusion in those who have had a lot of sex partners, especially if the relationship was not healthy. These cords can be cleared and cleaned so that the positive aspects of the connections remain and the negative are healed. They will never be completely dissolved.

The main causes of weakly developed or damaged second chakra cords that I have seen are:

- past life difficulties with regard to sensuality and sexuality, with which the child is born
- general disregard or degradation of sensuality or sexuality in the child's environment
- direct rejection of the child's sensual or sexual expression by parents or other close adults
- childhood sexual abuse
- rape by a person of the same or opposite sex
- invasive medical procedures on the young child
- mistreatment by a sexual partner

Common illnesses that result from damaged second chakra cords: The problems that I have seen result from damage to the second chakra cords are:

- depressed sexuality that results from sexual abuse
- sexual perversion (from all types of sexual abuse)
- inability to achieve orgasm
- inability to conceive
- impotence with a particular person
- prostate cancer
- vaginal infection
- vaginal cancer
- ovarian infection
- pelvic inflammatory disease
- homosexuality from repeated rape by a person of the same sex

This does not mean to imply that homosexuality is an illness. According to Heyoan:

~

One incarnates for a life task that is best served by all one's physical parameters, including the body. Many individuals may choose a male or female body without the traditional sexual attraction toward the opposite sex, simply because that is not the type of life experience needed by the individual in that particular lifetime. There are no judg-

ments in the spiritual world as to how one chooses to express one's sexuality. Rather, the goal is to express one's sexuality with love, truth, wisdom, and courage.

We can consider two types of homosexuality: one that is the result of free choice to create circumstances for life experience, and one that came from a trauma that resulted from the karma of past actions. (And let me remind you that karma is not punishment; rather, it is the rebound effect of a past action. All of our actions are causes that create effects that eventually come back to us. Sometimes it takes lifetimes before the effect comes back.) In a way, both types of homosexuality are the same, for both create the circumstances needed to fulfill the life task. In the second case, the trauma needs healing work, but that doesn't mean the healing work would necessarily lead to heterosexuality. Rather, the goal is wholeness for the individual.

~

I must make it clear that damaged cords are not the only general causes in the auric field of these problems. I am only listing examples from cases I have seen in working with people whose problem was mainly caused by damaged cords.

Examples of healings and their effects: In several cases I worked to rebalance channels of energy that connect the endocrine system on the auric level to help women be fertile. Sometimes unhealthy or embedded cords from past relationships prevent healthy cord connections to the person in the present sexual relationship from forming. In such cases, I have to clean and clear the old cords before new, appropriate cords can be connected properly. Once the cord connections for the present sexual relationship are repaired, pregnancy can occur. When both parties of the couple cooperated, I have been successful many times.

On the other hand, if both parties do not cooperate and healing is needed in both, connecting the cords doesn't work. For example, one woman came for healing to be able to get pregnant. Her field configurations related to endocrine balances were very distorted and disconnected. I worked on her about three times, and they all straightened out. She was ready.

At the end of the last session, her husband came to pick her up. He came into the healing room for a few minutes, and I saw that the cords between their second chakras were not connected. I began to try to connect the cords. But as I did so, I saw that there was much deeper work to be done in his field, especially around his genitals. There was damage deep inside the first and second chakras. I could see that his sperm were very weak and would not be able to penetrate the egg well. Unfortunately, the husband was very skeptical and a bit hostile about the work and wanted nothing to do with it. Since he didn't want healing, there was nothing I could do. I knew that when they went for testing, it would show a low count of very weak sperm.

Later, through a friend, I heard that they had tried artificial insemination, which didn't work either because of the husband's auric and physical difficulties. I have always felt rather sad about that interaction. Perhaps I shouldn't have kept quiet. Perhaps the bridge of skepticism could have been crossed. But I wanted to respect his opinion and choice.

Problems with Third Chakra Cords

Cords from the third chakra represent the clarity and appropriateness of caretaking of self and others in relationship. Taking care of a child means being there for the child for everyday needs—washing, dressing, feeding, reading bedtime stories, and putting to bed. There are parents who love their children deeply but do not know how to take care of them in these ways. Or vice versa: There are parents whose love connection is weak but do know how to take care of the child.

During trauma in relationship the cords can get badly damaged. Usually this trauma is from lack of contact and nurturing or from overcontrol by a parent. In either case, a child's reaction is to tear the cords between its third chakra and the third chakra of the parent involved. If the trauma was from lack of nurturance, the ends of the torn cords that come out of the child's third chakra usually end up floating around in space. It is as if the child were trying to find someone else to attach the cords to. When the trauma is from overcontrol, the cords usually get embedded into the child's third chakra. I would guess this is a protective means to keep anyone else from trying to control him or her in this way. This same trauma will most likely occur in other relationships as the child grows up and goes through life.

Usually, over time, these cords get tangled and embedded in the third chakra, causing it to dysfunction. In the long term, the process goes like this:

1. First being overcontrolling, the parent grows very controlling cords into the child.

2. Then the child tries to get away and tears the cords out.
3. Then the child gets entangled in the self, and the child's cords get entangled in his or her third chakra.
4. Then the child can't connect well with others because the cords are too unhealthy to connect to others.

People who live this process go through life without being connected to their parent(s) and have difficulty in connecting to other people. They never feel that their parent recognizes or understands them for who they are. They probably resent their parent and are unable to recognize the parent as a human being who is also going through life.

Through hands-on healing, these cords can be pulled out, untangled, cleaned off, and reconnected in a healthy way by a healer. It is actually quite easy for a trained healer to do this. The cords will remain healthy if the clients are ready to create healthy relationships. On the other hand, they could damage them again through negative relationship. But they are less likely to do so because the healthy cords provide them with the experience of a healthy relationship, something they have perhaps never had before in this lifetime.

Common illnesses that result from damaged third chakra cords: The most common illnesses that result from damage to the third chakra cords are illnesses of the organs in the area of the third chakra. Broken or embedded cords on the left side of the third chakra that originate from problems in the relationship with one's mother result in a problem such as hypoglycemia, diabetes, pancreatic cancer, indigestion, or ulcer.

Broken or embedded cords on the right side of the third chakra that originate from problems in the relationship with one's father result in a problem such as sluggish or underfunctioning liver, infectious liver disease, or liver cancer.

Examples of healings and their effects: In a demonstration during a workshop I worked with a student named Carey. Carey, a tall, thin, beautiful young woman is from the Boston area. She was very quiet all year in class, so I decided to work with her to help bring her out. I could see that she had cords embedded deep into her third chakra. One end of the cords was connected to the inner tip of her third chakra, and the other end, which would have normally been connected to her mother, was embedded into her third chakra. In the work I cleared the embedded cords from the left side of her third chakra to the left side of her mother's third chakra. As I took the bundle of entangled cord ends from her third chakra, she took a deep breath and stretched up in response to the room that she now felt in that space in her body.

Next I cleaned the cords. When this was done, I connected some of the loose ends, which represented dependence, down deep into Carey's third chakra, bringing them down through the haric level and rooting them deep into the core star. In other words, I rooted her cords deep into the core of her being. Since these cords represent caretaking, it means that her caretaking of both herself and others will now come from the core of her being.

Next I reconnected the rest of the cords back into the left side of Carey's mother's third chakra. Her mother was not physically present in this healing, so this was done with the same kind of connection as is used in long-distance healing. This gave Carey a very different feeling of connection with her mother.

The feedback on these types of healings has been amazing. It is more or less the same from most of the people on whom I have worked. The relationship changes very drastically. Usually people leave a healing with a mindset that now they will finally be able to act differently toward their parent. They are surprised to find not only how different they are but how different their parent is.

Not only is Carey's relationship to her mother changed, but her mother's way of relating to Carey is changed. The very next time Carey saw her mother, her mother welcomed her and recognized Carey in a way Carey had always wanted her mother to. After years of feeling alienated, Carey felt that her mother finally saw her as she is rather than as what her mother wanted her to be. Since then, their relationship is still unfolding and growing.

Confusion in relationship is sometimes caused by distorted cord connections. What the aura shows and what clients think the cause of their problem is many times will be opposite. A client may have gone through life thinking that the problem was with his or her father, when all along it was with the mother. Many women appear to have problems with men. They just can't seem to get what they need from a relationship with a man. But when I look at their auric field, the torn, tangled cords from the third chakra are on the lefthand side, indicating that the problem originated in their relationship with their mothers.

For example, my client Joyce learned at a very early age that she was not getting what she needed from her mom. This was an extremely painful and frightening experience, since from a child's perspective, Mother is the giver and sustainer of life. In other words, to the child it seemed to be life-threatening. In order not to feel this threat, Joyce tore the cords of the third chakra out of connection to Mom. She displaced her needs for mothering onto Dad. From the auric field perspective, that meant all her needs became focused through the cords connecting through the third chakra to her dad. Joyce got nurturing from Dad. Dad did as well as he could, but he just couldn't be Mom.

Later in life, the same relationships are re-created. Joyce, now a grown woman, tries to get mothering from her man. It never really works. So she assumes something is wrong with her relationship with men, which is true, of course, so she works on it in her sessions. Very logically, she chooses a male therapist to help her work on her relationships with men, to learn to get her needs met from the man in her life. She doesn't have much problem with women at this stage of the game because she doesn't expect much from them anyhow. She doesn't go to them to get anything, not even healing or therapy.

If this situation continues, Joyce will never really get much better, even though she may seem so from the outer level. She will stay in the transferential position of being a good girl and become an even better girl. She is in awe of her male therapist, praises him profusely, and will do anything for him. Unfortunately, sometimes he unconsciously enjoys this so much that he doesn't see the greater picture of what is going on.

A smart healer will know that a female client needs to work on her relationships with women with a woman therapist and/or a woman healer who is trained to deal with psychological issues, before the problem can be healed. She needs to open up the existential terror that she cut off when she broke her connection with her mother. Through this process she will begin to understand that the women in her life have a lot to give to her and that many of the needs she has placed on her man do not belong there. This is what will heal her relationship to her man. A healer can properly untangle, repair, and reconnect the client's torn cords to her mother. This will change the relationship drastically so that it can unfold and develop from the point at which it was frozen so long ago.

I demonstrated a healing on a freshman student I'll call Grace that also shows the strong effect of clearing relational cords. In Grace's case, I worked on the cords from the first chakra, and then the third; then six months later, it was time to work on her heart chakra cords. This example shows the progressive action of the healing process.

Grace is of light frame, blond, and quiet and gentle in nature. She works as a financial manager and book-keeper for an architectural firm. The healings lasted about forty-five minutes.

First, I worked on the first chakra, opening and grounding its cords deep into the earth. Then I restructured the etheric body of the left leg, which according to my HSP needed work. (Grace later commented that it was her weak leg.) Then I cleared the bladder meridian going up her left leg. Next, I cleared and restructured the second chakra.

I then spent the most time on Grace's third chakra. The cords were very damaged. I untangled them and cleared them. Some were so indrawn that they had gone in and wrapped around the central vertical power current. The guides took out the old cords and put in brand-new ones. I had never seen that before. I had only seen guides clean and repair cords. The guides put a prosthesis into the third chakra that looked like a badminton birdie. The guides said it would dissolve in three months.

Six months later, I interviewed Grace on the phone about the results of the healing I did with her. Here is what she had to say:

My relationship with my parents changed after you worked on the cords. After the healing my first chakra was very open. I felt more grounded than ever. When I came home, my mother embraced me and looked at me with so much love, which I had never seen before. The love that she had for me was profoundly transformed. Before, she never expressed it. She wanted to be with me all that weekend. She was gardening outside, and I just sat out in the grass and she kept asking me questions about healing. She was more open to me and more open to who I am.

I felt the same from my father. I felt a real heartfelt love coming from him. He's not one to express himself openly as much as he could—that's something that changed. And I also felt that over the summer, because I wasn't so defended. I didn't trigger them, and they didn't trigger me. Then I realized how much of the intimacy that existed between us was the patterns of triggering each other. With the new cords connecting to them, those patterns seemed to be completely gone, all through the summer.

The chakra stayed stable for five months. Now in December, the chakra has started wobbling again. I've been doing a lot of desk work and have a lot of pressure. I'm not getting any exercise.

Grace also said that her relationship with her parents had become more "dormant" since her third chakra had started wobbling again. It wasn't as it had been before the healings; rather, there was much.less outer expression of the love.

So I read Grace again, over the phone. The first chakra was becoming less open than it was after the healing, but it was much stronger than before it. The third chakra was wobbling a bit, but that was caused by a dark red plug of stagnant energy in its center. I described several ways that she could heal it. I also saw that her relationship with her parents was going deeper and that it was important for Grace to work to clear, repair, and make stronger connections with the heart chakra cords between herself and her parents. This she did, and once again her relationship with her parents has gone to another deeper level of intimacy.

Problems with Fourth Chakra Cords

Cords from the fourth chakra represent loving and the mystery of the balance between loving and willing in relationship. These cords between heart chakras are what is being referred to when we talk about "heartstrings." Most of the people I have worked with have some sort of problem with their heartstrings or fourth chakra cords. The fourth chakra cords are damaged during unhealthy love relationships. The unhealthy configuration starts in childhood and is repeated as the person grows up. Whatever the problem, it gets amplified each time the trauma is repeated.

Common illnesses that result from damaged fourth chakra cords: The most common cause of damage to the heart chakra cords I have seen in clients and students is from being hurt in an intimate love relationship. The diseases that result from this are heart pain, palpitations, atrial fibrillation, and damage to heart tissue that later results in heart attack.

Examples of healings and their effects: In the summer of 1991 I asked a person who was attending an introductory workshop if I could work on her for a demonstration of advanced healing techniques, and she agreed. Earlier during the workshop, I noticed that the cords that connected her heart chakra and that of her deceased father were very damaged. Most of them were entangled deep in the heart chakra. Some were hanging out in space. I also saw several psycho-noetic energy-consciousness forms left over from past life experiences in the heart chakra. As a result of all this, her heart chakra was wobbling around rather than spinning in an even, clockwise motion.

I asked her what she would like to be called for this case study, and she chose the name Esther because she relates to the biblical Esther. Esther, who lives in the midwestern part of the country, is a lawyer and free-lance writer.

In 1976, when she was in law school, Esther had been diagnosed as having a defective mitral valve. The doctor said that it was a fairly mild kind of defect and that unless it interrupted her daily activities she shouldn't be put on medication. Then a couple of years ago Esther started a vigorous exercise program. During one of those programs, problems began.

Esther explains:

My heart tripped out on me and I couldn't get it to stop. It was ongoing for over thirty minutes. That was when I was diagnosed as having atrial fibrilla-tion. I went to a cardiologist and he said, 'No, you don't have a defective mitral valve; you have atrial fibrillation.' And he said that I have an unusual type of it, in that part of it is positional. It can be caused simply by turning over on my left side. I had two symptoms. One was that it would beat at a higher rhythm. The other was that it would sometimes start missing beats. So the doctor prescribed Lanoxin, because when your heart does trip out, it can create an embolism, which then could create a stroke. So in order to prevent the risk of stroke, this was the safer thing to do.

I spent most of the time I worked on Esther on her heart chakra. First I cleared the stagnated energy away. Then I loosened the damaged cords, pulled them out, untangled, cleaned, cleared, charged, and strengthened them, then reconnected them appropriately to her father's heart chakra. Once this was accomplished, configurations from past life experiences began to unfold on the fourth level of the field, which were also in the heart chakra. I pulled a long sharp object that looked like a lance out of the left side of her heart. With HSP, it looked as if she had been betrayed and killed in a past life conflict. There were also two very heavy, dense shields over her heart, which had been placed there in a

ceremony during the ancient Goddess religion times. To be a priestess in these ancient times meant to dedi-cate one's life to the Goddess and vow to give up any relationships with men. The shields were inscribed with some sort of ancient writing. Shields such as these were placed over the heart in a ceremony to help pre-vent a priestess from falling in love with a man. Once I was able to remove the shields, I also could remove a suit of medieval-looking armor.

Past life objects such as these remain in the auric field as unresolved psycho-noetic energy-consciousness and influence present-day life. The spear could give Esther the tendency to expect betrayal of the heart; the shields would tend to interfere with her ability to relate to men. The suit of armor showed a strong psychic con-nection to Joan of Arc and martyrdom.

Once these objects were removed, a great deal of light emerged from Esther's chest. I have never seen anyone's chest radiate such a beautiful, brilliant light before. After the healing, Esther asked if she could go off her medication. I said no for several reasons. First of all, I had no authority to say yes. The doctor would have to decide that. And I had no plans to follow up the healing, as I do not have a healing practice. It turns out that Esther did go off her medication on her own.

Five months after the healing, I interviewed Esther to find out her experience during the healing and to follow up on what had happened since.

ESTHER: What I remember most vividly is feeling lighter and lighter as you removed the shields. I was never aware of the feeling of heaviness beforehand, but I remember feeling lighter as they were being re-moved. . . . The connection with Joan of Arc made a lot of sense to me because I have the tendency to martyr-dom. I tend to martyr myself for causes. . . . All of my friends would tell you that I'm a very intensely commit-ted person in terms of being very active in a number of causes. It's an area in which I've had to pull back at times, because of my intense overinvolvement. I'm codependent about it. I just throw myself into these things sometimes to the detriment of my energy state. I'm a peace activist. I'm a lawyer, and I was actively practicing law in civil rights cases. Most of the cases that I took were underdog cases. I represented many women who felt they had been discriminated against, such as sex harassment in the workplace, employment discrimination, race or sex discrimination. . . . Anita Hill was a lot like a lot of my clients. . . . I'm a femi-nist. . . .

What the healing did for me is that my heart problem

is ninety-five percent gone! I'm still experiencing a little bit of the, not the atrial fibrillation, but the other—it skips a bit every now and then. What I've learned to do when that happens is place the palm of my right hand over my heart chakra and just rotate it clockwise. It just regulates the energy field. You saw the heart chakra wobbling around, and what I picture is this wobbling heart chakra and I'm then able to just get it to calm down and go back into its regular clockwise pattern. That doesn't happen very often, but it does every now and then. But that's the only thing I do for it.

I tapered off the Lanoxin over the next ten days to two weeks. I think I was taking about one and one-half pills a day. I cut back to just taking one and then I took a half of one. Then I took a half of one every other day. Eventually within about two weeks, I was completely free of the medication.

I think the most exciting thing for me was that for several months after the thing had gotten rediagnosed, even with taking the Lanoxin, I was not able to turn over on my left side in bed without it kicking into the fast heartbeat. After this healing, I was able to just turn over on my left side. At first, it would feel like the heart didn't quite know what to do. And then it would just settle down and be itself, a normal heart. And that's the way it is today. I can turn over on my left side, and there's maybe a three- or four-second period of time, a very very brief period of time, when my heart seems to be remembering that it used to do this. But then it doesn't do it anymore. I don't know how else to describe it. It's a very funny feeling.

BARBARA: So during that time when you turn over, you're with your heart. It sounds as if you bring your conscious awareness to be with your heart. Bringing a new pattern there is what it sounds like you're doing automatically.

ESTHER: Yes, I do, I'm there and I'm with it. I guess I'm sort of reassuring it that it doesn't have to go crazy on me anymore. And it works.

But the most exciting thing for me was waking up one morning and realizing I had been asleep on my left side, and I had obviously just turned over in my sleep in the middle of the night, and my heart didn't trip out the way it used to when I did that. It would just wake me up immediately and drive me crazy until I turned over. But now I was obviously able to turn over in my sleep and sleep on my left side with absolutely no consequences and wake up in the morning a new person.

BARBARA: Great!

ESTHER: So that was really really exciting. But I get frustrated because I feel that I should be completely cured of this, with this wonderful healing. I wanted it to be totally, totally gone. I went through a period of time of being frustrated with that because it was ninety-five percent gone.... Because when it happened on the table, like this great miracle, I really felt like—like you had been the shaman. You were the person who did this, and you took all of this stuff off and you took it away. I was so much lighter. I remember the next day, I doused my heart chakra with a pendulum, and it was the entire width of my chest. It was just huge, and it was a wonderful feeling just being that open.... But then there was this, almost a ghost-pattern that would still be there at times. My husband tells me I'm too hard on myself, probably my martyr complex again.

But for now, I've really learned so much from that about the relationship between who I am emotionally and what my body is. And that the energy field is a real communication tool for me. And that was the most learning ... I finally realized that this whole thing for me had been a real learning experience. First of all, taking responsibility for my own healing and for teaching me that I'm responsible on a day-to-day basis. I'm responsible for my energy field, and there are some days when I don't take care of my energy field the way I should. I allow myself to get overstressed or overfatigued, and that's when I start feeling this ghost-pattern. My heart is trying to again tell me, "Hey, you're being a martyr. You're being too committed to this. You're too intense. You're too involved. Slow it down."

And I remembered you saying something about that in the workshop, about what our bodies tell us, what our disease processes tell us, and it's almost like I still need some piece of that to serve as my thermostat, as my warning bell, I think. Does that make sense?

BARBARA: That sounds great. Yes, that's true and that's probably why you've kept the ghost-pattern there, because you still need that protection for yourself.

ESTHER: Yes.

BARBARA: And someday that may go away too. Because you may get to the place where you automatically stop when your body tells you to in a more subtle way, like simply feeling it's time to quit.

ESTHER: Now I still have this need for a warning system to tell me when I'm scattering my energies. Then I know that it's time to stop, refocus, center my energy field, and work with my heart chakra, and I have the tools to do that now.

I'm working to get to the place where I can anticipate the dissipation of my energy. If I can anticipate that before it happens rather than after the fact, then I don't think I will have any need for this. I think it will be totally gone.

BARBARA: Good for you. Have you noticed any changes in your relationship to your father?

ESTHER: Oh, wow, that is interesting. The healing came in the middle of a journey that I began in April, in which I had joined, for the first time ever, a codependency therapy group working on early-childhood issues in family relationships. The most important piece of work that I did was after I came back from the healing. It was confronting my father on some things. I've had a history of not having a very good relationship with my mother, and I've struggled with that relationship for a lot of years. I have done all this work with my mother. But I always left my father alone. He was too scary to me or something to really be angry at, until I was able to do this work then, and that was after the healing. I had never had the courage to go ahead and be angry with him before. Some of the stuff that I had been blaming my mother for, I found out really belonged to my father. And so I gave him back his own stuff, and I was able to see my mother in a much more sympathetic light and how much she had struggled in her years of being married to this alcoholic man who was a womanizer and pretty selfish, who did his own thing. And so I was able to shift some of that over to him and confront him and, I think, come a lot closer to forgiving him. So yes, my relationship to my father definitely did change!

Problems with Fifth Chakra Cords

Cords from the fifth chakra represent secure trusting in the higher will of the relationship. They also represent giving and receiving in truthful communication through sound, words, music, and symbols. How communication and higher will interrelate is very interesting. When the throat chakra is open and functioning well, we speak our truth in the moment. That truth is automatically aligned with the higher will. In the beginning was the word, and the word was God. The word was made manifest. What we speak becomes manifest in the physical world. When our relational cords are healthy, the truths we speak to each other in a relationship bring about a positive manifestation of the relationship, which is aligned with the higher will of the relationship. Then we are able to accomplish our purpose in relating.

When our fifth chakra cords are not functioning, we don't know how to speak the truth of the higher will of our relationship. We have a difficult time completing the purpose of our relationship, and the relationship becomes painful.

All relationships are formed for the purpose of learning. The higher will of each relationship is always related to whatever is to be learned from that relationship. Some relationships may be formed just to complete karma. Karma is simply lessons that aren't yet learned that are carried over from one life to another. They are experiences that have not been completed. In the past, one has set an intention to complete a lesson, and when the lesson isn't learned, it gets carried over into another lifetime. We create a life plan, and within that plan are the types of significant relationships we will have to learn our lessons. We choose our parents and our family. The question is, do we also choose our "mates to be" way ahead of time? Do we have soulmates?

Heyoan says:

~

In the great wisdom of the Universe, there are many, many individuals who carry the desire to complete a particular learning, the wisdom, and the karma, who are compatible to your needs and who are available for you to meet. The universe is not so inefficient as to provide you with only one possibility. In any case, the individual that you will meet is someone you will recognize as the one, the mate, for that particular time in your life. In our view here, to a certain extent every individual on the planet is your soulmate and indeed also those that may not be in incarnation at this point. However, if you have come into a particular life with a major purpose, a major task, then the propensity for a particular mate will be higher if that individual has a life task that meshes completely with yours. In that sense, yes, you are soulmates. So you will recognize a soulmate from the perspective of being perfect in terms of energy vibrations, energy exchange, connectedness, and higher ideals and also in terms of who you are and where you are moving in the moment and over a particular period of time. When the lesson is learned, the karma is completed, and the relationship may no longer be active. The relationship will never end, since the connection remains forever. Or you will take on a new learning together and stay with each other for a lifetime if you so choose. It is completely up to you, for from our perspective there is no separation anyway.

Another way to look at it is in terms of how many times you have been together before. If you have been together before, you will recognize the other as yourself. The more times you have been together, the more you will recognize the other as yourself. Perhaps there is some particular moment when the number of times you have been together will bring you to the belief that this is indeed a soul twin. Once connected, always connected, and the more times you are connected, the more similar you become in experience and wisdom and in the level of integration of consciousness and individuality.

Relationships continue beyond the physical world. They also continue between an individual who is in the physical and one who has released the physical. They are very much the same as they are in the physical. That is how it is with one's relationship with God. You see, the human romantic relationship is one of the closest ways to experience the divine, for one experiences the divine in the individuality of the other. This is a prologue to how good it will be with God. The human romantic relationship is the first step of many mergings that you will experience before you unite with God in relationship. You never lose the eros and the beauty and the wonder of recognizing the other.

~

The cords in the fifth chakra can be damaged in harsh interactions regarding the truth and the higher will in relationship. They can be carried over from past lifetimes in which the individual was betrayed or betrayed others. They can be damaged in childhood through harsh interactions with regard to truth, such as a parent or other authority not believing children when they are telling the truth. They can be damaged by parents who don't take responsibility for their role. For example, one of the roles of a father is to protect the child from harm. But if the father doesn't protect the child and even takes his frustration out on the child by physically mistreating it, he is betraying the higher will of their relationship. The child will not trust relationships with other male authorities.

Common illnesses that result from damaged fifth chakra cords: The illnesses I have most often seen include hypoactive thyroid, goiter, misalignments in the neck, and lung diseases.

Examples of healings and their effects: A woman I shall call Lorie came to me in her early fifties, after having gone through many years of therapy in which she had cleared a lot of problems in her life. Her present complaint was a hypoactive thyroid. She still had one central issue: She didn't trust relationships. I will give a longer history in this case, because it gives a clearer idea of how someone can, step by step, clear many of the chakra cord problems that were developed during childhood. Although some parts of Lorie's story are more drastic than what you might consider normal, her chakra cord problems were not much worse than the so-called normal state of most people who are having problems. In other words, most people have difficulties in their cord connections in many of their chakras. And it is usual to take very long periods of time to heal them if they don't know they exist and therefore do not work directly on them. Although Lorie was unaware of relational cords for most of her life, I will tell her story in terms of them.

Lorie grew up in a conservative midwestern farm culture. She was a quiet girl, had few friends, studied a lot, and excelled in school. She didn't feel very connected to her mother, who chose her older brother and younger sister over her. She connected to her father, whom she adored and for whom she would do anything—even become the son to her father that her brother refused to be. She didn't play with dolls much, she loved to make things, and she assisted her father in many things. She felt terrible jealousy toward her little sister, who got all the adoration, while Lorie was made to work long hours helping her parents.

These experiences in her early life brought about a distortion of the cords to her parents in many of her chakras.

The first chakra cords grew pretty well into the earth, since she did a lot of work with her family members on the land at the farm.

The second chakra cords were damaged on the left side, the ones that connect to the mother, because she couldn't connect to her mother in terms of sensual and sexual pleasure, which her mother denied in her own life. Lorie also had a very strict sexual upbringing because of the culture she grew up in. Sex was a duty that was to be put up with.

The third chakra cords of caretaking developed well between Lorie and her father, but she tore the ones to her mother out. Her father paid attention to her and took care of her, but the roles were reversed with her mother. Lorie did the caretaking. Lorie tried to get her mothering needs from her father.

Lorie's fourth chakra cords became a bit embedded in the left side of her heart because she also disconnected her heart from her mother. She felt guilt because she competed with her mother for her father.

Over time, Lorie's fifth chakra cords were entangled on both sides because she was so confused about her identity and her true needs. She had no models in her family for asking and filling needs. No one really knew how to do it. Most personal needs were also overridden by economic hard times.

The sixth chakra cords developed fine. There was a lot of freedom within the family structure with ideas. Actually, there was very little intellectual discussion about anything in the family, but both parents had a great respect for knowledge. The cords of creative ideas were strong and healthy, although there weren't many of them.

Lorie's seventh chakra cords were also fine. She connected with her mother in her spirituality. Her mother had "the faith of a grain of mustard seed." She also learned the benefits of being silent while spending time fishing with her father. This was actually his method of meditating and feeling God. Lorie emulated her mother's faith and her father's practical use of meditation. She was thus able to make very strong connections through her seventh chakra.

As a result of Lorie's reactions to her childhood life and how she developed her relational cords because of it, she most naturally began to concentrate on the areas of her life where her cords were the healthiest. She slowly began to withdraw from family life and concentrate on school, where she could make a mark for herself. It was the main area left to her as a young teenager where she could find recognition and respect. This worked for her. She excelled in school and went on to college. Everything was fine until she got into relationships with men. Actually, she was fine as long as she could help them with their homework. But she could not take the role of a female caretaker or lover, because she had no direct model of it from her mother.

Lorie went through two marriages in which she was unable to get her needs met, or trust that the relationship was right for her, or support her in her life. She had difficulties for years communicating her needs in her relationships with both of her husbands.

First she married someone much older than herself. She was quite young and in a sense, wanted someone to take care of her. As she said to her friends at the time, "He is offering me my life on a golden platter." She hardly knew the man but married him out of fear of being alone. The week after the marriage she spent feeling completely trapped and sat staring out the window of the one-room apartment in which she now found herself. After several months of discovering that she had very little in common with her husband, who would sit for hours playing with his ham radio, she began to focus on her career as a way to make something in her life worthwhile. During the next five years, she built up a career and became financially independent. Although her husband was very nice to her, the marriage never really developed. Their sex life was more or less nonexistent. There were not many friends or pastimes, and no children were born. Lorie did not want to have children. She didn't have the faintest idea of how to mother them, and she didn't want to. After five years, she had an affair with someone at work, which she used to get out of her rather boring, unfulfilling marriage.

During the first marriage, what Lorie did accomplish was more development and strengthening of the cords from the sixth chakra that gained her financial independence. Because her husband was so loving, she was also able to begin working on her sexuality. So those cords began to be loosened and healed, especially the ones that had represented sex as a duty to put up with. Even though sex may not have been that interesting, at least it was no longer a duty.

Lorie had so many guilt feelings about the affair that she decided to try to make a go of it and moved in with the second man. There was immediate trouble in the relationship. By this time, Lorie was desperate to get some of her relational needs met, but she didn't understand this. She didn't know what her needs were. Neither could she communicate them in a way that worked. Instead, she was once again with someone who was very different from her. Lorie started demanding attention, caretaking, and sex. The new husband, who was a child of alcoholic parents, reacted by becoming abusive. The more she demanded, the more scared her husband got, the more abusive he became. Each year the abuse got worse, and Lorie became more distressed. She had no idea of what to do. She didn't even know she was creating this situation in which she seemed like a victim. She was successful in her career but miserable at home.

In this abusive situation, she grew very distorted cords. Her second, third, fourth, and fifth chakras became worse. Her agony finally forced her to get help. She began therapy and made great strides in clearing away a lot of issues. She found out how to stop the abuse by creating clear boundaries she didn't cross. In the process of creating boundaries, she used her seventh chakra spirituality connection, which her husband also had, to help herself stay on track. With this new safety, she found much more love for her husband and healed many of her heart chakra cords. She maintained the clarity of the sixth chakra cords in the process. But she still was unable to heal the second, third, and fifth chakra cords. She was very sexually incompatible with her husband, who was afraid of sexual passion and avoided it. The only way Lorie knew how to get sex was to demand it. This scared her husband even more. Soon their sex life became dormant.

She was unable to learn to take care of herself, and her husband could not deal with her demands. So he still continually either avoided her or rejected her. The left side of her third chakra began to tear open, causing weakness in the pancreas and then in her whole digestive system. She became food-sensitive and had to go on special diets to prevent exhaustion and bloat. Her fifth chakra got worse. She had regular fights with her husband, who still threatened physical abuse but turned it into verbal abuse, cruelty, and overcontrol.

During this time in her life, Lorie also did a lot of personal and couples therapy and body work. She continued to ground down strongly into the earth. Through this work, she strengthened her first, fourth, sixth, and seventh chakras.

After much struggle and soul-searching, she finally decided to end the marriage to work on herself alone. So by the end of her second marriage, she had many of the cords from her first, fourth, sixth, and seventh chakras well functioning. But the cords from her second, third, and fifth chakras were worse.

During her time alone, she worked on her second, third, and fifth chakras. She gave herself space to find out what her needs were, to find trust that they could be met, and to begin asking for them in a nondemanding way. This began to strengthen her fifth chakra, where she had had the most trouble since early childhood. She also began to take better care of herself, and this strengthened her third chakra. She began to explore her sexuality in a freer situation than she had ever been able to do before and discovered that she functioned quite well in that area. The second chakra cords also now began to heal.

After two years she met and married her third husband. Their heart and sexual connections were immediately felt. Because she had done so much work on her chakras, this time she was able to couple herself to someone much more compatible. She married a man who had very few difficulties with sexuality and was a caretaker. Her second chakra was now well on its way to health. Her husband spent years going with her through all her sexual pain left over from the two previous relationships. He took care of her in ways she

didn't even know existed. This was natural for him, having been brought up in a family that did this. Lorie began emulating him. She began making stronger connections to her original family, especially to her mother. And her third chakra cords to her mother began to heal. As she cleaned and strengthened her third chakra cords to her mother, she also revised her relationship with her father. She began creating healthy third chakra cords to other people with whom she was in relationship.

By the time Lorie came to me, most of these problems had been taken care of. But she still had a lot of problems in her neck, jaw, and thyroid. She still did not trust relationship. She still found it impossible to trust her husband enough to allow herself to admit any dependence on him. Her solution to problems was to stand on her own two feet and never to really rely on another person, to never really surrender to the higher will of a relationship and trust the relationship to carry her through.

As her relationship grew deeper, she was challenged more and more to do this. Her reaction, again, was to concentrate on her work life and to overwork. Thus, after years of overworking, her thyroid, which sits directly in the fifth chakra—where her cords had been entangled since early childhood—began to give out. This distrust in relationship was now interfering with her work life also. She found it difficult to delegate work to her employees. Many times she just did it herself. By the time she came to me, she had worked an average of sixty to eighty hours a week for about twenty years. She was very successful and still had lots of energy, but she was wearing out her body. The issue was whether she could surrender to the higher will of the relationship that she had created and learn to see it as an ongoing co-creation that she and her husband were doing.

As I worked on her fifth chakra and cleared the cords, Lorie began to let up a little. She began to quit work at five or six o'clock every day and just watch TV with her husband. She began getting more involved in her home life and painting and other pleasures that fulfilled her. She spent more time with her husband, even going on his business trips. And he went on hers. As she healed herself, she realized that she had had a tendency to malign people or employees who didn't meet her needs. She realized that she had difficulties in communicating duties to employees without anger or blame because she assumed they would not do what she wanted. All of it was wrapped up in her fifth chakra and her disbelief in the higher will of any of the relationships she was in.

As her fifth chakra cleared with several healings, her thyroid shrank in size and functioned normally. She focused on her communication skills with people who knew how to manage employees so they felt good about what they did and got things done. She used them as models to learn to communicate her needs. She practiced communication skills with friends. She tried new ways of verbalizing what she wanted to say. She realized she had to go over all the relationships that she had ever had, see the higher will in each, and find what she had learned through each so that she could feel safe in a relationship now. She is spending her daily meditation time for one year doing this. At the time of this writing, Lorie is in the process of doing this and is making great strides. Everything in her life is coming together in new ways, and she is trusting all her relationships much more.

Problems with Sixth Chakra Cords

Cords from the sixth chakra represent the ecstasy of seeing higher concepts in the exchange and interplay of ideas while at the same time experiencing unconditional love with whomever this exchange is taking place. They represent the pleasure of recognizing your loved one as a beautiful being of light and love. They represent the ability to love from a spiritual perspective, as did many of our religious figures such as the Christ and Buddha.

The cords of the sixth chakra can be damaged from past life experiences where people were forced to practice religions they did not believe in.

Common illnesses that result from damaged sixth chakra cords: Damage to cords from the sixth chakra can result in headaches, confusion, disorientation, brain disorders like schizophrenia, and learning disabilities.

Examples of healings and their effects: In February 1992, in an introductory workshop, I had the privilege of working on cords from the sixth chakra. I shall call the client Aida. During the break of a lecture I was giving, Aida came up to me and asked about her daughter's and her own dyslexia. I checked out Aida's sixth chakra and its cords. Sure enough, the sixth chakra was damaged on the right side. The cords that would normally connect from the center of the sixth chakra out into the corpus callosum did not connect at all. I rolled backward in time and saw that some of the damage was from when she was very young, and that part of the damage had occurred a couple of years before Aida got pregnant with her daughter, when she

had a fever of about 105. She had her tonsils out at that time. The cords that were supposed to connect from her sixth chakra to her father's sixth chakra were damaged. I could see that her father had tried to force his negative ideas about life into her mind through his sixth chakra cords, so she had torn them out. I asked if she would like to participate in the demo. She agreed.

First, I worked to help Aida ground herself, to strengthen her weak first and second chakras. Then I worked on the third chakra, which was not functioning properly. I cleared the clogged vortices in each of these chakras. I then cleared the vertical power current of energy up the spinal cord all the way up through the head. I lifted a dark shroud, somewhat like a cloud, off her head and shoulders. It had been there a long time. She began to feel much lighter, freer, and relieved as it came off.

Because of her father's economic difficulties, he had a pessimistic attitude about life, which he conveyed to Aida. However, as a child, Aida knew that it was very important to get to the heart of any matter before going to the solution. That is what was missing in the concepts that came from her father. Heyoan said that as a child, Aida had disconnected the cord pathway from the sixth chakra into the corpus callosum because she was afraid that she would take up her father's pessimistic attitude about life. Using her child's reasoning, she became wary of taking in information from anyone for fear that it would be pessimistic. To do this, she had to disconnect the sixth chakra cords from her corpus callosum, and thus she had created her dyslexia.

As I described what had happened to Aida, I untwisted her vertical power current.

Then Heyoan explained to her:

~

Anyone has the incarnational option open to them to create dyslexia in order to maintain the knowledge that it is very important to get to the heart of the matter before making an intellectual judgment about any situation. Given the structure of the school system in America, it would have been very difficult to keep your heart first. So you chose to give up, at least for the time being, the ability to take in information from a perspective that you thought would lose the heart. For you saw the need upon the earth, and in descending into incarnation you decided to give the gift to teach others to keep the heart first, before the rational mind. Now that this gift is clear, we shall work on these cords.

~

As I worked on the sixth and seventh chakra cords, Heyoan continued:

~

All the cords that go out the back of the chakras relate to past relationships that are not right now actively affecting this incarnation, and the front ones are actively affecting this incarnation.

~

I connected the cords from the inner tip of the sixth chakra down into the corpus callosum. Then I untangled and cleaned the cords from the front of the sixth chakra and asked Aida if she would be willing to deeply reconnect to her father. She agreed. As I made telepathic connection to her father, I could see that he had a heavy heart from the burdens of his life and that he was sad from many unfulfilled longings. He (telepathically) said that he is better now. I worked (long distance) on his third eye to help relieve some of the negative ideas, and I connected his head to his heart. At that point some of the cords from the front of Aida's chakra went to the rear. Heyoan explained,

~

Some of these issues are now behind you.

~

As the cords began to reconnect between Aida's and her father's sixth chakras, a new relationship began to form. I then worked on Aida's heart chakra cords to her father. I could see that earlier in life she had gotten very angry at him and wouldn't let him in. Aida said, "I pretended that my father was dead."

Heyoan said:

~

Over time you will see why it is so important to accept the love from your father the way it is. The way he expressed it and expresses it now. You need to accept the way each individual expresses his essence. In the past you have said, "Your love is not the way it ought to be, so I won't accept it." There is a deep lesson here for you to learn: how to accept the essence of each individual. This is what blocks you in your relationships to men and with a mate. They can never live up to how you deem they should be.

~

At this point, Aida stopped the cords from entering her heart, so I said, "Can you let your father walk toward you? Your father wants to walk into your heart exactly as he is with all his human frailty. That's good, let him walk right into you. Your child is saying, 'It will hurt, it will hurt. It will hurt because he hasn't been there for so long.'"

As the cords connected deep into Aida's heart, her breathing deepened.

"It feels pretty new, huh?" I said.

"Pretty alive!" Aida exclaimed.

Heyoan continued to speak as I worked:

~

Connect this deep into the soul seat. Connect it to your life's work. For it is directly connected to your life's work: accepting another individual's reality, finding the truth in it, and finding the bridges to commune from one to the other. It can only be done through the heart, by allowing the other into your heart. It is the way you can think for yourself and also allow the other to think for him/herself. Thus individual truths can exist side by side with apparent differences or even disagreements from the perspective of duality, and at the same time, from the higher spiritual truth, they would not be different.

~

I completed the connection into Aida's soul seat on the haric level and then switched to the core star level to expand her core essence out into the room, 360 degrees. I said, "Feel who you are that is different from anyone else on the earth. Feel the light going all through your body. It is coming from the inside of your body, from your core star."

Aida's light beamed out over the audience. She felt brilliantly alive. It was visible to everyone.

As we closed, Heyoan added,

~

This particular pattern is handed down through generations. It is only one type of dyslexia. There are three kinds. I will speak about them in the future.

~

I like to follow up healings at several-month intervals for as long as possible, to see the long-term effects of a healing. It has been five months since Aida's healing, but since this book needs to go to print, I cannot allow a longer time period to pass before followup. Here is what she said about the effects of the healing on her relationship with her father and on her dyslexia.

AIDA: Well, it's affected my relationship with my father a great deal. It's certainly a lot more loving and a lot more supportive. It's almost as if I've forgiven a lot of the past issues, and I feel a lot more connected with my father. There definitely has been some wonderful experience as a result of the healing.

BARBARA: Does he treat you any differently?

AIDA: Yes. In the past I always felt that he wasn't there for me; he wasn't available to me. And now, the least little bit of anything I need, he's right there to help me. He's very supportive. In the past, I would have said something, and a week, a month, a year would have gone by, and he would never have heard me. Now I just say one word, and within a matter of hours, it's done, and I'm thinking, "My goodness. This is definitely a change." So I'm feeling loved the way I had never felt it before because my father was just not available. Also, the communication between him and me has gotten better. He's been able to tell me about his childhood. He experienced a great deal of abuse as a child. He was battered a great deal both by a stepfather and by a mother who was in turn also abused. And she was an alcoholic. So in seeing and understanding where he came from, I was more able to accept and forgive the way he treated me and us—my brothers and my sister. Because there was a great deal of abuse and harshness and total rage, out of control, on his part.

BARBARA: That's great!

AIDA: Now the dyslexia part. There's a part of me that feels real organized, but I'm noticing some more disorganization. It's almost as if it's coming more to the surface. I'm becoming more aware of it. I'm more conscious of the difficulty that I have. I do see myself turning things around. I do see myself stumbling on new words that I have not seen or am real familiar with. In the past I would get frustrated and angry at myself, and now I'm a little more forgiving and tolerant of myself.

BARBARA: So the improvement is that you're consciously aware of when you're doing it. Were you consciously aware of it when you were doing it before?

AIDA: No, I was not.

BARBARA: Well, that's interesting because usually the first step in changing something is to become consciously aware of when you are doing what you want to change.

AIDA: Well, yes. I have been experiencing a lot of things that seem to be moving toward transformation. I had a vision of myself as being like an old twig. I could see my arms and my legs as an old dried-up twig. It was a vision because I wasn't asleep. Then I could see or feel or I recognized that the light was within me to rejuvenate or reignite, redevelop those twigs. And then the next picture was again my face, but I was with a vibrant alive body. I didn't realize what that was all about until just recently. It's almost as if my life is organizing itself so that I'm not so much the focal point for my children. My daughters are going away to college and summer school in July. My other one's in college, and I'm thinking of going back to school. I'm being drawn to a possible new area. . . . Perhaps I would have powers to do a lot of healing. There is a great deal of confirmation within me, and I'm wanting to do this, but there is fear on my part to surrender. I want to be willing to do God's work. I'm signed up for a communicative disorders course. Can I get any guidance? Is that in keeping with what my life purpose is?

BARBARA: Oh, yes.

Heyoan says:

~

Clearly, communicative disorders are right on the line of what we've been talking about.

~

Problems with Seventh Chakra Cords

Cords from the seventh chakra, which also connect up into the higher realms, represent the power to be within the divine mind of God in relationship to God, the universe, and another human being. They represent the ability to understand the perfect pattern of a relationship. They also represent the ability to integrate the physical and spiritual worlds in relationship.

Common illnesses that result from damaged seventh chakra cords: Damage to cords from the seventh chakra can result in depression, inability of the physical body's normal development through the maturation process, headaches, and mental disorders like schizophrenia.

Examples of healings and their effects: The seventh chakra cords connect to relationships that exist in the soul's life between incarnations in human form. They connect up to our spiritual heritage. Sometimes that heritage is related to our relationship to God or spiritual beings that are accepted by the organized religions of the world, such as the Christ, the Buddha, guardian angels, and spiritual guides. Sometimes they connect to beings in realities that may seem outrageous to those of us who have been brought up in the Western Hemisphere.

Seventh chakra cords tend to get damaged before birth, at conception, or in the womb. They are always related to difficulties with bringing the consciousness of the incoming soul into the body and the process of incarnation. Damage to the seventh chakra cords results in our either being stuck inside our bodies with no spiritual connection, or being stuck in the spiritual world and not being able to come down fully into the physical.

For example, retarded children have not been able to completely come down into their bodies, and they seem to have a great deal of fear to do so. I have not had the privilege of working with retarded people, so I do not know if the body was damaged first so that they couldn't get into it, or if the body became retarded because they were unwilling to come down into it. I would guess that either is possible. Probably the cause varies with the case and, of course, the life task. Retarded children are great teachers and sometimes volunteer to incarnate in that way to help the family into which they are born. I know of one case where a healer was able to bring a retarded child into normal development through years of daily hands-on healing work.

For those of us who call ourselves normal, there is usually one major reason why we haven't come completely down into our bodies and therefore have problems with our seventh chakra cords. We use the spiritual connection to escape from incarnation and avoid dealing with life as human beings on earth now. To do this, we simply keep shifting our consciousness out the top of our heads, or "going out the top of our heads." This is simply a defensive maneuver from fear.

This defensive maneuver is very popular with many healing students! When the cords are worked with and the fear dealt with, these students understand that since they are human now, their spirituality can be realized only from the perspective of being within a human body. They change their lives and begin to spiritualize matter rather than escape it.

An interesting seventh chakra cord problem is common among people who believe that they are from another star system. These people feel that they are not really human beings but have been forced to come here from an advanced culture, usually outside the solar system. They miss their "true" home and have a rough time getting into and staying in a physical body. HSP reveals that the seventh chakra cords from these people relate to these other star systems and connect to highly evolved beings from advanced cultures on planets in these star systems. These clients commonly call themselves star children and claim never to have been incarnated as humans before. In such cases, healing takes on a different flavor. The problem is usually that these people, in denying their connection to the earth, also deny their connection to the other place. They have torn their cords that connect to the other systems, yet they seek to leave their bodies to return "home" via their broken cords. (That won't work.) The result is that they find it very difficult to connect to anything in a stable way.

So in this way, they also resist incarnation. I have found that the best way to help these people come down into their bodies and connect down into the earth is to repair these torn cords and make the connection to the other star system stronger. To do this, they must connect to the part of them that volunteered to come here out of love and power. They then get nourished through these cords. Once the full connection is made, these people come down into their bodies and claim their humanness, even allowing for the very strong probability that they have been incarnated as human beings before. By reconnecting their star cords, they have a strong connection to the stars through which they can be nourished.

This may seem totally preposterous to some readers, but I remind you of my motto: "Don't ask if it is real. Just ask if it is useful." It works! Usually, part of the channeling that goes with such healings is to teach clients to perceive themselves as originating holographically out of the whole of the universe rather than just one planet or a particular star system. Since we are all holographically connected to everything, we can theoretically remember every life that ever was lived on this planet, as well as others, as if we were the one who lived it.

I have worked on seventh chakra cords on a number of occasions. The healing work is the same as with all the cords. They are cleared, untangled, cleaned, and reconnected appropriately.

In one case in my class, the student had cord connections to the planetary beings of a particular star system through all the chakras. In the healing I began with the seventh chakra and worked down the body to repair and connect all the cords that she had cut. She felt much better later and was much more in her body than I had ever seen her. At the time of this writing, she is much more grounded into her body, being surprised at how much she is enjoying it, feeling much safer in her body, and doing just fine.

Another time I worked on damaged cords from the seventh chakra in order to heal a depressed client. Before the healing series, the client felt connected to his fellow humans but experienced life as a finite, rather senseless passage to nowhere. He felt no connection to God. As a result, he was depressed. After spending several sessions repairing these cords, the client began to have a sense of connectedness to all that there is, including the divine. His depression went away, and he began to enjoy life at a deeper level of meaning. He began making choices about how he wanted to spend his time, and over a period of time, his life changed a great deal. He changed his attitude about work. Previously, he had been an accountant; now he chose to become a professional therapist, specializing in helping people understand the broad-scale aspects of their lives, in order to help them find what they want to do with their lives.

As I conclude this chapter and look at the compiled information, I am surprised at how important all our past and present relationships are in our health and healing as well as our personal development. Since it is now in vogue to say we each create our own reality, there has been a swing toward isolationism in many spiritual groups in dealing with this issue. It seems that some people work on "how I create my own reality" in isolation from everyone else. But in fact, holistically speaking, our reality is deeply intertwined with others, through our auric interactions and connections, through our past history of relationships, and through our genetic cords. We are products of millions of years of evolutionary development of the physical body, as well as of the auric connections. Undoubtedly, our auric cords develop over evolutionary time as well, since we are always evolving in our ability to relate.

We know that we create our own experience of reality, but who is the "we" or "I" that is creating? Probably the best practical context in which to work with the concept of creating one's own reality in self-transformation work and healing is that *what makes us sick is not our relationships per se but our energetic and psychological reactions to these relationships*. None of these auric interactions could occur without agreement between the people involved, yet they are usually automatic and unconscious.

Our negative interactions to relationship result in healing cycles in which we reflect upon ourselves more and thereby move through an individuation process that, as I stated in the beginning of this chapter, is the prime purpose of life experience on the fourth level of the field.

So from the broad-scale view, self-development or individuation through the incarnation process is working. Illnesses that result from our negative reactions to relationship help us sort out who we are from who we are not. Successful relationships teach us who we are, even if they are difficult and lead to illness. If we are not growing by learning about ourselves in a relationship, then the relationship is not successful.

This does not imply that people should stay in painful relationships. In such cases, usually part of the learning is to find out that we deserve and can create a much better situation in our lives.

The more we know ourselves and heal our codependency, the more we can learn about ourselves in a happy, smooth, flowing relationship. The more individuated we become, the more interdependence we achieve.

FIFTEEN

Observations of Auric Interactions During Relationships

Love is created when we come together, merge in communion, and then move apart again. The effects are immediately positive, and we experience more joy in our lives. When we come together and clash, we create life lessons or healing cycles that may be experienced negatively. But eventually, once lessons are learned or healings completed, they bring us back around to the positive. All this shows in auric field interactions.

We use all of the three major ways of influencing each other's fields that were discussed in Chapter 14. Some of these ways are positive; some are negative. In the positive interactions, we get along fine. We make positive connections with people with the chakra cords. We exchange positive energy with each other through our bioplasmic streamers. We lift each other's vibrations and bring clarity and lightness to each other through harmonic induction. We accept each other as we are and do not try to manipulate each other for our own purposes. In these positive interactions, we also do not allow other persons to mistreat us. We remain centered within ourselves and communicate well.

Negative Auric Interactions in Relationships

We also have habitual negative ways of interacting and manipulating each other through our fields. We usually do this out of fear and ignorance. We usually are not consciously aware that we are doing it. We try to make other persons' fields pulsate like ours through harmonic induction because we are not comfortable with their vibrations. We pull and push each other's fields with the bioplasmic streams of energy that flow between, or we stop the bioenergy flow altogether. We use the cords that are connected between us to get what we want. We try to hook or entangle each other with them. All this auric interaction is usually unconscious and invisible to most people, but anyone can learn to become aware of it and sense it by developing Higher Sense Perception.

There are really only four modes of energy flow that we use in these interactions: We push, pull, stop, or allow the energy flow. If one person pulls, the other may pull back or stop the energy flow completely. If one pushes, the other may push back or dig in their heels and stop.

A typical intimate relationship may go like this: She wants love from him, and she reaches out and tries to pull it out of him. He wants to be left alone for a while and pushes a powerful blast of energy at her so that she will go away. Or he may simply go into stop with his field and not respond, so that nothing she does gets through.

Think about how you interact with others. For example, when someone pushes energy at you, do you push back? Do you pull that energy into you? Do you go into stop, or do you yield and allow the energy to flow into you as it is being pushed into you? Most of us either stop the energy flow or push back.

We have all created some rather standard ways of interacting with each other through our energy fields. The standard energetic interactions correspond to the mutual agreements or contracts we all make with each other, described in Chapter 13. We do this unconsciously and habitually. Sometimes it works, and sometimes it doesn't. The way some people use their fields to interact with us is fine with us, and the way others do so is not fine with us. All of our habitual interactions are really energy field defense systems that we use to defend ourselves from an imagined dangerous world. Sometimes we are able to "handle" somebody else's defense system, and at other times we find ourselves very intolerant of it.

When we don't learn how to handle somebody's negative energetic actions in a positive healing way, a negative feedback loop can start. Each person may escalate defensive distortion until imagination and projection completely take over. In such cases, very painful damaging interactions can result. This happens on the personal level, between two people; it happens between groups of people; and it happens between nations, many times resulting in war. If we can learn to prevent it on the personal level, we will eventually know how to prevent it on the national level.

Extremely negative harsh interactions can wreak havoc in the auric field and leave people the job of repairing themselves afterward. Some of the repair occurs quite automatically, like the way the body repairs itself. Some auric wounds and psychic scars can remain in the auric field as long as a lifetime or even be carried on into future lifetimes, depending on how deep they are. Wounds remain in the field so long because people usually avoid directly experiencing their wounds but suppress them deeper into the field and then bury them

with an energy block. Deep wounds of this sort occur from one extremely harsh interaction or from habitually repeated negative interactions. All such wounds can be healed through hands-on healing and personal process.

According to what I have observed in auric fields over twenty years, all deep wounds are created through negative relational interactions that occurred in this lifetime or in a past lifetime, which are then carried forward into the next life experience. Or they are created through some sort of physical trauma, such as a natural disaster or accidental injury. In addition to that, I have been able to trace most accidental injuries in my clients back to a delayed reaction from a harsh interaction with another person. Good interactions are basic to our health; negative ones create disease or injury.

For example, recently in a workshop I was giving a healing demonstration on a young woman from Germany. I noticed that her left knee had been injured a few years earlier. With internal vision I could see that one of the ligaments that criss-cross under the kneecap was pulled and torn a bit, making it weaker. As I worked on the ligament, I rolled backward in time to see how it had been injured. With HSP, I saw the young woman riding a bike. She bumped into a fairly low object and flew headfirst over the right side of the handlebars. However, the reason she didn't see the object was that she had been preoccupied with an argument she had had with a young man a short time before. The next day, after the healing, she confirmed the information I had read with HSP.

Since all illness is related to a negative relational experience, it is of the utmost importance for us to learn to interact with each other in healthy, healing ways. In this chapter I will elaborate on some typical forms of energetic defense systems and the typical negative ways we react that eventually cause problems for us in our own energy fields and our health. I will then show positive ways to respond to the same energetic defense systems that create health for everyone.

A Framework to Resolve Negative Energetic Interactions

As a framework with which to organize the material and to describe the typical energetic defense patterns we all habitually use to some extent, I will use the five basic standard character structures that are used in the study of bioenergetics. You will find that some energetic defense patterns are very much like you, and others not so much. You will probably relate to a certain degree with each of them.

Character structure is a term that many body psychotherapists use to describe certain physical and psychological types in people. Although we inherit our physical makeup genetically, how our physical bodies develop depends on our childhood circumstances. People with similar childhood experiences and child-parent relations have similar bodies. People with similar bodies have similar basic psychological dynamics. These dynamics are dependent not only on types of child-parent relations but on the age at which children first experience life so traumatically that they begin to block their feelings. To do this, children block the flow of energy through their auric fields and begin to develop a defense system that will become habitual throughout the rest of life. A trauma experienced in the womb will be energetically blocked or defended against very differently from one experienced in the oral stage of growth, in toilet training, or in latency. This is natural because individuals and their fields are so different at different stages of life.

From my perspective, the circumstances and experiences of our childhood are determined by the belief systems that we carry forward from past life experiences, as well as by experiences of life on other planes of reality. Life events are effects from causes that we have set into motion long before our birth into our present physical bodies. Some people call this "karma" and call "bad karma" punishment for what we have done. But karma is not punishment. It is the law of cause and effect at work. It is simply life circumstances or events coming to us as a result of our past actions.

How those events affect us is completely based on how we experience them through our images and belief systems. We carry the tendencies toward certain images and belief systems over from life to life until, through experience, we are able to clear and heal them. Each time such events come back to us, we have a chance to learn how to heal. If we carry negative images and belief systems about a particular set of circumstances, we will experience them as terribly painful. We might even interpret them as punishment for something we feel we have done. Since we can't remember doing anything particularly bad in this lifetime, perhaps it was from long ago in the past.

If we don't have a negative belief about something, its occurrence does not bring us self-judgment and debilitating pain. Of course, there is pain, but it is not debilitating pain.

Heyoan says that we are here on earth because that is our choice. We do not have to be here. He says that anytime we choose to, we can leave. There are no judgments on that.

The only reason we experience a certain event as punishment is because our belief system tells us it is punishment. For example, I have heard many people who do not allow themselves their power say that in the past they have misused power, so it was taken away, and now they are being punished so they don't have any. It could very well be that they misused power in the past, and that certain life events come to them as a result of their past misuse of power. But those events are precisely what they need to learn how to use power well. The universe is much too efficient and balanced to use punishment. Rather, it brings the precise lessons we need to fill our needs.

So character structure is the pattern of energy field distortion and the imbalance in our physical form that results from our negative images and belief systems, which have most likely been in place for many lifetimes. In other words, character structure is the effect of our negative beliefs and images on our psyches, our auric fields, and our physical bodies. Our parents didn't do it to us. Our childhood circumstances and relationships serve to bring forth and crystallize the negative images and beliefs that we brought with us to be healed. That is why we chose these parents and circumstances in the first place.

The five major character structures used in bioenergetics are called the schizoid, the oral, the displaced or psychopathic, the masochistic, and the rigid characters. These terms do not mean the same thing as the standard Freudian terms. They were evolved from the standard terms by Dr. Alexander Lowen, who studied with Dr. Wilhelm Reich, who was a student of Freud. After studying Freudian psychology, these innovators went on to study the relationship between Freudian psychology, the physical body, and its bioenergy. Thus the new terms were born. In my book *Hands of Light*, the auric field structure of each of the five major character structures is discussed, as well as the development of the auric field in different stages of growth. Here I shall focus on new ways to look at each character structure and the energetic defense system used by each structure.

Just what is meant by character structures? Many times people who study them begin to define themselves according to the characterology. Someone might say, "I'm a schizoid," or "I'm a rigid." People even take pride in these personal definitions. So the first thing I

FIGURE 15–1 DEFENSIVE ASPECTS OF THE CHARACTER STRUCTURES

	Schizoid	Oral	Psychopathic	Masochistic	Rigid
Main issue	Existential terror	Nurturance	Betrayal	Invasion and theft	Authenticity; denial of real self
Fear	Living in human body as an individual	Not enough of anything	Letting go and trusting	Being controlled; loss of self	Imperfection
Experienced	Direct aggression	Lack of nurturance; abandonment	Was used and betrayed	Invaded; humiliated	Denial of psychological and spiritual reality
Defensive action	Leaves body	Sucks life	Controls others	Demands and resists at same time	Acts appropriately rather than authentically
Results of defensive action	Weaker body	Inability to metabolize own energy	Aggression and betrayal drawn to self	Dependence; inability to differentiate between self and other	Inability to experience self; world is false
Relationship to core essence	Can experience unitive essence; is afraid of individuated essence	Experiences individuated essence as not enough	Is afraid that essence is bad or evil	Individuated essence is not differentiated from others	Does not experience individuated essence—it doesn't exist
Human need	To individuate; to surrender to being human	To nurture self; to know self is enough	To trust others; to make mistakes and still be safe	To be free to feel and express self	To put self into life; to feel real self
Spiritual need	To experience individuated essence	To experience individuated essence as infinite source within	To recognize and honor core essence and higher will of others	To recognize self's core essence as self's own and claim God within self	To experience unitive and individual core essence in self
Time distortion	Experiences universal time; is unable to experience linear time or be in the now in the physical world	Never has enough time	Rushes into the future	Experiences the unfoldment of time as stopped	Experiences the constant rigid, mechanical movement of time forward

must say is that character structure does not help you define who you are. Rather, it is a road map of who you are not. Many times it is actually who you fear yourself to be. Character structure shows you how you block the essence of who you are from being expressed. It describes the way you distort who you are. It shows you how you are not being who you are. Each character structure has a pattern of defense that distorts who you are and then expresses who you are in a distorted way.

This expression is immediate. It happens so fast on the energetic level that we cannot stop it just by deciding to with our minds. We will react according to our habitual defense system when we are under a certain degree of stress. Remember, our character defense was built when we were very young. It has been very useful to us in defending ourselves in situations that we could find no other way to handle when we were very young. It has served all of us well. It still shields the vulnerable child within us from the hostile world that we create for ourselves from our negative belief systems and our images. However, it also helps create the hostile world because it acts as if our negative beliefs about reality were true, thus drawing to us the negative experiences in life in which we believe.

A character structure defense is the result of feeling unsafe. It is a result of some kind of fear. Each character defense has a basic issue related to a specific fear. The energetic defense is a reaction to that specific fear. The weaknesses in the auric field and physical body are a direct result of the habitual distortion caused by the energetic defense. With our defensive actions, each character creates a way of living that then creates life experiences that verify that the fear is right. The way of living of each character defense also generates a specific negative relationship to time. Each character defense distorts the relationship to the core essence. Each character defense has a specific physical human need as well as a spiritual one. Both need to be filled to help heal it.

The different defensive aspects of each character structure are listed in Figure 15–1. We will discuss each aspect as we discuss each type of character defense. We will explore how to make each person feel safe in interaction that will then lead to a more permanent feeling of safety and bring about a healing of the habitual defense distortions that cause so much psychological and physical trauma in life. Remember, the purpose of a positive healing response to a defense is to help both of you get back to reality and communion as soon as possible. People with character structure defenses will demand that you agree with their distorted view of the world. If you do, it only strengthens their defense. It is also important to not let someone take advantage of you through their defense because that also helps strengthen their defense and supports their remaining in the illusion of a distorted view of the world.

You will find all of these typical auric defense patterns happening all around you, in yourself, and in your intimate relationships. You probably use different defenses in different situations. You will find that you and your friends use a combination of defenses. You can estimate how much you use each one on a percentage scale. For example, you may use thirty percent schizoid, ten percent oral, five percent psychopathic, fifteen percent masochistic, and forty percent rigid. This means that you are carrying the main issues of each character structure to that degree within yourself.

You will also go through different life stages in which you will find yourself dealing with the main issues of a particular character structure. It is in these times that you will use that defense most often. Then, after some time, you will be dealing with a different character structure issue. This is perfectly normal. In general, the type of character defense we use stays pretty much the same as we go through life, but we use it much less often, much less forcefully, and it softens so that more of who we truly are is expressed. It is important to keep in mind that these defenses are used by both men and women.

The Defense System of the Schizoid Character

The Main Issue of the Schizoid Defense

The main issue of those who use a schizoid defense is that of existential terror. Schizoid characters have probably had many lives in physical pain and trauma and usually have experienced death by torture for having particular spiritual beliefs. The way schizoid characters dealt with the torture was to find ways to escape the body. Given such a past, they now believe that living within a physical body is a dangerous and terrifying experience. Because of their past, they will not be too interested in coming into the earth at all. They will not want much contact with other human beings. They will expect direct hostility from them. And that is the way they will experience them at times, no matter how they really are. They are already programmed to experience others that way. For example, if a mother happens

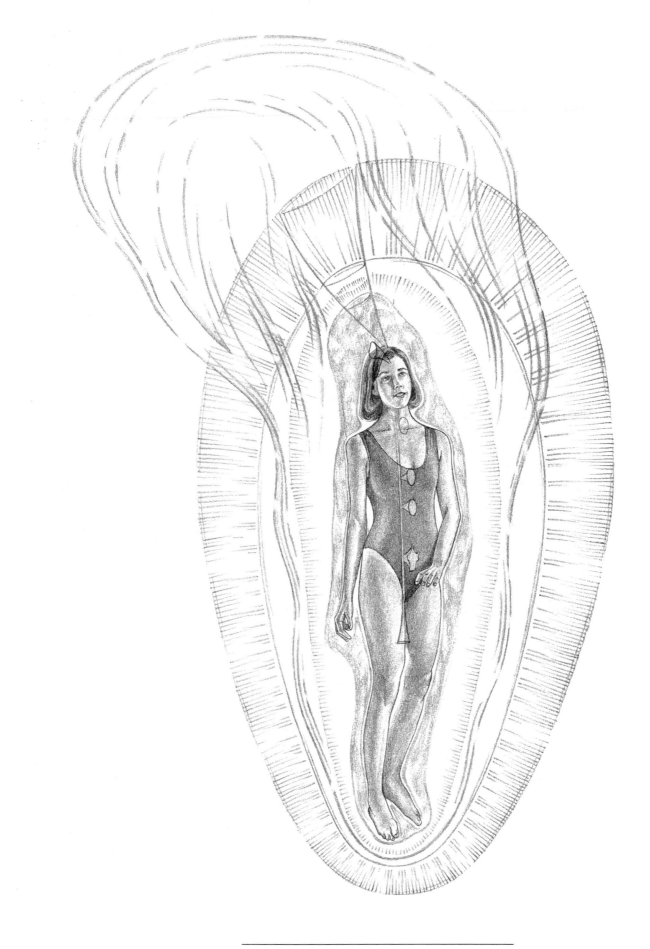

Figure 15–2 The Schizoid Character's Auric Defense

to be angry about something that has nothing to do with her child and happens to look at him in the crib, he will experience her anger as dangerous killer rage directed personally at him and will feel attacked. In the real situation, perhaps, she was angry at the carpenter for overcharging her.

On the other hand, these people's choice of parents will in some way reflect their belief that human beings are dangerous. Some parents do get enraged at their children, and some do abuse their children. What ultimately formulates the schizoid character defense is the way the child experiences reality, not necessarily the facts of a situation, although they usually are very similar.

In either case, people with a schizoid character defense are afraid of other people and have a rough time connecting to them. The third and fourth chakra cord connections to their parents never formed in a healthy way, so they have no model with which to connect to other people. Such people are afraid to completely incarnate; that is, they are afraid to bring consciousness and energy firmly into their physical body.

The Defensive Action the Schizoid Character Takes Against Fear

The defensive action schizoid characters take against fear is to vacate the physical body. They have found a way to first split and then twist energy-consciousness in order to allow a large portion of it to escape out the top. They usually exit out to one side of the top or the back of the head. Since they do this repeatedly from their very early childhood, sometimes beginning before birth, they create habitual twists in the energy body, which becomes lopsided and never develops a strong outer boundary for the aura. The eggshell of the seventh level is very weak.

The Negative Effects of the Schizoid Defensive Action

As a result of these defensive actions, the physical world feels even more unsafe to schizoid characters. Schizoid characters have very weak boundaries, which will be penetrated very easily by others. Their physical bodies follow twists in the energy field, so that they will probably have some sort of twist in their spine that weakens it. The lower levels of their auric fields will probably not be strong or developed, resulting in a very weak, sensitive body. Thus, in the long run, their defensive action actually makes things worse. It helps

create life experiences that prove to them that life in the physical body is dangerous because they are so sensitive and vulnerable. So they are caught in a vicious cycle.

In order to avoid incarnation into the physical world, of which they are afraid, people who use the schizoid defense spend as much time as possible in the higher spiritual realms in a diffuse state of unity in which their individuality is not experienced. As we have said before, life in the physical world serves as our mirror of self-reflection, so that we can learn to recognize the individuated divinity within us. Thus, people using the schizoid defense avoid the individuation process of incarnation through which they could recognize their core. Therefore they know themselves to be all that there is, but they do not know the individuated God within. Since they spend so much time in the higher realms, they will relate to time as it is there. There, time is experienced as all of time at once. So schizoid characters do not experience the moment of time that is now; nor do they experience time as linear. Rather, their home is in all of time. That is easy for them to experience. Figure 15–2 shows the schizoid energetic defense of withdrawal.

How to Tell If People Are Using a Schizoid Defense

It is easy to tell when people are actively using the schizoid defense of withdrawal because their eyes will be vacant. They won't be in their bodies. You will also be able to feel the fear all around them. You may see a twist in their body stance.

The Human and Spiritual Needs of People with a Schizoid Defense

Such people need to feel safe in the physical world on earth. They also need to learn how to connect to people in human relationships. They need to learn to live in the time of the moment, with a past and a future. On the spiritual level, they need to know that there is a God within and that that inner God is each person's unique divine essence.

What's Your Negative Reaction to the Schizoid Defense?

Let's explore what your negative reaction might be when people defend in this way.

What do you do when you are interacting with a schizoid character who leaves you? Do you get angry because they are not paying attention to you and push

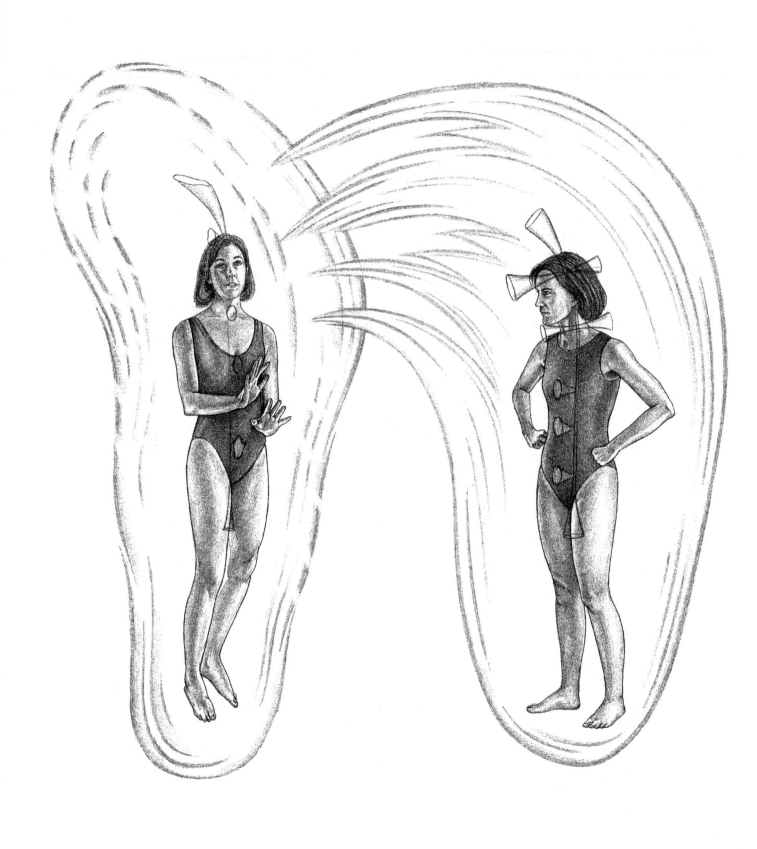

Figure 15–3 The Schizoid Defense and a Push Reaction

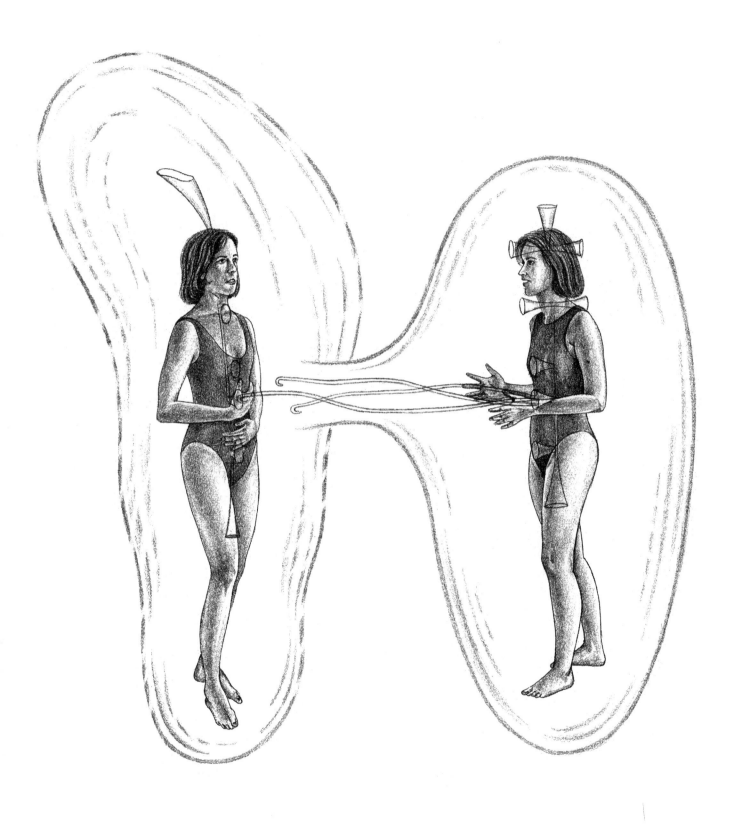

Figure 15–4 The Schizoid Defense and a Pull Reaction

more energy? If you do, they will get even more afraid of you and will go further off. It will be harder to reach them the next time. Figure 15-3 shows what could happen in your field when you get angry and push, and what the schizoid character does in reaction to anger.

Do you react by feeling abandoned and grab onto the person? Do you go into pull? If you do, they will go further away. What will you do then? Pull harder? Figure 15-4 shows what you do when you grab and pull, and what the schizoid character does in reaction to it.

Do you go into stop and stop your energy flow? When you go into stop, do you sink way down deep inside of yourself? So the schizoid character is way out there, and you are way in there. Do you miss each other when you do this? Or do you stay present while you are in stop and just wait? Perhaps with an impatient demand for the person to hurry up and come back? They won't. See the results of this in Figure 15-5.

Do you go into denial and allow? Do you simply allow what is happening, go into denial about it, and continue to carry on a conversation as if you were being heard, and waste your time? Did you get your purpose accomplished? I doubt it. See Figure 15-6.

Or do you go away too, so there is nobody there communicating? Figure 15-7 shows both people gone. Here we have space cadet city!

Many times schizoid characters will use arrogance and let you know that they are more psychic, evolved, or spiritual than you are in order to intimidate you and keep you away. How do you react then? Do you agree that "spiritual" and "psychic" mean "more evolved," and that they are better, so you withdraw contact? Or does it make you angry, so you come on stronger? Or do you stay as you are and not buy the pretense? If you get through that one, you still need to change your energy field. If you wish to help the schizoid character feel safe and come off guard, get down to earth, and begin to communicate so that you can accomplish whatever it is you are doing together.

How You Could Respond in a Positive Healing Way to the Schizoid Defense

Figure 15-8 (in the color insert) shows how you could regulate your energy field to interact with people in schizoid defense to make them feel safe. It is a response that is designed to bring both of you out of fear and your defense and back to reality and communion as soon as possible. We will use different variations of the three major types of field interactions (harmonic induc-

tion, biostreamers, and cords) and the four energy flow modes (push, pull, stop, and allow) to create a safe space for our friend with the schizoid defense.

Rule number one is to not go through the vulnerable boundary with any bioplasmic streamers. Think of the seventh level of this person's auric field as a broken eggshell. That means if you send any bioplasmic streamers over, they will go right through, and he or she will be gone in a flash. The second thing to remember is that schizoid characters run energy-consciousness on the high frequencies of the higher levels of the field. Therefore, to reach them, you must lift your vibrations to high frequency and let them feel them through harmonic induction.

Do this by focusing your attention on the highest spiritual reality you know. Bring your consciousness to the most complete experience of your higher spirituality by imagining it, seeing it, feeling it, hearing it, smelling it, and tasting it. If you can do this and at the same time prevent yourself from producing any bioplasmic streamers, the other person will begin to feel safe. To prevent yourself from projecting any bioplasmic streamers, keep your mind focused spherically in all directions at once. Feel the egg-shaped form on your field. Feel its pulsations. Feel the edges of your boundaries, and keep them contained. Do not bring your mind to focus on any one thing. Do not go out with your mind to any one thing.

You may not be able to directly face the person or have eye contact while you do this, because it will be threatening. That's okay. Once you are in sync and have contacted the person through harmonic induction, you may gently decrease the frequency of vibration of your field. Keep using harmonic induction to influence the other's to decrease with yours. To do this, simply relax all over and make yourself very calm. It will make the person feel calm. Imagine walking on nice green grass through trees. This will move your frequency down to a balanced earth frequency.

This next interaction requires much more advanced control of your energy field, so don't be upset if you can't do it. I add it for those readers who have an advanced level of auric control and may find it useful. Once you have accomplished a feeling of safety, ask permission to touch. If it is granted, ask the person to stand up and bend his or her knees. Then carefully put your right hand on the back of the second chakra. Be sure you are holding a calm vibration in your hand to do this and are not sending biostreamers. Then very carefully allow a bioplasmic stream to flow from your hand. With your intention, direct it down the inside

Figure 15–5 The Schizoid Defense and a Stop Reaction

Figure 15–6 The Schizoid Defense and an Allow or Denial Reaction

Figure 14–1
The Auric Fields of a Couple in Love

Figure 15–8
A Healing Response to the Schizoid Defense

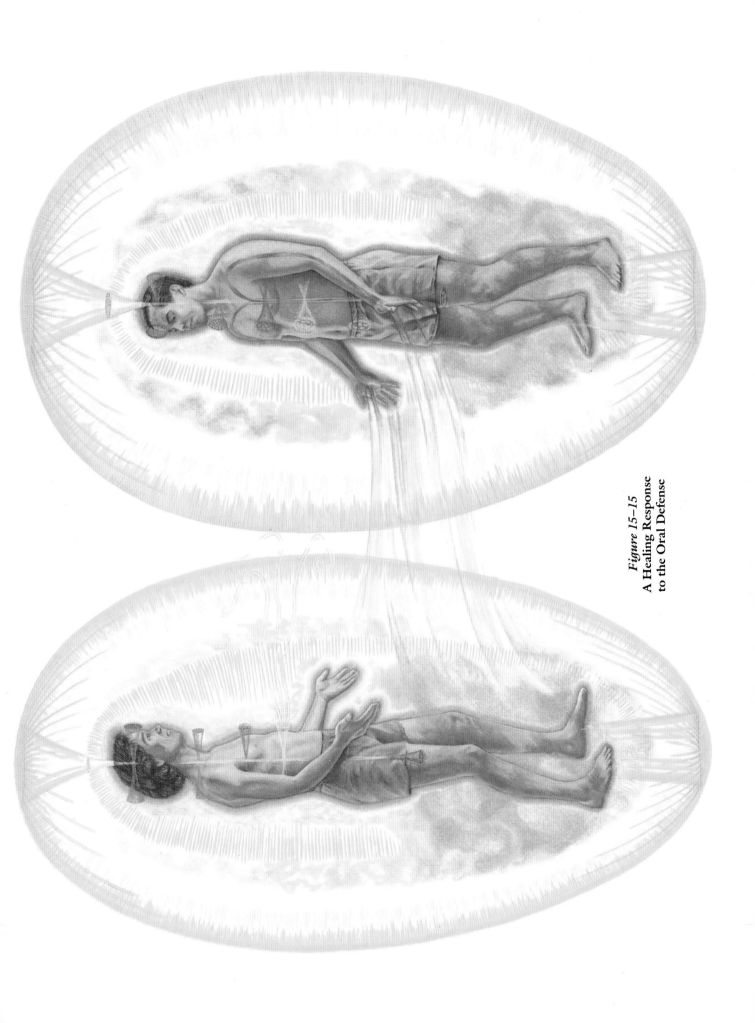

Figure 15–15
A Healing Response
to the Oral Defense

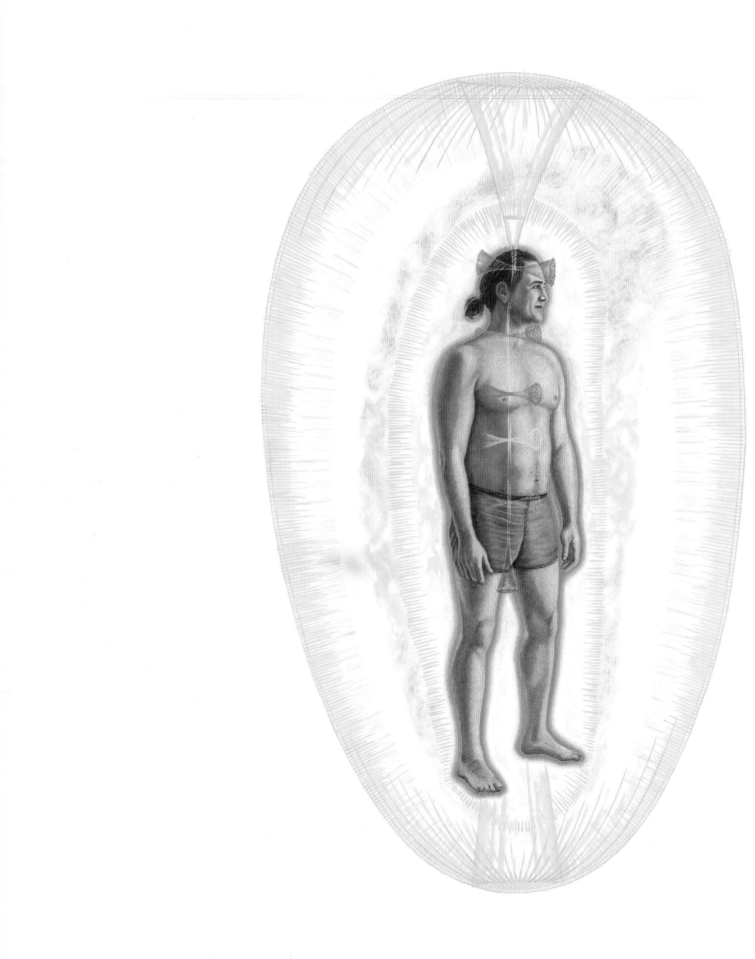

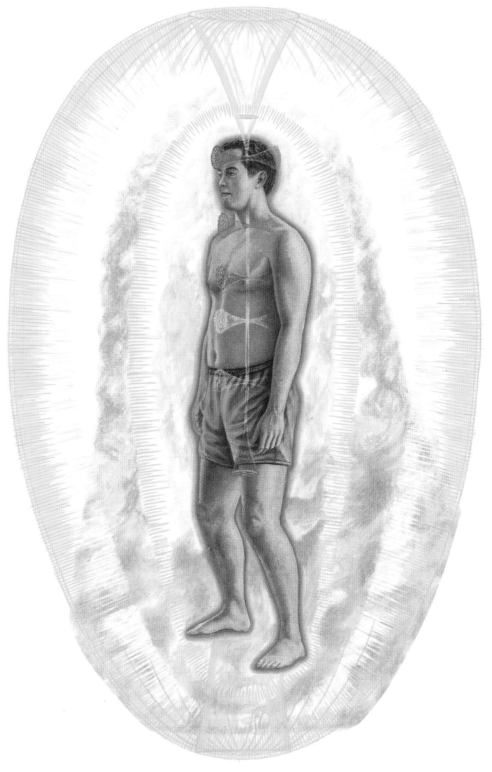

Figure 15–22
A Healing Response to the Psychopathic Defense

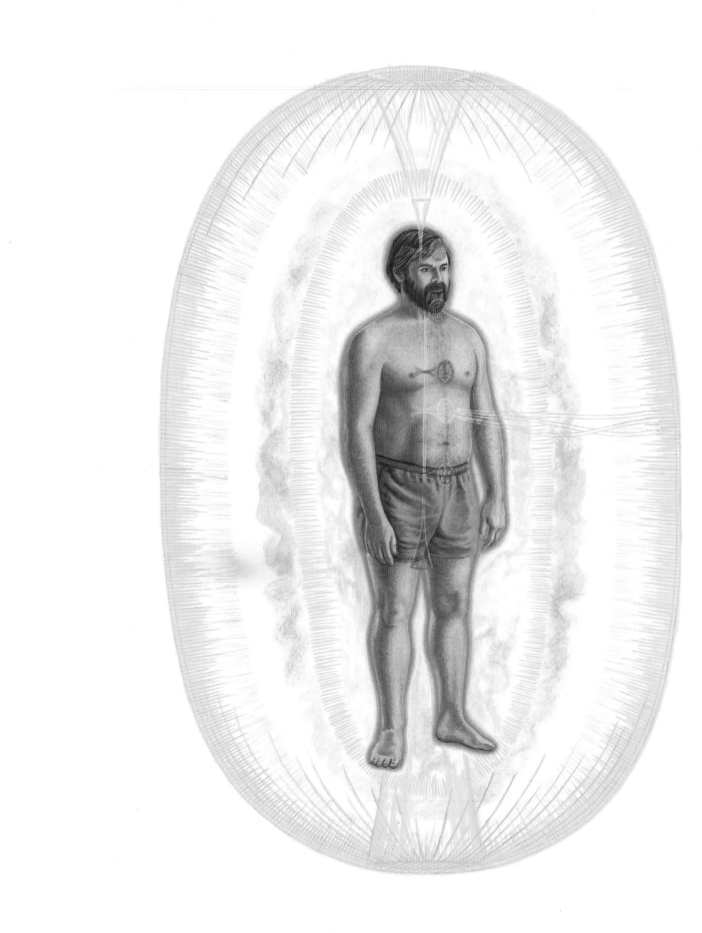

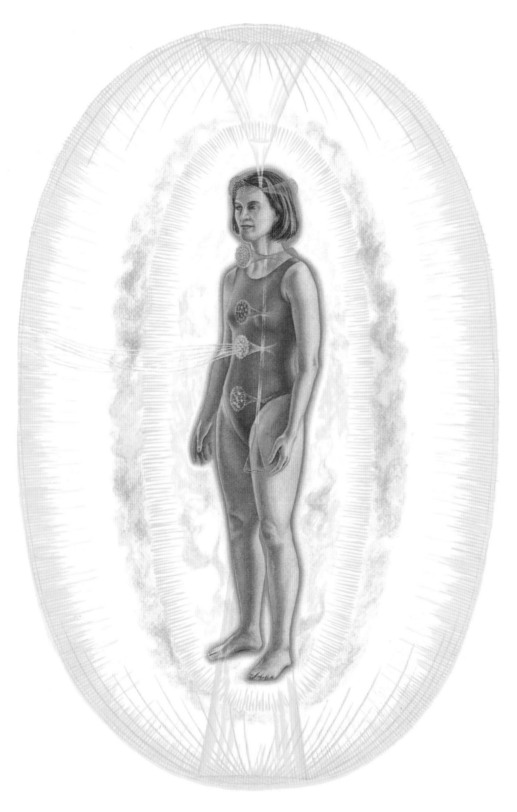

Figure 15–29
A Healing Response to the Masochistic Defense

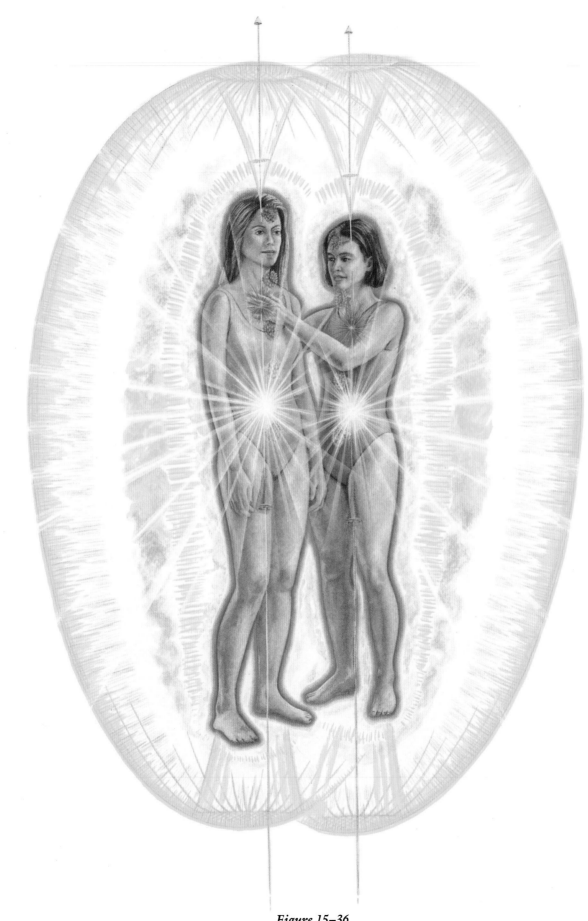

Figure 15–36
A Healing Response to the Rigid Defense

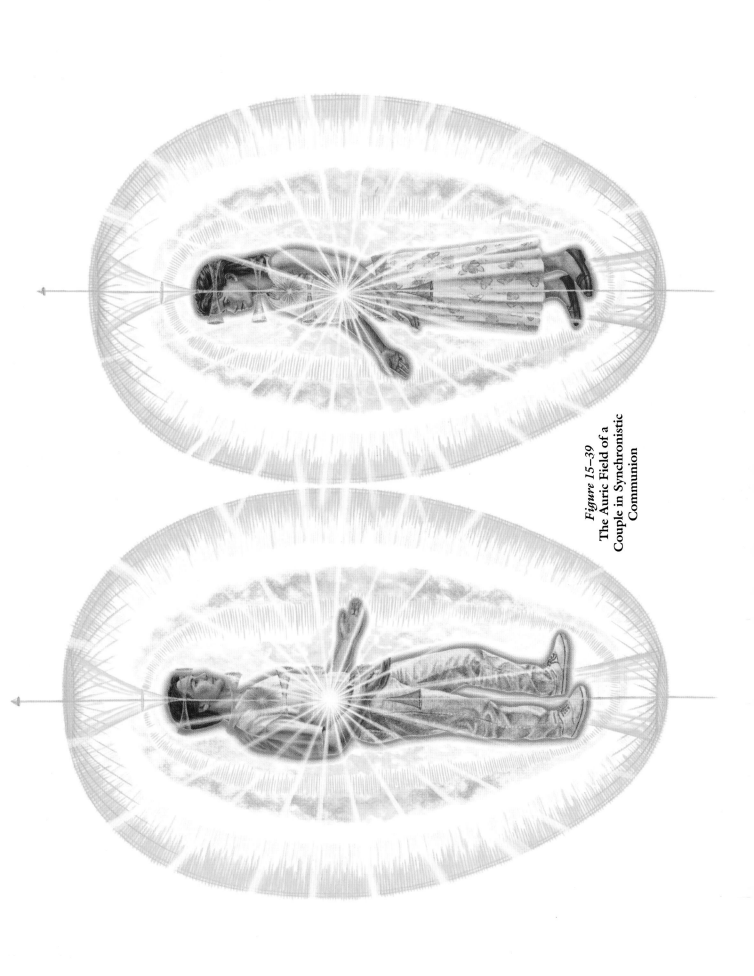

Figure 15–39
The Auric Field of a
Couple in Synchronistic
Communion

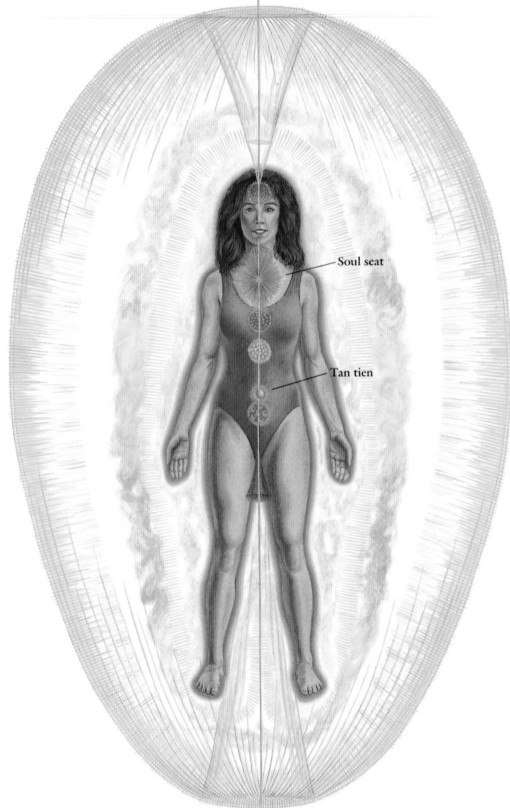

Connection to Godhead

Soul seat

Tan tien

Connection to Molten core of earth

Figure 17–1
The Hara of a Healthy Person

Figure 18–1
The Core Star

Figure 18–2
The Core Star Level of a Group of People

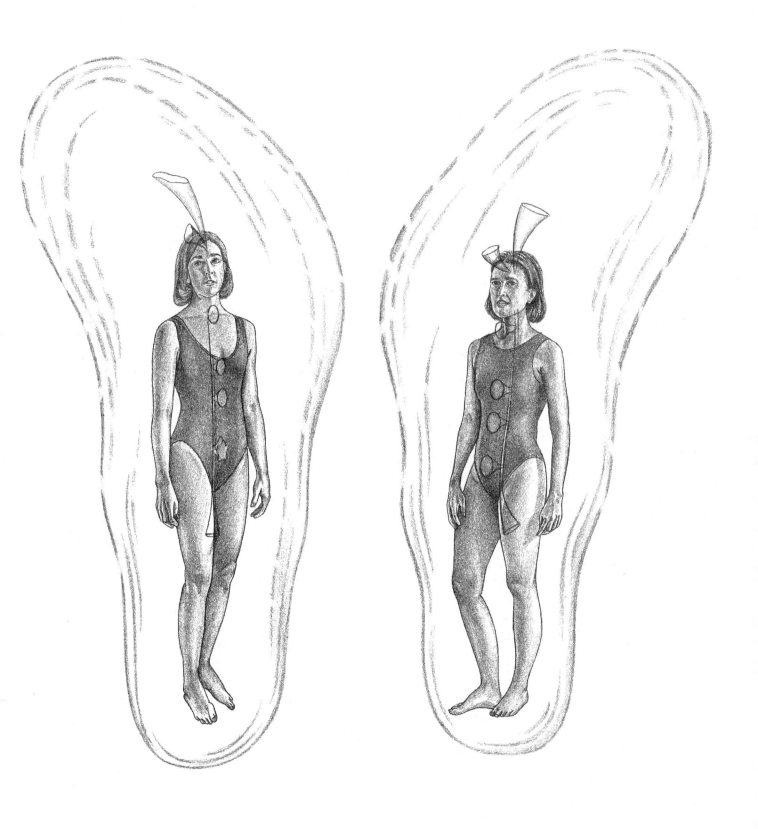

Figure 15–7 The Schizoid Defense and a Withdrawal Reaction

center of the person's body into the earth. This stream will connect him or her to the earth. Once that is accomplished, allow cords to connect from your heart and third chakra to theirs. The cords will have to come from the center of your chakras and sink all the way into the person's because he or she doesn't know how to connect them.

The Results of a Positive Healing Response

If you are able to accomplish part of the above, you will have greatly helped the person to find relationship more safe. It is important to remember that someone with a schizoid defense most likely has not experienced safety in human interactions or the connectedness that we are capable of feeling when our cords are connected through the heart and third chakras in a healthy way.

Learning to connect in relationship is essential for schizoid characters because it is only through relationship that they can fill their deepest spiritual need to experience their own individuality as godly. They experience God in the unitive state but not in the individuated state. They need to find the individuated God within. They can only learn that through communication with other human beings. Your holding a safe space for them to do that with your auric field will help them a great deal!

So next time your loved one beams out on you, it's okay if you react in your normal habitual way. It will probably be too fast a reaction to prevent. But as soon as you catch it, remember that the cause is fear—both your friend's beaming out and your defensive reaction. Bend your knees, ground down into the earth, take a deep breath, and start helping, as in Figure 15–8 (in the color insert). Your friend will come back, and you will both communicate again! At first this can be very difficult, because you probably will automatically go into your character defense. But the more you practice, the easier it will become, and instead of wasting your valuable time and energy in defense, you will move into a much fuller experience of life and communion.

How to Take Yourself Out of a Schizoid Defense

If you find yourself out in the stratosphere, the first thing to do is to notice that you are out there. Then realize that you are there because you are afraid. In order not to be afraid, you need to change what you are doing. First bend your knees and take a deep breath. Be sure to keep your eyes open. Keep your knees bent, and focus on the top of your head. Bring your conscious-ness to the top of your head, then down into your face, then your neck, your upper chest, and so on and so forth, until your consciousness is at the bottom of your feet. Feel the bottom of your feet, and then keep going down into the earth. Repeat the mantra, "I am safe. I am here." When you feel the earth firmly beneath your feet, try feeling the person who is conversing with you. If he or she seems warm and friendly and is trying to reach you, help. Try opening up your heart and your solar plexus to your friend and allowing him or her to connect to you in a warm, human way.

The Defense System of the Oral Character

The Main Issue of the Oral Defense

The main issue of a man or woman who uses an oral character defense is nurturance. Oral characters have had many lifetimes in which there wasn't enough to go around. They probably lived during famine and were left to starve to death or had to make terrible choices with regard to who got the little food there was. Oral characters have not had the experience of being completely filled, and they fear that they will never get enough.

Because oral characters have come into this life to heal this belief, they will draw childhood circumstances that bring this belief forward to the self in this life. They experienced abandonment early in life and fear it will happen again. Usually they experienced parental abandonment. To what extent they actually did is not as important as how they experienced it.

The classic example of creating an oral character defense is with a mother who doesn't have the time she needs to complete breast-feeding. If the baby is taken away from the breast before being filled, it will not have the experience of being filled and satisfied to the point when it would automatically pull away. In suckling, the baby fuses with Mother. It is the closest thing to being back in the womb. In this fusion, the baby experiences itself as Mother. It experiences Mother as God and self as God, which is Mother. Mother's, God's, and baby's essence are one. In order for the baby to feel its own essence, it must be filled with the essence of Mother/ God. Then on its own, the baby must have enough to move away into individuation to experience his or her own divine core essence. It is through being filled in breast-feeding that a baby learns to do this.

If Mother has a rough time with breast-feeding or takes the baby away from the breast before it is finished, or if she is in a hurry, is impatient, and wants the baby to hurry up, she is in a sense abandoning the infant. If this happens repeatedly, the baby will be nervous and will not be able to take in the milk very fast, thereby prolonging the feeding time and making the situation worse. Eventually, the child learns to abandon the mother before she abandons him or her. But in the process, the child doesn't get the experience of merging with all that there is (Mother's essence) and then individuating into their own. Such people grow up without a clear, full experience of their own essence, the source of the divine within. Rather, it is experienced as weak and not enough.

Such babies also experienced their parents as sucking energy from them. They probably did. Unfortunately, either their mothers or both their parents used the third chakra cord connections to them to take nurturance rather than give it. The parents also took energy from them through bioplasmic streamers which they attached to them. They never learned how to connect down to the earth.

The Defensive Action the Oral Character Takes Against Fear

As a result, oral characters' defensive actions are to suck energy from others. They will do this unconsciously in several ways: trying to connect third chakra cords to others in order to draw energy through them as the parents did; trying to suck energy through the bioplasmic streamers that are made with eye contact with their "vacuum cleaner eyes"; or by long boring conversations in which they talk too softly. When they talk too softly for others to hear clearly, the others will send out bioplasmic streamers to them in an effort to hear them. They then suck energy through the streamers by continuing the soft talk. Figure 15–9 shows the oral character defense of sucking.

The Negative Effects of the Oral Defensive Action

The result of these defensive actions is to make the physical world feel even more unnurturing to those who use the oral defense. Actually, people who use the oral defense refuse nurturance and don't know it. Since they use their energy system to suck energy from others, they never develop their chakras into the normal large chakras that would naturally fill their field with energy. They are focused on getting filled from the outside rather than from chakras or their inner source. Either they can't contact the source inside, or it feels too weak. Thus their field remains perpetually weak and dependent on predigested energy from others, creating a negative feedback loop that keeps them undernurtured and dependent on other people's energy. These actions cause people to dislike being around oral characters very much, so their abandonment is realized because people avoid them. Thus, they create life experiences proving that they will never have enough. So they are caught in a vicious cycle.

How to Tell If Someone Is Using an Oral Defense

It is easy to tell when people are actively using the oral defense because they will act helpless and want you to do things for them or take care of them in ways that are not normal for an adult. They may speak too softly for you to hear or may do a lot to have eye contact. But what you see in their eyes is a helpless type of pleading that says, "Do it for me. Take care of me rather than have a give-and-take adult exchange."

The Human and Spiritual Needs of Someone with an Oral Defense

Such people need to have an experience of being completely filled, in which they are the person who can do the filling. They need to learn how to do it for themselves. They need to experience the full and powerful source of life that exists within them in their core star.

What's Your Negative Reaction to the Oral Defense?

Once again, we will explore the major reactions people have to character defenses in terms of the five energy flow modes of push, pull, stop, allow, and withdrawal.

What do you do when you are interacting with people who act helpless and take and take and take and do not give back? Do you get angry because they are sucking energy from you and push more energy at them in a negative way so they stop? Do you get angry, insult, or put them down and blast them with energy? This will make them feel worse about themselves. If you do, they will probably collapse and become even more helpless. It will be harder to reach them the next time. Figure 15–10 shows what could happen in your field when you get angry and push, and what oral characters do in reaction to anger.

Do you react by feeling abandoned and grab onto

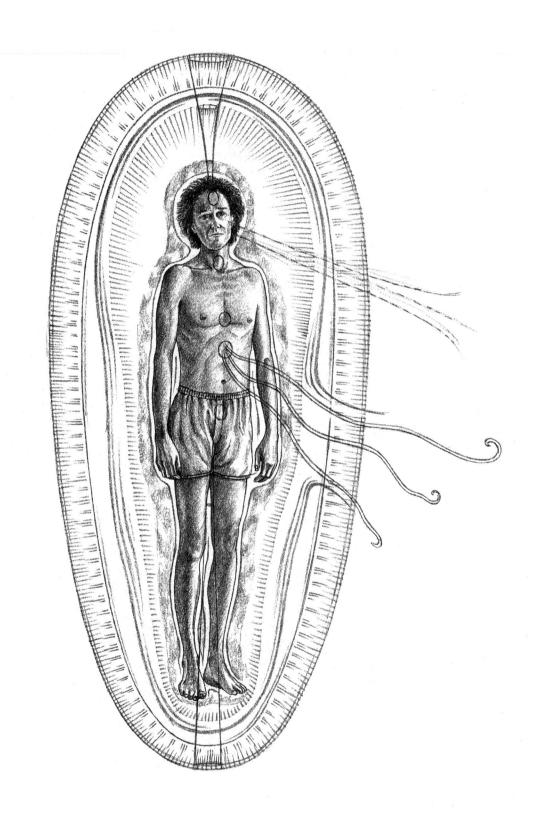

Figure 15–9 The Oral Character's Auric Defense

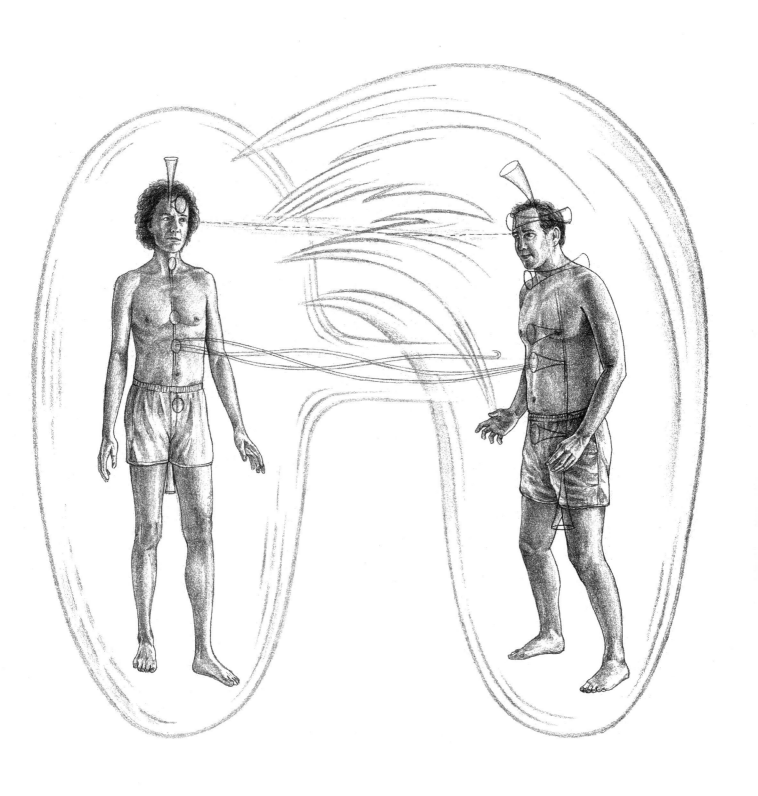

Figure 15–10 The Oral Defense and a Push Reaction

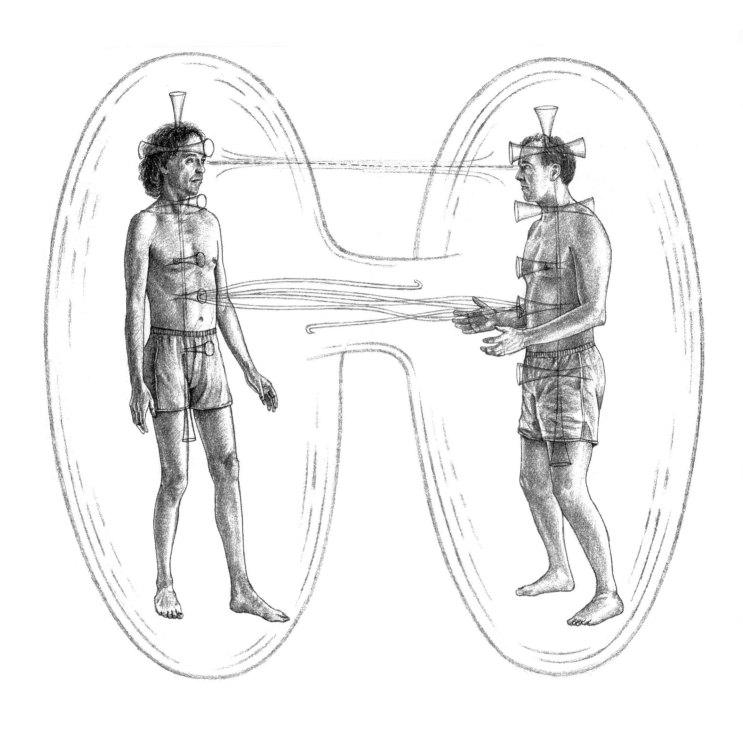

Figure 15–11 The Oral Defense and a Pull Reaction

them? Do you go into pull too? If you do, they will either pull harder and outsuck you, or they will collapse. What will you do then? Pull harder? Figure 15–11 shows what you do when you grab and pull, and what they do in reaction to it.

Do you go into stop and stop your energy flow, so they can't get any of your energy? When you go into stop, do you sink way down deep inside of yourself? So the oral character is out there trying to reach you and suck, and you are way in there. Do you miss each other when you do this? Or do you stay present while you are in stop and just wait for them to stop sucking—perhaps with an impatient demand for them to hurry up and give? They won't. Do you go into stop with your energy so no more gets sucked? Do you stop listening and abandon them? See the results of your stop in Figure 15–12.

Do you go into denial and allow? Do you simply allow what is happening, go into denial about it, and continue to carry on a conversation as if the surface level were what is really happening? Does it make you tired? Do you react by being a caretaker? Do you allow the person to attach the third chakra cords to suck your energy from your third chakra? If so, you will probably be able to feel it. Do you pour lots of energy into them with your bioplasmic streamers that you give to them in the way they manipulate and demand from you? Do you lean forward toward them so that you can hear them better in an effort to caretake? Do you allow the helpless look in their eyes to take your energy and thus psychically agree that they can't do it for themselves, but you have a lot to give? Do you get off on this? Does it help them? Not really—it helps them continue the way they have been since early childhood. That's not the solution. Figure 15–13 shows the caretaking reaction to the oral defense.

Do you react by avoiding the person and thus abandoning them? Or do you withdraw away so there is no energy left in your body to suck? They will experience it as abandonment, and they will either suck harder or collapse and give up, having had their worst fear confirmed once again. Figure 15–14 shows this combination of defenses.

How You Could Respond in a Positive Healing Way to the Oral Defense

Figure 15–15 (in the color insert) shows how you could regulate your energy field to interact with people in oral defense to make them feel safe, to help them have an experience of truly being filled, and to show them that they can do it themselves.

Rule number one is to not allow them to suck energy in habitual ways. Therefore do not allow them to connect the cords from the third chakra into yours in order to suck energy from you. A good way to avoid this is to not stand directly in front of such people. Do not face them. Stand side by side, and imagine a nice strong screen over your third chakra that prevents them from connecting their cords. Do not make eye contact or allow bioplasmic streamers to go out of you at their demand. However, it is beneficial to fill their auric field with the use of bioplasmic streamers. This is actually very easy to do on purpose. Simply relax and imagine beautiful, colored bioplasmic streamers of energy pouring out your hands and into the other person's third chakra. Do this without touching them physically. While you do this, keep encouraging them to stand on their own two feet. Do this with encouraging verbal statements in which you tell the person that they have strong legs and a strong inner source of life. Tell them that they can do it. In this way, you will give them an experience of being filled without reinforcing habitual defense that keeps them undercharged.

Now you will run into another problem that is also related to their defense. The main way that people who use an oral defense receive is through controlled sucking. By sucking, they are controlling how energy comes in. When you give to them outside of this controlled way of receiving, they will go into stop and not be able to receive much energy. After a while, they will allow a little to flow in. Then they decide that it is not enough, or it is taking too long, so they will go into stop again; that is, they will abandon you before you abandon them. And in doing so they abandon themselves. This back-and-forth movement will continue during the filling process and make it take a long time. As soon as you get frustrated, they will go into stop, and it will take even longer. They will get into a fight with time as the enemy. In their struggle, there will never be enough time for them. So you will be challenged to be able to stay there, be there for them, and continue the work until the filling process is completed.

When such a person's field is pretty well charged, focus your mind and your intention to move the energy inside of their field down into the earth to make a strong connection to the earth. Imagine their first chakra opening to allow more energy to come up into it from the earth. This is not difficult if you stay connected with your bioplasmic streamers. It does help to look at the part of the body you are focusing on. If the person is able to ground down into the earth, the energy will automatically flow up into their body like an artesian well. They will not have to suck it into

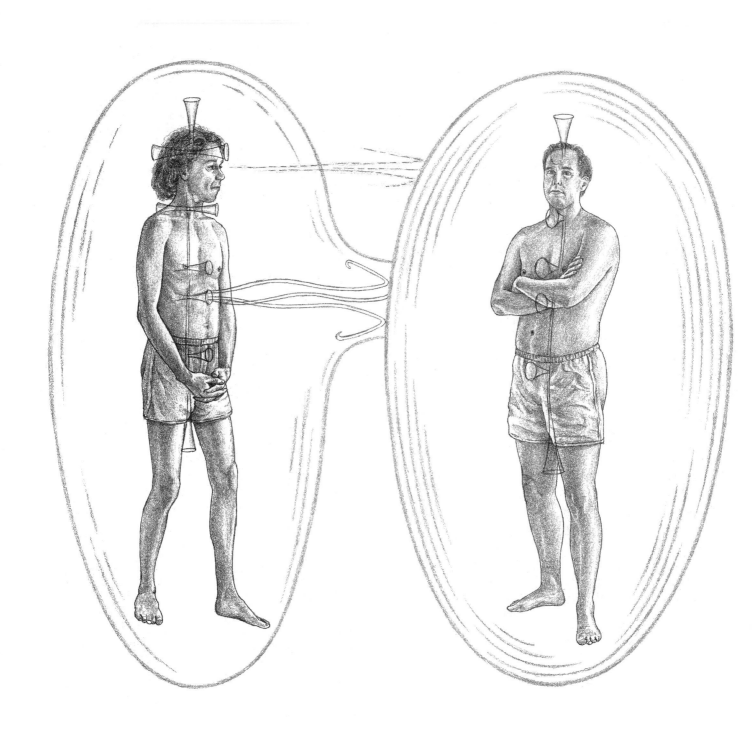

Figure 15–12 The Oral Defense and a Stop Reaction

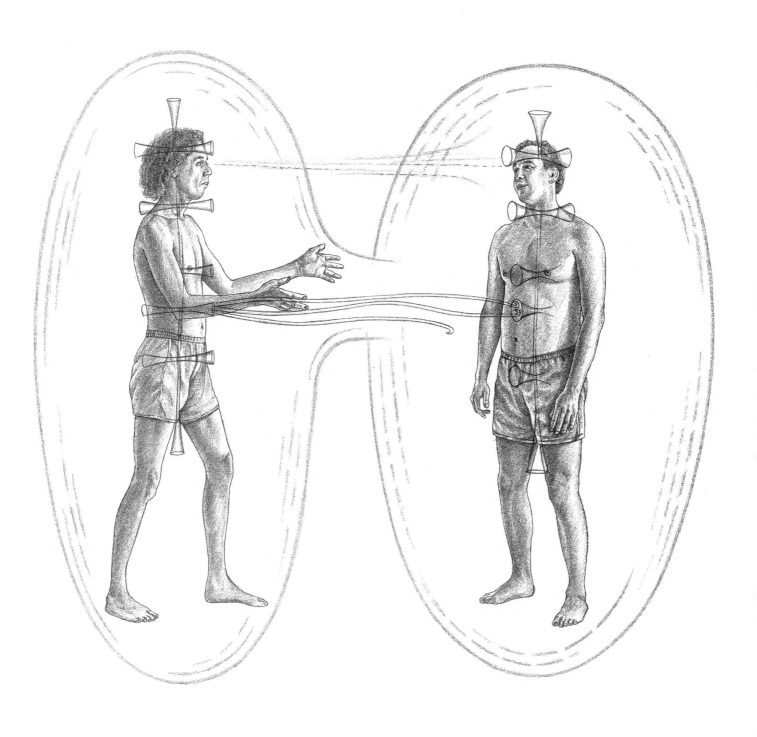

Figure 15–13 The Oral Defense and an Allow or Denial Reaction

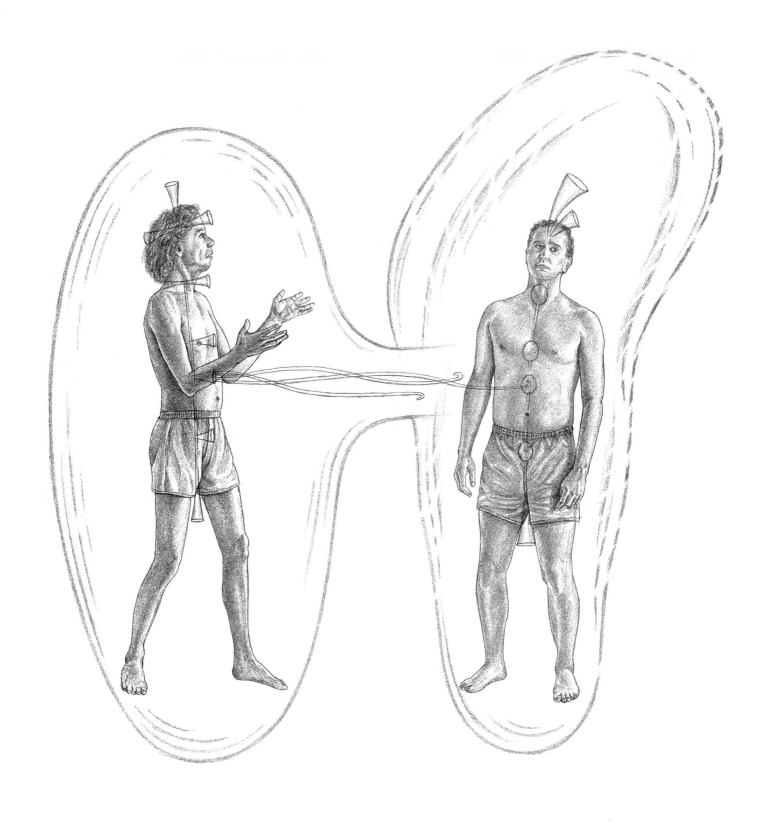

Figure 15–14 The Oral Defense and a Withdrawal Reaction

themselves. Once this occurs, stop your bioplasmic filling action and release your energetic contact with them so that they are self-filling.

The Results of a Positive Healing Response

If you are able to accomplish part of the above interaction, you will have greatly helped your oral character friend to find self-nurturance. This is very important, because as such people work, they will find that under their fear of not getting enough, they believe that they are not enough. At a very early age, they became convinced that their essence was not enough. Learning to fill themselves is the same as acknowledging that they are enough. Once they do this, they will be able to learn to connect in relationship without the habitual suck. Their relationships will become healthy exchanges of energy between two equal people. Their relationship to time will change. It will not be something to fight against, to get more of. Instead, they will have plenty of time for life.

On the spiritual level, such people's task is to learn to source the individual God within. It is only through relationship that they will be able to recognize that their divine core is as brilliant and full as anybody else's. Through relationship they will learn that the source of life is their timeless essence within.

So next time you notice your oral character friend or loved one acting helpless or sucking your energy, remember it means that he or she is afraid. Such people are afraid that they aren't enough. They don't believe their very essence is enough. If you react to fear, that's okay. As soon as you notice yourself defending against the sucking or helplessness they are expressing, take a deep breath and concentrate on relaxing. Bend your knees, ground down into the earth, center yourself and breathe. It's time to help—I'm sure you can!

How to Take Yourself Out of an Oral Defense

If you find that you feel helpless or are trying to get someone else to do something for you, take a deep breath and relax. Tell yourself you have all the time in the world. Get up on your feet. Bend your knees, ground down into the earth. Bring your focused attention to your core star. Here is the source of everything that you will ever need. You are not helpless. You can do anything. You are God. Repeat the mantra, "I am enough. I am enough."

The Defense System of the Psychopathic Character

The Main Issue of the Psychopathic Defense

Betrayal is the main issue for people who use the psychopathic character defense. They have probably experienced many lifetimes as warriors, standing up and fighting for a great cause. They sacrificed a lot on the personal level, fought, and won their battles. They knew their cause was right, knew they were right, and knew they were good, which was why they were so good at winning. The good cause made them good and the enemy bad. But in the end, these people were betrayed, overthrown, and probably killed by those they trusted most. Why? Because winning requires an adversary. If someone is right, then someone else is wrong. They are still good at winning.

Running a country requires leadership of a different kind. It requires teamwork and cooperation, where everyone is good and a lot of people are right, not just the leader. So people with a psychopathic structure never made it across the boundary from warrior to king or queen. Psychopathic characters are still warriors trying to win a war that no longer exists. As a result, deep inside they don't trust anyone anymore. Everyone is ultimately their enemy, even their closest associates. They see life as a battleground.

The family into which the psychopathic character chooses to be born becomes the next battleground. The people in it to whom they are closest become the next betrayers. They have experienced betrayal many times in life. They were betrayed at a very early age by one or both parents. In early childhood, winning was very important. Someone, usually a parent, had to be right and had to win. The person who won was proven to be good, and the person who lost was bad. Usually the parent of the opposite sex was having trouble with their spouse and transferred many of the needs that are supposed to be met by the spouse onto the child. That parent used seduction to control the child. The child became Mommy's "little man" or Daddy's "beautiful young woman" and was subtly told how much better than the other parent he or she was. The parent of the same sex was bad, and the child was good. The child was given responsibilities beyond his or her young age and encouraged to grow up fast. Such children gave their heart to the parent of the opposite sex, but sex was not in the picture.

Of course, when their sexuality came forth in puberty, all hell broke loose. The parent of the opposite sex was terribly jealous of any suitors. The child wasn't supposed to have sexual feelings and was only supposed to love the parent. Today, this makes it very scary for people with a psychopathic defense to have both sexuality and heart. To have them both is to betray a parent, and they themselves are bad. They are very vulnerable in this area. They are afraid of people of the same sex who remind them of the same-sex parent.

Of course, the true betrayal is from the parents, who used and controlled such children to fill the needs that they themselves were supposed to get from their spouse, with whom they couldn't resolve problems. So once again, people with psychopathic defenses fought for a cause (the "good" parent of the opposite sex against the "bad" parent of the same sex) and supposedly won (the love of the "good" parent). Then, in the end, they were betrayed by the parent they fought for, because after all the parent either stayed with the spouse or got a different one.

So these people carry a lot of fear and see the world as a battleground in which they are forced to fight. They are afraid of betrayal from closest friends, so they are afraid of them. They fear collapse under the heavy load that they must carry.

The Defensive Action the Psychopathic Character Takes Against Fear

As a result of their fear, the defensive action of psychopathic characters is to pull up and out of their bodies in an effort to be bigger and grow up faster than normal in order to take on the responsibilities of an adult. This ungrounds them and makes them feel less safe. Their energy fields are much more charged on the upper half than on the lower half. To maintain this displacement, they also push energy to the back of the body to increase their willpower. Since the heartstrings to the parent of the opposite sex are tainted with betrayal, they will be afraid to connect their heart cords to another woman or man.

Since life is characterized by fighting for what is right, psychopathic characters also tend to meet life in an aggressive manner. Seeing the world as attacking them, they throw their energy to the will in the back of the body, then up the back and over the head at the supposed aggressor. It is forceful and sharp, and it says: "You are the bad one." Figure 15–16 shows the psychopathic defense.

The Negative Effects of the Psychopathic Defensive Action

These defensive actions make the physical world feel even more unsafe to people who use the psychopathic defense. Actually, they are the aggressors and don't know it. Their aggressive behavior brings aggression back to them everywhere they turn. They must constantly fight and feel betrayed because they have fights with their closest friends. Their energy field is not grounded and they cannot source the life-force from earth energies, so they feel weak and unsupported. By displacing their energy upward, depleting their first and second chakras, these people make themselves more vulnerable to having the "rug being pulled out from under" their feet.

They have trouble with sexuality because their second chakra is undercharged. They are seductive, but the seduction doesn't lead to long-term relationships because the heart and sexuality don't work together. When they do connect heartstrings, they are preset to betrayal. A man will expect a woman to betray him; a woman expects a man to betray her. Each person helps set the other up for his or her betrayal. Or they do the betraying first.

The more their life experience is brought back to consciousness, the more they are caught in the struggle to win, to prove they are good. They see the world as being either good or bad, and they are afraid that perhaps they are the bad ones. When they win, they are good; when they lose, it proves they are bad. Therefore, they always pick fights to win so they can feel good, and they see the world as trying to prove that they are bad. But they never really win, because they are projecting the whole thing!

They also take on more than they can handle, having been taught to do this at a very early age. They take a heavy burden, give up personal needs, charge forward, and then eventually find some betrayal that lets them collapse. They work long hours and take more responsibility than is healthy because it is a way to control others. They think they must control those around them in order to survive. Physiologically, they are usually healthy and will work until collapsing, possibly with a heart attack, depending on how entangled the heart cords become from the experiences of betrayal that they store in them. They may have back or joint problems from taking on heavy burdens.

People who use the psychopathic defense rush forward in time. There is never enough time to do all that they need to do. They will not stop and be in the

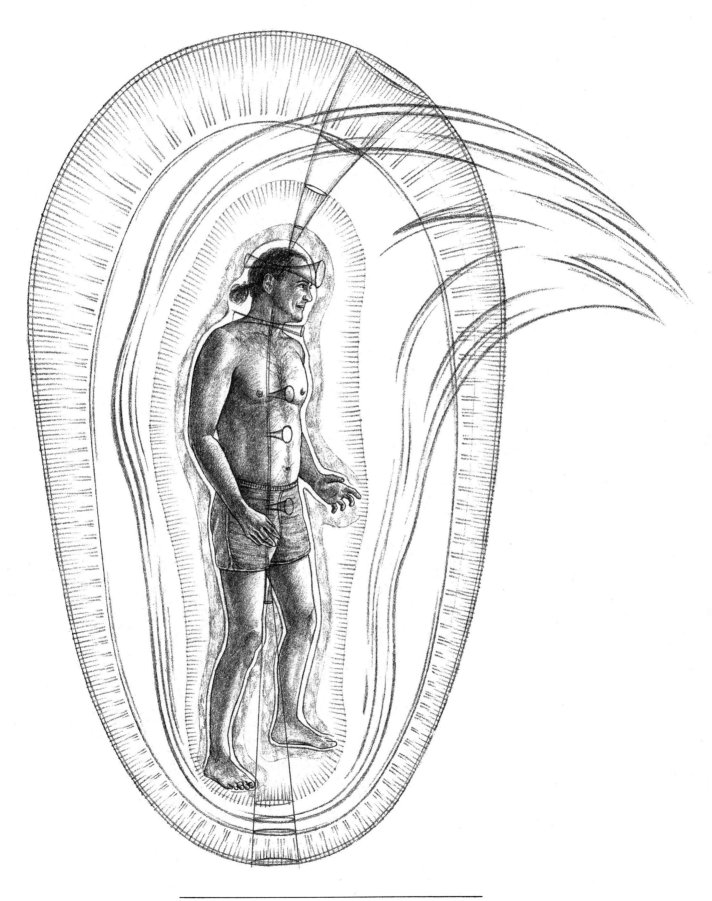

Figure 15–16 The Psychopathic Character's Auric Defense

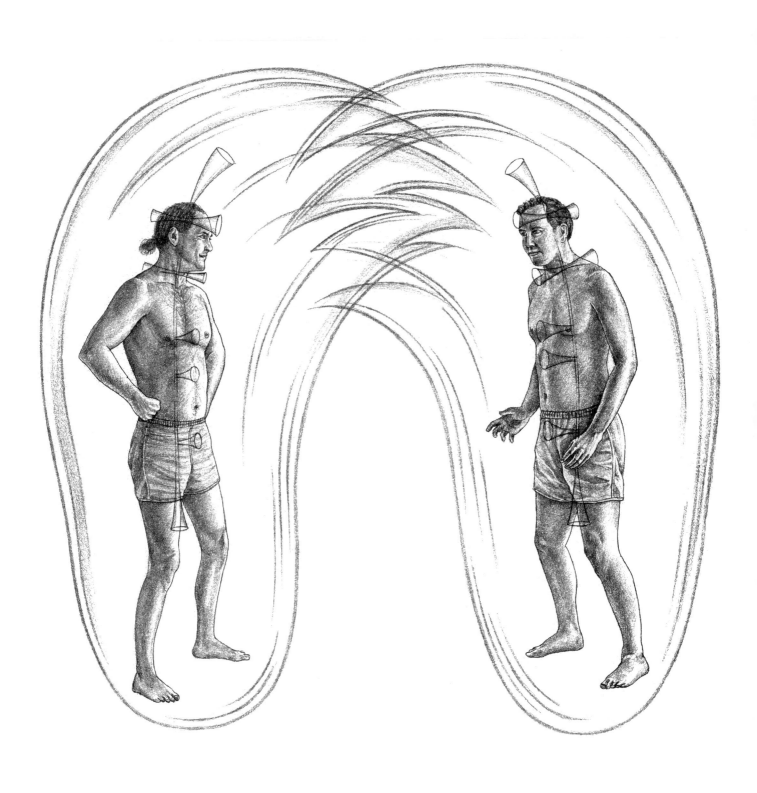

Figure 15–17 The Psychopathic Defense and a Push Reaction

moment, but live in a future that never comes. They experience their own essence as truth, and when aligned with a cause, they experience the unitive principle within that cause. But they do not experience or trust the divine individuality within others.

These people erroneously think their life task is leading the fight for some great cause. Later, we shall see that it is not.

How to Tell If Someone Is Using a Psychopathic Defense

The best way to tell if someone is using a psychopathic defense is to notice whether they try to pick a fight with you and then prove you are wrong. You are not only wrong, but there is an implication that you are really bad when you are wrong. They will also be very willing to help you with your problem. They themselves don't have a problem. (If they did, they would be bad. Bad is not just bad—it is evil.) For example, if you are a healer, they will be very glad to let you work on them so that you can learn your work better. They will be glad to critique it when you are finished.

The Human and Spiritual Needs of People with a Psychopathic Defense

Remember, all of the above is just a mask. And what's under it is extreme terror. People who use the psychopathic character defense need to be free of terror and to feel safe. They need to give up controlling others to feel safe. They need to learn to trust both themselves and others. They need to realize that earth is not a battleground. Rather, it is a place to commune with others, a place where others reflect the self. They need to give up the fight and let down the burden. They need to stop rushing into the future and surrender to the divine expression of the universe, which is life on earth as it is in the now. They need to surrender to imperfect humanness and find safety in that humanness. They need to let themselves make a mistake and feel safe and good. In doing this, they can recognize the divine within others.

What's Your Negative Reaction to the Psychopathic Defense?

Now let's explore what your negative reaction might be when people defend in this way. Once again we will explore the major different reactions people have to character defenses in terms of the energy flow modes of push, pull, stop, allow, and withdrawal.

What do you do when you are interacting with someone and they pick an argument with you to prove that they are right and you are not only wrong but bad? Psychopathic characters do this by throwing their aggressive energy at you from over the top of their head. It hovers over you. Do you get angry and fight back by doing the same thing? If you do, they will escalate. They will get more aggressive, clever, and even vicious. Remember, their experience of this is like that of a cornered wild animal that is fighting for its life. The more you fight, the less they will trust you and the more afraid they will be. So they will fight harder to win. Figure 15–17 shows what could happen in your fields if you get angry and push.

Do you react by feeling abandoned and grabbing onto the person? Do you go into pull? If you do, they will get more aggressive to push you away. What will you do then? Pull harder? Figure 15–18 shows what you do when you grab and pull and what they do in reaction to it.

Do you go into stop and stop your energy flow? If so, they will fight harder to reach you. When you go into stop, do you sink way down deep inside of yourself? If so, they are way up there, hovering over you— and you are way in there. Do you feel safer in there? You are still under attack. Do you miss the contact when you do this? Or do you stay present while you are in stop and just wait—perhaps with an impatient demand for them to hurry up and shut up? They won't. See the results of this in Figure 15–19.

Do you go into denial and allow? Do you simply allow what is happening, go into denial about it, and continue to carry on a conversation as if the conversation or connection were really happening? Do you let the person win and feel bad about yourself? Does it hurt? Does this really help them? Did they really win? Or did they just prove once again that they were right, the universe is a battleground? Did you get your purpose accomplished? I doubt it. See Figure 15–20.

Or do you withdraw and leave your body so there is nobody there to take the blame? They might get more aggressive and yell, "Look at me when I am talking to you!" Or, "Stop pretending you are afraid, I know what you are really feeling!" Figure 15–21 shows this combination.

How You Could Respond in a Positive Healing Way to the Psychopathic Defense

Remember, the purpose of the positive healing response to a defense is to help both of you get back to

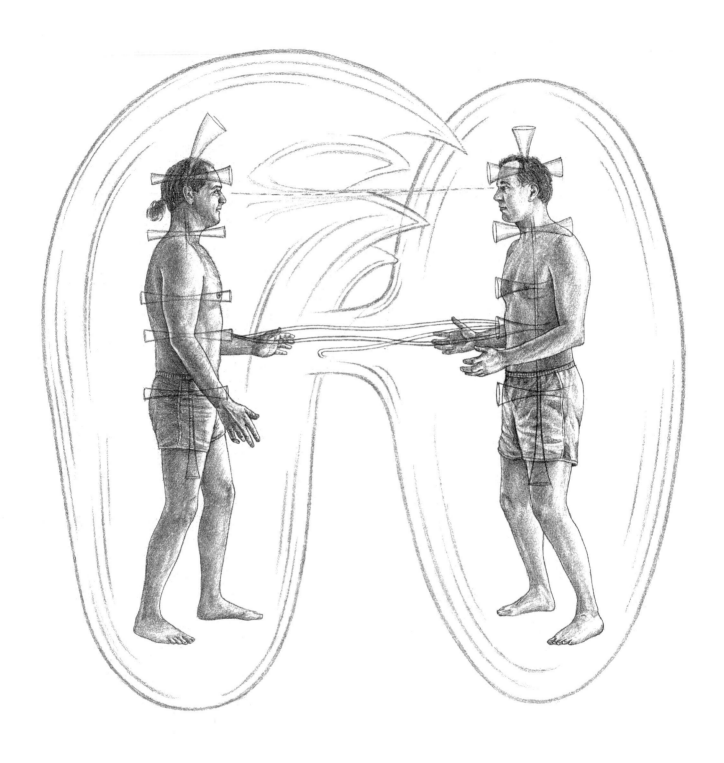

Figure 15–18 The Psychopathic Defense and a Pull Reaction

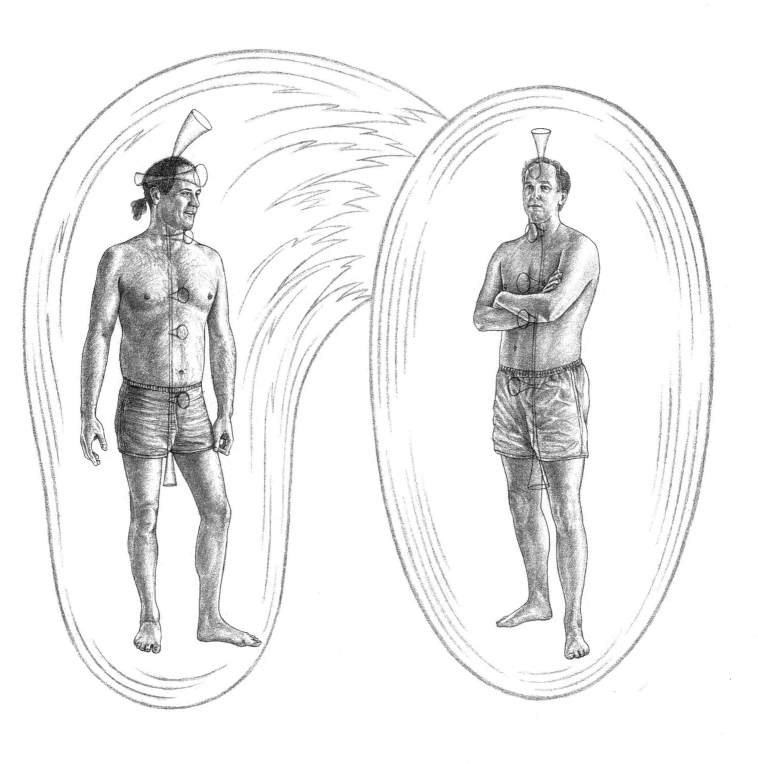

Figure 15–19 The Psychopathic Defense and a Stop Reaction

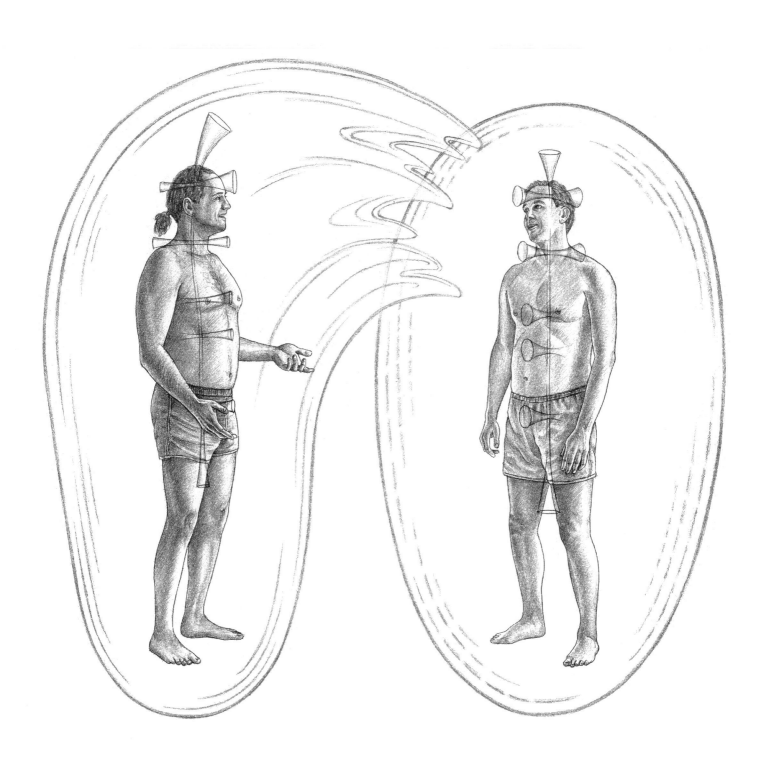

Figure 15–20 The Psychopathic Defense and an Allow or Denial Reaction

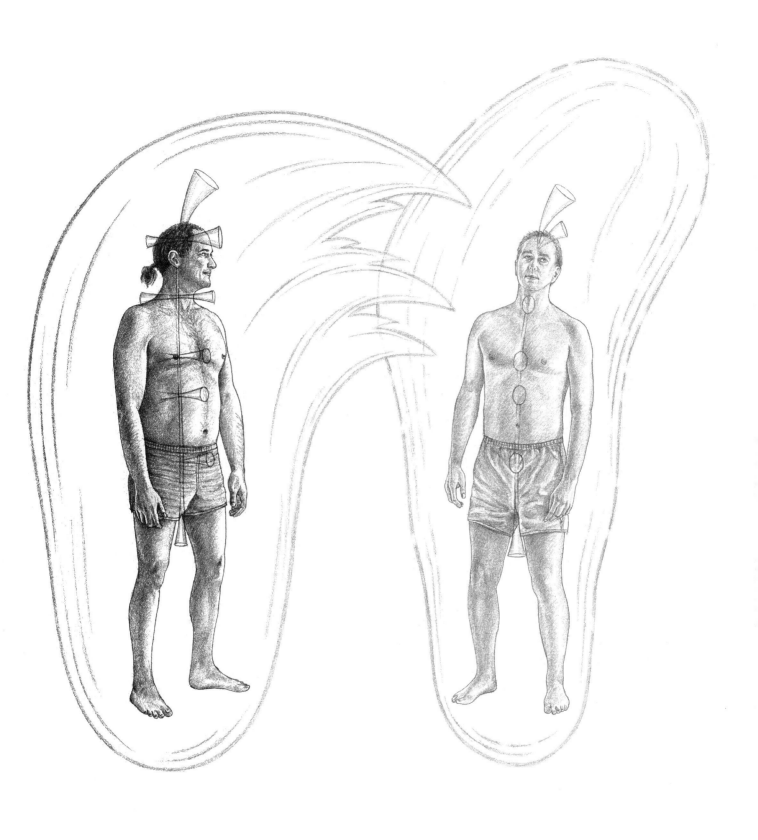

Figure 15–21 The Psychopathic Defense and a Withdrawal Reaction

reality and communion as soon as possible. Psychopathic characters' defense will demand that you agree with their distorted view of the world. Don't agree with their defense, because that only strengthens it. A primitive response is sometimes more difficult to do with people who use the psychopathic defense because they are so aggressive in asserting that they are right. However, if you get into an argument with such a person, you are, in a sense, also agreeing with their view of the world simply because you are arguing.

Figure 15–22 (in the color insert) shows what you could do with your energy field to help a man or woman with a psychopathic defense feel safe, get grounded, and reconnect for communion. Obviously, it is very difficult to respond immediately in a positive way when someone is attacking you. So after your first negative reaction, no matter what it is, take a deep breath and bend your knees. Remember, they see you as the aggressor who thinks they are bad. Any bioplasmic streamers coming their way right now will be experienced as an aggressive attack. Ground down into the earth, and pull back any bioplasmic streamers you may have sent out. Do this by becoming extremely passive and focusing your attention on yourself, while still listening to the person. You will probably have to break eye contact to do this. If they demand that you look at them, simply explain that you really want to hear what they have to say and you need to center yourself to do so. Move the energy in your field down into the earth, making the lower half of your field big with a wide base and the upper part of your field small. Do this by bringing your attention to your legs and a large area of ground behind you. Imagine it, feel it, and see it. Do not engage in a contest. Use the mantra, "No contest, no contest." Imagine yourself and your auric field to be made of Teflon so that any aggressive energy coming at you just pours off. Become rose and green.

Tell yourself to listen for the seed kernel of truth in the exaggerated accusations. The exaggerations are really expressing the other person's fear, not your badness or what you did or didn't do, even though that's what the person's words may be saying. Do not argue about any points. Just be there and listen to the argument, letting the negative energy slide into the earth as it reaches your Teflon aura. Remember, these people are terrified of betrayal, in self-hatred, and in denial of it. Let them go on until they finish. Do and say things that will let them know that you will not betray them. For example, speak about how good they are, how you trust them, and how you like being with them and want to continue that. Ask them to tell you more about the situation they are talking about. Let them know that you are really interested in changing the situation and your part in it.

Next, decrease the frequency of your field vibrations. In arguments, they get high, harsh, and jagged. Do this by concentrating on the earth and on how good it feels beneath your feet supporting you. Or you might want to think of things that make you feel calm, soft, and secure, such as a walk you took recently through nature, your favorite music, or someone who makes you feel very safe. Imagine that person standing next to you. It could be your guide. Keep slowing and smoothing your frequency until you match the earth's frequency, and hold it there. Simply be there, and allow your vibes to relate to the psychopathic character through harmonic induction. Soften your pulsations into a wavelike motion. Think of gently rocking in a boat on a calm lake on a sunny afternoon. But don't stop listening, being there for them, and seeing their beautiful core. Look for it, recognize it, and acknowledge it. As they calm down and you feel safer, allow the earth vibrations that you are making to include more and more of your heart energy. Accept them as they are now.

The Results of a Positive Healing Response

If you are able to do at least a part of the above work, you will have helped your friend find that the contest or argument is not as important as the acceptance of who they are as they are. Under this person's inability to recognize you lies an inability to recognize him or herself. As you simply are there recognizing them, they don't have to be anything else.

They will feel that they are heard, even though you may not even agree with them. They may assume that you do, but that really doesn't matter. They need to feel that you have heard them. This will make them feel safer next time, and maybe it won't be so important to get the point across. Their goodness will depend less on getting their point across than on your recognition of who they are, that you know they are not bad, and that you are not bad either! Your standing there in loving acceptance while they rant proves this. Thus they will have a new experience—that of communion.

Once they have that, they will begin to be able to recognize and trust the divine essence within you. Having done that, they will begin to trust you and the higher will of your relationship. That means they will be able to start giving up their control over you, which was the only way they could feel safe.

They can then begin to recognize their life task on the personal level as a surrender to the goodness within themselves and others. On the world level, it will probably be to work for a cause, but it will be through working as an equal with others that they will accomplish it. It is only through recognizing, trusting in, and helping enhance the divine in others that they can move from warrior to king. The king or queen is servant to all.

So next time your loved one picks a fight with you, blames it on you, and lists all the ways you are bad, just bend your knees, do a Teflon aura, and become a schmoo for a while. It won't last long. This is the best way for everyone to get back into reality, which is a much nicer place to be.

How to Take Yourself Out of a Psychopathic Defense

If you find yourself aggressively going after someone because you think that person has betrayed you, just stop a moment. Perhaps the situation is not so bad and you have overreacted. Try to feel your humanity as well as the other person's. Bend your knees, take a deep breath, and focus your attention deep inside. Are you afraid? Are you feeling hurt and betrayed? Has this happened to you before? A lot? Is this a repeated pattern? Are you defending your goodness? Is your energy all in the upper part of your body? If so, just back off a little and feel your feet on the earth. Bring your attention to the earth. Make your feet hot. Feel the energy in your legs. Center into your core star and repeat this mantra: "I am safe. I am goodness."

The Defense System of the Masochistic Character

The Main Issue of the Masochistic Defense

Remember, the masochistic character defense of bioenergetics or core energetics is not the same as the Freudian definition of a masochist. The main issue of a man or woman who uses a masochistic character defense is that of invasion and being controlled. Such people have probably experienced many lifetimes of being controlled and trapped in situations, not being allowed to express or exert themselves in ways they wanted to. In past lives, they probably suffered imprisonment, slavery, or some strong political or religious control by others. Self-expression and exertion

out of the accepted "norm" was dangerous. They had to submit.

As a result, deep inside they long for freedom but are afraid to claim it. They don't know how to become free. They are very resentful at not having freedom, blame others for their lack of autonomy, and stay trapped in dependence. They don't know how to get out.

The families they choose to be born into become their next prison and their parents their next captors. Their mother was dominating and sacrificing. They were given no personal private space, not even their own body. They were controlled, even to the extent of eating and toilet functions. They were made to feel guilty for every free self-expression. They were humiliated for feelings, especially their sexuality. They were not given the opportunity to individuate.

Their parents used bioplasmic streamers to swamp them in their energy or to hook and control them. The parents also used the cords that connect between third chakras to control the children. At the same time, the parents loved them dearly and made loyal, loving cord connections between the fourth chakras.

One or both of the parents treated these children as if they were part of themselves. Everything that went into the children was controlled, and everything that came out was controlled, including the children's thoughts, ideas, and creations. The parents interfered with their creative process. Whenever they created something, such as a drawing or painting, their parents would immediately take what was created and claim it as their own—the parents'—with such statements as "Oh, look what my child did! It's a picture of a＿＿＿!" The parents would then describe and define the created object rather than just let it be or let the child define it.

Remember, the spiritual purpose of what we create is to reflect back to ourselves who we are and to help us recognize our essence. These children's parents interfered with the step in the creative process in which the creative object reflects self-recognition back to its creator. Before these children got a chance to do that, their parents took the object and defined it according to the parents. In other words, the parents imposed their own face onto the created object by defining it. Thus, when the children who created an object looked into its reflective mirror, they saw the essence of their parents, not their own essence. In effect, the parents stole the children's essence, and now the children can't feel the difference between the essence of their parents and themselves. Another simple way this theft happened was by a parent finishing the children's sentences.

The Defensive Action the Masochistic Character Takes Against Fear

As a result of their fear of being controlled and humiliated and of having their essence stolen, the defensive action of masochistic characters is to retreat deep inside their bodies and build a massive physical fortress to keep the controlling invaders out. They do not bring out what is inside of themselves. After all, it will just be stolen or used to humiliate them, so they just keep it inside. Since not much is going out, their field gets very charged and big. However, since they were so psychically invaded, their auric boundaries never got a chance to develop and be defined. The diffuse unstructured levels became more highly charged and developed than the structured levels that create strong boundaries. So their auric fields are very porous. Unfortunately, this combination of a big strong heavy body and a large porous field gives the impression that masochistic characters are well protected. That is not the case. Psychic energy goes right in and can be felt very strongly, so they must retreat even more deeply into their interior. At some point or other in these people's maturation, they will also seek to destroy the third chakra cords with which the parents control them. Usually, masochistic defense people do this by pulling the cords inside and entangling them in a mass inside the third chakra.

People with a masochistic defense lack autonomy and are afraid to act on their own. They either stay hidden way deep inside or try to get permission from other people to come out. To get permission, they will send out bioplasmic streamers or try to connect third chakra cords into their friends' solar plexus to get the friends involved with their coming out in some way. Such people will make statements like "*You and I* have an issue to discuss," rather than just saying, "I have an issue I need to clear with you." Or if you happen to be in a therapy group with people like this, they will not volunteer to work in group alone but will always want to work with someone else. Figure 15–23 shows the masochistic defense.

The Negative Effects of the Masochistic Defensive Action

The result of these defensive actions makes the physical world feel like a prison, where autonomy is forbidden. These people's passive behavior, seeking to involve other people, constantly brings the experience of being controlled back to them.

Since they keep what is inside, it is as if time stood still. They live in the now, with not much of a future. They never really learn to self-express, and their creations get stuck inside. Their inability to bring forth self-expression puts them in situations in which other people will help them finish their sentences, interfering with their development and the formulation of their ideas.

This problem is easy to see in a group with masochistic characters. When it is their turn to speak about ideas, they will be able to bring out only partial ideas, usually in partial sentences. Then there will be a pause. During the pause, they are going back inside to bring out the rest of the idea that they wish to formulate and express. This pause happens right in the creative phase, which is where the parents grabbed their idea and defined it. Usually, during a pause in a group of people, a few people in the group will not be able to tolerate the silence and will jump in to help. This breaks their creative process; masochistic characters retreat deeper inside and take longer to come back out with more of their idea. Once again someone will fill the gap, and they retreat inside deeper and get more confused. Soon a conglomerate of everyone else's ideas is being discussed, and no one really listened to what they had to share. In this very painful process, they once again feel controlled.

Unfortunately, over a long period of time, they forget what is inside because it has been held so long. They create a large internal world of unclear, undifferentiated ideas and fantasies. Only through bringing them out can that be made clear. But since this process was interfered with, they don't know how to bring things out, to create. So they remain trapped in a prison of self, lonely and humiliated, resenting the world for keeping them there. Even if they throw a sharp hook at someone to provoke a fight in which they can get the anger out, it doesn't really work. The provocation is still a type of permission-seeking, and therefore they didn't express autonomy after all.

How to Tell If Someone Is Using a Masochistic Defense

Notice if they are able to bring forth ideas without great long pauses. Notice if they unconsciously try to get you to define their ideas. Are they giving you push-pull signals? Trying to get you involved but saying that they are trying to keep you out? Are they saying it is "our" problem, not "my" problem? Does the way they talk and interact display an inability to tell the differ-

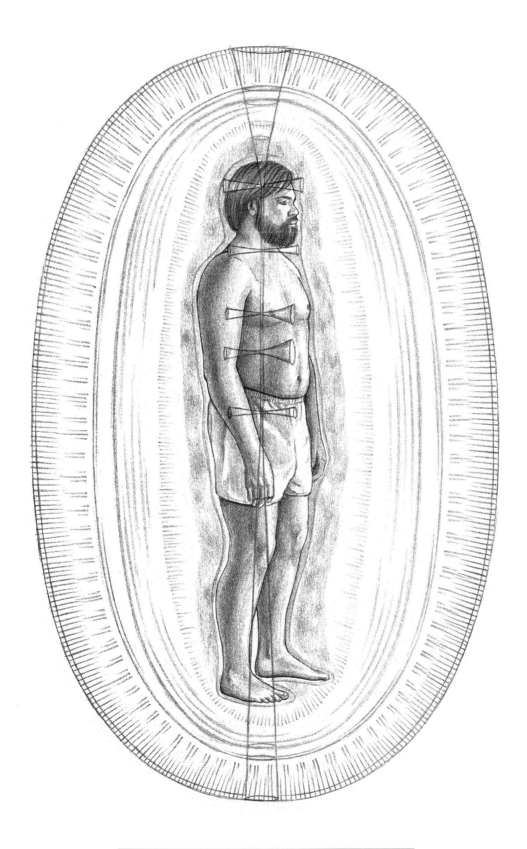

Figure 15–23 The Masochistic Character's Auric Defense

ence between themselves and you? How does your solar plexus feel? Does it feel as if someone were grabbing you there and entangling themselves in your guts? Notice that the conversation is heavy. It is serious. It is very serious! Notice if there is a sense of inertia and humiliation in the air, a sense that you are controlling the person and that they can't do anything without you. They want your advice. They can't move without you, but all your suggestions are wrong and won't help. Masochistic characters will reject everything you suggest, whereas oral characters will gladly suck in all the advice that you give, and ask for more.

The Human and Spiritual Needs of Someone with a Masochistic Defense

Remember, under all this prodding and poking at you, which expresses a lack of autonomy, is the desire to be self-sufficient. Masochistic characters need to claim themselves as individual human beings who are free to live their lives the way they want to. They need to claim and express who they are. They need to give themselves permission to have and express all their feelings, and then they need to learn how to do that. They need a lot of room and safe private space in which to bring out who they are and to look back at themselves in the self-reflective mirror of the physical world. (In Chapter 14, I spoke quite extensively about the physical world acting as a mirror in which we see ourselves reflected. There, I described the physical world as a material mirror that reflects aspects of the self.) These people need to bring out all those unclarified ideas and formulate them into clear, practical concepts to be applied in their personal lives. On the spiritual level, they need to recognize their core essence as their own and claim the individuated God within.

What's Your Negative Reaction to the Masochistic Defense?

Now let's explore what your negative reaction might be when a man or woman defends in this way. Once again we will describe the major different reactions people have to character defenses in terms of the four energy flow modes of push, pull, stop, and allow.

What do you do when you are interacting with people who retreat deep inside of themselves and at the same time grab onto you by provoking you, and then push you away? Then they reel you back in again, then blame you and describe how you are feeling, as if it were they themselves feeling? Do you get angry and push sharp, rejecting energy at them? If you do, they

will become even more afraid of you and will do more of what they are already doing. It will be harder to reach them the next time, because they will automatically go in deeper before you start the conversation. Figure 15–24 shows what could happen in your field when you get angry and push and what masochist characters do in reaction to anger.

When these people go deep inside, do you react by feeling abandoned, reaching in there to grab onto them to pull them out? That is just what their parents did! If you do, they will go deeper inside and hide. It will take longer for them to come out. What will you do then? Pull harder? Figure 15–25 shows what you do when you grab and pull, and what they do in reaction to it.

Do you go into stop and stop your energy flow? When you go into stop, do you sink way down deep inside of yourself too? Now they are way inside of themselves, and you are way inside yourself. Do you try to communicate through a vast distance? Do you miss each other when you do this? Or do you stay present while you are in stop and just wait—perhaps with an impatient demand for them to hurry up and come out? They won't. See the results of this in Figure 15–26.

Do you go into denial and allow? Do you simply allow what is happening, go into denial about it, and continue to carry on a conversation as if you weren't being messed with? How do you feel when this is happening? Tired? Helpless? Confused? Heavy? Do you need to rest now because you can't move? Did you get your purpose accomplished? I doubt it. See Figure 15–27.

Or do you withdraw out of your body so you are way out there, and they are way in there, and nobody is communicating? Figure 15–28 shows the outy and the inny—not reaching each other.

How You Could Respond in a Positive Healing Way to the Masochistic Defense

Figure 15–29 (in the color insert) shows how you could respond with your energy field to make people using the masochistic defense of hiding within feel safe and come back into communion. The first thing to remember is that even though they are unconsciously trying to get you to invade so that they can overcome childhood invasion and finally win, it won't work. So the first thing to do is not to accommodate them in this unconscious and ineffective plan. If it did work, they would have been finished with this problem long ago, because I am sure that they have succeeded in getting people to accommodate by invading them many times.

These people were totally invaded, and you do not

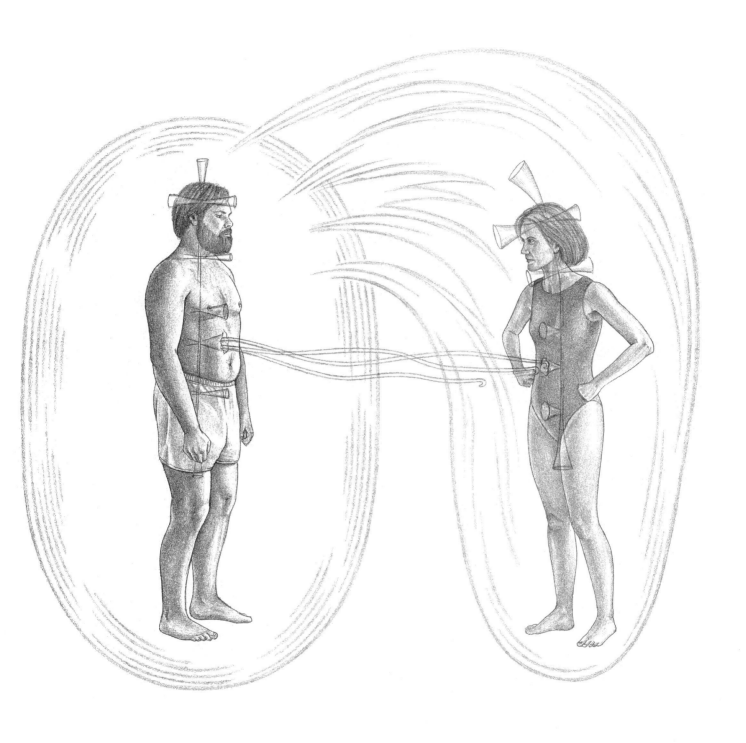

Figure 15–24 The Masochistic Defense and a Push Reaction

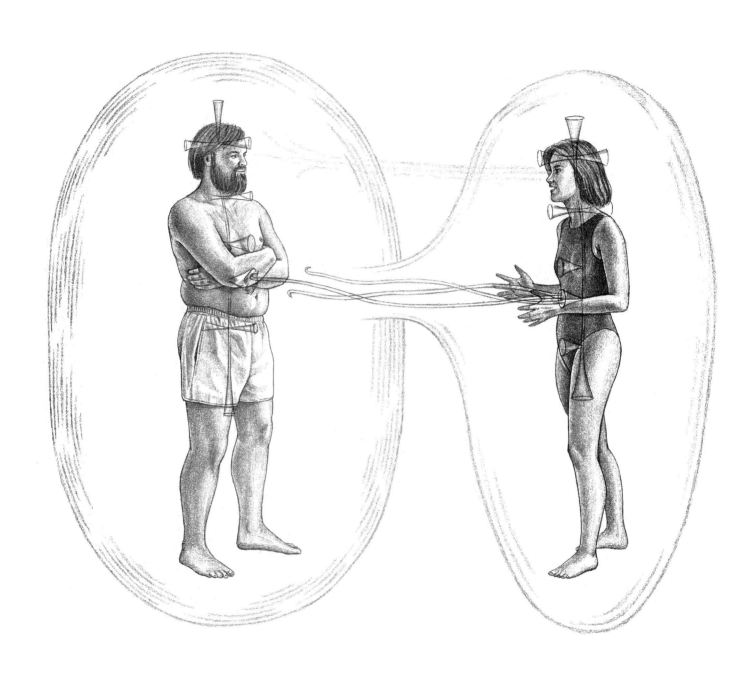

Figure 15–25 The Masochistic Defense and a Pull Reaction

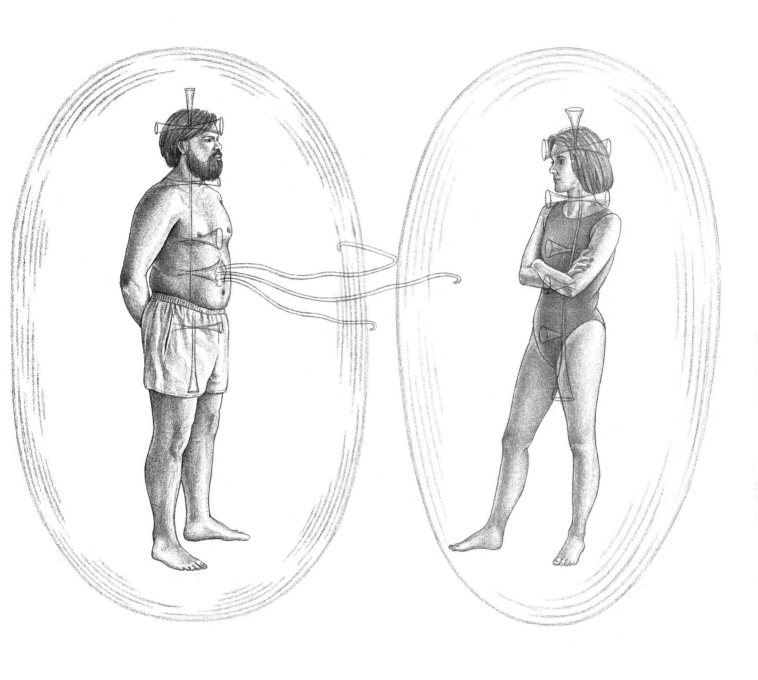

Figure 15–26 The Masochistic Defense and a Stop Reaction

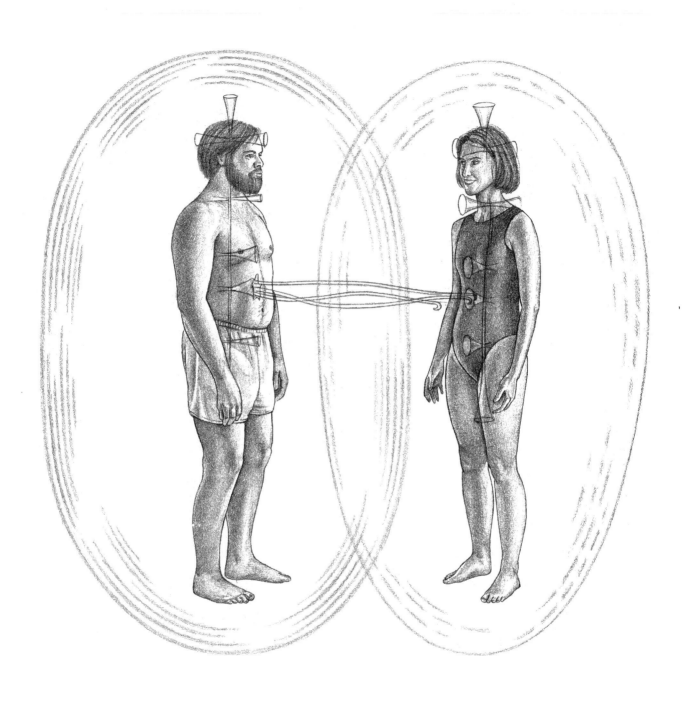

Figure 15–27 The Masochistic Defense and an Allow or Denial Reaction

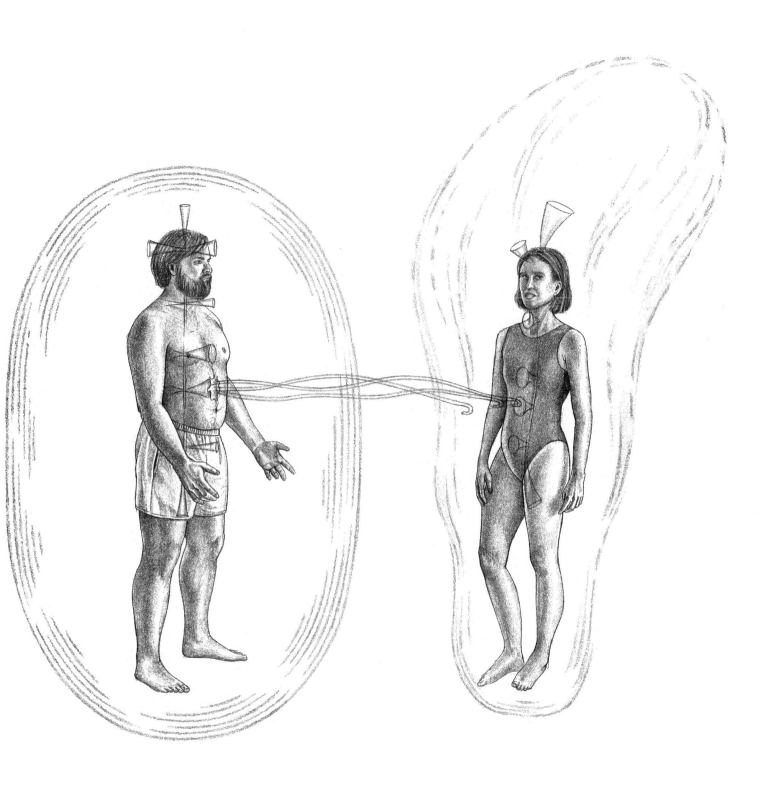

Figure 15–28 The Masochistic Defense and a Withdrawal Reaction

want to re-create their childhood situation. Rather, you must be very careful to not invade them with bioenergy streamers or third chakra cords. Do not make any bioplasmic streamers. Do not stand in front of them or send any third chakra cords to their third chakra. Do not let them invade your solar plexus with their third chakra cords. To prevent this, imagine a strong cap over your third chakra. If necessary, put your hands over your third chakra to help prevent this. It is very important. If they send out bioplasmic cords, imagine your aura to be made of Teflon, and let them fall to the earth.

Once you have the biostreamers and cords in control, begin to control the frequency of vibration of your field. Stand to their side, giving them plenty of space. Stand far enough away from them to be sure the seventh levels of your auric fields do not intermingle. If you can't feel this, stand about three and one-half feet away. This should be enough space for them; if not, move farther away.

Bring the frequency of your field to the same frequency that their field has. Do this by imagining yourself becoming them. Then lightly expand your auric field until it just touches the outer edge of theirs. They will be able to feel this. If they move closer, you know that you are a bit too far away. That is okay; let them set the distance. It will feel very comfortable to them, because it is like their field, yet separate and noninvasive. This will put them at ease. Just remain passive and do this. This will give them the safety of feeling the same as you, and the space for them to come out.

Stand there, with fields synchronized, honoring each other's core essence. At the same time feel your own essence and let it fill your field. One of the things that may happen in this configuration is that as you both stand there as equals, the cords from the third chakras may grow out of each of you and meet halfway between. This is true communion, and you will each feel the connection without control. Do not do this on purpose—just allow it to happen automatically.

The Results of a Positive Healing Response

If you are able to do at least part of the above work, you will have helped your masochistic character friend find that the world is not a place that only controls people. You will have helped them have an experience of their own essence and how it is different from yours. They will feel respected. You will have allowed them all the space to express themselves, without filling in the spaces that they need to find themselves or their next

idea. In this way, they will learn the creative process that unfolds from within. They will then be able to free themselves to create the life they want.

So next time your loved one pushes and pulls at you seeking freedom, give him or her plenty of space to find it. You will be giving the greatest gift of all, the road home to the real self: the road to claiming who they are, and the essence of their core. They will be able to move from the perpetual changing now into the future, based on what they have learned in the past. The now will be experienced as a constantly changing, unfolding moment. It is only through relationship that they can be given the chance to recognize their core and uniqueness because they need someone else's core with which to compare it!

How to Take Yourself Out of a Masochistic Defense

If you find yourself using a masochistic defense, bend your knees and breathe. Ground into the earth, and let the energy come from the earth up through your second chakra. Let the enormous energy that you are hanging on to begin to flow in your field by allowing yourself to feel connected to everything around you. Put your hand over your third chakra to protect yourself there. If you feel attached to anyone through the third chakra, imagine yourself pulling the cords that come from your third chakra to the other person, letting go of the other person, and coming back into yourself. Let these cords connect down into your core star, by visualizing and feeling them do so. This will bring your attention to the essence of your core. Keep your attention there, and be with yourself focusing on your own inner strength. Repeat one of the following mantras to yourself: "I am free, I am free," or "I regulate my own life."

You are very complicated, and your ideas are complicated and need plenty of time to incubate. They will come out piece by piece, like fitting a puzzle together. I highly recommend that you use a private journal in which to put your ideas. Let them come out one by one at their own pace. Don't try to make sense of them right away. They will not come out in a linear manner—that's not the way you function. They will be more holographic. You may even take two years or more to put the entire picture together. Do not show your journal to anyone during this time. You don't need anyone interpreting your ideas before they are jelled. That will only throw you off track. Only when you have had a good look into the material reflective mirror of your journal and are ready and have experienced the whole picture should you share it with anyone. Give yourself the honor and respect that you deserve.

The Defense System of the Rigid Character

The Main Issue of the Rigid Defense

The main issue of people with rigid character defenses is authenticity. This is caused by separation from their core essence and complete focus on keeping their outer world appearance perfect. This split is held so strongly that they have no idea that a core essence exists. People with rigid character defenses have had many lifetimes in which they had to keep up the appearance of being perfect, with no faults or weaknesses, in order to survive. Rigid characters probably were in charge of running things then, as they probably are now.

In growing up, there was a great deal of denial of the inner personal world. All negative experience was denied as soon as possible, and a positive false world was focused on. No matter what may have happened within the family in terms of arguments, ill health, alcoholism, or personal tragedy, by the next morning everything was cleaned up. A perfect meal was served, and it was off to school in perfect-looking clothes to excel. The philosophy was to focus on the good stuff and deny the bad. This denies children's perceptions, and they unconsciously think, "There is really nothing to be concerned about. That fight last night didn't really happen. Mommy doesn't really have cancer. It must have been my imagination!" The only way to do this is to deny the real self that is experiencing the negative events in a personal way. Since it didn't happen, the person who experienced it isn't real, was only imagining the event. In other words, don't feel it—it's not real.

Parents do this in a way that does not directly invade the children's boundaries or use humiliation to control, as the parents of masochistic children do. Here the whole outer environment is controlled to create an illusion of perfection. Children are treated and taught to act according to the facile illusion of perfection. They are taught to dress well, brush their teeth, do their homework right, go to sleep on time, eat a good breakfast, and so on.

So to sum up the world of the rigid character, the outer world is perfect, the inner psychological world is denied, and the core essence doesn't exist. Underneath the veneer—or shall we say gilded facade—of people with rigid character defenses is the vague distant fear that something is missing and life is passing them by. But they are not sure. After all, maybe this is all there is to it.

The Defensive Action the Rigid Character Takes Against Fear

As a result of their fear of a personally meaningless and unfulfilling world, the defensive action of rigid characters is to become even more perfect. They excel at work, they have a perfect spouse and a perfect family. They make a good amount of money. They dress well—everything matches. They do everything appropriately. Their physical body looks balanced and healthy. They regulate the auric field very well—it is balanced and healthy. Most of their chakras function well. They connect appropriately and lightly with other people through their chakra cords. They rarely throw any bioplasmic streamers at others.

In order to be perfect, they create two very severe internal splits. They control any outer effects of emotional response so that what goes on inside of them on the psychological level is split from the outer world. And they split their deeper core essence away from themselves. In fact, these people don't know their core essence exists. Figure 15–30 shows the rigid defense.

The Negative Effects of the Rigid Defensive Action

These defensive actions only make rigid characters more inauthentic and the world less meaningful. Everyone envies them for their apparently perfect, problem-free life. They have no one to go to for help. Instead, others tell them their problems. It seems that they can do anything. They will take many things on, do them well, and never collapse, but they never get much satisfaction in doing them, because it never seems that it is they that are the ones that are doing it. These people seem to be a blank.

They experience time in a linear march forward, never to be experienced again. Sometimes they may feel that they are being swept helplessly along in this march of time. Or at other times, time is just marching right past, carrying all of life with it. Psychologically, on the inside, they feel a lot, but it doesn't get expressed

Figure 15–30 The Rigid Character's Auric Defense

on the outside. Because of this, they are not quite sure if they are even feeling or not.

They have absolutely no clue as to the existence of their core essence. Either they haven't heard of it, or it is just someone's Pollyanna fantasy. They have absolutely no way to reach their core without help from another person because as children it was never confirmed for them as a reality. They can't even imagine what their core is. The only thing that is missing in these people's lives is themselves.

As a result of not experiencing themselves as real, it is impossible for them to integrate their heart and their sexuality. Their heart and sexuality do not function at the same time. They love an ideal person who doesn't exist, so they have short-term sexual relationships until that perfect person comes along. They are prone to having affairs that last only through the initial period of eros. Then the imperfections of the partner come to the fore—she's not his ideal, or he's not her ideal—and that is the end of that. Or they go into another denial, and the relationship begins to be outer-oriented. Actually what really happens is they are unable to sustain a deep personal relationship because they cannot source from the essence of the core within. They need another outer distraction.

How to Tell If Someone Is Using a Rigid Defense

The best way to tell if people are using rigid defenses is to check their authenticity. Is the person to whom you are talking involved in a personal way with what is going on? Or are they completely removed from the conversation and on automatic? Can this person handle everything, and yet you get the feeling that the real person is not there? Are they the type of person who never has anything wrong? Or whatever the problem, can they fix it in a perfectly appropriate way? Is everything perfectly reasonable, but you can't really reach them? Do you believe what is being presented is the whole picture? If this authenticity is missing, you are probably communicating with someone in a rigid character defense.

The Human and Spiritual Needs of Someone with a Rigid Defense

The human need of people who use rigid character defenses is to be real rather than appropriate. They need to come out of denial and express their inner feelings. They need to stop controlling themselves to be perfect and let down into the fear that is beneath their perfection so that they can heal it. They are afraid that they are not real, don't know who they are, and need to find out who they really are. They need to experience time in the now rather than only linear time. On the spiritual level, they need to experience their core essence, which they don't know exists. The only way they can fulfill any of their human needs is to experience their core essence. Once they do this, everything can come together.

What's Your Negative Reaction to the Rigid Defense?

Now let's explore what your negative reaction might be when someone defends in this way. Once again, we will use the major different reactions people have to character defenses in terms of the four energy flow modes of push, pull, stop, and allow.

What do you do when you are interacting with someone and they are inauthentic? Do you get angry because they are not really there and push more energy at them? If you do, they will get even more afraid of you and will become more perfect. They even may want to know what your problem is so they can help you with it. This is a good way to deny fear. If it works and you do talk about your problem, it will be harder to reach them the next time, because they will be ready to deflect the conversation onto you. Figure 15–31 shows what could happen in your field when you get angry and push, and what they do in reaction to your anger.

Do you react by feeling abandoned and grab onto this person? Do you go into pull? If you do, they will build the two inner walls even stronger, get further away, and become even more efficient and reasonable. What will you do then? Pull harder and get confused because they are denying it? Figure 15–32 shows what you do when you grab and pull, and what they do in reaction to it.

Do you go into stop and stop your energy flow? When you go into stop, do you sink way down deep inside of yourself away from the falsity of the conversation? Do you tune them out and pretend you are listening to them while you think about something else? So they are way in there, and you are way in there. Do you miss each other when you do this? Or do you stay present while you are in stop and just wait? So now both people are false. See the results of this in Figure 15–33.

Do you go into denial and allow? Do you simply allow what is happening, go into denial about it, continue to carry on a conversation as if it were really happening, and waste your time? Did you get your purpose accomplished? Did you commune with your

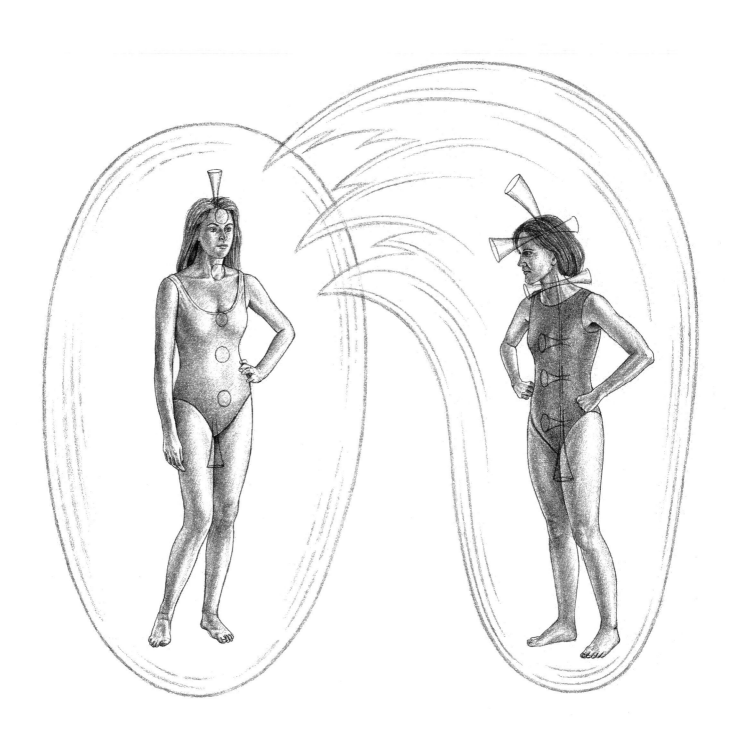

Figure 15–31 The Rigid Defense and a Push Reaction

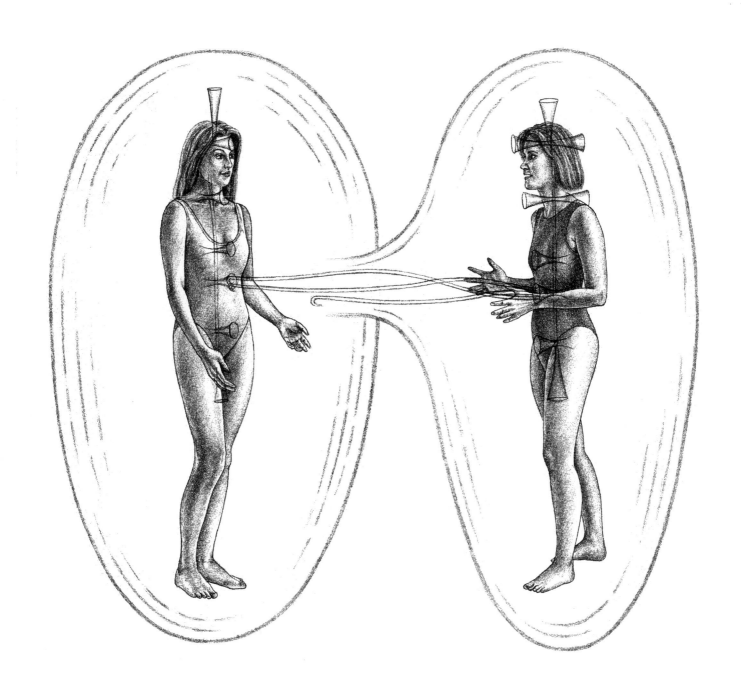

Figure 15–32 The Rigid Defense and a Pull Reaction

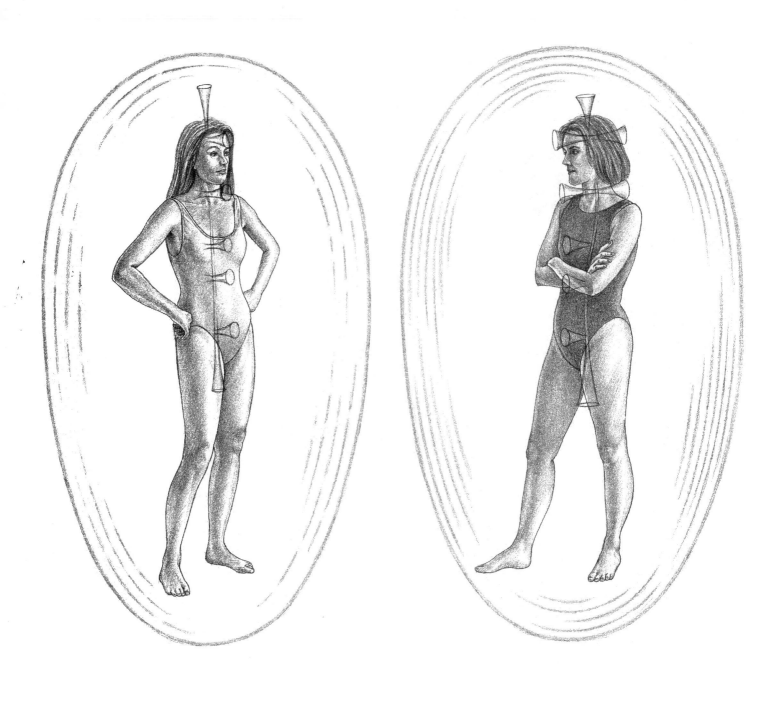

Figure 15–33 The Rigid Defense and a Stop Reaction

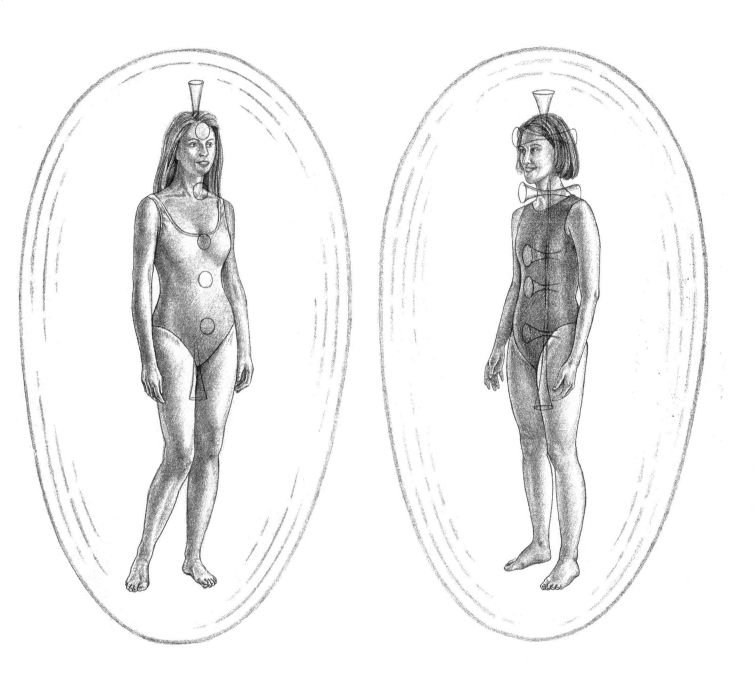

Figure 15–34 The Rigid Defense and an Allow or Denial Reaction

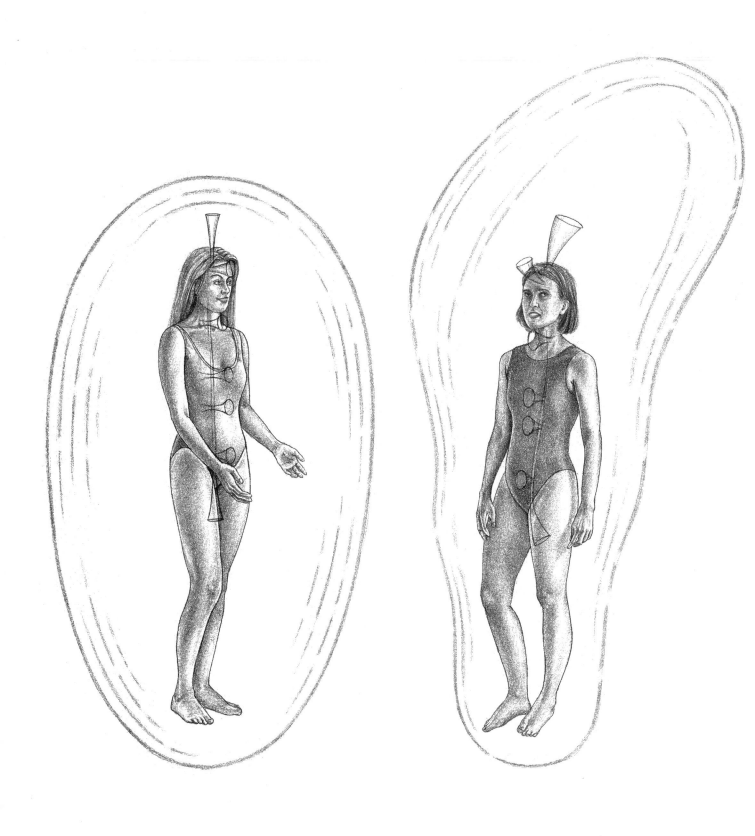

Figure 15–35 The Rigid Defense and a Withdrawal Reaction

friend? Did you get to know them better? Did fusion happen? I doubt it. See Figure 15–34.

Or do you withdraw away, so an inauthentic person is being perfectly reasonable to someone who isn't there communicating? Figure 15–35 shows this.

How You Could Respond in a Positive Healing Way to the Rigid Defense

Figure 15–36 (in the color insert) shows how you could help people with rigid defenses feel the reality of their own core essence. This response is the most difficult because it requires of you a great deal of ability to experience your own essence and theirs. But I am sure you can learn it with practice.

The first thing to remember is that since a rigid character defense has a strong balanced auric field, with boundaries well in place, you don't have to worry about boundary. So stand up close. There is a good chance they will be more comfortable being close than you are. You also don't have to worry about controlling your bioplasmic streamers or the vibrational frequency of your field. But standing in a state of loving kindness and acceptance helps a lot. What you do need to learn how to do is to feel the essence of your core within you and to fill your whole auric field with this essence. There are specific exercises in Chapter 17 on the core that teach how to bring the core essence up into your auric field. Please follow them to learn how to do it.

Once you have done that, then also feel their essence at the same time you feel your own. To do that, focus your attention on their core star, which is located one and one-half inches above the navel on the center line of the physical body. When you bring your conscious awareness there, you will be able to experience their essence. Once you know what it feels like, put your hands on their upper chest and feel their essence there. The only way you can feel another's essence is with your own, so you are automatically doing that. Hold your essence right at the edge of the other's to feel it. Now describe what you are feeling, keeping your hand on their chest. Encourage them to feel the difference between their essence and yours. This is very subtle, delicate work. It will take a lot of patience in being there. If you pull back, they will retreat. Remember, this is very important to them. So please take the time.

The Results of a Positive Healing Response

If you are able to do at least part of the above work, you will have helped your friend to find their core essence,

perhaps for the first time since very early childhood. They have never had an experience of essence being confirmed. They have no framework in which to experience essence because as far as their upbringing went, it didn't exist. In effect, you are holding up the reflective mirror to them so that they can find their individuality. They can only find individuality by experiencing essence.

When you do this, everything will change. They will be able to move out of the inexorable march of time into the presence of the now that encompasses all of time. They will be able to express feelings on the outside because they will know who it is that is doing the feeling, and that will make them authentic. They will be able to be appropriate and authentic at the same time. They will connect their sexuality and heart through their core essence because it is in both. They will have a self and know who they are.

Next time your friend disappears from your conversation into perfectionism, it's okay if you react in a negative way. But as soon as you notice it, take a deep breath, bend your knees, and ground down into the earth. Feel your own core essence, and fill your field with it. Move up closer, ask permission to touch, and describe what you wish to do. You will give them a great gift. For it is only in the communion of being touched and touching at the level of the core essence that they will accomplish their deepest purpose on earth: to know the individuated God within.

How to Take Yourself Out of a Rigid Defense

If you find yourself missing from a conversation you are having with someone, stop, center within yourself, and bring your attention to your core star, one and one-half inches above your navel on the center line of your body. Simply stay there till you feel yourself. Then very delicately bring this self into the conversation. Repeat the mantra, "I am real. I am real. I am light." You will be surprised at the results.

Auric Observations of a Couple in Dispute and How They Energetically Resolved It

A good example of a couple moving from character defense clash into healing synchronicity happened one evening when I was visiting a couple who are friends of mine. When I arrived, they had been stuck in an issue for a few days. As they started relating their positions to me, I observed their fields interacting. Here is what happened.

The husband, who was in an oral defensive action, complained of wanting and needing more contact and intimacy. The wife went into her psychopathic defense and said that they already had a lot of it. She began subtly acting as if it were his problem, trying to get him to explain more and more. She listened while he tried to explain but at the same time energetically pulled back from him. First she pulled her field back; then she started disconnecting her bioplasmic flows of energy that connected them between their hearts and their third chakras.

This confused him. She seemed to be earnestly listening, but at the same time she energetically withdrew from him, right when he was trying to get more of her energy. See Figure 15–37.

While the husband continued to try to explain his situation, he fell into the oral defense more and more. He became more and more confused and less confident that what he was talking about was real. The woman escalated her psychopathic defense by disconnecting her field from his. She pulled her energy up her back and started sending an aggressive bioplasmic streamer up from her back, over the top of her head, and over his head in an effort to control him, deny his reality, and yet still remain connected in the aggressive way that she felt safe. She was unaware of doing this.

Her auric field reaction to her husband's statements showed that she was frightened by them and by his desire for more intimacy. She used her psychopathic defensive stance to control him by pulling her energy back and yet appearing to be there for him, so that she wouldn't feel her fear. As a result of her energetic actions, he began to doubt that what he was saying had any truth in it. He thought that perhaps the problem wasn't real. Perhaps it was all "just his stuff." Her defense was to convince him that the issue was not real so that she wouldn't have to deal with it. Unconsciously, she was denying her own perceptions. Deep inside somewhere, she knew he had a point to make that was very real, but she blocked it from her awareness. Consciously, she was only aware of being "helpful," of trying to understand what he was saying. By keeping her energy to the back of her body and in the will chakras, she was using her will to be there for him but without allowing herself to have feelings and to be vulnerable. If she were to allow her energy to move to the front of her body, she would feel her feelings and her vulnerability. This would bring her into more intimacy. But more intimacy for her would mean surrendering down into deeper levels of herself, where she was afraid to go.

As this process continued, the husband began to be afraid. He reached a long hook out of his third chakra into hers and started grabbing and pulling her energy in order to stop her from disconnecting and leaving him. She reacted with even more overhead pushes and controls. See Figure 15–38. The more each person got into their defense, the more distorted their energy fields became.

The more distorted an energy field becomes, the more that person goes into a negative image about reality, the less present that person is, and the less able they are to relate to what is happening in the now. In the situation with my friends, the more defended each became, the more painful the situation became. Less and less of each true person and more and more of just their defenses was there.

At this point, I described what their fields were doing to make them feel worse. They both began to work on pulling their fields back into themselves, centering into their core, and grounding into the earth. I read their fields as they worked, guiding them into their respective centers. When they were centered and grounded, they each worked to align and enhance their haric line. Then they worked together through each level of the field, clearing, balancing, and charging it. As I read their energy fields and guided them, they brought the core star essence up through the haric level and each level of the field. By the time this was done, the defenses were gone, each field was coherent, and the room was filled with the essence of each of them.

Then, the most wonderful thing I have ever witnessed between two people's fields happened. I saw all the great arches of colored bioplasma flowing between them dissolve. What was left was two people with coherent fields, pulsating at their own frequencies and in synchronicity with one another. They were communing without an energy flow exchange. There was no dependence at all. There was simply self-expression, with acceptance, acknowledgment, and delight in each other. This beautiful dance of light continued for some time. Everyone was in ecstasy. It is shown in Figure 15–39 in the color insert.

This is the only time I have ever seen such a sight. I believe it to be an unusual state of relationship, one for which we all long and strive, one that, perhaps in the future, will become the norm. We will do it automatically when we learn to believe in ourselves and in the core of our being, as well as honor each other, respect each other, and delight in our differences.

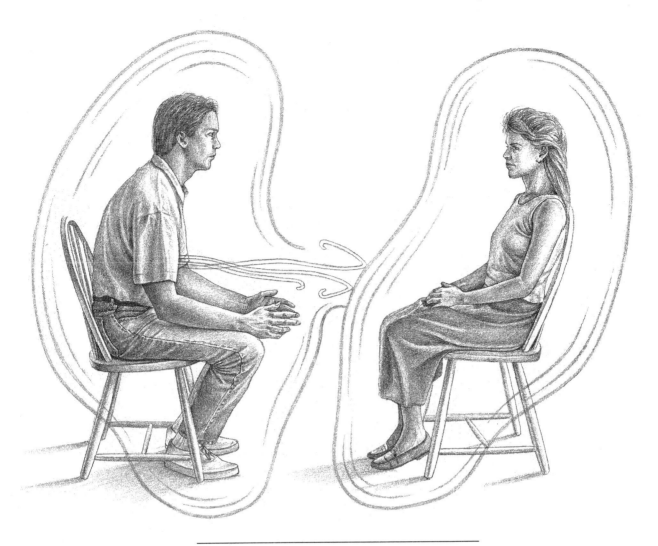

Figure 15–37 The Auric Field of a Couple in Defense

Introduction to Healing Through Forgiveness

I would like to close this chapter with one of the most powerful healing meditations that Heyoan has given. It is the "Healing Through Forgiveness" meditation. This meditation brings you into a deep contemplation, with which you will be able to heal the internal wounds you carry from past relationships. The most important factor in healing past wounds in relationships is forgiveness.

Usually, we are more conscious of not being able to forgive someone else than of not being able to forgive ourselves. All of us have known that it makes a big

difference when we forgive someone for hurting us. Most of the time, we remember painful situations in the light of someone else hurting us and blame the other person.

Our blame is on the surface; deeper inside, there is usually a nagging guilt to which we may not admit. Many times, the other person did not experience the situation as we did and may not even know we are hurt. In fact, at times the other person thinks we should apologize so that they can forgive us. In all of these situations we are locked in duality. Forgiveness lifts us beyond that duality into love.

In his "Healing Through Forgiveness" meditation, Heyoan gives us a broad view of forgiveness. He helps us transcend the blame of "he/she did it to me," with its

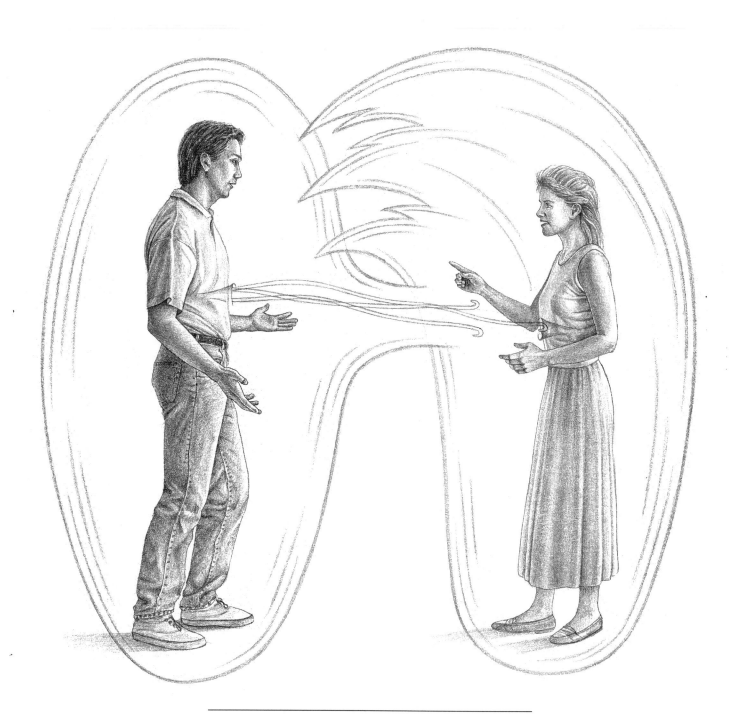

Figure 15–38 The Auric Field of a Couple Escalating Defense

deeper nagging guilt, and brings us to a unitary understanding of why forgiveness works.

Before you begin, I suggest you create a list of people in your life whom you have not been able to forgive. Then do the following meditation on forgiveness. It is very nice to have someone read the Heyoan material to you, or get the tape of this channeled material from the Barbara Brennan School of Healing. Or read it out loud into a tape recorder yourself. On tape, it is much more personal, and you will be able to absorb it more easily by simply resting back in your bed with your eyes closed.

~

HEALING THROUGH FORGIVENESS
Channeled from
Heyoan

Feel a pillar of light within. Feel a star of light in your center, just above your navel. It is no accident that you are here. You have brought yourself to this very moment in your life, for your own purposes, which arise out of the deep and sacred longing that you carry above your heart. The more that you honor that longing, the more you will find yourself directly on your path in a life that is joyous and fulfilling, in a life that is creative and forgiving.

I would like you today to take one person with whom you are having difficulties in your life and begin working and praying to align yourself for forgiveness and healing. Healing requires forgiveness of both yourself and that individual. As you may know, healing encompasses the entire life—indeed, all your lifetimes—and that which is beyond lifetimes. You exist in a realm much greater than the physical, which is defined by time and space. Time and space to you are only commodities of limitation that you have placed in this schoolroom, that you have created for yourself to learn within. You have created your lessons, you have created your schoolroom, you have created your teachers within that schoolroom, and yet you are the master of all of this creation. You have come to this earth for your own purposes that are carried in your sacred longing.

Now I ask you, with regard to the person you have chosen, how have you betrayed your sacred longing and thereby created a situation in which self-forgiveness is needed? This may not be an easy answer that comes immediately. But if you focus on it and pray about it and connect it to your healing work, you will begin to understand. Through your life experience, a deeper understanding of what is being said here will well up from the fountain of life within you.

Yes, it is true that you create your experience of your life. It is of your design. You have designed it from the utmost wisdom within you. If there is pain, then ask what that pain is saying to you, for pain arises out of forgetting who you are. Pain arises out of belief that the shadow reality is the true reality. The shadow reality is a result of forgetting who you are, which is based upon the belief that you are separate, or separated from God.

I tell you, dear ones, all disease, no matter what its form or manifestation, is the result of this forgetting. You have returned here, to this earth plane, to remember. Do not be distressed by this. Set your life-force in the direction of remembering, and its illumination will awaken the portions of your psyche that exist in shadow and in pain.

When you illuminate them with the light of the divine, which exists within every cell of your body, within every cell of your being, the light shines into the shadow and the shadow begins to remember. Re-membering means to bring your members back together. Through illumination, you will re-member the portions of yourself and your body that have become dissociated and therefore dis-eased. It is a new beginning; yes, some pain is experienced, but it is a healing pain. The tears will wash your soul clear and clean, like fresh-fallen rain. Your cries will release what has been held for centuries, awaiting emergence. All of those blocks that have been talked about will flow and fill with life renewed. You will find yourself filled with much more energy. You will find your life moving into creativity and joy. You will find yourself being filled in a natural dance with all those around you, and with the universe.

But this requires forgiveness: forgiveness first of the self. What have you to forgive yourself for?

If you were to spend five minutes—and I will ask you to do this at the end of my little talk—writing a list of those things you must forgive yourself for someday, you will find it quite extensive. But it is not so difficult. If you take each item and meditate on it for a few minutes several times a day and forgive yourself for it, you will lighten the burden on your heart. Forgiveness comes from the divine within. By praying for and experiencing your forgiveness, you connect with the divine within you. You become the divine within you.

The next questions are: How does each item that you forgive yourself for show in your psyche and in your physical body? How does it show in your energy field? Trace it through all seven experiential levels of your field.

Where is the pain in your body that is associated with that unforgiving attitude that you have held toward yourself, and thereby maintained a negative connection with a particular individual that you find difficult to forgive? You see, healing always begins at home.

Within you, in the place an inch and a half to two inches above your navel, there is a beautiful star, the core star. It is the essence of your individuality. This essence is your divine individuality. It is the center of your beingness. It is the center of who you are in complete peace before, during, and beyond all lifetimes that you have ever experienced on your mother the earth. Feel this place within you. You existed before this life. You existed before all of the chaos and pain and strife that exists upon this earth, and you will continue to do so.

This center of your beingness is the center of your divinity. From this place you are the center of the entire universe. It is from this place that you will heal. You will remember who you are, and you will help others remember who they are. For it is from the center of your being that all of your actions arise. As soon as your actions become disconnected from the center of your being, you are no longer aligned with your divine purpose. Action disconnected from divine purpose creates pain and dis-ease. So, dear ones, center yourselves into your core. It is from this center that all forgiveness arises.

I should like you now to take the first item you found to forgive yourself for to your core. Whatever it was that you created that needs forgiving was created in a manner that was disconnected from your center. As you moved to create, you disconnected from the center of your being; your actions became unaligned with your divine purpose and moved, perhaps ever so slightly, into shadow and forgetting. So if you take that which needs to be forgiven, bring it to the core star and simply hold it there, surround it and infuse it with love, you will, through this love, bring it back to the light. You will find your original purpose that arose from your center. Once having found this, you can move forth with the original creation. For in finding, surrounding, and infusing it with love and light, you will find forgiveness within yourself. I will give you a few moments now to bring forth self-forgiveness in this manner.

As this forgiveness streams through your being, you will find yourselves automatically forgiving others that may be involved in this particular situation that calls for forgiveness.

~

HEALING THROUGH OUR HIGHER SPIRITUAL REALITIES

"In each and every moment, we have the freedom to choose,
and every choice determines the direction of our lives."

—Olivia Hoblitzelle

Integrating Your Higher Spiritual Aspects and Deeper Dimensions into Your Healing Plan

As I continued to teach and practice, I found that our spiritual needs and a connection to our deeper realities are just as important in our healing process as our physical needs. In fact, it became obvious that they are primary, and that without them life is merely three-dimensional and very limited. In order to understand who we are and our life purpose, and to experience life as a safe, benign, loving passage, we must have spiritual communion as well as human communion.

As I worked with the higher spiritual levels of the auric field and the deeper dimensions beneath the auric field, my whole concept of health and healing changed. In fact, my whole concept of life in the physical world

changed. I began to see healing as a beautiful creative process that is most natural and most universal. We are guided every step of the way through this beautiful life process. In it, we find ourselves to be both individual and universal. We find ourselves held completely safe in a benign abundant universe where life and healing are one.

We will start with the experience and purpose of spiritual guidance in our lives. That will most naturally bring us to the higher spirituality that is experienced in the higher levels of the auric field. Then we will move on to the deeper dimensions that form the very foundations of our being.

The Process of
Guidance in Your Life

Quietly moving into a spiritually centered life requires a great reorientation of consciousness into the transcendent realities of the higher vibrational levels—five, six, and seven—of the auric field. In these higher ranges of consciousness and energy, whole worlds of nonmaterial spiritual beings exist. Many people do not experience these levels of consciousness at all; to them, even the existence of these levels seems highly speculative, absurd, or even ridiculous. In the healing process, however, if you continue on the upward path through levels of consciousness, you will automatically begin to have experiences involving these higher levels and eventually encounter such beings.

As you move your conscious awareness into the three higher levels of your auric field, you move into the higher aspects of your will, emotions, and reason. Each of these three levels is a template for the lower three levels of the field. The higher will, called the divine will within, is the template for the first level of the field, which contains the will to live in the physical world. The higher emotional level, sometimes called the inspirational level or the level of your divine love, is the template for the second level of the field, your feelings about yourself. The higher reason of level seven, called divine mind, which gives an understanding of the perfect pattern of all things, is a template for the reason of level three, the mental level. This relation-

ship has been stated since the days of old as: "As above, so below."

The correspondence between levels seven and three, six and two, and five and one provides a way to heal the lower levels by bringing the values from the higher levels down into the lower ones. To do so, we must reach up or transcend into the higher levels. This is called the transcendent process. We reach up into our higher realities and claim them as our own. When we do this, our reason becomes truth, our emotions become love, and our will becomes courage. If we continue this transcendent process, our truth becomes wisdom, our love becomes unconditional love, and our courage becomes power. We claim our spiritual reality as our own and find God within.

The best, most practical way to enter into the transcendent process is through guidance. Guidance is available to all human beings from their higher self within, their guardian angel, or in more popular terms, their spirit guide. Usually people start by getting guidance from their higher self, then later expand into receiving it from spirit guides.

Getting guidance and channeling spirit guides is a very popular activity in some circles now. Many people ask guidance for all kinds of things but generally to find out how to deal with life issues, what to do for a particular day, or how to solve a problem. Guidance is even used to get information to cure illnesses. Guidance is so popular that some try to use it to win the lottery, get answers to tests, and even to find parking places. Some people misuse guidance to try to get out of real responsibilities. They break commitments in irresponsible ways, saying that their guidance told them to do it. They seem to think that that justifies unethical and irresponsible behavior. Many people who use guidance fail to see its deeper function and the great benefit it has in their life learning process.

Guidance is an integral part of the unfoldment of your life. It is the key to the development of your heart's desire and your life task, no matter what it is. Guidance is more than communicating with guides, more than channeling information; it is a life process. HSP and the ability to get precise information come from following guidance over a long period of time. In observing the effects of guidance in my own life, I have discerned the following information about how guidance works.

How Spiritual Guidance Works

1. Guidance never lets you off the hook. It keeps you responsible in many ways: responsible to who you are, to not betraying yourself, and to keeping your commitments. If your commitments need to be changed, guidance will never let you change them without responsibility. In other words, if you make a commitment that later is not healthy for you, that commitment is changeable but not irresponsibly.

2. Guidance does not absolve your karma. Rather, it gives you a tool to handle it, even possibly for enjoying its clearing. You must go through the balancing of the karmic scales. Balancing your karmic scales does not mean karmic punishment. It means learning what you did not learn in life experiences of the past that still affect your life in a negative way now. Usually this learning is done through life situations that you experience according to how clear you are from images and misconceptions.

3. Following guidance brings you life experiences that you need in order to develop your life task or your healership.

4. Living a spiritual life and finding your life task requires a willingness to follow guidance and live by the truth, no matter what the price appears to be when you get the guidance.

5. Guidance gets personally harder and the apparent price increases as you follow it.

6. Guidance and faith go together. You have to have a lot of faith to follow your guidance, and in turn, following guidance builds your faith. Guidance is designed to take you through areas of your personal psyche where you have previously refused to go but must go in order to unfold. It takes you through your deepest fears into your deepest faith.

7. Faith is a state of being that sets, balances, and charges the auric field into a healing state. It connects the small ego part of you to the greater you, the God within. It is a process of holographically connecting to all that there is—you to the universe.

8. Your separated ego will doesn't have a lot of chance to interfere with systematic guidance because many times you don't know why you are doing what it tells you to do.

9. As you surrender or let go of your separated ego will and follow divine will as communicated to you through your guidance, others trust you more.

10. Guidance automatically and systematically builds both physical and spiritual endurance for your life task.

11. The more endurance you build, the more love, power, and support you will get and the greater and more effective on a broader scale will be the unfoldment of your life task. As you solve problems, you will proceed to more responsible and difficult ones.

12. The act of following your guidance builds your healing vessel for the healing life energies. It builds your vessel for the divine task you have chosen to come in with. Guidance releases the involuntary creative principle into a safe vessel. Only by the surrender to guidance, the surrender of the ego to the greater holy spirit, or God within, can your involuntary life-force be released into a safe vessel. The involuntary life-force is everything that comes out of you automatically when you don't block your energy flow. Sometimes it is positive; sometimes it is negative. Guidance systematically clears your negativity so that more and more of the positive life-force can be released. It releases this powerful flow of life-force into your vessel in exact proportion to its ability to handle it. Therefore your vessel is safe.

13. The powerful flow of life-force that comes with the involuntary divine creative principle cannot be commanded by the ego. Another way to say this is that the goodness within you flows of its own

accord; it reaches out in wisdom, love, and caring of its own accord. It does not flow on the command of the ego. The only thing the ego can do is stop it from flowing or get out of its way.

14. Guidance takes you by the hand and walks with you into a state of surrender to your true human fragility and vulnerability, which is centered in the little ego. When following it, you immediately face the fact that you do not have life in your hands, that your ego does not control your life, and that guidance will not help it do so. That is it—you simply can't. To me, that is what is meant by surrender of the ego. To what do you surrender? You surrender to a deeper power within you. Following guidance is a systematic letting-go of an outer ego that may try to make you safe but cannot. Guidance reconnects you to your original power. You become a child of God. In this surrender, you find another power—the power of God within. You become an instrument of God. You find all the power, wisdom, and love of God within you.

15. There is no punishment if you don't follow guidance. You have all the time in the world, since time is an illusion. If you get guidance and you don't follow it for three months or two years, that's all right. But to the degree that you do follow your guidance, to that very degree, you gain spiritual power within because following guidance automatically helps you surrender to the greater divinity within you. This spiritual power helps you complete your life task.

16. Following guidance allows the holy spirit to combine with your core essence to give you power. This power is not accumulated in your ego. Rather, it works to connect your inner core essence or divine individual spark with the universal God.

17. Guidance builds freedom and independence by shifting life's focus to reliance on the reality of inner divinity rather than on outer values.

18. The best things in life are free.

How Guidance Has Led Me Through My Life

As I look back over my life, I find that every major turning point was very specifically and precisely guided. Sometimes I followed guidance that seemed totally outrageous. People around me were telling me not to do it, but I did.

During the time when I was living in Washington, D.C., training to be a bioenergetic therapist, a wonderful guidance event occurred. It happened at Easter. Some new friends said they heard about a miracle that was to take place in West Virginia on Easter morning. They said, "Do you want to come?" I said sure and then thought, "What do I wear to a miracle?" I decided on white pants and a shirt with sandals! We drove five hours and arrived at the apple orchard early, before the sun rose. There were TV cameras. The woman who had predicted the miracle had set up the whole thing with different stations representing the Christ's life, including the garden of Gethsemane. We were to be pilgrims and bring roses to put in the garden.

We all anxiously awaited the sunrise to see the predicted miracle. Finally the sun came up. I looked at the sun as it rose, and it swirled off lots of red streamers and moved around a bit in the sky. I said, "Ooh, just like the miracle of Fatima, when thousands of people saw the sun spin in the sky!" Then I thought, "What an interesting retina effect. So that is what happens when you look into the sun." All around me, people were shouting, "Look at the sun spin! Do you see it?" Others grumbled, "I can't look, I can't look—it's too bright." Again, it was just like what had happened at the miracle of Fatima. Another person was saying, "There's a cross in the sky." I couldn't see it. That was it. So I put my rose in the garden and we drove home. While going home, I said to myself, "Why don't I just let it be a miracle? I don't know what a miracle looks like. Maybe it was real." So I said, "I'm going to test this out."

The next morning I got up at the same time to look at the sun to test what would happen in terms of the retina effect. I couldn't look into the sun—it was too bright. I said, "That's interesting. Now I can't look into the sun at all. I'll just be patient and wait to see if anything else happens, since I don't really know what a miracle is."

It didn't take long for the so-called miracle to show itself in new phenomena. What happened from then on, I consider part of the miracle, because what began for me was a whole unraveling of the mystery of life. What happened was simple: Whenever the sun was at a certain angle in the sky, I would hear a clear verbal message instructing me what to do. Sometimes it was "Calm down. Your mind is exaggerating everything." Or, "Your healing teacher is ill, and you need to give her a healing rather than receive one today." I would hear a voice, as if it were coming from the sun. The sun would reflect upon me and get my attention, and I would get a message. It seemed that even if the sun could not get to me directly, it would find a way. Once I was sitting in a chair rocking my baby daughter. The sun was over on the opposite side of the house, and it reflected over to the next-door neighbor's window and came through my window and hit me at the right angle. This communication from the sun has continued for years.

Another example of guidance happened after I had been trained as a bioenergetic therapist and was giving sessions as a therapist in Washington, D.C. I had started to see past lives. I didn't know what to do about this. So I started praying for help about what to do. I went camping on Assateague Island. It was raining, so I was lying on the beach with a plastic tarp over my head. In the middle of the night I heard my name called three times so loudly that it woke me up. I looked up at the tarp. It was translucent, so I thought I was looking up at the clouds. Suddenly I realized it was just the tarp, so I pushed it off of me to see where the voice was coming from. The whole sky was completely clear, and I fell back in awe because I could hear the stars singing back and forth to each other across the heavens. I knew my prayers had been answered. I had been called, and the answer would come.

A short time later I found the Center for the Living Force (now called the Pathwork Center) in Phoenicia, New York. I went there for a workshop and knew that the answer to my prayer was that I needed to move there. It took a year before I could accomplish this. My husband didn't want to move to the center, but I did with my four-year-old daughter, because it was guidance. Later he came.

After moving to Phoenicia, I worked in process group on my channel because I was getting a lot of psychic information like other people's past lives that I didn't know what to do with. At one time I had a broken leg and was stomping around with a cast on, loudly yelling that I wasn't angry. The head of the center, Eva Pierrakos, who channeled the Pathwork guide lectures, said, "The problem with you is that your channel opened too fast, and you are too angry inside, and you can't handle it. You need to close your channel." My guidance confirmed this. I was getting a lot of pleasure from being psychic. I was getting off on being special and was using it to avoid dealing with important issues in my life. The only acceptable use of my channel was for my own personal work. So I closed my channel except for personal work. I didn't know how long it would have to be this way. My guides simply said for as long as it takes.

Shortly after my vow, I was tested. One day I accidentally started to leave my body. I saw beautiful guides with jewels all over their robes standing nearby. I was very curious as to who they were, but I remembered my vow and quickly forced myself back into my body. My psychic gifts were a lot to give up, but I let go and concentrated on my personal work. I spent the next six years focusing on my own transformation. I focused for the first two years on divine will. To do this, I made sure that everything I did was aligned with God's will. Every morning when I got up, I prayed and meditated to commit myself to and align with God's will. I had private sessions in which I tried to understand what is meant by God's will. I felt a conflict about what God was going to make me do next. Was I his slave? I dealt with everything in my life from the perspective of being in divine will. Slowly, over time, I found that whatever I wanted to do at any moment from the deepest clearest part of me was also God's will. I was able to find the will of God singing within my own heart.

The next two years, I concentrated on divine love. I focused on being loving in everything I did. Every morning I prayed and meditated on learning about divine love. In doing this, I found that many of my actions were not so loving. I worked in my private sessions on bringing love into my life. During those two years things began to change, and I was able to be and express loving much more in my life. My work for the next two years was to concentrate on divine truth. I followed the same pattern as before, praying and meditating every morning to find what divine truth is. I spent a great deal of time concentrating on exploring its function in my life, where it was missing, and how to bring more of it into my life. Was I willing to find and stand up for the truth in all situations? Since I lived in a spiritual community all this time, I was always offered life situations to practice all three of these divine aspects of ourselves.

Everyone in the resident community at the Center for the Living Force was working on themselves in this way for self-transformation. It was a real boiling pot of people seeking spiritual truths and struggling with each other every day in running the community. We all learned a lot in those days. We thought we were creating a city of light, but later, as we scattered all over the world, we realized that we each had gotten what we came there for. We embodied the work. We filled our beings with the work, so that we lived according to the higher spiritual principles that we believed in. Finally, after six years of deep work and struggle, I knew I was ready to open my channel again because I was trustworthy. People simply trusted me because I was willing to let go to whatever the truth was and follow it. Of course that didn't mean I was finished with personal transformation. The work still continues to this day, and it will for the rest of my life. But I knew I had reached a turning point in my life and that things would begin changing drastically, which they did.

I knew I was supposed to go to Findhorn. I did. When I was there, I stood on a nature power point called Randolph's Leap, a place near Findhorn where the Druids are supposed to have worshiped and communed with nature spirits. I asked to have access to the nature spirits. Nothing appeared to happen. I went to Holland to run an intensive workshop, and then to Switzerland to ski. I totally forgot about my request. After I was back about a month, I started waking up at five-thirty every morning writing reams of information of guidance. I started seeing little nature spirits everywhere I went. They would follow me as I walked around the property. They were always a bit shy and would stay a few feet behind me, giggling.

Through the contact with the nature spirits I got a lot of information about the Center for the Living Force, such as the location and placement of where the sanctuary building was to be built. It came in very small, sweet doses in daily meditations. I was walking down the upper road at the center on my way to work in the kitchen when a voice called my name. I ignored it. It called again. I told it that I was late for my job and kept walking.

It called a third time, and I said, "Oh, okay. What do you want?" It led me to a meadow and to a rock.

I said, "So?"

It said, "Sit." So I sat.

Then I said, "Now what?"

It said, "Sit." So I sat and meditated.

Every day for the next year I went to the rock to meditate. Each day during my meditation, I was given small pieces of information about the land. I was told that the rock I sat on was the altar rock. The voice pointed out another rock directly down the hill and then two others on each side that were marker rocks. A line could be drawn between the altar rock and the first marker rock. Another line could be drawn between the two side marker rocks. The two lines crossed each other in the middle of the meadow. On that exact spot two small trees had fallen and crossed. A year or so later, when it was time to find the spot for the sanctuary building, everyone was asked to lead the sanctuary committee in charge of the construction to their favorite places on the center property. A place was chosen.

I was sure it was wrong, but I kept quiet. On our way back to the main hall someone asked me to show them my secret place of daily meditation. I reluctantly led the group of people to the altar rock. Everyone sat on it to meditate. Everyone instantly knew that this was the place. Then I shyly started sharing the information I had gathered over the last year of meditations. Later, when I went there with a surveyor, it turned out that the lines defined by the marker rocks were in the exact position of the maximum solar angle for a solar building. The fallen trees turned out to be the exact location of the joining of two large walls of glass on the front of the seven-sided building.

I was part of the committee that helped design the building. Since the terrain was mountainous, we had to blast the rock bed with dynamite to build the foundation. I tried in vain to shoo the deer away before the blast, but they wouldn't go. They only moved five or ten feet away when the dynamite exploded, then proceeded to graze as if nothing had happened.

During my years at the center, I went through a long period of testing of very simple things. The guides would give me instructions like, "Go saw the dead limb off that tree." Sometimes it would take me three months to do it because I thought it was stupid—a little resistance there! But finally I did it. I began to notice that if I didn't do it, no new instruction would come until I did it. As soon as I would do it, I would get the next instruction. Now I realize that I was being trained to follow instructions exactly and precisely. This built up trust so that I could do fifth-level spiritual surgery with the guides. Fifth-level surgery, described in *Hands of Light*, is a way to restructure the fifth level of the auric field, with guides doing most of the work. It began one day for me when I still had a massage practice.

I was giving someone a Swedish massage, and a guide appeared and said, "Hold up two green stripes," to get me to take my hands off the body. My client had come in for a massage, but now I sat there for forty-five minutes with my hands above her body, holding up two green stripes. I saw guides come in under the green stripes and do an operation on my client. That is when I started to learn about fifth-level spiritual surgery. I observed the operation. I kept waiting for my client to say, "Hey, where's my massage?" But she didn't. The next week she came back complaining of postoperative symptoms. I could see the stitches on her spleen that the guides had put there. Again, I had to hold up two green stripes. This time they took out the stitches. And again, she didn't complain that I didn't touch her body for her massage. She said whatever I was doing felt wonderful. That is how I began learning to do fifth-level spiritual surgery.

One day, after doing my morning writing at five-thirty, guidance told me to buy a typewriter. I didn't know how to type, but I was getting guidance so fast that I couldn't write it out in longhand anymore. So I was to type it. I learned to type. After some time of typing, I couldn't type fast enough. I was told to buy a tape recorder, so I started recording it. Without knowing it, I had started my first book.

I worked on my first book, *Hands of Light*, for fifteen years. Twelve publishers refused the manuscript. I didn't know what to do. I got guidance to publish it myself. I sold the house I owned but didn't live in anymore and got $50,000 for it. Everyone thought I was totally nuts to take my entire life savings to do the book. But I said, "Either this is my life's work or it isn't. It's time to give everything to it." It cost me $50,000 to make a thousand books. By the time the book was published, I had a few hundred dollars left to my name and a daughter to support. I wrote a letter to people I knew explaining that I had published my book. "I paid fifty dollars a book. I'll sell it to you for fifty dollars." The book sold out in three months, and then I got the next batch. Someone suggested I take it to a publisher. I said, "But they all refused it already." But I did, and Bantam bought it. The book is now in nine different languages and distributed all over the world.

When I first started communicating with guides, I did not particularly distinguish between the ones who were with me all the time and those who came for several-month intervals to teach me new techniques and then left. I could always see them. After I had done all those years of preparation by working with the guides by myself, they started making suggestions as to how to work with my clients during sessions. This continued as my massage and therapy practice slowly turned into a healing practice. The guides would tell me what to do with my hands. They would also give me information about clients that I had no way of knowing otherwise. They would tell me the physical cause of a client's problem as well as the psychological cause and how both related to certain relationships the client was in now and had been in in the past. I slowly, shyly, and embarrassingly introduced the information into the session. I would say things like, "Have you ever thought of this . . ." and then add the guides' information.

Soon the psychic pressure of so much information more or less pushed me into channeling it. I never told

the client it was a guide—I just talked in a little different voice. I said that my voice changed because I was in an altered state. After a few years of this, a client said, "You were channeling a guide, weren't you?"

"Who, me?"

"What is his name?" the client asked.

"I don't know."

I usually paid more attention to the guides my clients brought with them to a healing session because the clients would always want me to describe their guides to them. I would convey information to clients from their guides as well as from mine. I even began speaking in strange accents for a while, but I found it rather embarrassing. Finally, I said that I only wanted to channel one guide that had a more normal voice. If somebody else's guide wanted to convey information through me, I would listen and then repeat it.

I could always see five guides around me when I worked—they are still with me. By this time, guides were in vogue. Everyone was channeling, and I still didn't know who my main guide was. So I decided to find out. I asked my guides one day when I was giving a healing/channeling workshop with Pat Rodegast, a well-known channeler and author of *Emmanuel's Book* and *Emmanuel's Book II*. I heard the word "Heyoan" or "Heokan." I said, "Yuk! I want a guide with a nice name like Pat's Emmanuel." I didn't like the name at all and tried to change it, to no avail. Then I forgot all about it. Six months later, I was giving another workshop on channeling and healing with Pat. Whenever we worked together, we always asked to learn something during the work. This time, in frustration, I said, "Why does everyone know the name of her guide but me? I want to learn the name of my guide." Sure enough, during the workshop, Heyoan once again leaned over me when I was demonstrating a healing and said,

~

My name is Heyoan—remember, I told you six months ago. It's from Africa and means, "The wind whispering truth through the centuries."

~

Well now, that was really embarrassing. I had actually been told and had completely forgotten the incident ever happened. That was my formal introduction to Heyoan. We have been great buddies ever since. In my state of conscious awareness that I call Barbara, I usually "see" Heyoan standing to my right and slightly behind me. He appears to be about ten to twelve feet tall and light blue, gold, and white in color. When I channel Heyoan, our consciousness fuses and becomes one consciousness. I "become" Heyoan. When I do this, my auric field stretches out to a diameter of about twenty feet. Many times after channeling Heyoan for an hour or two, I am taken up into a room of light where there is a large long table, with many guides around it. Here they show me a large blueprint of plans of what is to be in the future. I don't usually understand much of what is on these plans, but I am trying. Little by little, I think I'll learn how to read them.

Different groups of guides joined the programs I have run through the years. About five years ago, I started channeling another spiritual being who appeared to be very feminine. In the beginning, we called her the Goddess because she appeared to be the feminine aspect of God. The energy field from this being is white and gold and has increased over the years. She is so large that it is impossible to tell her size. My dear friend Marjorie Valeri, a professional harpist, and I go into trance. Marjorie channels the harp. A wall of white light, much larger than the room, rushes in from behind Marjorie and me and lifts everyone's consciousness. I go into trance and walk around the room giving healing and channeling for people. The power is so great in this work that I have actually been able to give healing to as many as 280 people in one hour.

What is more, the healing power is so great that the effects of the healing unfold over a period of several months' time. The most outstanding case was of someone who came to a workshop at the Omega Institute. She was carrying oxygen on her back. She was waiting for a heart and two lung transplants. The Goddess worked on her for about five minutes. This, and her longing to heal herself, helped her turn her illness around. The oxygen level in her blood began to increase until it was higher when she was off the oxygen than it was when she was on it. The donor organs never came through. She later got married and moved out west somewhere. The last I heard, her physicians said that she only needed one lung transplant. It has now been three years since the Goddess touched her.

Through the years, the healing energy that we called the Goddess has now become much more balanced in both masculine and feminine energy. And I was told recently in guidance that it really is the holy spirit. I now have to deal with my shyness at claiming to channel the holy spirit. Somehow, the feminine aspect of God seems more permissible. I'll have to work on that one. In the last workshop I did in Santa Fe, I also picked up a new group of guides that call themselves the Council of Light. They seem to have a great deal of power. They sit around in a circle with a candle at each one's feet. They seem to have big plans about building healing centers around the world. I'm curious as to how this one will unfold. It will, in its own time.

So that is how guidance has worked in my life. In doing those things, even though some were rather outrageous, ridiculous, or apparently foolish, I built my faith. It took faith as I was continually tested to do exactly what I was asked to do or to give the exact information and not expound on the information that I was given. That is why I eventually got to the level of channeling specific treatments and how long a person should take them. Guidance took me step by step into my Higher Sense Perception, channeling, and the higher three levels of the auric field. It took me into my spirituality and the spirit world and made it real. Guidance has brought me many wonderful experiences and has taken me to a broader understanding of my own divinity.

Following guidance and entering into the spiritual side of life is not always easy because it is so challenging. We tend to ignore it, put it off, or just plain think it is not real. Learning to follow guidance is a step-by-step process that brings us into our higher spiritual realities. Each time we choose to follow guidance, we choose our higher divine will. By repeatedly doing this, we begin to experience the higher levels of our spiritual realities that correspond to the fifth, sixth, and seventh levels of our auric field. Let us now go to the higher levels of the field.

The Fifth Level of the Aura: Divine Will

The fifth level of the auric field is associated with divine will. It is the primal level of all form and symbols. As soon as you lift up into the fifth level with your Higher Sense Perception, you will see cobalt-blue light. It may be a bit confusing at first because the fifth level is the template or blueprint for all form. That means that it is like the negative of a photograph or a stencil for an airbrush. Everything is reversed. What you would expect to be solid is empty, clear space. What you would expect to be empty, clear space is solid cobalt blue. After you have spent some time on the fifth level, you get used to this reversal and don't notice it so much. Since the fifth level is the template for the first, you can think of it as made of grooves into which the lines of the first level of the auric field fit. Or you might think of the bed of a river in which the water (energy lines of the first level) flows. The fifth level of your field is the template for the first level, which is then the template for your physical body.

The fifth level is usually hardest for people in our culture to understand. In our culture, we let reason rule. If we are asked to do something, we want to know why. We want to understand what it is all about. The problem with this is that with our reason we can understand only things that are within our definition of reality. If we have not experienced the spiritual realities of the higher dimensions, they are not real for us. And we have to be taken by the hand and led into them step by step. We won't recognize the landscape for a while because it is new territory. We need to let go of our preconceived ideas of how it will be and allow the experience simply to unfold.

In order to walk into the spiritual world described in my books, I had to trust and follow divine will when I didn't understand what it was all about. Understanding came later. It is no accident that one of the first things the guides told me to do was a very simple harmless act. They were accommodating my reason. I needed to be led step by step. With divine will I was able to do this, even though my reason constantly demanded to understand something it did not have enough information to understand. The only way to gather enough information was to just do what I was told to do and to trust.

Our Negative Images About Divine Will

Divine will, also known as God's will, is often not understood and has been misused a great deal. The old way of experiencing divine will reflects an authority issue. Our main negative image is that God's will is pitted against our own, because most likely it isn't what we want. It is something we must defy in order to be free. Yet we are given free will to choose. So we are in a double bind. We have free will, but if we don't use our willpower to force ourselves to choose God's will—which we don't want to do—we are in trouble.

Therefore, we have another image: God's will is something to fear, because if we don't do God's will, we will be punished. So if we don't know what it is, maybe we won't be punished so badly. So we'd better stay away from knowing what it is.

Another image about divine will that we use to re-sign ourselves to painful situations is: There is nothing I can do to change God's will. That gets us nicely out of the responsibility to do something about a situation that is painful.

Divine will is also a nice catchall to explain anything we don't understand. Once again, we don't have to understand it! It is mysterious. In fact, it may even be sacrilege to try to understand it!

In our religions, God's will has been used to control people with the idea that only a few know what God's will is. Therefore, the rest of us have to do what those few say. Essentially, those few people have turned our main image inside out and acted, perhaps unconsciously, as if their will were God's will. They have used the main God image of their followers for their own advantage. God's will has been used to give excuses to kill and take territory. In fact, God's will has probably been used as an excuse for all the terrible things that different peoples have done to each other throughout history.

If we see our desires as being at odds with God's, then we can blame God for our problems. It is God who won't give to us. This places power outside of us. All we need to do under this system is to be good, according to a particular religion's rules, and then he may give us what we want. Our negative image of good is that it is rather boring, hard to do, and definitely not free. God is rather like our parents, isn't he? "If you behave, we can go for ice cream." No wonder people shy away from the idea of divine will.

Our negative images of divine will also cause confusion in us as to what will is. Most of the time, we think of willpower as something we need in order to get things done, because it is hard to get things done. There is always something or someone that we have to push or get out of our way. In other words, another negative image we have about will is that it is needed to fight resistance. Will gives us the power to win over an obstacle. Within the old system, the resistance is always seen as outside of us.

In fact, all these images about divine will separate us not only from others but from ourselves. If we're doing God's will and it's different from what we want to do, we're separated from ourselves. When we're separated from ourselves, we're also separated from others, and the battle begins.

The fact that we have to work so hard to make our will agree with God's will implies that our will is not so good. Where does the idea that our will might not be good come from? It comes from the idea of separation and that there is something wrong with us. Such vestiges of old religious values are outmoded and no longer work for us. They exist under the old regime of power-over. The underlying image in this old way of being is that we need a God to keep us responsible and good. But is that really so? Heyoan says:

~

All of this, my friends, is an illusion. By virtue of your pushing, you create the resistance to push against. Without the resistance, what would the will do?

~

Connecting to the Divine Will Within Your Own Heart

We are moving into a new way of being that is based on power and responsibility from within. Consider the possibility that will has nothing to do with overcoming resistance, but rather acts to find our way. Let us look at a different metaphysics in which this will make sense.

If we recognize ourselves as having a good, responsible God within that lives in synchronicity with and is holographically part of the great universal God, then our inner will is the same as that of God. It simply is. There is nothing to fight against, nothing to push against. There is only action to be done to accomplish that which is willed. Will evokes action.

Our need is to be able to know what our good will is. Where does it come from? How do we recognize this good will within us? How do we know that it is the right one? What does it feel like?

Again, it is time to turn to the new M-3 metaphysics, introduced in Chapter 3. Within this framework, all things physical are born out of mind or consciousness. Thus, our physical lives are born out of mind. Mind was there before matter. If we assume mind indeed created our physical lives, it must have had a purpose in doing so. The universal mind's purpose in doing so is divine purpose. The divine purpose for which we were created is our life task. Divine will puts divine reason into action.

The physical world is constantly held in creation by universal or divine mind. Our purpose is ongoing. It is, so to speak, alive. Our purpose extends not only across the broad expanse of our lifetime but functions in the here-and-now moment. Our purpose in this very moment is always connected with our life purpose, no matter what situation we find ourselves in. Our inner divine will functions in all tiny moments, in all grand time scales, in little actions, and in large long-term projects. It functions holographically to serve divine purpose.

The Relationship Between Free Will and Divine Will

Our confusion about will comes when we do not understand that our free-will choice of any moment is always challenged to serve our internal divine will. The degree to which we freely choose our divine will within is the exact degree to which we express and act according to our true self. This will is based on power-from-within rather than power-against or -over another. It is based on self-responsibility rather than on blame. It is based on freedom for all, rather than control of others. In divine will, there is no place for blame or the illusion of something outside us to fight against.

In areas of our lives where we have pain and trouble, we have acted out of fear and not followed our inner divine will. Perhaps we are confused about what we want to do with our lives. We act out of fear and do what we think will please other people. Here our actions are still functioning from the perspective that we must fight against something outside us to get our way, so we don't bother to follow our true will. We are not doing what we truly want to do. We may even create an apparent outside resistance to prevent us from doing what we want. It is really ourselves that we fight—other people are just "stand-ins." At times, we say things calculated to get someone else to protest, so that we can get out of doing something we want but are too afraid to take the chance to do. Of course, it certainly doesn't seem so at the time of our decision making. We just focus on the protest from people around us as a diversion from what we know we must do. But in the long run that never really works. Happiness will not be ours until we do what is right for us.

For example, writing my first book was a very difficult task. I was constantly fighting myself on it. I spent a lot of time in doubt and avoidance, committing to too many things at once so there was no time left to write. I was too afraid to admit that what I was doing was very important work and that the world really wanted this material. Most people didn't even know that I was writing a book. Almost everyone I spoke to about publishing a book on my own thought it was a pretty crazy idea. "Who in their right mind would take their entire life's savings and put it into a book that twelve publishers have already refused?" they asked. But I knew that it was my divine purpose to bring this work into the world, so I did it and trusted. Doing it myself was a great act of faith and extremely empowering. It changed my life because I knew that my work had been done out of love.

Our divine purpose in the moment is always aligned

with the universal whole. People may not know that and may protest what we have decided to do, but it is our full responsibility to decide and to then follow through. What our divine will says to do is not usually the easiest solution. Many times it is very difficult, as when I moved to the center without my husband. Had I not done so, however, my life would have been very different.

Some good questions to find out if you are aligned with your divine will:

Does my will interfere with someone else's freedom?
Am I trying to control someone?
Is my will based on blame and therefore defiant of an imagined authority?
Is my will pitted against someone else's and therefore expressive of an inner resistance?

If your answer is yes to any of the above, you are still thinking or acting out of M-1 metaphysics.

Is my will in this moment connected to the purpose of my life?
Does my will turn me in the direction of my own self-responsibility and therefore my freedom?
Does my will help me open my heart and love?
Does it empower me to move ahead to fill the deepest longing of my soul?

If your answer is yes to any of the above, you have shifted your perspective to the new M-3 metaphysics. It will work better for you.

Daily Affirmations to Keep Aligned with Your Purpose

To keep your life and your health running smoothly, it is a very good practice to align yourself consciously with your divine or positive will. What is it that you wish to accomplish? This question holds not only for your personal life and health but for your whole life as well. As we have already said, our purpose in life is synchronistic with our purpose in this very moment. They are holographically connected. Whatever it is you want to accomplish in any given moment is directly connected to your greater purpose in life. It may not always seem so, but it is.

If your purpose in life is to be a healer, for example, then how you take care of your health right now matters because it affects your energy field and your ability to heal others. If your purpose in life is to express

yourself in words, then speaking your truth right now is a way to stay aligned with your expression. If feeding the poor is your life task, then your relationship to food and nurturing is very important. What you do right now to nurture others is practice for your larger life task and affects it directly. How, what, and how much you eat right now matter. If your life task is to simply find pleasure in living, then how you approach your life in this very moment is a very important step in that task. If you see the glass as half empty now, you are further from pleasure in living than if you see the glass as half full. If you feel deep inside that you are to be a great leader of many people, then how you act right now to those near you who have the least power matters a great deal. If you do not treat them with love and respect now, you will not get closer to your leadership. Your task now is to practice higher principles in the things that you do every moment. Your greater life task is actually just a result of your moment-to-moment practice of higher life principles. The real work is right now, wherever you are, whatever life brings.

If your purpose in the moment is a distorted version of your original purpose and therefore causes pain and dis-ease in your life, it needs to be placed in direct alignment with your greater purpose, so it can create health and balance in your life.

A way to align your will is with affirmations. If the idea of following God's will sounds like a struggle to do something imposed from the outside, then you still carry the negative authority image that God is a deity that gives rules. The truth is that God's will rests within your own heart. Listen to the will of God as it speaks through your own heart.

Here is the affirmation I used several times every day for a period of two years, right after I was asked to close my channel and concentrate on my own inner work. I used it to bring about the shift within myself from the small ego will to the divine will within my own heart. It is a great affirmation to dispel the notion that God's will is an outside rule. It is taken from a Pathwork guide lecture channeled by Eva Pierrakos.

Affirmation to Align with God's Will

I commit myself to the will of God.
I give my heart and soul to God.
I deserve the best in life.
I serve the best cause in life.
I am a divine manifestation of God.

The Mechanics of Getting Guidance

The mechanics of getting guidance are actually rather simple. It is best to start very simply. You may do it in a group or alone. It is important to experience getting guidance in both ways during your training period. Simply sit down with a notebook and pencil. Sit in a meditative position and consciously align with divine will.

You may silently say to yourself, "I align myself with God's will. I want to know the truth, whatever it is. I let go of my personal stake in the answer. In the name of God [or Christ, Buddha, Allah, or whatever spiritual figure is meaningful to you] I want to know." Write down your question on the paper, then simply wait for an answer. Your pencil will not move automatically. You are not doing automatic writing. Rather, you are telepathically listening. Write whatever comes into your mind without discrimination. You may judge what comes out as stupid or wrong, but write it anyway. After the writing is ended, put it away without reading it for at least four hours. Then you may read it and analyze it.

It is important to write down everything that comes into your mind when you are practicing. If you do so, with practice, you will begin to recognize what you are making up with your mind and what you are hearing telepathically. There will be a distinct difference in the quality of information, the language it comes in, and its tone. True guidance is always loving, supportive, non-judgmental, and truthful. It will not betray your integrity, your honesty, or your honor.

If you are practicing in a group, have one person ask a question. Everyone can get guidance for the answer. Share it right away, and compare answers. You will be surprised at how they agree and complement each other. Do not be afraid to speak up in the group if you think an answer is wrong. Now, in the beginning, is the time to learn to keep the channel clear. If you are criticized, find the seed kernel of truth in the criticism and take it to your next guidance session. When you find something in yourself to clear that relates to the criticism, take it to a session to find out what your bias is that influenced your channeling. This is difficult work and usually needs to be done with another person who is skilled in psychological functioning and in finding spiritual truth. I have always found it necessary to get regular help from another person. The more honest you are with yourself, the clearer your channel will be.

Following my guidance for so many years has brought me great reward and many experiences of spir-itual ecstasy. As I used to say when I had a healing practice, "It is a great privilege because I spend all day working with angels and being in a state of love." It was the most effective tool in helping me lift to the sixth level of the auric field, divine love.

The Sixth Level of the Aura: Divine Love

Unlike level five, level six is very familiar to us. We are inspired by the beauty of a sunrise or sunset, by the beauty of sunlight on water or of moonlight on a lake. The stars lift us into the indigo of the night sky, and we are in wonder. We listen to music in a cathedral or chanting in a temple, and we are brought to spiritual ecstasy. We feel as if we are brought home to ourselves, and we love all that there is. These experiences are unique to each of us. There is no way words can convey the depth and breadth of spiritual feelings. Poetry brings us to the door, but we walk through it.

The sixth level of the aura looks like beautiful bright opalescent rays of light that reach out in all directions in a general egg shape. It has all the colors of the rainbow and is perhaps the most beautiful level of the aura to look at. Bringing our conscious awareness to this level brings us into spiritual ecstasy.

We all have a need to experience this regularly, like breathing. Many people do not know this. But it is as essential to feed the human soul as it is to feed the body. When the human soul is not fed, we become cynical about life. Life becomes just one hurdle after another, and there is a lack of well-beingness. Many times we try to replace the something-is-missing feeling with material wealth. It doesn't work. The only way to fill sixth-level needs is through sixth-level experience. That means lifting ourselves to this level of experience. This means giving time and energy to this part of ourselves in our daily lives.

It may mean regular meditation. It may mean regular silent sunrise walks on the beach or in the mountains. It may mean going regularly to a religious service of your choice. It may mean regular poetry readings or regular attendance at the symphony. It is simply a matter of giving it time and focus. If silent meditation is not for you, try playing inspirational music when you meditate.

Your job in your self-healing is to provide yourself with this kind of nourishment. What music lifts you to these levels? What type of meditation do you prefer that lifts you into spiritual experience? Do you have other ways to do it? What are they?

When you do this regularly, you will awaken vast parts of yourself that are full of beauty and love that you get to know. They will become part of your normal self.

On the sixth level, you will experience unconditional love, both for yourself and for others. Unconditional love is the experience of caring completely for the well-being of another person without wanting anything in return for it. You give your love without placing any conditions on it. That means completely accepting them exactly as they are. It means giving your love in a way that stands in honor and respect for who they are, delighting in their differences from you, and supporting them to move into their excellence. It means acknowledging the source of life within them as the source of the divine.

The Importance of Desire

The even-numbered levels of the aura are all feeling levels. All carry our desires. On level two—our feelings about ourselves—we carry the desires to feel good about ourselves, to love ourselves, and to be happy. On level four, our desires center on our relationships with others: our desires for intimacy, for a loving home, and loving friends. On the sixth level, our desires are to feel connected to all that there is, connected to God. These are our desires for spiritual communion.

Some spiritual or religious groups say that desires are not good, that desires get you in trouble and need to be controlled or turned off. All the world's major religions have rejected a part of the human experience, whether it be sexual desire, our desire to be connected to God directly instead of going through some particularly chosen person, our desire to know who we are, our desire to remember our past experience, our desire to commune with the angels, our desire to know good and evil, and our desire to know reality—how it is created and our part in it. Every religion has labeled some of these desires as bad, dangerous, or ridiculous.

Heyoan, however, has a different viewpoint. He says that the prime problem is not the true desires themselves but the distortion or exaggeration of them. All of these desires are connected to a deeper desire, or our spiritual longing carried inside us on deeper dimensions of who we are. (These dimensions will be discussed in Chapter 17.) This spiritual longing leads us through our lives. It keeps us on our path. It helps us complete our purpose in being upon the earth. Recently, during a meditation, Heyoan explained how our personal desires are very helpful to us and need to be listened to, clarified, and followed through on. Here is a little lecture he gave that explains the causes of the distortion and exaggeration of our true desires. It shows us how to separate the true desires from the distorted ones and how to heal the distorted ones that bring us so much frustration and a sense of unfulfillment.

~

CONNECTING PERSONAL DESIRE WITH SPIRITUAL LONGING
Channeled from
Heyoan

Set your purpose of personal healing for what you wish to receive, and connect to the greater plan that is being directed by the spiritual world. When you continue to align with your task that is synchronized with the task of the spiritual world, the work will be much lighter and easier. You will be connected to the deeper meaning of any event that you experience as you go through your healing process. You will be able to settle into the purpose that you have set and let go the desires of the personality that do not synchronize with those of your life task.

You see, not all desires are negative, as some groups perhaps say. Rather, some desires are a distortion or exaggeration of your deeper spiritual desire that rests within your life plan. The unfulfillment or frustration that you feel comes from the unfulfillment of the deeper spiritual work that you have come to accomplish, not from the apparent unfulfilled desire that rests on the surface of your consciousness. Your personal work, then, is to find and understand the root of your distorted desires that rest within the life plan, then manifest those deeper desires, or spiritual longings as we call them, in accordance with that plan.

And so, dear ones, what are your true needs? Here is how to allow the feelings and the longings for those real needs to fill your being so that they can be fulfilled. First make a list. What do you wish to create for yourself? Keep it simple and profound. As you make that visualization clear, *do not send it up to us as if we will give it down to you, but rather seed it deeply into the core of your being so that it can emerge from your inner fountain.* Whenever you have a desire that is clear and synchronized with your life task, take it to the inner fountain of creativity.

As you move into yourself and expand your conscious awareness to a greater level of being, you will experience at first hand the connection to the great plan of salvation and to the hierarchy that runs it. For there is a plan that involves many, many people. This plan will continue to unfold over the face of the earth to a greater extent and intensity and with a greater clarity as the years progress.

What you read today may not be immediately understandable to you. Understanding may come perhaps in the next three, seven, ten, or fifteen years. Hold these teachings in a personal, sacred place within. Keep a sacred personal journal, so that as the years progress and your personal path unfolds, you will have reference to earlier occurrences that did not make sense or were not understandable to you at the time of occurrence, but that will later become a key piece in the puzzle of your life task. These journals can also be for private guidance that you receive for your personal process. We seek to help you recognize the power and the light and the responsibility for that power and light within you, for that is where it already rests.

Now we will lead you to a deeper understanding of the wound that you carry that we spoke about in the first chapter in this book and to a deeper understanding of your intent not to feel that wound. This intent is called negative intent, for it does not serve you. It just brings more pain into your life. This will bring a greater understanding of self and the overall process of personal transformation. The work of transformation is to move into the self and discover the inner landscape. You have already traversed such landscapes. You have traversed inner tunnels of darkness that lead to more light. Through this transformation process, you find greater love, integrity, power, and innocence within the self. You discover that the world inside is just as large as that outside, and then you might ask again, "Who am I?"

In the beginning of your life, there came unexpected pain. You reacted to this pain by trying to stop it. In doing so, you stopped the creative impulse within you. Perhaps it was as simple as the pain you felt when you touched the hot burner of a stove, or perhaps it was an angry look from a parent. In the moment pain came, you stopped the creative force within you and covered it with shadow. In doing so, you disconnected from your center, and a part of you forgot who you are.

As you discover more inner landscapes through the personal transformation process, you bring back the memory of who you are. The original love and spiritual longing that you carried in your emotion, the original courage of your will, the original truth in your reason is still within you. You may not be aware of your spiritual longing directly, but it makes its way through your inner shadows as personality desires. There is nothing wrong with personal desires on the human level, for they are a reflection of the divine longing within, the original creative impulse.

The desires that you have as a human being for relationship, for love, for security, for finding your way to create your life as you wish are beautiful. Perhaps they are also not clear. Perhaps they are distorted. Perhaps you wish for a great deal of money because you do not feel safe. But it is not money that will make you feel safe. Perhaps you wish for a perfect mate who will completely understand you, not disagree with you, and take care of you. But what is under such a desire? The abdication of adult responsibility? The fear of change? In such conditions you would not grow through an exchange of ideas. That kind of "perfection" would not work in the human condition; it would neutralize your purpose of life in the physical.

If you wish to fulfill your true desires in your life, it becomes a matter of finding the parts of you that shadow and distort the original creative act coming from your inner fountain. You can do this by clearing the shadow and distortions and synchronizing your personal desires with your original spiritual longing that is held deep within the core of your being. They are directly connected. Your clear undistorted personal desires are the manifestation, on the personality level, of your deeper core's longing. They are your allies. They lead you to the deeper core of your life.

What is the desire that you feel now? Perhaps you think it's selfish. It may or may not be. Simply ask, "How does this desire of my personality connect to the original inner longing that leads me through my life?" Your work is simply to clear a path between the two so that the personality desire is a pure expression of the original creative impulse within.

There has been a lot of confusion over the earth about this issue. Much pain has come from this confusion because in some circles desires are regarded as sin. The only sin is forgetting who you are. The only sin is the illusion that you find yourself in. Do not judge your desires. Hold your desires as most holy precious parts of yourself, parts of the pieces of your life that need to be illuminated.

Now meditate to find a way from your personality desires to your deeper soul's longing. Remember, you are connected to the great plan of salvation that is unfolding on this earth. As you heal yourself, so earth heals herself.

~

It is at the sixth level of our being that we experience faith and hope.

A very important part of your healing process will be the building of faith and hope. The building of faith in yourself, in your internal resources, and in your ability to take care of yourself and create what you hope and long for in life: Hope for a better life. Hope for better health. Hope for a new world order. Hope for humanity, for the planet. Faith carries you step by step through the dark tunnels we all traverse in life toward the hope for the fulfillment of our longing.

We all go through periods of our life when we lose faith. This happens when we are in the darkest places of the internal tunnels we go through during the transformation process. When all else fails and we are sure we have lost, we finally surrender to faith and hope that we didn't even know we had inside.

A beautiful healing meditation came through in a lecture I gave in Denver in July 1988. It speaks of faith and hope, and it connects healing your pain to your life task. It is a wonderful thing to use when your faith is being tested. Here it is.

~

HEALING THROUGH FAITH AND HOPE
Channeled from
Heyoan

Allow the light to come through you and lift you while you have your feet firmly fixed upon the earth. For you stand most naturally as a bridge between heaven and your spirituality and the earth, your beloved home in the physical. The more you allow this reality to come through to your daily personality, the more you will begin living your true self—who you are and what you have come here for. Feel the energies in this room turn molten white as we join you for this communion. Open your eyes to see, your ears to hear, and your senses to feel our presence. We are not your imagination. Indeed, we are your brethren, and we have come here to work together, to bring peace and healing to this planet.

We have all agreed to do that before you were born. It was with a great deal of hope and faith that you came here and took over a physical body. For the longing that you felt to come to this planet and to serve her was so great that you agreed to take up some of the pain that exists upon this planet and to heal it. You agreed to take that pain into your own body and into your own psyche, so that it could be transformed into love.

So I say to you, you came with great hope in your hearts of a beautiful future and with the faith to guide you every step of the way to that transformation not only within yourself but of this planet.

So let us explore a bit more in detail just how this works. We call it connecting with the universal divinity. You have brought with you great wisdom and great power. You have brought with you tremendous amounts of love, much more than you have ever dreamed of having or receiving. It is with that love and wisdom and power that you came here to heal. You have brought up a body from the body of the mother earth. You have designed that body well. You have brought from the heavens an energy system of the perfect combinations of energies that will give you the tools to fulfill your deepest inner longing. For that is what you have come here for: that which you long to do more than anything. That most outrageous dream that you carry secretly locked away, in a little package, deep within your heart—that is what you have come here to do.

So perhaps now you can take that little package, open it, and look inside. Do not be ashamed. Do not think that what you see is egotistical. It is not—it is the truth. Do not think it too outrageous, for the only limitation that you have is the belief system that you have placed upon yourself. Do not think it too mundane to be in the now, to be connected and have all your actions come from your being. No matter what you happen to be doing at the moment, it is a most holy act. It is an act of faith.

If you haven't opened your little package yet, go ahead and do so. You will be delighted with that which you've packed away. I suggest to you that you take this package that is opened and put it upon an altar and meditate on it twice a day, at least five minutes each time. I'm sure you can find five minutes twice a day, when you get up in the morning and before you go to bed at night, to align yourself with this purpose. If you are shy about it, keep it a secret. If you wish to speak about it, feel free. But choose well those with whom you speak about it, choose those who will understand and will support you in your endeavor. For you have a job to do. I shall describe that job to you in the following way.

I would like you now to scan your life. Go back to your childhood to find the deepest pain that you have ever felt. Find that pain in its seed kernel. For every one of you carries a seed kernel of pain within you.

Once you have found it, follow where you have gone from the seed. Find how it has permeated every moment of your life, every area of your life. Find how you have carried this pain, year after year. Yes, it has changed. It has expressed itself differently in different areas, but I assure you it is the same pain.

It is precisely the pain, not only within yourself but reflected in the world, that you have come here to heal.

You have taken up this pain and placed it within your body and in your psyche. With great courage you have done this. There is no escape. Escape from the pain does not heal it. There is only the healing.

I would like you to take this pain and wrap it gently in love and acceptance. Treat it as a newborn child, a child who has forgotten who he is. This is a child of *hope*, a child of the bright, shining future, and it is you, the healer, that has the *faith* to heal this child of pain. The first step in your self-healing is to accept that this pain is yours to heal. It is your personal task that you have voluntarily accepted in service of not only yourself but the planet. You as healers have taken an oath to be meticulously honest with yourself, to love and honor the self, to follow and obey the divine wisdom that is inside of you, above you, below you, and all around you.

Feel our presence in the room. You need not pick up this burden alone. There is always guidance. Use your *faith* to heal your body. Make a habit of it. Do not wait until you are in pain. Do it with faith.

Upon your altar, place the pain of the child next to the love of the healer within: *One is hope and one is faith.* It is these two that will mold and transmute your energy so that you and the earth can become transfigured in light. Feel the love in this room. Feel the light that you are. Feel the light above you and below you. Feel the light all around you, and the light of those who have gone before you. Feel the light in every cell of your body. Be who you are. That is all that you ever volunteered for. Be who you are, that is all that was ever required. Be who you are, that is all that was ever needed. Be who you are.

The Seventh Level of the Aura: Divine Mind

It is said that the highest form of ecstasy is pure, divine creative thought. This is the gift of the seventh level. Here is where the creator soars, for it is here that he/she knows the perfect pattern and understands him-/herself to be God. Here he/she weaves his/her own golden thread through the perfect universal pattern of creation, bringing even more perfection to an alive, pulsating, golden web of reality.

This is everyone's birthright; it is everyone's most natural, normal state. The more we allow ourselves this, the more alive we become, the more healthy we become, and the more human we become. We could not exist without this seventh level. We will exist in much more happiness, ecstasy, and love when we give this to ourselves in simple regular daily meditation, and then integrate it into our daily lives. Do not underestimate yourself. It is already in you. It is a matter of bringing your conscious awareness to it, and being who you are.

Meditation to Reach the Seventh Level

Do this simple meditation for ten minutes daily each morning on rising, and you will be surprised how well your day goes. Simply sit in a meditative position and keep your back straight. Do not lean on anything with your upper back. If you need support, prop something behind your sacrum. Now simply repeat each word of the following mantra with each in or out breath that you take. Each time your mind wanders, simply bring it back to the words of the mantra, which is, "Be still, and know that I am God."

The level of divine mind brings us to our reason for being. The seventh level of the field is divine mind, knowing the perfect pattern. When we lift our consciousness to this level of our being, we enter into a state of clarity that brings us to the understanding that everything is perfect the way it is, even in its imperfections. It is only from this level of our being that we can understand this. From other levels, it may sound like a copout or just another airy-fairy idea that has nothing to do with reality. How could something that is imperfect be perfect?

It is from the seventh level that we understand that the earth experience is a schoolroom of lessons. The major lesson here is to learn love. It is easy to love what is perfect and gives us no problem. It is when we are in trouble

and pain that we need to learn to love ourselves and others. Therefore, the imperfections on the earth are the perfect situation in which to learn love. If we knew how to love under any conditions, we would not have created these conditions. When we learn to love under any conditions, the love we give will change the conditions.

On the seventh level, the aura is made of very strong brilliant lines of gold-white light. They hold the whole thing together. These lines of light are surprisingly strong. Meditation in which you lift your conscious awareness to this level will bring about a sense of strength, ease, and acceptance in your life. Since everything is perfect and is working within a perfect order of things, whatever happens must have a higher reason behind it, no matter what it is. Bad things don't happen because we are bad. We are not being punished. Many things happen out of a greater order that we may not understand. Whatever happens, no matter how much it doesn't make sense or makes sense only in a negative context, is a lesson in loving. No matter what.

Learning what the higher divine reason for any difficult situation is helps us deal with what is happening. If we know that a divine lesson is being learned through a difficult experience, it is easier to go through it, even if we do not know what that lesson is. Most of the time, we do not know what that lesson is because usually we can't understand it until we have learned it.

Two particular cases come to mind that show how an unacceptable event was made acceptable through surrendering to the healing process or life lesson being learned, and lifting to a higher level of understanding.

Healing Stephanie's Heart Heals the Heart of Her Family

In 1985, I gave a series of healings to a three-year-old and her mother. The little girl, Stephanie, had been born with atrial septal defect (ASD), a hole about the size of a quarter between two chambers of her heart. Open heart surgery had been scheduled for July 1985. The mother, Karen, had had several surgeries herself and was afraid for Stephanie of the pain that would follow surgery. Karen's initial motive for bringing Stephanie to the healings was to prevent the surgery.

Each session, Karen would ask Heyoan if her daughter really had to have open heart surgery. Wasn't there any way it could be prevented? I was also really into avoiding the surgery. Every time Karen asked Heyoan about it, I would get nervous. I didn't want to give any false predictions. At one point toward the end of a healing, Heyoan, as if he had had enough of our complaining, suddenly exclaimed to me, "Here, follow me."

I found myself rushing down a hospital corridor behind Heyoan. He flung open the doors to surgery, brought me up to the table, and said, "Here, look at this."

I found myself leaning over and looking down into the open cavity in Stephanie's chest. The operation was going well. Then the scene moved forward in time and switched to recovery. Stephanie was doing fine. Then it was a day or two after the operation. Already Stephanie was sitting in a chair in her hospital room looking very chipper. I saw her jump out of the chair and run to her parents when they came into the room. Next, the scene switched to Stephanie, at about thirteen years old, just moving into puberty. She was standing in front of a mirror, looking at the scar on her chest. She looked beautiful, healthy, and radiant. She was examining the scar in a curious and unconcerned way. The scar helped her connect with her heart and loving.

Then Heyoan said, "Now, is that so bad?"

I relayed my little adventure to Karen, and her fears abated for a while, but of course, by the next session, they were back.

It was still very difficult for me to stay unbiased in the healings. Since I am a mother of a daughter, too, I wanted to help avoid this operation. Having had a cesarean section with complications for the birth of my own daughter, I also found that I was biased against surgery, even though the surgery had saved my baby's life. Because of my own bias and the pressure from Karen, I again was having trouble keeping my channel clear. Finally, I was able to lift up through the higher levels of the auric field to Heyoan, and I received the following guidance from him:

~

The issues around loving for you relate to your being able to hold someone within the field of your loving energy and still let them experience their life as they had planned it for themselves. You cannot protect or save any child of yours from its own karma. Karma in this case means its own life plan that it has chosen. For this is a wise soul and has come in for a beautiful task and has chosen exactly how she will do it, and she continues to choose that moment by moment. She continues to remake her commitment to life in the physical world with every breath she takes, just as the two of you do.

[Here Heyoan refers to both Barbara and Karen.]

And so if we could enter into these discussions from this broader point of view, perhaps there will be less static in the channel. If the two of you were now to move to the place of wisdom within yourselves, you will both find the deeper wisdom within you that chose the operations that you each experienced. There was an enormous amount learned by each of you. Why, it started this one [referring to Barbara] on her road to becoming a healer, did it not? For before that, there was no experience of pain or illness, so therefore there was no empathy of those that were ill because her experience was lacking.

And with you, Karen, my dear, similar issues hold. You had never experienced being so well cared for until your surgery. It opened for you great vistas of the heart, of caring and being cared for, of giving in and trusting. But yet I'm hearing you say, "Trusting—are you kidding? I trusted and look at what happened!" And I say to you, do look at what happened. You ended up with two wonderful children. You were cared for. The closeness between you and your husband and between you and your greater family grew a great deal.

You are now caring for them. You understand their pain more. You are certainly well prepared to help carry your child through this operation, if it occurs, for you know what it's like. So ask yourself, "What would you have asked of others when you had your operation? What gave you the most pleasure—the flowers in the room, the people visiting, the loving hands placed upon you? How did your experience lighten itself? Through what experiences did your hospital stay become more pleasant?"

And so, if you have a child who goes into surgery, how can you be with her? Choose the hospital carefully, as you did for the birth. Be there in the hospital with her. Go through the experience. Have your feelings. Hold her in your field of love, knowing that whatever happens is God's will and her will. That is the most difficult. For whatever happens is what she has chosen. Therefore, respect the wisdom of the soul that resides within your child. Respect its choices and support those choices. Support the learning that this child has undertaken to do. If she chooses to go through the surgery, know that it is a statement from her of an increased trust in the family, in loving, and in the heart.

Now this may sound like a contradiction in terms, but look at the experience. Would one not need more trust in family, in loving, and in the heart to go through the experience than to not go through it?

And yes, Barbara would argue, "But why couldn't she avoid it? Why not?" And we simply say one way is no better than the other. Each teaches a different lesson.

Remember, keep complete respect and courage. She has so much courage. She will tell you, "Mommy, look—I am going to do this, and it will increase your faith as much as mine. I bring this to you as a gift. For the world is safe, although there be pain in it. The world is loving, although there be separation. The world is beautiful, although there be disarray. And I make this statement through these actions of my complete faith in the physical realm. I bring this to you as a gift. And so, dear Mommy, I have come to heal your heart as you have come to heal mine."

~

KAREN: In light of all this positive talk, and this has really touched me, my husband wanted to know if there are any psychological issues that will come out of it if she does have the surgery. She sounds as if she really is very together. It seems the difficulty is more for my husband and me than for her.

HEYOAN: We spoke to you today in the terms we did to echo the statements of Stephanie's broader and greater and deeper wisdom. But of course, there is the part that forgets. Of course, if she has surgery, when she wakes up there will be pain; and of course she will react in the pain; and of course she will say, "Mommy, take me home. Mommy, take me home." And you will not be able to. But you can stay with her and say, "The world is a safe place. I remember 'cause you told me so."

And the same goes for your dear husband. Trying to protect her from her own wisdom does not work, my dear son. Go with the deeper wisdom of her choice, and you will be strengthened by it. When she forgets her strength, you can give her yours. You simply are returning the gift. You see how beautiful the harmony flows between each of you in the family, and what a family it is!

KAREN: I don't have any more questions, I just want to thank your guides for suggesting we do laying on of hands and for all the help. It really has been a pleasure to do it this month. She likes it and I like it, and it's become a ritual.

[Heyoan had instructed Karen to do laying on of hands healing with Stephanie each evening at bedtime. They grew much closer through this process and had been doing it for several months at this point.]

HEYOAN: Yes, it is a beautiful communion, is it not?

KAREN: I also wanted to know if there was anything that happened today that we should know about.

HEYOAN: The heart was strengthened; her faith was strengthened; and you need to go through more time before you know the outcome. I'm sorry, my dear, but we respect again the wisdom of your soul, for there will be great rejoicing when you have come through your tunnel.

BARBARA: I'm trying to see what's in this tunnel here. [She looks in the tunnel.] It looks like one of those Lego block games, sort of a funny little game, a kid-adult game to play with. That's what's in the tunnel.

They're standing waiting as if there's more to say, only they don't have anything to say. I don't know if you have more questions.

KAREN: I have a lot of feeling. I can feel the tunnel. A lot of what I'm going through this last month is separation from my parents. I really finally am taking it in that my parents aren't here for me. And when they said the tunnel, I felt as if I'm having to be here for my family and be grown-up and be really separated from my dependence on my parents that was never . . . I was dependent on them, and they were never there. I'm having a lot of feelings about them. I don't know what to ask about it.

HEYOAN: We are sorry that you experienced this pain, and we are so sorry that it was not perfectly the way you wanted it, from the level of the child. And as we have already said, your greater wisdom chose your childhood experiences. If you were to look at your mothering now and see the wonder of it, of the self-expression and the enormous room that you have for your self-expression through mothering, you would understand some of the choices that you have made. For there is no one bending over your shoulder saying, "No, this is how a mother acts." Nor would you do that to your child when she becomes a mother.

KAREN: That's true. I forget the freedom.

HEYOAN: And so remember when you are in the hospital, don't let anyone stand over your shoulder and say, "This is how you should be acting." Be completely yourself, and if you need someone to hold you, then by all means ask for that, for no one ever really grows up, at least in those terms. Needs are real and they are beautiful, and they bring people together and create more love between people, more communication and strength. You might say that a need is a strength growing. Admitting a fear is finding love. Admitting that you are lost means you are finding your way home. A need is a statement of truth, of where you are along your path. When Christ was on the cross, he expressed his doubts. There was a moment of nonfaith, and he expressed it. Then later it was followed by a moment of faith. And so be completely in yourself and who you are in the moment. This will bring more courage and more strength to those around you. Lean on that dear husband of yours more. He's very strong.

KAREN: Really!

HEYOAN: Perhaps he forgets now and then. Try leaning a little more, and he'll remember it.

KAREN: I feel as if I'm going to burden him. I don't want to lean on him. It's amazing. Thanks.

HEYOAN: You are heartily welcome, and remember we are always with you. We will be there holding her gently when she leaves her body in the possible operation.

KAREN: Yes, I know. I don't want to bank on the fact that she might not have it, so I'm really like sort of preparing myself that—

HEYOAN: You're going through it. You need to go through your tunnel one way or the other.

Through guidance, it became clearer and clearer that the surgery would probably happen in order to help the whole family come together and learn to have faith in and trust in living in a physical world. Both parents were very spiritually oriented and somehow had equated the surgery to not having done something right spiritually. Through the series of guidances, it became clear that this was not the case. In the last session, Heyoan told Karen that shortly after the surgery, her husband Michael would get a new job and they would move out of Brooklyn and into a small town about an hour out of New York, where their life would take on new form. All this, he said, would be the result of the tremendous changes and growth in the family as it went through the family healing initiated by Stephanie's surgery. Karen said that her husband had been looking for a job for over a year and that they wanted to move to New Jersey. Heyoan said that it was not yet time for them to move, because they needed to complete the family healing that was taking place. It was important for Stephanie to complete her healing in

the old home and leave it all behind so that she would start a new life in the new one.

It is 1992 as I write this book. I have just interviewed Karen to check out the results of all the work. They are happy and comfortable. Karen says life is better than she ever dreamed it could be. She just confirmed the little trek that Heyoan took me on, through the operating room. Events unfolded just as he had said they would. Stephanie had open heart surgery in July. Her recovery was very fast. Two or three days after the operation, she was very perky. The minute the nurses took the tubes out of her, she jumped out of the chair and ran across the room to greet her parents as they walked into the room.

Karen said that Stephanie had had three emotional traumas during the hospital stay. They occurred when the staff had to take Stephanie away from her parents to have testing procedures, to have surgery, and then to remove the tubes. Karen said that Stephanie had three nightmares the first three times she slept at home, one for each of the emotional traumas. After that she was fine—no bad memories, and no problems about the hospital experience.

The family went on vacation in August, another thing Heyoan said would happen that they didn't believe. When they returned from vacation, there was a job offer for Michael in New Jersey. It was the job he wanted but had refused earlier because the salary was too low. Now they had increased the salary to meet his requirements. Karen said it had taken only a couple of days to find the house they bought. By October, they were living in New Jersey, and Michael was in his new job.

Karen says that the healing experience with Stephanie was a very important step in their evolution as a family. She says that three to four weeks after the surgery Stephanie was a different child. Before the surgery, she had been a wistful child, but afterward she came solidly into her body, and her color changed. She is now ten. She calls herself a Heart Child. She writes beautiful poetry and music, sings, and is interested in acting.

Karen says that, through the experience, she learned to trust much more in the synchronicity of the universe. Looking back, she can see that everything happened in perfect timing. For example, even though Michael had looked for a job for a year, the move could not happen until the healing was completed. Once it was, everything flowed easily and automatically into the new life the family made for itself.

Now Karen says, "I'm learning to trust in this greater plan. You have to put an effort out for anything. But when you put an effort out and you keep meeting resistance, you have to know that something else is going on. It might not be just that you are resistant; it might be that the timing is not right, and that something else has to happen, something has to be completed. Because once it was completed, everything fell into place immediately. I went house shopping for two days, Michael went one day, and we bought this house the day after we saw it. They had just lowered the price, so it fit at the top of our price range. Everything was like clockwork. I feel as if I learned to trust in that from the experience with Stephanie. And I have continued to have things like that. When something is right, it just goes along easily. You don't have to push upstream."

Andy Brings His Family Back Together

The second example that gives us the possibility to accept the unacceptable through lifting to a higher level of understanding and thereby transforming our life experience is that of a young man of about twenty-five who was dying of malignant melanoma. I shall call him Andy.

Andy lived about three hours away by car, and his lovely mother brought him to healings. When Andy came to me, he had, according to his doctors, less than a year to live. The fast-moving cancer had already spread all over his body and was now entering his brain. Later, as he worked with me, radiation was given periodically to reduce the size of the tumors, which then were beginning to give him pain.

No one told Andy what the real state of his health was, but deep inside he knew. What was very striking about Andy was that he was not really that concerned about his death. This was true even when he first started coming to me, and he was not yet in pain. From the first moment he walked into my office, he did not struggle much for life in the physical body. He admitted that he was very ambivalent about being in the physical world at all. He wanted to know more about the spiritual world. I channeled Heyoan a lot to Andy, and they became good friends.

Over time, Andy became more comfortable in the spiritual world and sought to reach his own guide. Andy became more and more concerned about love between people, especially about people in his family loving each other. Sometimes he would puzzle as to whether he would die soon, but each time he would state his ambivalence and a certain curiosity, as if looking forward to a great adventure.

Soon he had a prophetic dream that completely took him out of denial. He said that he was pretty sure he was going to die because he saw his guide. In the dream his guide got closer and closer to him, until he merged with and became one with his guide. Then, in this state of oneness, he watched people at his funeral lower his casket into the ground. Andy died a month or so later.

I was very sad. I knew this young man had a lot to teach me and others. I felt I had failed him because he died, even though it had been okay with him. I was rather shy about seeing his family again, when his brother and mother came to see me after a lecture I gave in their area. I assumed they would not be too pleased with me, having not been able to "save" him. But I had a great surprise. They thanked me profusely and told me that Andy's healing had had a profound effect of healing on the whole family. Through the healing process, Andy's surrender to truth and love had helped the family members open to each other so deeply that the entire family had changed.

His brother told me that there had been a severe break in the family around the time of Andy's birth, about twenty-five years earlier. Apparently the family had split in half, and one half had not spoken to the other half for years—that is, not until Andy, during his healing processes, started insisting that they heal the wounds. The two halves of the family that had split at his birth came together in love on the day he died, and they had been together ever since.

The family was convinced that one of Andy's life tasks had been to heal the family. Andy's whole life had been a momentous life lesson for the family. They were grateful for having had him with them, and grateful for all he had given them.

Healing Meditation for the Seventh Level

Sit up with a straight back, or lie down and relax on a comfortable surface. Slow down your breathing and relax. Center your focus inward; let go of the things you may have to do. Listen and feel inward.

First, feel your body as it is now. Bring your awareness to the particular part of your body you are concerned about. Bring it into integration with your body, by giving it your loving acceptance just as it is.

Next, visualize it in completeness and perfection. See it as a golden grid of perfection, bright, strong, and beautiful. With a sweep of your hand that is golden light, you turn the organ into its perfect state. Give thanks for its transformation.

Do several times a day. It only takes a minute or two.

A Healing Meditation That Integrates All Levels of the Field

A simple, deep relaxation and visualization technique helps you bring healing energy to specific areas of your body and all the levels of your auric field that are in need of healing. I call it "Traveling Through the Body." It consists of four major parts. The first part is becoming deeply relaxed; the second part is loving the self and connecting with your guardian angels; the third part is healing specific parts of the body; and the fourth part is coming back out of the deep relaxation while maintaining a healing state.

You can become very deeply relaxed by utilizing both kinesthetic feeling and visual imagery through audio suggestion, along with soft music. If you are primarily kinesthetic (meaning that you relate to the world through the physical sensation of feeling), then you will respond to suggestions of physical sensations, like lying on a bed of feathers or gently floating on a boat. If you are primarily visual, you will respond to the descriptions of beautiful skies, mountains, and lakes. It is best to use all five senses to help induce a relaxed state.

Once you have entered into a relaxed state, you have created a harmonious flow in your body that promotes healing. You can go on to the second part of the visualization. It is loving yourself and opening to help from your guardian angels.

Next, in the third part, you can get specific about what you want healed. You can keep it very simple and focus on a state of complete health for your whole body. Or you can be very specific about organs and even cells. For example, some people visualize white blood corpuscles eating the unwanted cells of a tumor. You will feel healing energy coming to the unhealthy parts of your body. It is important to stay in this state until you know that you have completed your work for the period of time allotted.

The fourth part of visualization is to simply come out of the deep relaxation and to create a nice closure to insure continuation of the healing process. Give yourself time to come out of your deep relaxation, and while you are doing it, be sure to give yourself the suggestion that you can return to that healing state within a matter of moments anytime you wish. Also include, in your closure, the suggestion that the healing that you have initiated will continue throughout the rest of your healing process. That way, each day you can build up more healing power in your energy system.

You can build your own visualization from the above format. Use your favorite music, your favorite images, and your favorite physical sensations. Here is an example of traveling through the body that I find effective. First, put on some of your favorite soft music. Then lie down on a couch, bed, or mat, and relax your breathing.

Traveling Through the Body

Stretch out on a comfortable surface, and loosen all tight clothing.

Feel your body resting on the surface beneath you. Feel warmth and energy flowing through each part of your body. Focus on your feet. Your feet become heavy and warm. Then move to your legs, and slowly work your way up the body. Each part becomes heavy, warm, and deeply relaxed. Feel the tension flowing off your body into the surface below you like thick honey. It oozes down through the surface, through the floor, and into the ground beneath. It sinks deep into the earth. Allow your breathing to continue to slow down to a nice healthy relaxed pace. Repeat to yourself, "I am at peace, no noise will bother me. I am at peace, no noise will bother me."

Imagine yourself very tiny, like a small gold light, and enter your body wherever you choose. Your tiny self flows to your left shoulder, relaxing all the tension in your left shoulder. Say to yourself, "My left shoulder is heavy and warm." Then move across into your right shoulder. Give your tiny self any tools it would like to use to relax the tension in your left shoulder, like squirting it with a hose or painting it with a brush. Say to yourself, "My right arm is heavy and warm. I am at peace, no noise will bother me." Your tiny self flows back up your right arm and flows into your chest, relaxing you even more. Your tiny self continues to move throughout your entire body, part by part, relaxing it. It becomes heavy and warm.

Pause for a few moments to go through your whole body.

Now if you really wish to go deeper, imagine that you are walking in a meadow with beautiful flowers. Look at the flowers and all their beautiful colors and shapes, smell their fragrance, feel the soft velvet petals. As you continue walking through the meadow, feel the light breeze on your face. You come upon your favorite fruit tree, and you taste your favorite fruit. The breezes rustle gently through the leaves of the trees that surround the meadow. The birds are singing. You look up and see a beautiful sky, with white puffy clouds. As you lie on the soft grass beneath the tree, you make shapes out of the clouds.

You feel good about yourself, your life, and your body. You begin to feel love for yourself. You begin thoroughly loving all of yourself, all of your personality, all of your psyche, each part of your body, all of your problems, and every aspect of your life. You gently enfold each aspect of yourself in loving acceptance, no matter how much you normally hate this part and reject it. Enfold each negative part in loving acceptance, and visualize it melting into whatever its original divine aspect was. It is okay not to know what that original aspect was. In the melting and remembering process, it will slowly and automatically revert to its original divine purpose, truth, and feeling. You recognize the deeper meaning of your life.

As you love yourself, you go through each part of your body loving it, and wiping away any pain that may be there.

If there is a particular part of your body that you are concerned about, send special love to that part. Enfold it in loving acceptance. Now it is time to do the specific work of getting rid of unwanted cells or microorganisms. Tell them that it is simply not appropriate for them to be there and that they should go elsewhere. Or put up a more aggressive fight—whichever feels right for you. You can imagine a hose of fresh water squirting away anything you wish to leave. If a particular organ is under- or overfunctioning, you can make contact with it and coax it into balance. Be as creative as you wish. Enjoy yourself.

Pause to have time to go through the body parts that are ill.

After you finish healing specific body areas, move through each layer of your auric field, bringing energy and loving acceptance to it. Each time you move up a layer, it is like tuning the radio to a station with a higher frequency. Or going up in an elevator and getting off on the next floor. Just set your dial a bit higher, and you are there.

Level one of the auric field: First there is the layer of physical sensation. It is beautiful blue gridwork of energy holding the cells together. Make it brighter. You feel a bit larger than your physical body because it extends out a bit from it. Now focus on each of the seven chakras.

They are located as follows: The first is in the perineum, between your legs. The second is just above the pubic bone, on the front and back of your body. The third is in the solar plexus area, in the hollow between and just below your ribs, on the front and back of your body. The fourth is on the heart and between the shoulder blades. The fifth is in front of and in back of your throat. The sixth is in the forehead and back of your head. The seventh is at the crown of your head. On this level of your field, they are all made of blue meshwork. Spin each one clockwise, as seen from the outside of your body on both the front and back of the body, so that they spiral in toward each other. Imagine a clock on your body in the location of each chakra, and spin the dials on the blue clock.

Level two of the auric field: Next go to the emotional level, where many clouds of color are moving over and through you. Enjoy them as they move, and make them brighter. Feel the love to yourself that flows here. On this level the chakras change color. The first is red, the second is orange, third is yellow. Next comes green, then blue, then indigo, and finally white at the top of your head.

Level three of the auric field: Now move to the light, delicate yellow of the the mental level. Feel the sense of clarity, appropriateness, and integration that is here, and enhance it. Now your boundaries are even larger. You must be at least six inches wider on each side. Each level of being you go to draws your consciousness into higher realms of self-acceptance and self-understanding. Spin each chakra clockwise on this level—they are all a fine bright yellow color.

Level four of the auric field: As you now move to the fourth level of your field, you will again feel colors flowing through and around you. Remember each level extends completely through the body. This time they feel a little thicker, more like fluid. You will find even more love in this layer. Let it flow through you as you feel your love for others. Again, enhance the colors of your field. Spin each of the fluid flowing chakras clockwise. Again, the colors change as you move upward. The colors are similar to the second layer, except that they have a lot of rose light in each of them.

Connect with guardian angels for help.

During this time, it is also good to ask for help from your guardian angels, for there is much help available to you through your greater spiritual connections than most people are aware of. I have seen personal guardian angels working on many patients without the presence of a spiritual healer. Knowing this help is available to you will help you feel supported and not alone in your struggle. With the help of your guides, now move through the higher levels of your being.

Level five of the auric field: First, feel the divine will within you. Feel its template all around and through you. It looks like a cobalt-blue blueprint of the first layer. Feel how it strengthens you and gives you form. This is usually the hardest for people to relate to, because on this layer, the background, the space, is solid dark cobalt blue, and that which is normally solid is empty space. Spin the chakras on this level. They are composed of fine lines of empty space.

Level six of the auric field: As you continue to move out now, to the sixth level, you begin to feel spiritual ecstasy. You are like the brilliant glow around a candle. You are opalescent colors streaming forth. Let your light shine. Your awareness of self now extends at least two feet from each side of your body. Each chakra again changes color, like before, but this time they are all full of opalescent pearly light.

Level seven of the auric field: Finally, you come to the golden grid of the seventh layer. Feel the strength of these fine golden threads of light. They wrap you inside a golden egg. Feel the strength of the eggshell as it protects you. Make it even stronger. Fill it in in places that need it. Spin each golden chakra clockwise. Feel how strong it is. Now you extend to about three feet beyond your physical body in every direction. Enjoy it. Rest in the serenity of your divine mind. Stay in the expanded relaxed state as long as you like. It is good for your healing. Go to sleep if you like.

Come back to a normal state of awareness.

When you are ready to come back to a normal state of awareness, give yourself a count back to assist. Simply say, "By the time I count back to zero, I will be wide awake and alert, self-confident and aware, but remain deeply relaxed, and my healing will continue." Then slowly start counting back from five or six. Each time you count the next number, remind yourself that you can return to this deep state of healing within a matter of minutes. Again say, "By the time I count back to zero, I will be wide awake and alert, self-confident and aware, and yet remain very deeply relaxed."

Finally you can say, "Zero! I am now wide awake *and* alert, and my healing continues!"

Our Intentionality and the Hara Dimension

Everything we do rests on the foundation of our intentionality in the moment we do it. For example, we can say any particular set of words has a normal meaning, but the way we deliver that set of words can change their meaning drastically. We fill our words with the energy of our feelings, and how we deliver those words conveys just what we really intend. We can say "I love you" with love, with disgust, with pleading, with a falsity of tone that really means "I hate you."

How we deliver the words conveys our intention in the moment we deliver them. When we say "I love you" with love, that is exactly what we mean. On the other hand, when we say "I love you" with disgust, we are intending to let our disgust be known without directly saying so. When we say "I love you" with pleading, our intention is not to convey love but to get something through the act of pleading. When we say "I love you" with falsity, we may be intending to convey that we don't love the person. Or we may have any number of different intentions.

In each of these instances, even though the words are the same, the energy that carries and delivers them is different and looks different in the auric field. What has changed is the intention under the words. It is our intentionality that creates the energy in the auric field that then conveys the actual message. The result is that we have accomplished what we intended—we have delivered the message.

I have already made reference to intentionality (in Chapter 12) when discussing reasons why not. Our reasons why not do not get us the results that we want, because our reasons why not are based on a different intentionality. They are based not on the intention to complete our original purpose but on the intention to make excuses for why we did not accomplish what we intended. Our reasons why not covered our original purpose by pretending to be in alignment with it. But they are really based on a totally different purpose. Thus we have mixed intentions when we allow reasons why not.

In Chapter 13, on creating healthy contracts in relationships, we saw that we confuse our purposes a great deal in relationships. We saw that sorting out our intentions in relationships can be very powerful and transforming work.

The lecture on world peace healing that Heyoan gave (in Chapter 13) shows how our individual wants or desires stem from different purposes. Some of our wants or desires serve the purpose of assuaging fear; some of our wants or desires come from our deeper spiritual longing or higher desires. When our purpose is also to assuage fear, we have mixed intentions or are at cross-purposes with ourselves. This interferes with the natural process of creativity in our lives, and we can't create what we want. Anywhere in our lives—including health and healing—where we have trouble creating what we want, is where we have mixed intentions or crossed purposes. To create what we want, then, it is essential to be able to find what our mixed intentions are and sort them out. We must clarify our true intentions so we can realign the ones that are not in keeping with what we truly want. What we truly want is always aligned with our highest spiritual longings. When our personal wants and desires are aligned with our spiritual longing or higher desires, our purposes are aligned and the creative principle in the universe can function unhindered. By fulfilling our spiritual desires, we are led step by step to fulfill our life's greater spiritual purpose, our life task.

After working with and observing the auric field for many years, I could see that a change in intentionality completely changes the balance of energy in the auric field as well as the type of energy that is released in the bioplasmic streamers. Chapter 15 shows many examples of interactions of the typical energetic defense systems we use related to what our underlying intentionality is. I could see these tremendous changes in the field, but I could not find any particular aspect in the field that corresponded to intentionality per se.

I wondered if intentionality could be worked on directly by a healer with laying on of hands. Why and how does it have so much power to change the auric field so drastically? How does our intentionality function? What role does it play, from the perspective of HSP and the aura, in our health and healing? I wondered if our intentionality is held in the auric field or somewhere else. Could it be that a whole deeper world beneath the auric field exists on a deeper dimension, just as the auric field exists on a dimension deeper than the physical body?

To get the answers to my questions, I needed a bit of a push. I got it from my students. With that small push, I found where our intentionality exists and why it has so much power to change the auric field. Heyoan also taught me how to work directly in the hara dimension with our intentionality for health and healing and our daily lives.

My entry into the realms of reality beneath the auric field began in 1987, when a student asked me to channel about the hara. I felt rather embarrassed, since I knew very little about the hara, having never studied martial arts myself.

I had read a little from the well-known philosopher and psychotherapist Karlfried Durkheim in his book, *Hara*. He had learned about the hara in his travels to the East. *Hara* is the term Japanese use when referring to the lower belly. *Hara* refers not only to the location of the lower belly but to a quality of having strength, energy, and focused power in that area. It is a center of spiritual power. For centuries the warriors of the East have developed martial arts, centering on disciplines to focus and build up power in the hara as a source from which to draw in combat. Within the hara region of the lower abdomen is a central point called the *tan tien*. It is traditionally referred to as the center of gravity in the body. The tan tien is the focal point of power in the hara. In the martial arts, it is the center from which all movement originates.

In addition to the little reading I had done on the hara, I also had the opportunity to use HSP to observe the tan tien inside the body. I noticed that in most Americans the tan tien was very dim and undercharged. However, in people who had practiced martial arts for some time, this place was a very bright ball of gold light. In fact, some of them had a very strong gold line of light running through their bodies from head to toe.

After many requests for channeling, I finally surrendered to the moment, and a new adventure began. I would like to share that adventure with you in this section. You will find it very important to your personal healing plan because it puts healing where it ought to be. It brings healing into the powerful act of evolutionary creativity. Here is what Heyoan said in the channeling on the hara:

~

The hara exists on a dimension deeper than the auric field. It exists on the level of intentionality. It is an area of power within the physical body that contains the tan tien. It is the one note with which you have drawn up your physical body from your mother the earth. It is this one note that holds your body in physical manifestation. Without the one note, you would not have a body. When you change this one note, your entire body will change. Your body is a gelatinous form held together by this one note. This note is the sound the center of the earth makes.

~

Well, that was enough to send me reeling. When I recovered from my normal reaction of, "Oh no, now what have I said?" I began searching for ways to apply the new information. If indeed this one note held our bodies in physical manifestation, then working directly with that note would be extremely powerful. The idea that our bodies are gelatinous is a very nice concept when we are trying to change something we think will take years to change. So the use of the idea of a gelatinous body in healing visualizations came in very handy.

In later channelings, Heyoan explained that our haric level, where our intentionality is found, is the foundation upon which the auric field is formed. To understand this more fully, let us review once again the relationship between the dimensions of the physical world and the worlds of the auric field.

The physical world exists in three dimensions. It behaves according to physical laws. Our physical body is related to our personality, but its reactions to what we do minute to minute in our psyche usually take a long time, sometimes decades.

There is a big difference between the physical world that we can see with our eyes and the world of the auric field that we can see with HSP. In order to move our conscious awareness from the physical world to the auric field, we must make a quantum leap into a deeper dimension, into what I believe is the fourth dimension. I think the auric field exists in four dimensions. It behaves according to the physics of bioplasma and light. On the auric level, time is much different from the way it is in the physical. We can be in the present time, or we can move along what many people are now calling a time line and enter past life experiences as if they were happening now.

The auric field exists on a dimension deeper into our personality than the physical body. It corresponds on a second-to-second basis with what is going on in our personality. This auric field correspondence is specific and immediate. Every thought, feeling, or other type of life experience shows immediately in the auric field as energy-consciousness movement in form and color.

Energy and consciousness are experienced differently in the auric dimension from the way they are in the physical. On the physical level they appear to be two different things. On the auric level, energy and consciousness cannot be separated. The human experience of this energy-consciousness depends on its frequency or vibrational level. We can move our consciousness from one level of the auric field to another. We thereby experience different aspects of human consciousness, as was described in Chapter 2. Even though we are moving from one level of energy-consciousness and human experience to another within the auric field, we still remain in the fourth dimension.

In order to move from the auric dimension into the hara dimension and our intentionality, we must make another quantum leap. Our intentionality exists on a dimension deeper into our basic nature than the auric field. Whether or not the hara dimension can be equated with the fifth dimension, I really don't know. It would take quite a bit of research into it to tell, so I hesitate to guess.

Our hara line has a specific, immediate correspondence with our intentionality. Just as the auric field has a specific immediate correspondence to our thoughts and feelings, any change in our intentionality corresponds to a shifting in the position and alignment of our hara line.

Figure 17–1 (in the color insert) shows the aligned hara level when it is in a healthy person. It is composed of three major points connected by a laserlike line which I call the hara line. The hara line originates in a point that is three and a half feet above the head, which I call the individuation point, or ID point. It looks like a very small funnel whose larger end, one-third inch in diameter, points down over the head. It represents our first individuation out of the void, or unmanifest God. Through it, we have our direct connection to the godhead.

The hara line connects down through a point in the upper chest area that I call the soul seat. Sometimes it is called the high heart and confused with a chakra. It is not. The soul seat looks like a source of diffuse light reaching out in all directions. It is usually one to two inches in diameter but can expand to a fifteen-foot diameter in meditation. Here we carry our spiritual longing that leads us through life. Within it we can find everything we long to be, do, or become from the smallest thing or moment in our lives to the grandest scale of life itself.

The hara line continues down into the tan tien in the lower abdomen. The tan tien is located about two and one-half inches below the navel. It is about one and one-half inches in diameter, and it doesn't change in size. It looks a bit like a hollow rubber ball in that it has a membrane. As Heyoan said, the tone of this note is the one note that holds our physical body in physical manifestation. That note is a harmonic of the sound that the molten core of the earth makes. Healers use this point as a way of connecting to a great deal of healing energy. It connects them to the power source of the earth.

The concept of sound holding shape in the physical world was discussed in Chapter 9. In this case, the one note is more than a simple tone that can be heard with normal auditory perception. Rather, this note also exists in the HSP range. I think it means even more than that, but I don't know what it is yet. The closest thing to it that I have heard in the normal sound range is the cry that a karate master makes when chopping bricks in half with a light blow.

The hara line continues down from the tan tien deep into the center of the earth's core. Here we are connected to the earth and to the sound that the center of the earth makes. Once again, sound means more than just sound. Rather, it probably refers to a vibratory life source. By connecting down into the center of the earth through the hara line, we can synchronize our field pulsations with those of the earth's magnetic field and therefore entrain energy from the earth's field.

A healthy hara line is located in the center line of the body and is straight, well formed, energized, and well rooted into the earth's core. Each of the three points along the line are in balance, in form, and firmly connected to each other along the laserlike hara line. People with the configuration shown in Figure 17–1 are healthy, centered in their purpose, and on line with their life tasks. When this alignment is held, it is holographically true both in the moment and for all moments of the person's life. The person is at once present for the small task at hand and is connected to each larger task that surrounds it, as in the holographic model discussed in Chapter 3. This person is able to do the task of the moment in the moment, when it needs to be done, because she or he knows how it is connected to all time and to the whole task.

When your hara line is aligned, you are synchronized with the whole. When your haric level is healthy, you will feel a lot of personal integrity, power, and personal purpose, because you are synchronized with universal purpose. That's when you have those wonderful days in which everything flows easily, just as it ought to.

The feeling of being in your hara is a very freeing one. In this position, there is no adversary. Once any two people align their hara lines with universal purpose, they are automatically aligned with each other. Therefore, their purposes are synchronized so that each fits with the other. Their purposes are also holographically connected. Each purpose of each moment connects to all immediate purposes and to all greater long-term purposes.

On the other hand, people who take adversarial positions could not possibly have aligned their hara lines, because in order to do so, they must be aligned with universal purpose, which has no adversaries. Anyone who aligns his or her hara line automatically aligns with others with aligned hara lines.

Therefore, to the extent that you have aligned your hara line, to that exact degree you are on line with your purpose and in positive Intent. To the extent that you are not on line in your haric level, to that exact degree you are in negative Intent. It is as simple as that.

The complicated part is, how do you tell if you are aligned or not? If you do have HSP developed, it is possible to tell by using HSP to look at the haric level to see if everything is well formed, aligned, charged, balanced, and functioning. Another way to tell is that someone who is in alignment will not argue about who is right or wrong. From that person's perspective, there is no adversary with whom to argue or fight.

If you find yourself arguing, it means that you are not in alignment. Neither is the person with whom you are arguing, if he or she is arguing back. This does not mean that when you are aligned in your hara, you simply say you are right and walk away. Rather, there just simply isn't anything to argue about or disagree on. Whenever you find yourself in an argument, your first act must be to center in and to align your hara line.

Arguments of right and wrong come from people working at cross-purposes within themselves. That is, part of them is aligned and part is not aligned. This misalignment shows in the hara line. These internal parts are at cross-purposes with each other. If we use the concepts of the higher self, lower self, and mask self mentioned in Chapter 1, we could say that part of the psyche may be functioning from any combination of each of these three aspects. That is usually the case. Very rarely are we totally functioning from our higher selves and, thus, from an aligned hara.

The internal disagreement between these parts of ourselves gets manifested on the outer level in the form of an argument with another person. Our cross-purposes will also be materialized in the outer world as problems in creating or accomplishing something. They may arise in such things as procrastination or sloppy work. They may also arise between two people who are working together on a project in such ways as misunderstanding, confusion, competition, and broken contracts.

For example, if each person's purpose is to get a project completed in the best way possible, on time and with the best quality, then it will probably happen. But if one employee wishes to take over the boss's job, the negative intention will change the quality of work, automatically undermining the boss, even if the employee doesn't try to.

The Haric Level in Health and Healing

In health and healing, the same principle of aligning with your purpose holds true. To the extent that you stay on line with your purpose to maintain or regain your health, to that exact degree you will maintain or regain your health wherever it is humanly possible.

Distortion in the hara line and the points along it depict the tremendous pain of humanity. This is pain that humanity feels but does not understand. Dysfunction, in the haric level, is related to intention and life task. Many people do not even know, let alone understand, that we create our own experience of reality. They do not understand the idea of life purpose or life task. They do not understand the idea that our intentions have a great effect on our lives. They are not aware of the subtle but powerful shift that a change in intention causes in our auric fields and our creative energy flow.

In any serious or long-term illness, a dysfunction in the hara line will be apparent. A trained healer will be able to work on the haric level to heal it. Healing the haric level involves working on the deeper issues of the client's intention, including purpose at any one given moment, and life task issues. Before giving examples of what this means in practical healing sessions, let us first look at the types of distortions that can occur in the points along the hara line and in the hara line itself.

Dysfunction in the Tan Tien

Dysfunction in the tan tien shows in several ways. It can be displaced. It can be too far forward, backward, or to one side of the body. It can be misshapen. The membrane enclosing the tan tien can be torn, half of it blown open, or even worse. (See Figure 17–2.)

The result of tan tien dysfunction is chronic back problems. If the tan tien is too far forward, the lower part of the pelvis will be tipped backward. Such clients are trying to jump ahead of themselves. If the tan tien is too far back, the lower pelvis will be tilted forward. Such clients are "holding back" from their life task. Both of these will show in the body as lower back problems.

Since the tan tien carries the one note, or tone, that holds the body in physical manifestation, if the tan tien is torn or blown open, its tone will be way off. In such a case, the body and psyche can be badly shaken. I have seen people with such a condition go into hysterics and not be able to get out of it for several hours. I have seen

Figure 17–2 Distortion in the Tan Tien

the body become extremely weak and not be able to recover its strength for years. I have even seen cases where the legs deteriorate.

No matter what such people do for themselves, even physical exercises, nothing will help much until the damaged tan tien is repaired. Therefore work must be directed toward healing the tan tien by repairing it, positioning it correctly along the hara line, connecting it to the earth through the hara line, and charging it. A healer who is advanced enough to do hara healing can do this directly or with long-distance healing.

Healing the tan tien may also occur by doing martial arts with a good teacher. The practice of tai chi is very good for this. It is very important to learn martial arts from a good teacher so that it is done right. Otherwise, the healing effects won't happen.

After the tan tien is repaired, then physical exercise to maintain alignment is very effective. All physical exercise ought to be done with focused intent to bring conscious awareness into the body.

Dysfunction in the Soul Seat

The soul seat usually becomes disfigured by shrouding. That is, it gets covered by a dark cloud of energy. (See Figure 17–3.) The result of this is that people don't have the ability to feel what they want now or in the future in life. They have no feeling for what they want to do in their lives. Such people also usually have a sunken chest and display a "give up," "I don't care," or "life is boring and meaningless" stance. They carry a deep sadness.

When a healer begins to clear the cloud of dark energy and enhance the light of the soul seat so that it begins to expand and flow forth, clients usually have one of two reactions. In the first, they may suddenly feel a new lease on life and begin re-creating life accord-

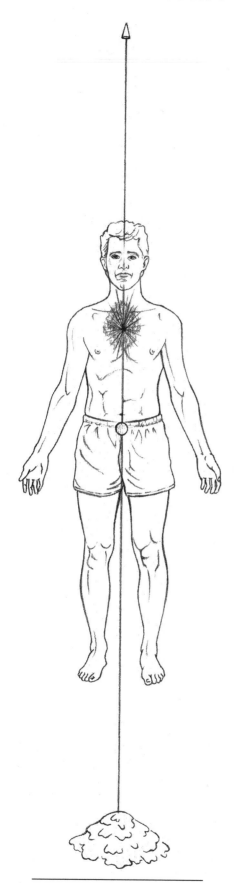

Figure 17–3 Shrouded Soul Seat

ing to spiritual longing of which they are now aware. The second is that they may go into mourning for all the lost time in life in which they have not been doing what they wanted to do. After a period of mourning, clients' lives begin to take on new meaning. New eros is born, and clients find themselves full of great excitement about what they can do with their lives.

Many people create a shroud of dark energy around their soul seat after they lose a loved one. This anesthetizes their feeling of loss. But it also stops the natural mourning process. If the couple had great plans with each other that were not fulfilled, many times the person who is left alone in the physical world thinks that continuing with the plans, as they were before the death, is an act of loyalty to the deceased. Unfortunately, since all plans are alive, constantly changing and unfolding, that doesn't work. Blocking the mourning will not allow the plan to be alive and changing. Refusal to mourn will eventually freeze all the life-force out of the plan. And after some time, no more unfoldment of the work will continue. People will focus on preserving the work, and it will take on a museumlike quality.

The way to heal this is to go through the mourning of the loved one. This will release the plans for unfoldment. It can be done at any time. This allows other people to enter into the plan for new life and companionship. It is never too late for anything. The plan can be accomplished, but in a different way than before, because different tools and people will be there for its accomplishment.

Dysfunction in the ID Point

The funnel-shaped individuation point above the head can get distorted in form or clogged up, as shown in Figure 17–4. This results in a disconnection from the ID point. Disconnection from the ID point also leads to a certain cynicism about life, because there is no understanding, no "knowing of God." People disconnected from their ID points probably think that people who believe in God have a very Pollyanna view of life and are in fantasy. To such individuals, organized religion is a way to control people because it defines and describes a God that, to them, doesn't exist. They have had no personal experience of God with which to compare and confirm any descriptions or definitions of God. They may be atheists or agnostics. They will accept M-1 metaphysics, which ignores the question of God's existence.

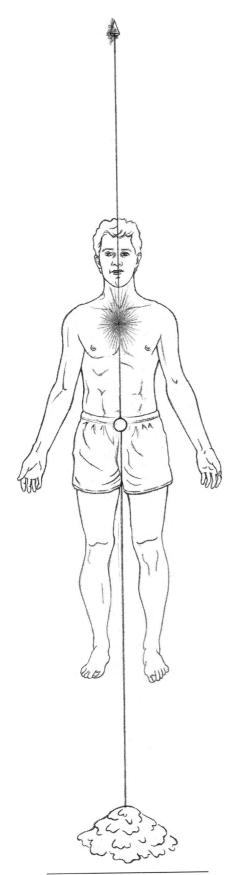

Figure 17–4 Blocked ID Point

When the healer clears and reconnects this point, clients will actually begin having childhood memories about being connected to God. They will also begin to develop a new connection to God through their personal experience, rather than accept God according to someone else's descriptions or rules, as in many organized religions.

Dysfunction in the Hara Line and Its Points

From my perception, the alignment of most of humanity's hara line is not ideal. I have never met anyone who is able to hold their hara line straight and in alignment all the time. Most people do not hold it in alignment at all. A few can hold it perhaps thirty percent of the time. A very, very few can hold it more than fifty percent of the time. Most martial artists, after years of training, are able to hold the lower portion of the line that connects between the earth and the tan tien. Some can hold the middle part of the hara line from the tan tien to the soul seat. But they do not know about the upper part of it. It takes years of training for anyone to connect to and hold the entire hara line in alignment for any length of time.

Instead, most people are misaligned most of the time and suffer greatly from it. Misalignment in the haric level shows as distortions in the hara line and the three points along it, as well as disconnection between each of the three points and/or the earth. Figure 17–5 shows the most common haric level distortion that many people of our culture have.

It shows that:

- The tan tien is off to the right of center, causing the person to be overly aggressive. (The right side of the body in general has masculine/aggressive energy.)
- The laser line is not connected to the earth, so that the person has no grounding to support aggression that is useful in a positive way. In other words, this person is dangerous and can be irrationally aggressive without power. Nor is this person connected to "being on the earth" with others and thus has a difficult time relating to other earth inhabitants.
- The tan tien is not connected to the soul seat, so that this person's physical existence is not connected to the spiritual longing that is designed to lead him or her through life. Thus, the person

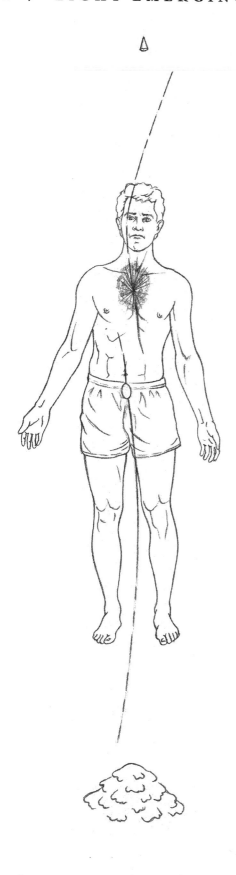

Figure 17–5 Distortion in the Hara Line

cannot feel and does not know what he or she came here for, so he or she cannot accomplish it.

• The laser line is not connected to the ID point, so this person is not connected to the godhead and thus has no true personal connection to spirituality or religion.

As a result of the above-listed distortions, many people in our culture are largely disconnected from the earth, from their fellow creatures, from God, and from their purpose, as well as from themselves. This causes great pain, both on the emotional and on the spiritual levels. They don't know why they are here, they don't believe there is a purpose to their lives, and they are very uncomfortable on earth. In short, as the popular saying goes, "Life sucks and then you die." This too can be healed through hara healing.

Hara lines of people of other cultures are different from those of Americans. People in different cultures distort their hara lines in different ways. People within the same culture distort their hara lines in similar ways. Therefore, people within the same culture suffer in similar ways. People of different cultures suffer from different kinds of pain. I have not had the time or privilege to make enough observations of different cultures around the globe to see this difference, but Heyoan has said that it is the cause of a great many international disputes and that, as we learn to heal the haric level, we will also make peace between the peoples of the earth.

Hara Healing

Once healers have determined the state of the haric level, they can work on the haric level for healing. This healing will bring it back to the state of healthy alignment, balance, and charge, as shown in Figure 17–1. It will also put clients squarely back on their life path, and their life will change, usually quite a lot in a very short time. As people return to their true life's path, all the material world around them that is not in harmony with that life path either changes or drops away. This includes material possessions, jobs, and living location, as well as friends and intimate relationships.

Hara healing is advanced work and requires a lot of training and practice. The healer must be able to straighten and hold his or her hara line, with all three points in the correct position, and be firmly grounded into the earth in order to correct clients' hara lines. Healers who are off can easily make clients ill, disoriented, and confused. I am not allowed to teach healers hara healing until they are ready. That is, they must be able to hold the hara line for one hour without dropping it. Then, if they do drop it, it must be recovered within less than a minute. This takes years of practice.

A good example of what can happen as a result of hara healing occurred in my work with a professional musician, whom I will call Thomas. Thomas's auric field was very dark and stagnated with dense, low-vibratory energy. From his field condition, I could tell he had been depressed for years. He was full of resentment and rage, and he had a great deal of masochism. So if I went in to pull it out and clear his field, it wouldn't have worked because I would have been doing the precise thing that his parents had done to him to cause the problem in the first place. (See the masochistic defense sections in Chapter 15.) On the haric level, his tan tien had been pushed down and to the back of his body and was disconnected from his soul seat. This meant that he was depressing his life task and backing out on it. He was also not connected into the first point of the individuation point above his head.

Knowing that the key to his release was to realign him with his life purpose, I concentrated only on the hara work during the healings. In a series of four or five hara healings, I aligned his hara line and all the points along it. I watched his aura straighten and clear as a result of the hara healings. The clearing of his auric field lifted his depression and allowed his psychological issues to rise to the surface of his consciousness to be worked on. He worked directly on these issues in his therapy sessions.

In an interview with him four years later, he stated:

Before the healings, I had a lot of trouble just living, as far as going into depression. I wanted to just hide a lot of things and not really deal with what was going on at the time. I was depressed a lot. The main reason I came for healing was to claim my own energy. There was a lot of turmoil, a lot of upheaval, and a lot of change after each healing session. I started dealing with a lot of family stuff, mother and father stuff, in my therapy. It was the usual life-parent stuff, a lot of anger. I had a tremendous amount of anger. Soon after that, the breakup of my marriage came. Plus, I was having all these career problems, financial problems, all happening at once. There was so much struggle and pain and confusion and sadness and all of that, that the conclusion that I came to was that my purpose in being here [on earth] was to resolve all of that. As long as I could keep things simple, if I could just remember that that's why I'm here now, I was fine.

As a result, I got through it. I lost about twenty pounds. I've been in a great relationship for about three years now, and I'm very good friends with my ex-wife and her family. There is nothing more there to be resolved. I'm also going to computer school as a way to learn to make more money. I'm still a professional musician. I still play and I have some students.

The main thing I took from the healings—the most memorable part of it—was feeling more centered in my own energy. So I'm now able to sustain my own energy and do what I feel I need to do for myself. I still would like to teach more music and go into more musical expression. I'd like to express the music that's inside of me without necessarily labeling it jazz or New Age. I want to tap into something inside of me. That's my big challenge now.

Aligning with Your Life Purpose

Aligning your haric level will align you with your life purpose. The exercise that follows will help you to align your hara line and heal any distortions in it or in the points along it. It will align you with your greater purpose. I suggest you do it each day in the morning to heal yourself and each time you set about accomplishing something. You will be amazed at the results you get. As you get used to holding the hara alignment, you will use it all the time. With it, you will be able to stay aligned with your greater life task in any small thing that you are doing in the moment. It is very applicable to your task of healing yourself.

An Exercise to Align Your Will with Your Life Purpose

Imagine a sphere of energy inside your body on the midline of your body, located about one and one-half inches below your navel. This point is the center of gravity of the physical body. It is the tan tien. It is the one note that holds your body in physical manifestation. The hara line and the tan tien are usually gold. In this exercise, you will make the tan tien red.

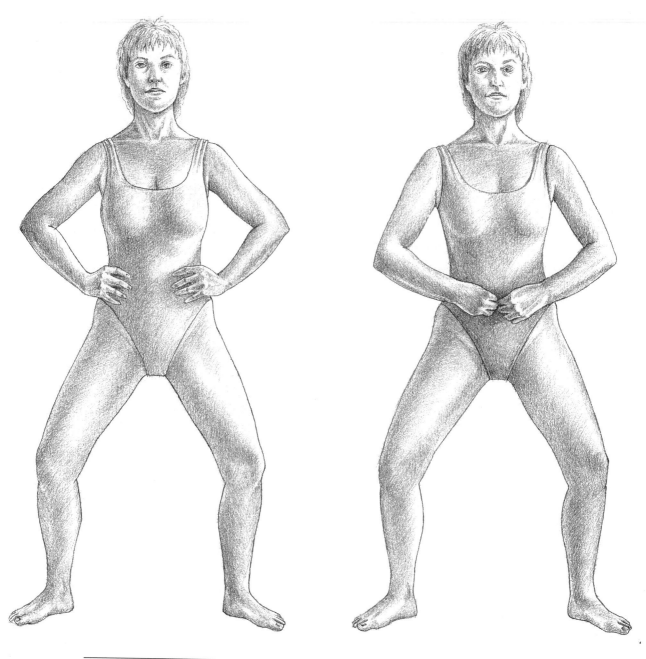

Figure 17–6 Hara Stance

Figure 17–7 Fingertips into Tan Tien

Stand with your feet about three feet apart, and bend your knees deeply, as shown in Figure 17–6. Let your feet splay outward so that you do not twist your knees. Align your spine. Pick up a piece of hair that is directly on the top of your head. Pull it so that you can feel the very center top of your head. Now pretend that you are hanging from this piece of hair. This will align your body on a plumb line with the earth.

Place the tips of the fingers of both hands into the tan tien, as shown in Figure 17–7. Keep your fingers together. Feel the tan tien within your body, and make it hot. Make it red hot. If you connect to it, soon your whole body will be warm. If your body does not get warm, you have not connected to it. Try again. Practice till you succeed. Once you have succeeded, move your awareness to the molten core of the earth.

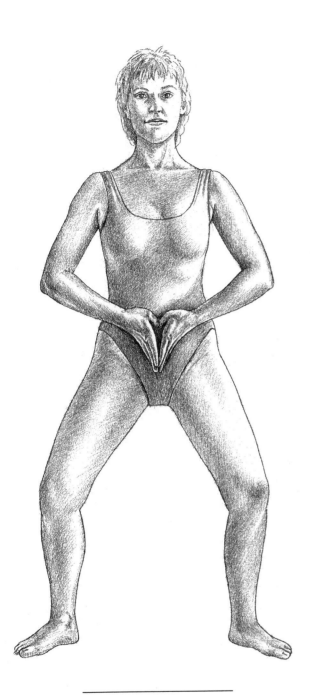

Figure 17–8 Triangle Down

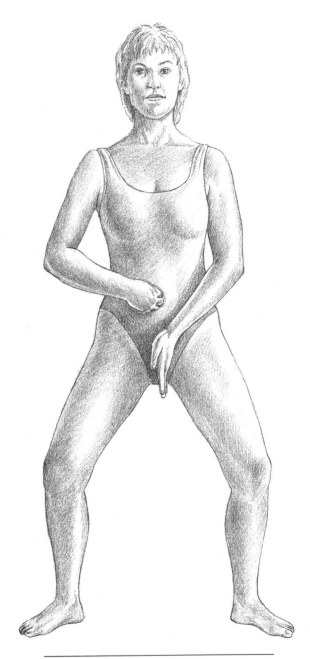

Figure 17–9 Right Fingertips into Tan Tien,
Left Hand over Tan Tien, Fingers Down

Place your hands in a triangle position, with finger-tips pointed down into the earth directly in front of the tan tien. (See Figure 17–8.) Feel the connection between the earth's core and your tan tien. Now you will really feel the heat, burning heat, so much that you will start sweating. You may even hear a sound similar to the one martial artists use as a cry when they are about to strike. If your Higher Sense Perception is open, you will be able to see the red color in your tan tien. You will also see a laser line of light connecting the tan tien with the molten core of the earth. I call this the hara laser line. If you don't see it, imagine it. You don't have to see it to make it work.

Now place the fingertips of the right hand into the tan tien, and point the left palm to the right side of your body with the fingers down. Hold the left hand directly in front of the tan tien. (See Figure 17–9.) Hold this configuration until you are stable.

Now bring your awareness to your upper chest area, about three inches below the hollow in your throat and again on the midline of your body. Here is a sphere of diffuse light. This light carries the song of your soul, your unique note that you bring to the universal symphony. It carries the longing that leads you through life to accomplish your soul's purpose for your life. Place the fingertips of both hands into the soul seat in the upper chest, as you did before in the tan tien.

When you connect to it, it may feel like a balloon is being blown up inside your chest. It may feel very safe and sweet there. Feel that sweet sacred longing as it rests within you. It may remain nameless, but you can still feel it. It looks like the diffuse light around a candle, but it is purple-blue in color. Expand the purple-blue light in your chest.

Next place the fingertips of the right hand into the soul seat and the fingers of the left hand, pointed down to the earth, over the tan tien. The flat open palm of the left hand faces the right side of your body. (See Figure 17–10.) Feel the hara line running directly down from the soul seat through your tan tien and down into the center of the earth. When you can feel this very strongly, then move on to the next step.

Leaving your left hand where it is, raise the fingers of the right hand over your head. Let the middle finger of your right hand point up to the ID point, three and one-half feet above your head. (See Figure 17–11.) Feel the hara line, which extends from the soul seat up through your head to the small upside-down funnel opening of the ID point. This small opening is really a small vortex, its open end facing downward. It is the hardest to feel. Try it. It may take some time. This vortex represents the first point of individuation out of the godhead, or is-ness. It represents the first point of individuation from the oneness of God. When you are able to get the hara line through the ID point, it suddenly disappears into formlessness. When it goes through the funnel, it may make an HSP sound like a cork coming out of a bottle. You will instantly feel the difference, because as soon as you connect it, you will have thousands of times more power. Suddenly everything will get quiet inside, and you will feel like a bridge of power. You have aligned your hara line.

Wait for several minutes until the hara line is stable. Then lower your right hand, with fingers pointed up and palm to the left side of your body, so that it is over your soul seat. That will be more comfortable for you.

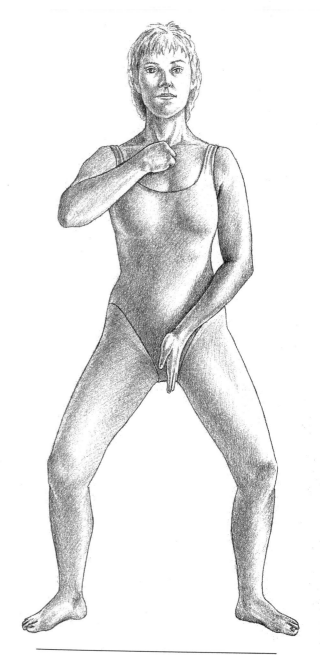

Figure 17–10 Right Fingertips into Soul Seat, Left Hand over Tan Tien, Fingers Down

Keep the left hand pointed down, palm to the right side of your body, held over the tan tien. (See Figure 17–12.)

Feel the hara line and the three points. Make it straight with your intention. Intend for it to be straight, bright, and strong. Keep your intention until you feel it get straight, bright, and strong. Straighten

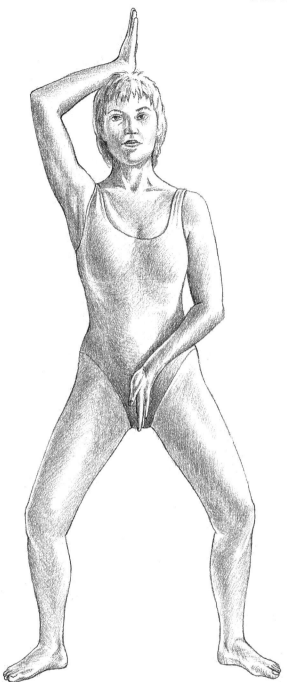

Figure 17–11 Right Hand Aligned with ID Point,
Left Hand over Tan Tien, Fingers Down

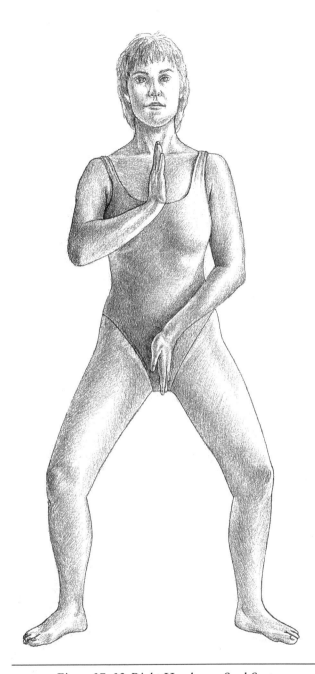

Figure 17–12 Right Hand over Soul Seat,
Fingers Up, Left Hand over Tan Tien, Fingers Down

your body again so that it is as if you were hanging from a hair on the middle top of your head. Tuck your buttocks under a bit, and deeply bend your knees, keeping your feet three feet apart and splayed out a bit to protect your knees. As you bend your knees, they should come down directly over your feet. Check to see, feel, and hear if the points are strong, firm, and charged. If there is weakness in any area, note which

area it is. This is an area that needs healing work. Concentrate on it longer. Align the hara line and enhance the points as best you can.

When you have aligned your first point of individuation from the godhead with your soul's sacred longing and with the one note with which you have drawn your body up from your mother the earth, you have aligned yourself with your life purpose. You may not even know what it is, but you are aligned with it, and your actions will automatically be synchronistic with it as long as you remain aligned.

The Group Hara Line

This technique can also be used with groups to set the purpose of the group. Here is how it works. The true individual purpose of any member of a group is holographically connected to the purpose of the group as a whole. Once all have aligned their haras, all have aligned their purpose in the moment with their greater purpose as individuals and as a group. Everyone's greater purpose is part of the great evolutionary plan of the earth, which was first mentioned in Chapter 13. This puts everyone into synchronicity, and the group becomes synchronistic. And as was said before, within this framework of reality no adversarial position is possible. The synchronicity can be felt in the room. The room fills with the power of the task at hand. Everyone has a part to do. The purpose of each part is connected to the purpose of the whole. It is surprising how well groups function when they are able to begin by aligning each individual will within the group. When this is accomplished, the group's will emerges.

Hara alignment can be used for any group. You can use it with your healing team, your research group, political group, or business group to set the purpose of the team. This model holds true everywhere, especially at the negotiating table between businesses, because it is based on unity rather than duality. If all align their haras and are connected to the universal purpose, there will be no win-lose situation. The transactions will be smoother.

I once gave a thirty-minute lecture to the Win-Win breakfast club in Denver on this subject. This organization is a group of heads of businesses and corporations dedicated to the win-win style of business, rather than the win-over-the-adversary style. It took them only a few minutes to change the energy in the room to a synchronized group purpose when I showed them how to align the hara. They learned it faster than any group I have ever had the privilege of teaching.

I recommend using this as a beginning meditation every time you work with a group. If disagreements arise, it means your alignment has gone off. I recommend repeating the meditation for realignment.

On the other hand, the presence of a leader whose hara is held in alignment will help all others around him or her to synchronize with their own purpose. I use

this regularly in preparing first myself, then the team of teachers with whom I work, and later the larger team of apprentices with whom I work in my training programs. I call it setting the group hara line. To set a group hara line, the first step is very important. The leader must first set her or his hara. This means personally going through the hara setting meditation just given.

I, as leader, do this alone, before my first meeting with the teaching team. Then when the teaching team first meets, we go through the whole meditation as a group. This synchronizes the purpose of each individual within the teaching team with the purpose of the team. Later, when the teaching team meets with the apprentice team that supports the teaching team, we once again use the meditation to set the purpose of that greater team.

The next day, early in the morning before class starts, this alignment is done again with everyone in the room. This aligned energy is then expanded throughout the room before the students enter the room. After the students are all settled into their seats, I once again lead the meditation to help them also set their hara lines. This process helps us regulate the tremendous amounts of energy released during the training class weeks.

The power, strength, and purpose that builds in the room can be felt as the group hara line takes shape. It is a beautiful thing to watch. Each line within each person connects to the earth, aligns, and gets brighter. As each does, it helps those who haven't been able to align to do so because of the power in the room. Then when the whole room becomes synchronized, a large group hara line, representing the group purpose, forms in the center of the room. (See Figure 17–13.)

In this way, we stay on purpose throughout the class. If we get unsynchronized, we simply repeat the alignment process. Aligning the group hara is one of the best results of holographic modeling I have seen. It is a very practical example of maintaining individuality and individual purpose while remaining connected to the larger groups that surround the individual. In this way, the individual connects to the love, support, power, and knowledge within the larger group. I believe this is why we get so much accomplished in our classes and learning and change comes so fast for students.

Aligning a Group of People with Its Purpose
To do this in a group, sit or stand in a circle and align your individual hara lines according to the instructions given in the hara alignment exercise. Be sure that everyone does this together, moving from one position to the next at the same time.

Figure 17–13 Group Hara Line

With each step, give time for each person to get aligned. You will feel the energy of the group shifting as this is done. It is very much like an orchestra tuning up. After some time, you will sense or feel, see or hear, the energies of the group stabilize. If you continue to sit in meditation, you will sense the hara line of the group form in the center of the circle. It is very similar to the laser line through your body. It represents the group purpose. It is a beautiful golden line of light, with the same three points described above. There will also be connections like the spokes of a wheel, from the tan tien of the group hara line to the tan tien in each body. (See Figure 17–13.)

Feel how strong and stable the energy in the room is. Now you can go about your work as a group without hassles.

Reincarnation in the Same Lifetime and the Transformation of the Hara Line

In *Hands of Light*, I spoke about the phenomenon of reincarnation in the same lifetime that occurs when someone finishes his or her life task and moves into another life task without leaving the body. I described a cocoon that forms in the auric field around the vertical power current at the spine. Since then, I have observed that within the cocoon, on the haric level, the hara line dissolves and reestablishes itself, thus establishing a new life task for the new incarnation without requiring starting all over with a new body. The process of dissolving the old hara line and reestablishing a new one usually takes about two years.

Since the points along the hara line also change when the hara line changes, the reincarnation in the same lifetime is usually accompanied by some physical problems. When the tan tien wobbles and dissolves, the physical body may go into chaos. The physical symptoms may be many, but none may be diagnosable. Or in other cases, you may have a life-threatening illness, a near-death experience, or a physical death-back-to-life experience.

Reincarnation in the same lifetime is very confusing for anyone to go through because you lose your sense of self, all the things with which you identified yourself, and your purpose. It sometimes appears that you are going to die. It is a time of deep personal change. It is a time of not knowing, a time of contemplation and waiting, sometimes in a black velvet void that is teeming with unmanifested life. It is a time of surrender to the greater powers that are at work within you.

Later, during this time, new energies from your core star begin upwelling into the haric level to create a new hara line that corresponds with the new task you have taken on. Of course, the new task will be related to the old one in the same way that past lifetimes are related to each other and the present lifetime. Reincarnation in the same lifetime is becoming more and more widespread as the number of people on paths of spiritual awareness grows.

During the two years that it takes to undergo reincarnation in the same body, everything in the life changes. This includes major shifts in profession, intimate partner, living location, friends, and finances. After the two-year period, usually life is very different. Reincarnation in the same body can happen more than once in a lifetime. But to my knowledge, that is extremely unusual.

Here is a good example of how a person's life changed as a result of the process of reincarnation in the same lifetime. I shall call her Rachel. Rachel was a brilliant corporate executive, running the human resources division of a large financial organization. She originally came to me for healing of chronic edema, which she had had for eighteen months.

After three healings spaced a couple of weeks apart, Heyoan said that she didn't need any more healings. It took a couple of months for the edema to clear, and it never came back.

During the healings, Heyoan didn't talk about her physical condition at all. Instead, he talked about the tapestry of Rachel's life, about weaving the golden threads of her life together. Rachel then began studying at the Barbara Brennan School of Healing, and after several years, she began helping me run programs. It was during one of those programs that I noticed that her tan tien was shifting and that she was going into the two-year process of reincarnation in the same lifetime. Here is how she describes her experience:

I had no idea what was going on. On my thirty-eighth birthday in February I cut off my long hair. I had had it all my life. But I felt that I had to absolutely change something in myself. A few days after that, I went to San Francisco to meet you for the introductory workshop. I walked into a hotel room, and you took one look at me and said, "Oh look, your tan tien is wobbling all over the place!"

I had no idea what that meant. You said, "That's what happens when you reincarnate in the same body. Your hara line disintegrates!" This freaked me out, because I had no idea of what it meant. Then you looked to see if there was a cocoon around my vertical power current. There was a cocoon. You drew a picture of it.

Then six months later, after the cocoon had started to dissolve, there was a section of the vertical power current in which the change had been arrested. You said that I had stopped the process. Later, when my back went out, you said that one of the reasons I was having so much trouble healing was that my tan tien was still wobbling, because the reincarnation process was still going on. I had been in perfect health all my life before that, so it was very difficult for me.

After the reincarnation process started, I also went through a bunch of past lives. I had never experienced them on a personal level before. I also had at least eight or nine experiences that I would call a dimension of time lapse, in which two times were overlaid. I could feel or experience another level totally outside of what was happening in the present. One of them, I remember, happened when I was sitting on the stage during class, looking at the students. I looked up at the balcony, and I knew it was empty. I knew it was 1989. But at the same time, I also had a vivid experience that the balcony was filled with a screaming crowd of people, and they were yelling for judgment. It was a whole trial scene. Those experiences began after this reincarnation-in-the-same-body process began.

Then about two years after it all began, you came up to me when you were doing channeled healings and said it was over.

Some of the external, obvious things resulted from this. One, I couldn't stay in my job anymore. I had to spend a lot more time learning about spiritual life, and that's when I quit my job and worked for the school. I had wanted to leave for a long time, but I had a lot of fear about security in terms of money and what safety really was. After the reincarnation process began, it became impossible to stay in that job, no matter how great my fears were. The impetus behind the change literally propelled me to move into a part of my life where I would feel better about myself, even though I didn't know what that meant, because I didn't. I just knew I had to stop feeling that every day when I woke up I couldn't bear going to work.

The reincarnation experience gave me a feeling that change is good rather than scary. Change became something very exciting, like looking forward to something. It felt very different.

I was the most incredibly healthy person before the reincarnation started. After it started, I hurt my back. That was the first major disease I ever had. It was almost exactly a year after the reincarnation started. Now my back is a thousand percent better than it was a year ago. Now I have only functional back pain. I had no other physiological effects.

The major difference I see in myself from that period is the big change in my relationship to myself. Once I went into the past life experiences, my relationship to myself got a lot deeper. I had a greater awareness of how I wasn't aware of myself. My biggest change is that I really notice now the part I play in everything. I really am much more aware of how I am at least fifty percent responsible for everything that happens. I have much less blame in terms of "it's me or them." I have much more awareness of the habitual pattern in my life that causes me to act the way I do through my defense system. My self-awareness went from nil to extreme. I'm very very aware now of my reaction. I'm much more aware of the role I play in my life in all my situations than I was before. Instead of my life being something that happens to me, I feel much more like I am a creator or co-creator. So any experience I have, I immediately find my part in it. This includes relationships—everything.

I notice my part in things, my role, my responsibility. If I'm having a fight with somebody, now I see what part of it is my fault. I see how everything is shared with all of us; everything is communal. And that feels real different. Take my family: Instead of just interacting with them, I have a second vision where I also notice, even if I'm talking with my mother while cooking or whatever, exactly what I'm doing that affects her and how it affects her in a certain way. And then she has a reaction to me and it comes back to me like a ping-pong ball, and I'll have a reaction, and so on.

So since this reincarnation in the same body, I notice that there's always this interaction stuff going on, and I actually can see my part in the play superimposed over my life. For example, my whole Christmas holiday was wonderful because I was completely aware of the energetic interactions I had that were absolutely habitual with my family. It was fascinating to watch. If I just stopped the energy, just stopped that interaction and replaced it with something else, everything changed.

I think that what is left of my back pain is connected to everything I just said about being responsible for my interactions. I think that it has to do with focus outward instead of inward, and the more I learn to focus inward, the more my back heals. And the more I look outward, for acceptance or whatever, the more I get myself in trouble. My back still has to do with holding back my spontaneous emotional reactions or responses. I know that I still hold back a lot of gut reactions, a lot of feelings. I doubt and question myself a lot, and I think that's when my back hurts the most. I don't always notice it right away, but I'm beginning to be aware of that. So my back doesn't hurt very much when I'm happy.

Introduction to Surrender, Death, and Transfiguration

The experience of reincarnation in the same lifetime requires a letting go and dying of the old, to allow space and time for rebirth. Here is a wonderful meditation given by Heyoan to facilitate the letting go of whatever it is in you that needs to dissolve. I suggest that you play music in the background. You can do this either alone, or in a group. It is designed to facilitate great change in your life.

~

SURRENDER, DEATH, AND TRANSFIGURATION
Channeled from
Heyoan

Feel the power of your divine grace. The power of the light has brought you here. It is through grace that you will experience this healing. This period of time in your life may be a very difficult one for you, but certainly a time filled with growth, a time filled with love, a time filled with brotherhood. It is:

- a time to be grateful for
- a time to give thanksgiving for
- a time to be moving onward from and outward from
- a time of forgiveness for that which remains to be forgiven
- a time of understanding for that which can be understood
- a time of surrendering to that which cannot be understood
- a time of following and a time of leading
- a time to be and a time to do

It is your time. You have created it for yourself, and so, it is you who will be in it according to your choice.

Dear ones, how do you wish to spend this time? It is your time. It is your time to follow your soul's sacred longing.

- a time of life
- a time of birth
- a time of renewal

The laboring of birth comes after the time of darkness. Within the darkness the womb grows full. Magic is accomplished. Life sprouts from the earth. You are being reborn to a fullness in new form, in new life. With you, new generation arises and blesses the face of this earth. Peace will come. Peace will reign.

Feel a star of light in the center of your body that represents your individual essence. We are all born into the light. You are of the light, you are the light, and the light will reign on this earth for a thousand years; all humankind will be one.

Allow the magic to enfold both you and the ununderstandable. Simply be within the womb of regeneration. Allow that which needs to die to dissolve into the magic—fodder for the fields.

- What is it that you will give to the earth for dissolving?
- What is it that must be let go of for regeneration to occur?

Place it now into the earth with love and sweet surrender and farewells, sweet farewells. Let it go with blessings of sweet remembrances, of that which has served you in the past and no longer serves you now. Place it deep within the womb of your mother the earth. As a seed. Let it roll off your body. Let it flow out of your consciousness. Let it dissolve out of your thought forms and flow down deep into the earth for a time of forgetting.

Then come to the star of light within you, deep in your belly. Deep within your body, about one and one-half inches above your navel, is the beautiful star of your unique essence. Simply *be here now*. That which was let go will be transmuted while you simply *be here now*.

That which dies of form is immediately reborn into the formless life of the void. What is death to form is birth to the teeming, formless life of the void.

Within the natural cycle, spring will touch that which dissolves. That which is forgotten will, in spring cycle, arise like a phoenix in your re-remembering of a different sort.

As life within the formless void surrenders to its death, form is reborn.

~

EIGHTEEN

Our Divine Core

After working on the hara line and on intentionality with many people and seeing the big changes in their lives, with their life purpose opening up and fulfillment coming to them, I asked, "Who is it that is being fulfilled? Who is it that has this life purpose? Who is it that has all this intentionality?" After all, our intentionality isn't who we are. Clearly our personality isn't who we are. It is only a signature expressing a bit of who we really are. Our physical body certainly isn't who we are. Then who are we? Where are we? From where does all this life stem? Who am I?

I reasoned that there must be another deeper dimension beneath the haric level, a dimension that is the foundation for the haric level: the dimension of the knower. Heyoan was quick to respond to my curiosity:

~

Beneath the haric dimension lies the dimension of your deeper core. The core is the eternal "I am what is, was, and ever will be." Here is the origin of your creative force. Your core is the internal source of the divine. With HSP, it looks like a star, a core star. This light is a signature of the eternal essence of each person. It exists outside of time, space, physical incarnation, and even the concept of the soul. It seems to be the source of life itself. It is the unique individual God within each of us. It is the source from which all incarnation stems, and yet it remains in complete peace and serenity. Where the core light emerges, it brings health. Where it is blocked, dis-ease occurs.

~

So I was off on another adventure looking for the core, finding it, and learning to experience and work with it. Working with the core star has been extremely rewarding. In all healings that I give now, I work with all three levels at once. So travel with me now, as we enter into the world of your essence, the most holy of holies within you. I'm sure you will enjoy it.

The Core Star: The Eternal Source of Your Essence

Using HSP, I was able to locate the core star within the body. It is literally in the center of the body. I realize that the essence of the core is everywhere, but focusing on this central location in the body helps one contact it. The core star is located about one and one-half inches above the navel on the center line of the body. It looks like a brilliant light of many colors. (See Figure 18–1 in the color insert.) This light can expand infinitely. It has a very familiar feeling of unhindered self within it. It is the you that you have been throughout this life. It is the you that you were before this particular life. It is the you that will continue to be after this particular life. It is the you that exists beyond time and space. This essence of self is different for every person. It is your unique essence. That is the individuated divine within you.

What may be confusing about the core essence is that it also exists in the divine unitive principle, or God. That is, it is both the individuated God within us and the universal God at the same time. It is this paradox that sometimes is not easy for us to understand. How can I be me and God at the same time? God is so vast. God is beyond human understanding. How could I call myself God when I know that God is much more than me? The only way to answer that question is through the experience of the core star. Through bringing conscious awareness to the core star, sensing it, and then discovering that this essence is the same as the self, we can resolve this human paradox.

Once you can experience your core essence, you will be able to find it everywhere. You will find it everywhere in your body. You will find it everywhere in your auric field. You will find it everywhere in your haric level. You will find it everywhere in your life. You will find it stretched out to the far reaches of the universe. You will find it everywhere you look for it.

Your core essence expresses itself to certain degrees everywhere. The places in your intention, your life energy fields, in your physical body, and in your life where it is most fully expressed are the places where you are healthy and happy. The places where it is expressed the least are the places where you are least happy, in discomfort, or have problems. It is as simple as that. Therefore, we have come around to the beginning of this book, where disease is described as a signal that we have in some specific way become disconnected from our core essence. We have disconnected from our inner divinity. We have forgotten who we are. Using HSP, we can "see" this as disconnection from the core.

Disconnection from the Core

In the core star level, dysfunction is almost always related to people being disconnected from their core in some way. It isn't that there is something wrong in the core itself; it is that something is wrong in the connection between the core and the other levels of their existence. In some way, the core essence is not being transmitted all the way through into the physical world. It could be caused by a dysfunction in the auric or haric level that does not allow the core essence through. Or the core star may be shrouded with dark clouds of energy or even encased in a very dense, resilient substance. The pulsations and light from the core star are not allowed to emerge.

People severely disconnected from their cores have no connection to their creativity. They do not experience themselves as having an inner divinity. They cannot experience themselves as a unique center of light in the universe. These people have forgotten who they are and have a great deal of trouble connecting to the higher self or even knowing that they have a higher power within them.

Healing with the Core Essence

It is clear, because of the importance of the core star level, that all healings should include some work to upwell the core essence into all the levels above it. Any parts of the haric level, the auric field, and the physical body that have been worked on in any healing should be flooded with the core essence before closing a healing. This is true because anywhere the physical body, the auric field, or the haric level has been distorted, the core essence is also prevented from coming forth in its full brilliance.

To give a healing, first the healer uses HSP to appraise the condition of the physical, auric, haric, and core levels. The healer gives healing on each of the levels, beginning with either the aura or the hara, whichever is appropriate for the client. After this work is completed, the healer uncovers and then upwells the client's core star into each of the levels above it. The core essence is first upwelled into the haric level, then into the auric, and then into the physical body. The healer expands the client's core star so that the individual essence of the client fills his or her intention on the haric level, personality in the auric field, and every cell in the physical body. Then the healer expands the core light from the body out as far as is comfortable for the client. It may be a few feet, or it may extend to the far reaches of the universe in this way.

A good example of such a healing took place during a sophomore class around December 1989, when a student from the West Coast came in on crutches with her left leg in a brace. I'll call her Sarah. She said she had been in a snow-skiing accident and had badly torn the anterior cruciate ligament in her left knee. A brief HSP appraisal showed me that she had torn ligaments inside the knee that needed to be repaired. I could also see that her hara had become misaligned and that the deeper issue was her relationship to her budding healership. I asked her if I could use her knee as a teaching tool for the class and worked on her in front of the class.

I began the healing by interviewing all the students who had worked on her before I was able to and discussed what the results of each healing were. I then proceeded to repair more of the auric field, do a hara healing, and then to upwell the core essence into the cells of her body. As a result of her healings, she did not need surgery, and her leg healed very well. I interviewed her two years later, in December 1991, to follow up on the effect of the healings she received. Here are some excerpts from what Sarah told me:

When it first happened, I was in Yosemite. I was way up on this mountain. It was the first time I was on snow skis. I was in a class. We had been skiing all day and had slowly worked our way up higher and higher on the mountain. When I fell, I felt my knee pop out. My class kept going down the mountain. Then they stopped. I knew I shouldn't get up, but I didn't want them to come up and get me, so I got up and slowly skied down the mountain. I turned in my rental skis hobbling and aching.

I stayed in my cabin that night. It was the most miserable night of my life. I was really sick. The next morning I went to the hospital. Driving back down the mountain I was throwing up. I was green. They gave me something for the pain. They said, "This is very serious. You need to see an orthopedist right away." They immobilized my leg.

I went to see an orthopedist. My knee was swollen so badly that he couldn't do the fancy X-ray they can do. But from his poking and prodding and trying to get some range of motion out of it, he said it looked very serious. Everything pointed to the fact that I would probably need surgery in about ten days. He said, "This is serious." He said that I would need to come back in five days, but I said I wanted to go back to the East Coast to healing class in two days.

He looked at me and said, "You're insane. You must really want to go. I'm not going to tell you not to go, but you are going to be pretty miserable being on planes. But I'll leave it up to you. Sounds nuts to me."

It turns out that the trip was fine. The airlines just gave me wheelchairs, and there were three seats in my row, so I was pretty comfortable. Of course, I was with Tony, a classmate, and she took care of my luggage.

Tony worked on me once before I went east, right after I saw the orthopedist. And that's when I actually saw, using HSP, that she connected two thread-like strands in my auric field. The cruciate is a cross. That's what *cruciate* means in Latin. It's a cross hinge on the inside of the knee. She connected two of the threads that were just kind of hanging out there. They looked, using HSP I learned in class, like white, snakish-looking threads. And she put those back in. That was actually pretty painful when she put that back together. I was really sweating when she got in there.

Then I came back to class and I had three different classmates work on it. Somebody just ran level one energy into it, which I felt starved for. It was the first time I really understood what is meant by physical energy. Then Martin did a little bit of work on it. Each day someone worked on me, my knee got a little better. But I was still in a lot of pain, and there was no way I could put weight on it.

Then you put me up onstage and used my knee as a teaching tool. You invited each person who had worked on me to come up and talk about what they had seen using HSP and what they did. And then you had me give feedback about how that was for me. Then I remember you started doing the hara work, because we hadn't known anything about that. You were standing at my feet and conversing with the class, and I remember the incredible sensations that were moving up my legs. I was thinking, "I don't know what this is, but whoa, something is going on here!"

A tremendous amount of sensation was running

up my legs and through my whole body, and I was really feeling very affected by that. And then you said, "Oh, yes. What I'm doing now is working with hara." I remember lying there on that table with such a powerful sensation going on in my body, and I kind of went out. You did a core star closing after you did the core star, which was new. We'd never seen that before, and I didn't really know what you were doing.

I was out for a long time after you worked on me. I stayed on the stage probably for an hour or two just lying flat. And I remember getting up and being able to walk on my knee after that. I wasn't bearing full weight. I was just doing a little bit of a limp, and I had walked about halfway across the floor. And you said to me, "Don't do that yet! Get your crutches and give it a little bit of time to solidify."

After you worked on me, I felt very good. I didn't need my brace after that. But it wasn't just my knee—my whole body felt very good. I felt very solid in ways that I hadn't before. A pretty major shift happened for me from that time. A lot of things happened. I was always a skeptic about this work, and I had been questioning my place and the reality of this work. Then to have such a major injury that looked like I was going into surgery and to have the work be so effective and so incredibly helpful meant a lot for me. It really did heal my knee. It's as if I had to let myself know from a real basic level, in spite of myself, what this work really could do. It felt like a whole shift happened for me in that I got very solid in my work. It helped me connect to this work. A lot got very clear and focused for me.

When I went back to the orthopedist, he was surprised and amazed at my healed knee. He watched my knee for a couple of weeks. I really went back for him. I was swimming to strengthen the knee. I worked on my own knee on level one of the aura a lot, mostly charging level one of my knee.

The deeper meaning? I had had a lot of left-side injuries. It was very connected to the woman side of me. I needed to be able to step out of the world and receive. I did a lot of work on my feminine principle. I had lots of dreams about my little girl inside. I needed to surrender and receive. It was about going home to that place inside, to that place of balance, that true place inside of me that I call true life. It was also about standing on my own and believing in myself and believing that I have something to offer. Shortly after it happened, my healership began to unfold. Doing this work is a way that I get to keep coming home, because to work with people, I have

to go to that place. For me, the challenge is how can I do that for myself!

Opening Corridors to Your Core

Spend a few moments now bringing your conscious awareness to the physical location associated with the core star in the center of your body, about one and one-half inches above your navel. In a short time you will feel calm, relaxed, full of light, and powerful, and your sense of self will be enhanced. Opening HSP to the core star level is a wonderful experience. First you may see your own core star, in all its unique brilliance. Then, if you look at a room full of people, what you see is a room full of stars—each one different, each brilliant and exquisite. It is as if the stars sing to each other through the space filled with core light that is known as the Almighty. (See Figure 18–2 in the color insert.)

If you give a few minutes a day (only five will have an effect) to focusing your attention on this central core of your being, your life will change. You will begin a conscious path of change in your life that will take you to places you have always wanted to be able to go but couldn't get to. You may experience great spiritual heights of wonderment. You will also release issues that you have avoided facing, sometimes for your whole life. They will come to the foreground of your life to be experienced and healed. You will begin to create the things you have always wanted but have not yet created in your life.

Opening the internal corridor to our core will allow the love, truth, and courage within us to come forth. This is the essential process in healing. By opening this internal corridor, healing energy automatically upwells through all four dimensions of our creative energy and flows forth to be given in healing to the self or to another person. Healing energy automatically flows from anyone who opens his or her internal corridor between the outer personality and the core star. It is easy to feel this healing energy when you are in the presence of such a person. You feel calm, relaxed, safe, and full.

You have already automatically made the connection from your personality to your core through your higher self. Most people are rather shy about the true nature of being in their higher self. It feels a bit like being unveiled. It is like being undefended. So spend some time getting to know your higher self. Which parts of you are already clear, pure, and loving? When you become more aware of what those parts are, you can allow them to express themselves more. You will become more used to expressing your love and caring for others without being so shy.

Our core star is our divine source. Opening the internal corridor to our divine source also automatically connects us to the external divine source of love and energy all around us, to what I call universal divinity. It is by accepting the divine within us, which is the individualized, localized God within, that we are brought to know universal God. Another way to say it is, opening the internal corridor to God creates an external boulevard to God. Or in reverse, it is by surrendering to God, or to the divine above us, below us, and all around us, that we are brought to the divine within us, or the God within. One is not possible without the other.

Everything that we do originates from the core star, as does every positive intention. Pleasure is its motivating force, and it creates only joy and fulfillment.

Here is the creative path that our core essence takes as it expands into the world of manifestation. As our creative force upwells from this core star, it brings great pleasure with it. As the core essence emerges into the hara dimension on its way to our physical world, it upwells into the center of the three points along the hara line. If all three points are in alignment, we have aligned our intent with the best in us, and we have synchronized with divine intent. In other words, God's will and our will are one. When we then allow the core essence to upwell into this divine intent, we also express our individual essence through our intent or our purpose. We express individual divine purpose.

As the core essence upwells into the auric level, it upwells into the centers of the chakras and expands to permeate the whole auric field with the essence of who we are. Then we express our divine essence with our personality.

When the core essence upwells into the physical level, it upwells in the nucleus of each cell, in the DNA. It expands throughout the whole body until divine light shines so brilliantly that it literally shines through our skin, and we are radiant. Then we express our divine essence through our physical bodies. It is a beautiful sight to see. Our essence fills the room, and all who are present can experience and delight in it.

Here is a meditation channeled from Heyoan to bring forth your essence through each level of your being.

~

CORE STAR MEDITATION
Channeled from
Heyoan

Step One: Hara Alignment

Bring your awareness to the tan tien, an inch and a half below your belly button on the midline of your body. Feel the power there. Feel the heat there. Feel how it is the same as the heat in the molten core of the earth. It is a harmonic of the sound the core of the earth makes. Stay focused there until it is very hot.

Bring your awareness to an area in the upper chest, about two and one-half inches below the hollow in your throat. Here, on the haric level, the soul seat in the chest is like the diffuse light around a candle. The soul's longing, the song of the soul, resides here. It is not the heart chakra. When you connect with it, sometimes it feels like a ball being blown up inside your chest. It has a very clear, spherical appearance. It carries the soul's longing.

Feel the laser line now that goes from the soul seat in your chest, down through the tan tien in your pelvis, and into the center of the earth. Feel the strength and silence in the room as our individual and our group purposes become synchronous.

Bring your awareness to the point above your head. Straighten your spine. Don't let your head hang. Imagine a fine thread through the very top of your head. If you don't feel it, pick up a hair right at the very top of your head, pull up as if there were a string on which your head is hanging. With your mind's eye, reach up to that very tiny opening, about a quarter of an inch in diameter, two and a half to three feet above your head. You will hear a very high-pitched sound if your auditory perception is open. When you are able to place that laser line through that hole, you will actually hear it as a pop. It kind of pops through. It's not easy to find that high point. It's like a little vortex. When you find it, it's like going through into a totally different reality, way above you. If you pop through, you will find yourself within the godhead, or undifferentiated "is"-ness. In order to get that line through, you have to completely align your physical body.

Feel that very tiny laser beam half the size of your little finger, going all the way through you from the godhead to the molten core of the earth. Feel the soul's song in your chest and the creative force in your tan tien. Feel that at the same time you feel the line all the way down to the molten core of the earth. Feel that power. That's the alignment for your task. This is the bridge. This is you and the bridge between heaven and earth.

Feel the synchronicity of the purpose now in the room. That same line going down right through the middle of the room is the hara line of the group. Feel the connection from your tan tien to the tan tien of the group—that's in the center of the room.

It is upon this level that your task and the task of the greater group of which you are a member synchronize. It is on this level that the task of this group will synchronize with that of the greater community around. That will then synchronize with that of the state, the country, the continent, and the earth. This is the way to connect to the power and truth of a system within a system within a greater system. It is the key to holographic universal alignment. There is no need to struggle or to worry that your task is difficult. It need not be. For when you align yourselves on these levels—the core star, the aura, the hara, and the physical body—then you are in synchronicity with the world around you as well as yourselves.

Step Two: Light Emerging from the Core Star
Move your awareness now to the core star, an inch and a half above your belly button. Here resides the essence of who you are beyond time, beyond space, beyond longing and desire. At this place you simply are. There is no need. There is no pain. You simply are creator. When you as creator move forth from the core star of your essence to create, you first bring creative energy into the level of the hara, your divine task. From the haric level, you bring energy to the auric level, creating your personality, template for the physical. From the auric level you bring energy into the physical, to create life in form in the physical body.

The creative force moves from the one (core star) through trinity (represented by the point above your head, the point within your chest, and the point within your tan tien on the haric level) through the level of seven (the seven layers of the auric field) and into the multiplicity of form in the three-dimensional world. When you have completed one plan of creation, you will then move forth more of your essence into the trinity, through which shines your purpose.

So allow your essence now to exude itself strongly and steadily from your core star, through your haric level and into your auric field. Allow that essence to flow through each layer of the field. Each layer of the field represents a state of being, a level of being in humanness. Bring the essence of your being through each of those levels of human being. Then bring it through to the physical, to crystallize in your body, through every cell of your body. It will create health, joy, and pleasure in your physical life and your life's work. Your body, your personality, and your life are all expressions of your divine essence.

And so the one has become the trinity has become the seven, and as you open the seals of the seven, you will know God within the human being. Look now within each cell of your body. You will find in the nucleus of each cell a configuration very similar to your core star—a point of light radiating forth the essence of your being within every cell of your physical body. Healing, then, is simply helping your self connect with the truth of your being. It is nothing more than that.

Where there is pain or illness, anger or fear, where there is suspicion or greed, where there is forgetting, remember your core star. Allow the light within your core star to emerge. Remember the light within every cell of your body. Remember your body. Bring the members of your body together within the light of your body, your altar in form. That light is the light of your core star, your essence, the God within.

Your task did not come from pain; it came from the desire to create. It came from the flow of love out of the center of your being, which in its creative movement out from the core became disconnected and forgot who it is. It is only a matter of reconnecting with the memory of who you are. Your life task is to remember that original creative urge and to complete your creation so that another will well up from the source within you.

Let the essence of who you are that rests within your core star shine forth through all levels of your being. Allow that original creative urge there to lead you through your life.

The Core Star and the Creative Pulse of Life

Recently, in a lecture on creativity, Heyoan described the phases of the creative process in relationship to the four dimensions of our being. He said that the creative pulse arises out of our core and upwells through all the levels above into the material world, as you just experienced in the meditation. Heyoan said that the creative pulse then manifests fully in our lives as our life creations. For example, we paint a painting, write a book, build a house, make a scientific discovery, or create an organization. When we are finished, we celebrate. We have great feelings of accomplishment and say we have done it!

But Heyoan says it is here, at the apparent height of our creativity, that we must be careful about how we view our accomplishment. He says that our work of art or discovery is not the final product of our creative process. He reminds us that the purpose of life in the duality of the physical plane is to hold up a mirror to ourselves so that we might recognize our divine individuality. Our final product of art or scientific discovery or organization is really our most highly polished mirror. It is the point of highest discernment that says, "Look, see yourself reflected here in this accomplishment." It is really only the midpoint of the creative process.

The creative process or pulse of life has four phases. First is the stillness of the empty void deep within the core star. This is a point of stasis. Then comes the expansion out of the core, as the essence of who you are expresses itself through the levels of intention (haric level), personality (auric level), and into the physical world. At the height of physical expression, when we look into our highly polished mirror, we go into the next phase. It is the stasis at the end of our expansion into individualism. Here we pause for self-observation. Then soon afterward, the creative pulse of life moves back inward from the physical world into the auric, down into the haric level, and then back into the core. It is here, deep within the core, that we reach the fourth and final stage of the creative pulse of life. We again move into stasis deep in the core.

So what really is our final product of creation? Once we have had a good look in our highly polished mirror of self-discernment, we bring our creations back through the level of personality, through intentionality, and into the deeper self. As the creative force jumps back down through each dimension, each phase brings our learning with it. That learning moves from the physical world, to the psycho-noetic world of feeling-thoughts, into the noetic world of pure ideas, down into the world of intentionality, and deep into our essence. *Our final creation then is the distilled essence of our core.*

This creative process is continually occurring. We continually create more individual core essence. We are always somewhere on this creative wave in every part of our lives. I would guess we are probably on every part of the pulse all the time but in different areas of our life experience.

We are surrounded and interpenetrated by a pulsating universal wave of creation. We are of it, we are it, it is us. It flows through us, and we flow through it. There is no end and no beginning. We create it as it creates us. There is no initiator. There is only the creative wave of life that is constantly unfolding and enfolding. In its unfolding time is created. In its enfolding time is dissolved. It is what David Bohm, the renowned physicist, calls the "implicate order."

The creative wave begins with enfolded stasis, then it unfolds up and outward from the core star through the dimensions above into the physically manifest world and expands outward to the far reaches of the universe. The expansion slows, stops, and rests in stasis. It has woven the golden threads of new creation through all that there is, through all the manifest world. Here it communes with all that it has merged with. In this merger, love is created. Love remains. And then it begins the long journey of contraction. It enfolds upon itself. It returns through the four dimensions of our creative energies back into our core star, bringing all that it has learned and created back into the individual self.

Most of us do not give enough time for the stasis part of our creative wave. There are two phases in the stasis part of the creative wave: the part before expansion, when we are contracted and merged within our deepest self, and the part after expansion, when we are expanded and merged with another.

In the first, we need quiet time alone to integrate who we are with what we have created in the past. We need to be alone to meet ourselves, to be with ourselves without doing anything. This time of centering is a time of gathering power without doing anything.

For the second type of stasis, we need time to be with others in quiet, nonverbal ways, so that we can experience the wonder of the other. We can do this in many ways, such as by being in one-on-one dyads of silent interaction or in large group meditation, simply being together without having to do anything.

Most of us really like the expansive part of the creative wave. We enjoy the tremendous amount of outward-going energy, and we feel great about ourselves. We enjoy going out into the world on an adventure to learn. We think it is exciting to go to workshops, to take classes, or to paint a picture. We feel high as we look into the creative mirror that reflects ourselves as we enter into the state of expanded stasis that follows an expansion. We want to stay there forever, and we resist a change from this state.

We resist coming back down and inward. But it is important for us to remember that we need to give equal time and attention to the contraction phase of the creative pulse and the silent void of the phase of deep inner stasis that follows contraction. Many of us do not like contraction. Many of us get upset after a large expansive project and go into depression when it is finished. This is because many of us do not understand the natural contraction of the creative process, do not know how to honor and savor it to its fullest.

The phase of the creative principle in which we are enfolding or contracting back into the self is the one we resist the most because negative feelings about ourselves are usually evoked in this stage. Let me explain why.

In the phase of expansion, a great deal of energy moves through our bodies and energy system. This powerful energy begins to bring light to our dark, stagnated energy blocks, which brings life and conscious awareness back into them. As a result, they loosen and begin to move. Then we experience the energy-consciousness in them as part of the healing or enlightening process. To say it more simply, in the expansion phase we are high on our new knowledge and our new creations. But with this new knowledge we also see our faults more clearly. It's okay as long as we focus on the mirror of our new creations, but as we contract our focus turns inward. We see faults that we perhaps have not noticed before. The problem is that we begin to judge and reject ourselves for what we can now see and feel. These judgments increase our negative feelings about ourselves, and we just don't want to feel them.

Therefore, we do not want to be present on the wave as it retreats back into ourselves through the second level of our field, where our feelings about ourselves exist. So we resist the contraction. We try to stop the enfolding pulse of the wave, or we jump off it, and we interrupt the creative process. To do this, we disconnect from what we have created. We either throw it away by devaluing it, or we give it away by saying that we did it for someone else. Eventually, we even begin to believe that we did the creation for someone else, not for ourselves. It is as if we believe it is wrong to create something for our own pleasure, as if it wouldn't benefit others. This causes more pain.

The reason why many of us avoid creating is because we do not know how to complete the creative process by bringing what we created back to ourselves to honor ourselves for what we have accomplished. The process of honoring and acknowledging ourselves is the process of looking into the reflective mirror of manifestation so that we can recognize the individual divine within us. It is a very important phase of the creative process. We need to learn how to experience a contraction in a positive way.

Heyoan says:

~

Contracting is the coming in to the self, drawing yourself within to the wisdom that has been there forever. After an experience, such as a great success or even a healing, in about three days' time, perhaps sooner, you will most automatically contract. This contraction need not be a negative experience. It is one where you go within the self to recognize the self and later to find the next land, the next inner horizon, the next secret sacred room within the self. It is from this inner place that you will find a new life. If you give yourself the time and the faith after each of your expansions to move inside, to sit in silence with the self and to rerecognize who you are from a new level, then the expansion emerges most automatically. If you allow the natural flow of the contraction that brings you inward and view it from the aspect of a positive experience, you will not need to create negative experiences in your outer life that force you to go within.

Thus, by scheduling time for yourself after an expansion to go within, you will find an automatic positive flow inward. There you reach a point of silence; of sitting in the black velvet void within you that is teeming with undifferentiated life waiting to be born into manifestation. You will find this void deep within your core star. Out of that life comes a reemergence of the phoenix. It is the new self that manifests with an additional aspect of your core essence that has never been added to the self before.

~

We do not always allow the creative pulse to move through us unobstructively because we are afraid to experience it. It brings life experience and change. We are afraid of both. We block it because we still believe that life experience can be dangerous. We go into defense and move out of the moment of the now.

Recently Heyoan gave a lecture about our choice for defense and how that choice creates healing cycles in our lives. He titled it "Whom Do You Serve?"

~

WHOM DO YOU SERVE?
Channeled from
Heyoan

Center yourselves, and run through the alignment of your field: by connecting down into the earth, aligning with your life task or the hara line; by moving through each chakra and clearing it; by bringing your awareness up through all the levels of the field; and by walking yourself step by step into the core of your being. Ask yourself, "Whom do I serve? Why have I come to earth? Not only my short minute-to-minute purpose, but also my longer-term one."

From the perspective of the space/time continuum, you are creating in an apparently linear, moment-to-moment fashion. These creations follow the line of your intent. Each of your actions, each of your choices reflects whom you have chosen to serve. When you are present in the unfolding moment, you remain connected to your core energies and your core purpose. Thus your creative energies flow forth from your core unobstructed. You create pleasure and joy in your life. You serve the divine within you, your core.

When you are not present, as in defense, you are not directly connecting with the creative energies that move forth from your core star. You are not directly serving your creative core. If you choose to "protect yourself" by going into defense, then you are serving the illusion that you need a defense. Your defense takes you out of the unfolding moment. It tries to freeze time to control events to stop or prevent something from happening. The intent to stop the creative flow is called negative intent. It is the intent to forget.

We do not say this to you in a reprimanding way. Part of your life task is to learn to let go of your defense and learn to stay centered within yourself. Once you do go into your defense and create from there, since you are always creating no matter where you are, you then create lessons for yourself to learn. These lessons will, in time, automatically take you back to the core of your being. Such lessons can be seen as healing cycles.

You exist in a fail-safe system of healing or learning cycles. It is a system that you have devised. When you blame the system, you move another step away from your core purpose or divine intent. Another circle is created. The secondary circle, of course, is another healing cycle. And in your creations, you create healing cycles that can be considered to be either of primary or secondary order.

In your moment-to-moment, back-and-forth movement between positive clear intent and negative intent, you create first joy and then more healing cycles, through which you will go in your healing process. One supports the other. The more joy and pleasure in your life, the greater the foundation upon which you will rest as you go through cycles of learning and healing. The more learning you achieve, the more faith you have in your healing cycles. The more you accomplish in your life, the greater the pleasure and joy you can create. Thus your moment-to-moment process of creating your experience of life always brings you ultimately more to pleasure and joy!

I am here today to tell you that your healing cycles need not be so painful. The natural process of creation includes the expansive, contracting, and static principles. Many of the problems that you have come from not understanding the creative process and how to assist yourself as you go through it. The new cycles of lessons that lie before you will be easier if you stay with the truth of the self; that is, the truth of who you are in the moment, what you are capable of doing in that moment, and what is right for you to do in that moment.

Beneath your inability to stay with yourself in each moment lies a distrust. But you resist contraction, assuming that it is going to be painful.

Consider the possibility that a contraction is defined as going inside or enfolding to bring all of the treasures from the world that you have touched while you were in your expanded state to your inner self. In contraction, you bring those gifts down and place them on your inner altar for self-acknowledgment of what you have accomplished.

Contraction is sitting in those gifts, sitting in those learnings and bringing them to the inner child. It is laying them on the altar of the inner child that was wounded long ago and saying, "Here, look what I brought you from the outer world." Just as an adult, a mother or father, brings gifts to a child, a contraction brings gifts to the inner child. One of the great traditions in this culture is that when parents go on a trip, they bring a gift home to the child. That gift is not only for their own physical child but for their inner child. Many times their child inside enjoys that gift as much as the physical child and indeed sometimes more, as you have undoubtedly experienced. So bring these gifts to the inner self.

If you are in a contractive phase because you have just had a powerful expansive life experience or deep learning, then allow yourself to be taught from the contraction. If you are experiencing pain, then allow that to be the teacher. Do not hide, do not force yourself into a defense that will cause you to hide. If you must do a job, then do it from that place. If you are a teacher, then teach from that place. If you hide, your work will not express your essence. It will not be full. By allowing yourself to be undefended while you work, you will move to a state of pleasure.

Now what I am asking you to do is indeed very difficult. I am, in a sense, asking you not to do what you have always done to make yourself feel safe when you do not feel safe. I understand this and say it with full compassion. We are here for you, with you. We move with you at the boundary of your creative wave. And as you may have experienced during a healing session, when your healer is with you moment to moment at the boundary of your creative wave, the pain is not so great. It simply becomes a wave of life that is expressing itself.

So when I ask, "Whom do you serve?" consider that who you serve is the God or Goddess within you. That the source you are serving is the core star, the expression of the true individuality of God. And that if you question what to do next, or where to go or what to say, then move to the center of your being. If you encounter the inner wounded child, as you move to your core star, take it up into your arms and take it with you.

Allow that core star to expand within. If that means that you need a few moments before you speak to answer a question or follow through with an activity, then take the time because that is how you can be in your truth no matter what is going on on the outer level [in the outer world]. Simply say, "I need time right now. I need to catch up with myself and find the edge of my wave. When I find it, then I can commune with you. But before so, I am not even in communion with myself. How can I commune with you?"

When you are in the moment, being with yourself, with your wave, you are most perfect and most synchronized with the world. If you wonder why certain days flow effortlessly, it is because you are in synchronicity with your creative expanding, resting, contracting, resting creative wave. And of course, when you are with yourself, you are with the universe, with all that there is, with the divine that is manifest in the physical as well as the spiritual. That is your most natural form. That is who you are. That is who we are. For we are a part of you, as you are a part of us.

As you descended into the plane of the earth that carries both joy and sorrow, you forgot these truths I have spoken. You split into duality, leaving your guide in the spirit world. We the guides can be considered to be that which you will become and that which you already are. Yet you are more. So if you hold your personal guide in high esteem, realize that he or she is you. The portion of you that is incarnated carries a bit more forgetting than that which is manifested within the guide. That is the only difference between us. And we are always here to remind you and to bring you into synchronicity. That is the nature of what this work is about. It is a gift that you bring to the earth and the gift that we bring to you.

So as you move through your healing process, walk with yourself. We walk next to you, close to you, within you. Move through the creative way that is you. You will be most delighted with what the creative force within you has for you.

Self-Healing by Being on the Pulse of the Creative Wave

Healing and remaining healthy means becoming consciously aware of and staying on our creative wave. It means being present in the unfolding moment. It means being who we are in each moment of time. We can consciously follow the life pulse as it moves up through our four dimensions of creative energy. We can be with it in each moment as it moves through our auric field, level by level.

To bring this chapter to a close, I would like to share with you a meditation that Heyoan gave toward the end of the 1989–90 training program. It is a meditation to keep your conscious awareness firmly placed upon your creative wave as it moves through you. It brings you to the center of yourself, which is alive, creative, and free. In it, you become the pulse of life.

~

THE UNFOLDING SELF
Channeled from
Heyoan

Listen to the internal music that plays who you are. Feel the light welling up within you, within every cell of your body. Connect down into the ground and connect with your purpose in being here. What is the task that is set before you in this very moment? What have you come for, and what is there to learn in this very moment of your unfolding? Rather than thinking of what must be next, bring yourself to the unfolding moment within you and sit sweetly within every cell of your body—not who you wish to be, but who you are in this moment.

As you move through your expansion, then stasis/communion, and then pull down into the self in contraction, ride the wave all the way in. You will find a layer of pain, but simply ride through it to the child. As you take the child in hand, go deeper to the core of your being, to your individuality, and move deep inside this core into the great void within the self. Experience this great void, for it represents your potential. Within this void all of life is pulsing, vibrating, full, yet unborn. Here is great peace. Sit in grace within this inner void. This void is not empty, although it may appear that way from the personality level. The more one enters into this void within the self, the more life one finds. Simply surrender to the safety and to the grace of this inner center, letting go of all attachments.

When there is movement out of seemingly nothing, simply ride the expansion of the pulse of life that comes outward, filling the space with manifest life, filling the space with understanding. As you go upward and outward, you will feel this life pulse moving through the levels of your auric field. There will be a level where the mind begins again. If you continue through, you will move onward and outward through all the levels of your field and all the personal experience within each level. You are experiencing life manifesting. You are experiencing the creative process. This expansion continues outward indefinitely. Allow your conscious awareness to ride this pulse as far out as it is able. Know that this pulse goes to the far reaches of the universe. It is only your images that limit you. Bring your conscious awareness to this process. As you expand, reach in a 360-degree sphere outward as far as you will go. Expand, reaching through the infinite universe. There, there will be communion with all that is outside or apparently outside. This is where fusion takes place. Sit in it. Then once again, as your creative wave enfolds, simply follow it back in.

This expansion and contraction takes place every moment. It is a multifold expansion/stasis and contraction/stasis pulse. There are fast pulses and slow pulses. There are pulses of which you will never be able to be aware with the conscious mind, for they are inconceivable.

And so as you travel inward again, once again you will move through the levels of the field. As what you have learned is brought back through all the levels of your field and thus your personality, the new gifts bring light into your individuality. As that light comes in through your field, those portions of your being that are stagnated within your negative image are enlightened. When the light first touches the forgetting, many times you experience pain. For it evokes memories. It evokes energy and consciousness that have not been clear. In the beginning of the process, as you go in through the emotional levels of the field, you will feel your emotional pain. Do not stop the movement. Continue to bring the light in and lace it through all of these disappointments; through the fears, through the sadness, through the grief, through the mourning that you have experienced in your life.

If you continue on the inward pulse down, bringing light and the understanding that you are one with all that there is, you become one with the pain. You are one with the individuals that are involved in this pain. And thus, in the fusion of the duality that apparently exists between you and those involved in a painful incident in your life, love is born. For what is touched with light will create love. For communion creates love. As you go deeper through the pain and the fear, the very process of this communion creates love. It is brought down into the inner child and placed at the feet of the child, and that love touches the original wound of the child and it is healed. It continues down into the core star, the essence of who you are. Once again you sit in the void, having brought more light to the inner light. Simply sit in the mother in grace. With this grace, you are in communion with the great mother, and again love is born.

Later the movement outward begins. The child having been nourished to fullness now moves away as its inner cup runneth over. Having been born out of love, it moves into its own, feels its individual self and its body. It likes and loves what it feels. It has more love for itself. It understands itself and thus has its value. Being valuable, it feels its love for others and continues outward. This love for others evokes their love. The child receives the love and validation back from others. Loving validation brings courage as the child's conscious awareness expands through divine will. It feels its wholeness and its divinity and enters into spiritual ecstasy. Entering spiritual ecstasy, the child is brought through to perceive the perfect pattern and the knowledge of the divine mind. It moves outward through the far reaches of the universe, out to that which has been called the father, once again approaching fusion. Your inner self moves through the manifest universe, creating more life as you go, bringing the gifts that the individual self has manifested to the universe.

This is the creative process. It dissolves dualism. Thus, you create your world around you: through the expansion, stasis, and communion with the universe around you; and the contraction, stasis, and communion with your interior individuality. It is you—
The Unfolding Self.

~

CONCLUSION

We have spoken much of creating your own reality and its connection with your health and well-being in this book. We have explained how creative energy originates in our creative core and that the impulse to create originates in pleasure. We have discussed the route that creative waves of energies take as they emerge from our core on their way into the physical world. We have shown that when this creative energy emerges into the physical world in a pure, unobstructed way, it creates health, happiness, joy, and fulfillment in our lives. When it is interrupted, blocked, or distorted, the result is negative experience and illness. Illness is a result of blocking the creative force. *Illness is blocked creativity.*

Each negative experience is a life lesson designed to bring us into our truth. Each negative life experience can be seen as a healing cycle that takes us into deep levels of the self that we have forgotten for a long time.

Creative energy from the core automatically wells up directly and creates more pleasure in our lives, or it is diverted and creates a healing cycle. It is one or the other: Either we are fully expressing our core essence in joy and pleasure, or we are in a healing cycle that brings about more conscious awareness of ourselves, which eventually, in a roundabout way, also allows more expression of our core essence, which then creates more

joy and pleasure in our lives. This is the new paradigm for the nineties.

On the spiritual level, our choice in the moment is the choice between love and fear. And we make it each moment of our lives, whether or not we are consciously aware of it. It is the choice between being undefended or defended, of being connected and individual or disconnected and separate. The choice for love is to let our core essence shine forth. If we can't make that choice in the moment, then the next choice for love is to accept our human condition as it is and to work through another healing cycle or life lesson and gain more self-awareness.

There are no judgments on which we choose. A healing cycle or life lesson is an honorable choice. Our choice to be in the physical world is a choice to go through healing cycles. It takes courage to be here. We are honorable and brave to choose to be here. Heyoan says that the only reason we are here is that every moment we make the choice to be here. No outer god is making us be here, no old karma is forcing us to be here. We have chosen this human condition. Part of the human condition is that we are unable in our state of evolution to always choose to express our core essence. We don't know how to do so yet. We haven't yet learned eternal love, but we are sure working at it and doing pretty well. We have decided the trip is worth it, so we are here. We all have hope for and desire self-improvement. We are all here to learn who we are, both on the most microscopic as well as the macroscopic level.

Thus allowing the *light to emerge* from the source of the core star is the healing process. The more you let your true essence shine through every cell of your being, through every cell of your body, the healthier and happier you will be.

Healing Session with Richard W.

To illustrate what a healing is like, I have chosen a healing session I gave to a physician whom I shall call Richard W. I usually have patients fill in an intake form and do an intake interview. Since Richard was curious about my work, he didn't give me any intake information at all. It was sort of a test on his part to see if HSP and healing are informative and helpful. He was satisfied by the healing and gave the transcript to his own physician, George Sarant, M.D. Dr. Sarant has written a letter comparing medical test reports and medical diagnoses to the information read with HSP during the healing session. His letter follows this transcript.

Transcript of Healing Session with Patient Richard W.

(*Richard W. and Barbara are seated in chairs facing each other about six feet apart.*)

BARBARA: You need a lot more strengthening in your lower half, in the first chakra and in the pelvic area. And the sugar metabolism is off a little; the thyroid is underfunctioning and probably could use some cleansing in the liver. Something's going on in terms of your assimilation of nutrients in the small intestine. It's not as efficient as it ought to be. Do you have trouble with constipation?

RICHARD W.: No.

BARBARA: Your coccyx needs to be a little more flexible. You know, the occiput and the coccyx move when you breathe. That's partly why there's a little less strength in your lower half than there could be. I'm sure you've dealt with it in terms of your character structure too. [Character structure is a term from bio-energetic therapy that relates the body's physical structure to the person's psychological makeup.] But the weakness is caused partly by the coccyx—it's not flexible enough. I'll work on that. The fifth chakra and the first chakra would be the ones affected primarily by the characterology of masochism. I want to work primarily on [the problem in] the third chakra, which I realize is a result of your childhood experience. In terms of psychodynamics, it is related to how you connect to people. There are some old issues in the third chakra relating to your mother and father that make this area the weakest area of your body.

Now, I think it wouldn't be hard for you to learn to see into the body. Your third eye is pretty open—you've got a lot of energy there. Have you tried? Did you see anything?

RICHARD W.: Just a faint outline. That's all. And sometimes I see things, and I'm not sure if it's real or not.

BARBARA: What you do with that issue of whether you saw it in a textbook or whether it's in the body is to look for anomalies that wouldn't show in the textbook. You've probably done autopsies. You have to separate that out too. But what you'll do when you keep looking in the body is that eventually you are going to find things that you didn't see before, and that's going to help you.

I don't know if this is normal or not, but the right side of your thyroid is a little smaller than the left. Do you mind removing your tie? It's a little hard to look. I'm looking to see if there's any physiological stuff going on in your heart.

So what are you doing about stress? Do you work long hours?

RICHARD W.: Nothing per se. Do you see anything physiological?

BARBARA: I don't right now. I'll go in deeper. . . . I do see you've been under stress. (*Pause; examining heart with HSP; still sitting six feet away facing him.*) When I look at the heart, the problem is actually on that side, in the back. (*Referring to the lower right back wall of the heart.*) That part on the back looks a little . . . the muscles look like they're harder. I'll find better words later. (*At this point holding back information, not wanting to disturb him.*)

(*Richard W. gets on the table, and Barbara starts to work. Some time passes.*)

BARBARA: I'll talk a little about what I'm doing right now. This is stuff that's not in my book. I'm going to work on something that I found that's deeper than the auric field. It's called the haric level. Martial arts people use it. You know about it. I'm going to go in and strengthen the point called the tan tien.

Just for your information, the reason I asked you about the constipation is, I think there's something going on with the fluid balance in your body.

So from the psychic point of view, when I do a hara healing, what happens is the whole lower half [of the body] starts letting go, in a sense kind of melting and reforming itself. So the sacroiliac joint on the right is out of alignment, and I'm working on it. The forward aspect of that joint is jammed together. . . .

(*Time passes.*)

What I'm doing now is, there is an acupuncture line, a meridian up here, that goes all the way right up into there, and I'm trying to energize it. . . . And I'm working into the ligaments, right in this area. Now the second chakra is beginning to get charged.

I've restructured the first chakra on the gold level of the field, which is the auric seventh layer. The first chakra goes right up to the coccyx and sits in the coccyx-sacral joint. There was a lack of energy there;

that continues up toward the right side of the sacroiliac joint, and that continues all the way up the body.

(*Time passes.*)

Where I am right now, from my perspective, is the gall bladder. . . . And now I'm moving into the third chakra area. Actually, the liver doesn't look bad; it looks a lot cleaner than I thought. There's one area back underneath here, the inside of the back of the liver is stagnated. . . .

What I am actually doing right now is trying to make the gall bladder dump some of the stuff that it's carrying. On the auric level, it's let go. But that doesn't necessarily mean on the physical level that it's let go. What I'm hearing is that it will respond overnight. I don't normally give a running explanation, but I'm going to do that since you are a physician.

I'm on the third chakra, working on the fourth level of the aura.

Do you have a brother? Somebody you were real close to when you were about twelve? Did he die or something happen? Fell out of a tree? Some sort of loss is involved. This is where it's left, or stuck, in your body. Sure feels like a brother. So the way that brother trauma is in your third chakra is in the form of a vortex here, that is kind of strung out and hung down. This is interesting. I've seen this auric configuration a couple of times, and it's always associated with overweight. (*Richard W. is overweight.*) But just now, when I first saw it connected with this friend or brother, that's new. Psychologically that's connected to Father. (*Refers to the right side of the solar plexus chakra.*) Then there's all this stuff with your mother here (*left side of the solar plexus chakra*). From what I can see, the relationship with your father was a lot healthier than the one with your mother. There is more left here [in the auric field] to deal with.

So what I am doing here is kind of lightly bringing this whole area back together. The third chakra has been torn in this area, near the pancreas area.

RICHARD W.: Is that the mother stuff?

BARBARA: Yes. I'm just beginning to move into this area [with healing energy] to knit it back together. If I work on it longer, I'll go deeper and deeper. I'm just kind of bringing it back, just the beginning of the knitting on the first level of the auric field. You might feel that it's kind of knitting through the whole thing. Just strengthening the whole area.

(*Time passes. Barbara is toning healing sounds into the solar plexus pancreas area.*)

Now it's affecting the second layer more, a lightening, actually kind of like a sweetening.

(*Barbara completes healing in silence and leaves. Richard W. rests about fifteen to twenty minutes. Then Barbara returns to discuss healing. Usually, healings are not so thoroughly discussed afterward. It is important for the patient to rest. In this case, since Richard W. is a physician, a longer, more detailed discussion takes place.*)

BARBARA: Okay, with the restructuring of the third chakra and the reactivation of those energies of the system, you will feel relief in the area of the heart chakra. The heart chakra was trying to do the work of two chakras.

RICHARD W.: Do you see anything around my heart chakra?

BARBARA: Yes, there are a few things that I haven't said. The weakness in the pancreas was affecting the left kidney. All of the organs have deep pulses that are all synchronized in health. [In dis-ease they are not synchronized.] Last month, a student and I were working on someone who had a liver transplant; we had to repulse all the organs back together. Because of your pancreas being off, it had to be repulsed with the liver, then with the kidney. It was almost as if energetically the kidney were stuck, pulled up and stuck, obviously not physically, onto the pancreas. And when I was working in there, I pulled it back.

There is stagnation in the heart. It was as if this side [left] of the heart had more energy than this side, but the primary cause isn't the heart. It's the weakness in the lower chakras so you overcompensate with the heart. And I kept hearing Heyóan saying, "When you connect with your patients, you need to begin focusing on the hara and the lower chakras." The reason there's a weakness and clogging that was deep in the heart was because this chakra [third chakra] is torn open. It was overcompensating by running energy through here. Remember that acupuncture line I said runs up through here?

Now there was less energy in the heart on the right side than on the left. So I moved it [the energy] over. So it wouldn't surprise me if you felt stagnation here. The other thing is, if you're worried about any arrhythmia, the cause is from the third chakra area rather than all the traditional things. I know that's not traditional. But of course I can watch all that stuff too, cholesterol and fats and all that kind of stuff. So there are some of those.

But the heart itself, when supported by the lower organs and the metabolism in the body and the lower chakras, will be fine. So my recommendation of what you need to do is to really strengthen in here [in your lower half]. Now this [chakras three and four] is all restructured, so you will feel different there. And I've put a lot of power into the hara, tan tien, and I worked on the coccyx. So [stay] down in your legs, and when you are in the hospital [working], really feel the hara and connect here. Instead of just connecting here [the heart and solar plexus areas] with the patients, make the hara strong. It is okay to use these chakras [the heart and solar plexus], but put a cap over these chakras, the third chakra and the fourth. Just imagine a little cap protecting you. And that's about it.

Do you have any other questions you want to ask me?

RICHARD W.: So my structure—I'm top heavy?

BARBARA: Characterologically? Yes, masochistic psychopathy.

RICHARD W.: And it's not flowing? There's upward displacement and energy trapped in the torso?

BARBARA: Yes.

RICHARD W.: Physically, I had a heart attack two years ago. What did you mean when you said the heart was doing the work of two?

BARBARA: Both chakras. The heart chakra was also doing the work of the third chakra. Remember I said those muscles [on the back of the heart] were—it was almost as if the word were *old*. I didn't want to say it because it was a pretty negative statement. But it was almost as if those muscles—you know how when people get old, they lose the connective tissue in the muscles, like it's stringy and hard? That's what the muscles on the lower right chamber of the heart look like on the back, like cardboard. I don't know if that correlates with anything.

RICHARD W.: Scar tissue.

BARBARA: That's what it is.

RICHARD W.: Because [the cardiologist told me that] the interior wall of my heart doesn't move well. It's hard. Scar tissue, dead heart muscle.

BARBARA: Just on that side or the whole heart? Because the top part looks a lot better.

RICHARD W.: The bottom part, the interior wall of the right atrium is stiff because . . .

BARBARA: I'm seeing it on the back on the right.

RICHARD W.: (*Points to the rear of the heart, correlating to the area Barbara was viewing.*) That's the scar tissue, so it doesn't contract vigorously. But [you say] the problem then is really lower.

BARBARA: The cause is, [it's] the weakness in here [solar plexus], the problem with the sugar metabolism, this whole chakra being torn out, and then you're not going down to really rest in your power which is down here [tan tien]. So something like tai chi would be really good for you because that would redistribute the power. What's not good for you is connecting to your patients too much through the heart. That's not good because it's already overworked because of the weakness [below], the way I see it.

So two years ago you had a heart attack?

RICHARD W.: I had surgery.

BARBARA: You had surgery? I missed that. Did you have a bypass? Well, you know what I saw? It was funny—it was almost as if your whole aorta were pushed over this way [to the right] too far, and I pushed it back. [On the energy level.] All the energy along the aorta, I pushed back to the left. I guess they moved it during surgery.

RICHARD W.: They probably did.

BARBARA: That's why there's such a difference in the right and left side here [in the heart area].

Many times surgery will move the organs out of their places held in the field structure. If the organs are not properly placed within this matrix-structure, they will not receive the life energy they need to function properly. This causes later dysfunction of the organs, since the energy bodies serve as an energetic matrix-structure in which the cells and organs are nourished and grow. So whenever anyone has had surgery, it is necessary to reset the physical organs into their energetic organs and realign the energy bodies with the physical body. That is what I did with this patient's aorta.

Unfortunately, at the time I gave the healing to Richard W., I was just closing my practice in order to have time for teaching and writing, and I did not see him again. It would be interesting to know how he would have progressed if the healings had continued.

I asked Dr. Sarant to write a letter giving medical information about Richard W. that could be compared with the reading. Here it is.

Letter from George Sarant, M.D., Commenting on Richard W.'s Healing Session

In the past, the relationship between healers and physicians has not been particularly fruitful or productive, and the history of the relationship between organized medicine and unorthodox healing systems has been even worse. I recall, as a medical student, the derisive and belittling remarks made by teachers and classmates about healers and other health systems. I think, how-ever, that traditional attitudes are beginning to soften. We are finding physicians who refer patients to alternative health workers and healers, and some physicians who become healers themselves. In this context, certainly the names of Norm Shealy, M.D., Bernie Siegel, M.D., and Brugh Joy, M.D. (among many others) come to mind.

I sent my patient Richard W. to see Barbara Brennan for several reasons. Richard W., himself a physician, has a great interest, as I do, in healers and healing that are unorthodox. Richard W.'s history is that, at the age of thirty-seven, he suffered from a huge inferior wall myo-cardial infarction [that is, a heart attack] and underwent coronary artery bypass surgery. He also infarcted and had considerable damage to his right atrium [the significance of which shows in the reading above]. Richard W.'s father had, himself, died at the age of thirty-eight, and at the time of Richard W.'s disease, he certainly suffered from a feeling of hopelessness, as if there were no way out of the emotional and situational morass in which he felt himself. He was interested in getting different perspectives on his disease.

We decided that the best tack in going to see Barbara would be to tell her nothing a priori and see what she came up with. Her reading was truly incredible and rather awesome. While she didn't come out and say, "Aha! I see you've had a heart attack," her reading revealed a valuable and rather incredible description of a myocardium that had been damaged by ischemia; that is, she described a heart that had suffered from a coronary attack. She describes a stagnation in the heart . . . and a weakness and clogging that was deep in [the] heart. . . . Very interesting is her comment that . . . [the left] side of the heart had more energy than this [the right] side. . . . For in fact, Richard W. suffered muscle damage to both left and right ventricles but also to the right atrium. The right atrium was the most damaged, and it is probably this that Barbara saw ("stringy and hard . . . the muscles on the lower right chamber of the heart"). Anatomically, if you look at the posterior of the heart, it is mostly made up of right atrium and ventricle. If you could see through someone's back and look at the heart, you would be looking at mostly right atrium and ventricle; and this stringy and hard part of Richard W.'s heart was his (damaged) right atrium and ventricle. It is impossible for Barbara to have known this except via her ability to see inside the body.

Other aspects of the reading are no less impressive: Barbara states emphatically that his "sugar metabolism is off a little," which, interestingly enough, did not become a clinical problem until almost two years after the reading. Richard W. does now, in fact, have type II diabetes mellitus. It is interesting to speculate that this delay in apparent clinical disease was perhaps secondary to some manipulations in his energy field. Unbeknownst to Richard W. at the time, he in fact does also have some biochemical evidence of slight hepatic dysfunction. His liver function tests are slightly to moderately elevated, confirming Barbara's statement ("could use some cleansing in the liver"). Her comments about the thyroid gland being underfunctioning could not be substantiated; his thyroid function tests have remained biochemically normal.

Other parts of the reading were functionally correct while formally incorrect. It is interesting to compare some of Barbara's reading with dreams, or with people who telepathically receive information. They are sometimes almost right. That is, while the overall validity of the reporting is undoubtedly correct, there are instances of slight exceptions.

Thus, it wasn't Richard W.'s brother who died when Richard W. was twelve; it was his father who died when Richard W. was nine. But Richard W. admits that his relationship with his father was like two brothers. It seems to me that some more work and research needs to be done on specific parts of some readings. While Barbara was completely correct in seeing and describing the anatomical and physiological abnormalities in Richard W.'s right atrium and ventricle, she made no specific comments about his left ventricle. Could this be because the left ventricle is tucked more laterally in the chest and thus one doesn't have as ready access to it? Some questions to ponder.

Bioenergetically, Richard W. certainly has a tight and spastic diaphragm—that is, he has a rather severe diaphragmatic block that Barbara certainly picked up on and expounded on at some length. It is interesting that she notes a heart stagnation, which she attributes to this block.

I believe physicians can best utilize the services of healers by keeping an open mind and remembering that physicians certainly aren't the holders of the first nor last word on illness and disease. We need to show some humility and to keep an open mind.

Richard W. had some interesting comments on the reading: He found himself incredibly and deeply moved by the experience, yet he could not consciously determine why or what it was about the reading that was so moving. And he told me that several hours after the reading, he became extremely tired and had to take an hour or so nap. He compared it to the fatigue he experienced after acupuncture treatment.

I certainly hope that there will be many more joint consultations between physicians and healers. Each can benefit greatly from such joint ventures.

Types of Health-Care Professionals

Holistic Physicians (M.D.)

What they do: Holistic physicians are medical doctors who practice some type of natural therapy, such as homeopathy, acupuncture, nutrition, or other specialty. Holistic physicians assume that all aspects of life create and comprise a total state of health. They analyze nutritional, emotional, environmental, spiritual, and life-style values of the client to treat the individual rather than the disease. The treatment usually consists of several procedures, each appropriate to a different aspect of the client's life. The goal is to achieve a fuller, more unified sense of well-being. A holistic physician forms a cooperative relationship with the client and assists him or her in the process of self-healing. The client learns that self-responsibility for health plays an essential role in the healing process.

National Organization

American Holistic Medical Association (AHMA)
4101 Lake Boone Trail
Suite 201
Raleigh, NC 27606
(919) 787-5181

Naturopathic Doctors (N.D.)

What they do: The scope of a naturopathic doctor's practice includes all aspects of family care from natural childbirth through geriatrics. Naturopathic doctors are licensed in a number of states and several Canadian provinces. These physicians are trained in natural medicine. Training involves four years of postgraduate study, including two years of medical sciences and a diversity of natural therapies. The therapies studied include herbal medicine, hydrotherapy and manipulation, with specialty areas of natural childbirth, homeopathy, and acupuncture.

National Organization

The American Association of Naturopathic Physicians (AANP)
P.O. Box 20386
Seattle, WA 98102
(206) 323-7610

Osteopathic Doctors (D.O.)

What they do: This discipline was begun by Andrew Still in the late 1800s to teach bone manipulation to promote natural healing. Osteopathy helps the body to stimulate and restore its own immune system and is very effective in treating many autoimmune disorders such as arthritis. These doctors use a system of healing that emphasizes realignment of the body through manipulation to correct faulty structure and function. They specialize in manipulating muscles and joints to treat problems. Doctors of osteopathy are fully trained and licensed according to the same standards as MDs and receive additional extensive training in the body's structure and function.

National Organization

American Osteopathic Association (AOA)
142 East Ontario Street
Chicago, IL 60611
(312) 280-5800

Doctors of Chiropractic (D.C.)

What they do: Doctors of chiropractic specialize in the manipulation and adjustment of the spinal column. This discipline was begun in 1895 by Daniel Palmer and is based on the theory of spinal subluxation to support natural health. Chiropractors analyze and correct vertebral spinal nerve interferences, which can be the result of physical trauma, interference during birth process, mental stress, faulty nutrition, or poor posture.

National Organization

The American Chiropractor Association (ACA)
1701 Clarendon Boulevard
Arlington, VA 22209
(703) 276-8800

Nutritionists

What they do: Nutritionists use diet as therapy. They determine a patient's individual nutritional requirements as well as whether he or she has food allergies. Nutritionists then provide specific dietary guidelines and food supplements, such as vitamins and minerals, to be taken at regular intervals over a long period of time in the maintenance of health and treatment of disease. Many common conditions can be treated effectively by dietary measures.

National Organization

The American Dietetic Association (ADA)
216 West Jackson Boulevard
Suite 800
Chicago, IL 60606
(312) 899-0040

Homeopaths

What they do: Homeopathy was begun in Germany by Samuel Hahnemann (1755–1845) and established as a major natural health-care force in the 1800s in America. It is a natural pharmaceutical science that utilizes substances from the plant, mineral, and animal kingdoms and is based on the premise that these naturally occurring substances can cure disease symptoms similar to those they produce if taken in overdose. Each medicine is individually prescribed according to how it stimulates the immune and defense systems of the sick person. Sometimes it is called the "royal medicine."

National Organization

National Center for Homeopathy
801 North Fairfax Street
Suite 306
Alexandria, VA 22314
(704) 548-7790

Acupuncturists

What they do: Acupuncture is considered by the Chinese to be a form of health maintenance that stimulates the body's ability to sustain and balance itself. It is based on the theory that an electromagnetic life-force is channeled in its continuous flow throughout the body by a network of "meridians." Needles are inserted at specific points along the meridians to stimulate or disperse the flow of life-force in order to correct an imbalance. Acupuncture treatment does not employ a standardized system of correlations between particular diseases and techniques but treats each individual as unique.

National Organization

American Association of Acupuncture and Oriental Medicine (AAAOM)
4101 Lake Boone Trail
Suite 201
Raleigh, NC 27607
(919) 787-5181

Structural Bodyworkers

What they do: They use a technique of stretching and moving the connective tissue (fascia) in order to lengthen and balance the body along its natural vertical axis. Distortions of the connective tissue may be caused by reaction and compensation due to accidents, emotional tension, past traumas, or patterns of movement influenced by early childhood conditions. A complete treatment consists of ten sessions progressing from superficial areas of constriction to overall reorganization of larger body segments.

National Organization

The Rolf Institute
P.O. Box 1868
Boulder, CO 80306
(800) 530-8875

Massage Therapists

What they do: Massage therapy has been used since the time of Hippocrates in the fourth century B.C. The basic philosophy of massage is to manipulate soft tissues to enhance the body's tendency to heal itself. It consists of physical methods that include applying fixed or movable pressure, holding and moving parts of the body.

National Organizations

Associated Professional Massage Therapists and Bodyworkers (APMT)
1746 Cole Boulevard
Suite 225
Golden, CO 80401
(303) 674-8478

Second office:
P.O. Box 1869
Evergreen, CO 80439-1869

American Massage Therapy Association (AMTA)
1130 West North Shore Avenue
Chicago, IL 60626-4670
(312) 761-2682

Psychotherapists

What they do: Psychotherapists work with clients' emotional makeup, as disturbed by childhood trauma and other causes. Some deal with such problems in relation to the mind-body connection. They are known as body psychotherapists.

National Organizations

Association for Humanistic Psychology (AHP)
1772 Vallejo
Suite 3
San Francisco, CA 94123
(415) 346-7929

American Psychological Association
1200 17th Street, N.W.
Washington, DC 20036
(202) 955-7600

C.G. Jung Foundation for Analytical Psychology
28 East 39th Street
New York, NY 10016
(212) 697-6430

Institutes That Train Body Psychotherapists

International Institute for Bioenergetic Analysis
144 East 36th Street
New York, NY 10016
(212) 532-7742

Institute of Core Energetics
115 East 23rd Street
12th floor
New York, NY 10010
(212) 505-6767

Healers

What they do: As explained in this book, healers work either by touching or by not touching the body to balance and charge the auric field. They channel healing energy into clients to bring about either full or partial healing to any part of the body.

National Organization

National Federation of Spiritual Healers
1137 Silent Harbor
P.O. Box 2022
Mount Pleasant, SC 29465
(803) 849-1529

To find a healer, contact the Barbara Brennan School of Healing to receive a list of graduates.

The Barbara Brennan
School of Healing

The Barbara Brennan School of Healing is a specialized and highly respected educational institution dedicated to the exploration and enrichment of healing science. Established in 1982, the Barbara Brennan School of Healing has attracted students of all professions and backgrounds from throughout the world to pursue studies in healing science. There are two components to the school:

Introduction to Healing Science
Through workshops, lectures, seminars, and healing events, students begin to delve into the intricacies of healing science, examine the principles of healing, and explore the myriad aspects of the human experience that are woven into the healing process.

The Certified Healing Science Program
This college-level training leads to the practice of professional healing science. Education extends over a four-year period of classroom training supplemented by home study and includes both written and practicum examinations. Teacher training is an additional two years. Continuing education credit for nurses, massage therapists, and acupuncturists is also offered. Joint enrollment in a certified alternate university allows students to use their study as the major portion of their masters or doctoral degree work.

The training includes the study of the human energy field (HEF), or aura, both from the scientific point of view and from that of clinical observations by healers. It teaches the anatomy and physiology of the HEF; psychodynamics of the HEF, including energy blocks and defense systems as manifested in the HEF; the development of Higher Sense Perception to perceive the aura and gain information about the cause of illness; channeling spiritual guidance; hara healing; core star healing; and a variety of other healing techniques. It explores individual issues through deep personal process work directed toward uncovering the unique healer within. Five-day classes are held five times a year on Long Island, New York.

For more information, write, FAX, or phone:

The Barbara Brennan School of Healing
P.O. Box 2005
East Hampton, NY 11937
Phone 0-700-HEALERS   FAX 0-700-INLIGHT
If you are calling from a phone that is not on the AT&T network: Dial 10 + ATT + 0 + 700 + the number. Follow prompts.

BIBLIOGRAPHY

Altman, Nathaniel. *Everybody's Guide to Chiropractic Health Care*. Los Angeles, CA: J. P. Tarcher, 1990.

Angel, Jack E. *Physician's Desk Reference*. Montvale, NJ: Medical Economics Company, 1983.

Aranya, Swami Hariharananda. *Yoga Philosophy of Patanjali*. Albany, NY: State University of New York Press, 1983.

Artley, Malvin N. Jr. *Bodies of Fire, Vol. 1: A Thousand Points of Light*. Jersey City Heights, NJ: University of the Seven Rays Publishing House, 1992.

Becker, Robert O. *Cross Currents: The Promise of Electromedicine*. Los Angeles, CA: J. P. Tarcher, 1990.

Becker, Robert O. and Selden Gary. *The Body Electric: Electromagnetism and the Foundation of Life*. New York: William Morrow & Co., 1985.

Berkeley Holistic Health Center Staff. *The Holistic Health Lifebook*. Berkeley, CA: And-Or Press, 1981.

Berkow, Robert. *The Merck Manual of Diagnosis and Therapy*. West Point, PA: Merck Sharp & Dohme International, 1982.

Bohm, David and David F. Peat. *Science, Order, and Creativity*. New York: Bantam, 1987.

Bohm, David. *Wholeness and the Implicate Order*. New York: Routledge Chapman & Hall, 1983.

Brewster, Letitia and Michael F. Jacobson. *The Changing American Diet: A Chronicle of American Eating Habits from 1910–1980*. Washington, DC: Centers for Science in the Public Interest, 1993.

Bruyere, Rosalyn L. *Wheels of Light: A Study of the Chakras*. Arcadia, CA: Bon Productions, 1989.

Burnham, Sophy. *A Book of Angels*. New York: Random House, 1990.

Burr, Harold Saxton. *Blueprint for Immortality: The Electric Patterns of Life*. Essex, England: The C.W. Daniel Company, Ltd., 1972.

Burt, Bernard. *Fodor's Healthy Escapes*. New York: McKay, 1991.

Campbell, Don, ed. *Music Physician for Times to Come*. Wheaton, IL: Quest Books, 1991.

Cousens, Gabriel. *Conscious Eating*. Coos Bay, OR: Vision Books, 1992.

Cummings, Stephen and Dana Ullman. *Everybody's Guide to Homeopathic Medicines*. Los Angeles, CA: J. P. Tarcher, 1984.

Diamond, Harvey and Marilyn. *Fit For Life*. New York: Warner Books, 1985.

Dunne, Lavon J. *The Bestselling Guide to Better Eating for Better Health*. New York: McGraw-Hill, 1990.

Durkheim, Karlfried. *Hara: The Vital Center of Man*. New York: Samuel Weiser, 1975.

Eisenberg, David. *Encounters with Qi: Exploring Chinese Medicine*. New York: Viking Penguin, 1987.

Epstein, Gerald. *Healing Visualizations: Creating Health Through Imagery*. New York: Bantam, 1989.

Estella, Mary. *Natural Foods Cookbook*. New York: Japan Publications, 1985.

Evans, John. *Mind, Body and Electromagnetism*. Dorset, England: Element Books, 1986.

Fremantle, Francesca, and Chogyam Trungpa. *The Tibetan Book of the Dead*. Boston: Shambhala, 1975.

Gach, Michael Reed. *Acu-Yoga*. New York: Japan Publications, 1981.

Gawain, Shakti. *Living in the Light*. San Rafael, CA: New World Library, 1986.

Gerber, Richard. *Vibrational Medicine*. Santa Fe, NM: Bear & Co., 1988.

Goldman, Jonathan. *Healing Sounds: The Power of Harmonics*. Rockport, MA: Element, Inc., 1992.

Goldstrich, Joe D. *The Best Chance Diet*. Atlanta, GA: Humanics, 1982.

Gottschall, Elaine. *Food and the Gut Reaction: Intestinal Health Through Diet*. Ontario: The Kirkton Press, 1986.

Grof, Christina, and Stanislav Grof, M.D. *The Stormy Search for the Self*. Los Angeles, CA: Jeremy P. Tarcher, Inc., 1990.

Harman, Willis. *Global Mind Change*. Indianapolis, IN: Knowledge Systems, Inc., 1988.

Harman, Willis, and Howard Rheingold. *Higher Creativity: Liberating the Unconscious for Breakthrough Insights*. Los Angeles, CA: J. P. Tarcher, 1984.

Hay, Louise L. *You Can Heal Your Life*. Santa Monica, CA: Hay House, 1982.

Hodson, Geoffrey. *Music Forms*. Wheaton, IL: The Theosophical Publishing House, 1976.

Hooper, Judith and Dick Teresi. *The Three Pound Universe*. New York: Macmillan, 1986.

Ivanova, Barbara. *The Golden Chalice*. San Francisco, CA: H. S. Dakin Co., 1986.

Jaffee, Dennis T. *Healing from Within: Psychological Techniques to Help the Mind Heal the Body*. New York: Simon & Schuster, 1980.

Jening, Hans. *Cymatics*. Basel, Switzerland: Basler Druck and Verlagsanstalt, 1974.

Karagulla, Shafica, M.D., and Dora van Gelder Kunz. *The Chakras and the Human Energy Fields*. Wheaton, IL: The Theosophical Publishing House, 1989.

Kowalski, Robert E. *The 8-Week Cholesterol Cure*. New York: Harper & Row, 1989.

Krieger, Dolores. *The Therapeutic Touch: How to Use Your Hands to Help or Heal*. Englewood Cliffs, NJ: Prentice-Hall, 1979.

Kulvinskas, Viktoras. *Survival into the 21st Century: Planetary Healers Manual*. Connecticut: Omangod Press, 1975.

Kushi, Aveline with Alex Jack. *Aveline Kushi's Complete Guide to Macrobiotic Cooking for Health, Harmony and Peace*. New York: Warner Books, 1985.

Kushi, Aveline and Michio. *Macrobiotic Diet*. New York: Japan Publications, 1985.

Lavabre, Marcel. *Aromatherapy Workbook*. Rochester, VT: Healing Arts Press, 1990.

Levine, Frederick G. *Psychic Sourcebook: How to Choose and Use a Psychic*. New York: Warner, 1988.

Levine, Stephen. *Healing Into Life and Death*. New York: Doubleday, 1984.

Liberman, Jacob, O.D., Ph.D. *Light: Medicine of the Future*. Santa Fe, NM: Bear & Company, 1991.

Mandel, Peter. *Energy Emission Analysis: New Application of Kirlian Photography for Holistic Health*. Germany: Synthesis Publishing Company, N.d.

Markides, Kyriacos C. *Homage to the Sun*. New York: Routledge, 1987.

_____. *The Magus of Strovolos: The Extraordinary World of a Spiritual Healer*. New York: Routledge, 1985.

McCarty, Meredith. *American Macrobiotic Cuisine*. Eureka, CA: Turning Point Publications, 1986.

Mitchell, Elinor R. *Plain Talk About Acupuncture*. New York: Whalehall, 1987.

O'Connor, John and Dan Bensky, eds. *Acupuncture: A Comprehensive Text*. Chicago, IL: Eastland Press, 1981.

Orenstein, Neil and Sarah L. Bingham. *Food Allergies: How to Tell If You Have Them, What to Do About Them If You Do*. New York: Putnam Publishing Group, 1987.

Ott, John N. *Health and Light*. Columbus, OH: Ariel Press, 1973.

Pearson, Carol S. *The Hero Within: Six Archetypes We Live By*. New York: HarperCollins, 1989.

Pierrakos, Eva. *The Pathwork of Self-Transformation*. New York: Bantam, 1990.

Pritikin, Nathan. *Pritikin Permanent Weight Loss Manual*. New York: Putnam Publishing Group, 1981.

Pritikin, Nathan and Patrick McGrady. *Pritikin Program for Diet and Exercise*. New York: Bantam, 1984.

Reilly, Harold J. and Ruth H. Brod. *The Edgar Cayce Handbook for Health Through Drugless Therapy*. New York: Berkeley, 1985.

Rodegast, Pat and Judith Stanton. *Emmanuel's Book II: The Choice for Love*. New York: Bantam, 1989.

Rolf, Ida P. *Rolfing: The Integration of Human Structures*. Rochester, VT: Inner Traditions, 1989.

Rubin, Jerome. *New York Naturally*. New York: City Spirit Publications, 1988.

Satprem. *The Mind of the Cells*. New York: Institute for Evolutionary Research, 1982.

Schechter, Steven R. and Tom Monte. *Fighting Radiation with Foods, Herbs and Vitamins*. Brookline, MA: East-West, 1988.

Schwarz, Jack. *Voluntary Controls: Exercises for Creative Meditation and for Activating the Potential of the Chakras*. New York: Dutton, 1978.

Seem, Mark. *Acupuncture Energetics*. Rochester, VT: Inner Traditions, 1987.

Shealy, Norman C. and Caroline Myss. *The Creation of Health: Merging Traditional Medicine with Intuitive Diagnosis*. Walpole, NH: Stillpoint Publishing, 1988.

Sheldrake, Rupert. *A New Science of Life*. Los Angeles, CA: J. P. Tarcher, 1981.

Siegel, Bernie S. *Love, Medicine & Miracles*. New York: Harper & Row, 1986.

Simonton, O. Carl, and Reid Henson, with Brenda Hampton. *The Healing Journey*. New York: Bantam, 1992.

Steindl-Rast, Brother David. *Gratefulness, the Heart of Prayer*. New York: Paulist Press, 1984.

Talbot, Michael. *The Holographic Universe*. New York: HarperCollins, 1991.

Ullman, Dana, ed. *Discovering Homeopathy: Your Introduction to the Science and Art of Homeopathic Medicine*. Berkeley, CA: North Atlantic Books, 1991.

Upledger, John E., and Jon D. Vredevoogd. *Craniosacral Therapy*. Seattle, WA: Eastland Press, 1983.

Werbach, Melvin R. *Nutritional Influences on Illness: A Sourcebook of Clinical Research*. New Canaan, CT: Keats Publishing, 1989.

Wilber, Ken. *The Holographic Paradigm and Other Paradoxes*. Boston: Shambhala, 1982.

————. *No Boundary: Eastern and Western Approaches to Personal Growth*. Boston: Shambhala, 1979.

Wilhelm, Richard and C. G. Jung. *The Secret of the Golden Flower*. New York: Harcourt Brace Jovanovich, 1970.

Woolf, Vernon V., Ph.D. *Holodynamics: How to Develop **and** Manage Your Personal Power*. Tucson, AZ: Harbinger House, Inc., 1990.

Woolger, Roger J. *Other Lives, Other Selves*. New York: Bantam, 1988.

Zerden, Sheldon. *The Best of Health: The 101 Best Books*. New York: Four Walls Eight Windows, 1989.

Zukav, Gary. *The Seat of the Soul*. New York: Simon & Schuster, 1989.

I N D E X

BARBARA ANN BRENNAN is a healer, therapist, and scientist who has devoted more than twenty years to research and exploration of the human energy field. Following an advanced degree in atmospheric physics from the University of Wisconsin, she worked as a research scientist at NASA's Goddard Space Flight Center. She trained in bioenergetic and core energetic therapy at the Institute for Psychophysical Synthesis and at the Community of the Whole Person in Washington, D.C. She was in the first graduating class of Dr. John Pierrakos' Institute for the New Age, now known as The Institute of Core Energetics in New York City.

Her first book, *Hands of Light,* is recognized as one of the primary texts for alternative healing in our time. She is the founder and director of the Barbara Brennan School of Healing in East Hampton, Long Island, where she has developed a four-year certification program in healing science. Her workshops, lectures, and demonstrations have taken her throughout North America and Europe.